FUNDAMENTALS OF PHILOSOPHY

Fundamentals of Philosophy is a comprehensive and accessible introduction to the major topics in philosophy and is designed to be used as a companion to any undergraduate philosophy course.

Based on the well-known series of the same name, this textbook brings together specially commissioned articles by leading philosophers. Each chapter provides an authoritative overview of topics commonly taught at undergraduate level, focusing on the major issues that typically arise when studying the subject. Discussions are up to date and written in an engaging manner so as to provide students with the core building-blocks of their degree course.

Helpful exercises are included at the end of each chapter, as well as bibliographies and annotated further reading sections.

Fundamentals of Philosophy is an ideal starting point for those coming to philosophy for the first time and will be a useful complement to the primary texts studied at undergraduate level. Ideally suited to novice philosophy students, it will also be of interest to those in related subjects across the humanities and social sciences.

John Shand is Associate Lecturer at The Open University. He is series editor of the *Fundamentals of Philosophy* series (Routledge), author of *Arguing Well* (Routledge 2000) and *Philosophy and Philosophers* (2002).

FUNDAMENTALS OF PHILOSOPHY

Edited by John Shand

Routledge
Taylor & Francis Group

LONDON AND NEW YORK

First published 2003
by Routledge
11 New Fetter Lane, London EC4P 4EE

Simultaneously published in the USA and Canada
by Routledge
29 West 35th Street, New York, NY 10001

Routledge is an imprint of the Taylor and Francis Group

Typeset in Sabon and Frutiger by
Keystroke, Jacaranda Lodqe, Wolverhampton
Printed and bound in Great Britain by
TJ International Ltd, Padstow, Cornwall

British Library Cataloguing in Publication Data
A catalogue record for this book is available from the British Library

Library of Congress Cataloging in Publication Data
Fundamentals of philosophy / [edited by] John Shand.
p.   cm.
Includes bibliographical references and index.
1. Philosophy–Textbooks. I. Shand, John, 1956–

BD31.F86 2003
100–dc21

2002044529

ISBN 0–415–22709–7 (hbk)
ISBN 0–415–22710–0 (pbk)

TO SARAH WITH LOVE

CONTENTS

CONTRIBUTORS

Piers Benn is Lecturer in Medical Ethics at Imperial College, London. Previously he lectured in Philosophy at Leeds and St Andrews. He is author of *Ethics* (Routledge 1998) and much of his writing is in applied ethics. His interests within philosophy range widely and he has published in popular as well as scholarly outlets.

Alexander Bird is Lecturer in Philosophy at the University of Edinburgh, and has held visiting positions at the Universities of Caen, Siena and Cambridge, and at Dartmouth College. He was educated at Westminster School and the universities of Oxford, Munich and Cambridge. He is the author of *Philosophy of Science* (Routledge 1998) and *Thomas Kuhn* (2000).

Stephen Burwood was born in London in 1959 and now teaches philosophy at the University of Hull. He is co-author of *Philosophy of Mind* (Routledge 1998) and is currently working on books on the self and competing conceptions of human embodiment.

Richard Francks was born in Leicestershire in 1950. He has taught English in Spain, Japan and Scotland, and Philosophy at The Open University and University of York. He is currently Director of Undergraduate Studies in Philosophy at Leeds, and not very good at cricket.

Simon Glendinning is Lecturer in Philosophy at the University of Reading. He is the author of *On Being with Others: Heidegger–Derrida–Wittgenstein* (1998); and the editor of *The Edinburgh Encyclopedia of Continental Philosophy* (1999) and *Arguing with Derrida* (2001). He has published articles on perception, animal life, and the end of philosophy.

Alan Goldman is William R. Kenan, Jr Professor of Humanities and Professor of Philosophy, College of William and Mary, Virginia. He is the author of six books, including *Empirical Knowledge*, *Moral Knowledge*, *Aesthetic Value*, and *Practical Rules*. He loves to play tennis.

Michael Jubien is Professor of Philosophy at the University of California, Davis. He studied mathematics and philosophy at Dartmouth College and The Rockefeller University, and is the author of *Ontology, Modality, and the Fallacy of Reference* (1993) and *Contemporary Metaphysics* (1997).

Dudley Knowles is Senior Lecturer in Philosophy at the University of Glasgow. He is the author of *Political Philosophy* (Routledge 2001) and *Hegel and 'The Philosophy of Right'* (Routledge 2002).

Colin Lyas is Senior Lecturer in Philosophy at the University of Lancaster and the author of *Aesthetics* (Routledge 1997).

Alexander Miller is Senior Lecturer in Philosophy at Macquarie University, Australia. He is the author of *Philosophy of Language* (Routledge 1998) and co-editor (with Crispin Wright) of *Rule-Following and Meaning* (2002). He is currently working on a book on Michael Dummett and a book on metaethics.

Dermot Moran is Professor of Philosophy at University College Dublin and author of *John Scottus Eriugena: A Study of Idealism in the Middle Ages* (1989) and many articles on medieval philosophy. He is author of *Introduction to Phenomenology* (Routledge 2001) and Editor of *International Journal of Philosophical Studies*.

Greg Restall was born in Brisbane in 1969. He studied mathematics and philosophy at the University of Queensland. He is an Associate Professor in Philosophy at the University of Melbourne, and is the author of *An Introduction to Substructural Logics* (2000) and *Logic* (Routledge 2003).

John Shand studied philosophy at the University of Manchester and King's College, Cambridge. He is an Associate Lecturer in Philosophy at The Open University and is the author of *Philosophy and Philosophers: An Introduction to Western Philosophy* (2003) and *Arguing Well* (Routledge 2000).

Suzanne Stern-Gillet is currently Professor of Philosophy at the Bolton Institute. She holds degrees in Philosophy and in Classics from the Universities of Liège (Belgium) and Manchester (UK). She is the author of *Aristotle's Philosophy of Friendship* (1995). She is currently working on a history of ancient philosophy, *From Thales to Iamblichus* (Routledge).

W. Jay Wood received his PhD in philosophy from the University of Notre Dame, and has taught at Wheaton College since 1982. He is the author of *Epistemology: Becoming Intellectually Virtuous* (1998) and other articles on epistemology and the philosophy of religion.

PREFACE

Putting together this book has been interesting and rewarding. Most of all I should like to thank the authors of the individual chapters for their hard work, cooperation, care, and indeed the insightful skill with which they wrote each of their contributions. Individually and collectively I think they have done a great service for philosophy by presenting core aspects of the subject in such an accessible, thoughtful and well-written way. It should open doors for many. Their accomplishment is nothing like as easy as it may look.

I should like to thank Siobhan Pattinson at Routledge for being so easy to work with as she helped ferry the book through. I should also like to express as always my appreciation to my wife Judith whose eagle eyes and intelligence improved the text. Personal thanks go to my young daughter Sarah for being a delight. The book is dedicated to her.

John Shand
Manchester
2003

INTRODUCTION

John Shand

THE AIM OF THIS BOOK

This book is an accessible stimulating gateway to the central areas of philosophy. The chapters are carefully arranged to begin with what are usually regarded as the core areas of the subject and then extend out to other important subjects of less generality, not, one should emphasise, of less importance. The prime purpose of the chapters is not to give comprehensive coverage of each subject, but rather to open the door on the subject for the reader and encourage thought about all the ideas within. Someone once said to me that studying philosophy had 'opened doors'; if this book does that, it will have succeeded.

WHAT IS PHILOSOPHY?

Philosophy is a great intellectual adventure while at the same time what it discusses is one of the most important things we can do with our lives.

There is a standing joke among many professional philosophers that involves one of them being cornered at a party by someone, and on hearing that he is a philosopher, being asked, 'Well, what is philosophy then?' The joke in fact reflects the unease of many philosophers and the discomforting awareness of not being able to come out with a straight clear answer. Many philosophers resort to the list-method of answering, saying that it's about 'fundamental issues' such as 'truth', 'What can be known?', 'What is the nature of a good and bad action?', 'What is the nature of mind and how is it related to body?' The other way of dealing with the question is somewhat evasive and involves saying as little as possible, something like: 'well, the best way to understand what philosophy is is to do it'. Both these answers, neither of which is without truth, are likely to leave the original questioners rightly bewildered, dissatisfied and quickly heading off to get another drink – much to the relief of the philosopher.

1

I think it is incumbent on professional philosophers to tackle this question head-on. After all we do get paid. My immediate answer to the question, requiring a little refinement later on, is:

Philosophy is what happens when you start thinking for yourself.

A bit more may then be added. Once one frees oneself from the habits of received belief, those that one just happens to have acquired even about basic issues, and really starts to think about what one ought to believe, judged by reason (argument) and evidence, then one has started to do philosophy. The 'tradition' of relying instead on 'authorities' and 'holy text' is the usual state of affairs rather than the exception in history – for many it still is the natural way of going on. Moreover, thinking for oneself is not something easily taken on by mere momentary act of will, but rather something to be strengthened like a muscle through good mental habits. Philosophy is a way of life to be built up over years; philosophical thinking is a cast of mind that becomes part of a person's very nature.

Philosophy is often thought to be an unnecessary impractical luxury. A sort of futile, at best entertaining, addition to life after one has dealt with the practicalities. But this is a mistake.

Far from being unnecessary philosophy is unavoidable just as soon as people cease taking their received beliefs for granted and instead start thinking them through for themselves. The glory of philosophy – and certainly one of the original attractions for many drawn to it – is that nothing is out of bounds, not even the value of reason, or indeed (although this may seem paradoxical) the status of philosophy itself. No holds are barred. Only something like argument and debate without boundaries seems to be a constant. It's a wonderful freedom. Either one is a slave to the beliefs one happens to have acquired through the contingent circumstances of how and where one is brought up, or one is to some degree a philosopher. Philosophy is the bastion of free thought and of the exploration of ideas above all others.

What of the charge of it being an impractical luxury? This is a mistake too. This is because beliefs lead to actions (and inaction), and badly thought out ideas lead often to terrible actions. Our responsibility for what we believe, and what we leave ourselves open to being capable of believing, cannot be divorced from our responsibility for our actions. Ideas that in untesting times can even seem benign, in extreme circumstances lead to awful actions.

Philosophy sometimes addresses the question as to how one should live. It can be argued that keeping a philosophical stance itself is exactly how one should live – anything else is gullible slavery. Of course it's a matter of degree, but for the most part it's one-way to freedom of thought: after having it no-one wants slavery again.

It would be wrong to think that philosophy leaves one constantly in a state of vague doubt. One accepts one's beliefs on the basis of the best arguments. But one leaves the door ajar for further argument. In fact it is those who take on their beliefs as acts of will and faith that stand on a precarious escarpment from which they can be knocked by circumstance with the painful consequences of disappointment, emptiness and loss. The result may be catastrophic because they fall, if they do, from such a great height and from a place they thought absolutely secure. After which, what? Philosophy does not set its hopes so high. It's prepared also to live bravely with that. Even if one changes one's beliefs in the light of new arguments, one can tell oneself that last time one held a view one did one's best to really get to the bottom of the matter. Philosophy breeds neither empty doubt nor an unattainable certainty.

As a way of life philosophy and philosophical thinking do not promise happiness, but they do, I think, enhance what is best in human beings. Philosophy embodies that which is noblest in our species.

THE HOUSE THAT PHILOSOPHERS BUILT

Philosophy is rather like a house built on stilts in a river. In the house one can do all sorts of things – construct things, move things about – but one is always aware that the structure is supported by pillars that are driven into something potentially and often actually shifting. Philosophy goes down repeatedly to see how things are going on around the foot of the pillars and indeed inspects the pillars themselves. Things may need changing down there. For philosophers this is not just the nature of philosophy, it is the true intellectual condition of mankind. It is philosophy that pays that condition close attention and take it seriously. This rather than ignoring it or solving it glibly.

THE AREAS OF PHILOSOPHY

The range of philosophy is large and basically unified. However, to clarify issues and build up expertise it divides its energies into areas of specialisation. There are two characteristics of these areas. One is those that have a subject matter that seems to underpin most of what we think and do. The others underpin more particular concerns we have. The areas feed on one another and are interrelated. Philosophy is not built like other subjects from unquestioned basic foundation upwards. It does not consist of easy bits we can all assume out of which the more complex bits are made. There is, as they say, no shallow end in philosophy – when one starts all the deep issues come into play straightaway.

As far as the subjects of the chapters in this book are concerned, philosophy can be divided into three groups.

    Group I
        Logic
        Epistemology
        Metaphysics
    Group II
        Ethics

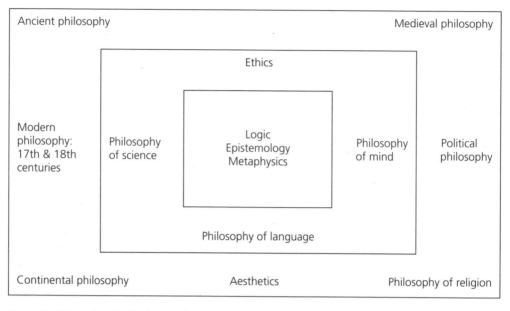

Figure I.1 Philosophy: the fundamentals

      Philosophy of mind
      Philosophy of language
      Philosophy of science
Group III
      Ancient philosophy
      Medieval philosophy
      Modern philosophy: seventeenth and eighteenth centuries
      Political philosophy
      Aesthetics
      Continental philosophy
      Philosophy of religion

The relation between these subdivisions of philosophy is not one of difficulty but one of generality, with lesser generality as one moves away from the centre. This is not to say the outer subjects are less important. Rather it is that those subjects in Group I underpin the problems considered in Group II, and have consequences for the conclusions one reaches in Group II – Group II finds itself referring back to Group I constantly. The subjects in Group III do not raise new fundamental philosophical considerations that are not dealt with in Groups I and II, but rather apply all the problems encountered in Groups I and II to specific areas. Here are some examples: Metaphysics may be concerned with what sort of entities fundamentally exist; aesthetics is concerned with thinking about in what way works of art exist; what sort of entities are they? Ethics examines what it is to say that we ought to do something, for something to be right or wrong; political philosophy studies the right way to organise society, if it should be organised at all.

The historical chapters listed here, such as Ancient Philosophy and Medieval Philosophy of course deal with all the central problems of philosophy as they are treated by a period or school of thinkers.

THE PROBLEMS OF PHILOSOPHY

Here is a list of some of the most commonly addressed and most basic philosophical problems. Do not worry too much about how one would address these questions as a philosopher – just look through them and consider how you might answer them in an immediate intuitive way – my guess is that you will soon find yourself in deeper water than you may expect, philosophical water in fact. In fact do not feel pressure to find *an* answer, but think of various ways one may answer the questions and what reasons one has for those answers being correct. The answers, or merely how one should even start to approach them, are a good deal less straightforward than one may suppose.

What is the nature of philosophy?
Are there philosophical problems?
What is the correct method for solving philosophical problems?
When are inferences sound?
What is the nature of rationality?
What is truth?
What is it to know something?
What are we perceiving when we claim to be perceiving the world?
Can we know the external world exists?
What is reality?
What is it for something to exist?
What sorts of things exist?
What is a cause?
What is it for something to be morally good?
What is the good life?
Can ethical judgements be justified?
What is the nature of mind?
What is consciousness?
What is the self?
What is it for expressions in a language to have meaning?
What is it to understand the meaning of a word?
Can induction be justified?

What is a scientific law?
How should society best be organised?
What justifies the power of the state?
What are human rights?
What is a work of art?
Can we justify the evaluations we make of works of art?
What determines the meaning of a work of art?
What is it to justify the existence of God?
What is the nature of God?
How ought we to live?

TIMELESSNESS

It is not uncontentious to say that philosophical problems are timeless. To some it looks like an excuse for examining problems which in fact can have no answer because there is something wrong in considering them as 'problems' in the first place. However, the subject of philosophy certainly acts as if philosophical problems are timeless. Certain topics may be more of a central concern at a particular time, but that is mainly a function of fashion. The central topics and questions come round again and again. Rarely is it the case that a matter considered by philosophy is wholly dismissed, or the way it was once treated regarded as valueless. Quite the contrary. Philosophers find themselves going back to philosophers of the past at the least to use their ideas on certain topics as starting points, but often much more than that. A book that considers the nature of justice will naturally find itself looking to see what Plato had to say. The problems of induction and causation normally involve discussing Hume in depth. The starting point for considering the nature of mind is often Descartes.

It's far from clear that progress is made in philosophy as in some other subjects. In this sense philosophy is quite unlike science – a chemist would rarely find any value in checking to see what another chemist said about something a hundred years ago.

So one may wonder what is the point of philosophy in this case if it does not definitively solve problems. As suggested already philosophical problems arise when we start to think deeply about our most fundamental beliefs. When we do so we often find that we neither fully understand the content of those beliefs, nor have any clear justification for holding them. For a certain kind of mind this is perplexing and the problems will not go away through the acceptance of glib answers or in response to a dismissive frame of mind. We may not be able to present final solutions, nevertheless we can come to a conclusion that is a result of the best thinking on a certain matter.

I would conclude that philosophical problems are timeless by virtue of their profundity, generality and, as a consequence of that, the uncertainty surrounding the very methods by which they may be best approached. The result is that the problems do not die, nor do the ways of attempting to solve them or at least deal with them.

One thing is pretty certain: the issue of whether philosophical problems are timeless is itself a philosophical problem.

BEYOND THE FACTUAL

Philosophy is not usually concerned with gathering facts. That can be left to other disciplines such as science, or history, or psychology or anthropology. The reason for this is twofold. First, philosophy usually deals with matters that have to be assumed in gathering the facts – questions about truth and the knowability of reality, for example. Any attempt to solve the philosophical problems by reference to the facts is therefore highly likely to be question begging. We cannot for example refer to the evidence gathered through perception about the world to solve the philosophical problem of what can be known, if anything, about the world through perception. Second, the facts are usually insufficient to deal with the philosophical problem. This is particularly obvious in ethics. It is generally argued that no reference to what people are like and what they actually do can answer the question of what people ought to do. This is not to say the facts are ignored, just that the facts are insufficient to allow us to come to conclusions about the matters with which philosophy deals.

THE SUBJECTS OF PHILOSOPHY

This section gives a thumbnail sketch of the subjects of philosophy discussed in this book. The book is not exhaustive of philosophy, but it can fairly be said that all the core areas are covered here.

Epistemology

The subject here is the nature of knowledge, and given that nature, what it can be truly said that we can know, as opposed to just having beliefs and opinions about. Can we counter views of sceptics who would claim that strictly speaking we cannot know as much as we claim to, or indeed anything at all?

Metaphysics

What sorts of things ultimately exist and how do they connect to each other and how things appear to us? Are all the things that appear to us real, or are they derived from something more fundamental? And what do we say about the existence of things that do not in the usual sense 'exist' but to which we nevertheless refer, such as unicorns or numbers.

Logic

This is concerned with the nature and identification of good inferences: those circumstances in which one statement is said to follow from another. It seeks to understand and classify the cases where statements, if true, justify to whatever degree the truth of other statements.

Ethics

This is concerned with values (normative as opposed to factual matters) with respect to human actions. What is it for something we do to be counted good or bad? What is it to say we ought to do or not do something? It is not enough to talk of what we do, we need to address what we should do and what saying this means.

Ancient philosophy

This is the study of the philosophers of the Greek and Roman world. The usual concentration is on Greek philosophy from c.624BC, marking the birth of the Presocratic Thales, to 322BC as the death of Aristotle. The most important figures are undoubtedly Plato and Aristotle. Often this period is extended to include the Roman world. The significance of thought in the ancient world cannot be overestimated. Here we find almost everything, developed to varying degrees, that characterises the Western outlook. Indeed it represents a watershed in human history, where for the first time reason alone is applied across the board to the solving of the deepest problems rather than appeal to mere authority or an idea's longevity.

Medieval philosophy

This covers, we should note, the study of philosophers over a vast time of around one thousand years, extending from St Augustine of Hippo (AD354–430) and William of Ockham (c.1285–1349), and continuing beyond until at least the Renaissance. The connecting thread is the rise and dominance of Christianity which permeates the philosophy done during this period. The other most significant link throughout the period is the interpretation and adaptation of Aristotle's metaphysics.

Modern philosophy: the seventeenth and eighteenth centuries

It may seem strange to call philosophy done in the seventeenth and eighteenth centuries 'modern philosophy'. It indicates a period of astonishing fecundity in philosophical thought and a new way of doing philosophy that was a significant break from what had gone before. Moreover many of the ways that philosophy is presently done still derive from thought in this period. The central figures are Descartes, Spinoza, Leibniz, Locke, Berkeley, Hume.

Philosophy of mind

What kind of entity are we referring to when we talk about the 'mind'? How does talk of the mind relate to talk of what we normally call our bodies? Are the mind and the body one or is the mind non-physical? How can conscious awareness and understanding whereby we refer to things arise from inert matter? What do we mean by, and can it justify, saying that someone is the same person throughout his life?

Philosophy of language

What is it for an expression, spoken or written, to have meaning and the capacity to refer to things? What constitutes a person's understanding the meaning of a word, at which point they know how it ought to be used correctly?

Philosophy of science

What defines a law of nature? How does it differ from other claims about the world? How if at all are scientific theories justified by evidence? How can we know that our laws of nature describe features of the world that will persist next time we examine it?

Political philosophy

How ought society to be organised? What justifies the existence of the state that can rightly usurp power from people? How should the state be controlled? What justifies private property, if anything? How do people acquire rights that cannot be transgressed apart from exceptional circumstances, if at all?

Philosophy of arts

Can what a work of art is be defined? What do we mean when we say some work has a certain aesthetic quality, such as beauty? What determines the meaning of a work of art? What, if anything, justifies our valuing works of art differently?

Philosophy of religion

How good are the arguments justifying the existence of God? Are arguments for the existence of God required, or is faith enough? What is the nature of God and how does that relate to the sort of creatures we are?

Continental philosophy

It is controversial to claim that the group of philosophers often brought together under this title can be done so coherently, and the chapter here deals mainly with this matter. Negatively the title may indicate a divergence of methods and philosophical concerns between philosophers in Continental Europe and English-speaking philosophers in Britain, North America, New Zealand and Australia. Positively there is perhaps a thread that runs from the philosopher Immanuel Kant (1724–1804) to the present with such thinkers as Jacques Derrida, and this can be seen as various ways of responding to the philosophical outlook of transcendental idealism. The recent philosophers here are often marked by the most fundamental questioning of the nature, and indeed existence, of philosophy itself.

THE FUTURE OF PHILOSOPHY

Philosophy will go on just as long as some people hold the view that thinking things through for themselves is important. It is hard to say what philosophical concerns will be the centre of people's attention in the future. But it looks as if there will always be someone trying to struggle with the deepest questions and unwilling to take on trust the answers that happen to be around.

1

EPISTEMOLOGY

Alan Goldman

INTRODUCTION

Epistemology is concerned with the nature, scope and structure of knowledge. As epistemologists, we want to know first what knowledge is, and we want our analysis of the concept to guide us in determining the scope of knowledge, in deciding how much knowledge we have. In determining the scope of knowledge, the epistemologist will attempt to answer sceptical challenges to the sources that are usually assumed to produce knowledge, sources such as perception, memory, testimony of others, and various kinds of reasoning. The sceptic will question whether the ways things appear in perception or memory, for example, constitute good evidence for the ways we take them really to be, and whether various kinds of reasoning produce true beliefs from their data. In attempting to provide answers to the sceptic's questions, we should be able to reveal not only the scope of knowledge, but also its structure. We will see whether knowledge has a web-like structure, in which beliefs reflect their status as knowledge by connecting with other beliefs in a set, or whether knowledge has foundations, special beliefs which attain their status independent of connections with other beliefs, and with which other beliefs must cohere.

We will take up each of these topics in turn, beginning with the analysis of knowledge. A particular approach to epistemology will be endorsed and briefly defended here. But we will also note difficulties for this approach, and the major alternatives will be considered and criticised as well. At the end, the reader should have both a feel for the general field and an idea of how one theory might be developed and defended against alternatives and against sceptical objections.

THE NATURE OF KNOWLEDGE

Knowledge is the goal of belief. It is what belief aims to be, or, more precisely, what we aim at in believing. There may be some types of belief, for example religious, for which knowledge is seen to be impossible and belief itself sufficient (in its effects). But knowledge is always to be preferred to mere belief where it is possible; it is, other things being equal, the ideal form of belief. An analysis of knowledge must reflect this fact. What must knowledge be like to function properly as our cognitive goal? We want our beliefs to be true, but we want more of them as well. We want not just truth, but secure truth, truth that will be resistant to pressures against its acquisition or retention. If the truth of a belief is not firm in this way, then changes in the world or in the subject that are unrelated to the fact believed will likely alter the belief and render the resulting changed belief false. Beliefs acquired similarly in the future will be likely to be false as well, and we will not be able to tell as easily whether they are true or false. Thus, we want our beliefs to be *non-accidentally* true, so that they will not be subject to such whims of fortune. We want to remove luck from the acquisition and retention of true belief, just as we want to remove moral luck from the actions of agents. Acting in a morally right way by accident (when rightness is no part of an agent's intention) does not produce faith in or praise for the agent; similarly, believing the truth by accident does not produce faith in one's cognitive abilities or positive grades for the achievement.

It is relatively uncontroversial among epistemologists that knowledge involves true belief, and most would accept the claim that the truth of a belief must be non-accidental if it is to amount to knowledge. But controversy will arise over how to understand this crucial requirement. Certain kinds of luck or accident can enter into the acquisition of knowledge, while other kinds must be ruled out. And the absence of accident in certain senses will not guarantee that a true belief counts as knowledge. Regarding the first point, I might be just lucky to run into a friend of mine in Paris and hence to know he is there; but despite the fact that my running into him was accidental, I do know he is there. Regarding the second point, a perverse epistemologist might deliberately trick me into believing the truth when my belief is based on the wrong reasons or is unconnected in the right way with the fact I believe. He might trick me into believing that *someone* in my department owns a Ford by convincing me that he himself does, when he but not I know that only another member of my department owns a Ford. There is a sense here in which it is non-accidental that I believe a true proposition, but I still lack knowledge.

These two examples can help us to begin to sharpen the sense in which knowledge must be non-accidental. In the first example, *given the context* in which I acquire the belief, that in which I see my friend, it is non-accidental that I believe he is there.

And in the second example, while my perverse colleague deliberately sets up the context in which I acquire my belief, given that context, my belief that someone in my department owns a Ford is only accidentally true. Thus, we can say that a belief must be non-accidentally true in the context in which it is acquired in order to count as knowledge. Beyond this point, however, it will remain a matter of great controversy how to interpret the requirement of being non-accidental.

Ordinarily, when our beliefs are only accidentally true, they result from lucky guesses. A venerable but suspect tradition in epistemology seeks to eliminate lucky guesses by requiring that believers be *justified* in their beliefs. This concept of justification has its origin and natural home in ethics. In morally judging persons by their actions, we demand that they be justified in acting as they do and that they act as they do because of this justification. Similarly, in judging persons by their beliefs, we may demand that they be justified in believing as they do and not achieve truth by lucky guesses. But it remains questionable whether justification is either necessary for knowledge or sufficient when added to true belief.

Before attempting to answer these questions, it is necessary to clarify the concept of justification to which appeal is being made. While we often talk in non-philosophical contexts of agents being justified in acting as they do, 'justification' is a technical term of art in epistemology, rarely used in reference to beliefs outside the context of philosophical analysis and debate. And it is a concept about which epistemologists themselves have conflicting intuitions. The analogy with ethics suggests that justification is a matter of fulfilling one's obligations as these can be determined from an internal perspective, from the subject's own point of view. Moral agents are justified when acting in a subjectively right way given the information available to them. Similarly, believers might be said to be justified when they have fulfilled their epistemic obligations given the evidence available to them, for example, when they have critically assessed the available evidence.

But there are many problems with this internalist conception, based as it is on what subjects should believe from their own perspective. First, the analogy with ethics may be out of place, since we do not have the same degree of control over the acquisition of beliefs as we do over our actions. If we cannot help believing as we do, then talk of epistemic obligations is suspect, although we can still exercise control over the degree to which we gather evidence, seek to be impartial, and so on. Second, it must be clarified to what degree the justification for one's beliefs must be available and able to be articulated from one's own perspective. On the most extreme view, in order to be justified in a belief, one must be aware not only of the evidence for it, but of the justifying relation in which that evidence stands to the belief. But, given the motivation for this view, it seems that one's belief in that justifying relation must itself be justified, and that one's belief that it is justified must be justified, and so on. Even if that regress were to end somehow, it seems clear that ordinary subjects are not aware of such complex sets of judgements and so could never fulfil this requirement.

A weaker internalism regarding justification would require only that evidence for one's beliefs be in principle recoverable from one's internal states. One question here is whether subjects must be able to articulate their evidence as such. This requirement would disallow the perceptual knowledge of children, for example, who cannot articulate the ways things appear to them as ways of appearing. Even without this requirement, there seem to be clear counterexamples to internalist concepts of justification as necessary for knowledge. (The internalist distinguishes between a person's being justified and there being some justification not in the person's possession, the latter being irrelevant.) A clairvoyant who could reliably foretell the future, an idiot savant who knows mathematical truths without knowing how he knows them, or a person with perfect pitch who can identify tones with almost perfect accuracy have beliefs that count as knowledge without having any apparent justification for those beliefs. Certainly they are not justified in their beliefs until they notice their repeated successes, but they have knowledge from the beginning. In more mundane cases, we all have knowledge when completely unaware of its source, when that source or the evidence for our beliefs is completely unrecoverable. I know that Columbus sailed in 1492, and I assume that I learned this from some elementary school teacher, but who that teacher was, or what her evidence for the date was, is, I also assume, completely unrecoverable by me. More generally, knowledge from the testimony of others requires neither that one knows the evidence for the proposition transmitted nor even that one have evidence of the reliability of those providing the testimony (what it does require will be discussed below).

Thus justification in the sense in which the concept is derived from ethics is not necessary for knowledge. It is more commonly accepted since Edmund Gettier's famous article that justification, when added to true belief, is not sufficient for knowledge (Gettier 1963). Many examples like the one cited earlier about the owner of the Ford exemplify justified, true belief that is not knowledge. They show that a person can be accidentally right in a belief that is not simply a lucky guess. Other examples that show the same thing include beliefs about the outcomes of lotteries, which falsify many otherwise plausible analyses of knowledge, and beliefs of those in sceptical worlds (also to be discussed later), such as brains in vats programmed to have experiences and beliefs, or victims of deceiving demons. A brain in a vat programmed to have the beliefs it does can occasionally be programmed to have a true belief grounded in its seeming perceptual experience about an object outside the vat, but that justified, true belief will not be knowledge. I can justifiably and truly believe that my ticket in this week's Florida lottery will not win, but I do not know it is a loser until another ticket is drawn.

Thus, justification in any intuitive sense is neither necessary nor sufficient, when added to true belief, for knowledge. Some philosophers have sought to beef up the notion so as to make it the sufficient additional condition for knowledge by requiring that justification be 'undefeated'. One's justification is said to be defeated when it depends on a false proposition, such as the proposition that my colleague owns a Ford in that earlier example (Lehrer 2000, p. 20). There are two fatal flaws in this position. One is that it takes justification to be necessary for knowledge, and we have seen that it is not. The other is that it cannot distinguish between examples in which one's claims to knowledge are threatened by misleading evidence one does not possess. Suppose in the Ford example that my colleague does own the car and gives me good evidence that he does, but that he has an enemy who spreads the false rumour that he is a pathological liar. If that enemy is also in my department and the chances were great that I would have heard his false rumour, then my claim to knowledge will be defeated. It will then be a matter of luck that, given the context of being in my department, I did not hear his testimony and so believe as I do. If, by contrast, my colleague's enemy is in some distant city, his attacks will be irrelevant to my knowledge. No way of unpacking the notion of 'depending on a false proposition' will distinguish correctly between these cases.

That knowledge is the goal of belief indicates yet again that the epistemologist's notion of justification is largely irrelevant. In a court of law, for example, where it is of utmost importance whether witnesses know that to which they testify, jurors must assess whether the evidence they present connects in the right way with the facts they allege. Jurors want to know whether the best explanation for the evidence presented by witnesses appeals to the facts as they represent them, or whether the explanation offered by the opposing attorney is just as plausible. They do not care whether the witnesses are justified in their beliefs, only again whether their beliefs hook up in the right way with the facts. Sceptical worlds also reveal that justification can be worthless, hence not a goal of belief, as firm truth is. One such sceptical world mentioned earlier is that of brains in vats programmed to have all the perceptual experiences that they have. Brains in vats are normally justified in their beliefs on the basis of such experience, but such justification is unrelated to truth and knowledge, not the sort of thing we seek for itself.

If justification is irrelevant to knowledge, we may wonder at the epistemologist's obsession with the notion. There are several explanations. One is that, while ordinary knowers need not be able to defend their claims to knowledge in order to have knowledge, it is one of the epistemologist's tasks in showing the scope of knowledge to defend it against sceptical challenges. In doing so, she will be justifying or showing the justification for various types of beliefs. Some epistemologists might confuse themselves for ordinary knowers, in thinking that ordinary knowers too must justify their beliefs in the face of sceptical challenge. Another explanation for all the attention to this concept is the practice of some epistemologists of calling whatever must be added to true belief to produce knowledge 'justification'. This practice might be excused by the fact, noted earlier, that the term in epistemology is in any case a stipulative term of art. But, if this term refers only to an external relation between a belief and the fact believed, or to a process of acquiring belief that is outside the subject's awareness, then it will lose its normative force and any connection with the ethical concept of justification from which it supposedly derived. It will then lead only to confusion to refer to such additional conditions for knowledge as justification. Externalists might retain the concept by requiring only that there be some justification that perhaps no one has, but again this invites confusion in seeming to be, but not being, a normative concept.

Externalist accounts of knowledge do not require that the condition beyond true belief must be accessible to the subject. They take that condition to be either general reliability in the process that produces the belief or some connection between the particular belief and the fact to which it refers. We may consider reliabilism first (Goldman 1986). Can reliabilists capture the requirement that the truth of a belief that counts as knowledge must be non-accidental? If so, they must take it that when subjects use reliable processes, processes that produce a high proportion of true beliefs, it will not be accidental that they arrive at the truth. But reliabilists who require only general reliability in belief-forming processes would be mistaken in assuming this to be universally true. If a process is not 100 per cent reliable, then, even when it generates a true belief on a particular occasion, it may be only accidental or lucky that the belief is true. I may be not very reliable at identifying breeds of dogs by sight, except for golden retrievers, which I am generally reliable at identifying. But I may be not very good at identifying golden retrievers when they have a particular mark that I wrongly believe to indicate a different breed. I may then fail to notice that mark on a particular dog that I therefore identify correctly, albeit only by luck or accidentally.

This example reveals several problems, some insurmountable, in the account of knowledge that takes it to be true belief produced by a generally reliable process. First, at what level of generality should we describe the process that generates this true belief (Feldman and Conee 1998)? Intuitively, we take processes that generate beliefs to be those such as seeing middle-sized objects in daylight, inductively inferring on the basis of various kinds of samples, and so on. But the former, although used to generate the belief in this example, seems completely irrelevant to evaluating the belief. Whether I am generally reliable in identifying things that I see in daylight has little if anything to do with whether I acquire knowledge that this dog is a golden retriever. Given our judgement that I do not have such knowledge in this example, that I am only lucky to believe truly that this dog is a retriever, we can choose as the relevant process the unreliable one of identifying dogs with the marks that tend to mislead me. This is a quite specific process, but, of course there is the yet more specific one of identifying retrievers with such marks without noticing the marks, which turns out to be reliable and to give the wrong answer in this case. By choosing the former process as the relevant one, we can make the reliability account appear to capture the example. In fact, we can probably do the same for any example, given that every instance of belief acquisition instantiates many different processes at different levels of specificity. But such ad hoc adjustments do nothing to support the reliabilist account. We need independent reason or intuition of the correct specification of the relevant process in particular cases, if not in general, in order for the account to be informative or illuminating.

Our example reveals the pressure to specify the relevant process more and more narrowly. But at the same time it shows that however narrowly we specify it in particular cases, as long as we leave some generality in its description, there will remain room for only accidentally true belief being produced by the process. This indicates clearly that what is important in evaluating a true belief as a claim to knowledge is not the reliability of any generalisable process that produced it, but the particular connection between that very belief and the fact believed. One might try to save the language of reliability by claiming that a process must be reliable in the particular conditions in which it operates on a particular occasion, but once more any looseness or generality at all will allow room for the type of accident that defeats a claim to knowledge. One might also demand perfect reliability, but then one would have to explain why we allow beliefs produced by perception and induction, both fallible processes, to count as knowledge. We do so when these methods connect particular beliefs to their referents in the proper way.

If the example discussed does not suffice, we can appeal to the lottery example once more to show the weakness of reliabilism as an analysis of knowledge. If one inductively infers that one's ticket will not win, we can make the reliability of this inductive process as high as we like short of 100 per cent by increasing the number of tickets. But one still does not know one's ticket will not win until another ticket is drawn. If one did know this, one would never buy a ticket. The problem is not the lack of high reliability or truth, but the lack of the proper connection between the drawing of another ticket and one's belief. Once one receives a report of the drawing of another ticket, then one knows, if the report is based on some witnessing of the event. One then knows even if the probability of error in such reports is the same as the initial probability that one's ticket would be drawn. Once more, it is not the probability or reliability of the process that counts, but the actual connection between belief and fact. Mere statistical inference about the future does not suffice in itself for knowledge, no matter how reliable, but one can have knowledge of the future if it is based on evidence that connects in the proper way with the future events believed to be coming. If, for example, one discovers that the lottery is fixed, then one can come to know that one's ticket will not win.

Given the failure of reliabilism to rule out accidentality in true belief, one might again explain the popularity of the theory among epistemologists as the result of their confusing themselves with ordinary knowers. While the general reliability of belief-forming processes is irrelevant to the knowledge of ordinary knowers in particular cases, the epistemologist, who is interested in defending types of beliefs against sceptical challenges, does try to show that certain sources such as perception or induction are generally truth generating or reliable. The project of seeking to improve our epistemic practices must also seek to establish first which practices reliably produce truth. But the analysis of knowledge must focus instead on finding the right connection between belief and truth or fact.

The first attempt to specify the connection between belief and fact that renders the belief knowledge was the causal theory (Goldman 1967). This account holds that a true belief must be causally related to its referent in order to count as knowledge. The account captures such examples as the lottery, which, given the failure of so many other theories to do so, indicates that it's on the right track, but it proves to be too narrow. One can have knowledge of universal and mathematical propositions, for example, but universal and mathematical facts or truths do not seem to cause anything. It is also too weak in failing to rule out cases in which there is the usual causal connection between a perceptual belief, for example, and an object to which it refers, but in which the subject could not distinguish this object from relevant alternatives (Goldman, 1967). I might see a criminal commit a crime but not know that he is the culprit because I do not know that his twin brother, also in the vicinity, did not commit the act.

This sort of case is handled by what is perhaps the best-known attempt to specify the crucial connection between belief and fact, the counterfactual account (Nozick 1981, ch. 3). This holds that one knows a fact if one would not believe it if it were not the case, and if other changes in circumstances would leave one believing it. In terms of possible worlds, one knows a proposition if and only if in the closest possible world in which the proposition is false, one does not believe it, and in close possible worlds in which it remains true, one does believe it. (We measure closeness of possible worlds by how similar they are to the actual world.) This account captures the examples so far considered, but unlike the causal account that proves to be too weak, this one is too strong, disallowing genuine knowledge claims. Many of the most mundane facts that I know do not obtain only in very distant possible worlds. In worlds so unlike this one there may be no telling what I would believe there. And it does not matter what I would believe in such worlds. I know that my son is not a knight of the round table and that it is not ninety degrees below zero outside. There is no telling what I might believe if those propositions were false, but this affects not the least my knowledge claims. Thus the first counterfactual condition is too strong. If the second requires retention of belief in all close possible worlds, then it is too strong also. An aging philosopher can still know this truth, although there are close worlds in which he cannot follow the argument that establishes it.

Thus, we need a specification of the relevant connection between fact and belief that counts as knowledge that requires that the connection hold only across close possible worlds, and only across most of them. Such a connection is what we would expect also from a naturalistic perspective, from the fact that the capacity for achieving knowledge is a likely product of natural selection. The capacity to achieve firm true belief is one that would be selected in slowly changing environments, so that true belief would be firm in situations close to actual, but not in distant possible worlds. An analysis that meets this condition and captures all of the examples so far discussed requires that the fact believed (the truth of the belief) enter into the best explanation for the belief's being held. The concept of explanation here can itself be explicated in terms of possible worlds. In this account A explains B if A raises the antecedent probability of B (given other factors, it will raise the probability to 1, where there is no indeterminism or chance involved), and there is no third factor that screens out this relation, that fully accounts for the difference. The last clause is required because evidence, for example, raises the probability of that for which it is evidence, but this relation is screened out by whatever explains both the evidence and that for which it is evidence. In intuitive terms, A explains B if, given A, we can see why B was to be expected. In terms of possible worlds, A explains B if the ratio of close worlds in which B is the case is higher in those in which A is the case than it is in the entire set of close worlds.

Let us review some of the examples that were problematic for the rival accounts of knowledge. When there is misleading evidence I am just lucky not to have noticed, then what explains my belief is the fact that I have not noticed this evidence. My believing the dog in that example to be a golden retriever is explained by my not having noticed the misleading mark. My believing as I do is not made significantly more probable by the fact believed, given all the close possible worlds in which I am aware of the misleading evidence. In the lottery example, the inductive evidence on the basis of which I believe that my ticket will lose does not explain its losing, since the probabilistic connection between that evidence and its losing is screened out by what does explain the latter, the drawing of another ticket. That drawing explains my losing but not my prior belief, which remains explanatorily unconnected to the fact to which it refers.

In regard to problems for the causal theory, the truth of universal propositions helps to explain our belief in them, or it helps to explain the inductive evidence that explains our beliefs. In the case in which I cannot distinguish the cause of my belief from relevant alternatives in the vicinity, the explanation for my belief lies in the broader context and not in the specific cause, just as we do not explain the outbreak of a war by citing only the specific event that triggered it, when any number of equally likely events would have done so in the broader context of latent hostility. In such cases the specific cause does not significantly raise the probability of its effect across close worlds in which alternative causes are also present. To be able to rule out relevant alternatives in claiming knowledge is to be able to rule out alternative explanations for the evidence one has.

In regard to the cases that were problematic for the counterfactual account, what explains the fact that my son is not a knight of the round table, the fact that he lives in the present time and is a tennis player attending Yale, also explains my belief that he is not a Medieval knight. What explains the fact that it is not ninety degrees below zero outside, namely the fact that it is ninety above zero, also explains my belief that it is not subfreezing. Finally, in the aging philosopher example, his belief that the counterfactual analysis is too strong is connected with the evidence that it is too strong in many, although not all, close possible worlds.

In many of these examples, appeal is made to explanatory chains. It suffices for knowledge if what explains my true belief also explains or is explained by the fact to which the belief refers, as long as a certain constraint on these chains is met. Each link in such chains must make later ones more probable. This constraint defeats some purported counter-examples that will not be considered here (see Goldman 1988, pp. 46–50), but its relevance is also clear in the case of knowledge from testimony mentioned earlier in discussing the issue of justification. A person may be justified in believing the testimony of another without any evidence of the other's expertise or sincerity, as long as there is no evidence that the testimony is likely to be false. Testimony can create its own justification, just as perception can, whether or not the testifier is herself justified in believing her own testimony. But this again simply contrasts justified true belief with knowledge, since one cannot transmit knowledge one does not have. Knowledge from testimony requires an explanatory chain in which the truth of the testimonial evidence enters ultimately into the best explanation for its being given and believed. If I am completely gullible and believe absolutely anything I hear, then I do not gain knowledge from testimony, just as if I see everything as red, then I do not know a red object when I see one. But the last two points imply a third, that a completely gullible person anywhere in the testimonial chain destroys knowledge in the later links. For each link, the fact that the belief was more likely because true must make its transmission more likely to be believed at later links, the constraint mentioned earlier. This does not prevent children from gaining or transmitting testimonial knowledge, since they tend to believe their parents, for example, more than they believe their peers (Schmitt 1999, p. 372).

This completes our brief account of the nature of knowledge. As we shall now see, it will prove to be highly suggestive for the task of determining the scope and structure of knowledge.

THE SCOPE OF KNOWLEDGE

In the first section we utilised intuitions about when knowledge is had in order to derive an account of its nature. This might seem to beg the question against the sceptic by guaranteeing that our criteria for knowledge are met for the most part. But we are not in fact assuming that scepticism is false. This is because we allow that purported cases of knowledge to which we appeal in analysing its nature can turn out under sceptical attack to be not genuine. Indeed, sceptics themselves must adopt the same procedure of analysis – first using ordinary intuitions to derive criteria – and then give us reasons for doubting that these criteria are really satisfied. Otherwise, they risk basing their sceptical attacks on an assumed analysis that is too demanding and so out of touch with our concept of knowledge. In that case we would not need to take them seriously. Here we will take them seriously by dismissing all claims that their doubts are necessarily misplaced.

Scepticism challenges us because our beliefs about the properties of real things transcend the evidence we have for those beliefs. Such evidence consists in the ways those things appear to us. But objective properties of real objects are what they are independently of our beliefs about them and the ways they appear to us. Thus, our beliefs are underdetermined by our evidence. There will be alternative possible explanations for all the evidence we have. If everything can seem exactly as it does to us and yet nothing be as we believe it to be, then how can we know that it is as we believe it to be? If all our evidence is compatible with alternative explanations of it, then how can we rule out all but one, indeed any, of those explanations? If knowledge is belief best explained by its truth, then how can we know we have knowledge when different explanations are compatible with all the evidence we have for our beliefs? How can we know that the explanatory chains end in the facts as we take them to be?

Sceptics dramatize this problem by presenting us with alternative scenarios or sceptical worlds in which everything appears to us as it does now, i.e. our experience remains exactly the same, and yet nothing in the world is as we take it to be. Descartes challenged us to show that we are not dreaming all that we currently experience, or that we are not being deceived by some powerful demon who causes us to have the experiences we do. Or, to take the contemporary version, suppose that we are brains in vats programmed by super scientists or computers to have exactly the experiences we do. We believe this scenario to be possible, since we believe that our experiences are immediately caused by happenings (neuronal firings) in our brains. How, then, could we know that it is not actual? If we cannot know that it is not actual, that we are not brains in vats, then it seems we cannot know that we have bodies surrounded by middle-sized objects with any of the properties we take them to have. Thus, the sceptic concludes, since his scenario is possible, we do not have any knowledge of real objects.

A recent trend among epistemologists who battle this sceptic is to grant that we do not know that we are not brains in vats, but then to argue that we do nevertheless retain ordinary knowledge of such things as the properties of middle-sized objects. This response is held to refute the brunt of the sceptic's argument while simultaneously showing the source of its plausibility, a goal now endorsed by anti-sceptical epistemologists as well. Both claims – that the sceptic's first premise must be granted, but his conclusion denied – are suggested by the counterfactual analysis of knowledge described in the first section. According to this account, we do not know we are not brains in vats because in the possible world in which we are, we do not believe we are (since everything appears as now). But this sceptic's world is assumed to be very distant from the actual world. It therefore does not affect the fact that in the closest possible worlds in which particular propositions now believed about ordinary objects are false, we do not believe them. Hence ordinary knowledge is retained despite the truth of the sceptic's premise and resultant plausibility of his argument.

There are nevertheless three crushing problems with this response to the sceptic. First, its dependence on the counterfactual account is itself problematic, since we saw earlier that this account is too strong, ruling out legitimate claims to knowledge. And, by its own lights, the response relies on the account in just the case in which it is most dubious, where our evaluation of a knowledge claim takes us to a distant possible world. Only in this way is the sceptic's premise endorsed. Second, the analysis implies that the sceptic's second, conditional premise (that if we do not know we are not brains in vats, then we do not know we are surrounded by middle-sized objects) is false, and it clearly seems to be true. If we do not know that we are not surrounded by a vat's clear liquid, how can we know that we are surrounded instead by tables and chairs? Third, and perhaps most important, in denying the sceptic's conclusion, the proponent of the counterfactual analysis simply assumes that the sceptic's world is a very distant one. But if, as the account admits, we cannot know that the sceptic's world is not actual, how could we possibly know that it is distant from the actual world? As an answer to the sceptic, this response simply begs the question. Even if accepted, it shows only that knowledge is possible, not that it is actual.

A yet more contemporary response, contextualism, builds upon the previous one by agreeing that we do not know that we do not occupy sceptical worlds even though we do retain knowledge in ordinary contexts. Contextualists differ from counterfactualists in holding that the sceptic's second premise is true also, as is their conclusion in the context of their argument (DeRose 1995). In the context of sceptical doubt, sceptical worlds such as that of the vatted brains become relevant alternatives that cannot be ruled out. And if they cannot be ruled out, then we do not retain knowledge of mundane facts with which they compete. But in ordinary contexts free from sceptical doubts, the sceptic's distant worlds are irrelevant, and our beliefs must vary with the presence or absence of the facts to which they refer only in close possible worlds. When judges of knowledge claims raise sceptical doubts, they raise the standards for evaluating beliefs; and when beliefs have to be sensitive to facts in the distant worlds of the sceptic, they cannot pass this unusual test. Recognition of such varying standards in different contexts of evaluation allows the contextualist to say that the sceptic's argument is sound but irrelevant to our ordinary knowledge claims. How better to show the plausibility of the sceptical position while defending the ordinary knower?

Despite this attraction, contextualism fares no better in the end than counter-factualism. It may improve on the latter by allowing that if we cannot know we are not brains in vats, then we cannot know that we are surrounded by tables and chairs. Once more, in the context of the doubt that the antecedent expresses, this conditional is held to be true. But the other problems facing counterfactualism plague contextualism too, and additional ones as well. First, the position still relies on evaluating beliefs in what it holds to be distant possible worlds, and we have seen that this demand is too strong in any context. Some of the most mundane truths that are easiest to know are false only in very distant possible worlds, where there is no telling what we would believe. The counterfactual account makes these the most difficult facts to know. Second, in defending ordinary knowledge the position once more simply assumes that the sceptic's worlds are distant while admitting that we cannot know they are not actual. This does not satisfy the demand to answer the sceptic by showing that we have knowledge. Third, there is the implausibility of the claim that we can destroy knowledge we have by simply thinking of sceptical alternatives. One unwelcome implication of this claim is that philosophers, who frequently entertain sceptical hypotheses, have so much less knowledge than their more fortunate, if more naive, counterparts in the real world. While ignorance may be bliss in some contexts, pursuing a profession that so systematically substitutes it for knowledge is probably not what young philosophy undergraduates have in mind. Contextualists who may be content to know so much less than anyone else nevertheless had better not advertise their position.

Can we then defend knowledge by rejecting the sceptic's first premise? Can we claim to know that we are not brains in vats? Can we show that the evidence we have from experience is evidence for the world as we take it to be, and not for the sceptic's worlds? How could we know or show this, when experience itself cannot differentiate between the world as we take it to be and the phenomenal world of a brain in a vat? One older answer favoured by some epistemologists is that we know this a priori, that its defence does not require any inductive argument since it *could* not be false. It is held that we *must* know it a priori precisely because experience in itself cannot distinguish these worlds and so cannot be the source of this knowledge. Defenders of this tradition give different but related explanations of how we have this a priori knowledge, of how we can know that the way something appears, for example, is *necessarily* evidence for how we take it to be.

Many of the arguments here begin from an account of how we learn to understand the terms in our language, how we learn to use them correctly or to interpret their use by others (Hamlyn 1970, ch. 3). If we learn to pick out tables, for example, by how they appear to us, how they look and feel, then it must be correct that whatever looks and feels to us continuously in those ways must be tables, or at least that such looks and feels are necessarily evidence for the presence of tables. In the language game in which we apply the term 'table' to tables, such ways of appearing are criteria for the correct use of this term. We therefore cannot all be mistaken in this use based on these experiences any more than we could all be mistaken in the way we play chess. Tables are whatever we call tables based on correct application of the term, and correct application is determined by the agreed upon criteria, in this case certain ways of appearing. Thus, these ways of appearing are necessarily evidence for tables and for the properties that define them to be tables. We can neither use the term correctly without accepting these criteria nor interpret its use by others without typically ascribing true beliefs about tables to them. Likewise, of course, for other middle-sized objects and their properties.

Is this argument sound? What it really establishes is only the way we must initially conceive of things. Once we develop the notion of objects whose properties are independent of our experiences and beliefs, once we develop theories of how these properties cause our experiences, and once we see that our experiences can mislead us as to the real properties that cause them, the possibility of wholesale error becomes intelligible. In fact this possibility is entailed by the notion of independence that defines the concept of realism about objects and their properties. That real properties are independent of the ways they appear and the beliefs they cause means that these appearances and beliefs can be misleading and false. Once we recognise the possibility of wholesale error on our part, we need not necessarily ascribe mostly true beliefs to others (although we will ordinarily do so). If, for example, we were to see some brains in vats and understood their situation, we would not ascribe to them mostly true beliefs about the objects around them. To interpret the language of others, we need to explain their utterances, but truth of the beliefs expressed need not necessarily enter into the majority of these explanations. Nor will we explain the brains' utterances as true of phenomenal objects instead of false of real ones, since they will have the same concept of real objects as we do and will intend to refer to them and their properties. What we and the brains take to be evidence for the objective properties of real objects cannot dictate what those properties are. Our shared concept of chess may determine the nature of that game, but this is what distinguishes games from reality.

Thus, premises about how we learn and interpret our language do not show that the evidence we have for our beliefs about real objects must necessarily be evidence for their objective properties as we take them to be. Is this notion of criteria as necessary evidence short of entailment even coherent? If we do not do away with real objects and their properties by reducing them to experiences or appearances, can the latter nevertheless necessarily be evidence for the former? To say that appearances are necessarily evidence for real properties is to say that they are evidence in all possible worlds. But in a world of brains in vats in which the brains were informed or knew of their own situation, their experiences would not be evidence of objects as we take them to be. This would be true of any sceptical world believed to be such by its victims. Such worlds are possible. The sceptic's descriptions of them do not involve logical contradictions. We could even grant that we could not *all* be brains in vats, but that would leave open the possibility that any one of us is and could possibly be informed of this by our programmers. Thus, there is no necessary connection between experiential evidence and the real properties of objects.

Do we have *any* a priori knowledge of reality, as opposed to that which reflects only definitions of terms, including logical connectives and operators? Is there any a priori insight into the necessary structure of reality, knowledge of what is real but not contingent, that needs no inductive confirmation? Well-worn examples that seem to express such knowledge include the claims that nothing can be red and green all over and that, if A is taller than B, and B is taller than C, then A is taller than C (Bonjour 1998, pp. 100–3). It turns out, however, that such examples express lack of experience or imagination, instead of a priori insight into necessary truth. When I was much younger and clothing styles were much different, I owned an iridescent raincoat that looked red and green (as well as tan) all over. Whether the effect was achieved with discrete red and green threads is irrelevant here, since on most accounts of colour, whatever looks a certain colour to normal observers in normal conditions is that colour.

I must admit that I have never seen three people or objects that disconfirm the example regarding tallness, but imagine the following possible world. Imagine a world with only three rods and one observer (you). When rod A is visually compared to B, A appears to be taller; when B is visually paired with C, B appears taller; but when C is compared to A, C appears taller. When you attempt to place all three in the same visual field, you cannot take them all in by sight. One always disappears out of the visual field. This world is possible: in fact, it is not so unlike the world of quantum mechanics, with its indeterminacy and measurement problem. And the world described seems not to be a world in which the supposed necessary truth about tallness holds true. Hence it is not a necessary truth (unless we simply stipulate a definition of 'tallness' in which only a transitive relation will bear that term).

Even if we are not so sceptical of necessary truths about reality, the relation between appearing and being a real property of objects seems not to be necessary. If we are to answer sceptical challenges to our beliefs about that relation, we therefore require an inductive argument, broadly construed. We have looked at the implications for the sceptical argument of the counterfactual analysis of knowledge. It is time to use the analysis we endorsed, that knowledge is belief best explained (in significant part) by truth. Here the question becomes whether the ways we are appeared to in experience are better explained by objects and their properties as we take them to be than by sceptical hypotheses such as the programming of brains in vats.

It will be objected to this approach right off that we cannot construe our beliefs about physical objects and their properties as a theory that best explains the patterns within appearances because we cannot even formulate such patterns without appeal to physical space and objects. We learn the language of appearing only after learning to hedge our claims about real properties, which we immediately and naturally ascribe without inference. More important, it is claimed, we know what experiences we have had and will have only by reference to locations in physical space among physical objects. Thus, to even formulate the supposed data we must presuppose the 'theory' that is supposed to explain the data, which 'theory' therefore does not require this explanatory justification.

The former point about learning, however, is again irrelevant to the question of justification, or demonstrating knowledge. Even if we must conceive of physical properties first, that does not show that there are such properties or that they are as we take them to be. Our evidence for our beliefs about them still consists in the ways they appear, although we don't initially conceive it that way. The latter point about formulating the data is first of all debatable. While we cannot translate statements about physical properties into statements about appearings, it is not so clear that we could not learn to weaken all claims about objects to claims about appearances, although doing so would be very cumbersome and awkward. Instead of talking of seeing an unsupported object fall, we could talk of a visual experience as of an unsupported object followed by a visual experience as of an object falling. But even if such reductions would not be universally possible for a skillful language user, this still only indicates a conceptual necessity, the way we must express ourselves. It still does not imply that the ways we conceive objects are the ways they are independent of our conceptions, and it still does not preclude the attempt to show that real properties as we conceive them best explain the ways they appear to us.

That physical objects and their properties do provide the best explanation we have for the ways we are appeared to seems easily established. Appeal to real physical objects first of all explains more deeply than do explanations for particular appearances in terms of regularities within experience itself. The former can explain the regularities themselves that are otherwise taken to be ultimate. And explanations in terms of physical objects and their properties are also superior to sceptical explanatory hypotheses such as programmes for brains in vats or deceptive Cartesian demons. The agreement of the different sense modalities on the qualities and dimensions of objects, for example, strongly suggests a realist explanation, and of course we also use the realist model successfully to predict future experiences. The physical realist picture explains both how physical objects interact with each other and, at least in part, how they cause experiences (by reflecting light, emitting sound waves, and so on). No such predictions or explanations are forthcoming from the brain in vat or evil demon hypotheses, which are therefore ad hoc and useless additions. The only way they have any explanatory power is by being parasitic on physical object explanations: the demon or programmer of brains must make it seem as if we are surrounded by interacting physical objects (Vogel 1990). Not only does this add nothing to the explanations available without these additions; it also raises natural but unanswerable questions, such as why the programmers or demon would deceive us in this way.

If the commonsense and scientific explanations for our experience are superior to the sceptical hypotheses, does this show that we know that we are not brains in vats? When a hypothesis is put forth only to explain certain data, and when a superior explanation is later offered, we have some reason to disbelieve the former hypothesis and the entities it posits solely for explanatory purposes. When the demon theory of disease was replaced by the germ theory, rational people ceased to believe in disease-causing demons. In that case, however, there was additional evidence against the existence of demons – the fact that no one has ever seen one (except perhaps in a highly irrational frame of mind). The best explanation for the latter fact is that there are none. In the brain in the vats case, we would not see ourselves as such if we were, and so we lack that additional evidence. Unlike the usual case of knowledge of negative existential propositions (propositions that certain things do not exist), we have no evidence against the existence of the brains (while also lacking evidence for their existence). It is this, we can claim, that explains the plausibility of the sceptical argument, while leaving it open to us to defend our knowledge claims against that argument via inference to the best explanation.

Two problems remain for this inference as an answer to the sceptic. The more tractable one is that an inference to the best available explanation at a given time is not necessarily an inference to the best explanation *tout court*, so that even if we can accept the latter as producing the true explanation, we cannot so easily accept the former as doing so. We need additional reason to think that the available explanations exhaust the field of plausible ones. Here that demand seems easily met, however. There does not seem to be the remotest possibility of an explanation for our experience being developed that rivals that which appeals to physical objects and the scientific theories of physical reality.

The far more difficult problem is that an inference to the best explanation defeats the sceptic only if we can defend the principle that underlies such inference against sceptical challenge. We must be able to show that what appears to us to be a best explanation is likely to be true. In general, the most difficult part of any anti-sceptical epistemology will be to defend the fundamental principles of reasoning or the basic sources through which we seek knowledge. We have seen that we can defend perception as a source of knowledge through an inference to the best explanation. Similar arguments will be available for memory, knowledge of other minds, and ordinary induction (for example, the best explanation for many coherent memory impressions will appeal to earlier veridical perception or testimony; the best explanation for an observed ratio of instances in a class may well be a deeper or universal regularity, and so on). But this leaves the formidable task of defending the principle of inference on the basis of which these other sources of knowledge can be defended.

In indicating the nature of this defence, we must note first that we cannot know a priori that such fundamental cognitive principles as inference to the best explanation lead to truth. This is not a necessary truth, since sometimes such inference fails; and whether it is generally reliable depends on the type of brains we have and on our relation to our environment. Nor can it be necessary that inference to the best explanation is likely to be reliable. It is hard to imagine how it could be necessary that anything is likely (contrast Bonjour 1998, p. 214). In terms of the possible worlds model of probability, this would mean that in all galaxies or groups of possible worlds, the number of worlds in which the proposition in question is true exceeds the number in which it is false. But how could that be necessary and how could we know that it was: what is to keep the worlds in which the proposition is false from clustering?

In the absence of an a priori defence of inference to the best explanation and other fundamental cognitive principles and practices, we would require an inductive or empirical argument. One promising approach might be to argue that for creatures with such limited physical capacities and instincts as humans, basic cognitive capacities would have been naturally selected for their capacity to provide information or truth necessary to survival. It is plausible that humans would have had to infer correctly the proximity of predators from tracks or predator noises, for example, in order to survive, since they could not outrun them or otherwise protect themselves. There are three major obstacles that a generalised version of such an argument would have to overcome, however. First, there is the question whether, in the environment in which our brains evolved or were selected for their cognitive capacities, truth was in general the key determinant of fitness or utility. Second, a natural next question is whether an affirmative answer to the first one suggests that inferences to explanations far removed from the environment in which natural selection took place continue to be truth preserving. And third, there is the problem of circularity in the argument.

We can only very briefly indicate answers to the first two questions here, since we will pay more attention to the third, which will introduce the topic of the structure of knowledge. In regard to the first question, it must be admitted that systematic distortion can be utile and even fitness enhancing, as when the exaggeration of colour contrasts enables us to see object boundaries more easily (not to mention that the perception of colour in itself may be a systematic distortion of objective reality). But such systematic distortions seem to occur precisely to enable us to obtain more vital veridical information about the environment, for example about the locations of various objects. It remains hard to see how creatures like us could have survived if our basic cognitive capacities did not generate true information about our environments. We must know the means necessary to our ends, including survival, as well as the consequences of our actions, and all this is a matter of inferences as well as perception and memory.

As for inferences far removed from contexts in which survival is at stake, we can ask generally whether there is reason to suspect that a cognitive capacity that produces truth in one context will cease doing so in another. More specifically, we can separate everyday inferences that can be later verified directly in perception from those which produce the more remote products of scientific theory. The former inferences are demonstrated to be true if perception is accepted as a source of knowledge, but the charge of circularity will be raised again, to be addressed shortly. Scientific inferences not only take explanations to deeper levels, but seek to correct for distorting subjective inputs into earlier, commonsense explanations. This gives us more instead of less reason to believe in the truth of such explanations, although there might be less reason here to believe that the best of available explanations at a given time is the best overall, hence the true explanation.

The problem of circularity can be pressed at every stage of this suggested defence of inference to the best explanation as a basic cognitive principle. First, it was suggested that brains with such cognitive capacities to provide truths necessary to survival were probably products of natural selection. But theory of natural selection, indeed appeal to the physical environment, is itself legitimated via inference to the best explanation. The attempt to legitimate a principle by appeal to the products of its own use is circular. Second, we noted that many such inferences can be confirmed by later perceptions, giving direct evidence of their truth-preserving nature. But once more perception itself is certified as a source of knowledge only via inference to the best explanation for the ways things perceptually appear, again using the very cognitive principle that perception is supposed to help legitimate.

Addressing this problem of circularity takes us to the question of the structure of knowledge, to which we now turn.

THE STRUCTURE OF KNOWLEDGE

In responding to the charge of circularity, we should note first that the argument defending inference to the best explanation does not beg the question against the sceptic in the way that it would if one of its premises simply stated that the principle of inference is sound or truth preserving. Any principle, indeed any conclusion, could be 'defended' in this way, since any premise implies itself. Here the principle of inference was used, not mentioned, in its own defence. Such use does not trivially result in self-support, as the sceptic might suggest. We do not normally dream, for example, that dreaming is a reliable source of knowledge or hallucinate that hallucination is reliable. In the case of inference to the best explanation, it is not a foregone conclusion that it will be self-supporting, and the argument from evolution is controversial even if sound. But the principle, when applied with critical care, does iterate, in that it is more explanatorily coherent to believe that it leads to truth. It is doubtful whether there are any obviously unsound principles that iterate it this way or cohere with other fundamental sources of knowledge.

This coherence with other principles or sources is also significant even if circular. Crystal balls might predict their own reliability, but their predictions fail to be regularly confirmed by perceptions. This kind of mutual support adds significantly to the self-support of the principle, since it strongly suggests a common cause in truth. Why should percepts confirm earlier inferences if they do not reflect the same facts believed? The more seemingly independent facts that an explanation unifies, the more reason there is for accepting the explanation. Of course, a non-sceptical answer to the question just raised simply applies an inference to the best explanation again. But the near ubiquitous nature of the principle does not more firmly support a sceptical attitude toward it, although it does make more clear that any defence of it will have to be circular. While we have not relied heavily on necessary truths, it is worth pointing out here that it is a necessary truth that basic or fundamental epistemic principles can be supported only by themselves or their products and other fundamental principles (otherwise they would not be fundamental). We cannot escape the totality of our cognitive resources to verify that they lead to truth. Such confirmation can come only from within the circle of these resources. In the case of inference to the best explanation, which is involved in the legitimisation of perception, memory, and simple induction, and in turn supported by them, the circle is certainly not narrow. Can we demand more of the epistemologist than the demonstration of such broad coherence in the set of our epistemic beliefs?

Circular reasoning is certainly not always vicious. We assess the skill of a tennis player, for example, by noting his execution of many skilful shots. But we judge a shot to be skilful and not merely lucky because it is made by a skilful player. The same shot made by a beginner would be just lucky. The reasoning is circular but sound and informative nonetheless (compare Sosa and Van Cleve 2001). That inference to the best explanation is supported by its own products makes for a circle, but not a vicious or self-defeating one. It is true that if the principle of inference did not lead to truth, then its being more explanatorily coherent to believe that it does would not seem to lend it much useful support. But in the absence of knowledge of the antecedent, the coherence of the principle with its products and with other basic epistemic sources can be seen to give us reason to accept it, just as inconsistency or incoherence with other principles would give us reason to reject a principle.

Sceptics, however, will have a strong rejoinder to this response to the charge of circularity. They will point out that perfect coherence in a set of beliefs, including epistemic beliefs, even together with truth, does not suffice for knowledge. Brains in vats may have coherent sets of beliefs, and when some of those beliefs about objects outside the vats also happen to be true, this does not give them knowledge. A coherent set of beliefs describes some possible world, but not necessarily the actual one. If we took the entire set of a person's beliefs and transferred them to another person in a different set of circumstances, the set would be equally coherent, but would contain much less knowledge (Sosa 1991, p. 203). It is clear once more from these examples that, in order to constitute knowledge, a coherent set of beliefs must be anchored to the actual world or surrounding environment in the right way.

Perceptual input in itself is insufficient to provide the required anchor. Such input could be provided by a deceiving demon or by the programmers of the brains in vats, and a complete madman could weirdly process perceptual input so as to make it cohere with his other mad beliefs. Such input and such processing would not help in the acquisition of knowledge even if it occasionally resulted in true belief. The perceptual experience must be of the right kind, and it must result in the right kind of belief to be of use in acquiring or demonstrating knowledge. But we cannot simply check this experience itself or the causal chains by which it produces beliefs in order to confirm that it and they are of the right kinds. The causal chains are largely inaccessible, and the experience must be conceptualised correctly in order to be of epistemic use. Experience itself need not be conceptualised (or it could not be the source of concepts), but until it is, it can play only an inaccessible causal role. To be of use in demonstrating knowledge, experiential input must be conceptualised in such a way that the best explanations for the beliefs it produces appeal to the truth of those beliefs. It will be clear that the madman's beliefs fail this test from the fact that they fail to cohere with the beliefs of others, despite their internal coherence.

In our own case, in order to demonstrate knowledge we must defend our beliefs against sceptical challenge. Normally we defend a belief by citing evidence for it that is part of an explanatory chain leading to the fact believed. We do so for simple perceptual beliefs as well. For example, I defend my belief that there is a red object before me by noting that I am appeared to redly (but not seemingly by red beams of light). The claim that there is indeed a red appearance that explains my belief in the red object can be defended not only by inferring it as the explanation for that belief, but also directly by appeal to the belief that I am appeared to in that way (which is not to imply that I normally infer the belief about the object from the belief about the appearance). But here I arrive at a point in the demonstration where I no longer defend my belief by appeal to evidence or an explanatory chain. The best explanation for my belief that I am appeared to redly is simply that I am so appeared to, that 'red' is the correct concept or term in my vocabulary to apply to this experience, that I apply this term consistently to this type of experience. The latter is all that is required for the truth of my belief, and the only evidence for its being the case is my having formed the belief itself.

These beliefs about certain appearances form the foundations for the demonstration of knowledge in two related senses. First, they are shown to constitute knowledge without appeal to evidence or coherence with other beliefs. Second, they make up a set of most certain beliefs which with others must cohere, picking out one set of coherent beliefs as true of the actual world of the subject. Once this anchor is in place, it is doubtful that there are equally coherent but incompatible sets of beliefs with equal explanatory coherence, and the main objection to demonstrating knowledge by showing coherence in a set of beliefs falls away. In clarifying the sense in which these beliefs are foundations, several caveats must also be mentioned.

First, the relevant beliefs about appearances are not infallible, in contrast to their characterization by traditional foundationalism. In order to pick out patterns in experience from which objective properties can be inferred as causes in the demonstration of knowledge, they must refer to properties that are instantiated on different occasions and in different objects. While 'appears red' (as opposed to 'appears to be red') refers to a phenomenal property, a property picked out by what it is like to experience it, it is not defined ostensively on each occasion as referring only to whatever property is present in the visual field. A belief employing the latter ostensive concept might be infallible, but it would not be of any epistemic use. Beliefs in reinstantiated or reinstantiable properties are always fallible, since the concepts they employ can be misapplied or applied inconsistently. But for certain properties that are naturally salient in experience, the best explanation for beliefs about how they appear will appeal only to the truth of these beliefs, as indicated earlier. The second caveat is that this will be true *only* for beliefs about how these naturally salient properties appear, for beliefs about red but not about C-sharp. The best explanation for my belief that I am appeared to C-sharply appeals to my musical training, and not simply to the fact that I am so appeared to. Third, it is not necessary in order to serve the function of foundations that the defence of every other belief trace a line back to one or more of these beliefs about appearances. Knowledge can have a web-like instead of linear structure as long as it is anchored to the world at key points.

CONCLUSION

At the end of the day, sceptics and non-sceptics can both stand their ground. Non-sceptics will hold that a set of coherent beliefs anchored to the world via suitable foundations, generated by a set of epistemic principles that are supported by their products and by each other, such that the best explanations for the beliefs being held appeal to their truth, constitutes the best indication we can have of knowledge of the real world. Non-sceptics will point out that nothing said earlier precludes the possibility that we are brains in vats or systematically deceived about the nature of reality. It remains possible that our fundamental epistemic principles and sources provide only a distorted view of the world independent of them. And the only argument to the contrary remains circular. The only surefire way to avoid these sceptical possibilities is to give up this notion of an independent world or the idea that we can intelligibly aim at knowledge of its properties. But if explanatory coherence among beliefs includes depth of explanations, and if appeal to real properties explains more deeply than explanations limited to the domain of experience, then this is not a viable epistemological option.

Absent this guarantee, we certainly have reason from within our world view for thinking that our epistemic principles and practices are sound and provide us with knowledge of the real world. But such reason must remain relative to those principles that determine what counts as a reason and so cannot convince the sceptic who will reject any principle that lacks independent support. Such fundamental and seemingly irreconcilable disagreement may be disappointing, but it keeps philosophy alive.

EXERCISES

1 Does contextualism solve the problems that face the counterfactual analysis of knowledge? Does the explanatory analysis fare any better?
2 Do we know that we are not brains in vats? So, how can we know this? If not, can we nevertheless have knowledge of the ordinary objects that we take to surround us?
3 Can fundamental epistemic principles such as inference to the best explanation be defended? How? Can their defence satisfy the sceptic?
4 Does knowledge have foundations? If so, what is their nature? If not, doesn't the possibility of equally coherent but incompatible sets of beliefs defeat any claims to knowledge?

BIBLIOGRAPHY

Bonjour, Laurence (1998) *In Defense of Pure Reason*, Cambridge: Cambridge University Press.
DeRose, Keith (1995) 'Solving the sceptical problem', *The Philosophical Review* **104**: 1–52.
Feldman, Richard and Conee, Earl (1998) 'The generality problem for reliabilism', *Philosophical Studies* **89**: 1–29.
Gettier, Edmund (1963) 'Is justified true belief knowledge?', *Analysis* **23**: 121–3.
Goldman, Alan (1988) *Empirical Knowledge*, Berkeley, CA: University of California Press.
Goldman, Alvin (1967) 'A causal theory of knowing', *The Journal of Philosophy* **64**: 355–72.
Goldman, Alvin (1986) *Epistemology and Cognition*, Cambridge, MA: Harvard University Press.
Hamlyn, D.W. (1970) *The Theory of Knowledge*, Garden City, NY: Anchor.
Lehrer, Keith (2000) *Theory of Knowledge*, Boulder, CO: Westview.
Nozick, Robert (1981) *Philosophical Explanations*, Cambridge, MA: Harvard University Press.
Schmitt, Frederick (1999) 'Social Epistemology' in John Greco and Ernest Sosa (eds) *The Blackwell Guide to Epistemology*, Oxford: Blackwell.
Sosa, Ernest (1991) *Knowledge in Perspective*, Cambridge: Cambridge University Press.
Sosa, Ernest and Van Cleve, James (2001) 'Thomas Reid' in Steven Emmanuel (ed.) *The Modern Philosophers: From Descartes to Nietzsche*, Oxford: Blackwell.
Vogel, Jonathan (1990) 'Cartesian scepticism and inference to the best explanation', *The Journal of Philosophy* **87**: 658–66.

FURTHER READING

Alcoff, Linda Martin (ed.) (1998) *Epistemology: The Big Questions*, Oxford: Blackwell. A collection of influential essays on the major topics in epistemology.
Alston, William (1993) *The Reliability of Sense Perception*, Ithaca, NY: Cornell University Press. An excellent discussion of the circularity problem for the justification of fundamental sources of knowledge.
Audi, Robert (1998) *Epistemology*, London: Routledge. A comprehensive introduction, containing discussions of the analysis of knowledge and its major sources.

Baergen, Ralph (1995) *Contemporary Epistemology*, Fort Worth, TX: Harcourt Brace. An introductory text with a good discussion of the internalism–externalism debate.

Dancy, Jonathan and Sosa, Ernest (eds) (1993) *A Companion to Epistemology*, Oxford: Blackwell. A comprehensive reference work with brief entries on numerous topics.

Goldman, Alvin (1999) *Knowledge in a Social World*, Oxford: Clarendon. A discussion of testimony and other topics in social epistemology.

Moser, Paul, Mulder, Dwayne and Trout, J.D. (1998) *The Theory of Knowledge*, Oxford: Oxford University Press. A contemporary introduction with emphasis on inference to the best explanation in the answer to scepticism.

2

METAPHYSICS

Michael Jubien

INTRODUCTION

Metaphysics is the part of philosophy that treats the concept of *existence* (or *being*) along with a host of related concepts. As we all know, remarkably different sorts of entities have been thought to exist. To mention a few: stones, tables, dogs, people, unicorns, phlogiston, quarks, spacetime, events, obligations, numbers, properties, propositions, thoughts, minds, souls, ghosts, and God. It's hard to think of any significant feature these entities would have in common, if they all really did exist, beyond simply *existing*. Such dramatic differences are reflected in different sorts of metaphysical questions, and metaphysics itself may be seen as divided into rather different (but generally related) areas or topics. In this introduction we will touch lightly upon a few examples just to give the reader a feel for scope of the subject. We will then look at three central topics in somewhat greater detail. That should give the reader a better sense of how metaphysics is actually conducted.

One striking difference among the (supposed) entities on our list is that some of them would evidently be physical in nature, located in space and time, while others – so-called *abstract* entities – seemingly would not. Many metaphysical questions concern physical entities and relations among them. We normally take for granted the idea that physical *events* occur, and that they somehow consist in physical entities interacting with each other. But it isn't easy to give a plausible analysis of the notion of an event, and this is a good example of a metaphysical question. We may gain a sense of the difficulty of the question as follows. First, consider the simple idea that an event is just the totality of what goes on in any specific region of spacetime. This is promising, but it doesn't actually square with our ordinary thinking, which allows that more than one event may occur in exactly the same spatiotemporal region. For example, a ball may be both *rotating* and *heating up* at the same time and place. As we usually think, these would be different events despite having the same spatiotemporal location. So it appears that we cannot correctly view an event simply as the contents of a specific part of spacetime. But then what *is* a physical event?

Events play an important role in another deep (and famous) metaphysical question. Built into our everyday thinking is the idea that some events *cause* other events to occur. But, as David Hume insisted, we never actually *perceive* any 'necessary connection' between events – what we perceive is simply one event followed by (and perhaps physically contiguous with) another. This is in sharp contrast with other physical relations, like motion, which we regularly perceive. So, is genuine causal efficacy really built into the physical world, as we normally presume, or is it just something we imagine to be present? It could simply be that we are psychologically incapable of repeatedly seeing events of one sort followed by events of another without thinking there is some necessary connection between them. On the other hand, if genuine causation really is embedded in the world, then finding a reasonable account of this elusive relation is a pressing philosophical challenge.

Another famous metaphysical question concerns entities whose existence we take for granted and also take very seriously: ourselves. Many philosophers have advocated the 'dualist' position that a person's mind (or soul) is a special non-physical entity, while others have held the 'materialist' view that we are simply physical organisms of a certain sort. These philosophers either view the mind as a physical part of the body, or else deny that there really are minds and try to explain the mental phenomena that prompt the postulation of minds some other way. This famous metaphysical issue is called the mind–body problem. It is so important and widely discussed that, along with a cluster of closely related topics, it has assumed the status of a branch of philosophy in its own right: the philosophy of mind.

Another question we might ask about the list is whether anything on it would exist *of necessity*. Certainly we usually think that a thing like a dog or a table owes its existence to sheer circumstance, and would not have existed at all if things had been somewhat different. And of course we also think that things really could have been somewhat different, even very different. On the other hand, necessary existence is part of the common conception of God. More generally, it is hard to imagine that anything not located in spacetime could be contingent. This is because the notion of contingency seems to involve coming into existence, and this is something that, by their very nature, entities not located in spacetime could not do.

Many philosophers hold that certain kinds of entities really do exist, but are not located in space or time. Two frequently encountered examples are *numbers* and *properties*. On the property view, for example, *being red* and *being a dog* are non-physical entities that have no spatiotemporal locations. Further, on this view, even if there had been no physical matter at all, there would still be properties like *having mass* and *being physical* (and even *being a dog*). These properties would have no *instances* in these imagined circumstances, just as the property of *being a ghost* presumably has no instances in our actual circumstances. *Properties*, on this 'Platonic' conception, would exist necessarily, and so would be no different in this respect from God (as God is often conceived).

The *modal* concepts of necessity and possibility are not restricted to questions of existence. We generally think that an ordinary thing like a dog or a table could have been different in many ways far less drastic than failing to exist. The dog could have been fatter, or better trained. The table might have been scratched, or polished. On the other hand, the dog could not have been a table, or a cyclotron. It's apparently *necessary* that the dog is an animal, not an inanimate object. But exactly what do these assertions of possibility and necessity mean? They're very different from *nonmodal* claims, which we're generally able to verify more or less by direct inspection. Whether the table is scratched is something we can settle by looking at it. But how do we determine that the (presently unscratched) table *could have been scratched* (at this very moment)? We certainly don't decide this by looking at it. And we certainly do take it to be obviously true. But thinking it's obvious doesn't settle the question of what it *means*. (Many of the deepest philosophical questions arise from things we normally take to be obvious. The question of causal efficacy mentioned above is an example. Another is the meaning of '2 + 2 = 4'.)

Analysing or otherwise explaining these modal notions is a pressing project in contemporary metaphysics. Its importance is due in large part to the fact that many other fundamental notions in widely different areas of philosophy are clearly modal in nature. The notion of causal efficacy is a good example. That events of type A *cause* events of type B appears to entail that it is somehow necessary that if a type-A event occurs, then it is followed by a type-B event. A very different example is provided by the notion of *moral responsibility*. We normally think that a person isn't morally responsible for having done something unless it was possible for that person not to have done it.

A final example inspired by our list is the general problem of *ontology*. Which of these items really do exist, and what are their essential natures? The problem is especially acute for abstract entities since we are unable to detect and inspect them directly. This has made it very difficult for some philosophers to accept abstract entities in the first place, and it has led others to hold that these entities don't exist in the same sense of the term that applies to dogs and tables. Despite these doubts and qualifications, the case for postulating entities like numbers or properties is logically on a par with the case for postulating entities like quarks in physics. In both cases, entities we cannot perceive provide the basis for a theory that explains phenomena that we can perceive. Such entities are 'theoretical' in the sense that they are asserted to exist in a theory, and the success of the theory is the best evidence for their existence that we can hope to find. Of course, if they really do exist, then their existence is just as genuine as that of things we perceive or otherwise experience and accept without theoretical support. Certain contemporary theories of particle physics, as typically formulated, are apparently committed not only to quarks, but also to numbers. If numbers really are indispensable in such theories, and these theories really do explain observable phenomena, then this should be viewed as significant evidence not only for the quarks, but also for the numbers.

In this introductory section we have indicated only a few of the topics that metaphysicians treat. The ones mentioned are closely related to the original list of possible entities and to the basic question of the existence of such entities. In fact, the nature of the concept of existence itself – so easily taken for granted – is an underlying metaphysical question of the most fundamental kind. Further topics of great importance include: identity, the nature of things (and substances), time (and spacetime), truth, freedom and determinism, and whether any genuine facts are specifically moral in nature. The topics mentioned so far of course do not exhaust the rich realm of metaphysics. We now turn to three very fundamental ontological topics that happen to have important mutual relations.

IDENTITY AND CONSTITUTION

In this section we will consider a famous metaphysical puzzle. Suppose there is a clay statue on an otherwise empty table before us. Let's imagine that it's a statue of a horse and rider. Then it's true that there is a statue on the table, and it's also true that there is a piece of clay on the table. Are the statue and the piece of clay just one physical thing, or are they two? Most people would say they are just one thing – a thing that (like just about anything) admits of different descriptions. So let's call this the 'Common Sense View.' It certainly has initial appeal. But we'll soon see that there is an important principle that appears to undermine the Common Sense View. To make matters worse, this principle draws its support directly from common sense.

The claim that the statue and the piece of clay are just one thing is sometimes expressed by saying that the statue *is* (or: *is identical with*) the piece of clay, or that the statue and the piece of clay are *identical*. Now, although the words 'is' and 'identical' are in fact often used in other ways, in this context they are being used to express a special *relation* that philosophers call *identity*. It is a matter of definition that the identity relation *always* holds between any entity and itself (no matter what that entity may be like), and also never holds between any entity and any *other* entity. (Mathematicians often express identity by using the familiar symbol '=', which they call the *identity* or *equality sign*.) It should be clear that if a thing x is identical to a thing y in the present sense of the term, so that the identity relation holds between x and y, then x and y are just one thing (and never two).

The principle that threatens the Common Sense View concerns the identity relation. It's called the principle of the *indiscernibility of identicals*, and we may state it as follows: (For any entities x and y) if x is identical to y, then whatever is true of x is also true of y and whatever is true of y is true of x. Alternatively: if x is identical to y, then for any property P, x has P if and only if y has P. And yet more compactly: if x is identical to y, then x and y have exactly the same properties. It is important to notice that this principle should not be confused with the 'converse' principle, that if x and y have exactly the same properties, then x is identical to y. The principle of the indiscernibility of identicals is sometimes called *Leibniz' Law*, and we will abbreviate it by 'LL'.

Although most people never have occasion to assert or even to reflect on LL in this very general form, it is nevertheless deeply embedded in our commonsense way of thinking about the world, and we rely on it tacitly in everyday life. To see this, notice first that LL is equivalent to the claim that if a thing x has a property that a thing y does not have, then x is not identical with y. It is this form of the principle that often underlies everyday reasoning. For example, suppose you and a friend see someone in the middle distance who looks a lot like another friend, Sue. You ask, 'Is that Sue?' and your friend replies, 'It can't be – Sue never wears a hat.' Your friend, in effect, has reasoned that since the person you now see has a property – *wearing a hat* – that (he believes) Sue doesn't have, it follows that the person you see isn't Sue. Given that he's right about Sue's dress habits, this reasoning is impeccable. In essence, it is an application of LL in a specific case.

This form of reasoning may often have very important consequences. For example, it might be used to exonerate a defendant in a murder case if his blood type or eye colour (etc.) didn't fit with facts presumed to have been established about the real killer. Given that the various factual claims were beyond dispute, the reasoning would again be impeccable, and really just a matter of common sense.

We may also argue from common sense directly in favour of LL, as follows. Suppose the principle is in fact false. Then some x and y are such that x is identical with y, but x has some property, say P, that y doesn't have. But since x is identical with y, x and y are just one thing. Therefore, there is some one thing that both has and does not have the property P. This is a contradiction. So the assumption that the principle is false leads directly to a contradiction. It follows that the principle is true after all. There is nothing even remotely suspicious about this argument. It is evidently an informal but entirely rigorous proof of the principle – one that relies only on simple logical steps accepted by common sense.

We have now seen that LL often underlies everyday reasoning, and we've also seen that it admits of a simple proof. We have ample reason to accept the principle in what follows.

Back to the statue and the piece of clay. Common sense says they're just one thing, they're identical. Common sense also endorses LL. If we accept both, then it follows that the statue and the piece of clay have exactly the same properties. But consider this. Suppose the piece of clay had been shaped like a sphere instead of shaped like a horse and rider. The sculptor might have taken the original blob of clay and simply worked it into a sphere instead of undertaking the more difficult task of producing a statue of a horse and rider. Certainly this might have happened. It just didn't. But if it had happened, that would be a situation in which the piece of clay existed but the statue of the horse and rider did not. The piece of clay would have had a shape different from its actual shape, but that is entirely beside the point, which is simply that the piece of clay would have existed and the statue would not have existed.

It therefore appears that something is true about the piece of clay – namely, that it *might have been spherical* – that *isn't* true about the statue. To put it a little differently, the piece of clay apparently has a property – *being possibly spherical* – that the statue does not have. But then LL should deliver the conclusion that the piece of clay and the statue aren't identical after all, that they are two things, not one.

It now looks very much like our ordinary ways of thinking about ordinary objects are paradoxical. It looks like we have to choose between Leibniz' Law and the idea that the statue and the piece of clay are identical. But we apparently have a clear proof of Leibniz' Law. Should we therefore resolve the puzzle by declaring that here is a case in which there are two physical objects in exactly the same spatiotemporal location, despite our original thinking?

Let's take a little time to consider some problems that arise for the two-object view. We begin with a dilemma. Are the 'corresponding' smaller parts of the statue (S) and the piece of clay (C) identical with each other or not? Neither answer will seem satisfactory.

Suppose we say *yes*. Then, for example, any individual molecule that is part of S is also part of C, and vice versa. (This is already very odd, for how can a single bunch of specific molecules comprise two different things at the same time?) Also, the rather large part of S that we would describe as 'the horse' is a part of C. Now let's fix on a very large part of S, say all of it except for a specific surface molecule, M. Call this part L. L, of course, is just an aggregation of molecules, related to each other in a certain specific way. Since L isn't all of either S or C, it is also a part of C. Notice that although L isn't a statue (since there's only one statue in the general region) it certainly might have been a statue. The molecule M might have adhered to the sculptor's hand instead of becoming an integral part of the statue. Now, suppose this had happened. Then there would have been a statue, S*, and a piece of clay, C*. According to the view under discussion, S* would not be identical with

C* though their smaller corresponding parts would be identical. Now, as we have described matters, L is identical with S* and hence not identical with C*. But we could have described the very same situation in terms that would have led to the opposite conclusion – that L was identical with C*, not S*! ('Consider all of C except for a certain single molecule. It might have been that this molecule adhered to the sculptor's hand and hence was absent from the piece of clay he was working with . . .')

The idea that the smaller parts of S and C are identical thus has the disconcerting consequence that if things had been only slightly different, then a certain specific aggregation of molecules, L, would have existed in precisely the same region as a certain statue and a certain piece of clay, but would not clearly have been identical with either one of them. (Yet all of its smaller parts would have been parts of both the statue and the piece of clay.) We can only conclude that either it is an insoluble mystery whether L is identical with S* or with C*, or else L is yet a *third* physical object sharing their exact spatiotemporal location. (At this point the three-object view might actually seem the least objectionable since it dodges the mystery of choosing between S* and C*.)

Two things should be noticed about our predicament. First, it is completely general. So there is *also* an aggregation of molecules A in exactly the same region as both S and C, and we have no good reason to think A is identical with S or identical with C. Second, if we avoid this mystery by adopting the three-object view, we will only produce more trouble. For the same sort of reasoning will apply with respect to the third object, and there will be no limit to the number of physical objects in exactly the same location. Surely this is too much to believe.

So now suppose we say *no* to our question, adopting the view that the corresponding smaller parts of S and C are not identical with each other. For example, let M be an arbitrary molecule that is part of S. Then there is a distinct molecule, say M*, in exactly the same location, that is a part of C but not a part of S. And similar conclusions hold for *any* parts of S and C, including ones that are much larger or smaller than individual molecules. For example, there is a horse-shaped part of C that isn't part of S, and vice-versa, and so on. This is a very strange view, and one that may not be attractive even to those initially inclined toward the idea that S and C are two different entities.

Here is one apparent consequence of the view. Consider a molecule M that is a part of S. Suppose we detach it from the rest of S (say in a laboratory) so that it's now just an isolated molecule. Then another molecule has automatically been detached from the rest of C as well. (Of course it isn't M, since M was never a part of C.) It seems to follow that we now have two molecules in exactly the same place, even though neither of them is attached to any other molecules in the way they formerly were. Now, suppose we arrange to 'vaporise' the rest of S (and so the rest of C as well). Although it might be consistent, it is very odd to think that this would have any effect on the molecule M, or on its inseparable partner. For example, it would be odd to conclude that when the rest of S goes out of existence, so does M, but that a like molecule comes into existence precisely in the region vacated by M at precisely the time of annihilation. It's far more natural to think that M and its partner still exist. But now consider isolated molecules that have never been bonded to other physical entities. Do they too come in inseparable pairs? If the histories of M and its partner are irrelevant, then so should be the histories of eternally isolated molecules, and indeed of any entities of any description at all. So it seems that the present view is best seen not just as a view about special entities like statues and pieces of clay, but about all physical entities in the universe: they just happen come in inseparable pairs. Many will find this unacceptable.

But nearly all will find it unacceptable if we have to go *beyond* pairs. The Common Sense View was that there is just one thing under consideration, a thing that we might describe as a statue or as a piece of clay. The trouble started when we noticed that when we *describe* it one way, some of its features seem to differ from ones it has when we describe it the other way. But obviously these are just two among many possible ways of describing this seemingly single entity. And some of these other descriptions may raise the same sorts of considerations that led us to take the two-object view seriously, thus raising the spectre of three, four, and even infinitely many objects in the same place at the same time. If the two-object view points inevitably in this direction, then we would do well to try to save the Common Sense View after all. And apparently it does point in this direction, as we will now see.

Imagine that the object in question was in fact the prototype for a famous Frederic Remington bronze. Then not only are there a statue and a piece of clay before us, there is also a statue-prototype. Originally, it seemed that the piece of clay could have been spherical but the statue could not have been spherical, and this (along with LL) led us to consider the two-object view. But now imagine that Remington had instead made the statue with no intention of making a model for a future bronze work, and in fact never produced any similar work in bronze. That would be a situation in which the statue existed, but the statue-prototype did not. So something seems to be true of the statue – it could have existed even though no prototype existed – that isn't true of the prototype. So it looks like the prototype and the statue are two different things. Since it is also clear that the piece of clay has properties that the prototype lacks (*possibly being spherical* will do), the original style of reasoning evidently yields the conclusion that we have *three* objects, not two. Discovering a fourth, a fifth, and so on, is now just a matter of finding new descriptions to support further applications of the two-object reasoning with respect to each of the objects already conceded to exist.

There is yet a further reason to think that the present view will result in far too many things. For consider any aggregation of molecules filling the entire location of S (and C), but some of which are parts of S and some of which are parts of C. It's very hard to deny that it's a physical object. But it can't be either S or C, since some of its parts aren't parts of S and others of its parts aren't parts of C. Either we have a new physical object (and hence many, many more, corresponding to the many different ways of combining parts of S with parts of C), or else we have to give up the initially compelling idea that any bunch of molecules that are stuck together in a given such region constitute a legitimate physical object.

We have mentioned only a few of the difficulties that confront the 'two'-object view, but they are clearly very serious. So let's try to save the Common Sense View. Of course we want to save it without abandoning Leibniz' Law, but also – if we can – without abandoning our ordinary beliefs about statues and pieces of clay. Thus we seek a solution according to which both

(1) The piece of clay could have been spherical.

and

(2) The statue could not have been spherical.

remain true even though the piece of clay and the statue are just one thing.

Our proposed solution depends on Plato's bold idea that the various properties that things have – like *being a statue or being made of clay* – are 'abstract' entities, entities that genuinely exist but are nevertheless not physical in nature. (Plato's own 'theory of forms' is the cornerstone of his metaphysics and epistemology.)

For now, let's assume in this Platonic spirit that for an entity 'to have a property' is for it to stand in a special relation to a specific such abstract entity. This relation is usually called *instantiation* (or *exemplification*). On this assumption, for example, for a thing to be a statue is nothing more nor less than for it to instantiate the property of *being a statue*. To put it a little differently, the fact that a thing is a statue, and the fact that it instantiates the property of *being a statue*, are *just one fact*.

On this view, to pick a different example, when a thing, x, is red, the basic metaphysical nature of this state of affairs is *relational*: it consists in x's bearing the instantiation relation to the property *being red* (or *redness*). Thus when we say 'x is red', we are really saying that x instantiates *being red*, that is, that the instantiation relation holds between x and the property of *being red*. So the proposition that x is red is really about *two* entities, not just one. It's about the physical entity x and also about an abstract entity, the property of *being red*. This metaphysical picture plays a crucial role in solving the puzzle of the statue.

Because any ordinary entity instantiates a multitude of properties at any given time, there is no difficulty in supposing that a single thing instantiates both the property of *being the statue* and the property of *being the piece of clay*. The way is now clear for the possibility of saving the Common Sense View. But first we need a further ingredient.

Suppose you are holding a red apple. Then you are holding something that has numerous properties, including *being red*, *being an apple*, and *being physical*. On our normal conception, these properties are related to each other in certain basic ways. For example, everyone will agree that something could be red without being an apple, and vice versa. And also that nothing could be red (or an apple) without being physical. And, of course, something could be physical though neither red nor an apple. What is the metaphysical source of these indisputable connections between these very familiar properties? The Platonic view offers an answer.

In a nutshell, the answer is that these connections are relations between the properties that depend only on how the properties are *in themselves* – their so-called *intrinsic* properties – and not on any instances that the properties may or may not have. Relations that hold between any entities strictly as a result of their intrinsic properties are also sometimes called *intrinsic*. To illustrate the general idea, suppose a given jockey is *shorter than* a given basketball player. Then that is a relation that holds between these individuals solely as a result of their respective heights. So it depends only on the athletes' intrinsic properties, and it is therefore an intrinsic relation.

Analogously, according to the Platonic view, if a property like *being red* or *being an apple* cannot be instantiated by a thing unless that thing also instantiates *being physical*, then this is a relation between the *properties* that depends only on how *they* are in themselves. It *doesn't* depend on there being any red things or any physical things even though some things do happen to be both red and physical. The property of *being a unicorn* in fact has no instances, but it is nevertheless true that it could not be instantiated by a thing unless that thing also instantiated *being physical*. If there were any unicorns then they would be physical in nature. So *being a unicorn* is related to *being physical* in the same way that *being red* and *being an apple* are.

According to the Platonic view, again, to be red is just to instantiate *being red*. Now, in keeping with the present idea, instantiating *being red* automatically involves instantiating *being physical*. It's no accident, it's something about *being red* in itself and *being physical* in itself that makes it impossible for anything to instantiate the former property without also instantiating the latter. When this relation holds between properties x and y, we say that *x entails y*. So *being red*, *being an apple*, and *being a unicorn* are three examples of properties that entail *being physical*. Obviously, *being physical* doesn't entail any of the other three, so entailment between properties may hold in one direction without holding in the other.

Closely related to entailment is a relation between properties we may call *compatibility*. Intuitively, two properties are compatible if there could be something that instantiated both. Thus *being red* and *being an apple* are compatible (though neither entails the other). And so are *being a unicorn* and *being physical*. *Being red* and *being green*, on the other hand, are *incompatible*, as are *being round* and *being square*. It isn't hard to see that the compatibility of *being red* with *being an apple* is just the failure of *being red* to entail *not being an apple*. Similarly, the incompatibility of *being red* and *being green* consists in the fact that *being red* entails *not being green*. So entailment and compatibility are, in a certain simple way, two sides of the same coin.

We are now able to state the Platonic solution to the puzzle of the statue and the piece of clay. Sentences (1) and (2) above do *not* just assert of a certain physical object, respectively, that it could, and could not, have been spherical. It is precisely the assumption that sentences like these merely assert that a given thing could have been one way or another that leads to all the trouble. The Platonic conception provides the possibility of a better interpretation. On this interpretation, sentence (1) is not only about the thing in question and the property of *being spherical*, but also about the property of *being the piece of clay*. Sentence (2), on the other hand, is not at all about the property of *being the piece of clay*, but instead is about the property of *being the statue*. Here, then, are the suggested Platonic readings of (1) and (2):

(1*) Something instantiates *being the piece of clay*, and *being the piece of clay* is compatible with *being spherical*;
(2*) Something instantiates *being the statue*, and *being the statue* is incompatible with *being spherical*.

Each sentence thus asserts the existence of a physical object with a certain property, and then goes on to assert either the compatibility or the incompatibility of the relevant property with *being spherical*. Intuitively, when we say, 'The piece of clay could have been spherical', we are saying that something could have been spherical while being the piece of clay. And when we say, 'The statue could not have been spherical', we are saying that nothing could have been spherical while being the statue. So, if the sculptor had used the clay to make a sphere, then a certain physical object would have instantiated the properties *being the piece of clay* and *being spherical*, but of course not the property of *being the statue*.

This solution conforms to the Common Sense View by allowing that the piece of clay and the statue are just one thing. And our intuition that 'the piece of clay' has a property that 'the statue' lacks is also accommodated, but with no danger of some one thing both having and lacking a certain property. The 'having' and 'lacking' of our intuition are accounted for by the compatibility and incompatibility of *different* properties with *being spherical*. These different properties, of course, are precisely the ones that are expressed by the different descriptions of what is in fact one single thing.

It is worth noticing that the present solution and the multiple-object solution have something important in common. They are both 'ontological' positions. They attempt to resolve a seeming conflict in our ordinary thought by claiming, in effect, that there are more things in existence than perhaps meet the eye. The multiple-object solution depends on accepting a multitude of *physical* objects that happen to occupy the exact same regions that other physical objects occupy. And the Platonic solution depends on accepting a multitude of *abstract* objects that aren't located in physical space at all. We now turn to some questions about existence itself, the fundamental concept of metaphysics and ontology.

EXISTENCE AND NON-EXISTENCE

What does it mean to say that something *exists*? To put the question a little differently: What is involved in the *concept* of existence? Many concepts may be explained by analysing them in terms of more basic concepts that we already take to be understood. For example, the concept *sibling* may be analysed by appeal to the simpler concept *parent*, as follows: to be a *sibling* is to be one of at least two individuals that have a common parent. Is a similar sort of analysis available for the concept of existence, or is this concept so basic that it cannot be analysed?

Materialist philosophers may be tempted to offer an analysis, in particular to hold that *to exist* is to occupy space and time. Since materialists hold that only material (that is, physical) entities exist, and since nothing could be material without occupying space and time, it's easy to see why this view might be tempting. It is nevertheless a very dubious view.

Millions of people have believed that various genuinely existing entities are *not* located in space and time. (Certainly this is part of many conceptions of God, and also of certain philosophically sophisticated conceptions of abstract entities like numbers and properties.) If 'existing' just meant *occupying space and time*, then these opinions would not only be wrong, they would be *self-contradictory*. They would be logically absurd just as a matter of definition. This would imply that their proponents' grasp of the concept of existence was dramatically incorrect. But surely it isn't self-contradictory to think that spirits or numbers exist. It may very well be wrong, but it isn't absurd. If spirits or numbers fail to exist, that is a matter of fact, not a matter of definition, and this is something that a reflective materialist will not dispute.

The concept of existence thus doesn't seem to be analysable by appeal to the notions of space and time. Are there any *other* notions that might do the job? It is very instructive to try to think of more basic concepts that might figure in a successful analysis. If you try to find such concepts you are very likely to draw a blank. This strongly suggests that the concept of existence is as basic as a concept can be, and hence that it is *simple* in the special sense of *failing to have any analysis in more basic terms*. It suggests that the millions of people who have thought that various sorts of non-spatiotemporal entities exist have grasped the concept of existence no less well than those who have rejected such entities.

Aristotle famously (and rightly) pointed out that not all concepts can be analysed, for to assume otherwise would produce circularity or infinite regress. It is very important to see that for a concept to lack an analysis in no way implies it is mysterious or incomprehensible. On the other hand, it doesn't imply it is unproblematic or easily understood either. (So a concept that is simple in the present special sense need not be simple in the everyday sense of being easily understood.) Existence is a concept that has in fact created a good deal of metaphysical confusion. Much of that confusion surrounds the logic of *assertions* of existence and non-existence, and we will now try to dispel it by offering an analysis. In conformity with our recent discussion, our analysis will not incorporate an analysis of *existence* itself, so it will be compatible with the view that this concept is simple.

Let's begin by thinking about sentences of *subject–predicate* form. For example, consider 'Mars is a planet'. What makes this sentence say something about the world? One very natural answer – variations on which are widely accepted – has two parts. First, the (grammatical) subject, 'Mars', refers to a specific entity; and second, the predicate, 'is a planet', says something about that entity. A Platonist, for example, might hold that the predicate attributes the property of *being a planet* to the entity to which the subject refers. This overall semantic picture is very appealing but it may not ultimately be accurate. For example, if there really are no Platonic properties, then some other way of understanding the 'attribution' made by the predicate will have to be found. Further, there may be problems with the idea that the function of the subject is just to refer to a certain entity. But – for the moment – let's set these issues aside and accept the picture provisionally, as an intuitively reasonable starting point. Certainly *something* along these lines really is going on, and that is how the sentence manages to say something about the world.

In fact there is a physical object, Mars, that does instantiate the property of *being a planet*, and since our sentence evidently asserts precisely this, it's *true*. If it had happened that Mars was *not* a planet, the sentence would still assert that it is, so it would be *false*. This sounds good so far. But now consider the false sentence, 'Mars does not exist'. *Why* is it false? It's tempting to answer in accordance with our provisional view. That would be to say it's false because the object that 'Mars' refers to instantiates the property of *existing*, and hence *doesn't* instantiate the property of *not existing*, with the result that the sentence is false.

But there is a huge problem with this answer. For sometimes sentences like this are *true*. For example: 'Zeus does not exist' or 'Santa Claus does not exist', or the like. The very fact that these sentences are true *seems* to entail that there simply are no entities for the terms 'Zeus' and 'Santa Claus' to refer to in the first place. This would make it impossible to account for their truth in the way we accounted for the truth of 'Mars is a planet'. The idea that there is an *entity* that is referred to by 'Zeus' *and* instantiates the property *not existing* seems paradoxical. This is the problem of existence and non-existence.

A more general consideration is this. It is uncontroversial that many *ordinary* things, like trees and houses, come into existence at given times and later go out of existence. So our problem isn't just about exotic mythical or fictional 'entities'. (Just *when* a specific tree or house begins or ceases to exist is perhaps unclear, but that is a different question.) Now, intuitively, if something doesn't exist, then it's very hard to see how it could instantiate any properties at all. Instantiation, on the Platonic picture anyway, is a relation between an *entity* and a property: no entity, no instantiation. This suggests immediately that *not existing* is not a property that any entity could instantiate. For example, no tree that has ceased to exist is now available to instantiate *not existing*. But then, what do we mean when we say that the oak tree that used to be in the yard no longer exists? The other side of this coin is that *existing* is a property that every entity instantiates. Even though many trees and houses have long since ceased to exist, it's still true, right now, that everything exists, because the 'everything' doesn't include these *former* entities. (Some philosophers have drawn the stronger conclusion that *existing* and *not existing* simply aren't properties in the first place. But this creates the problem of saying just what it is that these terms express if they don't express properties.)

Various ways of dealing with the problem of existence and non-existence have been proposed. Here we will only consider two. One of them is a surprising departure from our ordinary thinking. It's the view that even though Zeus doesn't *actually exist*, he nevertheless enjoys a certain sort of *being*, so that the term 'Zeus' really does refer to something. On this view (originating with the Austrian psychologist and philosopher, Alexius Meinong), there are two kinds or levels of being. One level, in effect, is *actual existence*. The other is *merely possible existence*. The planet Mars has being in the first and more robust sense. The god Zeus lacks this, but nevertheless has being in the second, less robust sense. Several different versions of this basic position have been offered and we won't go into their details. But all of them have the virtue of allowing for a *uniform* treatment of the sentences 'Mars is a planet' and 'Zeus does not exist'. They see these sentences as attributing properties to *real*, though not necessarily *actual*, entities. This general position is called *possibilism*, because it acknowledges 'merely possible' entities. Any view that rejects merely possible entities, holding that everything that exists is actual, is a species of the general position called *actualism*.

Possibilism is a genuinely exotic view, but of course that doesn't mean it's wrong. The mere fact that it allows for a uniform semantic analysis of the sorts of sentences we've been considering is surely a strong point in its favour. But it faces the very stiff challenge of explaining the second level of existence in a plausible way. This involves addressing many difficult problems. Here are two that are closely related:

1   It seems that merely possible entities must be *abstract*. Consider Santa Claus. If he were to exist in the more robust sense, he would be a physical entity (at least in part). So he (or at least his body) would, at any time, have a specific location. But since he doesn't exist in this sense, he doesn't have any physical location. So he must be abstract. It is certainly *very* odd to suppose that a given thing might or might not be abstract, depending on what sort of being it happened to enjoy. For example, this evidently entails that Mount Everest would have been an abstract entity if the geology of the earth had developed differently.

    One response might be that the abstract Santa exists even in possible circumstances in which Santa enjoys the more robust sort of being. In such circumstances there would be *two* entities, abstract-Santa and robust-Santa. But this really is hard to defend. Which sentences containing the term 'Santa Claus' refer to the abstract entity, and which refer to the robust entity? Intuitively, the 'Santa' of 'Santa is fat' would refer to robust-Santa if he were to enjoy robust being. But isn't 'Santa is fat' true even though he doesn't actually exist? And how can it be that in the actually false 'Santa exists', 'Santa' refers to abstract-Santa? Wouldn't it refer to robust-Santa if he did exist? Or would the sentence then be ambiguous? We are in serious danger of losing the semantic uniformity that recommended the possibilist view in the first place.

2   What are the limits of merely possible existence? Suppose both you and I have convincing dreams that there is a single golden mountain. Each of us has vivid visual images in these dreams. And suppose each of us is convinced of the actual existence of such an entity. Alas, we are both wrong. Yet we go around saying 'The golden mountain exists'. Do our respective utterances mean the same thing or not? It's difficult to believe that they do, for you might think 'the mountain' was on Mars, while I might think 'it' was in a remote Amazonian jungle, or below the sea on the lost continent of Atlantis. But then how many abstract, *unique* golden mountains are there? If there's just one, then how is it that our very different conceptions concern *it*? And what if a third person dreams that there are *many* golden mountains? What keeps the one we imagine to exist from being among the many the third person imagines? (After all, *ours* was supposed

to be unique.) On the other hand, if yours and mine are different, then they seem to be dependent on our imaginings. But it's very odd to think that *abstract* entities should depend for their existence on things that go on in the temporal realm. After all, they aren't located in space or time in the first place. And if these entities aren't dependent on our imaginings, then there must be many more that have never been and never will be imagined.

These problems pose a very severe test for any possibilist account. But addressing them would immerse us in more detail than we can undertake here. So instead we'll turn to an actualist approach to the problem of existence and non-existence. One such approach goes roughly like this. In the sentence 'Mars is a planet', the term 'Mars' *doesn't* refer to a specific object after all. (So the provisional view is held to be wrong on this crucial point.) Rather, it expresses a *property – being Mars –* which a single specific object happens to instantiate. The entire sentence means that *some entity instantiates both the property of being Mars and the property of being a planet.* Because some entity in fact *does* instantiate both of these properties, the sentence is true. Now, the proponent of this view surely owes us a clear explanation of the nature of properties like *being Mars*, and providing one might prove to be a difficult task. But, for present purposes, let's just assume an adequate explanation can be given and ask how things would then work with assertions of existence and non-existence.

Consider the true sentences 'Mars exists' and 'Zeus does not exist'. First we'll give an approximate analysis and then refine it. On strict analogy with 'Mars is a planet', the first sentence would mean that *some entity instantiates both being Mars and existing.* That seems fine. But the second sentence *can't* mean that *some entity instantiates both being Zeus and not existing,* since that would be an explicitly possibilist interpretation. Instead, suppose we take assertions of non-existence to be negations of assertions of existence. Then 'Zeus does not exist' is simply shorthand for 'It is not the case that Zeus exists'. Accordingly, it just means *it is not the case that some entity instantiates both being Zeus and existing.* This treatment doesn't require that there be anything for 'Zeus' to refer to, so it is fully compatible with actualism.

That is our first approximation. The problem is that it may not really provide a uniform *general* treatment. For it isn't clear that we can always 'move' an internal negation out to the front and preserve the meaning of sentences with predicates not explicitly expressing existence. (For example, 'Jones does not like Smith' and 'It is not the case that Jones likes Smith' apparently don't say the same thing. The first sentence strongly suggests that Jones dislikes Smith, but the second is compatible with a neutral attitude.) In other words, some predicates may not function like 'exists' and 'does not exist' in this respect.

Now, we have already noticed that existence and non-existence are rather unusual properties (assuming they are properties in the first place). No matter what the world might be like, it would still be true that everything exists. And no matter what the world might be like, it would still be true that nothing fails to exist. Parallel features don't seem to be shared by other properties. Moreover, it is also intuitively right that no property whatsoever can be instantiated by anything that doesn't exist. Thus it seems redundant to regard 'Mars exists' as meaning that *some entity instantiates both being Mars and existing.* If an entity instantiates *being Mars* – or any other property – then it *automatically* exists. So why not take 'Mars exists' to mean simply that *some entity instantiates being Mars?* That would remove the redundancy. And then 'Zeus does not exist' would mean *it is not the case that some entity instantiates being Zeus* or, in other words, that *no entity instantiates being Zeus.* This is our final actualist analysis.

This treatment takes existence as a special property that is expressed in English by 'something', 'some entity', 'someone' and so on. Expressions like these are called *existential quantifiers.* Thus, on the present account, *existence* is expressed by existential quantifiers, and *non-existence* by negations of existential quantifiers. To say that Zeus doesn't exist is, in effect, to say that none of the things that exist have the property of *being Zeus.* Because existence and non-existence are treated in this special way, the analysis makes no general commitment regarding predicates not explicitly expressing these properties (and it is therefore an improvement on the first approximation).

We conclude this section with a few remarks about a famous and fascinating problem about existence. Many people have gazed at the night sky and experienced a deep sense of awe that such a cosmos should exist *at all.* This sense of wonder is reflected in the familiar question, 'Why is there something rather than nothing?' In what follows we will content ourselves with trying to illuminate this 'cosmological' question, for it is significantly subtler than it might first seem.

When people ask the cosmological question, they are typically wondering only about the existence of the seemingly *contingent* reality that surrounds us. If there also exist *necessary* entities (like God or numbers), then their very necessity would evidently be the best possible explanation of their existence. So let's agree at the outset to understand the question as restricted to the case of contingent existence.

This question evidently asks for an *explanation,* but an explanation of exactly *what?* It's one thing to gaze at stars and ask why *our specific* universe exists, and quite another to ask why *any* universe of this general kind exists. It's actually fairly common to try to explain the existence of a specific contingent thing. For example, a certain dog's existence might be explained by pointing out that a mating of two other specific dogs occurred, with the given dog as a result. It's also common to try to explain why *any* entities of a specific general kind exist. Thus a well-known explanation for the existence of *dogs* posits that humans found that some wolves were not aggressive toward them, and they bred these wolves, rebred their offspring, and so on, intuitively selecting for friendliness and tractability at each stage. The ultimate result was *dogs*. This sort of explanation doesn't explain the existence of any *particular* dogs at all. (If the original individual wolves had been entirely different, it is very plausible to think that an entirely different genealogy of dogs would have resulted, so that no actual dog would have existed even though there would have been plenty of dogs.) If this explanation is successful, it merely tells us why there are some dogs rather than none.

So we are already familiar with explanations for both 'specific' and 'general' existence. Thus we have both a specific and a general interpretation of the cosmological question. In fact, there are three sorts of specialists with deep professional interest in this question: astronomers (including astrophysicists), metaphysicians, and theologians. Very roughly, the astronomers are mainly interested in the specific interpretation of the question, the metaphysicians mainly in the general, and the theologians are interested in both.

It's important to see that an answer to a specific existence question doesn't necessarily provide an answer to a corresponding general question (and that the reverse doesn't necessarily hold either). It's easy to see this in the case of dogs. My dog Jack exists (roughly) because two other dogs (both known to me) mated and Jack was in the resulting litter. This (perhaps) explains the existence of the dog Jack. It is a logical consequence of this explanation that dogs exist. But the explanation is nevertheless *not* an explanation of the general existence of dogs, for it *presupposes* that dogs exist. (Of course we just saw that although the wolf domestication story may explain why there are dogs, it doesn't explain the existence of Jack or any other particular dog.)

There is something else that complicates the cosmological question, whether we take it specifically or generally. It has to do with the concept of explanation. Our specific and general dog examples have something very important in common: they attempt to explain features of concrete reality by reference to *other* features of concrete reality. But the cosmological question seeks an explanation for *all* of (either specific or general) concrete reality. So appeal to other features of concrete reality is impossible. This suggests that no answer to the cosmological question would count as an 'explanation' in the ordinary sense of the term. But then would it really be an explanation and, if so, what kind of explanation? We cannot address these questions here, for the answers would depend heavily on the details of the candidate explanation.

Instead let us quickly survey the sorts of proposals that are associated with astronomers, theologians, and metaphysicians. It is often claimed that most astronomers hold that our (specific) universe originated in an awesome explosion – 'The

Big Bang' – that occurred some billions of years ago. It is certainly possible that there really was such a great explosion, and also that the specific array of matter (and energy) at each subsequent time in the universe may be traced to this singular event. That may be just what people who make this claim intend. But even though it may be correct (and if correct, extremely important), it isn't a satisfactory answer to the cosmological question. The reason is that the explosion *itself* would be a physical event, and hence it would be a (past) part of the physical universe. To claim that the explosion explained the existence of the universe would be to hold that the existence of a specific entity could be explained by appealing to a part of that very entity. But that seems entirely unsatisfactory. A general moral is that any attempt to explain the existence of the universe by appealing to *physical* events, conditions, or entities evidently fails to answer the cosmological question in a satisfying way.

Many theologians (along with many ordinary people) hold that the universe was created by *God*, a necessary being who is not part of the material realm. This approach avoids the 'Big Bang'-style difficulty of trying to explain the existence of an entity by appealing to a part of it. But for precisely this reason, it faces a number of equally vexing problems. For one, it is a radical departure from our usual concept of explanation as applied to material events and entities. As we saw earlier, our usual procedure is to explain one material circumstance by appealing to other material circumstances. Positing divine creation would clearly not provide an explanation in anything like this sense of the term.

And here is a closely related problem. Although we routinely understand cases in which a physical thing is *created* from other physical things (a fence from some boards, steam from water, etc.), it is hard to see how something physical could be created either from nothing or else from something nonphysical. Thus it has seemed to many critics that claiming the universe is God's creation is so far just a metaphor, and that it cannot be a plausible explanation until the metaphor is eliminated in favour of a genuine analysis. Many proponents of the religious answer to the cosmological question fully appreciate this problem, and some hold that divine creation is beyond human analysis or understanding, but that it is nevertheless true.

A metaphysician might survey these efforts and try to find a way to avoid the pitfalls of both. One way might be to conclude that the universe exists necessarily, despite our strong initial feeling to the contrary. This would be to explain the concrete universe without appealing to any entities at all, whether outside of it or part of it. It would also be a proposal that answered both the specific and the general version of the cosmological question. The main problem with this idea is that if our specific universe is indeed a necessary entity, then so is every part of it, including every proton, every grain of sand, every animal and human being, every artefact, and so on. This conclusion is very hard to accept since we normally think all such entities are contingent.

But it isn't just these familiar entities that would be necessary, for the universe isn't just a collection of individual entities. *Events* occur in the universe, and it would follow that they all occur of necessity, including those that seem intuitively to be actions we have freely chosen to perform. So the explanation from necessity faces the very high hurdle of replacing a great deal of our commonsense picture of ourselves and our world. An alternative in the same spirit might be to argue somehow that it is necessary that there be *some* contingent universe or other, leaving the intuitive contingency of the actual universe intact. This would be to propose a 'necessitarian' answer to the *general* cosmological question. But it is far from clear how such an argument would proceed, and it would still leave the *specific* ontological question unanswered.

We now turn to our third metaphysical topic, which will provide an excellent occasion for applying the actualist analysis of assertions of existence and non-existence discussed above, as well as the conception of properties developed in the section on identity and constitution.

LIFE AND DEATH

During the American election season of the year 2000, something interesting and unfortunate occurred. One of the two major candidates running for the (US) Senate from Missouri was killed in an aeroplane crash. His name was Mel Carnahan, and his death occurred after the ballots had been printed and distributed to precincts, but before election day. It was too late for his party to select a new candidate and for new ballots to reflect a change. On election day, a vast majority of voters were well aware that Carnahan was dead. But when the votes were finally counted, 'Carnahan' received more than 'his' major opponent, John Ashcroft.

If this is surprising, what followed may be even more so. For the news media reported, in complete sincerity, that Ashcroft had been 'defeated by a dead man', and Ashcroft himself conceded defeat. Then Carnahan's wife was appointed to serve the term in the Senate, as if Carnahan had died *after* winning the election.

But how can 'a dead man' win an election? By getting more votes? That's too simple; it just replaces one difficult question with another: how can 'a dead man' get more votes? *Winning the election* and *getting more votes* are evidently *properties*. In the section on existence and non-existence we endorsed the Platonic idea that instantiation is a relation that holds between *entities* and *properties*. Thus if it were true that a dead man won the election, then there would have to be a genuinely existing entity – *a dead man* – available to instantiate that property. So the underlying metaphysical question is whether dead people really do exist.

If dead people exist, what are they like? A common religious answer appeals to a species of mind–body dualism. It holds that a dead person is an immaterial soul (or mind) that has been 'separated' from the human body it once 'inhabited'. This view is compatible with each of two very different accounts of *living* people. On one, a living person is an immaterial soul that happens to inhabit a human body. On the other, a living person is the 'sum' of a soul and the human body it inhabits (and so only a *part* of the living person). But on either view, a *dead person* is taken to be a soul that once inhabited a human body (but doesn't now). Thus 'religious dualism' offers entities to instantiate such properties as *winning the election* and, in general, *being dead*. (It is worth noting that dualism *per se* is not committed to the view that the 'separated' soul is a *dead person*. In fact, dualism is logically compatible with the idea that the soul ceases to exist when the body dies. But of course religious versions are typically very much committed to the continued existence of the person.)

Dualist views about *living people* face their own distinctive problems, which we will not discuss. But the one that is likely the most pressing is worth mentioning briefly. We need a plausible explanation of what it means for an immaterial soul to *inhabit* a material body. Does this notion involve immaterial entities having spatiotemporal locations? If it does, then we need an explanation of how this can occur. And if it doesn't, the notion of inhabiting may seem merely metaphorical.

The religious doctrine of *death* also faces problems. The most important is probably this. Even if there are immaterial souls, somehow associated with our bodies when we're alive, to hold that death is the separation of the soul from the body is a considerable departure from how we ordinarily think about death in general. The departure has two closely related aspects. First, many entities besides humans live and die, but most of us are not at all inclined to think, for example, that simple plants and animals have souls. Of course if they don't have souls, then their deaths consist in purely physical events not involving any relations between immaterial and material entities. It is very odd to think that death should be dramatically different *metaphysically*, depending on which species of things are doing the dying.

The second aspect is that our actual assessments of the occurrence of death in humans are *always* made on purely physical grounds. We don't have any means for detecting a cessation of inhabitation of a body by a soul. We don't even think about this. When we look for evidence of death we're concerned with the state of vital organs (namely the heart and the brain). In short, our evidence for human death is completely analogous, given differences of biological makeup, to the evidence that bears on the death of, say, a geranium or a salamander.

So it seems that the concept of death is one that applies in a uniform way across all species of living things, including ours, and that this is entirely independent of the truth or falsity of the religious doctrine of dead people as souls. A religious dualist and a non-religious materialist should have the same conception of death even though they have dramatically different conceptions of what it is to be a human being (living or dead). Death, on this account, is something entirely *physical* that happens to human (and other) *bodies*. When we say that a *person* has died, we are claiming that something has happened to the person's *body*. It is crucial to see that in saying this, we do not thereby make any commitment as to whether or not a dead person exists as a consequence of the death. Both materialists and dualists may either affirm or deny the existence of dead people (though, again, a *religious* dualist will not be tempted by the latter option).

There are compelling reasons for a materialist to deny the existence of dead people. Having rejected immaterial souls, a materialist who favours dead people must take them to be physical entities. But what physical entities? The answer may at first seem obvious: it's human bodies that die, and a dead human body is a corpse. So the corpses are the dead people. In fact we commonly both think of and refer to corpses as 'dead people'. (Of course this may just be a loose and unreflective way of thinking and speaking about *dead bodies*.)

But sometimes people die in cataclysmic ways, with the result that there is no physical entity that can plausibly be called a corpse – there simply is no dead body. It's extremely odd to think that if a 'natural' death occurs during sleep, we have a dead person, but if someone is annihilated in a nuclear catastrophe, we do not. The doctrine of dead people is intuitively implausible if some deaths result in dead people but others do not. Death should be entirely egalitarian.

Earlier we considered two rival accounts of what it takes for subject–predicate sentences akin to 'Smith is dead' to be true. Though they differ in the details of how the subject 'Smith' functions, both views as they stand require that there be an entity that instantiates *being dead*. As we have just seen, a sentence like 'Smith is dead' *ought* to be true *no matter how Smith died*. This is certainly how we normally use such sentences. But if Smith was blown to smithereens, 'Smith is dead' winds up being *false* on either of the unmodified accounts. This outcome seems clearly unacceptable, and it strongly suggests that such semantic accounts of 'Smith is dead' need revision.

Of course one might hope for a conception of dead people that is both materialist and egalitarian. We might decide to count not only corpses, but also certain piles of ashes, certain 'sums' of widely scattered atoms (or even subatomic particles), and so forth, as dead people. Most would probably find this extension of the original idea too far-fetched to accept. Furthermore, it would do nothing to address the remaining, inegalitarian *possibility* of the complete annihilation of the body, in which nothing at all survives the event of the death.

A more promising way for a materialist to preserve egalitarianism is to deny that there are any dead people in the first place. On this view, a sentence like 'Smith is dead' is synonymous with 'Smith died', and makes no commitment to the existence of a dead person. This idea is somewhat parallel to the treatment of assertions of existence and non-existence we considered in the second section. Just as 'Zeus does not exist' was held not to entail that some entity instantiates *not existing*, 'Smith is dead' is held not to entail that some entity instantiates *being dead*. But death is a little more complicated than non-existence since it has to be preceded by life. So let's try to develop the details of the suggested view carefully, recapitulating some of what was discussed before.

Our original model subject–predicate sentence was 'Mars is a planet', and we ultimately analysed it by:

(1) Some entity instantiates *being Mars* and *being a planet*.

But this model was found not to work well with claims of existence and non-existence, and we finally analysed 'Mars exists' by the simpler:

(2) Some entity instantiates *being Mars*.

and 'Zeus does not exist' by:

(3) No entity instantiates *being Zeus*.

Now, *being alive* and *being dead* are surely genuine properties that various things may or may not have. But, they don't work quite as smoothly as *existing* and *not existing*, because (as just noted) *being dead* isn't simply *not being alive*. Tables and chairs aren't alive, but they aren't dead either since they never were alive. Corpses and autumn leaves, on the other hand, really are dead. To be dead, roughly, is to fail to be alive *after* having been alive. Of course, nothing can be either dead or alive unless it exists. Let's put these thoughts together while retaining the egalitarian goal of avoiding commitment to dead people.

Suppose a human being, Smith, dies while sleeping. During the period when Smith is alive, the sentence 'Smith is alive' is of course true. Following the pattern of (1), we may analyse it by:

(4) Some entity instantiates both *being Smith* and *being alive*.

A materialist believes this entity is nothing more nor less than Smith's warm body. For a while after Smith expires, his corpse remains. And of course it *is* a dead human body, so *some* related entity does instantiate *being dead* during this period. This might tempt us to analyse 'Smith is dead' by: *once some entity instantiated being*

Smith and being alive, but now that entity instantiates being dead. This view might seem promising for the egalitarian since it makes no commitment to the dead entity's being the person *Smith*. The trouble is that we've already agreed that 'Smith is dead' would be true even if his death involved the complete annihilation of his body. So this·analysis just isn't right. We need an analysis according to which 'Smith is dead' – despite its superficial appearance *and* despite the convenient but misleading presence of Smith's dead body – *does not* assert that some entity instantiates *being dead*. So we need to get the irrelevant dead body out of the picture entirely. This suggests a departure from the model of (1) analogous to the earlier departure captured in (2) and (3). It suggests that we take 'Smith is dead' to mean:

(5) Once an entity instantiated both *being Smith* and *being alive*, but now no entity instantiates both *being Smith* and *being alive*.

Given that (4) correctly analyses 'Smith is alive', analysis (5) says, in effect, 'Once Smith was alive, but now it is not the case that Smith is alive.' This, of course, is just a roundabout way of saying that Smith has died. So (5) captures the fact that Smith is dead, but it does so without requiring the existence of anything instantiating the property of *being dead*. It's just what our egalitarian materialist needs.

But notice that (5) should also be perfectly acceptable to others, even to religious dualists who believe that Smith still exists and that he's dead. Analysis (5) is logically compatible with this view since it doesn't require the property of *being Smith* to be uninstantiated. It only requires that nothing instantiate both *being Smith* and *being alive*. Since a religious dualist of course doesn't think Smith is alive, the overall view is fully consistent with (5). Our dualist and our materialist can both accept the analysis, but their acceptance of the second part will be for very different reasons.

The idea that there are dead people stems from three or four misleading sources. First, it is clearly true that people die. Second, when a person dies, a dead human body usually remains. Third, the belief that an immaterial soul survives the death of the body is very widespread. Finally, we commonly report the fact that Smith has died by saying 'Smith is dead', and then our ordinary understanding of present-tense, subject–predicate sentences leads us to think this requires that there be some entity that is dead. Between the dead body and the disembodied soul, there is a good deal of pressure to think that this must be right, and that one or another of these very different entities (or something closely related) really is Smith and, of course, really is dead. But our analysis has shown that a very reasonable account of human death requires no such thing. It is perfectly consistent to hold that although many people have died, there really are no dead people.

CONCLUDING NOTE

In this chapter we have considered several important metaphysical concepts, including *existence*, *identity*, *properties* and *death*. And of course many other important philosophical concepts are treated in the other chapters of this book. But what are *concepts*? Are they just ideas in our minds? And do philosophers treat concepts in a distinctive or unusual way? Let's try to shed a little light on these questions.

The words 'concept', 'idea', and 'notion' (along with a few other synonyms) are confusingly ambiguous. Sometimes they are used to express something that is going on 'in the mind'. This sense is intended, for example, when we say things like 'He has no concept of fairness' or 'She sometimes had delusional ideas'. Here concepts and ideas are evidently *mental* events or representations (or processes or the like), and we may think of them as *subjective* in the sense that they *depend for their existence on a thinking subject*. Whether subjective concepts are physical events in our brains or non-physical phenomena occurring in immaterial minds doesn't matter for present purposes. What matters is that they are 'private': you and I may have subjective concepts that are somehow similar, but it is impossible for us *both* to have what is literally a *single* such concept. Whether our minds are physical or not, different minds have no parts in common, so what is going on in one mind automatically *isn't* going on in another. (Furthermore, because they are mental events or states, the concept of, say, fairness that you have on one occasion cannot be identical with the one you have at another time. They are distinct events no matter how similar they might be.)

But on other occasions these same three words evidently mean something that is not at all subjective. For example, when a physics professor says, 'We now turn to the concept of gravitation', it isn't something *mental* that's being introduced. The topic is not going to be one of the professor's own mental representations, nor will it involve our own mental activity. Instead the topic will be a concept in a *non-subjective* sense of the word, something 'public' that we are all capable of thinking about, but that *doesn't depend for its existence on any thinking subject* at all. Gravitation, after all, is a concept that is realised in the physical world in complete independence of any mental activity. This is potentially confusing because the very act of thinking about the *non-subjective* concept of gravitation involves having a *subjective* concept of gravitation. When we think about gravitation we are thinking about a certain non-subjective concept, and our various subjective concepts represent it. They're like different photographs of a single specific object. (Matters are even more confusing when the non-subjective concept is of something subjective, like *consciousness*. Thinking about the non-subjective concept of consciousness involves having in one's own consciousness a subjective concept of consciousness.)

We do not have space to discuss the nature of non-subjective concepts in detail. (One promising view is that they are Platonic properties and relations. For example, the concepts of *existence* and *mass* are properties that things may have; the concepts of *identity* and *gravitation* are relations that things may bear to one another.) For now let's just assume that such concepts really do exist, and that existence, mass, identity, and gravitation are among them.

Two of these concepts are from physics and two are from metaphysics. Although it may be initially surprising, a little reflection reveals that theoretical scientists and philosophers are engaged in very much the same sort of activity. They are trying to formulate theories that analyse and connect the non-subjective concepts that are specific to their disciplines. Here are two simple examples. Newton's law of gravitation holds that the strength of the gravitational force between two bodies is directly proportional to the product of their masses and inversely proportional to the square of the distance between them. This theory (now supplanted by more modern views) postulates explicit connections between the concepts of gravitational force, mass, and spatial distance. But it is not a mere report of how *actual* bodies are related in these ways to each other. It is 'universal' in the sense that it asserts an unwavering connection among these concepts, one that is supposed to hold no matter how the matter in the universe might actually be arranged. It's a *theory*.

Our philosophical example is drawn from epistemology. It was once widely accepted that the following three conditions were necessary and (jointly) sufficient for a subject S to *know* a proposition p: (1) S believes p; (2) p is true; and (3) S is justified in believing p. This theory connects the philosophical concepts of *knowledge, belief, truth* and *justification*. It is a very appealing view, but most contemporary philosophers agree that although the three conditions are indeed necessary, they aren't sufficient for knowledge.

Physicists and philosophers go about their business in very much the same way. They think about the concepts they are working on, formulate hypotheses, and subject them to critical scrutiny. In physics, the scrutiny often ultimately involves empirical evidence obtained from experimentation or observation. But it can also rest on purely conceptual considerations made independently of empirical evidence. (Many physical theories have in fact been overthrown on purely conceptual grounds.) In philosophy the balance is tilted the other way. It is comparatively rare (though not unheard of) that empirical evidence plays an ultimate evidential role, and very common that the critical scrutiny of theories is based on purely conceptual considerations. In this respect philosophy is more like pure mathematics than physics. This difference between philosophy and mathematics, on the one hand, and physics and other natural sciences, on the other, is largely just a result of the sorts of concepts that are involved in the various theories.

Somehow all of us have access to the basic non-subjective concepts that philosophy treats, and we are able to formulate and criticise theories largely by reflection on these concepts and how they are related to one another. Many examples of this 'analytic' philosophical approach may be found in this and other chapters of this book.

EXERCISES

1 If abstract entities like numbers (or properties) exist, do they exist in the same sense of the word in which concrete entities exist? To put it a little differently, when the word 'exist' occurs in sentences like 'Numbers exist', does it mean what it means in sentences like 'Dogs exist'?

2 Leibniz' Law evidently admits of a rigorous proof. What about the converse of Leibniz' Law? Is it even true?

3 Assuming that Platonic properties exist, it is clear that some *actually* have no instances (*being a female US president in 1999*) and some *necessarily* have no instances (*being a round square*). With this in mind, discuss such properties as *being a Martian*, *being a unicorn* and *being Sherlock Holmes*.

4 Did John Ashcroft really lose the election? Approach this question from a strictly metaphysical (rather than legal) perspective.

5 Any two entities are similar in some respects, different in others. For example a tennis ball and a golf ball are similar in shape but different in size, and so on. Platonic properties provide the basis for an explanation of this phenomenon: things are similar when there is a property that they both instantiate, different when there is a property that one instantiates but the other doesn't. How might a philosopher who rejects abstract entities go about explaining similarity and difference?

FURTHER READING

Hamlyn, D.W. (1984) *Metaphysics*, Cambridge: Cambridge University Press. A sophisticated introduction to metaphysics, with chapters on such basic topics as ontology, substance, appearance and reality, and mind.

Jubien, Michael (1997) *Contemporary Metaphysics*, Oxford: Blackwell. A contemporary textbook that contains chapters on several fundamental metaphysical topics, including the cosmological question. It also contains a few chapters on more specialised topics, such as colour, modality, and truth in fiction.

Kim, Jaegwon and Sosa, Ernest (1999) *Metaphysics: An Anthology*, Oxford: Blackwell. This anthology offers an excellent array of important articles on basic metaphysical topics. It also contains extensive references to other important sources in the field.

Taylor, Richard (1992) *Metaphysics*, Upper Saddle River, NJ: Prentice-Hall. Originally published in 1963, this classic textbook treats central topics in metaphysics, including the mind–body problem, space and time, causation, and God.

van Inwagen, Peter (1993) *Metaphysics*, Boulder, CO: Westview Press. A contemporary textbook that presents a distinctive overall view of the nature of reality and rational beings.

3

LOGIC
Greg Restall[1]

INTRODUCTION

Logic is the study of good reasoning. It's not the study of reasoning as it actually occurs, because people can often reason *badly*. Instead, in logic, we study what makes good reasoning *good*. The *logic* of good reasoning is the kind of connection between the *premises* from which we reason and the conclusions at which we arrive. Logic is a *normative* discipline: it aims to elucidate how we *ought* to reason. Reasoning is at the heart of philosophy, so *logic* has always been a central concern for philosophers.

This chapter is not a comprehensive introduction to formal logic. It will not teach you how to use the *tools* and *techniques* that have been so important to the discipline in the last century. For *that* you need a textbook, the time and patience to work through it, and preferably an instructor to help.[2] The aim of this chapter is to *situate* the field of logic. We will examine some of the core ideas of formal logic, as it has developed in the past century, we will spend a significant amount of time showing connections between logic and other areas of philosophy, and most importantly, we will show how the philosophy of logic contains many open questions and areas of continued research and investigation. Logic is a living field, and a great deal of interesting and important work in that field is being done today.

This chapter has five major sections: the first, *Validity* introduces and demarcates the topic which will be the focus of our investigation: *logical validity*, or in other words, *deductive logical consequence*. The most fruitful work in logic in the twentieth century has been informed by work in the formal sciences, mathematics throughout the century, and computer science in the second half of the century and into the twenty-first. So, the nature of *Formalism* will take up our second section. I will explain why logic as it has been studied is a *formal* discipline, and what that might mean for its techniques and applications. Work presenting formal logical systems generally proceeds in one of two ways, commonly called *syntax* and *semantics*, though I will explain below why I think that these terms are jointly a misnomer for the distinction between *Interpretations* on the one hand and *Proofs* on the other. There is no doubt that *Interpretations* and *Proofs* play an exceedingly important role in logic. The relationships between the two general modes of presenting a logical system can be presented in *soundness* and *completeness* results, which are vital to logic as a discipline. Finally, a section on *Directions* will sketch where the material presented here can lead, both into open issues in logic and its interpretation, and into other areas of philosophy.

By the end of this chapter, I hope to have convinced you that logic is a vital discipline in both senses of this word – yes, it is *important* to philosophy, mathematics and to theories of computation and of language – but just as importantly, it is *alive*. The insights of logicians, from Boole, to Frege, Russell, Hilbert, Gödel, Gentzen, Tarski to those working in the present, are alive today, and they continue to inform and enrich our understanding.

We will start our investigation, then, by looking at the subject matter logicians study: logical consequence, or valid argument.

VALIDITY

An *argument*, for philosophers, is a unit of reasoning: it is the move from premises to a conclusion. Here are some arguments that might be familiar to you.[3]

> **Nothing causes itself.**
> **There are no infinite regresses of causes.**
> **Therefore, there is an uncaused cause.**

> **It is a greater thing to exist both in the understanding and in reality, rather than in the understanding alone.**
> **That which is greater than all exists in the understanding.**
> **Therefore, that which is greater than all must exist not only in the understanding but in reality.**

The first argument here has two premises (the first states that nothing causes itself, the second that there is no regress of causes) and one conclusion (stating that there is a cause which is not caused by something else). Arguments may have many different virtues and vices. Some arguments are *convincing* and others are not. Some arguments are *understandable* and others are not. Some arguments are *surprising* and others are not. None of these virtues are the prime concern in the discipline of logic. They bear not only on the argument itself and the connections between premises and conclusions, but also on important features of the *hearers* of the argument. Issues like these are very important, but they are not *logic* as it is currently conceived. The central virtue of an argument, as far as *logic* is concerned, is the virtue of *validity*. To state things rather crudely, an argument is valid just when the conclusion *follows from* the premises: that is, in stating the premises, the conclusion follows inexorably from them.

This 'definition' of the term is no more than a hint. It does not tell us very much about how you might go about constructing valid arguments, and nor does it tell you how you might convince yourself (or convince others) that an argument is not valid. To do that, we need to fill out that hint in some way. *One* way to fill out the hint, which has gained widespread acceptance, is to define the concept of validity like this:

> **An argument is valid if and only if in every circumstance in which the premises are true, the conclusion is true too.**

This way of understanding validity clearly has *something* to do with the initial hint. If we have an argument whose premises are true in some circumstance, but whose conclusion is not true in that circumstance, then in an important sense, the conclusion tells you *more* than what is stated in the premises. On the other hand, if there is no such circumstance, the conclusion indeed does follow inexorably from the premises. No matter what possible way things are like, if the premises are true, so is the conclusion: without any exception whatsoever.[4]

This understanding of the concept of validity also at points you towards solutions to the two questions we asked. To show that an argument is *invalid* you must find a *circumstance* in which the premises are true and the conclusion is not. To convince yourself that an argument is *valid* you can do one of two things: you can convince yourself that there is no such circumstance, or you can endeavour to understand some basic arguments which preserve truth in all circumstances, and then string these basic arguments together to spell out in detail the larger argument. These two techniques for demonstrating validity will form the next two parts of this chapter. *Interpretations* provide one technique for understanding what counts as a circumstance, and techniques in logic from model theory will give techniques for constructing interpretations which demonstrate (and hopefully contribute to an *explanation* of) the invalidity of invalid arguments. *Proofs* are techniques to demonstrate validity of longer arguments in terms of the validity of small steps that are indubitably valid. We will see examples of both kinds of techniques in this chapter. Before this, we need to do a little more work to explain the notion of validity and its neighbours.

Validity is an all-or-nothing thing. It doesn't come in grades or shades. If you have an argument and there is just *one* unlikely circumstance in which the premises are true and the conclusion is not, the argument is *invalid*. Consider the cosmological argument, inferring the existence of an uncaused cause from the premises that nothing causes itself, and there are no infinite regresses of causes: one way to point out the invalidity of the argument as it stands is to note that a circumstance in which there are *no* causes or effects renders the premises true and the conclusion false. Then discussion about the argument can continue. We can either add the claim that something causes something else as a new premise, or we can attempt to argue that this hypothetical[5] circumstance is somehow impermissible. Both, of course, are acceptable ways to proceed: and taking either path goes some way to explain the virtues and vices of the argument and different ways we could extend or repair it.

The conclusion of a valid argument need not actually be *true*. Validity is a *conditional* concept: it is like *fragility*. Something is fragile when *if* you drop it on a hard surface it breaks. A fragile object need not be broken if it is never dropped. Similarly, an argument is valid if and only if in every circumstance where the premises are true, so is the conclusion. The conclusion needs to be true, unless *this* circumstance is one in which the premises are in fact true. Another virtue of arguments, which we call *soundness*, obtains when these 'activating conditions' obtain.

> **An argument is sound if and only if it is valid, and in addition, the premises are all true.**

Of course, many arguments have virtues without being valid or sound. For example, the argument

> **Christine is the mother of a five-month old son.**
> **Therefore, Christine is not getting much sleep.**

is reasonable, in the sense that we would not be making a terrible *mistake* of inferring the conclusion on the basis of the premises. However, the argument is not valid. There are circumstances in which the premise is true, but the conclusion is not. Christine might not be looking after her son, or her son *could* be unreasonably easy to care for. However, such circumstances are out of the ordinary. This motivates another definition of a virtue of arguments:[6]

> **An argument is strong if and only if in normal circumstances in which the premises are true, the conclusion is true too.**

This definition picks out an interesting relationship, which we can use to understand ways in which arguments are good or bad. However this kind of *strength*, commonly called *inductive strength* in contrast to *deductive* validity, will not be the focus of our chapter. By far the bulk of the work in logic in the twentieth century is in studying the notion of *validity*, and in particular, in using *formal* techniques to study it. So, we will turn to this new concept. What is it that makes formal logic *formal*?

FORMALISM

The *form* of an argument is its shape or its structure. For example, the following two arguments share some important structural features:

> **If the dog ran away, then the gate was not closed.**
> **The gate was closed.**
> **So, the dog didn't run away.**

> **If your actions are predetermined, then you are not free.**
> **You are free.**
> **Therefore, your actions are not predetermined.**

You can see that both of these arguments are valid, and they both are valid for the same kind of reason. One way of seeing that they are both valid is to see that they both have the following *form*:

> **If *p*, then not *q*.**
> **_q_.**
> **Therefore, not *p*.**

We get the first argument by selecting **the dog ran away** for *p* and **the gate was closed** for *q*. We get the second argument by selecting **your actions are predetermined** for *p* and **you are free** for *q*. Whatever you choose for *p* and *q*, the resulting argument will turn out to be valid: if the premises are both true, then *p* cannot be true, because if it *were* true, then since *p* implies the falsity of *q* we would have contradicted ourselves by agreeing that *q* is true. So *p* isn't true after all. As a result, we say that the argument form is also *valid*.

> **An argument form is valid if and only if whenever you substitute statements for the letters in the argument form, you get a valid argument as a result.**

The result of substituting statements for letters in an argument form is called an *instance* of the form. As a result, we could have said that an argument form is valid if and only if all of its instances are valid. Here is an example of *invalid* argument form.

If *p*, then *q*.
_q_.
Therefore, *p*.

This looks a lot like the previous argument form, but it not as good: it has many invalid instances. Here is one of them.

If it's a Tuesday, then it's a weekday.
It's a weekday.
Therefore, it's Tuesday.

This is an invalid argument, because there are plenty of circumstances in which the premises are both true, but the conclusion is not. (Try Wednesday.)

We shouldn't conclude that *every* instance of this form is invalid. An invalid argument form can have valid instances. Here is one:

If it's a Tuesday, then it's a Tuesday.
It's a Tuesday.
Therefore, it's Tuesday.

This is not a particularly informative or helpful argument, but using the definitions before us, it is most certainly a valid one. (This will hopefully make it clear, if it wasn't already, that validity is not the only virtue an argument can have.) You might object that the argument doesn't have the form requested. After all, it has the form

If *p*, then *p*.
_p_.
Therefore, *p*.

Which is valid (though not informative, at least in most instances). And that is correct. An argument can be an instance of different forms. This argument is an instance of the first form by selecting **it's Tuesday** for both *p* and *q*, it is an instance of the second form by selecting **it's Tuesday** for *p*.[7]

Formal logic is the study of the validity of argument forms. Developing formal logic, then, requires giving an account of the kinds of argument forms we wish to consider. Different choices of argument forms correspond to different choices of what you wish to include and what you wish to ignore when you consider validity. Think of the shape of an argument as determined by the degree of *ignorance* you wish to exhibit when looking at arguments. In the examples considered so far, we ignore everything except for **if . . . then . . .** and **not**. One reason for this is that we can say interesting things about validity with respect to arguments formulated with these kinds of words. Another reason is that these words are an important sense, *topic neutral*. The word **not** is not about anything in particular, in the way that the word **cabbage** is about a particular kind of vegetable. We can use the word not when talking about anything at all, and we do not introduce *new* subject matter. Whenever I *use* the word **cabbage** I talk about vegetables.[8]

Another way to think about the choice of argument forms is to think of it as the construction of a particular language that contains only words for particular concepts we take to study, and letters or variables for the rest. This is the construction of a *formal language*. Sometimes this construction of a particular formal language comes with high philosophical expectations. An important case is Frege's *Begriffschrift* (Frege 1972, 1984). Of course, commitment to the importance of formal logic need have no such hegemony for formal languages. Formalism may be important in gaining insight into rich natural languages, without ever endeavouring to *replace* messy natural languages by precise formal languages.

In this chapter, I will give an account of two different choices of formal languages: a smaller one (the language of *propositional logic*) and a larger one (the language *predicate logic*). Let's start with the language of propositional logic.

Propositional logic concerns itself with propositions or statements, and the ways that we combine statements to form other statements. The words or concepts that we use to combine or modify statements are called *operators*. We have already seen two: **if . . . then . . .** combines two statements to form another, which we call a *conditional* statement. The statement **if *p* then *q*** is the conditional with *p* as the *antecedent* and *q* as the *consequent*. On the other hand, **not** does not combine statements, it modifies one statement. If *p* is a statement, then so is **not-*p***, and we call this the *negation* of *p*.

In formal languages, it becomes convenient to use a shorthand form of writing to represent these forms of propositions. Instead of **if *p* then *q***, logicians write $p \supset q$. Instead of **not-*p***, you can write ~*p*. The use of symbols may be frightening or unfamiliar, but there is nothing special in it. It is merely a shorthand convenience. It is much easier (when you get used to it) to understand:

$(p \supset q) \supset (\sim q \supset \sim p)$

than it is to understand:

If (if the first then the second) then (if it's not the case that the second then it's not the case that the first).

The second sentence is no less *formal* than the first. The *formality* of logic arises from the study of forms of arguments. The symbolism is just a convenient way of representing these forms. The use of symbols for the operators and letters for statements makes it easier to see at a glance the structure of the statement.

Other operators beyond the conditional and negation are studied in propositional logic. Two important operators are *conjunction* (*p* **and** *q*) is the conjunction featuring *p* and *q* as its *conjuncts*: we write this (*p* & *q*) and *disjunction* (*p* **or** *q*) is the disjunction featuring *p* and *q* as its *disjuncts*: we write this (*p* v *q*).

Together with conditionals and negations, conjunction and disjunction can represent the structural features of a great deal of interesting and important reasoning. These operators form the basis of the *language of propositional logic*. In the following two sections, we will see two different kinds of techniques people have used to determine the kinds of arguments valid in this formal language. Before that, however, let's consider a larger language: the language of predicate logic.

If you think of the statements in propositional logic as *molecules*, then *predicate logic* introduces *atoms*. Consider the following short argument:

Horses are animals.
Therefore, heads of horses are heads of animals.

This is a valid argument, and it possesses a valid *form*.[9] It is a form it shares with this argument:

Philosophers are academics.
Therefore, children of philosophers are children of academics.

There are a number of things going on in these arguments, but nowhere inside the premises or the conclusions will you find a simpler statement. The premises and conclusions are combinations of other sorts of things. The most obvious are *predicates*. **Philosopher** is not a name: many things are philosophers, and many things are not. **Philosopher** is a term that *predicates* a property (being a philosopher) of an entity. The same goes with **horse**, **animal** and **academic**. These are all predicates. Sometimes we can use **child** and **animal** to predicate properties too, but this is not how these terms work in our arguments. The relevant property we care about is not that this is a head, or that this is a child: it is that this is a head *of some animal*, and that that is a child *of some philosopher*. These parts of the language **head of** and **child of** in these arguments predicate relations between things. Just as **philosopher** divides the world into the philosophers and the non-philosophers, **child** of divides *pairs* of things into those where the first thing is a child of the second, and those where the first is not a child of the second. So, **Greg is a philosopher** is true, but **Zack is a philosopher** is not (yet); and **Zack is a child of Greg** is true but **Greg is a child of Zack** is not.

Predicates can be one-place (like **philosopher**), two-place (like **child of**), or three-place (try . . . **is between** . . . **and** . . .) and of higher complexity.

We have already seen one thing that you can do with predicates. You can plug in *names* that pick out individuals, and combine them with predicates to make statements. However, in our arguments we are considering, there are no names at all. Something else is going on to combine these predicates together.

The traditional *syllogistic* logic due to Aristotle took there to be primitive ways of combining one-place predicates (in Aristotelian jargon, these are *subjects* and *predicates*) such as **all F** are **G**, **some F** are **G**, **no F** are **G** and **some F** are not **G**. Many arguments can be expressed using these techniques for combining predicates. However, our arguments above do even more with the language. The premises indeed do have the form **all F** are **G**; they say that all horses are animals, and that all philosophers are academics. To put things more technically, they say that for anything you choose at all, if it is an *F* then it is a *G*. The conclusions also have this form: in the first argument it says that, for anything you choose, if it is a head of a horse it is also the head of an animal. But what is it for something to be the head of a horse? Expressing this using the two-place predicate **head of** and the one-place predicate **horse**, you can see that a thing is the head of a horse just when there is another thing that is a **horse**, and this thing is a head of that thing. There is a lot going on here. We are showing that for anything we choose at all, if we can choose something (a horse) such that the first thing is the head of this thing, then we can choose something (an animal) such that the first thing is also the head of this thing. Making explicit the way that these choices interact is actually quite difficult. We can get by if we are happy to talk of *this thing*, *that thing*, and *the other thing* all the time. But just as we introduced letters *p*, *q* and so on to stand for statements, it is very useful to introduce letters *x*, *y* and so on to stand in the places of these pronouns. These are the *variables* in the language of predicate logic.

The only remaining pieces of the language we need to express this argument form are ways to express the kinds of choices we made for each pronoun. Sometimes we said that for *anything* we choose, if it is a horse, it is an animal. At other times we said that there was *something* we could choose which was a horse and had our other thing as a head. We have two ways of choosing and stating things: either we say that *everything* has some property, or we say that *something* has that property. These two ways of choosing are called *quantifiers*. Each comes with a variable: The *universal quantifier* (**All** *x*) – symbolised as (∀*x*) – indicates that our statement is true for any choice for *x* at all. The *existential quantifier* (**Some** *x*) – symbolised as

($\exists x$) – indicates that our statement is true for some choice for x. (You must be careful here: in English we almost always read 'some' as meaning 'a few'.) Given the language of predicates, variables and quantifiers, our arguments then have the following form:

(All *x*)(if *Fx* then *Gx*)
So, (All *y*)(if (Some *z*)(*Fz* and *Hyz*) then (Some *z*)(*Gz* and *Hyz*))

Or, using the symbols at our disposal:

($\forall x$)(*Fx* $\supset$ *Gx*)
So, ($\forall y$)(($\exists z$)(*Fz* & *Hyz*) $\supset$ ($\exists z$)(*Gz* & *Hyz*))

This notation makes very explicit the dependencies between the choices made in quantifiers. For example, it makes clear the two different claims: *someone robbed everyone*, and *everyone was robbed by someone*.[10]

($\exists x$)($\forall y$)*Rxy*   **($\forall y$)($\exists x$)*Rxy***

In *someone robbed everyone*, the choice of *someone* happens first, and we state that that person robbed everyone. In *everyone was robbed by someone*, we consider each individual person first, and for each person, we state that someone robbed this person. The person who robbed this person might not have robbed anyone else.

Some predicates have special properties. A very special predicate, from the point of view of logic, is the identity predicate, most often depicted by the '=' sign. A statement of the form $a = b$ is true if and only if the names a and b denote the same object. A language with identity can state much more than a language without it. In particular, in the language of predicate logic with identity, we are able to *count* objects. For example, we can say that there is exactly one object with property F with the expression

($\exists x$)(*Fx* & ($\forall y$)(*Fy* $\supset$ *x* = *y*))

which states that something is F and that if anything at all is F it is the same object as the first object we chose.

There is much more that you can say about formal languages, but we must stop here. It is not clear that *all* of the structure relevant to determining the validity of arguments can be explained using the techniques we have seen so far. Some arguments utilise notions of possibility and necessity (It *could* rain and the game *has* to be played, therefore we *could* be playing in the rain), predicate *modifiers* (She walked very quickly, therefore she walked) and quantification over *properties* as well as *objects* (The evening star has some property that the morning star doesn't, so the evening star and the morning star are different objects). Various *extensions* of this formal language have been considered and used to attempt to uncover more about the forms of these kinds of arguments.

INTERPRETATIONS

Given a formal language, we have a precise grasp of the kinds of assertions that can be made and the features we need to understand in order to give an account of validity. Recall that we take an argument to be valid if and only if in any circumstance in which the premises are true, so is the conclusion. As a result, to establish which arguments are valid in a formal language, it suffices to give an account of what these circumstances might be, and what it takes for a sentence in our formal language to be true in a circumstance.

Of course, in our *formal* languages, sentences are not genuinely true or false, because they do not *mean* anything. If we were to be precise, formulas such as $p \mathbin{\&} q$ or $(\forall x)(Fx \supset Gx)$ have a meaning only when meanings are given to their constituents. However, we can think of formulas as *derivatively* true or false, because they might be used to stand for true or false sentences in the language in which we are interested in expressing arguments. With this in mind, let's continue with the fiction of thinking of formulas as the kinds of things that might be true or false.

One way to think of circumstances appropriate for the analysis of arguments in *propositional* logic is to think of what they must do. A circumstance must decide the truth or otherwise of formulas. The language of propositional logic makes this task easy, because many of the operators of propositional logic interact with truth and falsity in special ways. The simplest case is negation: if a formula p is true, then its negation $\sim p$ is false, because it 'says' that p is not true – which is wrong, because p is true. On the other hand, if p is false, then its negation $\sim p$ is true, because it 'says' that p is not true, and this time this is correct. This small piece of reasoning can be presented in a table, which we call a *truth table*.

p	$\sim p$
0	1
1	0

Here, the number **1** represents truth and the number **0** represents falsehood. The two rows represent two different circumstances. In the first, p is false, and as a result, $\sim p$ is true. (We can say that in this circumstance the truth value of p is 0 and the value of $\sim p$ is **1**.) In the second, p is true, and as a result, $\sim p$ is false.

The fact that the truth value of a negation depends only on the truth value of the proposition negation means that negation is *truth functional*. More involved truth tables can be given for the other operators of propositional logic, because they are truth functional in exactly the same way.

We can present truth tables for other operators, by giving rows for the different circumstances – now we have *four* because there are four different combinations of truth or falsity among p and q – and a column for each complex formula: conjunction, disjunction and the conditional.

p	q	$p \& q$	$p \lor q$	$p \supset q$
0	0	0	0	1
0	1	0	1	1
1	0	0	1	0
1	1	1	1	1

Two of the three columns are straightforward: a conjunction is true if and only if both conjuncts are true, and a disjunction is true if and only if either disjunct is true. Here, disjunction is *inclusive*: $p \lor q$ is true when p and q are true. Another operator, *exclusive* disjunction, is false when both disjuncts are true. The column that causes controversy belongs to the conditional. According to this column, a conditional $p \supset q$ is false only when p is true and q is false. While it is clear that a conditional with a true antecedent and false consequent is false (we learn that **if it is cloudy it is raining** is false if it is a cloudy day without rain, for example) it is no means as certain that it this which is the *only* way that a conditional can be false. (After all, **if it is cloudy it is raining** certainly *seems* false even on a fine day when it is neither cloudy nor raining.) However, if we are to give a truth table for a conditional, it must be this one. (A conditional must be true if the antecedent and consequent have the same truth value, if $p \supset q$ is to always be true. A conditional must also be true if the antecedent is false and the consequent true, if $(p \& q) \supset p$ also is to be true when p is true but q is false.) Much has been said both in favour and against this analysis of the conditional. We will see a little of it in a later section. For now, it is sufficient to note that these rules for the conditional define *some* kind of **if** . . . **then** . . . operator, which happens to suffice for many arguments involving conditional constructions.[11]

It is also common to define another operator in terms of the conditional. The *biconditional* $p \equiv q$ can be defined as $(p \supset q)$ and $(q \supset p)$, that is, it says that if p is true, so is q and vice versa. Equivalently, you can define the biconditional by requiring that $p \equiv q$ gets the value true if and only if p and q get the same truth value.

Given this understanding of the interaction between operators and truth values, it is a very short step to using it to evaluate argument forms. After all, in any *circumstance* statements receive truth values. So, to evaluate an argument form involving these operators, it suffices to consider all of the possible combinations of truth values to the constituent atomic formulas that make up the argument form. For then, we can spot precisely the kinds of circumstances in which the statements are true, and those in which they are false. Since validity amounts to the preservation of truth in circumstances, we have a technique for testing validity of argument forms. Let's examine this technique by way of an example. Consider the argument form

p or q therefore if q then both p and q

with one premise and one conclusion. We can test it for validity by considering each of the possible combinations of truth values for p and q, and then using the truth table rules for each operator to establish the truth values of the premise and the conclusion, given each choice for p and q. This data can be presented in a table.

p	q	p	v	q	q	⊃	(p	&	q)
0	0	0	0	0	0	1	0	0	0
0	1	0	1	1	1	0	0	0	1
1	0	1	1	0	0	1	1	0	0
1	1	1	1	1	1	1	1	1	1

The two columns to the side list all the possible different combinations of truth values to p and q. As before, each row represents a different kind of circumstance. For example, the first row of truth values represents a kind of circumstance in which p and q are both false. Then, the other two sections of the table present the values of the premise and the conclusion in each of these rows. The values are computed *recursively*: in the first row, for example, the value of p & q is 0 because p & q are both 0: the value is written under the ampersand, the primary operator of this formula. The value of $q \supset (p$ & $q)$ is 1 because q and p & q both have the value 0. The other values in the table are computed in the same fashion.

In the table, the values of the premise and the conclusion are found in the two shaded columns. So, for example, in the first row, the premise is false and the conclusion is true. In the second (shaded) row, the premise is true but the conclusion is false. In the last two rows, the premise and conclusion are both true. Each row is an *interpretation* of the formulas, sufficient to determine their truth values. This information helps us evaluate the argument form. Since there is an interpretation in which the premise is true and the conclusion is not (that given by the second row) the argument form is *invalid*.

This is a sketch of the truth table technique for determining the validity of argument forms in the language of propositional logic. You can see that for any argument form, featuring n basic proposition letters, a truth table with 2^n rows is sufficient to determine the validity of this form. This means that we have a process that we can use to tell us whether or not an argument is valid. Validity in propositional logic is *decidable*. We will see more about decidability in the final section of this chapter.

There are a number of ways that these techniques can be extended further. One way we will not pursue here is to extend the class of truth values from the straightforward *true* and *false*. A popular extension is to admit a third value for statements that at least *appear* to be neither true nor false (think of borderline cases such as *Max is bald*, when Max is not hairless yet not hairy; or think of paradoxical sentences such as *this very statement is false*): you can think of adding extra values as extra *truth* values. However, this is not the only way to view modifications of this simple two-valued scheme. We may use more than two values to evaluate statements, without thinking of those values as extra truth values. Perhaps more values are needed to encode different kinds of semantic information. At any rate, *many-valued logic* is an active research area to this day (Urquhart 1986).

Another way that interpretations such as truth tables can be extended is to incorporate the predicates, names, variables and quantifiers of *predicate* logic. Here, we need to do a lot more work than with truth tables. To interpret the language of predicate logic we need to decide how to interpret *names*, *predicates*, *variables* and *quantifiers*. I will spend the rest of this section sketching the most prevalent way for providing interpretations for each semantic category. This technique is fundamentally due to Alfred Tarski, who pioneered and made precise the kinds of *models* for predicate logic in widespread use today (Tarski 1956).

In the case of truth tables, an interpretation of an expression was a simple affair: we distribute a truth value to each basic proposition letter, and we get the truth or falsity of every complex expression as defined out of them. We need something similar in the case of the language of predicate logic: we need enough to determine the truth or falsity of each expression of the language of predicate logic. But how can we do this? There are connections between different expressions such as *Fa*, $(\forall x)Fx$ and $(\exists x)Fx$. It will not suffice to distribute truth values among them. We need some way to understand the connections between them, and this will require understanding the ways that names, predicates, variables and quantifiers function, and how they contribute to truth.

A natural way to interpret names is to pair each name with an *object*, which we interpret the name as *denoting*. The collection of objects that *might* be used to

77

denote names we will call the *domain* of the interpretation. Then, to interpret a *predicate*, we need at the very least something that will give us a truth value for every object we wish to consider. Given that we know what *a* denotes, we wish to know if it has the *property* picked out by *F*. This is the very least we need in order to tell whether or not *Fa* is true. So, to interpret a one-place predicate, we require a *rule* that gives us a truth value (true or false; or equivalently, **1** or **0**) for each object in the domain. The same thing goes for two-place predicates, except that to tell whether or not *Rab* is true, we need a truth value corresponding to the *pair* of *a* and *b*: so a two-place predicate is interpreted by a rule that gives a truth value for every *pair* of objects in the domain.

Names and predicates are the straightforward part of the equation. The difficulty in interpreting the language of predicate logic is caused by quantifiers and variables. The major cause of the difficulty is in the behaviour of variables. Variables by themselves are meaningless. Even if we have an interpretation of each of the names and predicates in our language, variables don't mean anything in particular. In fact, variables don't have any interpretation at all in isolation. If we know what *F* means, it does not help in answering the question of what *Fx* means, and in particular, whether or not it is true. Variables have meanings by themselves only in the context of *quantifiers*. For example, given an interpretation, $(\exists x)Fx$ is true if and only if *something* in the domain of that interpretation has property *F* (as given by that interpretation). What we need is a rule that can tell us whether or not a quantified formula is true, in general. There are two general ways to do this. One, due to Tarski, keeps variables in the formula and adds exactly what you need to interpret them. The other expands the language to incorporate names for every object in the domain, and dispenses with variables when it comes to evaluating formulas involving quantifiers.

Tarski's approach notes that you can interpret variables 'unbound' by quantifiers, like the *x* in *Fx* if you already know in advance what we take *x* to denote. If we proceed with the fiction that *variables* can denote, we can say whether or not *Fx* is true. The way of maintaining the fiction is to introduce an *assignment* of values to variables. An *assignment* α is a rule that picks out an object in the domain for every variable in the language. Then we can say that a formula like $(\forall y)(\exists x)Rxy$ is true, relative to the assignment α when the inside formula $(\exists x)Rxy$ *is true for every value for* *y* – which now means that it's true for every assignment β that agrees with α, except that it is allowed to vary the value assigned to the variable *y*. Tarski said that a universally quantified formula is *satisfied* by an assignment, just when the inside formula is satisfied by every *variant* assignment. Similarly, an existentially quantified formula is satisfied by an assignment just when the inside formula is satisfied by *some* variant assignment, as it says that *something* in the domain has the required property.

Another way to go in interpreting a formula like $(\forall y)(\exists x)Rxy$ is to ignore assignments of variables, and to make sure that our language contains a name for every object in the domain. Then $(\forall y)(\exists x)Rxy$ is true just when $(\exists x)Rxa$, $(\exists x)Rxb$ $(\exists x)Rxc$ and all other *instances* of $(\forall y)(\exists x)Rxy$ are true. Similarly, $(\exists x)Rxa$ is true just when *some* instance such as **Raa**, **Rba**, or **Rca** is true.

Both techniques result in exactly the same answers for each formula, given an interpretation, and each technique has its own advantages. Tarski's technique assigns meanings to each expression in terms of the meanings of its constituent parts, without resorting to any *other* formula outside the original expression. The other technique, however, is decidedly simpler, especially when applied to interpretations where the domain is *finite*.

The rules we have discussed here suffice to fix a truth value for every complex expression in the language of predicate logic, once you are given an interpretation for every predicate and name in the language. Predicates, names, variables and quantifiers are interpreted using these techniques, and the operators of propositional logic are interpreted as before. Therefore, we have a technique for determining validity of arguments in the language of predicate logic. An argument form is valid if and only if every interpretation that makes the premises true also makes the conclusion true.

Let's see how this technique works in a simple example. We will show that the argument form

$(\forall y)(\exists x)Rxy$ therefore $(\exists x)(\forall y)Rxy$

is invalid, by exhibiting an interpretation which makes the first formula true, but the second one false. (To guide your intuitions here, think of **R** as 'is related to': The premise says that for everyone you choose, there's someone related to them. The conclusion says that someone is related to everyone.) Consider a simple domain with just two objects *a* and *b*. There are no names in the language of the argument, but we will use the two names *a* and *b* in the language to pick out the objects *a* and *b* respectively. To interpret the two-place predicate **R** we need to have a rule that gives us a truth value for *every* pair of objects in the domain. I will present a rule doing just that in a table, like this:

R	a	b
a	0	1
b	1	0

This table tells us that Raa and Rbb are false, but Rab and Rba are true. As an example of how to read tables for two-place predicates it is not particularly good, since I haven't told you which of the **1**s is the value for Rab and which is the value for Rba. The answer is this: The **1** in the first row and second column is the value for Rab.

Now, in this interpretation, $(\forall y)(\exists x)Rxy$ is true, since $(\exists x)Rxa$ and $(\exists x)Rxb$ are both true. (Why are these true? Well, $(\exists x)Rxa$ is true since Rba is, and $(\exists x)Rxb$ is true because Rab is.) However, in this interpretation $(\exists x)(\forall y)Rxy$ is not true, since $(\forall y)Ray$ and $(\forall y)Rby$ are both not true. (Why are these not true? $(\forall y)Ray$ is not true because Raa is not true, and $(\forall y)Rby$ is not true because Rbb is not true.) Therefore, the argument is invalid.

This very short example gives you a taste of how interpretations for predicate logic can be used to demonstrate the invalidity of argument forms. Of course, doing this at this level isn't necessarily an advance over simply thinking $(\forall y)(\exists x)Rxy$ could be true if every object is related by R to some other object: it doesn't follow that $(\exists x)(\forall y)Rxy$ because objects could be paired up, so that nothing is related by R to everything. Demonstrating invalidity by dreaming up hypothetical examples still has its place: the techniques of formal logic don't replace thought, they simply expose the structure of what we were already doing, and help us see how the techniques might apply in cases where our imagination or intuition give out.

You may notice that interpretations of the language of predicate logic differ from truth tables in one very important respect. We could easily *list* all of the possible different interpretations of an argument in propositional logic. In predicate logic this is no longer possible. We could interpret an argument in a domain of *one* object, of *two* objects, of *three*, or of 3088, or of a million, or of an infinite number. There is no limit to the number of different interpretations of the language of predicate logic. This means that our definition of validity for expressions in predicate logic does not give us a recipe for determining validity in practice. If we chance on a counterexample showing that an argument is invalid, we might be able to verify that the argument is invalid.[12] But what if there is no counterexample? How could we *verify* that there isn't one? Going one-by-one through an infinite list is not going to help. Finding an alternative way to *demonstrate* validity requires a different approach. We need to go back to square one, and examine an alternative analysis of validity.

PROOFS

Interpretations are one way to do *semantics*: to give an account of the *significance* of an expression. In doing this, models work from the *inside out*. In truth tables for propositional logic, the truth value of a complex proposition is determined by the truth values of its constituents. In models for predicate logic, the satisfaction of a complex formula in a model is determined by the satisfaction of its constituents in that model. In other models for other kinds of logics, the same features hold.

This is not the only way to determine significance. Another technique turns this on its head: you can work *outside in*. We may determine the significance of a complex expression in terms of its surface structure. Let's start with an example. Consider the argument form:

_p_ therefore (if _q_ then both _p_ and _q_)

One way to deal with the argument is to enumerate the different possibilities for *p* and *q* and consider what this expression might amount to in each of them, in terms of these possibilities. This is proceeding *inside out*.

On the other hand, we might work *outside in* by *supposing* that the premise is true, and then seeing if we can show that the conclusion is true. We might ask what we can do with the conclusion, an **if . . . then . . .** statement, by asking how we could show it to be true (or in general, how we could show that it follows from some collection of assumptions). It is a plausible thought that **if . . . then . . .** statements can be proved by *assuming* the antecedent (in this case, *q*) and then by *deducing* the consequent (in this case: **both *p* and *q***). To prove this on the basis of the assumptions we have, it suffices to look back and see that we have assumed both *p* and *q*. So, our argument seems valid: we have shown that the conclusion **if *q* then both *p* and *q*** follows from the premise *p*.

What we have just done is a *proof*: it is what is called a *natural deduction* proof. We can present that proof in a diagram. Here is one way of presenting what has gone on in that paragraph.

$$\cfrac{\cfrac{p \qquad \overline{q}}{p \ \& \ q}}{q \supset (p \ \& \ q)}$$

We start by *assuming p* and *q* at the top of the diagram. Then we deduce the conjunction *p* & *q* at the next line. Then in the last step, *we discharge* the assumption of *q* to deduce the conclusion *q* ⊃ (*p* & *q*).

This is a *natural deduction proof* in the style of Prawitz (1965). There are many other different styles of presenting proofs like this (Fitch 1952; Lemmon 1965), and it is most common to be taught logic by means of one of these kinds of systems of proof. Natural deduction proofs have a virtue of being very close to a natural style of reasoning we already use.

The rules for each operator can be supplemented with rules for quantifiers, which results in a proof system for the whole of predicate logic. For example, here is a proof showing $(\forall x)(Fx \ \& \ Gx)$ that follows from $(\forall x)Fx \ \& \ (\forall x)Gx$.

$$
\frac{\dfrac{\dfrac{(\forall x)Fx \ \& \ (\forall x)Gx}{(\forall x)Fx}}{Fa} \qquad \dfrac{\dfrac{(\forall x)Fx \ \& \ (\forall x)Gx}{(\forall x)Gx}}{Ga}}{\dfrac{Fa \ \& \ Ga}{(\forall x)(Fx \ \& \ Gx)}}
$$

The interesting moves in this proof are those involving quantifiers. In the left branch we move from $(\forall x)Fx$ to Fa: from a universal quantifier to some instance of it. Similarly in the right branch, we move from $(\forall x)Gx$ to Ga. Then, after deducing $Fa \ \& \ Ga$ from the two conjuncts, we deduce the final conclusion $(\forall x)(Fx \ \& \ Gx)$. This move is valid not because $(\forall x)(Fx \ \& \ Gx)$ follows from $Fa \ \& \ Ga$ – it doesn't – but because we proved $Fa \ \& \ Ga$ without assuming anything about a. The only assumption the proof made was $(\forall x)Fx \ \& \ (\forall x)Gx$. So, a was arbitrary. What holds for a holds for anything at all, so we can conclude $(\forall x)(Fx \ \& \ Gx)$.

There are other kinds of proof system beyond natural deduction. Hilbert-style proof theories typically have a number of *axioms* and a small number of rules, and construct proofs in a similar way to natural deduction systems. Tableaux or tree proof theories are somewhat different: instead of attempting to *demonstrate* statements, tableaux systems aim to show that statements are *satisfiable* or *unsatisfiable*. They are still *decompositional* theories, decomposing statements into their constituents, but instead of asking 'how can I *prove* X?' you ask 'what *follows from* X?' You show that an argument is valid, using a tableaux system by showing that you cannot make the premises true and the conclusion false: that is, the premises and the negation of the conclusion, considered together, are *unsatisfiable*.

Overleaf, for example, is a tableaux proof showing that $(\forall x)(Fx \ \& \ Gx)$ follows from $(\forall x)Fx \ \& \ (\forall x)Gx$: that is, that $(\forall x)Fx$ and $(\forall x)Gx$ and $\sim(\forall x)(Fx \ \& \ Gx)$ cannot be true together.

In this proof, as in the natural deduction proof, we deduce $(\forall x)Fx$ and $(\forall x)Gx$ from $(\forall x)Fx \ \& \ (\forall x)Gx$. However, from $\sim(\forall x)(Fx \ \& \ Gx)$ we deduce that there must be *some* object which doesn't have both properties F and G. We call this object a.

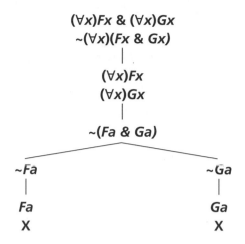

$(\forall x)Fx$ & $(\forall x)Gx$
$\sim(\forall x)(Fx$ & $Gx)$
|
$(\forall x)Fx$
$(\forall x)Gx$
|
$\sim(Fa$ & $Ga)$

$\sim Fa$ $\qquad\qquad\qquad$ $\sim Ga$
| $\qquad\qquad\qquad\qquad$ |
Fa $\qquad\qquad\qquad\qquad$ Ga
X $\qquad\qquad\qquad\qquad$ X

Now, since $\sim(Fa$ & $Ga)$ is true, it follows that *either* $\sim Fa$ or $\sim Ga$. Our way of representing this is by *branching* the tree into two possibilities. But now in the left branch we can use $(\forall x)Fx$ to deduce Fa which conflicts with $\sim Fa$, and in the right we can use $(\forall x)Gx$ to deduce Ga which conflicts with $\sim Ga$. Neither case is satisfiable in an interpretation, so there is no interpretation at all in which $(\forall x)Fx$ & $(\forall x)Gx$ and $\sim(\forall x)(Fx$ & $Gx)$ are true together: the argument is valid.

Proofs like these are one way to demonstrate conclusively that an argument in the language of predicate logic is indeed *valid*. To use proofs as a technique for determining validity of arguments, where validity is defined in terms of *interpretations* you need to have some connection between proofs and interpretations. Such a connection is provided by *soundness* and *completeness* results. A system of proofs is *sound* if any argument you can show to be valid using the proof system is indeed valid (according to the definition in terms of interpretations.) You can show that a system of proofs is sound by going through every rule in the proof system, showing that they are valid, and by checking that stringing together valid arguments in the ways licensed by the proof system results in more valid arguments. Soundness results are generally straightforward (if tedious) to demonstrate.

A system of proofs is *complete* if any argument that is indeed valid can be shown to be valid by some particular proof. Completeness results are typically much more difficult to prove. It is usually possible to demonstrate the equivalent result that if some argument cannot be proved by a particular proof system, then there is some interpretation that makes the premises true and the conclusion false. The techniques for demonstrating completeness are beyond the scope of this chapter, but they are some of the most important techniques in twentieth century logic.

DIRECTIONS AND ISSUES

I have attempted to give a general overview of some of the motivations, tools and techniques that have been important in the study of logic in the last century. In this remaining section, I will consider a few issues that arise on the basis of this foundation. These issues each form the core of distinct research programmes that are alive and flourish today.

Decidability and undecidability

We have already seen that the classes of interpretations appropriate for propositional and predicate logic differ in one important respect. To check a propositional argument form for validity, you need only check finitely many interpretations. To check a predicate logic form for validity you may need to check *infinitely* many interpretations. It has been shown that this is not an artefact of the way that interpretations have been defined. There is *no* recipe or algorithm for determining whether or not an argument form of predicate logic is valid or invalid. To be sure, some valid arguments can be shown to be valid, and some invalid arguments can be shown to be invalid. However, there is no single process which, when given any predicate logic argument form, will determine whether or not the argument form is valid. This result follows from Gödel's celebrated *incompleteness* theorem, which I will discuss below. To defend the claim that there is no algorithm determining validity, however, you need to have a precise account of what it is for something to be an algorithm. The clarification of this notion is another of the highlights of twentieth century logic. It has been shown that different explanations of what it is for a process to be an algorithm – a mathematical definition in terms of *recursive functions*, and different concrete implementations of algorithms in terms of *Turing machines* and *register machines* – are all equivalent: they pick out the same class of processes. This lends support to *Church's Thesis*: all computable processes are computable by Turing machines (Boolos and Jeffrey 1989). Given such a precise identification of the range of the computable, it follows – after some work (Boolos and Jeffrey 1989) – that there is no algorithm for determining validity in predicate logic. This means that no computer can be programmed to decide validity for arguments. Any theorem-proving software expressive enough to handle arguments in predicate logic, will encounter arguments that it will not be able to determine for validity.

Contemporary work in computer science aims to understand not only the border between the computable and the uncomputable, but also different grades of computability. Distinctions may still be drawn between problems that are solvable by algorithm. Some problems, such as evaluating propositional validity, are decidable by *exponentially difficult algorithms*. Here, the number of cases to check grows exponentially in terms of the length of the problem itself. (A problem in 3 sentence letters requires checking $2^3 = 8$ cases. A problem in 100 sentence letters requires checking 2^{100} cases. That is, you must check

1,267,650,600,228,229,401,496,703,205,376

cases, which is a great deal more. (Checking a billion cases a second would still leave you with 4×10^{13} years of work to complete your task.) So, an exponentially difficult problem like this can in practice be impossible to carry out.

Completeness and incompleteness

The insight that validity in predicate logic is *undecidable* followed from Kurt Gödel's groundbreaking work showing that elementary arithmetic is *incomplete*. That is, he showed that any collection of premises about numbers (expressed in the language of predicate logic, with enough vocabulary to express identity, addition and multiplication) would be *incomplete* in the sense that not every truth about the natural numbers (the whole numbers 0, 1, 2, 3 . . .) would follow from those premises. This is not quite right as it stands, of course, because you could take the premises to be the collection of *all* of the truths about whole numbers, and this would be trivially complete, at the cost of being uninteresting. No, Gödel showed that provided you had an *algorithm* for determining whether or not something was a premise for your theory of numbers, then your theory of numbers (the collection of conclusions provable from your premises) could not be complete, at least, not if it was consistent. If it were consistent, it would always leave *some* truth about numbers out.

Gödel's technique for demonstrating this is his celebrated encoding of statements about *proofs* and other *statements* into statements about *numbers*: what we now call a *Gödel* numbering. Arithmetic happens to be expressive enough to ensure that any statements about proofs checked with an algorithm can be encoded into statements about numbers. (The technique is not altogether different from the encoding of a document on a computer into a string of digits in ASCII or in Unicode.) Then statements about statements and proofs can be manipulated in a theory designed to talk only about numbers. In particular, you can get a theory T of arithmetic to express a statement G that would be true if and only if the theory T cannot prove that G is true. (The statement G basically 'says of itself' that it is not provable in T.) Now consider what the theory T can say about G. If the theory

T can prove G, then the theory T proves some falsehoods, since G is true if and only if it *cannot* be proved in T. So, if the theory cannot prove G then G must be true (because it is true if and only if it cannot be proved). So the theory T is incomplete.

This technique is general and it applies to other theories beyond arithmetic. An important branch of mathematics studies the relationships between different mathematical theories of increasing strength, and ways to extend incomplete theories in natural directions.

Gödel's results also have important philosophical consequences. Hilbert's program of finding a philosophically acceptable *foundation* of mathematics in terms of logical consistency ran aground because logical consequence and consistency was shown by Gödel not to be a finitary algorithmically-checkable notion. Logic, in its complexity, remains useful as a tool for the analysis of arguments. It is less appealing as a straightforward foundation of mathematics or any other discipline.

Which are the logical constants?

We have shown that a lot can be done by focusing on the propositional operators and quantifiers. These expressions are logical *constants*. Their interpretation is held fixed in every model. We can vary propositional letters, names or predicates, but an interpretation is not allowed to model *conjunction* as *disjunction*. Is this simply a matter of convenience, or is this a matter deeply embedded in the notion of logical consequence? There is no settled answer to this question. Some take the logical constants to be privileged symbols in our language because of some special feature they have, such as truth functionality or some analogue (see, for example Quine 1970). Others take the distinction between the logical and non-logical vocabulary to be a conventional one (Etchemendy 1990).

Conditionality and modality

When we considered the truth table for the conditional, we saw that it appears to leave a lot to be desired. After all, if I assert

If it's Sunday, it's a weekday

on a Wednesday, we would not be inclined to say that my statement is *true* just because the antecedent is false and the consequent is true. We'd much more likely think that if it *were* a Sunday, it would be a weekend, and not a weekday, and so, the statement is actually *false*. What we have done in considering this statement in this way is to consider *alternative circumstances*. We have asked ourselves what the world *would* have been like had the antecedent been true, and in particular, we consider if the consequent would have been true in those circumstances. In doing this, we need to move beyond the simple evaluation of propositions just in terms of their truth or falsity to consider their truth or falsity in other circumstances. We have done this already to a small extent in the evaluation of arguments (which is, after all, a *conditional* notion: we want to know whether or not *if* the premises are true, *then* the conclusion is true). A *modal* account of the conditional says that the same must be done for (at least some) *if . . . then . . .* statements. A conditional statement depends not only on the truth or falsity of the antecedent and consequent here and now, but also on the connections between them in *alternative* circumstances.

This makes the conditional a kind of *modal* operator like *necessity* and *possibility*. It is *necessary* that *p* if and only if *p* is true in all alternative circumstances (so *p* is not only true, but it is in some sense *unavoidable*). It is *possible* that *p* if and only if *p* is true in some alternative circumstances (so *p* might not be true, but were things to turn out like *that* circumstance *p would be* true). Similar logical features are displayed by other operators that pay attention to *context* such as *temporal* operators (*always p* is true at some time if and only if *p* is true at all times) and *location* operators (*around here p* is true at some location if and only if *p* is true at all locations near that location). In each case, we see that the semantic value of an expression depends not only on its truth or falsity, but its truth or falsity in some kind of *context*. The study of these kinds of operators has flowered in the latter part of the twentieth century. See the further reading list for some places to pursue this material.

Relevance

Some arguments seem to be invalid, despite coming out as valid according to the definitions we have given. Some particularly tricky arguments are the *fallacies of relevance*:

p therefore q or not q   **p and not p therefore q**

The first argument turns out to be valid because *every* interpretation makes *q* **or not** *q* true, whether or not *p* is true. So in every interpretation in which *p* is true, so is *q* **or not** *q*. Similarly, no interpretation makes *p* **and not** *p* true, so there is no interpretation in which *p* **and not** *p* is true but *q* isn't, so there is no counterexample to the validity of the second argument. A minority tradition in twentieth century logic has argued that something is mistaken in the dominant account, because it does not pay heed to the norms of *relevance*. These arguments are invalid because the premise has nothing to do with the conclusion in each case. In the first argument, the conclusion is true (and necessarily so) but it need not *follow from* the premise. In the second case the premise is false (and necessarily so) but again, the conclusion need not follow from it (Read 1995). *Relevant* logics attempt to formalise a notion of validity that take these considerations into account.

Vagueness

Another issue with the standard account of propositional logic arises from the assumption that every interpretation assigns exactly one of the values *true* and *false* to every expression. This is certainly less than obviously true when it comes to *vague* expressions. Consider a strip of colour shading evenly from fire engine red on the one side to lemon yellow on the other. Consider the statement 'that's red' expressed while pointing to parts of the strip, going from left to right. The statement is true when you start, and false when you finish. Where along the strip did it change from true to false? It is difficult to say. This is one way to think of the problems of *vagueness*. One option is to say that logic has nothing to do with vagueness. Logical distinctions apply only when we have precise notions and not vague ones. This seems like an unpalatable option, because our languages are *riddled* with vague notions, and there seems to be no way to eliminate them in favour of precise ones. It would be dire indeed to conclude that there is *no* distinction between validity and invalidity for arguments involving vague notions.

So, let's consider options for considering how logic might apply in the context of vagueness. (Williamson (1994) gives a good overview of the issues here. Read (1995) supplies a helpful shorter account.) One option is to say that logic applies but that the standard *classical* two-valued account does not apply to vague predicates. A vague predicate is not interpreted as a rule giving just *true* or *false* for every object: it must do more. One simple account is to say that a vague predicate supplies the value *true* to every object definitely within the extension of the predicate, *false* to every object definitely outside it, and a third value, *neither*, to the rest. This might be appealing, but it almost certainly doesn't give the right answer in general. One problem plaguing this three-valued approach is the way that it trades in *one* sharp borderline (between the *true* and the *false*) for *two* sharp borderlines (between the *true* and the *neither* and between the *neither* and the *false*). If there is no sharp borderline between the red and the non-red in the strip of colours, there is no sharp borderline between the definitely red and the neither definitely red nor definitely non-red, and there is no sharp borderline between the neither definitely red nor definitely non-red and the definitely non-red. The distinctive behaviour of the strip of colours is that there appears to be *no* sharp borderline, not that there are *two*.

A more popular modification of classical predicate logic to deal with vagueness is to take predicates to be interpreted by *degrees*. The predicate *red* is interpreted not as dividing things into the red and non-red, and not as dividing things into the definitely red, definitely non-red and the neither, but rather as assigning a number between 0 and 1 to every object: its *degree* of redness. Canonical red things get degree 1, canonical non-red things get degree 0, and other things in between get an in-between value, such as 1/2, 0.33, or any other number in the interval [0, 1]. This is the approach of *fuzzy logic*. If we leave things as I have explained them, we are in no better situation than in the three-valued case: we have traded in one or two borderlines for *infinitely many*. Now there is not only a sharp difference between things which are definitely red (red to degree 1) and not quite definitely red (red to some degree less than 1), there is also the sharp difference between things which are more red than not (red to a degree greater than 1/2) and things which are at least as non-red as they are red (red to a degree no greater than 1/2), and infinitely more borderlines besides. Again, the strip of colours doesn't seem to exhibit *this* structure. Proponents of fuzzy logic respond that the assignment of values to objects is *itself* a matter of degree, and not an all-or-nothing matter. Whether this can be made coherent or not is a matter of some debate.

The alternative is to think that the classical two-valued approach still works in the case of vagueness, but that it must be interpreted carefully. There are two major traditions here. The first, *supervaluational* approach, due to van Fraassen and Fine (see Williamson's book for references) takes an interpretation to still assign one of the two truth values to each predicate/object pair, but vagueness means that our language doesn't pick out one interpretation as the *right one*. There are a number of ways that you could acceptably draw the borderline between the red and the non-red. Something is *true* if it is true in any acceptable interpretation. A *supervaluation* is a class of interpretations (or valuations). Again, supervaluational approaches face a similar problem with borderlines. The very notion of something being an acceptable interpretation seems to be a vague notion. Another kind of problem for supervaluational approaches is the fact that they seem to undercut their own position: it is true on any acceptable interpretation that there is a last red spot on the spectrum: a red patch where the very next patch is not red.[13] For any interpretation at all draws a line between the red and the non-red. So according to supervaluations there is a sharp borderline, but there is no line such that *that* is the line between the red and the non-red.

The major alternative approach is to bite the bullet and conclude that there *is* a borderline between the red and the non-red. However, the fact that the predicate is vague means that the borderline is impossible to discern. While there is one correct interpretation of the predicate *red*, the class of acceptable interpretations might be the best we can do in actually *determining* what the extension of *red* might be. Vagueness, then, is a limitation in our *knowledge* rather than our *semantics*. The meaning of the term *red* is picked out precisely, but our capacity for recognising that meaning is not complete. So goes the response of the *epistemicist* about vagueness. Williamson's book (1994) is a spirited defence of epistemicism.

Meaning

Vagueness is just one phenomenon alerting us to the fact that the interpretation of logical techniques is fraught with philosophical issues. So is the relationship between *proofs* and *models*. A number of deep philosophical concerns about *meaning* hang on the way we ought to analyse and understand the meanings of statements. Broadly *realist* approaches enjoin us to analyse meaning in terms of truth conditions (Devitt 1991) or what we might see as *models* or *interpretations*. Broadly *anti-realist* approaches enjoin us to take *inference* or *proof* as primary (Brandom 1994; Dummett 1991). It is not my place here to determine the virtues or vices of either side in this debate (to do so would take us away into concerns in the philosophy of language). Committed realists will take models or interpretations as primary, and view proof theory as derivative. Committed anti-realists will take proof theory as primary, and take models as derivative.[14] *Logicians* who start with a thorough grounding in the techniques of models and of proofs, and who know that they can be shown to be equivalent, might ask different questions. In what sense might proofs be primary? In what sense might models be primary? In what sense might they do exactly the same job?

EXERCISES

1   Is validity always a matter of logical form? Can you think of any genuinely *valid* argument that doesn't exhibit any kind of *form* or *structure* responsible for its validity?
2   What is special about the logical operators of conjunction, disjunction, negation and implication? What other operators, if any, have any of these special features?
3   What is special about the *existential* and *universal* quantifiers? Do other quantifiers like *most* (think: *most* of the beer is gone, instead of *all* of the beer is gone) have interesting logical properties?
4   We have seen proof systems like *natural deduction*, which aim to *demonstrate* formulas, and *tableaux*, which aim to *satisfy* formulas. Is there any other kind of goal a proof system might have?

5   Which has priority: proofs or interpretations? Or can one technique have priority in *one* sense, and the other in a *different* sense?

NOTES

1   Thanks to my students in logic classes at Macquarie University for their enthusiastic responses when I have to taught logic and shared some of why it is so interesting. Thanks, too, to John Shand for detailed comments on an earlier draft of this chapter.

2   Of course, I recommend my textbook Logic in this series. However, the Further Reading list contains a number of books that also serve as excellent introductions to the techniques of formal logic.

3   These are, of course, two arguments purporting to demonstrate the existence of God. The first is found in the second of Aquinas' *five ways*, and the second is Anselm's ontological argument.

4   'Circumstance' here, is *very* broadly construed. In fact, it is so broadly construed as to incorporate any consistent circumstance at all. As a result, we could also think of valid arguments as ones in which the premises are *inconsistent with* the denial of the conclusion.

5   For the circumstance is indeed hypothetical, because presumably there *are* causes and effects. Hypothetical or non-actual circumstances are always within the remit of our discussion, even if they seem crazy or unexpected. The way we demonstrate the invalidity of arguments is to ask 'but what would happen *if* . . .?' One does not have to argue that there *actually* are no causes or effects to show that this argument is invalid.

6   I am indebted to Graham Priest and his paper 'Validity' (Priest 1999) for this way to consider these kinds of *non-monotonic* virtues of arguments.

7   There is no more problem for picking the one thing to instantiate different *variables* in logic than there is in mathematics. After all, if $f(x,y) = x + 2y$, we want to be able to say that $f(3,3) = 9$, but in doing that, we're instantiating the variables x and y both to 3.

8   However, presumably I can *mention* the word cabbage without talking about vegetables.

9   The validity of these arguments cannot be shown using Aristotle's *Syllogistic*, and it was arguments like these that helped fuel the development of modern predicate logic.

10 Interestingly, the grammar checker in the software package I used to write this chapter does not know the difference: it prompts me to replace the passive voice in 'everyone was robbed by someone' with the active-voiced 'someone robbed everyone.' If 'someone' were grammatically a *name* this would be acceptable. The grammar checker does not understand the difference between names and quantifiers.

11 It also seems to suffice for the kinds of conditionals used in mathematical reasoning, which perhaps explains why logicians such as Frege and Russell saw this understanding of the conditional as adequate.

12 Even this might be difficult, if the domain is infinite. Consider statements about numbers. It might be that the domain of the natural numbers is a counterexample to Goldbach's conjecture (that every even number is the sum of two primes) but verifying this fact, if indeed it is a fact, is a difficult mathematical problem.

13 Let's presume that the spectrum is divided into a finite but very large number of patches, such that each patch looks indiscernibly different from the patches immediately to its left and to its right.

14 And in fact, some take constraints on an acceptable proof theory to be so stringent as to motivate us away from classical predicate logic to some weaker logic, such as intuitionistic predicate logic (Dummett 1991).

BIBLIOGRAPHY

Boolos, George and Richard C. Jeffrey (1989) *Computability and Logic*, third edition, Cambridge: Cambridge University Press.

Brandom, Robert (1994) *Making it Explicit*, New Haven: Harvard University Press.

Devitt, Michael (1991) *Realism and Truth*, second edition, Oxford: Blackwell.

Dummett, Michael (1991) *The Logical Basis of Metaphysics*, New Haven: Harvard University Press.

Etchemendy, John (1990) *The Concept of Logical Consequence*, Cambridge, MA: Harvard University Press.

Fitch, F.B. (1952) *Symbolic Logic*, New York: Roland Press.

Frege, Gottlob (1972) *Conceptual Notation and Related Articles*, translated and edited with a biography and introduction by Terrell Ward Bynum, Oxford: Oxford University Press.

Frege, Gottlob (1984) *Collected Papers on Mathematics, Logic and Philosophy*, edited by Brian McGuinness, translated by Max Black, V.H. Dudman, Peter Geach, Hans Kaal, E–H.W. Kluge, Brian McGuinness and R.H. Stoothoff, Oxford: Blackwell.

Lemmon, E.J. (1965) *Beginning Logic*, London: Nelson.

Prawitz, Dag (1965) *Natural Deduction*, Stockholm: Almqvist and Wiksell.

Priest, Graham (1999) 'Validity', in Achille C. Varzi (ed.) *European Review of Philosophy* volume 4: *The Nature of Logic*. Stanford, CA: CSLI Publications. pp. 183–206.

Tarski, Alfred (1956) *Logic, Semantics, Metamathematics: papers from 1923 to 1938*, translated by J.H. Woodger, Oxford: Clarendon Press.

Quine, W.V.O. (1970) *Philosophy of Logic*, Englewood Cliffs, NJ: Prentice-Hall.

Read, Stephen (1995) *Thinking about Logic*, Oxford: Oxford University Press

Urquhart, Alasdair (1986) 'Many-Valued Logics,' in Dov. M. Gabbay and Franz Günthner (eds) *Handbook of Philosophical Logic*, volume 3, Dordrecht: Reidel, pp. 71–116.

Williamson, Timothy (1994) *Vagueness*, London: Routledge.

FURTHER READING

There are many books you could use to further your study of logic. This list of recommended reading contains just a small sampling of what you can use to get started on more.

Introductions to Logic

Hodges, Wilfrid (1977) *Logic*, New York: Penguin.

Forbes, Graeme (1994) *Modern Logic*, Oxford: Oxford University Press.

Howson, Colin (1996) *Logic with Trees*, London: Routledge.

Restall, Greg (2003) *Logic*, London: Routledge.
Shand, John (2000) *Arguing Well*, London: Routledge.

Philosophy of Logic

Etchemendy, John (1990) *The Concept of Logical Consequence*, Cambridge, MA: Harvard University Press.
Priest, Graham (2000) *A Very Short Introduction to Logic*, Oxford: Oxford University Press.
Read, Stephen (1995) *Thinking about Logic*, Oxford: Oxford University Press.
Sainsbury, Mark (1991) *Logical Forms*, Oxford: Blackwell.
Quine, W.V.O. (1970) *Philosophy of Logic*, Englewood Cliffs, NJ: Prentice-Hall.

Special Topics

Bell J.L., deVidi, David and Solomon, Graham (2001) *Logical Options: An Introduction to Classical and Alternative Logics*, Peterborough: Broadview Press.
Boolos, George and Jeffrey, Richard C. (1989) *Computability and Logic*, third edition, Cambridge: Cambridge University Press.
Chellas, Brian (1980) *Modal Logic*, Cambridge: Cambridge University Press.
Dummett, Michael (1977) *Elements of Intuitionism*, Oxford: Oxford University Press.
Hughes, George and Cresswell, Max (1996) *A New Introduction to Modal Logic*, London: Routledge.
Girle, Roderic (2000) *Modal Logics and Philosophy*, Chesham: Acumen.
Jeffrey, Richard C. (1991) *Formal Logic: Its Scope and its Limits*, New York: McGraw-Hill.
Priest, Graham (2001) *An Introduction to Non-Classical Logic*, Oxford: Oxford University Press.
Restall, Greg (2000) *An Introduction to Substructural Logics*, London: Routledge.
Shapiro, Stewart (1991) *Foundations without Foundationalism: A Case for Second-order Logic*, Oxford: Oxford University Press.

4

ETHICS

Piers Benn

What are philosophers doing when they 'do ethics'? What is philosophical about their enterprise, and what qualifications do they bring to it? The layperson, who may not be particularly reflective or analytical, faces moral questions about what to do, and more generally about what things should be valued. Depending on temperament, the questions people think about may be straightforwardly practical (How should we deal with our child who has been caught stealing at school? Should we offer a room in our house to my sick mother-in-law?) or more abstract (What is the good life? What is justice? Why should we be moral?). Questions of both kinds, and many others, are discussed by philosophers. The vast and expanding branch of ethics known as *applied ethics* (one might ask how ethics could *not* be applied?) deals with issues of practical concern that arise in medicine, business, warfare, politics, sex and countless spheres besides. It is important to add, however, that merely because moral philosophers formulate and defend views on these issues, it does not follow that all such issues are genuinely in the province of ethics. For example, although many people defend moral positions concerning sex, it is a further question whether sex, in and of itself, raises any special ethical problems. In fact, many philosophers think it does not, and that the morality of sexual acts derives entirely from more general considerations such as benevolence and respect for others.

Discussion of issues in applied ethics often draws upon a more abstract kind of moral philosophy, which may roughly be called *moral theory*. Questions about whether we should be concerned only with the consequences of our actions, questions about rights, or the nature of justice come under this heading. More abstract still, there is a third area of moral philosophy, sometimes called *metaethics*, which includes notoriously intractable questions about the objectivity of moral claims and the nature of moral discourse. Thus, when someone says that morality is 'all relative' or 'all a matter of opinion' he or she is making a metaethical claim, whether knowingly or not, and however naively. Similarly, when it is said that no moral claim can possibly be true or false, or at least that no one can know any moral claim to be true or false, we are in the area of metaethics.

Questions of these kind, as we saw, are asked by many different kinds of people and certainly not only by philosophers. In this respect moral philosophy is unlike, let us say, the higher reaches of theoretical physics, whose problems are explored only by people with the appropriate qualifications. What then do the techniques of philosophy bring to the ethical questions we have mentioned?

This is a complex question, but we can begin by saying that philosophical thinking about any question involves critical thinking about foundational issues. That is to say, it tends to examine the presuppositions and starting points of our thinking, in the hope of understanding them better, or clarifying the concepts involved, or even asking whether they are rationally justified. Thus, in politics, a philosophical approach examines ideas such as justice, rights and equality in the hope of shedding light on what these things are and what value, if any, they might possess. The concepts of justice and rights (and many besides) are foundational because they lie at the foundation of positions advanced in politics, such as socialism or liberalism. The socialist might see 'social justice' as the proper aim of political action, just as the liberal might emphasise rights. But these concepts are far from simple, and invite philosophical theorising. Similarly, in ethics there are myriad foundational concepts that invite philosophical enquiry – the idea of reasons for action, virtue and vice, good and evil, human flourishing, the notion of objective value, the possibility of moral knowledge, to name but a few. There is also much scope for examining the moral attitudes and emotions that are inseparable from the moral life: esteem, admiration, guilt, shame, resentment and forgiveness, and it is to the credit of much recent moral philosophy that these things have been given the attention they deserve, helping to dispel the image of moral philosophy as something dry and detached from the ethical concerns of people who have no interest in philosophy. Although moral philosophy is theoretical and unavoidably concerned with precision and rigour, this is a *formal* feature of any good philosophical enquiry. There is no reason why the subject matter, the substantial *content*, of such enquiry should not be interesting and richly concerned with the human world.

How, then, is the subject best introduced? It is useful to start by removing some common obstacles to serious reflections about ethics, or more accurately, about particular practical issues. Such issues are sometimes called normative or 'first-order' questions, in contrast to metaethical or 'second-order' questions. The obstacles to reflection that will be briefly discussed can themselves be elaborated as metaethical positions, and are worthy of discussion in their own right.

RELATIVISM

Perhaps the best place to start is with the stance, less popular among philosophers than others, known as *moral relativism*. People use this term with a variety of meanings, some very loose and vague. Opinion-formers of a conservative bent often use the term pejoratively to mean a 'permissive' or 'anything goes' stance on particular moral issues, to be contrasted with something they call 'moral absolutism'. Sowing further confusion, the phrase 'moral absolutism' is employed to mean at least two very different things. Sometimes it turns out to refer to the opinion that morality is *objective*, that there are moral requirements and values that are independent of human opinion, and perhaps even involve the existence of special entities or properties; at other times it turns out to refer to the view that there are specific moral requirements that are binding *without exception* – for example, that you should *never* steal, *never* have premarital sex, and so on. These two views are, of course, compatible, but they are different claims. Logically speaking, you can be an objectivist without believing that there are any exceptionless moral requirements; indeed, this is the position of many philosophers, particularly consequentialists (a view we shall return to).

Philosophers usually mean something more precise by the term moral relativism. In essence, it is the doctrine that there is no *one* true moral system, binding on all people at all times. A relativist might say that infanticide is *wrong for* the people of the twenty-first century in the West, but *permissible for* the ancient Spartans and perhaps even for contemporary cultures in which it is practised, for example, to ensure that girls do not survive after birth. Relativists might also claim that morality literally changes, so that practices like corporal or capital punishment which were permissible in the nineteenth century are wrong in the twenty-first. Roughly speaking, relativists claim that what is right or wrong, better or worse, virtuous or vicious in a particular culture depends on what is accepted *in that culture* as right or wrong (etc.) Hence, for moral relativists, there is no transcultural perspective from which moral judgements can be made, in such a way that all such judgements legitimately apply to all cultures, regardless of what is accepted or practised in each culture. For example, a relativist might say that it is wrong (morally wrong? It is hard to be sure) for people in twenty-first century Western democracies to condemn practices widespread in sub-Saharan Africa, such as female genital mutilation, just because they are not accepted in Western cultures. Those practices are accepted in sub-Saharan Africa, and who are we to judge them? Female genital mutilation is right for the people in those cultures, or at least in small sub-cultures within them, and since terms like 'right' or 'wrong' can only mean 'right *for*' or 'wrong *for*' the people who live in such-and-such a culture, there is no more to be said. Similar things are sometimes said about attempts by organisations with morally universalist aspirations, like Amnesty International, to persuade all governments to respect the human rights allegedly possessed by all individuals. A relativist might point out that the very notion of human rights stems from the individualism that arose from the eighteenth-century European Enlightenment, and that it is parochial at best, and imperialist at worst, to demand that all cultures look to the Enlightenment for their moral inspiration. Some societies barely understand the notion of human rights, and, for the relativist, there is no legitimate transcultural perspective from which we are entitled to judge that they are wrong.

Such a relativist stance is a familiar part of the contemporary intellectual landscape. Relativism is less popular in philosophy departments than it is in departments of cultural studies, literature, or social sciences, but it raises basic philosophical issues. Before looking at the central issues, we need to clear up a number of confusions along the way, and make some crucial distinctions.

First of all, we can recognise the general spirit leading most expressions of relativism, and it is important to see how this spirit can be allowed some life even if we reject relativism. At its best, this spirit is one of intellectual humility and moral toleration.

The humility is shown in unwillingness to be dogmatic about the validity of the standards we happen to have been brought up to respect, without giving proper thought to other ways of doing things. We should not be parochial. Once we realise that, had we been raised in another culture, we would probably have internalised the values of that culture, we should wonder whether the standards we were actually brought up to believe in are right after all.

The moral toleration amounts to a rejection of rigid and dogmatic 'judgementalism', especially when we realise the vast impact of non-rational factors on our own moral outlook. The findings of anthropologists in the nineteenth and early twentieth century had an important influence in this respect, in making the citizens of the imperial powers see that other societies functioned perfectly well although in many respects their mores and moral outlooks were different from their own.

All this is important. It is good to see that one's own way of doing things may not be the only proper way, and good (at least sometimes) to cultivate toleration towards those who do things differently. Equally important, however, is to see that none of this entails moral relativism. You can be *fallibilist* about the best way to lead your life – that is, you accept that your moral judgements may be mistaken – without being remotely *relativistic* about morality. The distinction is subtle but crucial. The fallibilist says, in effect, that he or she is unsure of the nature of the good life, or of the best moral codes to live by, because other cultures probably have important things to teach us and we simply don't have enough opportunity to learn from them. This is different from saying that all cultures possess some kind of moral equality, in that nobody from one culture has any business judging the practices of another. The moral fallibilist says: there *is* a best way to live, but I may be mistaken as to what it is. The relativist says: there is no best way to live, because that very idea is inherently culturally relative.

A similar point may be made about toleration. To the extent that you are morally agnostic, it makes sense to be cautious in passing judgement on those who seem to be very different, since you don't know that they haven't important things to teach you. But in fact, this isn't really what is meant by toleration. Toleration implies, not moral relativism, but the very opposite. If we tolerate something or somebody, we are putting up with what we do *not* like or approve of. If I tolerate a taxi driver's racist banter, that means I decide not to get into an argument with him, particularly if that would cause me to be dumped somewhere miles from my intended destination. It doesn't mean I approve of what he says. If I tolerate a bore at a social event, that means I don't ignore him or let him know I think he is a bore. It doesn't mean I don't think he is a bore.

This helps to highlight a common confusion among those who describe themselves as relativists. They believe in toleration and respect for different lifestyles, and they probably believe in the values of a multi-cultural society. Indeed, they think that this moral stance is somehow mandated by relativism. If relativism is correct, they say, then we ought to tolerate difference. We have just remarked that toleration is not something we extend to things we approve of or are indifferent to – rather, we extend it to what we disapprove of. But there is a yet more important problem, which is that when we challenge the relativist to tell us *who* should be tolerant, or *in which societies* ought this to be a value, he or she will find it difficult to give a coherent answer without compromising the relativism. If the claim is: relativism is true, therefore *everyone* should be tolerant, if follows that a *non-relative* value – that of toleration – has been inadvertently introduced. But how can this be, if the relativism is to remain intact? Surely the relativist should be saying that toleration is right in societies where toleration is generally valued, but not elsewhere. This would be the most consistent stance, but would go against his or her instincts towards toleration.

This difficulty, in fact, points to a quandary relativists often find themselves in when they are asked about cultures where toleration is largely absent. As I write, a court in Pakistan has just passed the death sentence on a doctor who supposedly told his students that the Prophet of Islam was not a Muslim before he was forty (which is when he is said to have started receiving divine revelations), and in Afghanistan several foreign aid workers who have been accused of spreading Christianity face the death penalty. Some relativists find such cases embarrassing, as they tear their instincts in different directions.

However, this is not enough to refute relativism. We can imagine a relativist 'biting the bullet' and stating that toleration is not a universally binding value – that there is no non-relative requirement to be tolerant. So we come to ask what positive arguments there are in favour of relativism. The arguments come in varying degrees of subtlety, and the fact that some arguments are unsound does not imply that there aren't better ones. Here I simply wish to concentrate on an argument commonly invoked in favour of relativism, which may be called the Argument from Cultural Diversity.

The Argument from Cultural Diversity starts from the uncontroversial fact that different societies and different historical epochs have different moral codes. Of course, it may be debated to what extent this is true. Relativism is sometimes criticised for exaggerating the extent of these differences, and failing to see that some of them are no more than different conventions upholding the same moral values. It is also pointed out that there are core values that are essential to the survival of any society – for example, it is almost unknown for a society to show complete indifference towards the welfare of infants.

There is truth in these remarks, but they are not central to the issue here. Let us take it that there are some genuine moral differences between different societies, for example in the weight they accord to individual rights as opposed to community values, in their attitudes to sex, women or the elderly, in the amount of political freedom allowed, or in their treatment of prisoners. The question is, can the fact of these differences provide a cogent ground for moral relativism?

The argument often starts with the fact that different things are accepted in different cultures, and then leaps to the conclusion that no culture's core values are superior to those of any other. But it is hard to see how this inference can be justified. The starting point (in fact, the *only* premise!) states the factual, anthropological claim that different societies have different beliefs about what is morally right and wrong; the desired conclusion is that no society's beliefs about right and wrong are better than any other's. But how does this follow? The premise and the conclusion state different things, yet without an additional premise the inference is mysterious. Why can't some core values in a society be morally bad, and inferior to those of another society? Indeed, this possibility is widely taken for granted in non-moral spheres. Most people in the Western world are prepared to say that medieval theories of astronomy were overturned by Copernicus and Galileo, and that modern scientific medicine is more efficacious than witch-doctoring. I say 'most people', because there are those who subscribe to a relativist view not only of morality, but of any claims to truth; indeed, their ideas (sometimes described as postmodernist) are sometimes the driving force behind moral relativism. But many others are happy to be non-relativist about science, but relativist about morality, and this invites us to consider why morality is meant to be so different.

If the driving force behind moral relativism is, indeed, a more global relativism, involving scepticism as to the very possibility of objective truth or rationality, then such a position assumes an apparent invulnerability to rational refutation. Indeed, advocates of postmodernist notions are apt to charge their opponents with begging the question against relativism in their very attempts to argue against it – for it is the very possibility of rational argument that is in question. And in a sense, they are right; for fruitful argument to be possible, all parties to a dispute must take for granted the value of argument. But the relativist victory is hollow, since this stance makes it impossible to accept rational argument and objective truth, even if these things *should* be accepted. And to embrace, without argument, the stance that argument is impossible, is itself a way of begging the question.

In this short discussion I do not claim to have refuted moral relativism. However, I have suggested that it faces some serious obstacles, and that one of the most poular arguments in its favour is flawed.

EGOISM

Relativism is sometimes perceived, whether with relief or anxiety, as a threat to serious moral engagement. Another such supposed threat is in various theories described as egoist. All who teach ethics come across people who profess a theoretical egoism. Some of them claim that all human motivation is really self-interested, in spite of appearances to the contrary. Others claim that all human motivation *ought* to be self-interested, even if some people are genuinely but misguidedly altruistic. Egoists of either kind may appeal to the way the world (allegedly) works, perhaps as shown in the harsh realism of business, commerce, politics or warfare. The more theoretical among them might appeal to Darwinian evolution by natural selection, or to the modern discipline of evolutionary psychology. Is there anything to be said for egoism?

First let us distinguish *psychological* egoism from *ethical* egoism. Psychological egoists, the first sort described above, think that all our motivations are exclusively self-interested, whether or not we acknowledge the fact. That doesn't mean that we are always trying to do others down. Often self-interest coincides with the interests of others, and co-operative enterprises are set up to ensure that several people's interests are satisfied. However, according to psychological egoism, an individual enters into co-operation with others only when it is in his or her interest to do so.

As the name suggests, this theory is a psychological theory; it is about what *does* motivate us rather than what *should* motivate us. It is a familiar view. We all know people who think that when we give to a beggar, we are really doing so to avoid feeling guilty rather than because we genuinely care about him; that when we return borrowed property or own up to something embarrassing, we are doing so only because we would be caught out otherwise. Indeed, one of the attractions of this theory is that it seems consistent with everything we actually do. You refused to give to the beggar? That's because you preferred to spend your money on yourself. You gave to the beggar? That's so you wouldn't feel guilty for refusing. We have before us an elegant, plausible, catch-all theory.

Before looking at criticisms of this theory, we should note that as an empirical hypothesis, there is some truth in it. Most people often weight their own interests above those of others, or at least over those outside their circles. One's own interests often present themselves with an urgency that the interests of others lack. And often, when we seem to be doing something for another's benefit – like consoling someone after she has been treated badly – we do so partly for undeclared reasons, such as satisfying curiosity about people's motivations. But psychological egoism would not be interesting if it amounted only to this. What the theory says is not that we often put our own interests first, but that we always and necessarily do so. This is a much stronger thesis, and needs a strong defence.

How might such a defence go? It is best expressed in the first person. A common argument stresses that whenever I do something, I do it only because it is what I most desire to do. Even when my choices are severely limited by external factors, I always opt for what I most desire. If all the options are pretty dreadful, I most desire the least dreadful of the options, and that is what I choose to do. So desire is what motivates action, and is all that motivates action. Furthermore, the argument goes, all my desires are exclusively for the satisfaction of my interests. Again, it is often impossible to obtain what I most want, but my interests are satisfied as well as they can be whenever I obtain what I most desire, out of the options actually available.

Put more formally, then, the premises of the argument are:

1   All I do is motivated exclusively by my desires.
2   All my desires are for the satisfaction of my interests.

From these premises, the conclusion is drawn that in all action my actions are exclusively self-interested.

The argument is clearly valid – that is, if the premises are true then the conclusion is true. The question to ask, then, is whether the premises are true. Each is open to serious challenge, especially the second one.

We might challenge the first premise, asking why we should believe that all action springs from desire alone. In doing so, we would be entering a long and complex debate brought to prominence in the eighteenth century, concerning whether 'reason alone' can ever motivate action, as opposed to desire. In fact, the more we enter this debate, the less clear the concepts of reason and desire become. Immanuel Kant (1724–1804) insisted that any action with real moral worth must be motivated by reason, and indeed that only such actions could be genuinely free. David Hume (1711–76) by contrast, held that reason alone is totally inert, meaning that no recognition of truth, just by itself, could ever produce an action; what is always needed is a 'passion'. We shall look at this in more detail later. The immediate point is that the first premise of the argument can be challenged by pointing out that, very often, I do *not* do what I most want to do. If I stay at work late marking exams, I am certainly not doing what I most want to do. Concern for duty can militate against the satisfaction of desire.

No doubt the notion of desire can be refined to accommodate these examples, but we can leave this on one side, because most of the trouble, I suggest, comes with the second premise – that all my desires are for the satisfaction of my interests. Why should we believe this? It is the driving force behind the psychological egoist's insistence that whenever I help a beggar, repay a debt or go out of my way for a stranger, I am doing so because I wanted to, and that *therefore* my action is in fact self-interested. For by helping the stranger, I am satisfying a desire of *mine* – and isn't this a paradigm case of acting on self-interest? This idea, in turn, generates the particular accounts offered by the psychological egoist about what is really going on – for example, that I am only trying to avoid a guilty conscience, or wish for a good reputation, or am afraid of being caught out.

But this seductive chain of thought is surely flawed. Let us concede the first premise, for the sake of argument. Let us accept that all actions are motivated only by desire. Still, there is a distinction to be made between self-interested desire and desire to further the interests of others. My desire to visit the doctor is self-interested (though note, not *selfish* unless I deprive someone else of a similar benefit) because I want to look after my physical health. But my desire that my father should visit the doctor is other-interested – after all, it his welfare I am concerned with here, not my own. In both cases, I have a desire – but one is for my own benefit, and the other is for someone else's benefit.

This is a remarkably simple point, but many people have great difficulty seeing it. (Perhaps that is partly because they are egoists themselves?) They think that even if I do want my father to be healthy, there must also be something in it for me. However, if all they mean is that my father's good health satisfies a desire of mine, then I can happily agree: I want my desire for my father's benefit to be satisfied. But we still lack an argument for supposing that this desire is really self-interested. The psychological egoists might amplify the point, claiming that I desire my father's benefit only because if he became ill, it would be a nuisance for me to look after him, or if he died, my grief would be painful *for me*. But the answer should be clear: the very fact that I would bother looking after him, or would be sad if he died, suggests that I have a genuine concern for him. Otherwise, why would I bother about him at all?

In short, the immensely popular thesis of psychological egoism suffers from serious shortcomings. It might conceivably be true, but the popular arguments for it are unsound.

What about ethical egoism, the other kind of egoism we mentioned? This is a normative thesis – i.e. one that tells us how we ought to behave. Note that if psychological egoism is true, then ethical egoism becomes somewhat uninteresting. For there is little point in recommending that we be self-interested, if we have no other choice. But suppose that we can choose whether to be wholly self-interested, or to be altruistic to some degree. Should we be self-interested?

The ethical egoist likes to present himself as realistic, seeing himself surrounded by other egoists who are all only too ready to make mincemeat of him unless he uses his strength and cunning to the full. Such a world, admittedly, need not be a complete jungle, for it can be in a person's interest to enter into co-operation with others; there is no necessary conflict between self-interest and co-operation. One venerable theory with origins in this vision is Hobbesian contractualism, which claims to provide a self-interested basis for caring about morality. But the picture of human nature it starts from is too extreme. Even if self-interest is a dominant motive in many people, it is rarely the only motive. Besides, look around you and you will find many unsung people who do a lot of good for others, without seeking attention or external rewards. And even if the world were full of rampant egoists, this would not provide a moral justification for egoistic behaviour. It would not be enough to say (perhaps correctly) that only by being an egoist will I serve my own interests, for the question at issue is *whether* self-interest alone provides individuals with sound reasons for action. No doubt it is both prudent and sometimes morally permissible to look after our individual interests when they conflict with those of other people. But ethical egoism says more than this – it says that, ultimately, it is all an individual should be concerned with.

Another familiar claim is that well-meaning attempts to be altruistic often back-fire. 'Do-gooders' frequently do more harm than good, helping neither themselves nor others. For example, it may be said that if you are always trying to help others, your efforts will soon become intrusive and unwelcome, and may even undermine the autonomy of the intended beneficiaries. In particular, this is sometimes said of aid to developing countries and charitable giving: it lines the pockets of dictators and creates a culture of dependency. On the whole (the argument continues) individuals are the best judges of their own interests and are best left to pursue their interests in the way they see fit. In any case, unless you look after yourself, you will be in no position to look after others. If it is noble to give large amounts of money away to worthy causes, you can do this only if you have money in the first place, and you won't have it unless you are in the habit of looking after your own financial interests.

But note that these observations are irrelevant. For it is one question *whether* we should promote the interests of others, but another question *how* best to do so. The observations only tell us that many efforts to help others are counterproductive. They provide no case for *not* trying to help others. Thus, we do not escape any duties we may have to help the poor, merely by observing that charitable giving is no use. If that is the case, comes the reply, then find out what really does help them and go ahead and do it. Of course, we may also dispute the truth of these observations – maybe charitable giving does good, after all – but it is more economical in argument not to be side-tracked by this debate.

We might also try to dispose of ethical egoism by appealing to the Golden Rule that we should treat others as we would like them to treat us. Admittedly, a determined egoist can resist this, pointing out that although he would *prefer* others to treat him altruistically, while he treats them egoistically, he does not *morally object* to others putting their own interests before his. Indeed, he thinks that others ought to put their own interests first, just as he ought to put his interests before theirs. This is a consistent position, compatible with holding egoism as a universal principle rather than one that only applies to him. But it comes at a price. First, this stance is psychologically difficult to maintain and quite rare. Whatever we say in theory, we do feel moral resentment when others do us down; we feel their behaviour is not merely unfortunate for us, but reprehensible. And since we think this, we should realise that others are also entitled to feel resentment when we do them down. If we do not admit this, then we are treating ourselves as exceptions to a moral code we think others should abide by. Second, and related to this, is the difficulty of coming up with any convincing case for ethical egoism. Even if we avoid double standards by steadfastly claiming that everyone should be egoists, it is hard to see why such a view has any plausibility. Why should I, as a matter of principle, always put my interests before those of others?

In summary, we have noted two alleged obstacles to serious moral engagement: moral relativism and two types of egoism. Let us put them on one side and consider some more substantive moral theories.

CONSEQUENTIALISM

A popular theory with a venerable history is consequentialism. An important consequentialist theory is utilitarianism – indeed, the two terms are often used interchangeably. However, consequentialism, strictly speaking, is the view that actions should be judged entirely by their consequences; it does not itself specify what kinds of consequences are desirable. Classical utilitarianism specifies that the only thing ultimately valuable is pleasure or happiness, and all actions are to be judged in terms of their conduciveness to this. This was the thesis defended by the two great classical utilitarians, Jeremy Bentham (1748–1832) and John Stuart Mill (1806–73). However, modern day utilitarians place less emphasis on pleasure or happiness, preferring to adopt preference satisfaction as the ultimate goal of action (leaving it theoretically open as to what those preferences are).

The attractions of consequentialism are clear. It seems to provide a rational basis for many of the moral principles we take for granted. If someone tells us that we shouldn't behave cruelly, or tell lies, cheat or steal, it is natural to ask why we shouldn't do these things. To be told 'you just mustn't' may be rhetorically effective, but leaves us none the wiser. Surely, however, we can supply a reason just by looking at the consequences of doing these things. People prefer not to be cheated, hurt or lied to, and will often feel distress if they are. The frustration of their preferences is a bad thing, and so actions that promote it should be condemned. The satisfaction of a preference is a good thing in itself, even if its goodness may be outweighed by greater evils. Satisfying some people's preferences – like the preferences of sadists to see their victims suffer – causes far more evil than good, but this fact is entirely consistent with consequentialism, which says that whenever it is wrong to satisfy a preference, this is because doing so would frustrate a greater number or intensity of *other* preferences. For consequentialists, this serves only to reinforce the idea that preference satisfaction, in itself, is good – that indeed it is what morality is ultimately about.

Moreover, the contemporary emphasis on preference satisfaction rather than on pleasure or happiness avoids some notorious difficulties with classical utilitarianism. For example, Mill was a philosophical hedonist – that is, he espoused the view that the only thing good in itself, and not on account of its conduciveness to other goods, is 'pleasure or happiness'. However, the hedonism supported by Mill failed to register the highly significant differences between pleasure and happiness. He writes as if the two notions stood more or less for the same thing, which they obviously do not. Someone whose life is brimming over with pleasures may yet be unhappy – drugs, drink and orgiastic sex failing to supply a sense of meaning to her life – while the ascetic recluse, innocent of such indulgences, may still be happy (which is not to say that a life without pleasure cannot also be utterly miserable). Furthermore, Mill himself was convinced that some pleasures were far more worthy of pursuit than others, and faced the problem of reconciling this observation with his own theory that the pleasure produced by actions was the only ultimate criterion of their moral worth. He tried to get round this by claiming that there were 'higher' and 'lower' pleasures, in other words that pleasures differed in quality as well as quantity. However, although he was doubtless correct in this (even if his views on the lower pleasures were a touch priggish) such a distinction is ruinous to his hedonism – for it entails that pleasures are to be judged according to separate, non-hedonistic moral criterion.

Consequentialism's appeal partly derives from its claim to base morality in things whose value seems obvious. By contrast, a moral system whose primary emphasis is on doing or avoiding certain types of action – e.g. keeping promises, or never lying – runs the risk of *arbitrariness*, of issuing moral requirements that have no rational basis, *unless* they can be given a consequentialist justification. Such theories are often called deontological, meaning they emphasise specific rights, duties, obligations or rules. They may be enshrined in religion, as are the Ten Commandments, but they may also be given a non-religious basis, as is Kant's Categorical Imperative (of which more later). Consequentialists deny that these rules or codes should be obeyed just for their own sake. When they should be followed, this is because they promote a favourable net balance of preferences satisfied over preferences frustrated. But – and this is where some versions of consequentialism acquire notoriety – whenever following such a rule would not be beneficial in this way, then it should be disobeyed. If keeping a rule, such as a rule against lying, causes an unfavourable balance of good and bad, then the rule should be broken.

Critics of consequentialism are quick to protest that in that case, no type of deed is ruled out of court. It is conceivable, even if unlikely, that consequentialism would support killing the innocent, torture, rape and pillage if these deeds promoted the overall good (as conceived by consequentialists). Suppose you find yourself in a situation in which you can save a hundred innocent people from near-certain death only by killing ten innocent people. Or suppose you are poor, and someone offers you a good salary for helping to manufacture biological weapons, and you know that if you don't accept the post, then someone else will. What should you do? Critics of consequentialism claim that according to this theory, any action, however appalling in isolation, can become not only permissible but obligatory if someone makes a credible threat to do something worse if you don't comply. Similarly, it may become obligatory to inflict great suffering on people if this is 'compensated' by others' pleasure. No doubt the gladiatorial contests of Imperial Rome, where slaves and convicts had to bludgeon one another to death in front of large crowds, gave considerable amusement and pleasure to the spectators. If the net balance of suffering over pleasure was favourable, it would appear that consequentialism would endorse these contests. Indeed, we can imagine Romans justifying these spectacles as a way of keeping trouble off the streets and providing hot-headed youths with a chance to let off steam.

Unsurprisingly, consequentialists regard these criticisms as unfair. A common response is that we should not judge the theory in terms of what it might say about wild, unlikely theoretical possibilities. Even if, in theory, it could be right to kill ten people to save one hundred, in practice situations are rarely if ever like that. We often do not know whether our actions will have the desired effects, especially in the long term. If someone were callous and brutal enough to threaten that unless you killed ten people, he would massacre one hundred, he could surely not be trusted to spare the remaining ninety even after you have killed ten. It is far more likely that he is amusing himself by inveigling others into his evil plans, and undermining their sense of integrity. As for the Roman gladiators, most consequentialists would attach far greater importance to the alleviation of suffering than to the promotion of pleasure. What the spectators lose by forgoing the pleasure of the shows is far less than what the gladiators lose by being forced to kill and maim one another.

Furthermore, and powerfully, consequentialists point out that it even if we should accept that it is not only in theory, but also in practice, that we should break 'rules' or 'principles' in certain circumstances, this is accepted by almost everyone. Indeed, even those who try to rescue principles often buy their moral rigour by restricting the scope of those principles. Hardly anyone thinks it is *always* wrong to lie, that it is forbidden to lie even to the secret police who are looking to kill the innocent person you are sheltering. Hardly anyone thinks that all promises should be kept, come what may. Suppose you promise your partner that you will return home one evening with a copy of that celebrated intellectual journal *Loaded*, but you discover that all the shops in the vicinity have run out of it. No one would expect you to trek to the nearest shop, miles away, where there might be a copy. It would be reasonable to protest that you made reasonable efforts but couldn't get hold of a copy. Indeed, it is normally implicitly understood by all parties that promises like this are not binding if it would be unexpectedly burdensome to keep them. (In that case, you may protest, no promise has been really been broken, so no promise-breaking has been justified by the example. The obvious reply, though, is that this shows that sensible people do not think it reasonable to place these burdens on others – a point that applies to other 'absolute' principles as well).

If this is on the right lines, the best strategy for the consequentialist will be to point out this *practical* rapprochement between consequentialist and non-consequentialist theories, and then claim that consequentialism has *theoretical* superiority in explaining the basis of generally agreed practical principles. Various strategies have been tried. I shall briefly mention one, and then say a little more about another.

One consequentialist strategy is known as rule-consequentialism (some writers prefer to call it rule-utilitarianism). The idea here is that there is a proper place for rules in a consequentialist framework. We do not have to abandon the idea that it is wrong to kill, rape or steal, because rules against these things can be given a sound consequentialist justification. A world in which everyone obeyed such rules, even when in some cases it appeared that breaking such a rule would be beneficial overall, would be better than a world in which people decided on every individual occasion whether the rule should be kept or not. This stance is usually contrasted with the act-consequentialist (or act-utilitarian) position, which is what, in effect, we have been discussing so far. Act-consequentialists think that the notion of rules should pull no independent weight in deliberation; whenever it is right to act as the rule-utilitarian would act, it is because we can judge independently that acting thus would produce the best possible net distribution of benefits and harms. Rules are irrelevant. Either they tell you to do what act-utilitarianism tells you to do anyway, or they are not truly utilitarian rules.

Interestingly, both views are plausible. It is very likely that if the only principle people lived by were 'Do what seems, in the circumstances, to maximise utility' (i.e. produce the best possible balance of good over bad) then utility would not be maximised. People would make stupid miscalculations, or allow their personal biases and interests to distort their decisions. On the other hand, if this is correct, then we can expect an act-consequentialist to make the same point – and hence end up endorsing the more or less unreflective following of rules.

The matter is further complicated by the fact that almost everyone would agree that occasionally a rule should be broken, even if we should be pretty reluctant to do so as a matter of policy. If the so-called rule-consequentialist doesn't even accept this, then we must wonder whether his position is consequentialist at all!

One attempt to circumvent this is in a position that bears certain affinities to rule-consequentialism, but which allows the reflective breaking of rules. R.M. Hare (1919–2002) developed a 'Two-Level' consequentialist theory.[1] Rather than ask ourselves, on every occasion for action, what the proper utilitarian course would be, we should usually be content with following the precepts of commonly accepted morality. We should be trustworthy, keep our promises, be truthful and kind, pay special attention to those with whom we are in special relationships. A sound moral education will instil dispositions to follow such precepts without too much reflection. This is moral thinking at the 'intuitive' level. For the most part, it serves us well. However, it is only one 'level' of moral thinking, and not always sufficient. There can be occasions when we have to think at another level to solve moral problems. This is the 'critical' level. If we encounter conflicts between 'intuitive' principles, or if we encounter genuinely new kinds of situation, we may have to think from scratch.

Hare illustrates the distinction between the two levels of moral thinking by imagining two kinds of deliberator, the 'archangel' and the 'prole'. The archangel's deliberation is always at the critical level, and unlike ordinary humans he can be trusted to think all the time on this level. This is because he is not subject to temptations or self-serving biases. He is utterly impartial between everybody's interests and preferences. He knows every relevant fact and makes no errors of reasoning. By contrast, the prole is inclined to irrational thinking, partiality, self-deception and limited sympathies. If he were to attempt to think at the critical level, he would probably make a mess of it and do wrong things. That is why it is safer if he confines his thinking to the intuitive level, sticking with basic principles of truthfulness, unreflective kindness or loyalty.

Hare thinks the hypothetical archangel would reason as an act-utilitarian. He can be trusted to do this, because of his intelligence and impartiality. The prole should stick with something more simple. Where, however, does that leave us ordinary people? Many of us are somewhere between the archangel and the prole, and there are considerable individual variations. We are prole-ish enough to need intuitive thinking much of the time, but we can sometimes see clashes between principles, or even disasters looming if we stick by a principle. Then, cautiously and reluctantly, we should override the intuitive level with the critical.

This is probably the best account the utilitarian can offer. It helpfully reminds us that utilitarianism can endorse relatively conservative positions, contrary to its popular image. But for many critics, Hare's account is structurally unstable. How do we know when to 'go critical', so to speak? People no doubt have different thresholds; which are the right ones? To know when to switch to the critical level requires accurate insight into our individual limitations – something we all lack to some extent, especially those of us who most need it. A deeper worry is that although Hare provides a role for intuitive thinking, with all its vocabulary of duties, rights, and so on, his theory latches onto the wrong sort of reason for moral behaviour. Certain acts, we might want to say, are intrinsically wrong; there are certain intrinsic goods and evils. This is more than saying that it is useful to think and talk in this way. Certain preferences really are good or evil, and whatever it says, utilitarianism cannot ultimately make sense of this idea. For that theory, no type of deed or thought is ultimately ruled out of court.

There is an extensive literature on consequentialism, as it refines itself in ever more ingenious ways. Other controversial features of the theory include its denial, in most versions, of any intrinsic moral difference between an act with a certain consequence, and an omission with a similar consequence. This has led to an extensive literature in applied ethics, in which consequentialism is applied to such matters as killing and letting die in medical practice, and our obligations to help the starving. Let us leave the discussion here, however, and see how some of its rivals fare.

DEONTOLOGY

Another dominant moral theory, or cluster of theories, goes under the heading 'deontology', after the Greek word for duty. The deontogical approach has a flavour lacking to consequentialism, and probably appeals to a different moral temperament. The stress on absolute or nearly absolute specific obligations, rather than the general obligation to promote the overall good, is quite distinctive. It is characteristic of deontological ethical theories that they regard certain types of action as required or forbidden in themselves, simply because of the kinds of deed they are, and not because of their consequences.

It is important to remember that merely adhering to a deontological moral framework does not in itself tell us what to do or avoid. The theory does not determine the normative content of ethics. However, it is probably no accident, psychologically speaking, that traditional deontological theory has been more emphatic about what we should *not* do rather than our positive obligations, and has included in its list of prohibitions a familiar range of actions, such as lying, theft, promise-breaking, various sexual misdemeanours, and killing the innocent.

Kant is the best known exponent of a deontological ethics, and he employs a complex and sophisticated theory in its defence. His most famous work in ethics is his short book *Groundwork of the Metaphysic of Morals* in which he tries to place such an ethical system on an entirely rational footing. Not for Kant the appeal to mere authority, whether human or divine, nor the appeal to our desires. The moral law, which is described as the Categorical Imperative, can be known a priori – that is, by reflection alone, independent of empirical observation, religious revelation, or the desires we happen to have.

By calling the moral law categorical, Kant means to contrast it with another type of imperative, which can be called hypothetical. Hypothetical imperatives are valid only on condition that those to whom they are addressed already have certain desires or aims. Thus, if someone said 'If you want the bus to Oxford, go to Bay 16', or 'If you fancy her, then ask her out', she would be expressing hypothetical imperatives. (If you don't want to go to Oxford, but Newcastle, then catching the bus at Bay 16 is likely to end up in grief, and if you don't fancy the woman in question, then you may have no particular reason to ask her out.) Kant is adamant that moral imperatives are not like that. On the contrary, they are binding on us quite regardless of what desires we happen to have. They are categorical. But how can any imperative be categorical? How can someone have an inescapable reason for doing something that answers to no desire, interest, or end that she has?

A parallel may be useful here. Compare the moral law, which Kant thinks is inescapable, with the physical laws of Newtonian mechanics. Newtonian laws (or so Kant thought, writing before the advent of quantum theory) were deterministic and exceptionless. If I drop an apple, it must fall. If someone else drops an apple, under similar conditions, it too must fall. It cannot be otherwise. These are physical laws. But is there a universality to the moral law in the way that there is to the physical laws? For Kant, the moral law has a universality, but in a different way; it cannot literally ensure its own observance. We can ignore the moral law in a way we cannot ignore the law of gravity. Nevertheless, we cannot escape the rationally binding claim it has upon us.

It is not surprising, then, that the first formulation of Kant's Categorical Imperative is called the Formula of Universal Law. It states that 'I ought never to act except in such a way that I can also will that my maxim should become a universal law'. A 'maxim' is a subjective principle on which I act. Kant's thought is that an action is morally wrong if I cannot prescribe ('will') that not only I, but anyone else too, should act similarly in similar circumstances. Thus he asks whether it is permissible for me to obtain a loan by making a false promise that I shall repay it. The question is, can I will that the principle involved (that I should escape difficulties by false promising, whenever I am in need) be adopted as a universal law? Kant thinks it cannot, since if everyone availed themselves of this option, their promises would eventually not be believed – hence there would be no advantage in making a false promise. A universal law permitting lying promises would soon 'annul itself'. It would lead to the collapse of the institution of promising, thus making lying promises futile.

It is hard not to feel a sense of anti-climax here; a sense that an intriguing theory purporting to defend the inescapability of the moral law has been given such an implausible defence. It is also initially difficult to see to what extent this argument differs from a consequentialist one – after all, Kant seems to be appealing to consequences when he asks whether he could will the consequences of everyone making lying promises to get out of difficulties. But in fact there is a difference between this argument and standard consequentialist ones. Kant is not suggesting (which would be absurd anyway) that my making an insincere promise will somehow cause everyone else to do the same. The point is that if I consider myself morally permitted to perform some action, then I am bound to accept that anyone else in similar circumstances is permitted to do likewise. This is what it is to accept a moral imperative: it is to will it as a universal law, whether one realises this or not. The lying promiser wills lying as a universal law, but at the same time depends on the truthfulness of others. There is thus, as Kant puts it, a contradiction in his will.

Am I, however, willing a universal law whenever I prescribe an action for myself? In one obvious sense I am not. If I decide to go to a certain shop to buy some goods, I am clearly not prescribing that everyone else should go to that same shop, at the same time, to buy the same goods. That way lies chaos. But this point does not destroy the appeal of the thought that moral principles are, in some sense, universalisable. The point is that there are no special permissions, obligations or prohibitions that apply just to me, solely on account of my identity. Of course, there may be special facts about me, such as that I am extraordinarily talented in some way, that make it permissible for me to undertake tasks that no one else could be trusted to do. There is indeed a romantic strain in some ethical thinking, partly traceable to the German philosopher Friedrich Nietzsche (1844–1900) that stresses the liberation from ordinary ethical constraints that should be enjoyed by the 'Übermensch' ('superman') with special power and creativity. But whatever this somewhat vague idea amounts to, it is possible in theory to see it as universalisable: let *anyone* with such special characteristics behave differently from ordinary mortals.

There is far more to Kant's deontological theory of ethics than can be summarised here, but another important feature that must be mentioned is his second formulation of his Categorical Imperative, known as the Formula of the End in Itself. This tells us to 'Act so that you treat humanity, whether in your own person or in that of another, never as a means only but always at the same time as an end.' (It is important to stress the word 'only', for otherwise almost every interpersonal activity would be ruled out. I use a shop assistant as a means to buying the groceries, but do not thereby treat her as a *mere* means, as if she were good for nothing except serving me.) This idea has been extraordinarily influential both in ethics and in political philosophy, providing a basis for respect for individual rights and autonomy. Its relationship to the Formula of Universal Law is not at once obvious, but the thrust is that since all persons are rational beings, capable of formulating the moral law and then imposing it on themselves, they must never be treated as a mere extension of the will of another. To do this is to subvert the moral law within them; to fail to respect the autonomy that comes from being a rational self-legislator. Coercion and deception are two ways in which this might be done. If I force you to do something against your will, I am overriding your capacity to decide what you ought to do and then do it. Similarly, if I get you to do something by deception, then I am also subverting your rational will; although you consent to do as I ask, you would not consent if you knew the truth (we might then debate at length whether the 'consent' was ever genuine).

But suppose we are using coercion to stop people performing wrong deeds? One of the problems Kant gets himself into, probably unnecessarily, is that he believes that actions are autonomous only if they are both objectively right and performed from a sense of duty. In this, of course, he is not alone among philosophers; Plato, Rousseau and Spinoza had roughly the same idea. If that is correct, then forcibly preventing people from doing wrong is no violation of their autonomy, since the actions they would have performed without our intervention would not have been autonomous. Admittedly, what we force them to do instead would not be autonomous either, since it would not be self-legislated. But at least there would be no net loss of autonomy. Kant's theory would be more convincing if he admitted that wicked deeds can be just as free and autonomous as good deeds; the reason he doesn't is that he is wedded to a theory of freedom according to which dutiful actions performed for duty's sake are explained by the mysterious intrusion into the world of a 'noumenal' faculty of pure practical reason, whereas all other actions are explained by empirical (or 'phenomenal') causal laws. It is hard to make sense of this admittedly intriguing and attractive idea.

Nevertheless, there is still considerable appeal in Kant's notion of ends in themselves. It is probably the most plausible basis for a theory of natural rights, conceived as protective boundaries around persons that govern what we may do to them. It also gets at the heart of a crucial difference between most humans and (as far as we know) all non-human creatures: non-human animals have desires but not ends, and we do not subvert their autonomy by using them for our purposes, since there is no autonomy to subvert. Our ascriptions of moral responsibility to persons arguably depends on our regarding their actions and desires as their own, somehow originating with them rather than mediated through them. All this suggests that respect for autonomy is an essential part of morality, even if it is not the only part, and even if other values can sometimes override it. This has seemed so clear to some thinkers that they conceive the Kantian Formula of the End in Itself as capturing the essence of the moral law.

Is this true, or adequate? One influential critique of this system questions whether the whole notion of law – or deontology – is central to ethics. Some critics, indeed, want to remove the concept of law altogether from our ethical thinking. But we need not go this far to see the limitations of Kantian thinking.

VIRTUE

There is a well-established movement in moral philosophy that goes under the heading of 'virtue ethics'. There is, in fact, nothing new in this: Aristotle (384–322 BC) is seen as the main progenitor of this way of thinking. But the revival of this general approach over the past thirty years or so arose from dissatisfaction with utilitarian and Kantian theories of ethics – widely seen as the two main rivals to virtue ethics.

We should be wary of artificial distinctions between these theories. There is no reason, for example, why utilitarians should not help themselves to the idea of virtue – in fact, they tend to emphasise the importance of the virtue of benevolence and sympathy, as they are what motivate us to the impartial promotion of well-being. But there is at least a difference of emphasis between the different theories. Very loosely, we can say that whereas utilitarian and Kantian theories take the concept of right action to be fundamental to ethics, virtue ethics place great importance on individual character. 'What sort of person should I be?' rather than 'What is the right thing to do?' becomes the central question of ethics.

The Aristotelian doctrine holds that virtue is a stable state of character that predisposes us to seek the good for Man, or human flourishing. We flourish if we live according to our nature. This flourishing he calls *eudaimonia*, often translated as happiness, but consisting in objective well-being rather than any psychological state. We find out what sort of life makes for our flourishing by discovering what function Man uniquely performs. This turns out to be rational activity, or 'an activity of soul exhibiting excellence'. This is not mere contemplation, but practical reason (*phronesis*) that enables us to make right choices. The virtues, primarily courage, justice, temperance and wisdom, are what we need to engage in the 'activity of soul' that constitutes our flourishing, but this is not a simple means–end relationship. Rather, virtue is internal to our well-being – it is an indispensable part of it. To be happy is to live well.

Our post-Darwinian scepticism about whether there is an objective 'good for Man', or whether Man and other creatures are 'for' anything, should not blind us to the appeal of virtue theory. For there is something anaemic about a moral theory that simply tells us what to do, or merely provides algorithms for dealing with moral conflicts. It is natural to think that the moral life consists in something more than this – that we can evaluate our motives, desires and characters as well as what we do. No doubt those who reject virtue ethics will accept this, up to a point; for example, a utilitarian might well accept that it is good to desire the well-being of others, and to cultivate benevolence. But he will probably add that such virtues are valuable, in the last analysis, only because of the actions to which they tend to lead. For the virtue theorist, this leaves out something important. The desires we harbour, or at least those we voluntarily wallow in, can be indicative of a good or corrupt character, quite apart from any tendency we have to act them out. Someone who plays out sadistic fantasies on a virtual reality machine reveals something bad about himself, even if his behaviour towards others is impeccable. To the question: what does such a person do wrong? the answer would be: he *does* nothing wrong (unless we count fantasising as a deed) but this is not the point. Our moral evaluations should not extend only to our actions or their results, but to our characters, which are largely shown by what we take pleasure in. And our moral understanding is greatly enriched by virtue and vice concepts: loyalty, courage, honesty, temperance, stinginess, cowardice, dishonesty, intemperance. Moreover, the attitude we bring to our actions has moral significance. Aristotle thought it more virtuous to take pleasure in doing the things dictated by virtue, than it is to do them grudgingly. In this he surely comes off better than Kant, who thought that only a sense of duty could make a right action morally praiseworthy, and that the pleasure you take in it is morally irrelevant.

Recent virtue theory has also inspired and enriched certain areas of applied ethics, especially feminist ethical theory. It is ironic that although Aristotle thought the virtues could be fully displayed only by free men, some theorists have looked to virtue ethics to uphold feminist insights. Thus it has been claimed that there are distinct male and female perspectives on ethical problems, and that the male perspective (very broadly speaking) is legalistic, focusing on rights, justice and specific obligations, as befits the areas of life where men are dominant, such as business, politics, warfare and sport. By contrast, the female perspective is more focused on an 'ethics of care' than an 'ethics of justice', and gives priority to relationships, nurturing, and sensitivity to particular circumstances rather than rules. Women's experience of childbirth, in particular, is said to fashion their moral perspectives in the direction of 'care'.

There are thinkers who believe that this confirms virtue ethics – that the soundness of virtue ethics is the best explanation of the insights offered by 'female' ethics (which is supported by some feminists). But it would be unwise to rely on this too heavily. For one thing, there are reasonable doubts about whether women's approach to ethics (it is unclear whether this refers to all women, most women or some women) is really so different from the 'male' approach. And if they are different, this is probably because for most of history women have been pressurised to occupy the spheres where the 'care ethic' seems more appropriate. We simply do not know how women would have handled business and warfare, if they had had the chance. Second, although superiority is usually claimed for the ethics of care, this surely has to be argued for; it is not enough just to note that this is the way women think.

So feminist thinking fails to lend much support to virtue ethics. There is also a difficulty with virtue ethics that some adherents of other, 'action-based' theories regard as fatal. This is that virtue ethics is trivial, in that it cannot specify any content to the notion of virtue that other theories cannot also supply. Put simply, we want to know how to identify the virtuous agent. Surely we can only say that the virtuous agent is one who does the right things. But then, the right things would have to be specified independently, perhaps in Kantian or utilitarian terms. Thus the contrast between virtue ethics and other theories turns out to be illusory. The idea that virtue ethics' distinct contribution is in the emphasis on the sort of person I should be, becomes trivial. Surely I should just be the sort of person who *does the right things*. And no Kantian or utilitarian would disagree with that!

I think this objection shows that it is misguided to appeal to virtue ethics in order to abolish 'ought' concepts in favour of 'virtue' concepts. But that is not the complete end of virtue ethics. This approach can shed important light on what our obligations are, by asking what states of character various actions (or omissions) would show. This is perhaps brought out most clearly when we consider actions that cause neither hurt nor harm to anyone, but which we might, intuitively, wish to condemn. Consider someone who spits on graves when no one is looking. The dead, let us assume here, are neither hurt nor harmed by this action, and no living person is offended by it, since no one witnesses it. Yet there still seems to be something wrong; a deliberately disrespectful act is performed, which manifests a bad aspect of someone's character.

More generally, considering the virtues can help shape our principles of action, by bringing some explanatory simplicity to them. We might get a sense of the moral shape of an action if we see in it a similarity to other acts whose moral complexion we already understand. This similarity is often captured by the use of virtue terms. Thus we might want to say that what deception, cheating, stealing and fraud have in common is that they are dishonest, and more generally unjust. Justice is the bridging notion here. If I am wondering whether I can justify a certain course of action, I have a better grip on the problem if I ask whether the behaviour is just, kind or generous than if I vaguely ask whether it is 'right'. Virtue concepts cannot replace deontic ones (e.g. to do with rightness or obligation) but they can make their use more intelligible.

But to repeat, whilst we should understand the differences of emphasis and indeed normative content between these theories of ethics, we should avoid erecting artificial distinctions. There are areas of life where each seems appropriate. Simon Blackburn suggests that 'these focuses of attention – duty, situations, and virtue – correspond, respectively, to the ethics of police and lawcourts, the ethics of planning and managing, and the ethics of educators and schoolteachers.'[2] Each has an important role. The danger is in attempts to reduce all ethical insight to just one of these things.

TRUTH IN ETHICS

But maybe we have avoided discussing something rather important, up to this point. Theories such as consequentialism crack themselves up to be superior and more worthy to be believed and acted upon than their rivals. But in what way can those claims be true, or warranted?

We are now in the realm of metaethics, which enquires into such things as the nature of moral claims, their objectivity and meaning, and what distinguishes them from other concerns. A perennially important topic, although formulated differently at different times, is that of whether, or how, moral claims can be objectively true. But of course, that very notion is obscure in the present context.

Some philosophers interpret the issue as one of whether there are moral facts. Is there a 'way things are', morally speaking, independently of human opinions and conventions? (and what does 'independently' amount to here?). *Moral realism* says there is, that it is no more problematic to speak of moral facts than of any other kind of fact (which is not to say that the idea of a 'fact', at least construed as an entity, is without its difficulties). Various opponents of realism deny this. In theory, an opponent of realism could be a nihilist, believing that morality is literally an illusion and that there is no reason to have any moral concerns. Significantly, very few philosophical opponents of moral realism actually take that view. They maintain that morality should matter to us, that there are better and worse ways to live. However, they try to understand these claims while eschewing the metaethical doctrine of realism.

Probably the most influential tradition supporting this view is Humean naturalism. Hume was particularly concerned to attack the prevalent view that moral claims were the deliverances of reason. Many theorists believed (and still do) that the moral law is as much part of reality as the laws of nature, and that careful reflection will lead us to discover objective reasons for action. One version of this approach is found in natural law theory, which maintains that there are human goods – love, friendship, work, etc. – that we have reason to pursue regardless of our actual desires; that certain ends are 'natural' for us, and (some maintain) that these natural ends are part of a benevolent and providential order. Hume, however, held that the promptings of morality are not to be found in the domain of reason, that 'morality is properly felt than judg'd of', that 'reason is, and ought only to be, the slave of the passions'.[3] He asks us to contemplate any action that we think of as vicious, such as murder, and examine it closely to find the quality of vice. We will not find it in the action, he maintains; all we will find there is various passions and motives and physical movements. But when we look inwards, to our own reactions, we shall find it. All that exists in nature are actions with purely natural properties, and our subjective reactions to them. We 'gild and stain' the world with our reactions, and come to think that we are reacting to objective moral properties. But all that is really going on, to use a modern idiom, is a process of projection of our passions onto the world.[4]

There is another important strand to the Humean critique of what is now called moral realism. This is that morality is essentially practical – it is about what we *ought* to do. But 'reason alone' can never motivate an action. It can tell us how to achieve our ends, but it cannot give us those ends. For that, we need the 'passions'. The argument here points to the oddity of there being states of affairs, or facts, that are intrinsically prescriptive. We form *beliefs* about facts, about the way things *are*, but we form *desires* about what to do, or how things *should* be. For Humeans, morality is squarely in the domain of desire; a moral conviction is not a cognitive state that focuses on purely descriptive properties of the world.

Do these arguments finish off the claim that morality is 'objective', that there are binding reasons for action that we cannot escape? We could distinguish the notion of moral facts and that of objective prescriptions or reasons for action. Thus we might say that although moral commitments always have an attitudinal and/or motivational aspect, they still answer to genuine norms of correctness. This idea, it seems, is similar to that of Kant, who although an objectivist is not so obviously a moral realist. Utterances about what we ought to do are not to be identified with factual statements, yet they still have their own kind of objectivity. In a roughly similar vein, recent philosophers[5] have said that there are objective *reasons for action*, and indeed that the doctrine of moral realism amounts essentially to this. We act as if we recognise such reasons; the existence of severe pain, for example, might be held to generate a reason to act to alleviate the pain, not only for the person suffering it but for anyone else in a position to help. Scepticism about such reasons, as about the authority of morality generally, seems to fly in the face of our everyday practice of evaluating and deliberating.

Morality is about what matters to us. It does not exhaust all that matters to us – other things do too. But it concerns things that we care about, and this suggests that whatever the affinities between desiring something and judging it to be good, there is more to it than that. We don't simply desire what we take to be good; we also think we should desire it. Not that we always succeed in forming such desires: there are some desires we have, although we wish we didn't have them, and there are some desires we don't have, although we wish we did. We take issue with those who disagree with us about moral issues. We form negative attitudes towards their attitudes. This suggests that a casual moral relativism will not do, as we saw. But does it show that we must think of morality as objective in any sense?

If we are looking for reasons for action that we must accept, on pain of being shown to be irrational, then it is doubtful that morality has this status. This is not to say we cannot reason about ethics – we clearly can and do. We can judge moral claims to be inconsistent with other moral claims advanced by the same person. We can detect logical errors, confused or incoherent concepts, factual errors, bias and disguised self-interest. We can try to educate people's imagination, so that they get a better sense of the moral shape of a situation. We can analyse virtues and vices, asking subtle questions about the nature of pride, envy, kindness or justice. We can insist that moral claims are universalisable. What this doesn't show, though, is that the person who says 'So what?' when a moral consideration is invoked is being literally irrational. Hume calls such a character the 'sensible knave', who reasons well but just happens not to share the moral concerns that most other people do. He fails to be moved in the way most of us are. Indeed, the modern term 'psychopath' captures something of the sensible knave, and there are such people. They are neither insane nor necessarily unintelligent, but they lack the emotional capacity for empathy with others, and have little or no conscience.

But if we can't convict him of irrationality, should we worry that there is nothing we can say against him at all, or indeed that his very existence shows the rest of us to be in the grip of a chimera? This does not follow. We can quite reasonably say that this character is vicious, uncaring, selfish, greedy and generally undesirable. We can be committed to avoiding becoming like him. All this will follow from the concerns we actually have, which cannot be indifferent to whether others share those same concerns. We cannot derive relativism merely from our doubts about the ultimate grounding of ethics in Reason. The concerns that we call moral, and perhaps some others like aesthetic ones, are precisely those that generate second-order concerns about whether our moral concerns are shared. If I prefer tomato soup to leek and potato soup, I am not bothered by your preference for the latter, but if I morally object to imprisonment without trial, I cannot be indifferent to other people's acceptance of it.

So far so good, yet our worries are not over. For I want my objection to imprisonment without due process to be *correct* – to measure up, in some way, to an objective standard. Can I make sense of my moral concerns if I don't suppose that there is such a standard? Humean naturalists tell a sophisticated story about the ultimate incoherence of supposing that moral concerns can be supported by Reason (capital R), and about why they need no such support. However, one doesn't have to be convinced by any existing attempt to produce such an account (and Kant's is one of the most popular) to worry about the implications of the lack of one. The spectre of the nihilist appears in the corner of our moral vision, insinuating that morality really is an illusion if there is no objective moral reality, and that we are too cowardly and self-deceived to face up to this fact.

The problem may well be intractable. It is largely one of interpretation, of understanding how to make sense of the idea of objective moral reality. Some people find the idea perfectly simple, and given to us in our mundane moral experience. We 'see' the wickedness of the act of 'wilful murder' mentioned by Hume, just by experiencing our reaction to it. Perhaps our moral experience does not give us access to a *metaphysical* reality – but then, why suppose that genuine moral reality has to be metaphysical? It could be analogous to something empirically given, like colour – an analogy that has indeed been defended by a few moral realists.[6] Others, however, think that any realist notion of moral values must be problematic, perhaps stressing the difficulty with the idea that practical motivation can be justified or explained by a descriptive feature of reality. Those taking this view may, like Blackburn, be content with it, seeing in it no threat to our first-order ethical commitments. Others, like the present author, wish they could be convinced of this, but are not so sure.

We have not (here) solved the problem of the ultimate ontological status of values, but it is worth noting that the question should not be looked at in isolation from other areas of philosophy where disputes about 'realism' versus 'anti-realism' arise – for example, causation, time, substance and identity. When we have a clear account of these issues, we may be in a better position to ask whether values are part of the totality of all that exists, or whether they are after all something separate, perhaps projections of human needs and desires. To look at 'second-order' issues in ethics can only be part of a much wider philosophical enquiry. Fortunately, to be able to reason about moral concepts and first-order, normative questions, this wider expertise appears strictly optional.

EXERCISES

1 'You say that abortion is wrong, but that's only *your* point of view'. What is the speaker driving at? How would you respond?
2 Compare and contrast self-interest and selfishness. Under what circumstances, if any, will people who are exclusively self-interested enter into co-operation with others?
3 'Utilitarianism should be rejected, because it makes excessive demands upon us. For example, it tells well-off people to give away most of their money to the starving.' Do you agree (a) that this is a correct account of what utilitarianism demands of us, and (b) that if it is, then it should be rejected?
4 Does Kant show that immoral acts are irrational?
5 Does virtue ethics have anything true and important to say, that cannot be said by any other theory?
6 Is there any reason for thinking that good moral philosophers are likely to be good people?

NOTES

1 R.M. Hare (1981) *Moral Thinking*, Oxford: Oxford University Press.
2 Simon Blackburn (1998) *Ruling Passions*, Oxford: Clarendon Press, p. 30.
3 David Hume (1978) *A Treatise of Human Nature*, ed. L.A. Selby-Bigge, Oxford: Clarendon Press. See Book III.
4 This Humean story of the explanation for our moral reactions has been named 'projectivism' by Simon Blackburn, who is one of the theory's most prominent contemporary defenders. See in particular his 'Errors and the phenomenology of value', in Ted Honderich (ed.) (1985) *Morality and Objectivity*, London: Routledge.
5 For example, Thomas Nagel (1986) *The View From Nowhere*, Oxford: Oxford University Press.
6 See John McDowell, 'Values and secondary qualities', in Ted Honderich (ed.) (1985) *Morality and Objectivity*, London: Routledge.

FURTHER READING

Baron, Marcia W., Pettit, Philip and Slote, Michael (1997) *Three Methods of Ethics: A Debate*, Oxford: Blackwell.
Blackburn, Simon (1998) *Ruling Passions: A Theory of Practical Reasoning*, Oxford: Clarendon Press.
Crisp, Roger and Slote, Michael (eds) (1997) *Virtue Ethics*, Oxford: Oxford University Press.
Foot, Philippa (1977) *Virtues and Vices*, Oxford: Blackwell.
Foot, Philippa (2001) *Natural Goodness*, Oxford: Oxford University Press.
Gaita, Raimond (2000) *A Common Humanity: Thinking about Love and Truth and Justice*, New York & London: Routledge.

Hare, R.M. (1981) *Moral Thinking*, Oxford: Oxford University Press.

Honderich, Ted (ed.) (1985) *Morality and Objectivity*, London: Routledge.

Hooker, Brad (2000) *Ideal Code, Real World: A Rule-consequentialist Theory of Morality*, Oxford: Oxford University Press.

Hume, David (1888) *A Treatise of Human Nature*, ed. L.A. Selby-Bigge, Oxford: Clarendon Press.

Hursthouse, Rosalind (1999) *On Virtue Ethics*, Oxford: Oxford University Press.

Kant, Immanuel (1964) *Groundwork of the Metaphysic of Morals*, transl. H.J. Paton, New York: Harper and Row.

Nagel, Thomas (1986) *The View From Nowhere*, Oxford: Oxford University Press.

Smart, J.J.C. and Williams, B. (1973) *Utilitarianism: For and Against*, Cambridge: Cambridge University Press.

Williams, Bernard (1985) *Ethics and the Limits of Philosophy*, London: Fontana/Collins.

5

ANCIENT PHILOSOPHY

From Thales to Aristotle

Suzanne Stern-Gillet

INTRODUCTION

Anyone embarking on the study of philosophy can expect frequent encounters with ancient thinkers. Socrates, Plato and Aristotle will become almost constant companions. Epicurus, the Stoics, and Plotinus, too, will be met repeatedly, albeit at more distant intervals. This, in itself, is a curious and crucial fact. Unlike philosophy students, budding geographers and medical students, for instance, are not expected to gain familiarity with the beginnings of their subject. In fact, amongst traditional academic disciplines, philosophy appears to be the only one to be centrally interested in its own past. As the example of respected practitioners in all domains of philosophical research shows, philosophy includes, as an integral part of itself, a reflection on its history. So much is this the case that the logician and metaphysician A.N. Whitehead was not taken to be more than mildly paradoxical when he famously described philosophy as 'a set of footnotes to Plato'.[1]

There are several reasons why philosophy is, in this sense, reflexive: to list them all here would be beyond the scope of this chapter. Yet two of these reasons are worth spelling out since they bear directly on the study of ancient philosophy. At the horizon of all thinking – theoretical as well as practical – are assumptions on such large issues as the nature of reality, the origin and the reach of human knowledge, and the best life for a human being to lead. These assumptions, which, by definition, are not justifiable by appeal to principles more basic or better grounded than themselves, all constitute answers to the most fundamental of all philosophical questions. Yet, precisely because of their fundamental character, they cannot be settled once and for all. To raise these questions anew, and to study the ways in which past philosophers dealt with them is therefore part and parcel of the philosophic life. Hence, those concerned to lead such a life, at whatever modest or high a level, will often find themselves turning to the writings of the giants of the past, amongst whom Plato and Aristotle figure prominently.

A second, and related, reason for studying ancient thinkers is that they were the pioneers who, in the West, charted the terrain of philosophy and produced its first, large-scale map. To this day, theirs remains, in essentials, the core map, even though later philosophers smoothed some of its rough outlines and drew more detailed versions of it. Between the thinkers of the ancient world and us there is therefore an (almost) uninterrupted tradition. We are their heirs. True, we are also indebted to other systems of thought and traditions but the basic categories through which we process our experience of the world, and the concepts in which we express our philosophical thoughts, bear unmistakable marks of their ancient Greek parentage.

To become conscious of these marks and thereby to gain a sense of one's intellectual history is a by-product of the study of ancient philosophy. To obtain maximum benefit from this study, however, one must be on one's guard against the dangers of misapprehension and over-simplification that are identified in the following cautionary remarks.

The context

For almost all of us, the first encounters with philosophy are in our mother tongue and the conceptual apparatus of our time. Often, when we are taken back in time, it is to be encouraged to approach past thinkers from the vantage point of our own time. This philosopher or that, we are told, first formulated this distinction, bequeathed us that question, inaugurated this method, anticipated that theory. Sometimes, the great figures of the past are reduced to a succession of mistakes and misapprehensions, each engendered by the one that preceded it. The temptation, therefore, is great for beginners to project present ways and preoccupations back on to the past. Thus Heraclitus becomes the first exponent of dialectic. Plato and Aristotle are presented as holding diametrically opposed views on the subject of universals. Plato is classified as a rationalist, Aristotle becomes a forerunner of empiricism. His ethics is interpreted as egoistic in outlook. As for Plotinus' investigations into the nature of the individual soul, they are briskly pigeonholed as introspective.

To the extent that they help beginners in making connections between the present and the past of their discipline, such *rapprochements*, provided that they are kept in their place, are helpful. Unfortunately, they are rarely kept in their place. From mere teaching aids, they are allowed to harden into a methodology, which is aptly described as a-historical. In this approach, time and place are almost irrelevant. Philosophers separated by vast tracts of space and time are made to become partners in discussion. Parmenides is turned into a *ur*-Heideggerian, Plato into a feminist, and Aristotle into an honorary analytic philosopher. Not only is this a-historical approach distorting, it is also, in its extreme form, counter-productive. By stressing the resemblances between philosophers at the expense of the very real differences between them, this a-historical method undermines the very purpose of studying the great figures of the past, which is to gain an insight in the history of one's discipline while stimulating fresh approaches and insights into philosophical issues as currently perceived.

To learn the past and from it, we must let ancient thinkers speak to us in their strangeness. We must not oversimplify them. We must understand that although the problems that they first formulated, or inherited from their own predecessors, turned into the perennial problems of philosophy, these problems had nonetheless an identity of their own, stemming from the historical and cultural context in which they arose. To this context the best clue is ancient Greek, the language in which most of these philosophers wrote.[2] True, all seminal Greek texts are currently available in translation. Most of these translations are sound enough. Yet, we must not delude ourselves that reading, for instance, Plato in English is the same as reading him in Greek. For Plato's Greek was a living language and should be treated as such, not as a code. Greek philosophers in general – including Aristotle, in spite of his occasional partiality to jargon – mostly expressed their thoughts in the words of everyday speech, which were also the words of the poets, the tragedians, the orators and the historians of their time. These words, loaded as they were with diverse and complex connotations, bore heavily on the philosophical thoughts which they served to express. Even the best of translations cannot bring out the full semantic weight of these words. As for the wealth of implicit allusions pressing behind the idioms, the metaphors and the proverbs regularly used by ancient philosophers, they will often elude translation. Translators, however deft and painstaking, are but interpreters who must render one word by another word with a different connotative density, one idiomatic construction by another one which is not a perfect match for it. A good translator is one who distorts and impoverishes less than other translators.

This may seem a counsel of despair. Yet it is not. The fact that modern philosophical debates are full of references to ancient thinkers is proof enough that their writings do somehow survive translation. Even so, the inevitable limitations of translation must be borne in mind. Greek-less readers of ancient texts should therefore be encouraged to use more than one translation, and to acquaint themselves, as far as they can, with the historical and literary context in which the philosophies of the ancients were worked out.

Scribes and scholars[3]

Cheap and plentiful though modern translations are, they are nonetheless the outcome of a long and hazardous process of retrieval. Take the example of Plato's *oeuvre* which, in many respects, turned out to be a fortunate case since all of his writings – as well as a few more whose authenticity is in doubt – have come down to us in a generally uncorrupted form. Our oldest Plato manuscript, which dates from AD 895, happens to be a particularly fine example of calligraphy, executed on parchment by John the Calligrapher for Arethas, bishop of Cesarea in Cappadocia (see Figure 5.1). Yet it was made some twelve centuries after Plato's death, twelve centuries which include the Roman conquest of Athens and the rest of Greece, the fall of Rome subsequent to the Barbarian invasions, and the subsequent so-called dark ages. Unsurprisingly, this ninth century manuscript is itself a copy of an earlier copy; it is, therefore, related to Plato's own text through many intermediaries of unknown reliability. Alexandrine learned editions (now lost[4]) notwithstanding, we cannot expect the standards of critical edition in antiquity and the middle ages to have been as exacting as they became after the development of textual criticism in the nineteenth century. To assume that every word in our Oxford edition is directly related to Plato's own manuscripts would therefore be naive in the extreme. During the middle-ages texts were copied and re-copied in longhand by monks, many of whom were ignorant of Greek, not all of whom were intelligent, unbiased or, for that matter, interested. Mistakes of various kinds crept in, omissions took place, and amendments – not always judicious – were made. In turn, these manuscripts (*codices*) were themselves copied; their assorted mistakes were mostly, although not unfailingly, reproduced. On such families of manuscripts our modern editions of Plato are based.

To gain an idea of the work undertaken by Plato's modern editors, take a look at the photographic reproduction of a page in John the Calligrapher's manuscript (*Cratylus*, 390c6–391d3), catalogued in the Bodleian Library as Clarkianus MS 39. Note the absence of capital letters and punctuation signs. Observe the marginal comment in a different hand. Scrutinise the interlinear addition: is it in the copyist's own hand? If, as seems almost certain, it is not, who inserted it and why? Does it reflect the reading of another manuscript? If so, what do we know of that other manuscript and its credentials? Lastly, bear in mind that some 170 manuscripts of Plato are extant, probably going back to three different 'ancestors' or sources. Most of these manuscripts are far less legible and reliable than the Clarkianus. Worse still, they often present variants. In choosing which reading to adopt, editors are guided by external (codicological) and internal (philosophical) evidence. The use of the latter evidence presupposes not only a detailed knowledge of the Platonic *corpus* as a whole – to judge which reading represents what Plato might have written

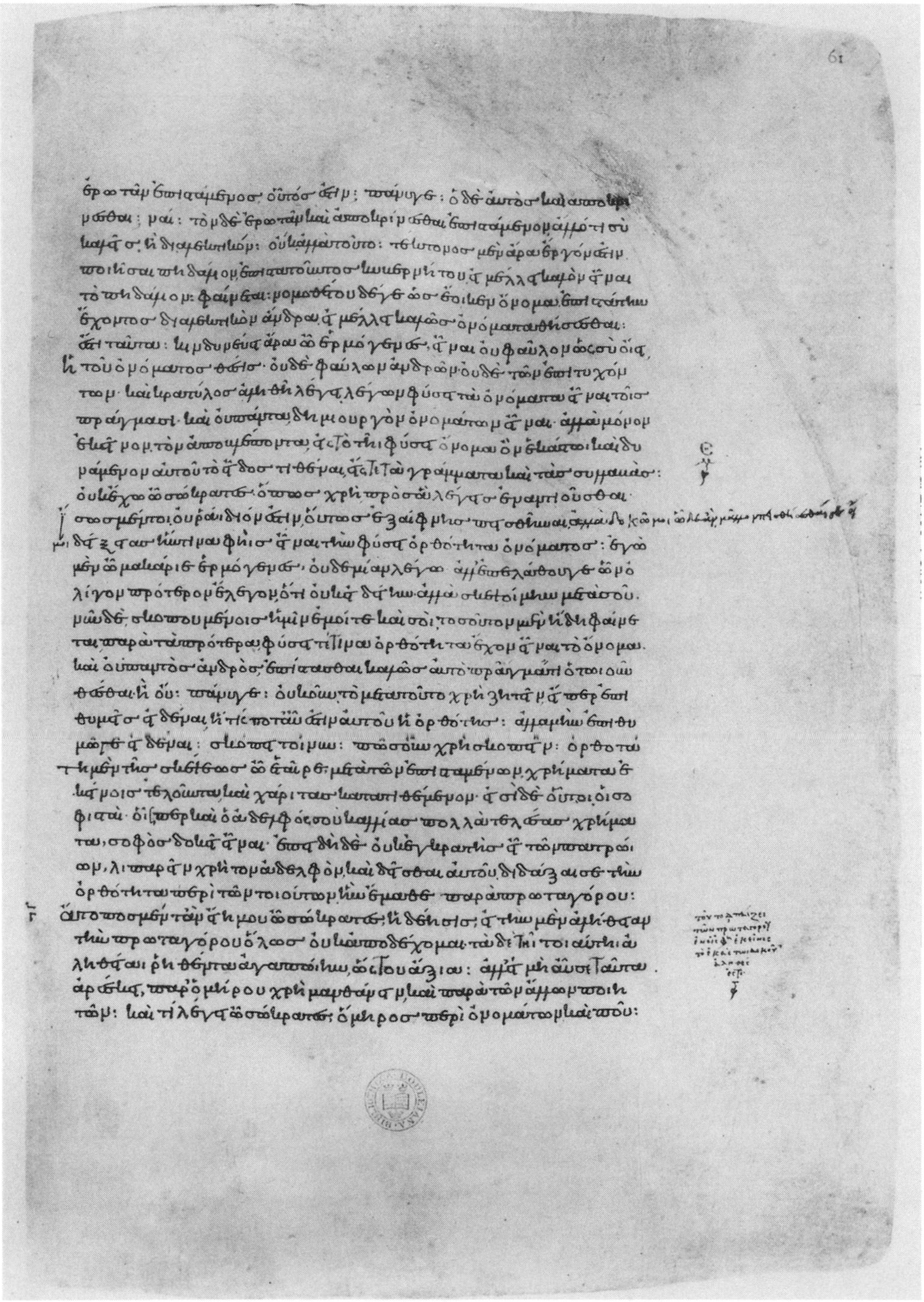

Figure 5.1 A page from the *Cratylus* in the oldest Plato manuscript dating from AD 895
Source: The Bodleian Library, Oxford

– but also considerable philosophical acumen – to select which reading best fits a particular argument in its context. To take into account new findings and methodologies, Plato's writings are periodically re-edited. A new complete edition, only one volume of which has so far appeared, is currently under way at the Oxford University Press.[5]

Awareness of the role of scribes, scholars and editors in the retrieval and edition of ancient Greek philosophical texts leads one to appreciate that any serious study of ancient philosophy is of necessity exegetical rather than merely expository. It also suffices to undermine the all too popular distinction between the 'merely scholarly' and the 'more philosophically original' approaches to ancient texts.

'The Greeks'

A phrase frequently encountered while dealing with ancient philosophy is 'the Greeks'. To those collectively designated by this phrase is ascribed a motley of views, beliefs, and assumptions which are taken to distinguish the ancient Greeks from other groups, most notably ourselves. While this blanket phrase is not exactly inapposite, it betokens intellectual laziness and must be used sparingly. Let us see why.

It is almost universally accepted that Thales, who was born in $c.624$ BC,[6] was the first Greek philosopher. It is not generally disputed that the last of the pagan Neoplatonists, Iamblichus, who died in $c.$AD 325, was the last of the Greek philosophers. Approximately 950 years of history separate these two dates. Translated into modern terms, this is the gap that separates us from Peter Damian, an obscure philosopher and theologian who was active in northern Italy in the middle of the eleventh century, around the time of the battle of Hastings. Presumably, Peter Damian's contemporaries and successors up to the present day would have to be labelled 'the Europeans'. Would the motley of beliefs and attitudes arguably held in common by the members of this class help to distinguish them collectively from other groups? The vast extension of either class alone suffices to throw serious doubt on their historical and exegetical usefulness.

Besides, not all 'the Greeks' were Greek although they mostly wrote in Greek. Several ancient philosophers came from Greek colonies on or off the coast of Asia Minor (e.g. Thales and Heraclitus), from Sicily (e.g. Empedocles and the Sophist Gorgias), from present-day Spain (Seneca), from Rome (e.g. Marcus Aurelius), from Thrace (Democritus and Protagoras), from Alexandria (several Neoplatonists including, probably, Plotinus), from Tyre in present-day Syria (Porphyry), etc. In fact, the areas from which the philosophers lumped collectively as 'the Greeks' came, covered practically the whole of the Western civilised world.

If dispersion in space and time was not reason enough to dismiss the label, let it further be pointed out that, in the dearth of easily available printed editions, such temporal gap and geographical dispersion was more significant in antiquity than it has since become. Public libraries, even when they were set up in the Hellenistic period, were rare, and critical editions of texts, which were late in being undertaken, were few and far between. Texts were manuscript on cumbersome papyrus rolls and therefore likely to be comparatively rare. Opportunities for travel and the exchange of ideas were less frequent and plentiful than they were to become in the middle ages and later. The homogeneity of belief, customs and attitudes necessary to give substance to the label 'the Greeks' was therefore lacking. The Stoic ideal of the *cosmic city* was precisely an attempt to formulate a moral and political ideal that did not presuppose such homogeneity.

By then, Greek philosophy was already some three centuries old. Let us now turn to its beginnings.

THE PRESOCRATICS

It has become usual to group the early Greek philosophers under the umbrella title of 'the Presocratics'. Convenient though this label is, it is important to realise that it is not historically innocent. To begin with, as Hegel is reputed to have warned his students, 'Do not forget that the Presocratics did not know that they were the Presocratics'.[7] So to lump together the early Greek thinkers is to embrace them in a category that they themselves could neither have chosen nor recognised. It is to view them mainly as precursors – for what they started – rather than as achievers in their own right. In fact, the thinkers so designated form a heterogeneous group covering a period of some two centuries and comprising the following main figures: the Milesians (Thales, Anaximander, Anaximenes), Xenophanes, Heraclitus, the Pythagoreans, the Eleatics (Parmenides, Zeno and Melissus), Empedocles, Anaxagoras, and the Atomists (Leucippus and Democritus). Let it lastly be noted that the label is not, strictly speaking, accurate in so far that not all the Presocratics were born before Socrates. Democritus, who was born in 460 BC, was younger than Socrates by some ten years, and some of the older Sophists, who were active a full generation before Socrates, are not unfailingly included among the Presocratics.

To the historian of philosophy the Presocratics present a particularly knotty problem in so far as they are known only through the good offices of later ancient writers who either quoted them directly or made reference to their views. Following Hermann Diels, the German scholar who, in 1903, produced the first critical edition of extant sources for the Presocratic philosophers, the former are called *fragmenta*, the latter *testimonia*.[8] Ancient sources for our knowledge of the Presocratics fall into three categories: philosophers engaged in working out their own system (e.g. Aristotle in the fourth century BC), philosophers for whom the sole form of philosophical activity was to write commentaries on the great philosophical works of the past (e.g. Simplicius in the sixth century AD), and doxographers, i.e. writers who were content merely to record, as they saw them, the lives and the views of past philosophers (e.g. Diogenes Laertius in the third century AD). How reliable are these various accounts? Are doxographers, who have no philosophical axe to grind, likely to be more objective than philosophers of either group, who are committed to a particular system? Not really. Great thinkers often elude the powers of understanding of their more literal-minded chroniclers; Diogenes Laertius, for instance, often flattens out the systems that he purports to describe. Besides, the doctrinal biases of philosophers can generally be inferred from their own works. Once these biases are identified, their capacity to mislead decreases. Aristotle, who presents his predecessors as his precursors and explicitly ascribes their 'errors' to an imperfect grasp of principles that he himself would be the first to formulate, is a case in point. His very openness in the matter often enables us to divest the arguments of his predecessors from the Aristotelian garb in which he clothes them.

Although the critical examination of several different sources constitutes the very basis of any serious study of the Presocratics, constraints of space force us to be highly selective. The brief account of Presocratic philosophies offered below is heavily reliant on a critical reading of the testimonies of Aristotle and his pupil Theophrastus. The volume and relative quality of their testimonies, as well as the philosophical importance of the Peripatetic school in general, have guided this decision.

When, in search of ancestors, Aristotle turned back in time, he identified Thales the Milesian as the first to have 'philosophised about reality'.[9] In this judgement, posterity has largely concurred, even if what Aristotle called 'philosophising about reality' then included also investigations which would nowadays be described as 'scientific'. The boundaries between academic disciplines were long in being drawn, and the further back in time we go the hazier they become. Unsurprisingly, therefore, the first Greek philosophers were also the first Greek scientists. Thus Thales is reputed to have predicted the solar eclipse of 584 BC and to have been able to calculate the height of pyramids and the distance of ships at sea. Likewise, his younger Milesian contemporary, Anaximander, is credited with drawing the first map of the earth, and inventing the gnomon (a vertical rod which, when inserted into the ground, projects a shadow which can be used to calculate the time of day).

Great as they were, the 'scientific' achievements of the Milesians are yet surpassed by their 'philosophical' significance. First in our tradition, they sought to explain nature by nature. Earlier cosmogonies, of which Hesiod's *Theogony* is the best example, had mostly relied on supra-natural factors, i.e. the capricious motives and intentions of anthropologically conceived individual deities, to account for the universe, its origin and diverse aspects. By contrast, if we believe Aristotle, the explanations of the Milesian thinkers mostly rely on general principles and are supported by arguments and empirical considerations. For these reasons they have a claim to being called theories.

Consider **Thales** (*c*.624–546 BC). Unfortunately, from an exegetical point of view, his is a particularly difficult case since it is unlikely that he wrote anything, or that, if he did, his work was still extant in Aristotle's day. Yet, for whatever knowledge we possess of Thales' philosophy we rely almost entirely on the account that Aristotle gave of it approximately two centuries after Thales' death. The testimony is extracted from the first book of the *Metaphysics*, a text that has a claim to being the first history of philosophy:

> Most of the first philosophers thought that principles in the form of matter were the only principles of all things; for the original source of all existing things, that from which a thing first comes-into-being and into which it is finally destroyed, the substance persisting but changing in its qualities, this they declare is the element and first principle of existing things, and for this reason they consider that there is no absolute coming-to-be or passing away, on the ground that such a nature is always preserved . . . for there must be some natural substance, either one or more than one, from which the other things come-into-being, while it is preserved. Over the number, however, and the form of this kind of principle they do not all agree; but Thales, the founder of this type of philosophy, says that it is water (and therefore declared that the earth is on water), perhaps taking this supposition from seeing the nurture of all things to be moist, and the warm itself coming-to-be from this and living by this (that from which they come-to-be being the principle of all things) – taking the supposition both from this and from the seeds of all things having a moist nature, water being the natural principle of moist things.
>
> (*Metaphysics*, I 3, 983b6–25, DK 11A12)

To yield useful information on Thales, this passage must first be scrutinised for signs of Aristotelianism. Let us note that the key technical concepts in it, i.e. substrate, substance, quality, and element are all Aristotelian.[10] In fact, the system here ascribed to Thales appears to be, from a structural point of view, a crude version of Aristotle's own; both the origin and the essence of the Milesian's physical universe are explained by means of a principle conceived as a material substratum that persists through the various changes brought about by the acquisition and the loss of properties. In other words, Thales' 'substratum' prefigures Aristotle's material cause, and is analysed in terms of the Aristotelian distinction between substance and accidents.

If we peel off these Aristotelian accretions, what does this passage tell us about its subject? It tells us that Thales thought that all existing things *originate* in a single material element which he identified as water or, perhaps more accurately, the moist. It traces this view to likely empirical observations, and also links it with Thales' description of the earth as floating on water.[11] This information is as likely to be accurate as any conveyed by one philosopher about another. Unfortunately, the rest of the passage may not be so reliable. Did Thales, as Aristotle claims, conceive of the moist, not only as the *origin* of all things perishable, but also as their ultimate *constituent* or *substrate* as well as their *final destination?* At this point, we must bear in mind that Aristotle may have projected his own theoretical framework onto Thales' system, with which, in any case, he was not directly acquainted. Unfortunately, we cannot be sure to what extent he re-interpreted Thales. Yet the matter is important. Indeed, if Thales thought of water as merely the originative stuff of the universe, then his monism is only a monism of origins: water mostly transforms itself into the other substances, solid and gaseous, of which our universe is formed, and, in the process, ceases to be water. But if, on the other hand, Thales thought of water as the persisting substratum of the universe, then his monism is all-embracing: as long as it lasts, the physical universe remains what it was first made of, i.e. water. This second, Aristotelian, interpretation lands Thales with a serious problem. How could fire, for instance, be generated from its opposite, i.e. water? How can the universe, which he describes as liquid, acquire solid or gaseous properties without ceasing to correspond to the description he had given of it? Unfortunately, in the absence of any substantial *testimonia* independent from Aristotle's, we are unlikely ever to know the extent of Thales' monism.

Frustrating though this conclusion is, it need not prevent us from appreciating Thales' singular genius. He was the first Western thinker to rely on empirical, natural, considerations to explain nature, and he effected the leap from these to speculation and theory. If Aristotle's report is wholly accurate, Thales is also to be credited for bringing the distinction between appearance and reality to bear on cosmological and philosophical speculation, when he claimed that although natural objects may *appear* solid (stars, stones and bodies) or gaseous (air and steam), they *are*, in fact, water under another name – or water modified. The fact that this move may have introduced a fatal incoherence into his system does not entirely detract from Thales' merit for making it.

It is likely that **Anaximander** (*c.*610–545 BC), the second of the Milesians, introduced the concept of *apeiron* (literally: the limitless) to avoid the problems involved in explaining the generation of the universe from a single definite substance. In Simplicius' report, written some eleven centuries later:

> Anaximander, son of Praxiades, a Milesian, the successor and pupil of Thales, said that the principle and element of existing things was the *apeiron*, being the

first to introduce this name of the material principle. He says that it is neither water nor any of the so-called elements, but some other *apeiron* nature, from which come into being all the heavens and the worlds in them. And the source of coming-to-be for existing things is that into which destruction, too, happens *according to necessity; for they pay penalty and retribution to each other for their injustice according to the assessment of Time, as he describes it in these rather poetical terms.*

(*In Phys.*, 24, 13; DK 12A9, my italics)

The Aristotelian veneer of this testimony, manifest in the anachronistic reference to a material principle and the 'so-called elements', is due to the fact that Simplicius' account closely follows that of Theophrastus, who was Aristotle's disciple. Yet, the mention of Anaximander's poetical style gives us confidence that the italicised part of the above quotation is likely to be Anaximander's own.

What more does this particular fragment reveal of Anaximander's thought? It tells us that, in his view, our world originates in some stuff which he called the *apeiron* and which he (most probably) conceived as material even though not as a single definite thing, such as water. A reservoir of virtualities, the *apeiron* also receives the outcome of the destruction and disintegration of the things which had first originated from it. Movement from the *apeiron*, as well as to it, is governed by a law which Anaximander conceived in evaluative and compensatory terms. From these points, it would appear to follow that the *apeiron* is eternal and that it generates a plurality of worlds, either successive or co-existent. On the internal composition of the *apeiron*, on the other hand, the fragment is not very informative. From the fact that it is described as neither one definite thing or quality nor another, it is not unreasonable to infer that it was qualitatively undifferentiated. This, however, does not explain what needs explaining, i.e. how definite substances and qualities came to emerge from such undifferentiated origin. Unsurprisingly, scholarly hypotheses, ancient and modern, abound to fill this gap in our knowledge of Anaximander's system.

If Anaximander's cosmogony is likely to remain an enigma, his reason for postulating the existence of an *apeiron* is clear – at least, if we can believe Aristotle:

there . . . cannot be one simple infinite (*apeiron*) body, and this is so not only if, as some say, it is an extra body over and above the elements, which acts as the source of the elements, but also on a more straightforward view. Those who suggest that the infinite (*apeiron*) is not air or water, but this extra body, do so because they want to avoid everything else being destroyed by an infinite element. The point is that the elements are related by mutual opposition (air is cold, for instance, while water is moist and fire is hot), and so if any one of them were infinite, the others would have been destroyed by now. So in fact, they say, there is this extra body which is the source of the elements.

(*Physics*, III 5, 204b22–29, trans. R. Waterfield)

If Aristotle is right, then the *apeiron* was postulated, at least in part, to account for what Thales had failed to render intelligible, i.e. the ever-changing diversity of our world. The *apeiron*, not being one definite substance but a qualitatively mixed reservoir, enabled Anaximander to explain the formation of the world and the composite nature of the things in it. It also accounts for its continuing existence or, at least, for the formation of others like it. On the assumption that Aristotle's report is accurate, one may also hazard the guess that the reasoning that led Anaximander to postulate the *apeiron* was an early form of what later became known as transcendental deduction, i.e. the deduction of what must be the case for what is the case to be the case.

Heraclitus (*c*.540–480 BC) is a transitional figure in the succession of Presocratic philosophies. His description of the cosmos as an eternal fire links him to the Milesians. Yet his concept of *logos* is evidence of a novel approach to the problem of identifying a unitary principle to account for the ever-changing multiplicity of appearances. Although a relatively large proportion of his writings have survived (some 120 fragments), he is not an easy philosopher to interpret. Not caring to be understood by the many, he wrote obscurely and, at times, incoherently.

Heraclitus is known mainly as the proponent of the doctrine of flux. Here is Plato's vivid, but perhaps not fully reliable, summary of it in the *Cratylus*:

Heraclitus somewhere says that all things are in process and nothing stays still, and likening existing things to the stream of a river he says that you would not step twice into the same river.

(402a8–10; DK 22A6)

The continuous flowing motion of the river is plain for all to see, but what of diamonds and temples? Are they a-flowing too? From the above fragment we infer that Heraclitus thought that they, too, like everything else in our surroundings, change constantly. This view, which interprets objects as successions of events, would appear to fly in the face of common sense. Did Heraclitus mean to challenge sense perception? To account for both the reality of continuous change and the appearance of permanence, Heraclitus evolved theoretical tools which later proved influential. Chief amongst these are strife as a dynamic principle and the unity of opposites.

'War', he wrote, 'is the father of all and king of all' (DK 22B53). Fathers beget and kings, at least in Heraclitus' time and in principle, rule. In this characteristically paradoxical aphorism, Heraclitus tells us that without the permanent dominance of strife in our universe, nothing would come to be and chaos would prevail. His concept of cosmic fire provides an illustration of this principle. Ever-moving fire, which needs air to burn its fuel and which yields smoke and ash, is the basic, though not the only, constituent of the universe. Eternal yet unable to consume all, presumably because of the presence and opposite action of the sea, fire goes out and is kindled 'in measures' (DK 22B30), i.e. in a proportionate and harmonious fashion. It becomes earth and earth becomes water; water, in turn, through a process of evaporation and under the action of the sun, turns into fire. This tension between the cosmic elements explains the appearance of permanence in some aspects of our universe, and ensures its continuing existence.

Heraclitus most probably accounted for the measured transformation of the elements into one another in terms of his principle of the inseparability of opposites. As he wrote, 'as the same thing there exists in us living and dead and the waking and the sleeping and young and old; for these things having changed round are those, and those having changed round are these' (DK 22B88). In this particular case what makes the opposites one is that they are mutually dependent and succeed each other in time. But the principle is protean. It also signifies that one and the same thing can be described or evaluated in opposite ways; 'the path up and down is one and the same' (DK 22A60) and 'Sea is the most pure and the most polluted water; for fishes it is drinkable and salutary, but for men it is undrinkable and deleterious' (DK 22B61).

Heraclitus did not expect to be understood. The constant flux, the antagonism and unity of the forces at work in the universe, he professed, remain hidden from all but the most penetrating reflection. From such reflection, humans, as a rule, shy away. They never learn the order of nature, which he famously called *logos*:

> Of the Logos which is as I describe it men always prove to be uncomprehending, both before they have heard it and when once they have heard it. For although all things happen according to this Logos men are like people of no experience, even when they experience such words and deeds as I explain, when I distinguish each thing according to its constitution and declare how it is; but the rest of them fail to notice what they do after they wake up just as they forget what they do when asleep.
>
> (DK 22B1)

From Heraclitus' description we infer that the *logos* is a universal law or principle which steers and governs all things. In so far as it is abstract, it is akin to what will later be called a law of nature. Yet in so far as it is occasionally identified with fire, the *logos* is also likely to have been, in Heraclitus' viewpoint, a concrete constituent of the universe. To object that the two conceptions are incompatible would be anachronistic since the history of science shows that the notion of a law of nature, which binds necessarily, was long in emerging.

If Heraclitus cared little about common sense **Parmenides** (*c.*515–450? BC) cared even less. His ruthless application of the as yet uncodified principles of logic,[12] and his lasting effect on ancient philosophers, from Plato to Plotinus, make him the central figure in Presocratic thought. In a long poem, some 130 lines of which survive thanks to Simplicius, he has a goddess instruct a young man in 'the unshaken ... heart of well-rounded truth', and discourage him from following the 'opinions of mortals' (DK 28B1). Of the former, the goddess states that '[it] is' and that 'it is impossible for [it] not to be'; of the object of the latter she states that '[it] is not' and 'it is needful that [it] not be' (DK 28B2).[13]

The first and major difficulty in the interpretation of these lines concerns the sense in which the verb 'to be' is used. Does the goddess mean to say that true enquiry must focus on (a) that which exists (existential use) of necessity or on (b) that which must bear at least one predicate (predicative use) or on (c) that which states what is the case (veridical use) of necessity? These interpretations, taken singly or in combination, have been debated at length. Briefly stated, my own view is that the 'existential' interpretation best fits DK 28B2 above while the 'predicative' interpretation is needed to make sense of DK 28B8, lines 3–4, in which 'what is' is described by means of the predicates 'uncreated', 'imperishable', 'whole', 'motionless', and 'perfect'. The veridical interpretation is the weakest of all: not only does it make DK 28B2 tautological but it also ascribes to Parmenides the view that the object of enquiry is of a propositional nature. Yet, this is invalidated by the goddess' assertion, in DK 28B6, line 1, that 'what is there to be said and thought must needs be'. If, as emphatically stated in this line, the order of thought is none other than the order of being, then thought, knowledge and discourse can have no other intentional object than what 'is', in Parmenides' austere understanding of being. For the above reasons, therefore, it seems best to assume that Parmenides' use of the verb 'to be', like our own, is at times existential and, at other times, predicative.[14]

Even this minimalist account of fragment DK 28B2 and of the difficulties involved in its interpretation suffices to show that Parmenides took a radical position on what was to remain a central philosophical problem, i.e. the relationship between language and reality. Holding that only the real can be the object of thought and discourse, he bequeathed us the problem of reference. Indeed, on his view, how can we speak of what is not, for instance the golden mountain (not to mention the present king of France)? Does the golden mountain not have to exist in order for us to utter truths about it, saying, for example, that it is not silver or that it does not exist? While it would be anachronistic to think that Parmenides considered this problem as such, it is certain that he meant to rule out as unintelligible all speech on 'what is not'.

As for ordinary descriptions of the world of sense, Parmenides placed no reliance on them. Things in this world are subject to generation and destruction, they move in space and, in the course of time, acquire and lose properties; the table, for example, which used to be smooth and clear, is now scratched and stained, and Socrates, once fresh-faced, has become wrinkled. Probably because Parmenides did not distinguish between the being of things to which properties are attached (the table, Socrates) and the being of properties (being scratched or wrinkled) – or between the 'is' of existence and that of predication – he concluded that the concrete particulars of our world have no ontological density. Like events, they lack permanence and fall short of the criteria of being. Being unreal, they cannot but be 'unthought and nameless' (DK 28B8, line 17) although the 'undiscriminating hordes', who foolishly trust sense perception, vainly attempt to think and to name them.

According to Parmenides, there is thus only one object of thought, namely 'what is'. 'What is' is whole, continuous and immobile. There is nothing outside it, not even the void.

Parmenides' ruthless logic and stark ontology brought ancient Greek philosophy to a point of no return. Material monism was no longer an option. Subsequent thinkers would have to question his premises, redefine his terms of reference, or embark on an altogether different path of philosophical enquiry. Let us first briefly turn to the atomists' attempt to reconcile Parmenides' conception of being with the testimony of our senses. In a remarkably economical system, revolving around the notions of atom (in its original meaning of 'the unsplittable'), void, infinite, and motion, **Democritus** (*c*.460–385), the best known and the most prolific of the atomists, sought to deal with fundamental questions of ontology, cosmology, philosophy of mind, epistemology, and ethics.

Atoms are the basic constituents of the universe; material yet physically indivisible, indestructible and imperceptible, all made of the same stuff and varying only in shape and size, atoms in their infinite number move eternally and in all directions in the infinite void. So moving, they collide. Through such contingencies as vicinity and congruence in shape they conglomerate for a time before dissociating under the impact of other moving atoms. From such temporary entanglements of atoms, worlds and their furnishings originate. Being uncreated, imperishable and unalterable, atoms meet *some* of Parmenides' rigorous ontological requirements while the void fulfils the dual function of making them discrete and enabling them to move. The void is thus a crucial feature in the atomists' system since it accounts for the fact that elements, which are individually invisible and indestructible, nevertheless come to form perceptible conglomerates of varying stability and duration. Whether Parmenides would have countenanced such an *ad hoc* and paradoxical notion as the atomist void is highly doubtful. Aristotle, who had reasons of his own for not believing in the void, denied any causal agency to the atomist void[15] and noted the paradox built in the very notion:

> Leucippus and his associate Democritus hold that the elements are the full and the void; they call them what is and what is not respectively. What is is full and solid, what is not is void and rare. Since the void exists no less than body, it follows that what is not exists no less than what is. The two together are the material causes of existing things.
>
> (*Metaphysics*, I 4, 985b4–10; DK 67A6)

The atomist universe is thoroughly materialistic. Souls, Democritus maintained, are made of light and spherical atoms which are distributed throughout the body. Perception, from which the mind takes its evidence, occurs through direct contact between the sense organs and the thin pellicles which are emitted by individual conglomerates of atoms. Even traditional deities are re-interpreted as atomic compounds. Crude as it may strike us, the atomists' brand of materialism turned out to be surprisingly successful. It furnished Epicurus and his followers with their basic physics and metaphysics. It resurfaced in the seventeenth century in the writings of Gassendi and, in a considerably modified and amended form, in modern atomic theory.

THE SOPHISTS

If the atomists tried to meet Parmenides' challenge on its own terms, the **Sophists** by-passed it by abandoning metaphysical speculation and turning instead to the consideration of moral and social problems. In this they were encouraged by political circumstances. In the second half of the fifth century BC, Athens, which became the centre of the Sophistic movement, was a direct democracy. Every citizen[16] had the right to vote in the assembly, and the assembly was sovereign in most matters, including the election to many of the offices of the state. Political success, therefore, depended on the ability to speak persuasively and pleasingly to a less than well educated crowd. Skilful public speaking was also vitally important to those who had to appear in the law courts since there were no lawyers in Athens and litigants had to present their own case. The Sophists, who specialised in the teaching of oratory and rhetoric, and boasted that they could 'make the weaker argument the stronger', were sought after and could command high fees. This, paradoxically, proved to be their undoing. To this day the word 'sophistry', although it derives from *sophos* (wise), remains a by-word for deceitful speech and captious argument. Yet, as will be shown below, the Sophists do not quite deserve their poor reputation. But let us first understand how they came to acquire it.

Plato is largely responsible for the Sophists' bad name. In several dialogues he has Socrates castigate the cupidity and insincerity of the Sophists, and show the vanity of their claim to wisdom. Sophistry itself, he defined as 'the art of contradiction making, descended from an insincere kind of conceited mimicry, of the semblance-making breed' (*Sophist*, 268c8–9). Aristotle, to whom he had passed this prejudice, wrote, more pithily, that 'sophistic is what appears to be philosophy but is not' (*Metaphysics*, IV 3, 1004b26). The combined authority of the two philosophers led their successors, immediate and distant, to neglect the writings of the Sophists. As a consequence, few of their writings have survived, and we have to rely on Plato's dialogues for our knowledge of them. Paradoxically, the Sophists as individuals come alive in this inimical context. Some are odious: Thrasymachus, for instance, is likely forever to remain in our minds the bumptious and confused young man who challenges Socrates in the first book of the *Republic*. Others, such as Protagoras, in Plato's eponymous dialogue, elicit our sympathy, if not our admiration, for their equanimity in withstanding Socrates' bullying argumentation. In only one case, that of Antiphon, do we possess substantial fragments.

The major figure in the Sophistic movement was **Protagoras**. The first serious relativist in the history of Western philosophy, he claimed that 'a man is the measure of all things – of those which are, that they are, and of those which are not, that they are not'.[17] As quoted in the context of Plato's *Theaetetus*, this somewhat mysterious sentence means that properties such as heat and cold, largeness and smallness, do not inhere in objects but arise from the encounter between percipient and object at the time of perception.[18] In this relativistic outlook, each thing is as it appears to each of us, there is no reality other than phenomenal reality, perception is knowledge, and truth is relative. Be it noted, however, that Protagoras' relativism did not extend to ethics and politics. As reported, again by Plato, Protagoras held that human beings are protected from the rigours of the state of nature by an innate moral sense, which it behoves educators and lawgivers to preserve, or to restore whenever it has been overshadowed by other innate drives.[19]

Protagoras' successors tended to be more radical than he had been. They opposed nature (*phusis*) to law (*nomos*) and, in so doing, brought relativism to matters of law and morality. Although different interpretations were given of this famous dichotomy, only the most famous can here be dealt with. Existing laws and moral rules, claimed **Callicles, Thrasymachus and Antiphon**, are not grounded in nature but are artificially and variously grafted on to it. Mere products of convention or custom,[20] they differ from age to age and from country to country. Justice, for instance, in the words of Antiphon, is but 'a matter of not transgressing what the laws prescribe in whatever city you are a citizen of'. Since there was then a considerable semantic overlap between the concepts of justice and morality, Antiphon's line can be interpreted as a statement of ethical relativism and hence as a challenge to the very existence of ethics. Indeed, if morality is merely a matter of convention, there can be no moral truths and, therefore, no objective moral standards. So to construe Antiphon's meaning, however, would be an over-simplification, just as it is an anachronism to attempt to map Hume's law ('no ought from and is') on to the *phusis* and *nomos* opposition. The following extract from Callicles' speech in Plato's Gorgias shows us why this is so:

> I believe that the people who institute our laws are the weak and the many. They do this, and they assign praise and blame with themselves and their own advantage in mind. They're afraid of the more powerful among men, the ones who are capable of having a greater share, and so they say that getting more than one's share is 'shameful' and 'unjust', and that doing what's unjust is trying to get more than one's share . . . I believe that nature itself reveals that it's a just thing for the better man and the more capable man to have a greater share than the worse man and the less capable man. Nature shows . . . that the superior rule the inferior and have a greater share than they . . . I believe that these men [great conquerors such as the Persian king Xerxes] do these things in accordance with . . . *the law of nature, and presumably not with the one we institute.*
>
> (*Gorgias*, 483b4–e4, trans. D.J. Zeyl, my italics)

Note the presence, in these lines, of two concepts of *nomos* or morality. One morality is a man-made institution, contrived by the weak to protect themselves by robbing the strong of their natural advantages. Being an artificial construct, this morality can take various forms, and its rules are relative to time and place. The prudent person would be well advised, therefore, hypocritically to comply with these rules whenever they cannot be transgressed with impunity. The values of the other morality, by contrast, are part and parcel of the fabric of the universe. Although they can temporarily be obscured by the impostrous rules of human device, they nevertheless are universal in the sense of applying to all of nature, and of being immune to spatial and temporal variations. Callicles' distinction between two concepts of *nomos* or morality is thus heavily polarised: morality as a human construct is, in his view, spurious because it reverses the order of nature in which alone values are securely grounded. Hence, if he is a relativist and an immoralist, it is only with reference to the first concept of morality. What he seeks to subvert is only an invented morality masquerading as the real thing, and his motive for subverting it is to allow the true morality or 'law of nature' to shine forth. Once it is realised that Callicles operates with two concepts of morality, it further becomes obvious that his dichotomy between *phusis* and *nomos* in no way prefigures Hume's distinction between description and prescription. A better match for the sophistic concept of *phusis* would be ethical naturalism. Nietzsche's contrast, in *The*

Genealogy of Morals, between the 'slave' and the 'master' morality is, of course, taken over from Callicles' speech in Plato's *Gorgias*.

SOCRATES

Close to the Sophists is the enigmatic figure of **Socrates** (469–399 BC). Forever locked with them in argument, he was yet not above borrowing their debating techniques. One of the most influential thinkers of all times, he yet advertised his ignorance to all and sundry. Ugly, seedy, and penniless, he yet fascinated the handsomest youths in Athens. The central character in the writings of others, he yet continues to generate exegetical controversies. A recognised master of irony, he yet eludes the earnest attempts of scholars to specify the nature of his irony. A martyr to his own cause, he conducted himself during his trial as if he had a death wish.

He was Plato's master and became his mouthpiece. And therein lies the problem: Plato, in the course of a writing career spanning over fifty years, gave us different portraits of Socrates. First came the *Apology*, written shortly after Socrates' condemnation to death by an Athenian jury on charges of irreligion and corruption of the young. In this short piece, which takes the form of a narrative of self-vindication, Plato's Socrates justifies his way of life as a response to what he describes as a religious calling. A friend of his, he reports, had gone to Apollo's temple in Delphi to enquire whether there was anyone wiser than Socrates. The god had replied that there was no one. This puzzled Socrates who went on to interview those in Athens with a claim to wisdom and knowledge. The exercise proved disappointing: all fancied themselves wise but were all in fact ignorant and foolish. Apollo's meaning then became clear to Socrates: his own wisdom lay in the fact that, unlike others, he knew that he knew nothing. Making light of his own growing unpopularity, especially with the old and the staid, Socrates interpreted the god's pronouncement as the conferment of a mission. He was to help the god by helping others to know themselves. This, he did by questioning them on their beliefs, usually regarding the nature of individual virtues. From the evidence of Plato's early dialogues – the so-called dialogues of definition (e.g. *Laches, Charmides, Euthyphro*) – it seems that Socrates' questioning was often so probing and pressing as to resemble a cross-examination followed by a refutation (*elenchus*). As each dialogue unfolds, Socrates' interlocutors find themselves progressively embarrassed, enmeshed, and trapped, before finally being driven to self-confutation, by Socrates' relentless search into the nature of their beliefs. While being induced to take the measure of their own ignorance or inconsistency, they are encouraged, in Socrates' estimation, to lead better lives since, as he held, 'the unexamined life is not worth living' (38a5–6). So closely did the Socrates of Plato's early dialogues relate intellectual and moral qualities that he later came to hold, most paradoxically, that no one does wrong knowingly (*Protagoras*, 357d–58d). Knowledge of one's own long-term self-interest (defined in terms of pleasure, happiness or good), he held, is sufficient motivation for refraining from doing what could jeopardise the achievement of that (paramount) end. To those who would object that the pursuit of one's own enlightened self-interest is not the same as the moral life, it can be retorted that Socrates, as Plato and Aristotle after him, construes self-interest so widely as to include the care of one's soul in general and one's reason in particular. As he had argued in the *Apology*, to harm others is ultimately to harm oneself. Socrates' idiosyncratic views on moral motivation led him famously to deny the very existence of weakness of the will (*akrasia*). The discussion generated by this denial continues to this day.

In Plato's writings this Socrates progressively gives way to a philosopher with definite views of his own. No longer content to investigate the nature of individual virtues, he has become interested in substantive moral issues such as the best way to live (*Gorgias*) and the constitution of the ideal state (*Republic*). More significantly even, he now addresses questions of metaphysics, epistemology and philosophical psychology. He discourses on the Forms (*Phaedo*, *Symposium* and *Republic*), distinguishes knowledge from belief (*Theaetetus*), outlines the structure of the soul (*Phaedrus*), and explains how the sensible world is related to the Forms (*Phaedo* and *Republic*). The likelihood is that this Socrates is mostly Plato's alias. In Plato's late dialogues, we encounter yet another Socrates. Diminished in intellectual stature,[21] this Socrates is given the persona of a young man, a philosopher's apprentice. This is appropriate symbolism since he is now at the receiving end of the arguments of others: Parmenides refutes him on participation (*Parmenides*), and the Eleatic Stranger, a philosopher in the Parmenidean tradition, shows him that there are two kinds of non-being (*Sophist*). In the *Laws*, Plato's last work, Socrates does not appear at all. So, we are led to ask, 'who was the historical Socrates?' Which of the views variously ascribed to him by Plato did he really hold? There is no reason to dissent from the long-held scholarly opinion that Plato's early works, especially the *Apology*, give us as good a likeness of Socrates as we can hope for. As Plato developed his own system, which he chose to communicate through the medium of the dialogue, it is likely that Socrates the literary fiction came progressively to overshadow the historical Socrates.

This leaves us with two interconnected problems. Where does Socrates' philosophy end and where does Plato's begin? In what way and to what extent did the master influence the disciple? For an answer to these questions, we could do worse than trust the testimony of someone who, though he can never have known Socrates in person, had a twenty-year long acquaintance with Plato and his works. Aristotle wrote:

two things may be fairly ascribed to Socrates – *inductive* arguments and *universal definition* . . . – but Socrates did not make the *universals* or the definitions exist apart; they [the Platonists], however, gave them separate existence, and this was the kind of thing they called Ideas.

(*Metaphysics.*, M 4, 1078b 27–32, trans. D. Ross)

If we bear in mind Aristotle's tendency to present the theories of his predecessors in his own terms (italicised above), these lines, and the whole passage from which they are extracted, give us a plausible account of Plato's philosophical debt to Socrates. The Socratic *elenchus* is based on the assumption that the various idiomatic uses of any given concept can be accounted for by means of a general definition of that concept. In Socrates' view – I here supplement Aristotle's account – such a definition, if it can be achieved, encapsulates the truth about the reality designated by the concept. Socrates probably went no further. **Plato** (*c.*427–347 BC) did. While Heraclitus had impressed upon him that our world is in a state of flux, Parmenides had convinced him that only what is unchanging can be known. Plato could not, therefore, have countenanced the view that the objects of Socrates' quest were in either the world of sense or the mind of the knower. He made them into real existents, the Forms.

PLATO

Or so goes a not unlikely version of events. . . . But let us turn to what is undoubtedly Platonic, that is, the twenty-four works which constitute the corpus. All save the *Apology* are in dialogue form, a medium which no philosopher, before or since, has used to such striking effect. The question as to why Plato wrote dialogues does not admit of an easy answer. The main reason seems to have been that this great stylist had a paradoxical distrust of the written word. Holding it to be but a dead residue of thought, unable 'either to speak in its own defence or to present the truth adequately' (*Phaedrus*, 276c7–8, trans. R. Hackforth), Plato dissuaded any serious person from 'making truth the helpless object of men's ill-will by committing it to writing' (*Seventh Letter*, 344c1–3, trans. W. Hamilton).[22] The dialogue form, one surmises, best fitted his view of philosophy as a cooperative activity, *elenchic* in nature. As he wrote,

It is only when all these things . . . are rubbed together and subjected to tests in which questions and answers are exchanged in good faith and without malice that, finally, when human capacity is stretched to its limit, a spark of understanding and intelligence flashes out and illuminates the subject at issue.

(*Seventh Letter*, 344b3–7, trans. W. Hamilton)

This being Plato's view, the dialogues should not be taken as repositories of a static body of doctrine but as invitations to follow in the footsteps of Socrates and, in his manner, to tend one's soul (or mind). Hence to read the dialogues philosophically requires subjecting oneself to the *elenchus*, disencumbering one's soul of hazy notions and received opinions, and collaborating in Socrates' energetic search for the truth, whether it be on the nature of knowledge, the function of philosophy or the best political constitution. In Plato's words, it is to receive the seed of intelligibility and to nurture it so that it may grow further.[23]

Far from being mere rhetoric to dress up the oft repeated (though not always heeded) point that philosophers must think for themselves, these metaphors take us to the core – ontological and epistemological – of the middle dialogues. Let us see how. It is often remarked that, strictly speaking, Plato had no *theory* of Forms. And it is true that nowhere in the *corpus* do we find a demonstration of their existence, followed by a discursive exposition of their nature and interrelatedness. Even in their first appearance, Plato has Socrates simply assume them to be familiar to his interlocutors.[24] Given Plato's strictures against dogmatic discourse, this is unsurprising. More to the point even is the fact that, in his view, the intelligible world of the Forms is the object of a quest that only those possessing the necessary moral and intellectual qualities are motivated to undertake and qualified to pursue. So much is clear from the elaboration of the theme of recollection (*anamnesis*) in the *Phaedo*, a dialogue likely to have been written early in Plato's so-called middle period.

The scene is set on the last day of Socrates' life. Socrates seeks to console his assembled friends and disciples by telling them that death is to be welcomed as it releases the soul from its association with the body. This remarkable proposition rests on three premises: the self is the soul, the body is a source of pollution and confusion for the soul, and the soul is deathless. While the first premise remains implicit,[25] the second is a *leitmotiv* of the dialogue, and the third is the object of several extended 'proofs'. Amongst these figures the argument from recollection in the course of which Socrates seeks to show that learning is nothing other than recollection (*anamnesis*, 74a–77a). Referring to our practice of describing sensible particulars by means of abstract concepts, Socrates claims that sense perception alone cannot account for the judgement that any two given wooden sticks, for instance, are equal in length. Why not? Like most sense objects, the sticks may appear equal to me (from where I sit) but unequal to you (from where you stand). It is also possible that each stick appears (or even is) equal in all (or most) respects to its pair yet unequal in some or most respects to a stone or a piece of cloth. Lastly, one may wish to add, the sticks are likely to fall short of strict mathematical equality. The sticks, therefore, are both equal and unequal or, in more technical language, they suffer from the *compresence of opposite qualities*.[26] By contrast, Socrates claims, as we shall see below, the Form of Equality is absolutely equal, as opposed

143

to perspectivally or relatively equal. It constitutes the standard of equality of which sense objects fall short. This is then taken by Socrates to constitute evidence that our concept of equality, far from being abstracted from the perception of relatively equal objects, precedes it. Prior to being united to a particular body and thus to having sense organs, he then explains, our soul led a divine existence amongst the supreme realities or Forms, i.e. the Beautiful itself, the Equal itself, the Just itself, etc. Living among them, it knew them, but forgot them at the moment of incarnation. But, he adds comfortingly, the soul can, and does, recover from this amnesia in its earthly life, at least up to a point and even if it is unaware that it recollects. Such process of recovery is initiated by sense perception: the sight of relatively equal objects jogs our soul into retrieving, to a greater or lesser extent, the knowledge of absolute equality that it possessed in its discarnate state.

This level of recollection is presupposed in the everyday use of concepts, and most people go no further. Those who do wish to advance further will need to promote the autarky of the soul by lessening its reliance upon the body, an end that is best achieved by the practice of philosophy:

> Philosophy . . . persuades the soul to withdraw from the senses in so far as it is not compelled to use them and bids the soul to gather itself together by itself, to trust only itself and whatever reality, existing by itself, the soul by itself understands, and not to consider as true what it examines by other means, for this is different in different circumstances and is sensible and visible, whereas what the soul itself sees is intelligible and invisible.
>
> (*Phaedo*, 83a6–b4, trans. G.M.A. Grube)

Knowledge of true reality, therefore, can be achieved only in so far as and to the extent that the soul liberates itself from what is alien to it, i.e. the sensible world, and returns to its own world, i.e. the world of the Forms, which alone is fully intelligible. To this world and its contents, i.e. the Forms,[27] we now turn.

There are Forms corresponding to qualities (e.g. Beauty), relations (e.g. Equality), numbers (e.g. Two), geometrical figures (e.g. Square), moral dispositions (e.g. Courage), natural kinds (e.g. Human Being), and artefacts (e.g. Bed). Contrary to the claim made by many writers of introductory manuals to philosophy, Forms should not straightforwardly be assimilated with the universals[28] of later philosophers. To begin with, Plato explicitly denied the existence of a one-to-one correspondence between Forms and universals when he ruled out that there be Forms of hair, cowardice or barbarity. Furthermore, as will presently be seen, self-predication makes Forms into individuals.

The Forms are existent entities, separate from each other and independent from our thoughts. They transcend the world of sense and exist in an intelligible elsewhere which Plato describes, metaphorically, as 'beyond the heavens' (*Phaedrus*, 247c1–2). Although their unworldly nature causes them to be inaccessible to our senses, they are accessible to the immortal part in us, i.e. soul[29] or intellect. The reason for this, as explained above, is that during their exile in human bodies, souls can recollect, with varying degrees of clarity, the intelligible realities that they knew in their discarnate state.

Being immune to change, the Forms are motionless and sempiternal; they abide constant in being. By contrast, the things of the phenomenal world are confined to becoming, falling short of full being though rising above absolute non-being. Since for Plato the order of knowledge follows the order of being, the Forms are the paradigmatic objects of knowledge while the phenomenal world can only give rise to opinion or belief (*Republic*, 476c–478d). In questions of value, the Forms are absolute standards: the Form of Justice, for instance, shows those who behold it what justice consists in. For this reason, in the *Republic*, Plato argues that philosophers are ideally suited to rule; their knowledge of the Just in itself would enable them justly to order their community and govern the state.

Each Form is a single-natured entity, undiminished by lack and uncompromised by the presence of its opposite quality. Mindful to stress the perfection of the Forms, Plato was occasionally led to say that each bears paradigmatically the quality of which it is the Form: the Form of Beauty is itself beautiful, the Form of Large is itself large, the Form of Justice is itself just, etc. This characterisation, which is labelled self-predication in current secondary literature, is evident in Plato's famous description of the vision of the Form of Beauty by a knower who has succeeded in reaching out to the intelligible realm:

> What he'll see is, in the first place, eternal; it does not come to be or cease to be, and it does not increase or diminish. In the second place, it isn't attractive in one respect and repulsive in another, or attractive in one setting at one time but not at another, or attractive in one setting but repulsive in another, or attractive here or repulsive elsewhere, depending on how people find it . . . he'll perceive it in itself and by itself, constant and eternal, and he'll see that every other beautiful object somehow partakes of it.
>
> (*Symposium* 210e6–211b3, trans. R. Waterfield)

Forms are causes upon which all individual existents in the phenomenal world depend for their nature and properties. As claimed in the above passage,[30] the relative and contingent beauty of phenomenal objects is due to their participation in the Form of Beauty whose perfect loveliness necessarily excludes any admixture of ugliness. Generally, Plato holds, the world of sense is as it is to the extent that its component parts partake (or participate) in the Forms. Later philosophers, from

Aristotle to Descartes, will generalise this principle, which he never spelled out, by stating that there must be more 'reality' in the cause than in the effects.

As described in the dialogues of Plato's middle period, the Forms are open to some serious objections. Chief among them are self-predication and the characterisation of the Forms as simple-natured.

To understand how self-predication turned out to be a liability for the theory of Forms, let us use the very argument that Plato himself later invoked against it and which Aristotle popularised under the name of 'Third Man Argument'.[31] Bearing its own character, the Form of Man is itself a man, a characteristic that it shares with all men in the sensible world. Yet, since the latter are men by virtue of participating in the Form of Man, a second Form of Man must be postulated to account for the manliness both of the first Form of Man and that of all phenomenal men. However, since this second Form of Man will itself be a man (in virtue of self-predication), yet another Form of Man needs to be postulated to account for the characteristic that the first two Forms of Man share with each other and with all men in the sensible world. The infinite regress is not only inevitable but also vicious since, in Plato's outlook, each Form is supposed to be a cause beyond which there need be no other.

A second problem concerns the interrelationships of the Forms. Although Plato had long held that the pious is a species of the just (*Euthyphro*), and that the Forms of Three and Oddness are necessarily related (*Phaedo*), his presentation of the Forms as singular, separate, and paradigmatically perfect had stood in the way of an account of the logical relations prevailing between them. Yet, such an account was needed to underpin his claim that meaningful discourse is grounded in the Forms. In the *Sophist*, in a bold modification of his ontology, Plato put forward the view that 'the interweaving of forms is what makes speech possible for us' (259e5–6). Although he does not there envisage that every Form associates with every other, he suggests that a few Forms do interweave with all, or with most, other Forms. They are 'the most important kinds' and include Being, Sameness and Otherness, Motion (or Change) and Rest. The first three interweave with each other and with all other Forms since each and every Form participates not only in Being, but also in sameness with reference to itself and in otherness with reference to all others. They are likened to the vowels of the alphabet whose function it is to bind consonants together and thereby to form words. As for Motion and Rest, they do not associate directly with each other, and the reason for their inclusion into the 'most important kinds' is unclear.

The principle of the interweaving of Forms enabled Plato to argue that everything that participates in Being participates also in otherness in relation to Being. Otherness is, however, itself a Form and, as such, it participates in Being. Hence, paradoxically, there is a part of otherness which both is and is the Form of

Non-Being. This account of non-being enabled Plato to dismiss as inconceivable a Parmenidean non-being that would be the contrary of being in so far as it would not participate in being at all.

Plato adapted this analysis to an explanation of how we can make meaningful false statements. He did so by introducing the distinction between subject and predicate. The predicates that are true of a subject are counted as so many beings for that subject. All remaining predicates, since they are other than these beings, are therefore counted as so many non-beings. A false statement puts non-beings, so defined, in the place of beings, so defined. So it is with the statement 'Theaetetus is flying'. 'Flying' is a Form, and does therefore exist, but it is other than the Forms which Theaetetus participates in, and which include, at the moment of utterance, 'sitting down'. In this particular context, 'flying' is therefore a non-being. Hence to ascribe this non-being to Theaetetus is to make a statement that is false. Plato's introduction of the distinction between absolute and relative non-being constitutes a rare example of progress in philosophy: Parmenides' ghost had finally been laid to rest.

ARISTOTLE

Plato's pupil, **Aristotle** (384–322 BC), reverted to the encyclopaedic mode of philosophy that had gone out with Plato. From his richly systematic *oeuvre*, which encompasses all branches of learning, only a few aspects can here be broached.

Unlike Plato, Aristotle took an interest in the world of sense. Having studied it, he held it to be both intelligible and good. He therefore saw no need of postulating a transcendent world to account for it, but argued that it forms part of a well-ordered universe or cosmos in which values are objectively grounded and whose elements are made intelligible through their relatedness to the whole. The living species that eternally dwell within this cosmos, he held, are well adapted to it: their members flourish whenever they grow and develop in accordance with their nature. Human beings possess cognitive faculties which can be tutored to apprehend the universe as it is. Such cognitive activity in all its forms, he maintained, fulfils their innate desire for knowledge and affords them unique joy and fulfilment.

Against Parmenides, as we saw, Plato had showed that the world of becoming shared in being. To avoid the difficulties of Platonic participation and to give a philosophical account of becoming, Aristotle distinguished ways of being. Holding that 'being is said in many ways',[32] he analysed predication and drew up a list of the headings under which individual existents, together with their various characteristics and properties, are classified. As featured in the *Categories*, his earliest technical treatise, these headings are: substance, quality, quantity, relation, time, place, position, condition, action and passion. Although these became the *praedicamenta* of medieval logicians, we should note that not all the categories are predicable: while substance *cannot* be predicated of the other categories, they *must* be predicated of substance. This asymmetry reflects the unequal ontological status of the categories. Substances, which in the philosophy of the *Categories*, are individual existents (e.g. John Paul II, Fido or the ring on your finger), differ from the other categories by being separate from each other and ontologically independent. The subsidiarity of the other modes of being relatively to substance justifies calling them 'things that happen' or *accidents* of the substance to which they are attached.

The distinction between substance and accidents plays a major role in Aristotle's account of change in the sensible world. Change, he held, can be substantial or accidental: substantial change consists in the coming to be or the passing away of individual existents while accidental change affects a pre-existing individual existent and usually consists in the replacement of some one of its properties by others. But change is not a matter of happenstance. Substances do not spring from any odd substratum, nor can they acquire just any property at any time: silk purses are not made out of sows' ears and garden gnomes do not acquire a tan. How individual existents develop over time and which properties they acquire depend on what they essentially are and what they are made of. As Aristotle puts it, they can only become *actually* what they are *potentially*.

Actuality, Aristotle holds, is prior to potentiality in three ways. It is *logically* prior in so far as the actualised state is that by reference to which the correspondent potential state is identified and defined. It is *ontologically* prior since it is the state at which the potential aims or to which it strives, and it is *chronologically* prior since what is potentially X can only become X in actuality through the intervention of an agent which actually is X or possesses X as an attribute.

To make intelligible the actualisation of the potential, which we witness every day of our lives, Aristotle invokes four principles of explanation, which are often but inaptly dubbed the 'four causes'. These are: the matter from which a thing or being is constituted (the material cause), the form or shape that makes it a thing or being of its kind (the formal cause), the agency through which it was brought into existence as a being of its kind (the efficient cause), and the goal or function (the final cause) that it furthers or fulfils.[33] Provided that one keeps to very simple examples, the theory is easily illustrated. Take a case of substantial change, i.e. the carving by Praxiteles of a statue of Hermes. Marble is the material cause of the statue, Hermes' conventional shape its formal cause, Praxiteles its efficient cause and the adornment of the temple its final cause. When one turns to living things, however, the theory becomes less clear and more puzzling. Take a human baby. According to Aristotle's picturesque theory of human reproduction,[34] the menstrual residue of the mother provides the material mass of the child, the father's semen contributes its form or soul principle, the father causes the form to bear on the matter, and physical maturity, as evidenced by the capacity for reproduction, is the end of the development of the child. This example presents three significant differences from the previous one. In living organisms the material cause of the embryo differs significantly from the material substratum (i.e. flesh and bones) of the adult that the embryo becomes, the final cause is immanent in the being caused, and, in so far as Aristotle defines women as incomplete (or mutilated) men,[35] the formal, efficient and final causes coincide in the person of the child's father.[36]

The theory of 'causal' explanation prompted Aristotle to revisit his earlier conception of substance. Indeed, if concrete individuals, as he had come to hold, are to be explained as the outcome of the operation of four causal principles then they can no longer be considered to be ontologically basic. The re-definition of substance, which is central to Aristotle's project of vindicating the intelligibility of the sensible universe, is undertaken in what is probably the most exegetically challenging text in the whole corpus, i.e. book VII of the *Metaphysics*. There the concepts of matter and form are crucially brought into play. Let's briefly consider how they bear on the issue.

Matter is the stuff that underlies change, the substratum of which concrete particulars are made up. Mere potentiality and contingence, it is indeterminate and, as such, beyond the reach of definition and knowledge. The causal intervention of form is needed to actualise the potentialities of matter and shape it into a concrete self-subsistent individual, which Aristotle, in his post-*Categories* writings, continues to call substance. While matter causes any concrete individual to be singular and thus different from all other members of the species, form gives it determination, shape, definition, and intelligibility. As Aristotle is at pains to stress, form plays the determinant role in the constitution of the furniture of our world: 'The form has a better claim than the matter to be called nature. For we call a thing something, when it is that thing in actuality, rather than just a possibility' (*Physics*, II 1, 193b6–8, trans. W. Charlton). Form, however, is common to all members of a species and therefore a factor of universality. As such, it combines uneasily with the singularity that Aristotle never ceased to regard as a central feature of substance.

Indeed, once form becomes the sole bearer of intelligibility, what makes Socrates, Hypatia and Callias, for instance, into unique individuals, different from all others, eludes intelligibility. This is not a conclusion that Aristotle could accept. To answer to his project of developing concepts and theories capable of capturing the intrinsic intelligibility of the sublunary world, forms should not be theorised as universals existing apart from their corresponding particulars. They must not be like Plato's. Book VII of the *Metaphysics* contains Aristotle's ingenious solution to this problem. First, he argues that forms are indwelling and that for each class of particulars there is a corresponding form. More importantly, he demonstrates that in the case of those classes whose defining properties collectively correspond to existing entities,[37] the form inheres *wholly and indivisibly* in each member.

To identify those classes, Aristotle invokes the method of classification that he had developed in the *Posterior Analytics*, II 13 and which, because of space constraints, can only here be illustrated. As a member of the human species, Hypatia is also included in the larger class of vertebrates which is itself a sub-group of the yet larger genus animal. In Aristotelian terms, the class of 'human beings' is an *infima species* since it cannot be subdivided into smaller classes without falling into *differentiae* that are merely 'accidental'. This means that the members of an *infima species* are actual individuals.

A basic principle of the Aristotelian logic of classes is that the extension or field of application of a concept is inversely proportional to its intension or internal content. Thus while the class of 'animals' is wider than that of 'human beings' in so far as it applies to more beings, 'human being' is a more precise classificatory tool than 'animal' in so far as it connotes a greater number of characteristics. It follows, therefore, that *infimae species*, which, by definition, cannot be further subdivided without ceasing to correspond to actual existents, are connotatively richest. For this reason, they furnish Aristotle with a tool with which to vindicate, as far as is possible within the limits of his system, the intelligibility of the sublunary world. Indeed, the defining principle of an *infima species* is the form which is both common to a group of concrete particulars *and* indivisibly instantiated in each of them. *Infimae species*, therefore, which account for the composite yet unitary nature of individuals, enable Aristotle to bring matter, in so far as it enters into the composition of concrete substances, within the orbit of intelligibility. The *infima species* 'human being', for instance, gives us the form, the substance, the essence, and the definition of any individual human being. Therefore, Aristotle argued, even if concrete substances are not fully intelligible, the form of the *infima species* to which they belong confers upon them a significant measure of intelligibility – all that they can have.

The principle of the inseparability of form and matter enabled Aristotle to formulate a new and highly original definition of the soul which eschews most of the problems traditionally associated with dualism and materialism:

> the soul is in the primary way that by means of which we live, perceive, and think . . . the soul does not exist without a body and yet is not itself a kind of body. For it is not a body, but something which belongs to a body, and for this reason exists in a body, and in a body of such and such a kind.
>
> (*De Anima*, II 2, 414a12–13, trans. D.W. Hamlyn)

The animating action of soul makes a lump of matter into a living body and progressively actualises its potentialities. These form a hierarchy of forms of life in which each level provides the foundation for the one above it. In its most basic manifestation, in which plants share, soul enables the individual organism to sustain itself by absorbing nourishment. Other living things have, in addition, the faculty of sense perception; some possess only one sense, namely touch, while others have all five senses. In turn, sense perception brings in its wake desire, pleasure and pain, together with, in most cases and with some help from the imaginative faculty, locomotion. Higher still are the faculties of imagination and memory. Highest of all are reason and thought, of which only human beings are capable.

If soul is thus formal and efficient cause of the body, it can also be said to be its final cause[38] in so far as the soul specific to each species constitutes the end, or perfected state, towards which each member of that species strives. Taking nourishment from the soil, growing towards the light, for instance, are what plants are meant to do, and these activities are precisely those which contribute to defining the kind of soul that plants possess. Human beings, on the other hand, have a soul which enables them to think, reason and understand the world around them; as a consequence, their optimal state of being or end (*telos*) is one in which these capacities are given as full a rein as possible. Since, as Aristotle puts it, 'it is right to call things after their end' (*De Anima*, II 4, 416b23–24), living things are to be defined by reference to the kind of soul that they possess.

To define a being by its end or final cause is to adopt a teleological point of view. In Aristotle's scheme of things, teleology has both a descriptive and a normative aspect. In its descriptive meaning, the end (*telos*) of a being is the stage of maturity that, as a matter of course, it will reach in appropriate surroundings and circumstances. In the case of human beings, however, Aristotelian teleology has also a strong normative component. It defines the end (*telos*) of human beings as the stage that they must reach on pains of remaining unfulfilled. In Aristotle's outlook, therefore, the good life for a human being is one in which the defining features of human nature, i.e. rationality and sociality, are developed. While morality promotes it in the private sphere, the nobler activity of politics secures and preserves it for the community.[39]

EXERCISES

1 Why, in your opinion, can the Presocratics be said to have engaged in an activity that we still identify as philosophy?
2 'After Parmenides Greek philosophy could never be the same, for everyone, even Plato and Aristotle, felt that they had to take account of him and, as it were, lay his ghost.' (W.K.C. Guthrie) Discuss with relation to Plato and Aristotle.
3 Assess the philosophical significance of Socrates.
4 What are Platonic Forms?

5 How and to what extent did Aristotle's concept of substance evolve from the *Categories* to the *Metaphysics*?

6 'The soul is in the primary way that by means of which we live, perceive and think' (Aristotle, *De Anima*, II 2, 414a12–13). Explicate and comment.

NOTES

1 A.N. Whitehead, *Process and Reality*, Cambridge University Press, 1929, p. 53.

2 A few ancient philosophers, of whom the main ones are Lucretius, Cicero and Seneca, wrote in Latin.

3 With apologies to L.D. Reynolds and N.G. Wilson whose *Scribes and Scholars*, Oxford University Press, 1991 (1st edn, 1968), is an excellent and accessible account of the transmission of classical texts.

4 The library at Alexandria burned down in AD 270.

5 *Platonis Opera*, vol. I, eds E.A. Duke, W.F. Hicken, W.S.M. Nicoll and J.C.G. Strachan, Oxford Classical Texts, Clarendon Press, 1995.

6 *c.* is an abbreviation for the latin *circa* which means 'around that time' when it precedes a date.

7 I have been unable to trace this quotation.

8 From 1934 onwards, the volumes were co-edited by W. Kranz: H. Diels and W. Kranz, *Die Fragmente der Vorsokratiker*, Weidmann, Berlin, numerous reprints. References to the Presocratics are commonly made through the numbering system that they used in this and subsequent editions. In their system, a number is assigned to each Presocratic, e.g. 12 for Anaximander. This is followed first by either the letter A for *testimonia* or the letter B for *fragmenta*, then by the number of the individual quotation or reference. Thus 12B1 refers to Simplicius' quotation of Anaximander's one extant sentence. Unless otherwise indicated, all translations are from G.S. Kirk, J.E. Raven and M. Schofield, *The Presocratic Philosophers*, second edition, Cambridge University Press, 1983.

9 Aristotle, *Metaphysics*, I 3, 983b2–3.

10 How and to what extent the theory here ascribed to Thales depends on Aristotle's own terminology and metaphysics will be more apparent in the section on Aristotle.

11 As further criticised by Aristotle in *De Caelo*, II 13, 294a28–b14.

12 The principles of logic were first spelt out and codified by Aristotle (q.v.) in the *Prior Analytics* and the *Metaphysics*.

13 The use of the square brackets here indicates that the verbs in both statements are without grammatical subjects. The repeated iteration of 'it' in the translation is therefore an interpretation.

14 This is not to say that he did so deliberately or even consciously since, as will be seen below, the distinction between the existential and the predicative use of 'to be' was not explicitly made before Plato introduced it in a late dialogue (the *Sophist*).

15 *Physics*, IV 8, 214b28–216a21.

16 The citizen body was composed of all free adult males born of Athenian parents. It has been estimated that approximately one fourteenth of the total adult population of the city enjoyed citizen rights.

17 Plato, *Theaetetus*, 152a2–4, trans. J. McDowell. 'Man' translates the Greek *anthropos* which is not gender specific.
18 Ibid., 157a.
19 See his myth of origins in Plato's *Protagoras*, 320c8–324d1.
20 Ibid., 172b. See also Callicles' claims in *Gorgias* and Thrasymachus' in *Republic* I.
21 In the *Philebus*, however, the *persona* of Socrates is consonant with that presented in earlier dialogues.
22 The most likely to be genuine amongst the thirteen attributed to Plato.
23 See, e.g., *Phaedrus*, 276e–277a.
24 See, e.g., *Phaedo*, 65d.
25 Indeed, it is conceivable that Plato could not have spelled it out in so far as the concept of self as such emerges only in Aristotle.
26 This should not be taken to mean that objects in the world of sense always possess the opposite qualities of all those qualities that they, as a matter of fact, do possess. Thus snow, being cold, cannot be said to be warm. Yet it is white and not white, solid and not solid.
27 Or 'Ideas', as Plato sometimes calls them. In so far as this appellation is apt to mislead the modern reader, for whom ideas exist only in the mind, I shall use 'Forms' throughout.
28 A universal is an abstract entity, essence or term to which corresponds a collection of sensible particulars.
29 Plato's concept of soul evolved: incomposite in the *Phaedo*, it is presented as tripartite in the *Republic*.
30 See also the *Phaedo*, 100c–101c.
31 See the *Parmenides*, 132a1–b3 and 132d6–133a3. Aristotle mentions the argument in the *Metaphysics*, I 9, 990b16–17 and VII 13, 1039a2–3.
32 *Physics*, 185a21, *Metaphysics*, IV.2, 1003 a 33; VI 4, 1028a25 and VII 1, 1028a10.
33 The *locus classicus* for this theory is *Physics*, II 3.
34 As described in the *De Generatione Animalium*, II 4.
35 Ibid., II 3, 737a27–28.
36 As theorised in, e.g., *Physics*, II 3, 195b17–18 and 198a24.
37 These are known as *infimae species*, i.e. species which have no sub-classes.
38 *De Anima*, II 4, 415b15–21.
39 Gordon Neal and Denis O'Brien made helpful comments on an early draft. I should like to thank them and to absolve them of any responsibility for the end result.

FURTHER READING

Secondary material is meant to place in context, to explain, or to comment upon, primary texts. It is never meant to take the place of reading primary texts.

For accessible anthologies of Presocratic fragments, turn either to

Kirk, G.S., Raven, J.E. and Schofield, M. (1983) *The Presocratic Philosophers*, second edition, Cambridge: Cambridge University Press. This sourcebook contains a comprehensive selection of Presocratic fragments and *testimonia*, both in Greek and in translation, together with an introduction and commentary.

or to

McKirahan, R.D. Jr. (1994) *Philosophy Before Socrates*, Indianapolis: Hackett Publishing Company. Together with a comprehensive selection of the fragments and *testimonia* in translation this guide provides an introduction, a commentary and a presentation of Presocratic views in context.

Amongst Plato's dialogues, you are advised first to read

The *Apology*, the *Phaedo*, the *Symposium*, and the *Republic* in either the Oxford Classics or the Hackett translations.

Central excerpts of Aristotle's works are provided in either:

Ackrill, J.L. (ed.) (1987) *A New Aristotle Reader*, Oxford: Clarendon Press (numerous reprints).

or in

Irwin, T. and Fine, G. (eds) (1996) *Aristotle: Introductory Readings*, Indianapolis: Hackett Publishing Company.

For a detailed survey and comprehensive survey of Greek philosophy from the Presocratics to Aristotle, it remains best to turn to the six volumes of:

Guthrie, W.K.C. (1963–83) *A History of Greek Philosophy*, Cambridge: Cambridge University Press.

6

MEDIEVAL PHILOSOPHY

From Augustine to Nicholas of Cusa

Dermot Moran

INTRODUCING THE MEDIEVAL WORLD: MULTICULTURALISM, MONOTHEISM AND RELIGIOUS PHILOSOPHY

This chapter is an introduction to the diverse, complex and exciting world of medieval thought and learning. It aims to provide a sketch of the historical development of philosophy and to give some specific examples of philosophical reasoning in that period. Medieval intellectuals were as active in philosophy as their classical counterparts and there is no good reason for the current neglect of this period in the undergraduate philosophy curriculum. On the other hand, it is not easy to read medieval texts; one needs considerable background historical knowledge of the classical philosophical tradition, familiarity with scripture, contextual awareness and linguistic expertise – not just in Greek, Latin or Arabic, but also modern European languages – in order to penetrate fully into the nature of medieval thought. Moreover, even with huge growth in our knowledge of medieval philosophy in the past 150 years, the extant corpus of medieval philosophy – by no means fully identified or complete – is far more vast than the entire classical legacy. Critical editions of the central writers (even those of Aquinas and Duns Scotus) are incomplete, and there is a paucity of English translations. Due to the neglect of medieval philosophy in the Anglophone world, most of the best scholarship is in German, French, Italian, or other European languages. Finally, there is no longer a single model of approach to medieval philosophy.[1] We can no longer categorise it in terms of a few central themes – Christian philosophy, the problem of universals, the revival of Aristotle, and so on. Medieval philosophy is as diverse as contemporary philosophy. In this chapter, therefore, we can only scratch the surface of the medieval philosophical heritage.

The term 'Middle Ages' (Latin '*medium aevum*', 'the middle period'), was first used in the Renaissance period in a disparaging sense to designate what was then considered to be the rather stagnant, superstitious period between the end of classical era and the enlightened 'modern' period. Seventeenth-century exponents of the New Philosophy – Galileo Galilei (1564–1642), René Descartes (1596–1650), Francis Bacon (1561–1626), and Thomas Hobbes (1588–1679) – all defined their new approach in opposition to the medieval scholastic tradition, denying the existence of Aristotelian forms or species, or the value of explanation in terms of final causes, and so on. Interest in medieval thought thenceforth declined until the Romantic movement again stimulated interest in it. Among Catholic scholars, the revival of interest in medieval philosophy was greatly encouraged by the anti-modernist movement. Pope Leo XIII, in his Encyclical *Aeterni Patris* (1879) recommended that all Catholic philosophers should give special consideration to the work of St Thomas.[2] The resulting intellectual movement, Neo-Thomism, portrayed St Thomas Aquinas as the highpoint of Catholic rationality whose views could be opposed to the secular rationalism and materialism of the so-called 'modernist' outlook. For Neo-Thomists, Aquinas was, to adapt Dante's phrase (originally applied to Aristotle), 'the master of those who know', and other philosophers of the period (e.g. both the nominalist William of Ockham and the Neoplatonic mystic Meister Eckhart) were deemed doctrinally suspect and ignored.

New research has entirely changed that picture. Careful scholarship and analytic philosophical methods have helped greatly to identify commonalities and continuities especially between the Scholastics of the thirteenth century and contemporary philosophy (in issues of logic, semantics, metaphysics, ethics, and so on). Furthermore, it is now recognised that this medieval period is characterised by extraordinary diversity; it is multi-cultural and multi-faith. It encompasses not just the mainly Christian culture of North Western Europe, communicated in Latin, but also the Eastern Byzantine Empire which stretched from Turkey through the Balkans, whose culture was also Christian but whose language was Greek (and hence preserved elements of late Greek Neoplatonic thought), as well as the Jewish and Islamic cultures of the Middle East, India and Central Asia – Ibn Sina, 980–1037, known in Latin as Avicenna, for example, was from Buchara in Uzbekistan – whose languages included Aramaic, Arabic, and Hebrew. Together, the Byzantine and Arabic cultures (both Islamic and Jewish) absorbed and continued the heritage of Greek philosophy in the new context of the religions of the Book.

The medieval period is also very long, extending well over a 1,000 years, roughly from St Augustine (354–430), writing in the latter years of the Roman empire[3] up to the end of the seventeenth century. Strictly speaking, Augustine and Boethius belong to the late Roman Empire, nevertheless, because of their attempts to synthesise classical wisdom with Christian faith, they had enormous influence on later philosophers in the Christian West and need to be studied by anyone interested in medieval philosophy. Augustine, for example, is the single most important authority for all medieval Christian philosophy. It is customary to divide medieval era into three periods: Early, High and Late Middle Ages. In the Early period – roughly from the fourth century to the middle of the twelfth century[4] – Platonism predominated in the Christian Europe while an eclectic Neoplatonism mixed with Aristotelian and other Hellenic elements was developing in the Middle East, chiefly in Baghdad. The High Middle Ages (roughly the late twelfth and thirteenth centuries) were characterised by the revival of Aristotle through the vast programme of translation from Arabic sources, the growth of the universities, the rise of the mendicant teaching orders (Dominicans and Franciscans), the development of philosophical schools (chiefly, Thomism, Scotism, nominalism), known collectively as Scholasticism.[5] Finally, Late Medieval philosophy (the fourteenth to seventeenth centuries) includes writers of the Italian Renaissance (Marsilio Ficino, 1433–99, Pico della Mirandola, 1463–94), who advocated a humanism inspired by Plato, as well as reformers such as Thomas More (1478–1535) and Desiderius Erasmus (1466–1536), who promoted a new religious humanism, and sceptics such as Michel Montaigne (1533–92). There also increasing recognition that the philosophy of particular periods, e.g. the Twelfth Century, or the so-called 'Northern Renaissance' (Nicholas of Cusa, the Rheinish mystics), constitutes unique constellations that deserve to be studied separately.[6] In Germany and in the Lowlands mystics such as the Dominican, Meister Eckhart, Tauler, Suso, and the Catholic Cardinal, Nicholas of Cusa (1401–64) were important for developing new ways of thinking about the divine, outside of the traditional Aristotelian categories. Reformers such as Martin Luther and Calvin are significant for their challenges to Catholic theology in a manner which continues the medieval tradition of disputation and debate. The counter-reformation also produced significant philosophers. In Spain, a writer like Francisco Suarez (1548–1617) produced one of the last great scholastic syntheses and influenced writers such as Descartes and Malebranche. There are Scholastic survivals well into the seventeenth century.

Whereas the issue of the existence and nature of the divine had been discussed by classical philosophers, including Plato and Aristotle, the emergence of the three monotheistic religions (Judaism, Christianity, Islam) meant that theological matters took centre field during the medieval period. Central to medieval philosophy is discussion concerning the existence and nature of God, the meaning of creation (creation *ex nihilo*), the nature and purpose of human beings. Augustine, Anselm, Maimonides, Averroes, Aquinas, Bonaventure and Duns Scotus, all offered proofs of the existence of God. But there was also a considerable sense of the fragile and contingent nature of creation. According to Augustine, for example, all created things bear the stamp of their maker and display traces (*vestigia*) of the divine

Trinity. Creatures testify to their very dependency on the divine. As Augustine puts it, each creature cries out: 'God made me' (*Deus me fecit*). Muslim philosophers, especially Avicenna, sought to draw a sharp distinction between the necessary being of God and the contingent nature of created beings giving rise to the distinction between essence and existence. Aquinas takes up this tradition and argues that in all creatures there is a real distinction to be found between essence and existence, between *what* a thing is (its quiddity, *quidditas*) and the fact *that* it is, a distinction not to be found in God. Some of the most exciting philosophical departures originated where the three great monotheistic faiths and cultures intersected, e.g. in twelfth-century Spain. The Islamic philosopher Abu'l Walid Muhammad Ibn Ahmad Ibn Muhammad Ibn Rushd (1126–98), known in the Latin world as Averroes, is perhaps the most famous of the Cordoba philosophers. There are examples in medieval philosophy of dialogues between Jews, Muslims and Christians concerning the nature of God and creation. Abelard for instance composed such a work.[7] Ramon Llull (1232–1316) was an important interface with Islam, and, in the fifteenth century, the Christian Nicholas of Cusa, influenced by Llull, wrote two works on the relations between Islam and Christianity, *De pace fidei* (*On Peaceful Unity of Faith*) and *Cribratio Alkorani* (*Scrutiny of the Koran*).[8] For Cusanus, Moses, Christ, and Mohamed are three divinely illumined, if unequal, bearers of a single revelation.

The revival of Aristotle in the twelfth and thirteenth centuries created a philosophical and scientific revolution of inestimable importance for the growth of European intellectual culture. In a few decades the Christian West assimilated what the Arabic tradition had built up over three centuries. This in itself was an extraordinary intellectual achievement. It laid the foundation for European pre-eminence in scientific knowledge right through to the twentieth century. Moreover, the rise of scientific knowledge was a particularly Christian development; even the universities are particularly Christian institutions, as Alain de Libera has emphasised.[9] But it is important not to see all of medieval philosophy exclusively in terms of the transmission of the Aristotelian heritage. Although the extremely rapid revival of Aristotle inaugurated a new philosophical tradition and reorganised the very structures of scientific knowledge and education, the more ancient tradition of Neoplatonic thought continued to flourish throughout the medieval period, often associated with the more conservative theological faculties in the university (e.g. Robert Grosseteste at Oxford). Platonism permeated the philosophy of the Church Fathers, the writings of Anselm and Abelard, the Twelfth-Century Renaissance and the Italian and Northern Renaissance.[10] Another version of Neoplatonism in the form of the Christian mystical writings of Pseudo-Dionysius influenced philosophers and theologians from John Scottus Eriugena to Aquinas and Grosseteste to Nicholas of Cusa.

The scientific advances of the modern period are not all to be credited to the revival of Aristotelian texts such as the *Physics*. Modern science has roots in the scientific practices of monks in Oxford, Padua, Bologna, and elsewhere. Indeed the mathematical treatment of nature, which inspired Kepler and Galileo, stems from late medieval Pythagorean Platonism opposed to Aristotelian empiricism, as the argument between Platonic Galileo and the Aristotelian Cardinal Bellarmine clearly shows. Whereas, for mathematical reasons, Galileo maintained that the sun did not really rise and set, Bellarmine maintained that our sense organs were reliable and would not mislead us about such a basic observable fact.

It is also important to remember that the doctrines and texts gathered under the names of Plato and Aristotle do not necessarily conform to our understanding of these figures. In general, up to the twelfth century, medieval philosophers tended to agree with Cassiodorus' maxim, '*Plato theologus, Aristoteles logicus*': Plato was considered primarily as a theologian, an expert on the divine, eternal, immaterial, intelligible realm, a classifier of the orders of angelic and demonic beings, whereas Aristotle was primarily a logician, a classifier of the forms of argument and of the categories into which everything real is divided. The 'Aristotle' that entered into Paris and Oxford through the Arabs in the thirteenth century was in fact a conglomeration of genuine Aristotelian texts together with a vast set of Neoplatonic commentaries compiled in the setting of Islam. It was not until the Renaissance that humanist scholars such as Lorenzo Valla began to separate out the genuine Platonic and Aristotelian texts, identify forgeries (e.g. the works of Pseudo-Dionysius) and establish the basis for the editions we know today (e.g. the Stephanus edition of Plato).

Medieval philosophy by its very nature is characterised by a very complex relation to the written word, to the text. Judaism, Christianity and Islam all believed in revelation in the form of the divinely inspired book (Torah, New Testament, Koran). Obedience to the divine required careful studying of the revealed word. There is therefore considerable stress on authority of the written text, and this reverence for authority was also applied to the classical heritage, e.g. to the writings of Aristotle and Plato in particular. Although there are genuinely original and novel forms of thought in the medieval period, in general a high emphasis was placed on securing arguments through appeal to learned authority. Since religious orthodoxy was enforced, often by secular authorities, dissent was severely punished, and thus there are no public declarations of atheism or even radical scepticism in the medieval period. Nevertheless, despite the reverence for tradition and the concern to be orthodox, philosophical debate was often extremely vigorous as is evidenced in the arguments between Abelard and William of Champeaux (*c*.1070–*c*.1120), for instance, or in the criticisms which Ockham levels against both the Thomists and the Scotists. It is entirely wrong to think of the philosophy of the period as lacking in intellectual sophistication, or slavish in following theological orthodoxy, or as monolithic in form or content. In the medieval schools and universities, philosophy was practiced in its own right and was not restricted simply to the service of theology. The thirteenth century produced the first modern intellectuals – individuals (e.g. Roger Bacon) capable of taking an informed critical stance towards the inherited body of learning, often at great personal risk (e.g. Ockham had to flee Avignon in fear of his life).

Although framed by theological interests, medieval philosophy is not exclusively theological in content. While the relation between God and creation was of special interest, within this overall framework questions could arise about being, knowledge, value, the nature of space and time, and so on. Medieval philosophy had a special preference for metaphysical issues, but there are treatises on cosmology, anthropology, epistemology, ethics and political philosophy. Great debates took place, and indeed were encouraged, in all the central areas of philosophy: on the nature of substance, properties and relations; on the nature of the intellect and the will; on freedom and determinism, on the nature of signs and words; on the morality of private property, on the nature of authority; on the relation between the individual and the state; on the eternity of the world; and so on and on.

Medieval philosophers were especially concerned with the preservation and transmission of knowledge. Considerable advances were made in the organisation of knowledge (e.g. the liberal arts), leading to the establishment (in the Christian West) of the university as the prime means for the transmission of scientific learning (a status the institution of the university retains today despite the application of business models). Typical of the Middle Ages is the treatise, the encyclopaedia or compendium of disputed questions. Enormous treatises, such as Thomas Aquinas' *Summa Theologiae*, were expected to treat on all questions relating to theological issues. Logic (or dialectic) also had an important place in medieval philosophy, both in the earlier commentaries on Boethius, in the dialectic of Anselm and Abelard, and in the later development in Ockham, Walter Burleigh, William of Sherwood and Peter of Spain. Nominalism produced analyses of the language of thought which anticipate contemporary methods of analysing propositions. Meanwhile, in Northern Italy in the late fourteenth century, the translation of the complete works of Plato by Marsilio Ficino and the re-discovery of Plotinus and Proclus led to a new Renaissance, characterised by humanism.

Finally, it should be borne in mind that studying medieval philosophy requires gaining familiarity with the world-view of the age. The medieval world is a closed, hierarchical and rather small place compared to the infinite space of Newton which so terrified Pascal. Medieval philosophy assumes the existence both of a sensible, temporal and an immaterial, eternal order. Human beings possess bodies and souls and hence belong in some way to both the temporal and the eternal orders.

Moreover, human reason is finite but is reliable and can achieve truth, and certainly is adequate to grasp the essential truths necessary for life in this world. There are no overt sceptics or relativists in the medieval tradition. In general, the medieval philosophy accepts a view of the universe as ordered hierarchically, from highest level, God, down to the lowest level, unformed matter or nothingness, in one great chain of being.[11] This hierarchical order was inherited from Neoplatonism but given a distinctive religious rendering. The term *hierarchy* means a 'sacred order' and was first used by the anonymous sixth-century, possibly Syrian, Christian Neoplatonist, Dionysius the Areopagite, to express the orders of angels and celestial beings who ringed around the Godhead. This celestial hierarchy, as Dionysius termed it, was mirrored on earth by the hierarchy of human nature, the animal, vegetable and mineral domains. Human social life itself mirrored this natural order so that kings, princes, noblemen, commoners, servants, etc. were all ordered in a natural hierarchy according to the natures. For instance, in his *Monologion*, St Anselm writes that anyone who does not understand that a horse is better than a tree and that a man is better than a horse is not rational:

> if anyone considers the natures of things he cannot help perceiving that they are not all of equal excellence but that some of them differ by an inequality of gradation. For if anyone doubts that a horse is by nature better (*melior*) than a tree and that a man is more excellent (*praestantior*) than a horse, then surely this [person] ought not to be called rational.[12]

FAITH AND REASON

During the late Greek and Roman periods, philosophy had come to be understood as the inclusive knowledge of everything. Cicero, for instance, had defined philosophy as 'the knowledge of all things divine and human' and this definition became an endlessly repeated truism in medieval writers such as Isidore of Seville, Alcuin and others, right down to Descartes. According to the Ciceronian model, philosophy was seen as an encyclopaedic wisdom – in line with the Hellenic educational ideal of *encyclios paideia*, an educational formation which encompassed everything. But the knowledge of everything (*cognitio omnium*) still had to accommodate religious faith. As religious philosophy emerged and struggled to accommodate the classical heritage, the issue of the relation between faith and reason became a central theme.[13]

Tertullian (*c*.160–220), born in Carthage, was the first Christian theologian to write in Latin. He strenuously opposed the articulation of faith in terms of philosophy in his *On Prescription Against Heretics* with his famous question: 'what has Athens to do with Jerusalem? What concord is there between the Academy and the Church? What between heretics and Christians?'[14] For Tertullian, faith was sufficient, the genuine Christian believer had no need of pagan eloquence and philosophy. Yet, Tertullian was not immune to philosophy. For example, in *Adversus Praxean* he conceived of God as a kind of vaporous material spirit (Greek: *pneuma*) in the manner of the Stoics, and in his *De Anima* argued for the soul as a kind of material substance (following the Stoics) against the Platonic conception. Tertullian thus illustrates a typical medieval dilemma. Even to oppose philosophy, as Peter Damian or Al-Ghazali did, meant to enter philosophical disputation.

Philosophy understood etymologically means 'love of wisdom' (*amor sapientiae*), and since, for Christians, Christ is the very incarnation of eternal wisdom, true philosophy meant the love of Christ. Augustine, following St Paul, contrasted the worldly wisdom or 'foolishness' of Greek pagan philosophy with Christian wisdom. Indeed St Paul refers to Christ as wisdom using the Greek word '*sophia*' in I *Corinthians* 1:24. St Paul had said that Christian wisdom founded on faith will appear to be a mere foolishness to those whose only standard is the wisdom of the world. Augustine expands on this idea: true wisdom cannot merely be knowledge of earthly, temporal things but actually must be the desire for eternal things. For Augustine, the philosopher seeks to transcend the world and not solely to know it. A Christian, Augustine, for example, maintained, must love Christ as much as anything, otherwise, his knowledge is vain and empty, mere *vana curiositas*.

For Augustine, particularly early in his career, true religion and true philosophy were one and the same, as he wrote in *Of True Religion* (*De vera religione*),[15] and by philosophy here he meant Platonism. In the same work (*De vera religione*, iv. 7), Augustine claimed one need only change a few words to see how closely Plato resembled Christianity. According to his *Confessiones* (*Confessions*) Book VII.xx.26,[16] Augustine's conversion to Christianity had been influenced by his reading 'books of the Platonists' (*libri platonicorum*) – most likely Marius Victorinus' translations of Plotinus and Porphyry – texts which convinced Augustine that truth was incorporeal, that God was eternal, unchanging, the cause of all things – in his mind paralleling truths revealed in St Paul's epistles.

It was Augustine who finally put paid to the view that faith could proceed without philosophy. For Augustine, the legacy of Plato and others should be integrated into Christian culture, just as the 'spoils of the Egyptians' were taken with them by the Israelites as they fled their captivity in Egypt. Augustine writes in *On Christian Doctrine* (Book II.XL.60):

> If those who are called philosophers, especially the Platonists, have said things which are indeed true and are well accommodated to our faith, they should not be feared; rather, what they have said should be taken from them as from unjust possessors and converted to our use. Just as the Egyptians had not only idols

and grave burdens which the people of Israel detested and avoided, so also they had vases and ornaments of gold and silver and clothing which the Israelites took with them secretly when they fled, as if to put them to a better use.[17]

Philosophers after Augustine no longer had any qualms about incorporating elements of classical philosophy, even if at times they used philosophical and dialectical techniques to draw attention to the limits of rational argument in trying to convey divine truth.

Christians who followed the Neoplatonic tradition tended to regard faith as preparatory to true knowledge. A line from Isaiah in the Latin version of the Old Testament, *'nisi credideritis, non intelligitis'* ('unless you will have believed, you will not have understood'), became a motto for medieval writers. For example, in a Sermon (No. 212, *Patrologia Latina* 35, Col. 1, 690) Augustine urged *'credite ut intelligas'* ('believe so that you may understand'), and St Anselm echoed this with his *credo ut intelligam* ('I believe so that I may understand'). But this stress on faith left considerable room for unaided reason, *recta ratio*. Followers of the Aristotelian tradition which re-emerged in the thirteenth century, on the other hand, distinguished between truths that were supremely intelligible in themselves (*per se*) and those which could grasped by our finite intellects, intelligible 'to us' (*quoad nos*). For Thomas, nothing in revelation could contradict reason in itself, although it might appear irrational to us. Some Parisian followers of Averroes – Siger of Brabant and Boethius of Dacia are usually mentioned in this context – on the other hand, have been associated with the notorious doctrine of 'double truth', i.e. the co-existence of two contradictory truths – truths grasped by reason and philosophy and truths propounded in theology.[18] While Christian philosophers struggled to interpret Aristotle faithfully, they were also constrained not to go against Christian doctrine and this often led to a tension between what Aristotle said and what the Church teaches as true. One way to deal with this, is to hold that Aristotle is right philosophically speaking but not theologically speaking. It is noteworthy for instance that when Ockham is commenting on Aristotle's *Physics* he makes it clear that he will expound what Aristotle said or what he ought to have said, consistent with his principles, and won't get into the issue of whether or not it is in conflict with Christian faith.

Another and less controversial claim in medieval philosophy (especially up to the twelfth century) was the commonplace that there were two non-conflicting sources of truth – the Book of Scripture and the Book of Nature – both of which need to be interpreted in sophisticated ways, but with a stronger emphasis on scripture than on nature. This hermeneutic approach, coupled with a Neoplatonic suspicion of the temporal and material, has led historians to see Christian philosophy as leading to what E.R. Dodds has called 'other-worldliness', devaluing the scientific study of things for their own sake which was at the heart of the researches of Aristotle for example, and focusing exclusively on the knowledge of God and the immortal soul. There is a certain truth in this characterisation especially when applied to Neoplatonic philosophers, nevertheless, the Neo-Aristotelian revival gave rise to a considerable interest in the sciences at Oxford and elsewhere, where there was a definite interest in the nature of the physical world, for its own sake.

In keeping with the theme of faith and reason was the related theme of the constraints on the interpretation of sacred texts. Medieval philosophers inherited from the classical era a vast and complex tradition of grammar, rhetoric, and hermeneutics. It was also generally accepted that texts were multilayered and poly-semic and could be interpreted in different ways. Efforts to harmonise the words of Scripture led to the development of sophisticated treatises on interpretation and semiology, e.g. St Augustine's enormously influential *De doctrina Christiana* (*On Christian Doctrine*, written between 396 and 427) which influenced Cassiodorus, Hugh of St Victor and Peter Lombard in setting down principles for reading scripture. In the theological tradition, four ways of interpreting Scripture – the literal, the allegorical, the symbolic and the anagogical – achieved something like canonical status.[19] But one must be careful – even the so-called 'literal' reading of Scripture could be highly speculative as Augustine's literal commentary on the meaning of Genesis (*De Genesi ad litteram*) shows.[20]

THE ORIGINS OF MEDIEVAL PHILOSOPHY

The foundations of medieval philosophy were laid during the late classical philosophy. In Alexandria, especially, religious scholars, steeped in Hellenism, sought to explore the meaning of the Jewish sacred writings using the grammatical and philosophical techniques of the Greek philosophers, drawing parallels between the creation accounts in Genesis and the stories of Plato's *Timaeus*.[21] Philo Judaeus (*c*.15 BC–AD 50), who had apparently no influence on the Jewish tradition, read the Bible in its Greek translation (*Septuagint*) and drew on Platonic and Stoic ideas to articulate his notion of the transcendence of God and of the nature of human beings as made in the image and likeness of God and aiming to achieve assimilation (*homoiosis*) with God. God is true being and 'He Who Is' (Exodus 3:4). God operates through the logos. God first created an intelligible world.

Initially, Christian writers, notably St Paul, show a marked hostility towards philosophy understood as pagan wisdom. Paul contrasted Greek philosophy (as arrogant foolishness) with the wisdom and truth of Jesus. Nevertheless, he absorbed philosophical conceptions current in his time. Thus, his epistles contain allusions to Greek (mostly Platonic and Stoic) philosophical ideas, e.g. concepts of natural law in the *Second Letter to the Romans*, the discussion of immortality in the *Second Letter to the Corinthians* 3–5, or the claim that existence of God may be proved by natural reason from the examination of natural things (*Romans* 1:20), a text much cited by medieval philosophy. St Paul employed a number of contrasts that are later taken up by Origen, Clement of Alexandria and Augustine, e.g. the contrast between the exterior and interior man, between the carnal and the spiritual, the old and the new.

As Christianity spread, Christians gradually began to address the surrounding Hellenic civilisation in its own terms. Within a century, Christian 'apologists' were arguing before hostile audiences for the truth and reasonableness of Christian revelation using arguments drawn from philosophy.[22] One such apologist was Justin Martyr (d. 162–8), who as a Greek philosopher, born in Samaria, but who converted to Christianity, possibly at Ephesus, relied heavily on Greek philosophical arguments in presenting the case for Christianity.[23] Three works survive: two Apologies, the first directed to the emperor, Antoninus Pius, and a dialogue with a Jew, *Dialogue with Trypho* where he compares the Biblical God with the god of the philosophers. *The First Apology* recounts his search for the truth, first with a Stoic teacher, then with a Peripatetic, followed by a Pythagorean and then a Platonist. For Justin it was obvious that philosophers must investigate the nature of the deity, the aim of philosophy was 'the vision of God'.

Christian philosophers borrowed heavily from ancient Greek and especially Platonic accounts of the immortality of the soul to spread the Christian message of personal immortal life. Clement of Alexandria (AD 150–215) wrote a number of works which advocated a philosophical approach to faith, notably *Stromateis* (*Miscellany*). Origen (*c*.185–*c*.254) combined Christian ideas with a philosophical structure derived from Platonism in his work, *On First Principles* which portrayed God as Oneness or Unity.[24] Clement and Origen saw no great clash between Platonism and Christianity, since both doctrines considered that this temporal world was not the whole of reality, that true reality was immaterial, timeless and perfect; that the eternal was to be valued over the temporal; the changeless over the changing. Both believed in the immortality of the soul and that it has the chance of eternal happiness. Both believed that there is a single source from which all things originate, and so on.

With the emergence of Christianity as the official religion of the Roman Empire in the era of Constantine, philosophical discussions of the Christian religion demonstrated a new confidence and sophistication. By 392, the Roman Senate had voted to abolish pagan cults. The division of the Roman Empire into a Greek East and a Latin West had the effect of partitioning the development of philosophy. Plotinus (205–70/71) was a typical example of the new hybrid – a Greek-speaking pagan, born in Egypt, who studied with Ammonius in Alexandria, and then lived and taught in Rome from 245 to his death. He attracted both vehemently pagan and Christian disciples. Porphyry, for example, wrote an attack on Christianity.

In the fourth century, in the Greek speaking Eastern part of the Roman Empire, Cappadocia, Gregory of Nyssa, Basil and Gregory Naziazen incorporated Plotinus in their development of a Neoplatonised Christianity, while in the Latin West, Hilary of Poitiers, Ambrose, Bishop of Milan, St Augustine, Bishop of Hippo, Jerome, and others, developed Christian philosophical cosmologies drawing from the writings of Clement of Alexandria and other earlier Christians. Ambrose's sermons, in particular, show heavy borrowings from Plotinus. These men came to be known as the Fathers of the Christian Church and they laid down the form that Christian philosophy and theology would develop in the succeeding centuries.[25]

PAGAN SURVIVALS: PLOTINUS, PORPHYRY AND PROCLUS

It would be wrong to characterise the development of Christian philosophy in the West as a long direct line of uninterrupted progress in the clarification and system-atisiation of basic Christian concepts. A vigorous pagan movement incorporating late Hellenistic religions co-existed side by side with Christianity during the early centuries. This counter movement reached its pinnacle in the third and fourth centuries CE with the writings of Plotinus, Porphyry, and Iamblichus. Various attempts were made to re-establish paganism, most notably by the Emperor Julian.[26] Plotinus (205–70 CE) was a pagan philosopher who taught at Rome, who knew a great deal about Christianity, but was not drawn to it. He systematised the thought of Plato into a monistic, hierarchical metaphysics where all things come from the One which in itself is above intellect and above all predication. His pupil and literary editor, Porphyry (233–309), who came from Tyre, was openly hostile to the Christians and wrote a treatise, *Against the Christians*, which unfortunately no longer survives.[27] Porphyry attacks the trustworthiness of the Bible as a prophetic document, concentrating on the Book of Daniel, which he claimed was not written in the sixth century BC as Christians believed, but in the second century AD. Rather than prophesying events it was actually describing actual events. He also attacked the allegorical method of reading the Bible which Philo, Clement and the Alexandrian school had popularised. Porphyry is dismissive of the Christian understanding of the *logos* as expressed in the prologue of the Johannine Gospel. Iamblichus (c.242–327), who taught at Apamea in Syria, was interested in the mystery religions, in the cult of Isis and Osiris and in theurgy, the practice of invoking demons. His *On the Mysteries* had considerable influence in Renaissance times.[28] Iamblichus' philosophical contribution included a programme for teaching Plato and Aristotle and a strong commitment to neo-Pythagorean number symbolism.

Proclus (*c.*410–85), head of the Platonic Academy at Athens, was the last great pagan philosopher practising in the West. While his own works (notably *Elements of Theology* and *Platonic Theology*)[29] did not have direct influence on Latin thought until translated by William of Moerbeke and commented on by Nicholas of Cusa, nevertheless he exercised a covert influence (circulating under the name of Aristotle) through an Arab compilation, *Liber de causis*,[30] translated into Latin by Gerard of Cremona in Toledo. Roger Bacon (*c.*1212–92), Thomas Aquinas, Giles of Rome (1247–1316), Henry of Ghent (d. 1293), Siger of Brabant, and Albert the Great all wrote commentaries on it.

Perhaps more importantly, Proclus entered the West through the writings of an anonymous fifth- or sixth-century Syrian Christian follower who went under the name of Dionysius the Areopagite. This author, while purporting to be the first convert of St Paul at Athens, mentioned in Acts 17:34, propounded a Proclean Neoplatonic Christian monism in his four treatises, which were first translated by Johannes Scottus Eriugena and later by John Saracen.[31] From Eriugena to Nicholas of Cusa, this author was wrongly identified with Saint Denis, patron saint of France and supposed founder of the important medieval French abbey of St Denis (Lorenzo Valla eventually showed the work to be a forgery). Dionysius' works had an important influence on medieval theology and spirituality. Eriugena, Albertus, Aquinas, Grosseteste and others wrote commentaries on him. In his *Divine Names* Dionysius argues that many of the appellations for the divine in sacred scripture cannot be taken literally. It is not literally true that God is a lion, or gets angry or has a face. For the God who transcends all predication, negations are often more true or more apt than affirmations. For Dionysius, it is more true to say that God is not rather than that God is, since God is 'above all the things that are and are not'. *The Mystical Theology* goes even further, God is to be thought of as above being and non-being.

The Neoplatonism of Plotinus, Porphyry and Proclus, influenced medieval philosophy in subterranean ways. Two extremely influential books in the medieval period – the *Theology of Aristotle* (actually a compilation from Plotinus) and the already mentioned *Liber de causis* (taken from Proclus) – both circulated under the name of Aristotle. Neoplatonism was Christianised especially by Augustine and Boethius. Coming towards the end of the Roman period, and representing a powerful if eclectic synthesis of Christian ideas, formulated in the language of Roman classical learning, the writings of Augustine of Hippo acted as a conduit for information concerning the opinions of the ancient Greek philosophers and in particular concerning the views of late classical writers such as Plotinus, Porphyry and other Neoplatonists (e.g. Marius Victorinus). That Augustine was not very impressed by the work of Aristotle is recorded in the *Confessions*. On the other hand, he was originally inducted into philosophy through the reading of Cicero's lost work

Hortensius and was deeply impressed by Neoplatonism, which he felt to be in sympathy with the intellectual and spiritual aims of Christianity. So close were the similarities between Plato and Scripture on the nature of God, the act of divine creation, the immortality of the soul, the corruptibility of the body, and the salvation of the good soul, that, initially, Augustine assumed that Plato must have learned from Moses. For Augustine, only the Platonists saw that God was eternal, immutable, immaterial, infinite and the creative source of all things. In the *City of God*, Book 8 Chapter 5, he writes: 'no one has come closer to us [Christians] than the Platonists . . . who have said that the true God is the author of all things, the illuminator of truth, and the giver of happiness'.[32] Augustine, above all, wants to combat the Stoic doctrine that God is a material body.

However, gradually Augustine began to realise that Neoplatonism had a deep distrust for the body and for human history which could accommodate neither the Christian concept of the incarnation of God the Son in the historical personage of Jesus Christ nor the notion of God's salvific role in human history. Augustine in his *Retractions* (*Retractationes*),[33] expresses regrets concerning various formulations of his belief that seemed too Neoplatonic; however he never abandoned Neoplatonism completely. Indeed, his own sanitised form of Neoplatonism was to become the standard cosmology for the medieval period until the rediscovery of the writings of Aristotle in the middle of the twelfth century.

Anicius Manlius Severinus Boethius (480–524) was the last philosopher to write within the framework of the Roman Empire, albeit an Empire now controlled by the Visigoths. Born into a patrician family, Boethius studied philosophy at Athens and possibly at Alexandria, and later, in 510, became an advisor to the Ostogoth Theodoric, Governor of Rome, but suspected of treason, he was arrested in 523, imprisoned and eventually put to death. Boethius' aim was to reconcile the philosophies of Plato and Aristotle, and, to this end, he translated and commented on Aristotelian works. His later influence came especially through his commentary on Aristotle's logical writings and on Porphyry. He wrote works explicating Christian theological concepts, *On The Trinity* (*De Trinitate*) and *On The Catholic Faith* (*De Fide Catholica*).[34] While in prison he wrote the dialogue, *Consolation of Philosophy* (524),[35] in five books, which extolled the value of philosophy in helping someone to face adversity, and became one of the most popular philosophical works in the medieval period. The 'consolation' of philosophy is that this world is a mere fleeting shadow compared with the true, timeless eternal world. The philosopher who knows this will not be perturbed by the vicissitudes of this world. Although the work is not explicitly Christian it was taken as extolling Christian virtues of resignation and fortitude. The fifth book contains an important discussion concerning divine foreknowledge and human freedom (paralleling the views of Augustine) which exercised a strong influence on Christian thought in the following centuries.

THE SOURCES OF MEDIEVAL PHILOSOPHY

The early medieval period in the Latin West is a period of beginning and recovery – a struggle to re-establish the very basics of knowledge lost in the decline of the Greek and Roman empires. Medieval philosophy grows upon the ruins of classical thought and one can apply to the Middle Ages generally the saying attributed to Bernard of Chartres by John of Salisbury in his *Metalogicon* III, 4, namely, that we [moderns] know more because we are like dwarfs standing on the backs of giants [the classical tradition].

Although philosophers in the Eastern or Byzantine part of the Roman empire continued to write in Greek up until the ninth century and beyond, most of this material was unavailable to the Latin-speaking West, and thus philosophers in the West had to rely on what could be gleaned from compilations found in the writings of Romans such as Cicero, Seneca, and in standard handbooks of the Liberal Arts such as the popular allegory, *The Marriage of Philology and Mercury*, written by the North African writer Martianus Capella, or another popular work by the fifth century writer Macrobius, whose *Commentary on the Dream of Scipio*, a discussion of Cicero's *Republic*, contained a discussion of the nature of the soul in Platonic terms. Cicero, for example, translated and summarised various Platonic dialogues including the *Republic* (*Res Publica*) as well as compiling a lot of information on the Sceptics in his *Academica*. But the majority of actual texts of Greek philosophy were not available to Western European medieval philosophers. In classical times, in the system of education, knowledge was divided into a number of different arts (Latin: *artes*) or disciplines (*disciplinae*), taught in a certain sequence. The Roman writer Varro puts these forward as a group of nine arts, including grammar, logic, rhetoric, arithmetic, geometry, music, astronomy, medicine and architecture. More frequently, following Martianus Capella, these arts were considered to number seven (arithmetic, geometry, music, astronomy, grammar, rhetoric and dialectic) – the seven bridesmaids of the woman Philology who is betrothed to the God Mercury in Martianus' popular allegory, *The Marriage of Philology and Mercury*. These arts were usually divided into two groups according to the focus of their subject matter: the group of three or *trivium* which dealt with words (*verba*) and the group of four or *quadrivium* which dealt with things (*res*). In the High Middle Ages the liberal arts were taught in the Arts Faculties of the Universities as a preliminary to the study of Theology. Medicine was taught in a separate Faculty as is the case in today's universities.

Of Plato's dialogues, up until the middle of the twelfth century, only a portion of the *Timaeus* survived in Latin translation (translated by Cicero in the second century, it circulated most broadly in the fourth-century fragmentary translation of Chalcidius).[36] Curiously, it was ignored until it suddenly came into vogue again in the twelfth century as philosophers developed Neoplatonic Christian cosmologies at the schools of Chartres and St Victor. In the twelfth century also, translations of the *Phaedo* and *Meno* became available, but again these did not have much impact until the full revival of Plato in Northern Europe which took place until the fourteenth century, largely through the efforts of Marsilio Ficino and the Florentine Academy, which contributed greatly to the development of the Renaissance.

With regard to Aristotle only a summary of his *Categories* was available in the earliest medieval period. Gradually, medieval philosophers (e.g. Alcuin in the ninth century), came to know Aristotle's *On Interpretation* (Greek: *Peri Hermeneias* or Latin: *De interpretatione*) as well as Porphyry's *Introduction* (*Isagoge*) and Boethius' logical commentaries. Taken together these works were collectively known as the *logica vetus* or 'old logic'. In the middle of the twelfth century, translations of Aristotle made from Arabic translations became available, largely through the endeavours of an important group of translators in Spain, including John of Spain, Gerard of Cremona and Gundissalinus among others. By the thirteenth century, scholars had become familiar with a larger range of Aristotelian texts, including the *Topics*, *Analytics* and the *Sophistical Refutations*, collectively known as the *logica nova* or 'new logic'. But it is noteworthy, that even Averroes did not have access to Aristotle's *Politics*, which did not become available in the West until 1260. In the thirteenth century these translations were replaced by new translations directly from the Greek, made principally by the Flemish Dominican, William of Moerbeke (d. 1286).

The absence of actual texts of Plato and Aristotle meant that medieval authors had to rely very heavily on secondary sources – most notably Augustine, whose *City of God* provided a very useful potted history of classical philosophy. But medieval philosophers proved to be remarkably adept at utilising these scant resources to develop speculative philosophical systems of extraordinary scope and vitality, as found, for example, in the *Periphyseon* of John Scottus Eriugena.

JOHN SCOTTUS ERIUGENA (c.800–c.877)

Although in general in North Western Europe, the so-called 'Dark Ages', i.e. the centuries following the collapse of the old Roman order, did not produce much intellectual or scholarly activity of any kind, one figure in particular stands out as a brilliant and sophisticated philosopher and theologian, namely, Johannes Scottus Eriugena, an Irishman who came to prominence in France in the ninth century, and is considered to be the most important philosopher writing in Latin between Boethius and Anselm. The revival of learning in ninth century France was stimulated by Charlemagne's educational reforms which sought to establish elementary schools attached to religious houses. Charlemagne's advisor Alcuin of York (died 804) began the tradition of Carolingian philosophy and theology which reached its heights with the philosophy of Eriugena.

John the Irishman (who signed himself 'Eriugena') was probably educated in the Irish monastic tradition (Ireland, being outside the Empire, had escaped the ravages following the collapse of Roman administration) but emigrated to France where he soon became palace master at the court of the Carolingian king, Charles the Bald. He wrote a *Commentary* on Martianus' *Marriage of Philology and Mercury* as well as a polemical treatise *On Divine Predestination*, which, on account of its optimistic interpretation of Augustine's concept of predestination, was condemned by several Councils in France as verging on Pelagianism.

A Christian Neoplatonist, Eriugena developed a unique synthesis between the Neoplatonic traditions of Pseudo-Dionysius and Augustine.[37] Most unusual in the Latin West at that time, Eriugena knew Greek and his translations of the works of Dionysius (especially the *Divine Names* and *Mystical Theology*), commissioned by the King of France, as well as other Greek Christian texts (notably Gregory of Nyssa and Maximus Confessor) provided access to a theological tradition hitherto unknown in the Latin West, namely the Eastern Christian tradition of negative theology (inspired by Plotinus). In his major dialogue *Periphyseon* (*De divisione naturae, On the Division of Nature*, c.867),[38] he developed an original cosmology with Nature (*natura*) as the first principle. Nature, the totality of all things that are and are not, includes both God and creation, and has four divisions: nature which creates and is not created, nature which creates and is created, nature which is created and does not create, and nature which is neither created nor creates. These divisions participate in the cosmic procession of creatures from God and their return to God. As everything takes place within Nature, God is present in all four divisions.

In the *Periphyseon*, Eriugena enthusiastically incorporated many Greek Christian theological concepts. God is conceived of as a nameless One beyond being, who cannot really be spoken of, whose first act is to create himself by a kind of self-externalisation or self-emanation, from non-being into being. The creation of the universe proceeds as a timeless unfolding (*proodos, exitus*) from this divine first principle through the Primary Causes into their spatial and temporal effects until the process reaches the limit with unformed matter. All things remain in being due to the first principle and all seek to return to it in the general return of all things (*epistrophe, reditus*). All created things are copies of the Ideas (called Primordial Causes) in the mind of God and so too human nature is originally a Platonic Idea in the divine mind. However the human failure to understand its true nature as from God due to the distraction of created, temporal images (*phantasiai*), leads to the Fall into the spatio-temporal realm of sense. However, through intellectual contemplation (*theoria*) and divine illumination (which is the divine self-manifestation, *theophania*), humans may achieve salvation and a return to their perfect state (also known as heaven). To the very few it will be given to achieve unification (*henosis*) with God, also known as *deification* (*theosis*, *deificatio*). This Greek Christian notion of deification emphasises the unity without remainder between the blessed and God. This is a radicalisation and interpretation of the Augustinian theme that God became man so that humans can become God.

Eriugena influenced contemporary philosophy in France, notably at Laon, Auxerre and Corbie but had no detectable influence on writers such as Anselm. The *Periphyseon* again became popular in the twelfth century, circulating in the paraphrase of Honorius Augustodunensis, *Clavis Physicae*. Eriugena influenced twelfth-century thinkers including Hugh of St Victor, Alanus of Lille, Suger of Saint-Denis and William of Malmesbury. In the thirteenth century, the *Periphyseon* was associated with the writings of David of Dinant and Amaury of Bène, two theologians at the University of Paris, and condemned with them in 1210 and 1225. In the later Middle Ages both Meister Eckhart of Hochheim (*c*.1260–*c*.1328) and Nicholas of Cusa (1401–64) were sympathetic to Eriugena and familiar with his *Periphyseon*, but others condemned his work as a form of pantheism.

THE ELEVENTH CENTURY: ST ANSELM OF CANTERBURY (1033–1109)

Eleventh-century philosophy continued to be framed within the outlook of Saint Augustine, since there was still no direct access to classical authors and Eriugena's Greek inspired Platonism were generally ignored. Instead the school curriculum was formed by various standard handbooks or compilations summarising the seven liberal arts. Despite this paucity of original material, a number of eleventh-century philosophers, most notably Anselm, Lanfranc, Peter Damian and Gaunilo, made important contributions by pursuing a rigorously dialectical (i.e. logical) method of argument based on rational premises which led to the twelfth-century flowering of dialectic in the work of Abelard and others. Peter Damian (1007–72), who raged against secular philosophy, actually made some significant advances. Discussing the question of whether God, who is understood to be all powerful, had the capacity to make something which has already happened not in fact have happened at all, i.e. whether God could change the past or whether the past had a certain kind of necessity, Peter Damian analyses the nature of possibility and necessity. He distinguishes between that necessity which is 'the consequence of statements' and actual necessity. If it is raining now then necessarily it is raining. This is the necessity of statements. Actual necessity, on the other hand, means whatever must be the case in all circumstances. God's power is not bound by the necessity of statements and hence God could change the past since the past is contingent and not something which must at all times be the case.

Anselm of Canterbury (1033–1109) is best known for his argument for the existence of God, versions of which re-appear in Bonaventure and Duns Scotus, as well as Descartes, Spinoza, Leibniz. On the other hand, it was rejected both by Thomas Aquinas and by Kant, who labelled it the 'ontological argument', meaning thereby that it is an argument from the mere conception of a thing to its reality or existence, a move Kant thought was illicit. Anselm's argument also brings to light difficulties in understanding the meaning of some of the basic philosophical notions like *existence*, *possibility*, *necessity*, notions central to metaphysics. In actual fact Anselm offers not one, but a number of different arguments for the existence of God in his *Monologion*.[39] In a subsequent work, *Prosologion*, he seeks to reduce his main arguments for the existence of God to a single proof.

In the *Monologion* Anselm claims to be following Augustine's *De Trinitate*, a work which examined the ways in which the mystery of the divine Trinity can be contemplated in the nature of created things. According to Augustine, all created things bear the stamp of their maker and display traces (*vestigia*) of the divine Trinity. Anselm, too, is seeking to discover the nature of God and his existence from created things. He begins with the Neoplatonic assumption that there is a hierarchy evident in nature: some things are better, more valuable, and so on, than other things. From the thought of this hierarchy of things, we can form the thought of 'that than which nothing greater can be thought'. The *Monologion* argument goes as follows: given that there are different goods in the world, although they actually differ in that some are better than others, nevertheless there must be some quality which they share if they are all to be called good. This quality they share must itself *cause* those things to be good in their respective ways. They are good *through* this cause, they participate in this quality. But this quality must be itself good on its own or *through itself* (*per se*) or else we would have an infinite regress of goods that were better than each other without a highest good. There must therefore be something which is perfectly good, and this we call 'God'. The form of this argumentation is clearly Platonic, going back to Plato's *Phaedo*, and indeed, in the thirteenth century, Aquinas will employ this form of argumentation in his fourth way of demonstrating the existence of God (*Summa theologiae*, Ia.2.3). Anselm concludes his argument in the *Monologion* as follows:

> Therefore, necessarily, there is a nature which is so superior to some [other] or some [others] that there is no [nature] to which it is ranked as inferior.

This prefigures the definition of God in the *Proslogion* as 'that than which nothing greater can be thought'.

While Anselm believed he had given a number of satisfactory arguments, a 'connected chain of many arguments' for the existence of God in the *Monologion*, in the *Proslogion* he announced that he now wanted to put forward a 'single argument' (*unum argumentum*) which on its own suffices to prove the existence of God.[40] Despite the fact that he begins the *Proslogion* saying he is following faith and seeking understanding, in fact he is offering a purely rational demonstration. He claims to proceed 'by rational means alone' (*sola ratione*) as he says in *Why the God-Man?* (*Cur Deus Homo?*). Indeed, Anselm often invokes the 'necessity of reason' indicating that he accepts that rational arguments in themselves are compelling.

Anselm's strategy in the *Proslogion* argument is to offer a definition of God which will be acceptable to both believer and non-believer, and then to show that what is referred to in the definition must exist, because the alternative is impossible. This kind of argument is called a reduction to absurdity, *reductio ad absurdum*. He begins by referring to 'the Fool' (*insipiens*), or ignorant one, in the Psalms, who has said in his heart that there is no God.[41] Anselm's Fool is a disbeliever who accepts that the very notion of God is coherent (i.e. not self-contradictory), and is merely asserting that no being answering that description actually exists. Anselm's next step is to try to get agreement about what the concept of God means:

> We believe that you are something than which nothing greater can be thought.

Medieval authors always relied heavily on traditional authorities and Anselm is no exception. For this definition, Anselm drew on the Roman philosopher, Seneca, who in his *Eight Books of Natural Questions*, answers the question 'What is God?' as follows: 'his magnitude is that than which nothing greater can be thought'. Augustine has several variations on this formula in his *On free Choice of the Will*, in *On Christian Doctrine* 1.7.7, 'something than which there is nothing better' (*aliquid quo nihil melius sit*), and in the *Confessions* Book VII.4.6.

Anselm employs various formulations: God is 'that than which nothing greater can be thought' (*aliquid quo nihil maius cogitari possit*) or 'that than which a greater can not be thought' (*quo maius cogitari nequit*). God is the greatest conceivable being, a greater being cannot be conceived. But Aquinas in fact was doubtful whether this was an adequate definition of God or even whether most people would regard it as the meaning of the term 'God'. In his *Summa theologiae* 1a. 2.1.2, he says:

> Someone hearing the word 'God' may very well not understand it to mean 'that than which nothing greater can be thought', indeed some people have believed God to be a body.

The phrase 'that than which nothing greater can be thought' (*id quo maius nihil cogitari potest*) in both English and Latin is deceptively complex. It involves a negative comparison: God is that being *than* which *nothing* greater can be conceived; no greater being than this is conceivable. Occasionally, Anselm reformulates it in positive terms: God is the greatest (most perfect) being conceivable. But his more considered position is found in *Proslogion* Chapter XV: God's being transcends our human powers of conceiving of Him; God is greater than can be thought, i.e. God is greater than any conceivable thing, and His greatness consists in part in being unthinkable. Indeed in his reply to a challenge from Gaunilo, an otherwise little known monk of Marmoutier, who wrote a refutation of Anselm, *Pro Insipiente* (*On Behalf of the Fool*) Anselm stresses that the positive version 'greater than everything' (*maius omnibus*) is not equivalent to the negative phrase 'that than which nothing is greater'. The first merely says God is the greatest being, and the second says God is greater than the greatest.

Anselm accepts the medieval hierarchical assumption that one thing may be said to be absolutely better than another thing: immutable things are better than mutable things. Incorporeal things are better than corporeal things (following Augustine). 'Better' here means possessing more perfections or attributes. In his *Reply to Gaunilo*, Anselm explains:

> For we believe of the Divine being, whatever it can, absolutely speaking, be thought to be better than not to be. For example, it is better to be eternal than not eternal, good than not good, goodness-itself than not goodness-itself.

Anselm's definition also contains a reference to human understanding or thinking. What does the phrase 'can be thought' mean? Anselm does not think he is using the term 'conceive' or 'think' here in the psychological sense, to mean mentally entertain or imagine. Rather he means what is logically or conceptually possible. Indeed, Anselm distinguishes between imagining and conceiving. Our imagination is indeed limited, but our ability to conceive is limited only by the law of contradiction. I can conceive of anything that is logically possible. Anselm thus identifies conceivability with logical possibility. God is the highest being conceivable hence God is the greatest possible being.

Anselm then develops the argument in the following way: to talk intelligibly about God requires understanding the term 'God' even if denying His existence. Second, the term 'God' means 'something than which nothing greater can be conceived'. Now, Anselm introduces a new premiss: 'but whatever one understands exists in the understanding' (*quod intelligit in intellectu eius est*). Anselm says explicitly that what is understood is in the understanding:

Observe then that, from the fact that it is understood, it does follow that it is in the mind. For, just as what is thought is thought by means of a thought, and what is thought by a thought is thus, as thought, in thought (*in cogitatione*), so also, what is understood (*quod intelligitur*) is understood (*intelligitur*) by the mind (*intellectu*), and what is understood by the mind is thus, as understood, in the mind (*in intellectu*). What could be more obvious than this?

This assumption is very problematic. Anselm appears to believe that whenever something is understood, then that thing itself exists in the mind. He admits that fictional or imaginary or 'false' things (*falsa*) have no existence outside the mind, but he appears to believe that they have something we might call 'mental existence'. But, from the fact that I understand what a table is, it does not follow that there is actually a table in my mind. Speaking of something being 'in' the mind is metaphorical. Anselm is operating with the assumption that there are at least two kinds of existence, which we might term 'mental' and 'actual' or 'real' existence:

For it is one thing for an object to exist in the mind (*in intellectu*), and another thing to understand that that object actually exists.

Anselm explicates this distinction with an example of a painter:

Thus, when a painter plans beforehand (*praecogitat*) what he is going to execute, he has [the picture] in his mind (*in intellectu*), but he does not yet think that it actually exists (*esse*) because he has not yet executed it. However, when he has actually painted it, then he both has it in his mind and understands that it exists because he has now made it.

The painting exists twice: first, as it is in the artist, and then again as it is in physical reality. Anselm assumes that somehow it is the same painting which has a dual existence: in the mind (in Latin variously *in intellectu* or *in mente*) and in reality (*in re*). By analogy with the painter who thinks beforehand of his painting, Anselm now suggests that someone who is considering the very notion of a God has actually got GOD (the entity) in his mind. Hence GOD has at least got mental existence or exists 'in the understanding' (*in intellectu*). Anselm here exploits an ambiguity. When we think about GOD, what have we got in our minds? Is it GOD – the actual entity – which is in our understanding? Or is it rather the *concept* of a God, that is *meaning* of the term 'God' which is in our understanding? Anselm wants us to believe the former; i.e. that GOD itself, is in our understanding and so to conclude that once we think of God we must admit that GOD exists – at least in our understanding; that GOD has at the very least got mental existence.

Anselm now proceeds: we can in fact think of something greater than mental existence. Whatever possesses *both* mental and real existence must be better than that which possesses mental existence alone. Sometimes Anselm is just claiming that something which exists in two ways is better than something that exists in one way. If we call mental existence 'a' and real existence 'b', then the argument is of the form: 'a+b>a'. But sometimes Anselm does argue that real existence is better than merely mental existence. Here the argument is of the form 'b>a'. Gaunilo reproduces this latter reasoning in his summary of Anselm's proof:

> For if this same being exists in the mind (*in intellectu*) alone, anything that existed also in reality (*in re*) would be greater than this being, and thus that which is greater than everything would be less than something and would not be greater than everything, which is obviously contradictory.

Since God possesses all perfections and those in the highest measure, God must possess the highest measure of existence as one of those perfections. That highest perfection is possession of both real existence and mental existence. Therefore God, if God is to fulfil the very definition we have accepted for Him, must have real existence as well as mental existence. We know already that God has mental existence and we have now proved that God has real existence. Therefore God exists.

A second version of this argument in *Proslogion* Chapter Three turns on the distinction between God possessing existence and God necessarily existing. This modal version on the proof is considered to be considerably stronger. Anselm himself elsewhere showed interest in the metaphysics of modal terms – the meaning of necessity, possibility, and so on, concepts that also received considerable attention among Muslim philosophers (e.g. Avicenna) writing roughly at the same time.

TWELFTH-CENTURY RENAISSANCE

The schools of Chartres and St Victor

The so-called twelfth-century philosophical 'renaissance' took place in France and was centred in the Cathedral schools of Notre Dame, Chartres and St Victor, and involved the revival of learning in a new institutional setting. The Cathedral schools – especially St Victor and Chartres – grew in importance and eventually would supply teachers to the new universities of the thirteenth century. The philosophy of the period is characterised by a vigorous Platonic cosmological speculation inspired by the *Timaeus* (renewing interest in a work that had been ignored for more than five hundred years), and also by an interest in dialectic and the liberal arts, based on readings of Boethius, Macrobius and Martianus Capella. The twelfth century also saw the dawn of a new understanding of nature, attempting to understand it for its own sake and not merely as a mirror of Scripture. Drawing on Calcidius' *Commentary on the Timaeus*, twelfth-century Platonists (Bernard of Chartres, Thierry of Chartres, and William of Conches) developed an account of the world in terms of the four elements and in terms of complex number symbolisms, stressing the relation between macrocosm and microcosm, and harmony between the divine and created spheres.

From the Middle Platonists onwards, Christians had noticed the parallels between Plato's *Timaeus* and the account of creation in Genesis. Moreover, Plato's literary method of exposition was similar to Christian parable; both use fables and symbols (*integumenta*, 'coverings') which require interpretation. The most prominent twelfth-century Platonist William of Conches, who probably taught at Chartres between 1120 and 1150, wrote the most extensive medieval commentary on the *Timaeus*. He also commented on Boethius' *Consolation of Philosophy* and composed two systematic works, *Philosophia mundi* and a revised version entitled *Dragmaticon*, set in the form of a dialogue between the Duke of Normandy and the Philosopher. For William, the *Timaeus* is a unified theological work displaying the beneficence of the creator. God has established an unvarying natural law which is discoverable at the heart of things. For William, God creates the intellectual realm and allows other causes (e.g. stars) to govern the lower world, thus proposing a doctrine of mediated creation at variance with Augustine's single-act view. William of Conches explicitly connects Plato with Pythagoras, and argues that since number possesses the highest perfection, nothing can exist without number.

William saw himself as expanding on the teaching of Plato:

> It is not my intention to expound here the words of Plato, but to set down here the view of natural scientists (*physici*) concerning substances; but even if I have not expounded Plato's words, I have said all that he said about elements, and more.
>
> (*Dragmatico*)[42]

He attempts to define the elements and addresses the question as to whether they are perceptible by the senses and corporeal and whether the division of matter ends with these indivisibles (atoms). William takes the view that the four elements are corporeal, unchanging substances which however are only found in combination. The elements then are corporeal but actually grasped by intellect since they are too small to be perceived by the senses on their own. Though they are unchangeable, they are created. God first made the four elements from nothing and then everything else out of the four elements, except the soul of man, which God made directly.

A major challenge to Christianising Plato's cosmology was to interpret the role played by the Platonic Demiurge. Christian Platonists were initially quick to identify the Demiurge with the Logos, the Second Person of the Trinity. This allowed them to make a further identification between the Holy Spirit and the world soul (*anima mundi*), which in the *Timaeus* enlivens the material cosmos. William of Conches initially, in his *Commentary on Macrobius*, I 12, 12, quite boldly identified the world soul of the *Timaeus* with the Holy Spirit, as Abelard was alleged to have done. The Council of Sens had condemned the identification, attributing it to Abelard. William appears to have grown more cautious, simply offering a number of different views in his *Philosophia* Book One (the world soul is the Holy Spirit, or a natural force implanted in things by God, or a certain incorporeal substance in bodies) and making no reference to the world soul in his *Dragmaticon*.

Bernard Silvestris' *Cosmographia* is a partly versified, allegorical account of the creation of the world that makes use of many Platonic ideas from the *Timaeus*, including that of a world soul, personified as Endelichia (who also appears in Martianus Capella and Cicero), but in a manner quite different from William of Conches. Bernard has a world of ideas (Noys) and a domain of unformed matter (personified as Silva – Calcidius' term for 'matter'). Gradually Noys imposes order on Silva until the whole world has been made. The sensible world imitates the intelligible; man is a microcosm of the macrocosm. Bernard portrays Plato as beginning with two principles: *unitas et diversum*, unity and diversity. Another Platonic cosmology in versified form was Alan of Lille's (*c*.1120–1203) *De planctu naturae*, a dialogue between the poet and Nature, influenced by Bernard Silvestris.

Peter Abelard (1079–1142): The Master of Dialectic

One cannot underestimate the importance of Abelard as providing the paradigm of the gifted, independently minded dialectician who revelled in disputation. He is also perhaps the most famous medieval philosopher, largely because of his doomed love affair with Heloise. We know a lot about his life because he left an autobiography, *Historia Calamitatum* (*The Story of My Misfortunes*).[43] Abelard was born into a noble family in Brittany in 1079, and while living in the house of Fulbert, the Canon of Notre Dame, he had an affair with Fulbert's niece, the young Heloise, when he became her private tutor. When she became pregnant, and following the birth of the child, Abelard secretly married her. He persuaded her to go to a monastery for her safety, but members of Fulbert's family attacked and castrated him. Heloise remained a nun after this and Abelard entered the monastery at St Denis where he became active in encouraging the monastic vocation. The bodies of Abelard and Heloise now rest in the Père Lachaise cemetery in Paris.

Abelard studied dialectic with Roscelin of Compiègne (*c*.1050–*c*.1120) and William of Champeaux (*c*.1070–1120), the most famous Paris master of his day and a renowned logician. Abelard sided with Roscelin and disagreed with William on the subject of the status of universals and eventually broke away to set up his own school of dialectic. William understood species and genera to be as real as individual things whereas Abelard, following Roscelin, saw them as mere verbal sounds that ultimately referred to individual things. He then studied with Anselm of Laon but also disputed with him. Dialectic at the time consisted of a sophisticated development of the classical logical corpus (the so called *logica vetus* or 'old logic') – Aristotle's *Categories* and *On Interpretation* together with Porphyry's *Isagoge* and Boethius' *De topicis differentiis* (*On Diverse Topics*) as well as the works of late classical liberal arts writers such as Martianus Capella. Abelard's logic held that logic was about things said (*verba*) as opposed to things (*res*), and on account of this Abelard has been seen as anticipating nominalism. It paid particular attention to the sentence (as did Stoic logic) and to what is asserted in a sentence, namely the *dictum* ('what is said') as opposed to the *dictio* (act of asserting). For Abelard, the force of the copula in a traditional judgement is to bring about the 'saying', otherwise the sentence would merely be a collection of words.

Abelard also wrote on theology and ethics. His account of the Trinity got him into trouble with Church authorities but he seems to have greatly enjoyed the controversy. His dialectical work, *Sic et Non* had a strong influence on Peter Lombard's *Book of Sentences* (*Liber Sententiarum*, *c*.1155–8) which became a standard introduction to theological reasoning in medieval universities. In this work in four books, Peter Lombard (died 1160), Bishop of Paris, compiled citations from the Fathers relating to various questions. Opposing opinions are ranked beside one another in a manner which would be copied by the Scholastics of the next century.

THE ISLAMIC TRADITION FROM THE EIGHTH TO THE TWELFTH CENTURIES

While all medieval scholars recognise the importance of the Islamic and Jewish contribution, there is great controversy over its precise significance.[44] There is even debate about whether it is more accurate to speak of 'philosophy in Arabic' rather than Islamic philosophy, since many of the writers in Arabic were Jews and Christians. Mohammed died in AD 632 and, in less than a hundred years, Islam had spread by militant conquest across North Africa to Spain and eastwards to India. Islam encountered Greek philosophy in the Greek intellectual centres in Mesopotamia, Syria and Egypt giving rise to a distinctive Islamic philosophy begins in the eighth century in Baghdad. All the works of Plato and Aristotle as well as their commentators were known in the Islamic world, and the emphasis was on finding agreement between these two authorities. Schools of translators translated this Greek science and philosophy into Arabic. Islamic philosophy emerged with the dialectical theologians in the schools of Baghdad and Basra. Great Islamic philosophers include the Neoplatonist Persian philosopher, Al-Kindi (796–873), who was active in Baghdad, Al-Razi (d. c.932), Al-Farabi (872–950) who developed Aristotelianism, Ibn Sina (Avicenna, 980–1037) who combined the Neoplatonism of Al-Kindi with the Aristotelianism of the Farabi school, Al Ghazali (1058–1111), and Ibn Rushd (Averroes) who lived in Cordoba in Spain.[45] Islamic philosophers were interested in the nature of prophecy and divine illumination.

Ibn Rushd was enormously influential in the Latin west in the thirteenth century and especially important for his refutation of Avicenna's views of the relevance of philosophy to theology. Thomas Aquinas and others regarded him as *the* commentator on Aristotle. His view of the nature of the separated intellect inspired a group of thirteenth-century philosophers known by modern scholars as 'the Latin Averroists'. Even in his life he was a controversial figure and was banished from Moslem Andalusia to North Africa although he was subsequently rehabilitated. Nevertheless, he lost the battle with the Muslim theologians who continued to regard him as doctrinally suspect (e.g. on the doctrine of personal immortality). By the eleventh century philosophy had already declined in Baghdad, and, after Averroes, Muslim philosophy generally went into a decline from which it has never recovered.

Islamic philosophy emphasised the unity of God and studied how God can be both one and also possess attributes such as omnipotence, omniscience and so on. The relation between the divine and human free will was also discussed as was the nature of the human soul, and the problem of the relation between divine creation found in the Koran and the Aristotelian teaching of the eternity of the world (Al-Farabi). It is within Islamic philosophy that the discussion of essence and existence emerged, an issue of central importance to Aquinas and Scotus. Avicenna is important for placing emphasis on the necessity of the divine existence which had important consequences for both Aquinas' and Scotus' proofs of the existence of God.

MEDIEVAL JEWISH PHILOSOPHY

Jewish philosophy emerged in the Middle Ages largely in consort with Islamic philosophy.[46] Jewish philosophy did not prosper in Byzantium but, as a protected minority in Islam, Jewish thinkers flourished in Baghdad and Egypt, and later in Andalousia in Southern Spain, writing in Arabic and familiar with both the classical Greek tradition as well as with Islamic philosophy. The growth of Jewish thought was hampered by persecution and the absence of dedicated institutions of learning such as universities. But Jewish translators in Provence and elsewhere played an important role in the transmission of classical texts into Northern Europe. Jewish philosophers included Isaac Israeli (*c*.855–*c*.955), Solomon Ibn Gabirol (1021–*c*.1070), Crescas, Gersonides (1288–1344) and Moses Maimonides. As we have seen, Philo Judaeus, although he may be counted as the first Jewish philosopher, had no direct influence on Jewish thought as such, although he had a considerable influence on the early Christian Fathers including Clement and Origen. The first Jewish philosopher of the Moslem period was Saadia Gaon (882–942), who was born in Egypt and headed the rabbinical academy of Sura near Baghdad. Jewish Neoplatonism is represented by Isaac Ben Israeli and Ibn Gabirol. Isaac Israeli was probably born in Egypt and has left four works, including the *Book of Definitions*, which shows similarities with the work of Al Kindi, and offers a version of Plotinian Neoplatonism where God is identified with the One. Isaac Israeli had an influence on Albertus Magnus. Solomon Ibn Gabirol (1021–51), known as Avicebron in the Latin world, who was born in Malaga and lived mostly in the towns of Andalousia. He wrote religious poetry and his *Fons vitae* (*Fountain of Life*), translated from the now lost Arabic original, circulated primarily among Christians. It was commented on critically by Thomas Aquinas in his *On Spiritual Creatures* (*De spiritualibus creaturis*) and denounced by Albertus Magnus in his *De intellectu de intellgibili* for preaching that the intellect was material. For Aquinas, the main import of the *Fons Vitae*, a work which sought to explain both the unity and diversity of all things, was its advocacy of a doctrine which became known as *universal hylomorphism*, the view that all things are composed of matter and form, and that spiritual creatures therefore possess a 'spiritual matter'.

Moses Maimonides (*c*.1135–1204) is the most important Jewish philosopher of the Middle Ages. He was born in Cordoba, but was forced to move from Andalusia. In 1154 he travelled to Jerusalem and then to Cairo, where he became a court physician. An important interpreter of Aristotle, his *Guide of the Perplexed* is a major summa, written first in Arabic in 1190 and translated into both Hebrew and Latin.[47] Aquinas was deeply influenced by Maimonides's discussions of the existence of God and the nature of the divine attributes. Following Maimonides, Gersonides attempted to refine problems he found in Maimonides's teaching, often making use of Averroes. Hasdai Crescas (*c*.1340–1410) began the critique of Aristotelian ideas. There were Jewish philosophers working in Spain until the expulsion of the Jews in 1492.

THOMAS AQUINAS (*c*.1224–1274) AND
THE NEO-ARISTOTELIAN REVIVAL

Aquinas's philosophy was shaped by the methods of teaching of the newly established universities as well as by his membership of the Dominican Order (founded in 1217). All the great thirteenth century philosophers – Alexander of Hales, Albert the Great, Aquinas, Bonaventure, Roger Bacon, Giles of Rome, Henry of Ghent, Duns Scotus – were all associated with the university of Paris. The University of Paris had received its Charter in 1200 and the first Dominican Chair was established in 1229. The university was a corporation, not unlike a medieval guild. While its main purpose was to produce theologians, it also was a centre for the production and transmission of scientific knowledge. Students like Aquinas first enrolled in the arts faculty and then progressed to theology. University instruction took the form of the reading aloud and exposition of classical texts (*lectio*) and the holding of vigorous debates (*disputatio*) where certain theses were defended or rebutted (e.g. 'that the world does not have a beginning in time'). A prerequisite for the Master's degree in theology involved writing a commentary on the *Sentences* of Peter Lombard. Aquinas not only wrote such a commentary, but also lectured on the *Sentences* in Paris from 1252 to 1256.

Thomas Aquinas wrote during the thirteenth-century revival of the writings of Aristotle in western Europe. Although he was steeped in the Neoplatonism of his teacher Albertus, and was familiar with the writings of Augustine, Boethius, Dionysius the Areopagite, and the *Book of Causes* (*Liber de causis*), his real interest lay in the interpretation of Aristotle and in reconciling his philosophical opinions with the truth as revealed by his Christian faith. Aquinas went to considerable effort to obtain reliable translations of Aristotle. William of Moerbeke helped to supply him with better translations. But in his writing, Aquinas was a radical Aristotelian.

Aquinas was born into a prominent political family in Roccasecca, near Naples. At the age of five, his family placed him in the Benedictine Abbey nearby in Monte Cassino where his uncle was the Abbot. In 1239, at the age of fourteen or fifteen, he entered the arts course at the University of Naples, where, under the tutelage of the Irish-born philosopher, Peter of Ireland (Petrus Hiberniae), he began the study of Aristotle, whose works had resurfaced in the Latin West. In 1244, he joined the newly-founded mendicant order, the Dominicans, against the wishes of his family who kidnapped and forcibly detained him for over a year in the family castle. He eventually persuaded them to release him and he rejoined the Dominican house in Naples. In 1245, his superiors sent him to Paris, where he remained until 1248, possibly studying with Albertus Magnus, known as 'the universal doctor' on account of his immense erudition. In 1248, Albertus was sent to Cologne to establish a Dominican *studium generale* (which, though not a university, became an important intellectual centre) and Thomas may have accompanied him. Certainly he studied with Albertus in Cologne after 1248. Sometime between 1248 and 1252 he was ordained. In 1252, Thomas went back to the University of Paris to continue his graduate study of theology. The Paris theology faculty was hostile to the new mendicant orders, the Franciscans and the Dominicans, and initially refused him his Master's degree, but, after papal intervention, they recanted. From 1256 to 1259 he taught as a Master of Theology at Paris, then he travelled in Italy to Orvieto, Rome, and Viterbo. In 1269, he returned to Paris where he taught until 1272. In 1274 he died in Italy near Naples, where he had been sent to set up a theology faculty at the University of Naples. Isolated statements from his writings were included in a general condemnation of 219 philosophical theses issued by Stephen Tempier, Bishop of Paris, in 1277. The Dominican order, however, adopted many of his works in their teaching and Aquinas's work was rehabilitated in 1324 by the Archbishop of Paris. Subsequently, he has been recognised as one of the foremost Christian philosophers, and, in the nineteenth century, Pope Leo XIII decreed that his works should form the basis of Christian intellectual formation, leading to the development of the Neo-Thomist movement. Central to the Neo-Thomist interpretation is the emphasis on Aquinas as a philosopher of being. God is understood as pure being, *esse purus*, pure act of existence, whose entire essence is realised in existing. All created things participate in being through an act of existing, *actus essendi*, which actualises their potential (but previously non-existent) natures. This distinction between essence and existence, superimposed upon the Aristotelian principles of form and matter, brings about a new metaphysical account of being.

Aquinas wrote commentaries on selected books of the Bible. He wrote important and original philosophical commentaries on Aristotle – twelve commentaries in all – of which the *Metaphysics* and *On the Soul* (*De anima*) are among the most significant. In these commentaries, Aquinas shows considerable knowledge not only of Aristotle, but also of his Muslim commentators, especially Ibn Rushd (Averroes) and also the Jewish philosopher, Moses Maimonides. Thomas himself is always a critical reader who shows his independence of these authorities. For instance, Averroes had interpreted a passage in Aristotle's *De anima* as meaning that there was a single intellect for all humans. Aquinas, on the other hand, defended the view that each human being has an individual intellect, a view which he took to be more in keeping with Christian teaching on the person.

In attempting to reconcile Aristotle with Christian faith, Aquinas also had to face the question as to whether the Aristotelian doctrine of the eternity of the world was compatible with the Biblically-inspired concept of creation from nothing (*creatio ex nihilo*). Aquinas argued that the concept of a creation does not in itself rule out the possibility that the world always existed in time. He argued that the concept of creation required only that the world have a 'total cause' for its being.

Aquinas held many disputations, including on the nature of truth (*De veritate*), on the power of God (*De potentia Dei*), on evil (*De malo*), and on the nature of the soul (*De anima*). Early in his career, he wrote his first purely philosophical treatise, *On Being and Essence* (*De ente et essentia*) which develops concepts found in Aristotle's *Categories*.[48] But his most important works are his two great summaries of philosophy and theology, the *Summa Contra Gentiles* (1259–65)[49] which summarised arguments to convince non-believers to convert to the Christian faith, and the *Summa theologiae* (begun 1266 and unfinished at his death), which addressed in systematic fashion questions concerning the nature of God, creation, human nature and the nature of salvation.

The *Summa theologiae* has a structure which reveals its origins in school discussion. A question is proposed, such as 'does God exist?', and then certain arguments are put forward opposing an affirmative reply (called 'objections'). This is followed by an opposing statement, called a '*sed contra*' ('but on the other hand . . .') which usually quotes an authority who supports an answer contrary to the opposing 'objections'. This is followed by a section where Aquinas articulates his own position, the '*respondeo*' ('I answer') and finally he gives a list of replies to the first set of objections.

Aquinas on the Five Ways

Aquinas's discusses the existence of God in many of his works, beginning with the *Commentary on the Sentences of Peter Lombard*, including the *Summa Contra Gentiles* (hereafter, 'SCG') and *Summa theologiae* (hereafter, 'ST'). The SCG develops two of the arguments at some length, whereas in *Summa Theologiae*, Part 1 Question 2 Article 3 (henceforth ST 1a. 2.3) Aquinas puts forward 'five ways' (Latin: *quinque viae*) to demonstrate the existence of God in an extremely condensed and sketchy fashion.[50] In this chapter we shall focus solely on the First Way. First of all, Aquinas disagrees with Anselm's *a priori* approach to proving the existence of God from the mere examination of what is entailed in the very concept of God. Instead, Thomas' proofs are based largely on his understanding of arguments found in Aristotle's *Physics* and *Metaphysics* and take the existing real world as their starting point (hence Kant called these kinds of arguments 'cosmological'). Aquinas wants to show that events in the real world, such as the existence of change, require causes and that by a chain of argument it can be shown that a first cause must exist. He takes it for granted that this first cause of all is what Christians call 'God'.

The First Way (the proof from movement)

The first argument is called the argument 'from motion' (Latin: *ex motu*) or change, and Aquinas thought this way was more obvious (*manifestior*) than the other ways. Aristotle (especially his *Physics* Book 5. 226a) distinguished between three kinds of change: (a) *locomotion*, i.e. physical change of place (such a stone rolling down hill or water flowing); (b) *change of quantity*, such as a plant growing larger or a leaf shrinking; and (c) *change of quality* which Aristotle calls 'alteration', i.e. a leaf changing colour. All kinds of change are included in Thomas' concept of *motus*.

Aquinas begins by claiming that it is evident to our senses that some things are in a process of change: 'Some things in the world are certainly in process of change: this we plainly see.' Change, as such, is an observable fact. In SCG 1.13 his example is the sun moving: 'That some things are in motion – for example, the sun – is evident from sense' (SCG 1.13.3). Aquinas believes that change requires an explanation – a cause. He next claims everything which is changed is changed by something else: 'Now anything in process of change is being changed by something else.' Aquinas, following Aristotle, believes that, in order for change to take place in the most general terms, something must come to have a characteristic it did not have before, for example, water boiled in a pot goes from cold to hot. Water gains the characteristic or property of 'being hot'. Aquinas says:

> it is a characteristic of things in process of change that they do not yet have the perfection towards which they move, though able to have it; whereas it is a characteristic of something causing change to have that perfection already.

A cause is that which *actually* possesses the characteristic (Aquinas uses the term 'perfection' to mean a property or characteristic) it is about to impart to the thing which will undergo change. Thus a hot ring on a stove is *actually* hot and it imparts heat to the pot which imparts heat to the water in the pot. Before the water becomes *actually* hot we can say that it is *potentially* hot; it is the kind of thing which is *capable* of being hot in the right circumstances. Something can undergo a specific change according to Aristotle and Aquinas, only if its nature is capable of supporting that change.

Aquinas assumes that nothing can change itself, since it would then both actually have the quality or characteristic it wanted to bring about in itself and also not have the quality (since change *means* that a thing gains a property it did not have before). This is impossible; if a wall is actually white it cannot change its colour to white. Aquinas concludes from this that nothing can change itself. Therefore everything which is changed is changed by another. Actually, Thomas Aquinas does acknowledge that some things do move themselves. Following Plato and Aristotle, he thinks

186

of the soul as a self-moving principle. So he could say that the stick is moved by the arm and the arm is moved by the soul but that the soul moves itself. But he finally thinks even self-moving causes require explanations and so posits a first cause. This move has got him into difficulty with some critics.

Aquinas recognises that there is a chain or sequence of changes and hence a chain of causes of change:

> Of necessity therefore anything in process of change is being changed by something else. Moreover this something else, if in process of change, is itself being changed by yet another thing; and this last by another.

Aquinas claims that an infinite chain of causes is impossible and the changing 'must stop somewhere'. For both Aristotle and Aquinas, if there is to be a genuine causal explanation, there must be a first cause. Aquinas takes an example from Aristotle's *Physics* 8.5 256a: a stone is moved by a stick and the stick is moved by a hand, which in turn is moved by a man. In this simple sequence the man is the first mover and without him moving, nothing else would subsequently move. Both Aristotle and Aquinas think that a chain of causes which went on endlessly would not be capable of being sustained, because unless there is a first cause there is no subsequent cause. It belongs to the very meaning of causation, that we explain everything with reference to a first. Aquinas then finds it inconceivable that an infinite series of causes could be possible.

Part of the problem is that there are at least two different ways in which a series could be infinite. The actual example which both Aristotle and Aquinas invoke (the hand moving the stick which moves the stone) illustrates the case of a chain of *simultaneous* movers. In other words there is no temporal succession: each cause acts simultaneously with the next. The hand is in motion at the same time as the stick and the ball. This kind of causation is often referred to as 'vertical': one cause underlies another in a vertical chain. Other kinds of causal chains would have temporal succession, often referred to as 'horizontal' causation. For example, the ancients considered the case of human reproduction, for every son there is a father, so the father causes a son and that son may himself go on (at a later time) to cause a son, and so on. But here not all the causes are simultaneous. Over generations, the earlier causes die off and cease to exist. Aquinas then had to face the problem of how this causal chain could keep going. Could there be an infinite series of fathers, especially since Aristotle taught that the world was eternal?

Muslim philosophers, notably Avicenna, proposed a solution to this problem, a solution which Aquinas adopted in SCG, based on a distinction between accidental (*per accidens*) causation and real or intrinsic (*per se*) causation. The father is the real cause of the son existing in the first place, so the father is said to be the cause of the son *qua* (as) human being. But the father is strictly speaking not the actual cause of the son himself going on to become a father. The father is the *accidental* (*per accidens*) cause of the son's becoming a father in his own right. A cause is *per accidens* when what causes it is not precisely responsible for what it appears in turn to cause the effect to do. Thus for example, if one person (A) is hammering and then passes the hammer to the second person (B), it is merely accidental that A is the cause of B's hammering. Similarly the father is the cause not of the son's ability to bring about another son but rather the father is the cause of the being of the son and only accidentally the cause that the son is himself a father to another son. For Aquinas, the real *per se* cause of the son's becoming a father is God. Therefore no matter whether there is an infinite series of fathers there is still only a finite chain of causation, since God is the first cause required to sustain the chain of causation. Clearly this view of causation is at the heart of Aquinas' proofs and it has been regarded as problematic by many philosophers.

Why does Aquinas hold that an infinite series of causes is impossible? We can easily imagine an infinite chain of causes stretching back endlessly with no first point. As a matter of fact, Aquinas himself was not completely opposed to the view that the world might have existed eternally and that there might always have been change. In ST 1.46.2. 7 he explicitly supposes that the generation of one human from another is endless. He is really arguing that an explanation which stays at the level of causes which themselves have causes (what Aquinas called 'intermediary' causes) is not a genuine explanation. For Aquinas, as for Aristotle, a true explanation must go back to a first cause or first principle. This is discussed in more detail in the *Summa Contra Gentiles*. Aquinas rejected an infinite sequence of causes on the grounds that an explanation that never terminates in a first principle is not an explanation. In the *Nicomachean Ethics*, Aristotle said that if we desired each thing for the sake of the next and this went on endlessly then we could never get started. There must then be something we desire for its own sake, and all other things are desired for the sake of that thing we desire for its own sake. In the *Physics*, Aristotle gives arguments against the possibility of an infinite series of movers or causes. Aquinas concludes that for any change there must be a first principle which causes that change, but which is itself unchanged, and this he says is God. God is the cause of change which is not itself changed. Aquinas says: 'and this is what everyone understands by God'. Hence he concludes that God exists.

Now, there are many problems with this argument. First we have the assumption that anything which changes requires a cause of that change. Why does Aquinas rule out random or accidental change? It might be that things start causing one another after a while but that the initial situation was one of mere chance occurrence. Second, we have the assumption that a chain of causes cannot go on *ad infinitum*, this assumption has been seen as untenable. Third, we have the assumption that all the causes go back to a single first cause. Why could there not be a whole host of different types of first causes? That which causes the physical material world to exist, need not be the same cause as that which produced living beings. Aquinas just assumes all chains of causation will dovetail back to a single starting point, but this assumption is not supported by argument. Finally, many people might not accept that this first cause is God. After all, a huge cosmic explosion or 'big bang' might be the cause of everything which subsequently exists in the universe, this does not mean that that first explosion is God.

A more grievous problem, which has been pointed out by Anthony Kenny,[51] is that Aquinas's argument depends on an analysis of causation which goes back to Aristotle. According to this analysis, it belongs to the meaning of the concept of cause that a cause will actually possess the property that it will impart to the effect. Thus fire must actually be hot to cause the stick which is put in the fire to become hot; but modern science has rejected this analysis of causation. The grain which makes a cow fat is not itself fat; microwaves can generate heat without themselves being hot and so on. Aquinas, according to Kenny, is not giving a straight-forward metaphysical analysis, but rather is giving an analysis which presumes a classical and discredited physics. His argument, therefore, does not stand alone but rather presupposes a whole world view.

THE LATER THIRTEENTH CENTURY AND THE RISE OF THE SCHOOLS

Late in the thirteenth century, especially at the University of Paris, philosophers began to organise into schools. In fact, the existence and uniformity of these schools has been challenged, but it is certainly the case, that the Franciscan and Dominican Orders which now controlled Chairs of theology, tended to have their own traditions of instruction and followed their own masters. Thus the Dominicans followed St Thomas whereas Duns Scotus and Bonaventure were the masters for the Franciscans. But one should not exaggerate this tendency; William of Ockham for instance was a severe critic both of Thomas and of Duns Scotus. Besides Paris, new centres of learning were developing, notably at Oxford and Bologna. Oxford especially produced Robert Grosseteste (1170–1253) who became Chancellor of the University. Born in Suffolk, he translated and commented on the books of Aristotle, but his own theological interests were Augustinian and Neoplatonic. He wrote an important work, *De luce*,[52] which makes light to be both the metaphysical and physical first principle of the cosmos – light is the first form of all things.

JOHN DUNS SCOTUS (c.1266–1308)

Little is known of the life of Scottish philosopher and Franciscan priest, John Duns Scotus, except that he achieved considerable renown as a teacher and commentator in the course of a short life, becoming known as 'the subtle doctor'. He entered Oxford probably in 1288 to study theology, and was ordained a priest in 1291. He was active in Oxford in 1300 as a bachelor in theology giving lectures on the *Sentences* of Peter Lombard and participating in disputes. He then went to the University of Paris in 1302 where he began new commentaries on the *Sentences*, but the following year was expelled from France, caught up in a dispute between the King and the Pope over the taxation of Church property. He may have spent time in Oxford or Cambridge, but he returned again in 1304 to Paris, when he was recommended for the Franciscan Chair of Theology. But within a few years, for unknown reasons, he was removed from the Chair and sent as lecturer to the Franciscan convent in Cologne, where he died in 1308. In his short life he attracted many disciples, and wrote a great many works, most of which were still being revised when he died. Many of his writings are in reaction to the works of Henry of Ghent (*c.*1240–93), the most important Paris master of his time.

Scotus' philosophical writings include discussions on Porphyry and on Aristotle's logical works, a lengthy set of questions, much revised, discussing Aristotle's *Metaphysics* (only books I–IX are authentic), and a short discussion of questions on Aristotle's *De anima*. His theological writings include various commentaries on the *Sentences* (including the *Ordinatio*, the *Lectura*; and the *Reportatio parisiensis*, recent scholarship is sorting out the various versions and editions) two sets of theological disputations, *Quaestiones quodlibetales* (Quodlibetal Questions), written at Paris and the *Collationes* (*Collations*), and two treatises, *De primo principio* (*On the First Principle*),[53] a lengthy proof of the existence of God, and *Theoremata* (whose authorship has been questioned).

It is impossible to summarise Scotus' philosophy. He wrote on metaphysics, on the nature of being, God, the transcendentals, on freedom of the will, and on many other issues. In metaphysics, he championed the univocity against the more standard analogical understanding of being. That is to say, Aquinas, Henry of Ghent and others followed Aristotle in holding that the meaning of being changes depending on the kind of thing of which it is predicated. God and creatures both have being but in different ways. Nevertheless, there is a relation or proportion or analogy between the manner in which God has being and that in which creatures have being. Scotus opposed this arguing for the *univocity* of being, that it has the same meaning for God and for creatures. Scotus' argument for the existence of God is the most complex of medieval arguments and has attracted a huge secondary literature. Scotus argues for the 'triple primacy' of God – as efficient and final cause and as most eminent of beings. Scotus is also known for his subtle discussion of the principle of individuation. He defends the need for a principle of individuation, whereby essences which in themselves are neither universal nor particular are instantiated through a specific principle which gives them their individuality of 'thisness' (*haecceitas*). His realist position on universals would be attacked by Ockham. Indeed, Scotus was the most quoted figure in fourteenth century Scholastic philosophy.

WILLIAM OF OCKHAM AND NOMINALISM

The growth of nominalism and of an interest in science is associated with the Merton School of Franciscans at Oxford. The so called 'problem of universals' first arose in relation to the interpretation of Aristotle's *Categories* and especially a commentary, the *Isagoge* or Introduction, written on that work by Porphyry, which was translated into Latin by Boethius. In the *Categories* Aristotle has claimed that a substance could be an individual entity, e.g. this man, but also that the general or universal term 'man' also indicated a substance. This raised the question as to whether universals were as real as individuals. A debate about realism and nominalism erupted in the ninth century and again in the twelfth century with the writings of Abelard, it continued through the fourteenth century and can rightly be seen to be a major theme of medieval philosophy.[54]

William of Ockham (c.1285–1347)

William was probably born in Ockham, a village in Surrey and probably entered the Franciscan order as a child. He would have followed the Franciscan plan of instruction, probably in London, where he was ordained. He also studied in Oxford where he completed his baccalaureate and between 1317 and 1319 lectured on Peter Lombard's *Sentences*, on which he wrote at least four commentaries. He also produced commentaries on Aristotle's logical works, probably while teaching in the Dominican *studium generale* in London and he may have begun his *Summa Logicae* around that time. However, he never became a Master and in 1324 he was investigated for heresy, an accusation made against him by a provincial in his own order who referred the case to the Pope then in Avignon. Ockham spent several years at Avignon before being forced to flee, together with the Franciscan General who supported him, Michael of Cesena in 1328. He took refuge in Munich under the protection of Louis of Bavaria where he spent the rest of his life writing theological and political tracts.

Ockham is best known for his reductionist metaphysics which rejected the Platonic reality of universals and sought to reduce ontological commitment. For Ockham, as he puts it in his *Commentary on the Sentences*, 'plurality is not to be posited without necessity', a saying which probably gave rise to the formulation usually associated with him, namely 'Ockham's razor': 'entities are not to be multiplied beyond necessity'. Ockham maintained that only singulars actually exist, and he denied the reality of all the Aristotelian categories except for substance and quality. There are strictly speaking no 'actions' although things act. Moreover, there are only singular substances or qualities, an individual white thing not 'whiteness' exists. He is opposed to the hypostatisation of qualities into universal entities. He offers a semantic theory for treating universals which does not give them ontological status. Universals are concepts, ways of speaking about things.

MEISTER ECKHART OF HOCHHEIM (1260–1327)

Eckhart is important as someone who was educated in the tradition of Paris philosophy but also went on to speak and write in the vernacular, in his local German, and some of his key concepts – detachment (*Abgeschiedenheit*) and releasement or 'letting be' (*Gelassenheit*) were first formulated in his Middle High German in sermons he gave mostly to convents of nuns. He was born probably around 1260 and joined the Dominican priory in Erfurt at the age of 15. By 1294 he was in Paris commenting on the *Sentences* of Peter Lombard meaning that he had already secured his Arts Degree at this time. At some point he left Paris to become Prior of the Dominican house at Erfurt, where he probably wrote his first surviving German work *Talks of Instruction*. In 1302 he returned to Paris to take up the Dominican Chair in Theology, previously held by St Thomas Aquinas (the other Chair of Theology was reserved for a Franciscan). Few works (aside from some *Questions*)[55] survive from this time although he probably wrote his Latin commentaries on Scripture at this stage. A year later, he was made Provincial of the new Dominican province of Saxonia, a post he held until 1311, when he returned to Paris to take up his Chair again. He held this post for two years during which he probably wrote his scriptural commentaries. However, he was moved again, this time to Strasburg, where he served as Vice-General with the responsibility of overseeing women's convents – including many Beguine communities. It was here that he wrote the *Liber Benedictus*. In 1323 he arrived in Cologne probably as Head of the Dominican *studium generale* there (founded by Albertus in 1248). In 1325 there was an investigation into his work by the theologian Nicholas of Strasburg, his junior in the Dominican Order, and it was found to be orthodox (this may have been an attempt to stave off a full inquisition). Nevertheless, the Franciscan Bishop of

Cologne ordered an inquisition into Eckhart's writings in 1326, and he was charged with heresy. Eckhart was the only Dominican ever to appear before the Inquisition. He responded to his accusations, arguing that he might be in error, but could not be a heretic, because he lacked the will. His case was referred to the Pope John XXII (then at Avignon and who was also reviewing the case of Ockham). Eckhart set out with some other Dominicans to walk to Avignon in 1327 to present his own case, but he died in Avignon probably in the winter of 1327/8. On 27th March 1329 the Papal Bill, *In Agro Dominico* (In the fields of the Lord) listed 28 articles, 17 which were said to be heretical and 11 of which sounded evil and gave rise to the suspicion of heresy.

A Dominican, Eckhart was influenced by Dominican thinkers such as Albertus Magnus, Thomas Aquinas, Ulrich of Strasburg (*c.*1220–77) and Dietrich of Freiburg (1250–*c.*1320), a tradition that stressed the importance of intellect. In his treatise *On the Intellect and the Intelligible*, Albertus had written: 'human beings, precisely as human, are essentially intellect'.[56] Both God and the soul are thought to be intellectual by nature and to be pure intellects, and it is in this respect that the human mind is the image of God (an important medieval theme). Intellect here means something like consciousness or awareness or grasp or understanding. And the highest form of intellection is considered to be self-knowledge.

Eckhart was also influenced by Augustine, Proclus, Avicenna and Maimonides. He belongs to the mystic tradition of Pseudo-Dionysius, Eriugena, Albertus, the author of the *Cloud of Unknowing*, Teresa of Avila, and John of the Cross. Following the Neoplatonic tradition, Eckhart emphasises God's unity and simplicity – likened to a 'desert' due its complete absence of features. God is not in any place, not 'here or there'. We only know what God is not and for that reason he says, quoting Augustine, 'all Scripture is vain'. Meister Eckhart has the strong conviction that we are blocked from appreciating the extraordinary transcendent and immanent nature of God by our limitations. This is why he prays: 'I pray God to rid me of God'.

Following Augustine, Eckhart claims that we must discover God within ourselves: 'I do not find God outside myself'. The metaphysical justification is Neoplatonic. For Eckhart, the soul in some sense remains a part of God or God remains in the soul; God is said to be the 'ground of the soul'. Eckhart's first principle is always this extraordinary transcendent goodness and grace of God, but he immediately adds to this principle the wondrous claim that the human soul has an equally high-ranking noble origin and dignified nature – an intrinsic nobility, which means that deep within each of us there is a perfect reflection of the divine purity; in Eckhart's terms: a 'little spark' in the soul, an 'interior castle', a 'nobleman'. The assertion that the human soul carries something divine within it – something 'uncreated' as Eckhart would often say – led to a suspicion that Eckhart was elevating human nature to the same level as God, and these accusations feature in his condemnation.

As with Eriugena, the act of God's creation is said to be timeless and eternal. There is a special event of understanding which he calls 'the birth of the Son in us'. According to Augustine, whom Eckhart quotes, this birth is always happening in us, it is an eternal birth. In an important sermon, number 53 in the critical edition of Joseph Quint, a sermon which dwells on the Scriptual text: *Misit dominus manum suam*, Eckhart focuses on detachment as one of the central themes of his preaching:

> When I preach, I am accustomed to speak about detachment, and that a man should be free of himself and of all things; second, that a man should be formed again into that simple good which is God; third, that he should reflect on the great nobility with which God has endowed his soul, so that in this way he may come to wonder at God; fourth, about the purity of the divine nature, for the brightness of the divine nature is beyond words. God is a word, a word unspoken.[57]

God is, in Eckhart's compelling image, 'an unspoken word', and hence all speaking must somehow be in vain.

NICHOLAS OF CUSA (1401–1464)

Nicholas of Cusa ('Cusanus') is an extraordinary figure. A reforming Catholic, eventually Cardinal, who participated in Councils of the Church and acted as a papal emissary, he was a scholar and book collector, a mathematician and scientist. Mostly self-taught in philosophy, and writing when nominalism was in the ascendancy, he wrote original works of Neoplatonic Christian mysticism, emphasising the infinity, transcendence, and unknowability of the divine. God is the 'Absolute Maximum', the 'coincidence of opposites' (*coincidentia oppositorum*), the 'not other' (*non aliud*), the unity of being (*esse*) and possibility (*posse*), for which Cusanus coins the term *possest*. Cusanus was an eager collector of manuscripts.[58] His eclectic reading and avid interest in new topics marks him out as a Renaissance man, indeed, he was known to the Italian Humanists who were his contemporaries. In his mathematical speculations he has been seen as a forerunner of the seventeenth-century Scientific Revolution.

Born in Cues, on the Moselle river east of Trier, Germany, in 1400–1, he may have studied at Deventer, founded in 1379 by Gerhard Groote, and run by the Brothers of the Common Life.[59] In 1416 he entered the University of Heidelberg, then a centre for nominalism and conciliarism, and then went to Padua, famous for law, medicine, mathematics and science, in 1417, where he received his doctorate in law in 1423. In 1425 he entered the University of Cologne, where the dominant tradition came from Albertus Magnus and there were vigorous disputes between the Albertists, Thomists and nominalists. As a secretary to a German Bishop, he participated in the Council of Basel (1431–37) and in 1434 wrote *De Concordantia Catholica* which included proposals for the reform of Church and state and is an important Conciliarist document. Later he shifted to the papal side. In 1437 he travelled to Constantinople to invite the Byzantine church to a council, while there he met the Emperor, and acquired the *Theologia Platonica* of Proclus. On his journey back to Venice he had a vision which inspired the treatise, *De docta ignorantia* (*On Learned Ignorance*, 1440, hereafter 'DI'), a work in which he developed the Augustinian view that God is better known by not knowing, by arguing for a kind of knowledge which recognises the contradictions of thinking about the divine and resolves them by considering God as the 'coincidence of opposites'.[60] Cusanus simply begins by characterising God as *maximum absolutum*, 'all that which can be' (*omne id quod esse potest*, DI I.iv.11). He is actually everything which is possible (DI I.xiii.14). God or the 'Godhead' (*deitas*) is 'infinite oneness' (*unitas infinita*, DI I.xiii.14). As such God is 'incomprehensible', because our minds must use oppositions and these do not apply to God. The maximum is 'incomprehensibly understandable and unnameably nameable' (DI I.v.13). God is 'beyond all opposition' and 'free of all opposition' (I.iv.12).

In 1444 he wrote his first dialogue, *De Deo abscondito* (*On the Hidden God*). In 1450 Cusanus went to Rome where he wrote *Idiota. De sapientia et de mente* (*The Layman on Wisdom and the Mind*, 1450),[61] and several mathematical works (including one on squaring the circle). In 1453 he wrote *De visione Dei* (*On the Vision of God*). In 1452 he became bishop in Brixen, where he enforced reforms but got caught up in local battles. In 1459 he returned to Rome, where he was held prisoner for a time by some of his Brixen enemies. After his release, he withdrew from politics. In his last years, he wrote the important works *Trialogus de possest* (1460)[62] and *De li non aliud* (1462), where he argues that God is 'not other'.[63] In 1464 he died in Todi. Cusanus' specific originality consists in his use of nominalist claims about God's infinite and unlimited power, combined with the Scholastic claim that God is pure being (*esse*) and pure actuality (*actus purus*), to make the claim that God is the infinite actualisation of all possibilities, and hence reconciles all oppositions and indeed in beyond all oppositions. Cusanus takes these themes from Proclus, Dionysius, Eriugena, Albert and Ecklhart, but wraps them in the language of late Scholasticism and presents them with scientific and mathematical embellishments. His writings break the form of Scholasticism and point towards the new philosophy of Descartes.

EXERCISES

1 Medieval philosophy has been characterised as 'faith seeking understanding'. Discuss.
2 The Platonic tradition prepared the way for Christianity since it held similar views on the nature of God, creation, the soul and the body. Discuss.
3 Explain and discuss Eriugena's fourfold division of nature. Does it amount to pantheism?
4 Outline critically one of Anselm's arguments for the existence of God.
5 Discuss the merits and defects of St Thomas Aquinas' First Way for demonstrating the existence of God.
6 Write an essay on the impact of the Aristotelian revival on Christian philosophy in the thirteenth century.
7 Write an essay on the conception of the divine in Meister Eckhart and Nicholas of Cusa.

NOTES

1 It has even been questioned whether it makes sense to speak of 'Christian philosophy' or 'medieval philosophy'. The very sense of philosophy has to be considered in discussing medieval authors.
2 For an account of this encyclical in relation to the debate over Christian philosophy, see Joseph Owens, *Towards a Christian Philosophy* (Washington, DC: Catholic University of America Press, 1990), esp. pp. 63–75.
3 It is difficult to set a precise date on the break-up of the Roman Empire; various dates are significant, e.g. the sack of Rome by Alaric the Visigoth, which took place in 410 and prompted Augustine to begin the *City of God*; or, 524 – the execution of Boethius, the last great Roman senator and intellectual, who was working in a Roman Empire governed by the Ostrogoth Theoderic; or, 529 – the date of Emperor Justinian's decree to close the pagan Platonic Academy at Athens.
4 For further information on this period see A. Armstrong (ed.), *The Cambridge History of Later Greek and Early Medieval Philosophy* (Cambridge: Cambridge University Press, 1967) and John Marenbon, *Early Medieval Philosophy 480–1150* (London: Routledge, 1983).
5 See A. Kenny, N. Kretzmann and J. Pinborg (eds), *The Cambridge History of Later Medieval Philosophy* (Cambridge: Cambridge University Press, 1982).
6 See, for instance, P. Dronke (ed.), *A History of Twelfth Century Philosophy* (Cambridge: Cambridge University Press, 1988) and Alain de Libera, *La Mystique Rhénane. D'Albert à Maître Eckhart* (Paris: Seuil, 1994).
7 See P. Abelard, *Dialogus inter philosophum, Iudaeum et Christianum*, ed. R. Thomas (Stuttgart: Fromann, 1970), trans. P.J. Payer, *Dialogue of a Philosopher with a Jew and a Christian* (Toronto: Pontifical Institute of Medieval Studies, 1979).
8 See Jasper Hopkins, *Nicholas of Cusa's De pace fidei and Cribratio Alkorani* (Minneapolis: The Arthur J. Banning Press, 1990). In the *Cribratio*, written after the fall of Constantinople, Nicholas traces the errors of Islam to the Nestorian heresy.
9 Alain de Libera, *La Philosophie médiévale* (Paris: Presses Universitaires de France, 1993), p. 367.

10 See Raymond Klibansky, *The Continuity of the Platonic Tradition during the Middle Ages* (London and Millwood, NY: The Warburg Institute and Kraus International Publications, 1982) and Stephen Gersh, *Middle Platonism and Neoplatonism: The Latin Tradition*, 2 Vols (Notre Dame, Indiana: Indiana University Press, 1986).

11 See A.O. Lovejoy, *The Great Chain of Being* (Cambridge, MA: Harvard University Press, 1976).

12 Anselm, *Monologion*, ch. 4, in J. Hopkins, *A New Interpretive Translation of St Anselm's Monologion and Proslogion* (Minneapolis: The Arthur J. Banning Press, 1986), p. 67.

13 See E. Gilson, *Reason and Revelation in the Middle Ages* (New York: Charles Scribner's Sons, 1938).

14 See E. Gilson, *Reason and Revelation in the Middle Ages*, op. cit., p. 9.

15 Augustine, *Of True Religion*, trans. J.H.S. Burleigh (South Bend, Indiana: Gateway Editions, 1959).

16 St Augustine, *Confessions*, trans. R.S. Pine-Coffin (London: Penguin, 1961), p. 154.

17 Augustine, *On Christian Doctrine*, trans. D.W. Robertson (Indianapolis: Bobbs-Merrill, 1958), p. 75.

18 Scholars now deny that Siger and Boethius actually taught the doctrine of two truths. The source of this accusation is Ernst Renan, *Averroès et l'Averroisme* (Paris: Durand, 1852). For a more critical view, see Alain de Libera, *Averroès et l'Averroisme. Que sais-je* (Paris: Presses Universitaires de France, 1991).

19 See Henri de Lubac, *Exégèse médiévale. Les quatres sens de l'écriture* (Paris: Editions Montaigne, 1959).

20 See St Augustine, *The Literal Meaning of Genesis*, trans. J.H. Taylor,. 2 Vols (New York: Newman, 1982).

21 See D.T. Runia, *Philo of Alexandria and the Timaeus of Plato* (Leiden: Brill, 1986).

22 '*Apologia*' meant a formal statement made before a judge on behalf of a defendant. See E. Gilson, *History of Christian Philosophy in the Middle Ages* (London: Sheed & Ward, 1955), p. 9.

23 On Justin Martyr, see Gilson, *History of Christian Philosophy*, op. cit., pp. 11–14; see also H. Chadwick, 'The Beginnings of Christian Philosophy: Justin: the Gnostics', in A.H. Armstrong (ed.), *The Cambridge History of Later Greek and Early Medieval Philosophy*, op. cit., pp. 158–67.

24 Origen, *On First Principles*, trans. G.W. Butterworth, introduction by Henri de Lubac (New York: Harper Torchbooks, 1966).

25 Although women were quite prominent in Greek and Roman life, and included many prominent Christians, they had no detectable influence on early medieval philosophy, until the twelfth century when we meet a figure such as Heloise. Augustine had serious intellectual conversations with his mother and both he and Jerome were in correspondence with prominent Christian women regarding theological and spiritual matters, but there is a general absence of women from Patristic philosophy. Indeed, one of the great pagan women philosophers – Hypatia – was murdered by a Christian mob incited by St Cyril.

26 See E.R. Dodds, *Pagan and Christian in an Age of Anxiety: Some Aspects of Religious Experience, from Marcus Aurelius to Constantine* (Cambridge: Cambridge University Press, 1965).

27 It was banned by a number of edicts of Christian emperors beginning with Constantine. See Andrew Smyth, 'The Pagan Neo-Platonists' Response to Christianity', *Maynooth Review* **14** (December 1989): 25–41.

28 Iamblichus, *On the Mysteries*, trans. T. Taylor (London, 1821, reprinted Hastings: Chthonios Books, 1989).

29 Proclus, *The Elements of Theology*, trans. E.R. Dodds, 2nd edn (Oxford: Clarendon, 1963).

30 See *The Book of Causes*, trans. from the Latin by Dennis J. Brand, 2nd edn (Milwaukee: Marquette University Press, 1984). The anonymous author probably worked in Baghdad in the ninth or tenth centuries. An alternative candidate for authorship is Ibn Daoud, a twelfth century Spanish Jew. Aquinas, following his contact with William of Moerbeke's translation of Proclus' *Elements of Theology* (completed 1268), recognised that the *Liber de causis* could not be an Aristotelian text and refers to its author as 'one of the Arab philosophers'. In fact, one of Aquinas' last works is his commentary on the *Liber de causis* (1272), see St Thomas Aquinas, *Commentary on the Book of Causes*, trans. Vincent A. Guagliardo, Charles Hess and Richard Taylor (Washington, DC: Catholic University of America Press, 1996).

31 See Pseudo-Dionysius, *The Complete Works*, trans. Colm Luibheid and Paul Rorem (London: Paulist Press, 1987).

32 Augustine, *The City of God Against the Pagans*, ed. and trans. R.W. Dyson (Cambridge: Cambridge University Press, 1998), pp. 318–19.

33 Augustine, *Retractions*, trans. M.I. Bogan, Fathers of the Church Vol. 60 (Washington, DC: Catholic University of America Press, 1968).

34 See Boethius, *The Theological Tractates and the Consolation of Philosophy*, ed. H.F. Stewart and E.K. Rand (Cambridge: Loeb Library, 1918).

35 See Boethius, *The Consolation of Philosophy*, trans. Richard Green (Indianapolis: Bobbs-Merrill, 1962).

36 Plato, *Timaeus* [Chalcidius' Latin translation], ed. J. Waszink (Leiden: Brill, 1975).

37 See Dermot Moran, *The Philosophy of John Scottus Eriugena: A Study of Idealism in the Middle Ages* (Cambridge: Cambridge University Press, 1989).

38 See I.P. Sheldon-Williams and J.J. O'Meara (eds), *Eriugena: Periphyseon (The Division of Nature)* (Montreal/Paris: Bellarmin, 1987).

39 A translation of the Monologion is to be found in S.N. Deane, *Saint Anselm: Basic Writings* (La Salle, Illinois: Open Court, 1962), pp. 35–144 and also in Jasper Hopkins, *A New Interpretive Translation of St Anselm's Monologion and Proslogion* (Minneapolis: The Arthur J. Banning Press, 1986), pp. 47–212.

40 M.J. Charlesworth, *St Anselm's Proslogion* (Notre Dame: University of Notre Dame Press, 1979).

41 It is noteworthy that his invoking a figure from the Psalms as public expressions of atheism or agnosticism would have been extremely dangerous in medieval times.

42 William of Conches, *A Dialogue on Natural Philosophy (Dragmaticon Philosophiae)*. Italo Ronaca and Matthew Curr (eds and trans.) (Chicago, University of Notre Dame Press, 1997). This passage is translated in P. Dronke (ed.), *A History of Twelfth Century Philosophy*, op. cit., p. 309.

43 See John Marenbon, *The Philosophy of Peter Abelard* (Cambridge: Cambridge University Press, 1997).

44 See S. Nasr and O. Leaman (eds), *History of Islamic Philosophy* (London: Routledge, 1996).

45 On Ibn Roshd see Dominique Urvoy, *Ibn Roshd (Averroes)* (London: Routledge, 1991).

46 See Isaac Husik, *A History of Medieval Jewish Philosophy* (New York: Athaneum, 1976).

47 See Moses Maimonides, *The Guide for the Perplexed*, trans. from the original Arabic by M. Friedlaender, 2nd edn (New York: Dover, 1956).

48 *On Being and Essence* is translated in Robert Goodwin (ed.), *Selected Writings of St Thomas Aquinas* (Indianapolis: Bobbs-Merrill, 1965), pp. 33–67.

49 St Thomas Aquinas, *Summa Contra Gentiles*, trans. Anton C. Pegis, 4 Vols (Notre Dame: University of Notre Dame Press, 1975).

50 Thomas Aquinas, *Summa Theologiae Volume One. The Existence of God: Part One Questions 1–13*, ed. Thomas Gilby O.P. (New York: Doubleday, 1969).

51 A. Kenny, *The Five Ways* (Notre Dame, Indiana: University of Notre Dame Press, 1980).

52 See R. Grosseteste, *On Light*, trans. C.R. Riedl (Milwaukee: Marquette, 1942).

53 John Duns Scotus, *A Treatise on God as First Principle*, trans. A.B. Wolter, 2nd edn (Chicago: Franciscan Herald Press, 1983).

54 See Paul Vincent Spade (ed.), *Five Texts on the Medieval Problem of Universals: Porphyry, Boethius, Abelard, Duns Scotus, Ockham* (Indianapolis: Hackett, 1994)

55 See the first two sets of questions (on the divine existence and understanding) in Meister Eckhart, *Parisian Questions and Prologues*, trans. Armand A. Maurer (Toronto: Pontifical Institute of Medieval Studies, 1974).

56 S. Tugwell, *Albert and Thomas: Selected Writings* (New York: Paulist Press, 1988), p. 59.

57 E. Colledge and B. McGinn (eds), *Meister Eckhart: The Essential Sermons, Commentaries, Treatises and Defence* (New York: Paulist Press, 1981), p. 203.

58 Nicholas' collection included Plato (*Phaedo, Crito, Apology, Republic, Laws, Parmenides and Seventh Letter*), Origen, Tertullian, Augustine, Ambrose, Calcidius's *Commentary on the Timaeus*, the *liber de causis*, part of Eriugena's *Periphyseon*, Avicenna's metaphysics, Albertus Magnus, Bonaventure's *Commentary on the Sentences*, Henry of Ghent's *Quodlibeta Theologica*, Moerbeke's translations of Proclus' *Elements of Theology* and *Commentary on the Parmenides*, as well as Grosseteste's translations of Dionysius's *Mystical Theology* and *Celestial Hierarchy*, and several works by Eckhart.

59 E. Van Steenberghe, *Le Cardinal Nicolas de Cues* (Paris, 1920), pp. 6–7. Thomas à Kempis lived at Deventer and later Erasmus went to school there.

60 J. Hopkins, *Nicholas of Cusa on Learned Ignorance: A Translation and Appraisal of De docta ignorantia* (Minneapolis: Arthur J. Banning Press, 3rd corrected edition, 1987).

61 Nicholas of Cusa, *The Layman on Wisdom and the Mind*, trans. M.L. Fuehrer (Toronto: Doverhouse Editions, 1989).

62 *De possest* is translated in J. Hopkins, *A Concise Introduction to the Philosophy of Nicholas of Cusa* (Minneapolis: University of Minnesota Press, 1980), as 'On Actualized-Possibility'.

63 J. Hopkins, *Nicholas of Cusa on God as Not-Other: A Translation and Appraisal of De Li Non Aliud* (Minneapolis: Banning Press, 1983).

FURTHER READING

Students who wish to gain an understanding of the philosophy of the Middle Ages should read at least one general survey of the period. It is also worth reading the entries for individual medieval philosophers in the *Routledge Encyclopedia of Philosophy*, 10 vols., ed. E. Craig (London: Routledge, 1998). They should also have a basic familiarity with the *Categories* of Aristotle, the *Timaeus* of Plato, and the main tenets of Neoplatonism. Augustine's *Confessions* is certainly worth reading to understand Augustine's early sense of the relationship between Christianity and Neoplatonism, while Book Eleven gives Augustine's famous meditation on the nature of time. Similarly, Boethius's

Consolation of Philosophy, especially Book Five, is a useful introduction to the problem of divine foreknowledge. Students should then read selections from Eriugena, Anselm, and Abelard, before studying the rise of Aristotle. The thirteenth century sees an explosion of authors but most courses concentrate on Aquinas with some reference to Scotus and Ockham.

General Surveys of Medieval Philosophy

Armstrong, A.H. (ed.) (1970) *The Cambridge History of Later Greek and Early Medieval Philosophy*, Cambridge: Cambridge University Press.

Copleston, F.C. (1972) *Medieval Philosophy*, London and New York: Methuen.

Copleston, F.C. (1983) *A History of Philosophy*, Volume II, *Augustine to Scotus* and Volume III, *Ockham to Suárez*, London and New York: Search Press and Paulist Press.

Gilson, Etienne (1955) *History of Christian Philosophy in the Middle Ages*, London: Sheed & Ward.

Gilson, Etienne (1966) *Reason and Revelation in the Middle Ages*, New York: Charles Scribners' Sons.

Haren, Michael (1992) *Medieval Thought: The Western Intellectual Tradition from Antiquity to the Thirteenth Century*, 2nd edn, London: Macmillan.

Kenny, Anthony, Norman Kretzmann and Jan Pinborg (eds) (1982) *The Cambridge History of Later Medieval Philosophy*, Cambridge: Cambridge University Press.

Knowles, David (1991) *The Evolution of Medieval Thought*, 2nd edn, London: Longman.

Luscombe, David (1997) *Medieval Thought*, Oxford: Oxford University Press.

Marenbon, John (1983) *Early Medieval Philosophy (480–1150)*, London: Routledge.

Marenbon, John (1987) *Later Medieval Philosophy (1150–1350)*, London: Routledqe.

Marenbon, John (ed.) (1998) *Medieval Philosophy*, Routledge History of Philosophy, Vol. 3, London: Routledge.

Price, B.B. (1992) *Medieval Thought: An Introduction*, Oxford: Basil Blackwell.

Wippel, John F. and Wolter, A.B. (eds) (1969) *Medieval Philosophy: From St Augustine to Nicholas of Cusa*, New York: Free Press.

The Platonic and Neoplatonic Background

O'Brien, Elmer (ed.) (1964) *The Essential Plotinus*, Indianapolis: Hackett.

Dillon, John (1977) *The Middle Platonists*, Ithaca, NY: Cornell University Press.

Gersh, Stephen (1986) *Middle Platonism and Neoplatonism: The Latin Tradition*, 2 Vols, Notre Dame, Indiana: Indiana University Press.

Gersh, Stephen (1987) *From Iamblichus to Eriugena*, Leiden: Brill.

Gerson, Lloyd (1994) *Plotinus*, London: Routledge.

Gerson, Lloyd (1996) *The Cambridge Companion to Plotinus*, Cambridge: Cambridge University Press.

St Augustine of Hippo

Augustine of Hippo (1984) *Selected Writings*, trans. Mary T. Clark, New York: Paulist Press.
Gilson, Etienne (1960) *The Philosophy of St Augustine*, New York: Random House.
Kirwan, Christopher (1989) *Augustine*, London: Routledge.

Boethius

Chadwick, Henry (1981) *Boethius: The Consolations of Music, Logic, Theology and Philosophy*, Oxford: Clarendon Press.
Gibson, Margaret (ed.) (1981) *Boethius: His Life, Thought and Influence*, Oxford: Oxford University Press.

Dionysius the Areopagite

Louth, Andrew (1989) *Denys the Areopagite*, London: Geoffrey Chapman.

John Scottus Eriugena

Carabine, Deirdre (2000) *John Scottus Eriugena*, Oxford: Oxford University Press.
Moran, D. (1989) *The Philosophy of John Scottus Eriugena: A Study of Idealism in the Middle Ages*, Cambridge: Cambridge University Press.

St Anselm of Canterbury

Henry, Desmond (1967) *The Logic of Anselm*, Oxford: Clarendon Press.
Hopkins, J.M. (1972) *A Companion to the Study of St Anselm*, Minneapolis: Minnosota University Press.
Southern, R.W. (1990) *Saint Anselm: A Portrait in a Landscape*, Cambridge: Cambridge University Press.

Twelfth-century philosophy

Dronke, Peter (ed.) (1988) *A History of Twelfth Century Philosophy*, Cambridge: Cambridge University Press.
Marenbon, John (1997) *The Philosophy of Peter Abelard*, Cambridge: Cambridge University Press.

Islamic and Jewish philosophy

Fakhry, M. (1990) *A History of Islamic Philosophy*, 2nd edn, New York: Columbia University Press.
Husik, Isaac (1976) *A History of Medieval Jewish Philosophy*, New York: Athaneum.
Leaman, O. (1997) *Moses Maimonides*, London: RoutledgeCurzon.
Nasr, S. and Leaman, O. (eds) (1996) *History of Islamic Philosophy*, London: Routledge.
Urvoy, Dominique (1991) *Ibn Roshd (Averroes)*, London: Routledge.

St Thomas Aquinas

Thomas Aquinas (1998) *Selected Writings*, ed. Ralph McInerny, London: Penguin.
Clark, Mary T. (ed.) (1992) *An Aquinas Reader*, New York: Fordham University Press.
Goodwin, Robert (ed.) (1965) *Selected Writings of St Thomas Aquinas*, Indianapolis: Bobbs-Merrill.
Kenny, Anthony (1980) *The Five Ways*, Notre Dame, IN: University of Notre Dame Press.
Kenny, Anthony (1980) *Aquinas*, Oxford: Oxford University Press.
Kenny, Anthony (1976) *Aquinas: A Collection of Critical Essays*, Notre Dame, IN: University of Notre Dame Press.
Kretzmann, Norman and Stump, Eleonore (eds) (1993) *The Cambridge Companion to Aquinas*, Cambridge: Cambridge University Press.
Kretzmann, Norman (1996) *The Metaphysics of Theism: Aquinas' Natural Theology in Summa Contra Gentiles I*, Oxford: Oxford University Press.
McInerny, Ralph (1982) *St Thomas Aquinas*, Notre Dame, IN: University of Notre Dame Press.
Wippel, John F. (2000) *The Metaphysical Thought of Thomas Aquinas: From Finite Being to Uncreated Being*, Washington, DC: Catholic University of America Press.

Robert Grosseteste

McEvoy, James (1980) *The Philosophy of Robert Grosseteste*, Oxford: Clarendon Press.
Southern, R.W. (1992) *Robert Grosseteste: The Growth of an English Mind in Medieval Europe*, 2nd edn, Oxford: Clarendon Press.

John Duns Scotus

Bettoni, E. (1961) *Duns Scotus: The Basic Principles of His Philosophy*, trans. and ed. B. Bonansea, Washington, DC: Catholic University of America Press.
Duns Scotus (1987) *Philosophical Writings*, trans. A.B. Wolter, Indianapolis, IN: Hackett.
Wolter, A.B. (1990) *The Philosophical Theology of John Duns Scotus*, ed. M. Adams, Ithaca, NY: Cornell University Press.

William of Ockham

Adams, Marilyn McCord (1987) *William Ockham*, 2 vols, Notre Dame: University of Notre Dame Press.

Spade, Paul Vincent (ed.) (1999) *The Cambridge Companion to Ockham*, Cambridge: Cambridge University Press.

Meister Eckhart

Davies, Oliver (1991) *Meister Eckhart: Mystical Theologian*, London: SPCK.

Meister Eckhart. *Selected Writings*, ed. Oliver Davies (1994), London: Penguin.

Schürmann, Reiner. *Meister Eckhart, Mystic and Philosopher* Bloomington: Indiana University Press.

Nicholas of Cusa

Hopkins, Jasper (1980) *A Concise Introduction to the Philosophy of Nicholas of Cusa*, Minneapolis: University of Minnesota Press.

7

MODERN PHILOSOPHY

The seventeenth and eighteenth centuries

Richard Francks

INTRODUCTION

The point of reading the history of philosophy – and the history of modern philosophy in particular – is not that it tells us what people who are now dead used to think, but that it helps us to understand what those who are now living currently believe. The attitudes and beliefs which inform and structure the lives we currently lead were not invented by us, but were inherited from our tradition: they are built into the language, conventions and institutions that we inhabit. Philosophers are the voices of that tradition: successful ones (which by definition any that we read today must be) have succeeded in articulating ideas which people have a use for, and which play some part in the evolutionary struggle between rival ways of thinking and living that has produced our current orthodoxies. By reading the philosophy of the past, therefore, we see something of how we came to be what we are; and more importantly, by understanding the views of the past, and comparing and contrasting them with what we take for granted, we come to understand our own positions the better, and therefore give ourselves the possibility of changing them.

The six philosophers we will look at in this chapter are Descartes, Spinoza, Leibniz, Locke, Berkeley and Hume – six people whose central works cover a period of more than 100 years from the mid-seventeenth to mid-eighteenth centuries, a time during which, it seems to me, the basis of the mind-set that we currently inhabit was laid down. I will make no attempt in these little sketches to try to summarise everything that these six authors wrote because (quite apart from the fact that I wouldn't know how) the result would only be a tedious and uninformative list. Instead, for each author I shall select one or two ideas which I think are central to their work, and which I think are important for the light they shed on our own attitudes and self-understanding. By the end I hope you will have a grasp of one or two important points that the authors in question tried to make, and will be able to start asking yourself whether and why you agree or disagree with them.

RENÉ DESCARTES: THE NEED FOR A NEW SCIENCE

Descartes (like others at the time) was far removed from the view that most people in our society today take, in that he believed that the established intellectual authorities, the experts in the universities, had no real understanding of the world around them and merely propagated outdated ideas which benefited no-one but themselves. At the same time, though, he shared with us the belief that if you want to develop a secure and lasting understanding of life, the universe and everything, the way to do it is through what we would call natural science. His whole philosophical effort was devoted to attempting to convince people of those two things.

The established learning of Descartes's day was an observational, descriptive study strongly influenced by the works of Aristotle and his later Christian commentators. The best way to understand it is through its survival in the kind of learning that is nowadays known as Natural History. In Natural History plants are closely observed, and classified on the basis of their observable characteristics (shape, size, colour, number and type of leaves, etc.), their behaviour (where they grow, when they flower, what conditions they thrive in) and their uses (which ones are good to eat, which are food for animals, which can be used as medicine, and so on). The outcome of such learning is a set of interrelated classes or categories which we still refer to by the Aristotelian terms of genus and species. Descartes's belief was that all such learning was valueless, and gave no real understanding of the world. At its best it produced nothing more than a catalogue of the way things look and the things they do, but it could offer no insight at all into what they really were, or why they are as they are. And at its worst it was no more than a mass of meaningless Latin jargon with which the so-called learned could intimidate the curious. His aim was nothing less than the complete reform of all learning. He wanted to sweep away the traditional categories, and to replace them with the new science which was being practised by people like Kepler, Galileo, and Descartes himself. Such knowledge, he tried to show, would be secure, reliable, useful, and completely compatible with the important truths of Christianity. I will try here to sketch out very briefly Descartes's ontology (i.e. what the world, according to Descartes, is really like) and his epistemology (his attempt to show that and how we can have knowledge of that reality – which in recent centuries has become the main focus of the work on him).

Descartes's ontology

I shall start by outlining Descartes's account of the natural, non-human world, and then explain how human beings fit into the story.

Non-human nature

According to Descartes, the natural world, when we look beyond superficial appearances and consider it as it really is in itself (scientifically, as we would say), actually consists of just one thing. What uneducated common sense sees as a rich and complex world of uncountably many individual objects located within empty space, the scientist Descartes understands as a single material continuum filling the entire universe. That continuum makes up all of physical reality, from the outer reaches of the stars to the Earth and all things on it and in it. The differences between things in the world, which common sense – and Aristotelian science – thought of as constituting different objects or different kinds of stuff, are really to be explained by the different ways in which that single object is arranged, or the different ways it acts in different areas and at different times. In Descartes's language, there is only one 'material substance' in existence; between what we call different objects there is no 'real' or substantial difference, only a 'modal' difference, or a difference in the way that single substance is, or acts.

That no doubt sounds like a strange and archaic story, the sort of thing that speculative philosophers used to believe, but which we now know to be false. Its purpose, though, is one we can understand and with which we can sympathise, and one which reveals our contemporary attitudes as clear descendants of the Cartesian story. In rejecting the Aristotelian system of individual and general substances and replacing it with his own account of a single all-encompassing material plenum, Descartes is making a crucial claim which we nowadays would accept without question. He is saying that to understand any individual thing – say this beech tree – we have to look for our explanation not in the particular characteristics of this unique individual organism, and not in the general characteristics of all trees, or of beech trees in particular. Instead the form our explanation must take is a *universal* one, in terms of the nature and behaviour of matter in general.

We nowadays take this idea for granted, even though it is a relatively new one, and it isn't at all obvious how we would argue for it if challenged. Of course it is useful to know about trees in general and about the particular characteristics of different kinds of tree – but ultimately, surely, we know that the reason this particular tree is as it is and does what it does is not because of some mysterious essence of its own, and not because it is made up of parts which are essentially treeish or beechy, but rather because of universal laws which apply to all physical objects (at least). That is the point which Descartes is making against the Aristotelian orthodoxy when he asserts that there is only a single material substance: there is only one matter, a seamless continuum of it filling the whole universe. And the way that matter is arranged and operates, in accordance with strict, deterministic, universal laws, explains everything that happens in nature.

For Descartes, the laws which govern the behaviour of the one material substance, and which therefore explain every physical process in the universe, are laws of motion. What makes the difference between what we call one object and the next is not that they are unique individuals, and not that they are made of different kinds of stuff, but that the universal material substance which makes up both of them moves in different ways. The particles of matter which make up this cup are arranged and fitted together in such a way that they move in unison – grab it by the handle and lift, and the whole thing moves. In the same way, the matter of the saucer is arranged in such a way as to give it a coherent identity and a relatively stable existence, even though we know that at the microscopic and sub-microscopic level particles are constantly being attached to or rubbed off it as the cup gets dirty or wears, and even though we know that all the matter which currently makes up both the cup and the saucer was once grains of sand under the ocean, and one day will be rubble on a demolition site, or dust in someone's eye. When the cup is lifted and the saucer stays on the table, the air that separates them, by contrast, has no such continuing identity. The matter which fills the 'empty' space between them is no less real and no less solid that that which makes up cups and saucers and rocks and mountains and beech trees, but it is disorganised, loose and separate, so that it offers little resistance to the motion of other matter through it.

The only properties that universal matter possesses for Descartes are simple mechanical ones, and incredible though it may seem, he held that all natural processes are the result of three simple mechanical laws: those of inertia, rectilinear motion and the conservation of motion. With those three simple laws – that things don't move unless pushed, or stop unless interfered with; that they travel in straight lines unless made to turn; that in collisions the motion lost by one body is exactly balanced by that gained by others – Descartes claimed that all natural processes could be understood. The motions of the stars, the creation of the Earth, the propagation of light, the eruption of a volcano, the weather, the growth of a flower, the beating of the heart – everything that happens in the material, non-human world is the inevitable consequence of the ways in which the different areas of the one material substance interact in accordance with the three mechanical laws of nature which God laid down at creation.

There is one particular feature of this story that I should make clear before we go on to see how human beings fit into it, and that is the role of mathematics. All physical processes can be explained through the mechanical properties of the different parts of matter. But those mechanical properties and interactions can all be stated mathematically. The only features of an object that are important for the scientist are size, shape and motion. We don't explain anything that happens to our beech tree by reference to its colour (colour is a function of the way light particles bounce off the particles on its surface), or by how beautiful it is (beauty is a relation between shapes and sizes), or by what it is made of (since everything is made of the same stuff, differently arranged). Rather, all scientific explanations will tell us about is the impacts between particles, and the outcomes of those impacts will depend only on how many there were, how big they are, what shape they are and how quickly they were moving. But all those properties can be stated as numbers – and that fact is an essential part of Descartes's story. What we see and hear when two billiard-balls collide is only the appearance of the event, detectable with the eyes of the body. The reality of that collision is a mathematical equation, stating how the motions were distributed before and after the impact. That latter, non-sensory, mathematical description is the only accurate description of the event we witnessed, and our initial description in terms of separate coloured objects rolling over a firm surface is only a very crude approximation to that underlying reality.

The place of human beings in Descartes's world

The mathematicisable, deterministic mechanical system of the material world accounts for all natural phenomena, including the lives of plants and animals, and the human body. But that is as far as it goes. The beating of the heart, the circulation of the blood, our sensory experience and our emotional lives can all, according to Descartes, be given a purely mechanical explanation, as can similar systems in the animal world. But some human characteristics are just not capable of that kind of explanation. The ability to reason, to understand, for example, he thinks cannot be accounted for by the mechanical interaction of particles. Mathematical knowledge, and the knowledge of God, are things which the laws of mechanical nature could never produce. And whereas all of physical nature is a deterministic, law-governed system, human beings can think about their actions, and their reactions, and can *choose* how to behave, and they are therefore, unlike animals and the rest of nature, capable of moral understanding and of responsibility. These characteristics are a result, Descartes thinks, of the fact that in addition to our living, functioning mechanical bodies, human beings also have something else, which follows different laws: we have – or more precisely, we *are* – a rational soul. That soul is closely associated with our physical body while we are alive on earth – we feel its reactions, and it responds to our decisions – but it is something quite separate, and immaterial.

It is because the soul is immaterial that it possesses the faculties of Will and Understanding that no purely mechanical system can achieve. And because it is immaterial it is not capable of being broken up and destroyed in the way that any material object can be, and so the soul of man is immortal. God, of course, is immaterial, and human souls are in fact little finite copies of God, united with an area of matter for the duration of their time on Earth.

In this way Descartes is able to defend himself against the accusation that by seeking to overturn established learning – primarily at the time the property of the Church – his new science is in danger of overturning religion. Quite the contrary, he says. A true, scientific understanding of nature is, as we saw at the end of the previous section, a non-sensory, mathematical understanding. Thus, in escaping from the sense-based understanding of the Aristotelians to the mathematical reading of the mechanical world, we are in fact escaping from our animal nature and recapitulating in our own small way God's own, non-sensory, understanding of his creation.

Descartes's epistemology

Descartes's epistemology is nowadays better known than the metaphysics it supported. His aim, as we have seen, was to show that the only safe and reliable knowledge is what we would now call scientific knowledge. Like many at the time, he held that the sense-based, classificatory knowledge of the Aristotelian orthodoxy was unreliable at best, but instead of giving up on natural knowledge and adopting the fashionable sceptical ideas of the time, he tried to show that genuine and lasting knowledge could be achieved, but only if we swept away the traditional learning and started again from scratch. By escaping from tradition, and ignoring what seemed to be the obvious evidence of our eyes and ears (ignoring, for example, the obvious evidence for the traditional view that the earth stood still while the sun was in motion) we could liberate the God-like power of the rational intellect to see behind appearances to the unchanging reality beneath. The irony of Descartes's writings is that in the course of trying to sell this message he established an epistemological tradition which has come to dominate our view of his work, and to obscure the very message he was trying to put across.

In order to make his point, Descartes hits upon a quite wonderful literary device as a way of dramatising his position and bringing home his conclusions to the lay reader. In his *Meditations on Philosophy* he presents his readers with a kind of diary, which purports to be the record of a spiritual retreat. Because he is confused and uncertain, he says, he has decided to withdraw from life for a week, in order to sort out his ideas and to try to come to some conclusion as to what to believe, whom to trust, and how to understand the world around him. The *Meditations* then presents the record of this fictional six-day journey, as each day he picks up from where he left off the day before to follow through the train of thought wherever it may lead. And it leads, of course, to the position Descartes has held all along. But the story he tells is so compelling, and his presentation of it so dramatic, that even now it strikes anyone with any philosophical imagination at all as instantly gripping and disturbing.

The story is well known, and I shall only sketch its basic outline here, without making any attempt to recreate the immediacy and engagement of the original. Descartes begins by the simple device of abandoning everything he has ever believed. Because he is unsure what he should believe and whose opinion he should trust, he resolves to try to pretend that everything he has ever accepted is false, and that all the world around him is an illusion. In this way he tries to find out whether there are any of his beliefs that he couldn't possibly give up in any circumstances. And in what is perhaps the most famous single move in the whole history of Western Philosophy, he comes to the conclusion that even if he is mistaken about everything else, he can still be certain of his own existence – because if he didn't exist, he couldn't even be mistaken. The mere fact that he is thinking, even if he is thinking falsely, means he exists: *cogito, ergo sum*.

The significance of this discovery for Descartes's overall project is twofold. First, the knowledge of his own existence is not something he has noticed, or something he has been taught, but something he has worked out for himself – something so obvious that it *must* be true. It is therefore an example of the kind of God-like rational understanding that enables men of science like Kepler and Galileo not merely to observe the way the world looks, but to work out rationally how it *must* really be. Secondly, the *Cogito* also enshrines Descartes's belief in the uniqueness of the human mind: because he can prove his own existence even when he is assuming that all the world around him is an illusion, he claims this shows that he himself, his own thinking soul, is not a part of that world, but a separate existent.

The rest of Descartes's narrative consists in developing the consequences of what the *Cogito* has shown, and he goes on to prove that there is an all-perfect God who has created him, and who has given him both the rationality to think clearly and truly, and also the free will to make mistakes and to be misled by appearances. He concludes that it is rational to believe that the world around us is not illusory, but that the correct way to understand it is through the rational judgements of a mathematical science, and not through common sense or through the views and methods of the traditional authorities.

In the last 200 years or so this attempt by Descartes to dramatise his epistemology has come to dominate our views of his whole philosophical project, and even to define the nature of philosophy itself. Many philosophers have seen epistemological questions as being the central part of philosophy, and the Cartesian struggle against all-encompassing doubt, conceived of as the attempt to work outwards from the contents of one's own consciousness, has been taken to be the basic form of all epistemological thinking. The irony is that because in the same period philosophers have tended to represent natural science as essentially an empirical investigation, they have often tended to miss Descartes's main point, and to represent his advocacy of reason over experience as an attack on the scientific knowledge that he spent his life trying to promote (and that he himself practised).

Descartes is the quintessential Modern philosopher, because he says that the world in itself is not as it appears, and is correctly describable only in objective, mathematical terms which are stripped of any reference to human subjectivity and are understood only by the expert. That belief has since become central to the way our society operates and understands itself. Is it true?

BARUCH SPINOZA (BENEDICTUS DE SPINOZA): SALVATION THROUGH UNDERSTANDING

Spinoza was enormously impressed by Descartes's belief that the task of science was to see beyond the world as it appears to the uneducated person in the street, and as it had been described by traditional learning, to an underlying reality which was not describable in the language of our day-to-day experience of it. But he wanted to go beyond Descartes in two crucial areas. Firstly, he held that Descartes's belief that the human soul was something wholly outside the natural order was absurd, and would make it impossible for us ever to give an objective, scientific account of the place of human beings in the world and of the best way for them to live their lives. Secondly, he thought that Descartes's belief in a traditional Christian God (Spinoza was an excommunicated Jew) meant that he would never be able to reconcile the life of science and the life of religion. The history of European thought since Descartes's day suggests that Spinoza was right on both counts; but his own attempt to resolve those problems proved much too radical, and his ideas were generally despised both in his own lifetime and after.

God and nature

Descartes, as we saw, held that mechanical laws explained all physical, non-human phenomena. Spinoza wants to go further, and to say that the whole universe, in all its aspects, must be explicable by a single set of laws which govern the behaviour of everything that is, ever has been or ever will be, whether human or non-human, natural or divine. But how exactly do those laws explain the phenomena?

Nowadays we tend to think of the relation between the laws of nature and nature itself as primarily a descriptive one. The laws of nature, we think, tell us how nature behaves: they tell us what it does and doesn't do, can and can't do. For Spinoza that relation is a great deal closer.

Consider for example the status of Cartesian laws of motion, and their relation to a particular physical event. Those laws never change, and they are universal. And every physical event that happens, anywhere and anytime, is a consequence of them, or derives from them. To understand any particular physical event at all, therefore, we need to understand how it arises from those unchanging facts of nature, or how those timeless generalities – the laws of motion – come to be manifested in this particular event at this time and in this place. For Spinoza (and for Descartes, too) this means that those underlying laws are the reality of the situation, and the particular event we started with is only a phenomenon, an appearance, or a particular way in which those basic facts are manifested.

For Spinoza then, what he called 'Nature as Cause' (*Natura Naturans*) is the basic facts which the fundamental laws of a unified science would state. That is the reality, the truth, behind 'Nature as Effect' (*Natura Naturata*), which is the sum total of what those underlying facts produce – the universe of time and space as we experience it. Those two are not separate things, but two ways of understanding the same thing – the world of science on the one hand, and the world of experience on the other. Spinoza, in standard seventeenth-century terms, calls Nature as Cause the one 'Substance' of the universe – the underlying reality of it – whereas any particular thing or event he refers to as a 'Mode' of that substance – a manifestation of it, or a way it behaves. His radicalism – and the reason why he was so widely hated – consists in the fact that he also called that substance 'God'.

The concept of 'God or Nature' (*Deus sive Natura*) is perhaps as shocking to us as it was to Spinoza's contemporaries, because most of us tend to think of God – if we think of it at all – as some kind of creative intelligence which made and maintains the world, in a way analogous to that in which an engineer makes and maintains an engine. Spinoza's God by contrast is the very world itself, the underlying reality of it, the truth of it. God creates the world not as the engineer creates the engine, but as the facts of meteorology create the weather.

Spinoza of course is aware that people will be shocked by this idea, but he puts that down to the fact that the majority of people don't understand science, and tend to think in childish, imagistic terms, which the traditional authorities have only reinforced. Religious documents in particular tend to be written for uneducated people in picturesque language which we must be careful not to take too literally. When we think about it carefully, he says, we can see that his God has all the attributes that more traditional conceptions of God have, but is not so easily represented in parables or in wall-paintings. God or Nature is the cause, the explanation, of the universe. It is infinite (it is boundless; there is nothing that is real that is not included in it) and eternal (it exists outside of time; it is the timeless truths which explain all temporal events). It is also omnipresent (there is nowhere it is not), omnipotent (everything that happens is God or Nature in action; everything that can be done, it does), and omniscient (it contains all truth, all knowledge). According to Spinoza it is God or Nature to which the prophets of the Bible were referring when they talked of God, and as we shall see later, it is God or Nature whom to love is perfect freedom.

In fact, according to Spinoza, the only properties of the traditional Judaeo-Christian God which his God or Nature lacks are specifically human ones such as personality, consciousness, and feelings. It is simply nonsense, he claims, to think of God or Nature as angry – or as loving, either. We can if we wish say that everything that happens is the Will of God, in the sense that it is God or Nature which is responsible for what happens at every moment in time and space; but we should remember when we do so that there is as much relation between the Will of God and a human will as there is between the Dog Star in the heavens and your friendly garden mongrel.

Spinoza's *Ethics* and the good life

Spinoza's metaphysics, then, closes the gap between God and Nature, and so identifies the life of science with the life of religion. The other crucial aspect of his belief in a single underlying reality which explains all natural phenomena is his conviction that human action is as much a part of nature, as much a part of that single deterministic system, as the movements of the planets or the circulation of the blood.

The human body for Spinoza is just as much a natural object as it is for Descartes. He describes it as a complex system of complex sub-systems which derives its identity not from the identity of the parts which make it up – as a living, developing organism its parts (cells, as we would say) are constantly being replaced – but from the organisation of those parts, the way they are put together, and function together. The life of the individual is the period of the coherent organisation of those constantly changing parts, and the individual's death occurs when that organisation breaks down and the parts begin to dissipate.

Having told this story about the body, Spinoza simply goes on to tell an exactly parallel one about the mind. We saw with Descartes that the difference between what we call a solid object and what we call an empty space is not that the stuff that makes them up is of two different kinds, but that the universal material substance which makes up both of them is arranged differently in the two places. In the same way Spinoza says that the difference between what we call a thinking thing like a human being and what we call an unthinking thing like a stone is not that – as Descartes said – there is an immaterial thinking soul in one case and not in the other, but just that the universal sensitive stuff is arranged differently in the two cases. Like the human body, the human mind is a complex system of complex sub-systems, and as long as those systems are operating together in the usual way we have what we refer to as a thinking mind. When the person dies and the system breaks down, that mind ceases to exist, even though the parts that had previously made it up continue in being. And just as after my death the parts of my body might break down and dissipate and blow away in the wind without thereby ceasing to be material objects, so those same parts, when considered as making up my mind, will break up into unconscious particles without thereby ceasing to be mental things.

It strikes us as a strange account, because it has never been very popular, and Cartesian ways of thinking have come to dominate our lives, our language, our institutions and our thoughts. But its advantages, if it could be made to work, as a way of fitting human experience into a unified account of nature, are considerable. And so perhaps are its disadvantages, in that it denies many assumptions that many people hold dear. Clearly, Spinoza's account leaves no space for any personal survival after death, for example. Equally, some will say that it seems to leave no personal survival even while we are alive, in the sense that there is on his account no such thing as the self, the thinking person, as opposed to merely the aggregate of thoughts which go towards making up my mental life at any given time. Most seriously of all, perhaps, by fitting the mind into a deterministic, law-governed system along with the body, it leaves no more room for the Freedom of the Will than it does for the freedom of the rainfall: human beings are natural objects, and as such are fully determined parts of the natural world.

Spinoza was quite aware of this consequence, and accepted it as a necessary part of the attempt to make human action explicable. The belief in human freedom, he says, is a childish mistake brought about by the fact that much of the time we are aware of our actions but not aware of their causes. As a consequence, he also denies the possibility of any system of morality. If human beings are parts of nature, and their actions are necessary consequences of the fundamental laws of the universe, then it cannot make much sense to say that some acts are good and some are bad, any more than it can make sense to say that some rainfall is better than some other. Of course, rainfall can be convenient or inconvenient, can help or hinder our plans, and in that sense we can call it good or bad. And the same is true of people's behaviour – things we want to happen we call good, and things we don't want to happen, things we don't like, we call bad; but in themselves, looked at objectively – as the scientist looks at them – they are all just neutral, natural events.

That position doesn't sound like the work of a man concerned to provide an account of the good life for human beings, and whose chief work was a book called

Ethics. Yet out of the cold objectivity of his account of human action as just one more feature of a deterministic universe, he develops a description of the kind of life most likely, as a general rule, to provide the kind of long-term satisfactions that human beings typically want. The key, he claims, is precisely to see our own thoughts and actions as the determined effects that they are. The way to escape from the sorrows and disappointments that are so much a part of human life is to understand both the world around us and our own reactions to it rationally, scientifically. That doesn't change what happens, of course – it doesn't make the sun shine on our holidays, or our friends live longer – but it can bring us a kind of peace of mind, a kind of independence of what happens to us, and a kind of control over our own thoughts and actions, which is as good as it gets for human beings.

Spinoza is in love with Descartes's Modernism, and with his conviction that science reveals the reality of the world. He develops that conviction to its logical conclusion by extending the world of science to include the two things Descartes that had deliberately excluded – human beings, and spirituality. Our tradition and our society are both Cartesian ones. Is that because Descartes is right, or because we've never really considered that he might be wrong?

GOTTFRIED WILHELM VON LEIBNIZ: THE NECESSITY FOR EXPLANATION

Leibniz thought Spinoza's monism was tantamount to atheism, and wanted to preserve a much more traditional Christian notion of God as a supremely good, rational intelligence which freely chose to create the world we know, and with which human beings could develop a personal relationship of love and obedience. He was committed to the Cartesian and Spinozan project of explaining the whole of nature through science, but argued that science on its own could never explain anything, but needed to be supplemented by an account of why the world is as science reveals it to be.

The centrepiece of Leibniz's thought is the great Principle of Sufficient Reason: that for everything that is so, there is an adequate reason why it is so and not otherwise. To us that seems at first sight like something we would accept; but when we see how far Leibniz is willing to pursue this principle – and the strange-looking conclusions it leads him to – we come to realise that in fact we treat the world and our lives in it as beyond explanation in most important respects.

Consider for example one of Leibniz's proofs of the existence of God. Take any event – like the fall of a tree in a storm. Why does it happen? We take it for granted that there must be a reason for such an event – it would be crazy, surely, to say that it just happened, nothing caused it, it was just a random event with no explanation.

And Leibniz would certainly agree. But if we managed to find the explanation – perhaps the roots had been loosened by the diverting of a stream, for example – then of course we would agree with Leibniz that there must be an explanation for that event, too. And so on, and so on, and so on.

Many people have of course argued that this process of explanation cannot go on indefinitely, but that is not the point Leibniz is making. His point is that even if we *do* allow that the chain of explanation goes on to infinity, we *still* won't have a real explanation, because we won't have explained *why* any single link in that chain is as it is. *Why is it* that trees without roots fall over when pushed? *Why* does gravity, for example, operate as it does? What we are looking for here is not something that produced gravitational forces, or an account of how those forces relate to others, but an explanation of why the world we live in has the laws it has, and not others. Until you have answered that question, Leibniz says, you haven't explained anything at all, because although you might have told us *how* the event in question was brought about, you have said nothing at all about why it happened in that way, and not otherwise.

At this point, we tend to come up short. We have no explanation for *why* the laws of nature are as they are – they are just facts, what the world is like, descriptions of how things just happen to be. Explanation stops at this point. The job of science, we think, is to tell us *how* things are, not *why*. But for Leibniz, that is every bit as nonsensical as saying that there was no reason why the tree fell in the first place.

According to Leibniz, the only way that this search for reasons can come to an end is if we can trace it back to something which itself stands in no need of explanation, and that, he claims, is God. But the chain of derivations from the Principle of Sufficient Reason doesn't simply end there. How, exactly, does this kind of metaphysical explanation, with which we have to supplement mere scientific explanation, work?

Consider our falling tree example again. We have now worked out, in principle, how its fall came about, by specifying the chain of preceding events that led up to it, and the laws that govern events of that kind, and we have also seen that the reason why those laws were in operation was because of a decision by God. God chose those particular laws, and those particular circumstances. And of course, in making those choices, he knew that as a consequence of those decisions it would happen that that particular tree would fall in just that way at just that time – not a second earlier or later, and not a millimetre to either side. So in choosing to create the world as he did, God chose the fall of that tree – along with every other detail of every other event in the whole history of time.

That is what it means to be omniscient and omnipotent. A being of that kind doesn't merely create a universe and let it run, and then keep an eye on how things turn out. In creating the universe, an omniscient God already knew, in the smallest possible detail, everything that would ever happen in it, and he chose to create that universe with every one of those infinite consequences in mind. Because he is also omnipotent he could, of course, have created a different universe – one, for example, in which our tree fell half a second later than it did in this world. But of course, in order to do that, unless he was going to create a random, inexplicable universe, he would have needed to create a *reason* why it fell at the new time and not at the old one, i.e. he would have needed to make adjustments somewhere else in the system to compensate for that change. And every one of those tiny adjustments would in turn have had an infinite number of consequences of its own, rippling out through all of time and space.

So why did God chose to create *this* universe, and not one of the infinite number of other possible worlds he could have made instead? Whereas Spinoza says simply that reality has this form, and could not be otherwise, for Leibniz the answer must be that God thought through all the alternatives, in all their infinite detail, and rationally decided on this one. He compared all the possible worlds together, and balanced out the competing demands of richness and diversity on the one hand, and simplicity and intelligibility on the other, and he came down on the side of the one that best reconciled those two principles, i.e. the one that was most perfect. And that was this world, which is therefore the Best of All Possible Worlds.

The same line of thought leads Leibniz on to his unique ontology. If what we have so far said is true, then God, in creating that particular tree which fell on that particular occasion, had an eye to every other thing in the universe, before and after, because if any tiny feature of the tree and of its history had been in any way different, then that change would have had to be compensated for by changes in the world around it, and those things would have impacted on their own environments in the same way, and so on and so on. It turns out, then, that our randomly-chosen example of a tree is actually crucial for the history of the whole universe, in the sense that the universe is as it is on account of the part that our tree is going to play in it; and our tree is the thing it is only because of the part it is going to play in that wider world. And what is true of that tree, of course, is true of every other thing in existence: they are all made for each other, with each other in mind, and none of them could have been otherwise unless God had chosen to create an entirely different universe from the one he in fact chose to create – and since God is good, he naturally chose the best one.

Fully to understand any particular individual, therefore, we would have to understand the entire universe and everything in it, because every individual, as Leibniz says, mirrors the whole universe from its own unique point of view. When we talk of one thing's causing another, therefore, we are speaking very loosely. It is of course true that the tree would not have fallen if the stream had not been diverted, and in that sense the one event is the cause of the other; but equally, if Leibniz is right, it is true that the stream would not have been diverted if it had not been going to undermine the tree, and so in that sense it is equally true to say that the fall of the tree was the cause of the diverting of the stream. All events are interconnected, all individuals are intimately bound up with each other, because they all play their own unique parts in the total system which God has designed. We speak for convenience of the moving of the stream as the cause of the fall of the tree, therefore, but it would be more accurate to speak of the tree as causing its own fall: it fell because it had to fall in order to be the tree that it is, and to play its assigned role in the overall system. And in just the same way the stream had to be diverted in order for it to be the stream that it is, and to play its part in the whole.

Leibniz's ontology is then the inevitable consequence of this line of reasoning. For him, the ultimate reality of the world consists not in separate things like trees and mountains and flowers, as common sense and Aristotelian science would have it; not in a material continuum and non-spatial minds, as Descartes had claimed, and not in the single infinite substance that Spinoza called God or Nature. For Leibniz, all that exists is a universe of reasons, or points of view.

Take our tree example again. If we are to understand that tree correctly, it is not enough for us to think of it just as a separate individual object, because as we have seen, everything that makes it what it is derives not from its character as one thing in isolation, but from the part that it plays in the whole universe, the way it is embedded in the universal system which is the Best Possible World. Yet equally it would be wrong to see the tree, as Descartes and Spinoza do, as merely a mode of matter – a particular local instantiation of more general laws. To do that would be to make the tree and all that happens to it seem unimportant, an unintended consequence of more general facts. For Leibniz, rather, that tree, like every other individual thing in the world, is a miniaturisation of the universe, specifically designed for its unique position in the universe – what he comes to call a 'monad'.

Monads are the ultimate reality of everything, of what the world really consists. They are 'soul-like' in that they are sensitive to, or express, the rest of the universe. They are not themselves material objects, but they provide the reasons, the explanation, as to why material objects are as they are and not otherwise. And everything that ever happens to each monad arises spontaneously from its being the monad that it is: it is pre-programmed from creation to play out its role in the great scheme of things that is the Best of All Possible Worlds.

Leibniz's world is a strange one, which few people have ever happily inhabited. The big question it raises for us is whether we can defend our conviction that the world is fully explicable – but only up to a point. Can we really justify saying that there must be laws which determine everything that happens, but that there is no reason why those laws are as they are and not otherwise? Is that a view we can defend, or just an attitude with which we have grown up, and have always taken for granted?

JOHN LOCKE: FREEDOM OF THOUGHT, AND THE LIMITS OF SCIENTIFIC KNOWLEDGE

One thing that Descartes, Spinoza and Leibniz have in common is their desire to look beyond the world of experience, their willingness to say that despite all appearances, the world is not as it seems: it is a spatial continuum with immaterial souls, it is a timeless psycho-physical totality, it is an infinity of interlocking perspectives, or whatever. Locke is sceptical of all such grand theories, and wary of their propensity to disempower decent solid citizens such as himself, and to place authority in the hands of the scientific élite. Although he was an enthusiastic supporter of the new science of the seventeenth century, therefore, he worked to show that all such knowledge was grounded in the common experience of ordinary human beings. Much of what he says about the nature of our experience and of our knowledge of the world we now take for granted; but it has important implications concerning the status of scientific knowledge that sit very uneasily with our current ways of life and thought.

Locke tries to ground an understanding of the new science on a comprehensive account of the nature of human thought and of our relation to the world around us. His first and most basic step is to say that everything we can ever understand, and everything we can ever know, is derived from our experience of living in the world, from the information we pick up through our senses. That means that no knowledge is innate, there are no principles written in the soul and discovered prior to or independently of experience: we come into existence with no knowledge and no understanding, and everything we ever manage to find out is built up on the basis of experiences we have in the course of our lives.

To many people that seems a fairly obvious, even a trivial, claim to make. For Locke it was politically very significant, and from it he derived conclusions about the possible scope and nature of our knowledge that we find hard to accept.

The political dimension of this 'empiricism' of Locke's is that if all knowledge comes to us through our senses, then all knowledge is in principle accessible to anyone who has the basic sensory capacity to perceive it. There are no arcane secrets, comprehensible only by the experts, or the élite, because everything is in principle accessible to us all. And there are no truths that are beyond question, which we must simply accept because they are delivered by Aristotle, or by God, or by the Government: anything that can be known can be known by any of us, so for any claim of yours that you want me to accept as true, you will have to give me reasons, and evidence.

The human mind, then, comes into being empty. It is a '*tabula rasa*', a blank sheet on which experience writes, an empty closet, which our experience furnishes with ideas. Anything you can ever understand, and therefore any thought you can ever think, is put there by experience, either through the sensations you receive via your eyes, ears, nose, etc., or through introspection – your awareness of your own mental states. What about fantasy, imagination, creativity? Imagination can never produce a wholly new idea, says Locke – you can't, for example, get an understanding of the taste of a pineapple without actually tasting one; a blind person can never grasp what a sighted person means by colour terms – all that your most creative imagination can do is to re-combine elements which you have already experienced: you can imagine a centaur by combining the head and torso of a person with the body of a horse, for example. And what about things we can't experience – abstractions, mathematics, God? We understand things like that, Locke says, because we can construct an understanding of them out of ideas of things we can experience: the idea of God, for example, is arrived at by taking observable human qualities like goodness, power, knowledge, and love, and raising them to the infinite level – which we do by taking the idea of an increase from for example addition, and taking away the idea of limitation or end, to produce the idea of increase without limit.

Having given that 'empiricist' characterisation of human understanding, Locke builds on it an account of human life and of human possibilities by way of a description of the nature and scope of human knowledge. Knowledge, according to Locke, is the interpretation of the concepts with which experience provides us. The clearest and most certain examples of such interpretation are what he calls 'intuition' – the immediate awareness of the relation between two ideas, such as 'white is not black', or 'two and two are four'. Once you have had the relevant experience to acquire the ideas of white and black, two and four, then you know those things, without the need for any further investigation. Other cases are far harder: I understand the concept of 13 and the concept of multiplication, but I can't see at a glance that $13 \times 13 = 169$: I have to work it out, follow up the chain of intuitions that lead from one to the other by the process Locke calls 'demonstration' (proof).

Apart from those two classes of purely conceptual knowledge, the only other things we can know are the things we can directly observe. I know there is a cat in the garden, because I can see it; I know there's music playing, because I can hear it, and so on. That kind of knowledge is not as certain as intuition or proof, but it is generally reliable, and deserves the name of knowledge. Anyone who questions it, who pretends, like Descartes, to doubt the immediate evidence of their own senses, is either a liar or a fool.

And that is it: those are the limits of human knowledge – that is the kind of creature that we are, and those are the kinds of things we can be sure of. Anything that doesn't fit into one of those three categories is either a hypothesis, a guess, or a lie.

The implications of that account of the nature of our thought and the range of our understanding are very important for Locke's account of our relation to the world around us, and of the kind of life we can and should lead. Locke was an enthusiastic supporter of the work of what became the Royal Society of London, and a believer in the theory that all natural phenomena are the result of the way things are put together at the microscopic and sub-microscopic level: the reason why gold is yellow, for example, is because the corpuscles which make up the surface of the gold are of such a size and shape, and are put together in such a way, that when particles of light strike them, the light particles bounce off with a particular kind of speed and spin which, when it strikes our eyes, leads to our having the sort of sensation we refer to as 'yellow'.

That seems like a fairly close relative of our own account of the matter. But when it is combined with the plausible-seeming theory of thought and of knowledge that we have seen, it produces some conclusions that we find less natural.

What status should we afford to our knowledge of the new science that Locke describes and that we have inherited? There can be no intuitive or demonstrative knowledge of the kind of account of the colour of gold that we have sketched, because there is no conceptual link, either immediate or indirect, between the idea of gold and the idea of this or that corpuscular structure, or this or that reaction to light particles. There is perhaps a conceptual link between the idea of gold and the idea of yellowness: we might say that it is part of the very idea of gold that it is yellow, and so we can know for certain, intuitively, that gold is yellow. But how does that help us? All it means is that it is part of the meaning of the word 'gold' that gold is yellow. But that kind of classificatory, definitional knowledge is precisely the kind of sterile, pointless erudition for which the Aristotelian orthodoxy were famous, and against which Locke and the bright new men of the Royal Society were rebelling. A systematic knowledge of the meanings of words – what Locke calls the 'nominal essences' of things – tells us only about the contents of our own ideas, and nothing at all about how the world is, and why it behaves as it does. To know that, we would need to know the 'real essences' of substances like gold – what we might call their molecular structures. If we knew precisely how gold is put together at the molecular level, we would then be able to derive intuitive and demonstrative knowledge of why it behaves as it does: we could understand in detail why it is soft and heavy, for example, because we could see why a structure of that kind must result in observable properties like those. But the problem is that we have no knowledge of the real essence of gold, or of anything else in the world, because our understandings are restricted to ideas we can acquire through experience, and our sensory capacities are not adapted to provide experience of the deep structure of nature.

In a classic passage Locke talks about our understanding of a clock. If we were a different kind of creature, he says, we would be able to see with our 'microscopical eyes' into the very structure of the metal that makes up the spring of the clock. If we could do that, we would be able to understand precisely why the metal was springy, and so why the clock worked as it does. And if we were such creatures, there is no doubt that we would be able to understand a whole world of secrets that we mere humans can never really grasp. However, if we were such creatures, the clock would be no use to us at all, because with a perceptual system of that kind we wouldn't be able to see what time it was.

Human beings, Locke thinks, are not made for knowledge. They are made for practical affairs, for social life, for religion, for morality, and of those things they can know all they need to know. They are not made for prying into the secrets of nature, and understanding how it works.

It seems odd that Locke combines this deep pessimism about the extent of scientific knowledge with his enthusiasm for the experimental science of the Royal Society. But perhaps it is not as odd as it seems. Science, for Locke, is a great tool, a wonderful device for making life better. We can never know the secrets of nature; but what we can do is to hypothesise – we can make theories, test them, develop them, and use them to generate a more and more sophisticated knowledge of what things can do, of what nature is capable of, and to make better and better devices for improving our practical lives.

Locke's pessimism with regard to scientific understanding survives today in the widespread acceptance of the idea that scientific theories are provisional, can never be proved, and may be falsified at any moment. Yet nowadays we combine that kind of empiricist rhetoric with a different, more Cartesian approach, which sees science as the pinnacle of human understanding, a God-like view into the truth of things. Locke would have said that the two are quite incompatible: that if science is infinitely revisable, for ever undecided, an endless adventure in thought, then it can never make sense to talk of scientific facts, and it can never be right to accord to scientific theories the kind of status and authority over other ways of thinking that Descartes had claimed. I think he was right.

GEORGE BERKELEY: THE INCOHERENCE OF OUR CONTEMPORARY WORLD-VIEW

Berkeley recognised that something like Locke's views were becoming very influential in early eighteenth-century Britain, and he saw this as another example of the corrupt and decadent state of European culture at the time. He had high hopes of the new, uncorrupted world of the Americas as offering a fresh start, where people could return to a simpler, more natural view of themselves and their relation to the world around them, and he tried in vain to turn the tide of opinion at home.

The problem with the Lockeian view was two-fold. First, it enshrined the Cartesian view – which we now take for granted – that the whole of nature was a vast mechanical system operating according to deterministic natural laws; a giant clockwork, as the popular contemporary image described it. For Berkeley that meant that people were in danger of coming to see their lives as ruled by nature, not by God; they would come to take their understanding of truth, of reality, of what is lasting, from the natural world, and not from God. Second, Locke's denial of the possibility of scientific knowledge and his insistence on the hypothetical nature of all scientific beliefs meant that our view of the reality which ruled our lives and informed our understanding of ourselves and of the world was inadequate, incomplete, uncertain. If such views took hold, he thought, people would grow up disaffected, alienated from the world around them, believing themselves to be of no more significance than a random collection of atoms, with no hope for anything beyond brief, short-term pleasures – pretty much like us, in other words.

To combat the dangers of the Lockeian view he tried to show that it was completely wrong, and to return us to a sense of the immediacy of our relation to the divine being. Hardly anyone believed him, but his arguments are maddeningly difficult to refute, and point, I think, to major flaws in our contemporary self-understanding.

Berkeley's central point is very simple: he says there is no such thing as a material world, and all the things we normally think of as things in the material world are really just our interpretation of sensory messages from God. In reality, all that exists is minds – of roughly the same kind that Descartes thought human beings possessed. There is the one infinite mind, which is God, and there are the uncountably many individual finite minds which are human beings (and angels). And that's it. The only other things that can be said in any sense to exist are ideas, thoughts, in those minds. Those ideas are not separate, extra existents in addition to the minds, but acts of willing and perceiving carried out by them.

So what becomes of the rest of the world? The trees and the flowers, the planets and the galaxies, the dust and the dog biscuits? The answer is that they are all just collections of ideas in our minds: God gives us various sensations – the sight of the stars, the smell of the flowers, the feel of the dust, the taste of the dog biscuits, or whatever – and we, through experience, learn to recognise patterns in those experiences, and we invent words to stand for those sets or patterns of experience. The smell of the flower, for example, we have learned to correlate with what the flower looks like and what it feels like, and we use the word 'primrose' to stand for those sets of experiences.

The first thing to make clear about this story is that, although he was often accused of it, Berkeley is emphatically *not* denying that there is any real world, or saying that everything is an illusion. Berkeley makes exactly the same distinction between what is real and what is illusory as we do: the real dagger is the one you can not only see, but feel in your hand, put in your pocket, and cut yourself with, whereas Macbeth's illusory dagger can be seen, but fails all the other tests for being a real thing. The only difference between Berkeley's position and ours is that we typically hold that the fact that in the case of the real dagger we have consistent sets of experiences, whereas in the case of the illusory one we don't, is because over and above all our actual and possible experiences of it the dagger actually exists as a real, mind-independent external material object in a three-dimensional world; Berkeley, by contrast, says that the real dagger just *is* the consistent set of experiences that we can have.

The idea strikes us as a very strange one. Is that because we have clear evidence that it is false, or just, as Berkeley would have said, because we have been corrupted by generations of thinkers who have taken something like the Lockeian model as natural? Our reaction to Berkeley's suggestion is to feel that suddenly nothing is secure, that everything solid has been taken away from us. But he claims that that is a mistake: what we are thrown back on is that of which we are actually most certain – the immediate evidence of our own experience; what we have lost is something of which we can never be confident – the supposed but undetectable three-dimensional world which lies beyond our sensations, and which is nothing more than a traditional but ill-founded hypothesis for explaining them. Berkeley's world, he will say, is much more secure than ours. The regularities that we experience in it – the laws of nature that control all of existence and which natural science aims to investigate – are grounded, not in the assumed nature of some hypothetical material substance which lies beyond experience, but in the nature of an omniscient and omnipotent God who is at every moment in direct communication with us through our sensations, and who we know will never vary, never trick us nor hide from us, and never change his ways.

The surprising and rather annoying fact seems to be that nothing in our experience can ever disprove Berkeley's position. If we believe that what we are immediately conscious of is sensations which are produced in us by our interactions with the material world around us, then we have no way at all of using anything in that experience to refute Berkeley's claim that those same sensations are produced by our interactions with an immaterial God. The experiences themselves are identical on either account; all that we are disagreeing with Berkeley about is our different *theory* as to what explains them.

If that is so, then a very important conclusion seems to follow, namely that an absolutely central part of our present-day self-understanding – the belief that we exist within a real world of physical objects – turns out to be a lot less firmly grounded than we thought it was. Our belief that the material universe exists is after all not the most fundamental, blindingly obvious, fact that no sane person could possibly deny, but a theory, an hypothesis, for which we seem to need to provide reasons.

How would you do it? How would you prove to Berkeley that your hypothesis of an extended material world is better than his of an omnipotent immaterial God as an explanation of life as we know it? Many people think they can answer that question, if only negatively: they would say that Berkeley's belief in God is itself unfounded, and so the alternative belief in a material world wins by default. It seems to me, though, that that is a very weak defence of so fundamental a part of our world picture, and that Berkeley has succeeded at the very least in shifting the burden of proof: it may be that there is no good reason to adopt his theory; but then, is there any good reason to adopt ours?

Berkeley, however, is not content to leave the position like that: that his theory and our broadly Lockeian common sense are alternative explanations, and that the job of the philosopher is to decide which is the more convincing. He thinks he can show that the Lockeian theory, the belief in a mind-independent material world, is obviously false, and it is only the fact that we have been brainwashed by centuries of corrupt Lockeian philosophy that has succeeded in concealing from us the obvious absurdity of what we take for granted.

The way he tries to show this is by arguing that the material world doesn't exist because it *can't* exist: that matter is *impossible*. And why is matter impossible? Because it is inconceivable: the whole idea of matter is an absurdity, a nonsense, a contradiction.

He develops a whole set of interlocking arguments to try to drive us to this conclusion. For the most part they turn on what he claims is the emptiness, the meaninglessness, of the concept of matter. Consider any material object – say, a brick. I can see its shape, its colour, feel its weight and its hardness, use it to build a wall, and so on. But all of those things in Berkeley's terms are just ideas in my mind. Its colour is a set of visual sensations, its shape is a set of visual sensations which are correlated with a set of touch sensations (I know what the corners feel like, as well as what they look like). Its heaviness and hardness are more sets of experiences, and its usefulness in building walls is a whole set of experiences I have had of building walls, knocking them down, looking at them, climbing on them, and so on. Berkeley asks: what is left of the brick if we take away from it all those things, which are clearly mind-dependent experiences, and not the brick in itself? What is the shape of the brick, for example, as distinct from the way it looks and the way it feels? What is shape *in itself*, as opposed to shape *in our experience*?

The question is not easy to answer. But if we can't answer it, then Berkeley's trap is sprung: as the arch-enemy Locke had himself shown, everything we can understand, we understand through experience: it is our sensations that provide all the concepts the mind can grasp. If that is so, then if 'matter' is to be intelligible to us, we must be able to translate the word into sensory terms – into feels, looks, tastes, and so on. But all those things are in Berkeley's terms ideas, and so not the matter we are looking for. And if matter is not translatable into sensory terms, then it is unintelligible, a nonsense, an absurdity. We bandy the word around, we feel as if we understand it, but as soon as we try to focus clearly on what we mean by the word, we find it means either sets of experiences, or nothing at all.

Berkeley's positive account of human beings as in constant sensory communication with an omnipotent and all-good God has never been popular. His negative critique of our own commonsense beliefs, though, is astonishingly difficult to resist. Is that fact merely an interesting historical anomaly, a game for philosophy students to play? Or does it suggest that the attitudes and beliefs that we currently inhabit are indefensible?

DAVID HUME: THE IMPOSSIBILITY OF UNDERSTANDING

Hume is an elusive philosopher. He sets out bold philosophical projects, and shows them to be impossible; he leads his readers to despairing conclusions, and then ignores them and carries on regardless. He writes knowing, witty texts which toy with his readers, mocking their hopes and their self-image. His main challenge to us is to call into question the very possibility of the kind of stable, well-grounded understanding of the world that we aim for and to a large extent think we possess, and to suggest instead that all our learning is in fact nothing but groundless, instinctive reactions and vain, self-important posturings.

Hume is deeply impressed by Berkeley's use of the Lockeian principle that all knowledge comes from what we can experience, and his development of it into a test for meaningfulness. For Berkeley we can only be said truly to understand something if we can cash it out in hard, experiential terms: you only know what a tree is if you can call to mind some appropriate tree-experiences, and you don't know what matter is because you can't call to mind any matter experiences, only shape experiences, colour experiences, hardness experiences, and so on. In Hume's hands this principle becomes a weapon with which to sweep away obfuscation and traditional ways of thinking, and to undercut the pretensions of the learned.

He starts out in the *Treatise of Human Nature* by saying he is going to analyse the human mind and its workings, as a way of unifying and grounding all human knowledge. All the disparate areas of knowledge have in common the very fact that they are items of human knowledge; if we can only understand, therefore, the way the mind works, and the way we come to conclusions, we will be able to bring together all the branches of learning into a single system – and thereby to sweep away everything that doesn't fit into that system as false, imaginary and unreal. The Lockeian/Berkeleian principle is a central part of this process of founding a new Science of Man.

The clearest example of Hume's method in action is his work on morality, of which he was especially proud, and which has been hugely influential. Moralists are fond of using words like good and bad; we often claim to know what is right and what is wrong, and try to teach it to other people. If such claims are to be legitimate, we will need first of all to establish what moral terms mean, i.e. to ascertain what experiences provide us with an understanding of them. What, then, is the meaning of a moral term like 'good'? What experiences does it derive from? What sensory 'impressions' give rise to this 'idea'? Hume invites us to consider actions we regard as good, and to ask what observable features of them lead us to describe them in that way.

So consider any good deed – giving money to charity, perhaps. The action might be done quickly or slowly, and it is easy to see how we give content to that judgement, or what experiences lead us to describe it one way or the other. Similarly it might be done willingly or unwillingly. Here it is less obvious, but we know from our own cases what it feels like to do something willingly, and we know how we behave when we do something that way, so we can recognise such behaviour in other people. And so on with other features of the action. But what of the *goodness* of the action? What feature of the act leads us to describe it as good? What sensory impressions do we derive that idea from? Hume's answer is that there is nothing at all that is discoverable in that action that leads us to call it good. The impression that gives meaning to the idea is not some observable feature of the act, but a feeling in us as observers: when we consider certain actions, we feel a kind of pleasure, or approbation, and when we consider others we feel a kind of displeasure – and that is what we mean when we say some actions are good and some are bad. Moral language, therefore, is misleading: acts, in themselves, are neither good nor bad; it's just that acts of certain kinds tend to give us good feelings. We misleadingly project those good feelings onto the acts when we describe them as good or bad.

To us that account of morality seems perfectly plausible, perhaps even obviously true. But when Hume applies exactly the same analysis to other areas of knowledge, his conclusions strike us as much less attractive. The most famous and most striking of these is his analysis of causation, which closely parallels that of morality.

Causation is important, Hume says, because all our knowledge of the world depends on it. Knowing how to do something is essentially a matter of knowing what causes produce what effects; knowing what something means is a matter of knowing what leads people – i.e. causes them – to say or write one thing rather than another, and, most obviously of all, our scientific knowledge is concerned with explaining the world around us, i.e. looking for the causes of what we experience. So, if causation is the basis of all our understanding of what happens in the world, we clearly need to analyse the idea of a cause and find out what it means.

The problem is that, just as with morality, it is very hard to find any set of experiences which we can point to as the origin of our idea of causality. Consider a causal sequence: the white ball rolls across the table, hits the black ball, and the black ball moves. What is it about that sequence that gives us the idea that the impact of the white ball *causes* the movement of the black ball? All we see, after all, is the one event followed by the other; but a sequence of events is not a cause. To say the impact of the white ball *caused* the movement of the black ball is to say not just that the one event followed the other, and not just that it always happens that way, but that the impact *made* the ball move, that it *had* to move – that there is some 'necessary connection' between the two events. But where do we get the idea of this necessity, as opposed to the mere regularity?

Perhaps the necessity is not something we see, but a matter of logic: perhaps it is a necessary truth that a black ball hit by a white ball in that way will move. But that isn't so. For the black ball to stand still, or jump upwards, or turn into a goldfish and sing, would be very strange, completely unprecedented, altogether bizarre – but it wouldn't be contradictory. And if there would be no contradiction in its not happening, then it isn't logically necessary that it should happen.

Hume concludes that the idea of a necessary connection comes neither from observation nor from logic. So where does it come from? He finds the answer in the same place as he finds morality: in our feelings. What happens is that from years of practice of observing event sequences we come to *expect* the effect to follow the cause, so that when we think of the one, we are automatically led to think of the other. Thus when the black ball moves we say it *had* to happen, it was *bound* to happen, the impact of the white ball *caused* it to move. But what we should say, if we were being more careful, is that the impact occurred – and we expected the usual consequence. The causation, like the morality, is not a part of the world around us, but a part of our reaction to it.

Whereas in the case of morality Hume's story seems quite natural, in the case of causality it seems quite crazy. The world, it seems, has no causal powers: all events are 'entirely loose and separate', mere regularities with nothing to maintain them, to bind them together. The world is causally neutral, just as it is morally neutral. We project our feelings onto it when we say otherwise. And having got so far, Hume proceeds by similar chains of reasoning to knock away much more of our self-esteem. If there are no causal powers, what reason is there to think that observed regularities will continue into the future? None – we are conditioned by our past experience to expect the sun to continue to rise, planets to continue to move in ellipses, sugar to continue to taste sweet; but there is no more reason to think those things will continue than to think they will change.

And it doesn't stop there. The world around us is an unwarranted and incomprehensible fiction, just as Berkeley had said. We feel as if there were an external world around us just because there are regularities in our perceptions – but as soon as we ask what that continuing thing might be like, we see that the idea has no content. And unlike Berkeley, Hume has no language of divine sensations to offer us instead, only the inexplicable sequences of our perceptions. And it gets worse. Just as the idea of a mind-independent world is shown to be incomprehensible, so too is the idea of the mind itself. What does it mean to talk of a mind? I know my thoughts, my feelings, my intentions, my perceptions, and all the so-called contents of my mind, but what of the mind itself? What meaning can we give to that? It seems that, like the external world, it is a nonsensical fiction, brought into being by our laziness and inattention to the true facts of our mental lives. Both mind and world are nothing but groundless inventions based on thoughtlessness.

In this way Hume uses his scientific, empirically-based theory to chop away all the foundations of our world picture. Even pure reason he claims, the truths of logic and mathematics, turn out to be based on a combination of laziness and rough-and-ready practical, social judgements. His attempt to carry out a rational, scientific investigation of human consciousness produces the conclusion that there is no rational basis to anything we do – including, or most especially, inquiries such as his own.

What are we to make of this stream of negative conclusions? At first it looks like the suicide of philosophy: a careful investigation that shows that careful investigations get you nowhere; a scientific proof that there is no such thing as a scientific proof. If Hume is right, then he is wrong – but there is no point in our trying to find a better position, because what he has shown is that trying to show anything is pointless. He reduces himself, he claims, to 'the most desperate condition imaginable', a hopeless scepticism that produces – in him, and in us, if we accept what he says – utter despair.

Yet an intriguing feature of Hume's position is that he himself admits quite openly that he doesn't believe any of it – or at least, not for very long. As soon as there is a knock at the door, he tells us, or he goes out into the world again, then all his carefully thought-out doubts and anxieties seem suddenly to disappear. He immediately slips back right into his old ways of thinking and acting, and all his painfully constructed philosophical angst seems only fantastic and absurd.

The conclusion he derives from this is that our nature is far stronger than our reasoning can ever be. He can see no flaw in his arguments, and yet, try as he might, he is just incapable of believing what they tell him. Where does he go from there? What does the unacceptability of his own conclusions show?

There are broadly two kinds of answer to that question. The older, more negative view of Hume is that his failure to believe his own conclusions only goes to establish them more firmly: we are so cut off from any reasonable view of the world, he is saying, so much the creatures of custom and habit, that we are incapable of believing the truth even when we see it. Human beings are just not built for truth, for understanding; they think what their mechanical minds make them think, and the final proof of that is the fact that when you present it to them as carefully as you can, it has as much effect on their behaviour and their thought processes as it would if you explained it to a rabbit, or an earthworm.

More recent commentators have read him in an altogether more optimistic way. The reason he cannot accept his own conclusions, he may be saying, is that the world-view that we inhabit is not any kind of conclusion that we have come to, or a judgement with regard to which we can give reasons, either for or against. The basic assumptions on which our lives are based – such things as the existence of ourselves and of the world we live in, the force of laws of nature, and the possibility of arriving at reasoned conclusions – all these things are not mere beliefs that we hold, or discoveries we have made, but are built into our very natures, hard-wired into the kind of creature that we are, so that we simply cannot exist without them. To question any of these principles is on this view simply nonsensical – as crazy as it would be for us to sit around and ask seriously whether we have any valid argument to convince us that it is a good idea for us to continue to breathe.

We all of us, all the time, act as if Hume's negative conclusions were wrong. Is that because they are wrong, or just because we are too set in our ways to do otherwise? Or are you happy to say that our most fundamental beliefs are constitutive of the kind of creature that we are, and as such do not admit of, and stand in no need of, any kind of justification?

If they are to be justified, it is perhaps not in any way that could have been considered by Hume, or by any of the six 'Modern' philosophers we have looked at. Immanuel Kant (1724–1804) claimed that it was the work of Hume that woke him from his dogmatic slumbers, and which led him to the 'Copernican Revolution' of his Transcendental Idealism. Kant said that Hume was quite right to point out that the fundamental concepts and judgements of our world picture are not self-justifying necessities, and also that they cannot be discovered or shown to be true by any possible experience. But Kant thought it was wrong to derive from that fact either a desperate scepticism or a robust but unargued assertion of the inescapability of Common Sense. According to Kant, although we can never show that in broad terms the world is as we take it to be, nevertheless it *is* possible to show that a view of broadly that form is essential to any account of the world that we could ever understand. Although such things as the self, the external world and causation cannot be shown to be genuine features of How Things Really Are, we can nevertheless resist the conclusion that they are mere subjective appearances, because we can show that they are necessary features of any possible human understanding of how things are, which for Kant means they can be objectively validated for all people and for all time.

Could such a manoeuvre work? Could it do the job of satisfying us, in the face of such problems as Cartesian Doubt, Berkeleian Idealism and Humeian Scepticism, that it is possible to achieve a well-founded and defensible view of the world and of our place in it? The answer will perhaps depend on the extent to which we are still in the grip of the 'Modern' viewpoint which Kant's predecessors invented, and which they have bequeathed to us.

EXERCISES

The question I have tried to raise in this chapter is this: is the way we see the world, our modern-day enlightened, scientific commonsense, a rational and carefully worked-out set of interlocking theories which we have discovered and can justify, and which enables us to live our lives to the full? Or is our world-view something over which we have no control, and which most of us have never thought about – an incoherent rag-bag of attitudes and beliefs which have been foisted on us by the history of Europe in the last few hundred years, and which get in the way of our understanding of ourselves and our place in nature: rather like an old and very dirty pair of spectacles which don't really fit us, but which we have grown used to and don't realise we are wearing? I think it is the latter. I have tried here to sketch some of the views of six people who wore different spectacles, and lived very different lives, because I think that is the best way to bring us to a consciousness of our own preconceptions. Here are some questions to help us clean our glasses.

1   Descartes tries to show that the scientist's mathematical understanding of natural processes is the only accurate and sustainable view of things, and that the ordinary person's view of the world is fundamentally mistaken. Is he right? If we deny his claim that scientific reasoning is a finite recapitulation of God's own understanding of creation, what grounds do we have for agreeing with him?

2 Is it simply misleading for Spinoza to use the terms 'God' and 'Nature' interchangeably, or does he indeed manage to reconcile the life of science with the life of religion?

3 Leibniz claims that for everything that is true, there is a reason why it is so and not otherwise. Is that true? Does there have to be a reason for the way things are, or do we at some point have to say 'That's just how it is'? If so, at *what* point?

4 Locke claimed that natural science could never, even in theory, be completed, but that the nature of human knowledge means that we can only ever know the way things act, and then develop plausible hypotheses as to why they do so. Has the history of science since Locke's day borne that out?

5 All we can ever immediately experience is our own sensations, and we can make no sense of something which is by definition beyond all possible experience. Does that mean that the idea of a material world makes no sense?

6 Is it conceivable that human beings have no good reason for any of the things they normally believe? Or does the fact that human beings normally believe them itself constitute a good reason for accepting them?

7 If it could be shown that the concept of an external world is an essential feature of any possible human understanding of things, would that prove that there is an external world?

FURTHER READING

Descartes

Descartes' most widely-read and most accessible work is his *Meditations on Philosophy* (or *on Metaphysics*, or *on First Philosophy*). More difficult and more wide-ranging is the *Discourse on Method*. His official *magnum opus* is the *Principles of Philosophy*.

Spinoza

For Spinoza the only thing to read is the *Ethics* – which unfortunately is presented in axiomatic form, which makes it very hard going. But it is worth the effort.

Leibniz

Leibniz has no single masterwork, but works out his views in a mass of articles and letters. A summary written late in his life is the *Monadology*, but much of the same story can be read in the much earlier *Discourse on Metaphysics*.

Locke

Locke's main theoretical work is the *Essay Concerning Human Understanding*. For his important political views, see the *Two Treatises of Government*, especially the second.

Berkeley

Berkeley's main work is the *Principles of Human Knowledge*. The same story is presented in dialogue form in *Three Dialogues Between Hylas and Philonous*.

Hume

Hume's most radical views are to be found in the *Treatise of Human Nature*, especially Book 1. The *Enquiry Concerning Human Understanding* is a later, somewhat sanitised, reworking of many of the same themes. His views on morality are in Book 3 of the *Treatise*, and in the *Enquiry Concerning the Principles of Morals*. For his views on religion, see the *Dialogues Concerning Natural Religion*.

Kant

Kant's ideas on these topics are set out in the *Critique of Pure Reason*, a work which he described as 'dry, obscure, opposed to all ordinary notions, and moreover long-winded'. He later summarised his views in the much shorter *Prologomena to Any Future Metaphysics*.

8

PHILOSOPHY OF MIND

Stephen Burwood

INTRODUCTION

When doing philosophy one sometimes cannot avoid the feeling that one is running just in order to stand still; and no more so than in philosophy of mind. Currently this is one of the most imaginative, fertile, and hotly contested areas of research. Nevertheless, I think it is fair to say that, despite this productivity, we are still just as far from a solution to its central problem as we ever were. What, then, is this problem that appears so intractable? Philosophy of mind, as most professionals presently working in the field conduct it, is almost exclusively concerned with the mind–body problem. Like many philosophical problems, it is surprisingly easy to set up but is something for which it is considerably harder to find anything like a fully satisfying solution. Human beings are minded creatures: we believe and disbelieve things; we agree and argue about these; we fall into love and despair; we enjoy the caress of our lover's hands and suffer agonising pain, we savour and find repulsive the flavour of coffee; and so on. Yet, we are also material creatures, made up of flesh and bone, themselves made up of nothing more than the same physical stuff as all other physical things. In fact, as educated modern people, we believe that we are either *principally* or perhaps even *entirely* material creatures, subject to the same natural laws as everything else in the world. How is it that mindedness, with its apparently intangible characteristics such as meaningfulness, rationality, and conscious experience, inhabits a material world that is exhaustively governed by natural laws and is, in itself, devoid of such characteristics? How is it that creatures of mere flesh and bone are minded? The French philosopher Merleau-Ponty neatly captures this puzzlement when he says 'How significance and intentionality could come to dwell in molecular edifices or masses of cells is a thing that can never be made comprehensible' (Merleau-Ponty 1962, p. 351). Of course, scientific investigations of these 'masses of cells', especially advances in the brain sciences and associated disciplines, help us to better understand the workings of complex human physiology, but can they dispel the philosophical puzzlement: how is it that *this stuff* is responsible for mindedness? This question is of the utmost moment in philosophy and its importance lies in the fact that it goes to the very heart of who we think we are, our conception of the world around us, and our understanding of our place in that world.

It is not my aim in this chapter to offer a solution to this puzzle, though I will volunteer some, alas all too perfunctory, remarks of my own in the last section. Nor is it my aim in a work of this length to review the many solutions attempted by others, though it will be necessary to rehearse, at a quick canter, some of the key moves made recently by different major theories. The aim is, rather, to explore some motivations and assumptions informing the current debate. This means briefly looking at two important intellectual developments; the Cartesian turn in philosophy in the seventeenth century, and twentieth-century developments in the philosophy of science. I have chosen these two, from a host of alternatives, because these are probably the most specific and direct influences on the present scene – though others are undoubtedly important background influences. In doing this I hope the reader gets something of the flavour of that debate as well as gaining a purchase on why the mind–body problem is considered a problem, why it has become the central problem in this field of study, and why the debate is conducted in the way that it is. If we seem overly concerned with a particular view known as physicalism, this is because that is where the subject mostly is nowadays. Any modern theory in the philosophy of mind is either within the physicalist framework, or has to position itself against that framework. Physicalism is also interesting because it represents the purest statement of the naturalising project that currently dominates the subject and is a manifestation of a powerful *Zeitgeist* within modern philosophical thought and our general culture.[1] What the majority of philosophers working in the field believe is that we need a theory that will facilitate and promote further scientific investigation of the mind. The mind, and what constitutes mentality, has become one of the last great frontiers for science. The game is now afoot and the goal is a fully-fledged science of the mind. Thus, the dominant view in the philosophy of mind sees its task as articulating a conception of the mental consistent with the investigation of the mental by natural science.

DESCARTES' LEGACY

To begin to see what motivates this naturalising project and to understand why the mind–body problem has become so central to the philosophy of mind, it is necessary first to look at the Cartesian turn in philosophy in the middle of the seventeenth century. The mind–body problem in its present form is a problem we owe almost entirely to Descartes and his contemporaries. Although the mind–body problem can be, and often is, profitably addressed in the context of thinkers prior to this period, we should note that for the most part their concerns were not ours. However, it is almost impossible to introduce someone to this debate without saying something about Descartes. He is perhaps best known for his own eponymous solution to the problem, a form of psycho-physical dualism in which body and mind are considered as distinct and autonomous substances that are able to causally interact. In his view, to have a mental or psychological state involves the modification of this mental substance, which may result in, or be the result of, modifications in the physical substance. This position became known as Cartesian dualism. But this is not the source of his continuing relevance to the debate. Although this sort of solution still enjoys evident popularity with the general public, and is occasionally defended by practising philosophers (e.g. Popper and Eccles 1977; Madell 1988; Foster 1991), the simple fact is that most professionals working in the philosophy of mind do not see any form of psycho-physical dualism as a going concern. The reason for this is that it runs up against a legion of profound philosophical difficulties and, not least, given the distinct whiff of supernaturalism that accompanies it, it offends against most modern philosophers' strongly materialist sensibilities. The consequence is that a vanishingly small number of philosophers will now argue for a philosophical position such as this, though it has become almost *de rigueur* to provide a chapter arguing against. Descartes' relevance lies rather in the way that his explication of the issues continues to shape our understanding of the problem and informs attempted solutions to it – even where these stand in opposition to his own solution.

Descartes' answer, then, was that we are not entirely or even principally material creatures but an amalgam of two distinct substances: an extended material substance (our bodies) and an unextended immaterial substance (our minds). However, this is only Descartes' 'official' view: it is possible to also read Descartes' work in such a way that he is much less of a pure Cartesian in this respect than many who came after him. It is true that he says his intention was to prove the immortality of the human soul; but in many ways this is a distraction.[2] Descartes had other philosophical motivations for his dualism; motivations still relevant in these less religious times. We should not forget that he was not only the father of modern philosophy, as he is often called in introductory textbooks, but also one of the architects of modern science. During the late Renaissance and the Baroque (the historical period in which he lived) people were beginning to investigate the natural world in new ways and this required them to formulate new ways of modelling its workings and their relations to it. Part of this conceptual shift was a remodelling of the material world and the human body, with the invention of new discourses by which they could be described and understood. Descartes recognised that the mind has certain distinctive features, such as its rationality and subjectivity, that does not allow it to fit neatly with the view of the world and the body proposed by this 'new science', and yet it has others, such as its causal efficacy, which suggest that it should. As we shall see, accounting for all these features in one encompassing theory continues to offer a challenge to philosophers. Before exploring the modern scene, however, we need to unpack this insight.

In many ways, therefore, Descartes' philosophy of mind grew out of the new science he and others, such as Bacon and Galileo, were endeavouring to establish and was an attempt to accommodate the mind's distinctiveness within this new framework. They conceived of the natural world as being subject to complete mathematical description and governed exhaustively by physical laws discoverable by science. This new dispensation did away with Aristotelian notions such as a 'vegetative' or 'sensitive soul', or a 'principle of movement', as a *causa vitae* and explanation of the movement of complex organisms or objects. The dominant metaphor informing it was the clock: the material world was understood in terms of a large clockwork-like mechanism and causal relations within it as a function of material objects' extension; as the push of one thing on another. Thus, Descartes occasionally indicates that complex bodies could be thought of in analogous terms to watches or other automata; i.e. machines that are able to move themselves by the mere arrangement of their internal organs, as watches move themselves simply by the arrangement of their counter-weights and wheels. As both human and animal bodies are material objects, their movements too could be understood mechanistically.

Descartes has become notorious for apparently claiming that non-human animals are mere unfeeling and unthinking automata, whose behaviour could be completely understood mechanistically. This is only half-right: he did think they are unthinking but not unfeeling. Furthermore, for the most part, the accounts he gives of sensation and perception apply equally to humans and non-human animals alike. In fact, he sometimes suggests that both human and animal bodies can be thought of as 'sentient machines'. Given that phenomena such as sensation and perception involve specialised bodily organs and require physiological changes to take place, they can only be understood in the context of a body and are largely susceptible to mechanistic explanation. He thought that many forms of bodily movement, human and non-human, could be explained mechanistically without invoking conscious states. Here he has in mind the automatic functioning of the body's internal organs as well as what he calls 'waking actions' such as walking (which can occur without our conscious attention) and reflex actions such as sticking out one's hand in order to protect oneself in a fall. What makes humans unique, according to Descartes, is that they have a wider behavioural repertoire than non-humans; one that includes types of behaviour for which this sort of explanation cannot fully account.

He thought that there were two principles governing bodily movement; the first is simply a causal–mechanical principle by which the motion of a body can be explained without reference to the mind, and the second is the will, which he calls a faculty of the rational soul. Descartes seems to have thought that the distinction between an action (i.e. behaviour directed towards a goal or object) and a mere bodily movement lay in the fact that actions have their origin in a certain mentalistic event, an act of will, which then produces the required physiological changes in the body. Humans are unique because we are agents capable of performing actions. So, while some of the movements of our bodies can be explained in purely causal–mechanical terms, there are many others that require a quite different economy of explanations. What Descartes grasped was that, as thinking beings and agents, the behaviour of humans enters into the domain of reason: their beliefs and actions may be considered as justified or unjustified, appropriate or inappropriate – normative concepts quite out of place in causal explanations. As rational, purposive creatures with goals of our own, we are not, he argued, merely machines performing set tasks. Human reason is, he thought, a 'universal instrument' which allows us, unlike machines, to respond to an almost infinite number of different circumstances in different and appropriate ways. Another way of putting this is to say that a large part of human behaviour consists of more than mere bodily movement.

The second distinctive feature Descartes thought a theory of mind should accommodate was its subjectivity. In these terms the difference between humans and animals was, for example, that not only do we see or feel something (which may be purely bodily) but that we can also *think* we see or feel something. In other words, we are consciously aware, as well as being rational beings. However, in explicating this he left us with a particular model of the mind whose influence has been enormous but not necessarily benign. What Descartes assumes is that the content (e.g. in the case of a belief, what it is about or, in the case of a sensation, how it feels) of a person's psychological states could be what they are irrespective of how the world is. The world may be radically different from how it appears and, indeed, may not even exist. In other words, even though her intentional states (i.e. those states, like beliefs, that are *about* something) fail to refer to anything real, or her phenomenal states (i.e. those states, like sensations, that have a qualitative aspect) do not have the physical cause she supposes, or no physical cause at all, they nevertheless have the content they do simply because they seem that way to her.[3] This is the model of the mind as the Cartesian theatre, something like a self-contained black box. It is a view that has given rise to the peculiar philosophical vocabulary of the 'inner' and 'outer': a private world of subjective conscious experience and a shared public world of objective facts. This model of the mind leads to an obvious scepticism about the minds of others: we cannot ever know directly what someone is thinking or feeling for her mind is shut away, hidden from view. All we have access to is her body described simply in terms of a physical, mechanical system. It also raises questions concerning the nature of mental states and not simply our knowledge of them. As far as Cartesian dualism is concerned, the mind is self-contained because it is an immaterial substance and thus a psychological state is essentially a modification of this immaterial substance.

However, even if Cartesian immaterialism is rejected as a way of picturing the mind as self-contained, this latter idea continues to influence the way philosophers understand the nature of the mind. If the idea of the mind as a Cartesian theatre assumes that our mental states have the content they do irrespective of how the world is, then it assumes that these states are 'narrow' as opposed to 'broad' in terms of what determines their content. This is a question about what sort of facts are constitutive of, say, a belief. Are they a narrow range of facts only about you – for Descartes an extremely narrow range of facts about how things seem to you – or do they include other sorts of facts as well, facts about things external to the mind's black box? Nowadays the view that mental states are narrow is often termed 'individualism' or 'internalism'; its opposite 'externalism'. Caution is needed here because, for the present-day internalist, the relevant facts about you may also include facts about the internal states of your body such as states of the central nervous system. As far as they are concerned the boundary between the 'inner' and the 'outer' lies at the surface of someone's skin, or somewhere within its surface (e.g. at the boundary of the brain). Thus, for these philosophers, certain physiological facts may be constitutive of what a mental state is; indeed, for some these may be the only relevant facts.

> The reason for this is that it may be these that underlie and explain the causal efficacy of our psychological states. This brings us to the last of Descartes' insights, that psychological states are causally linked to action. Accounting for this caused what was probably the greatest problems for his dualist solution to the mind–body problem. Despite the fact that his dualism regarded the mind as something autonomous and distinct from the body and the material world, he also recognised that, in practice, the mind was able to causally engage with world through an enigmatic union with the body. He was never able to explain the nature of this union and it remained a mysterious and brute fact in his philosophy. Under pressure to clarify it he concedes that human reason cannot provide an adequate account of the causal interaction between mind and body, though he continued to argue that experience teaches us that it is nevertheless true. Thus, in a famous reply to a persistent critic, he suggests 'That is why people who never philosophise and use only their senses have no doubt that the soul moves the body and that the body acts on the soul. . . . [I]t is the ordinary course of life and conversation, and abstention from meditation and the study of things which exercise the imagination, that teaches us how to conceive the union of the soul and the body.'
>
> (Descartes 1991, p. 227)

Apart from the inability to say how two distinct substances causally interact, there is a another problem with dualist interactionism; one which flows partly from the conception of the physical Descartes himself initiated. This is the problem commonly known as the over-determination of the physical. To grasp what this means, consider the case of the unlucky golfer who is simultaneously struck by a meteor and a bolt of lightening while having a heart attack. If each of these events is sufficient on its own to kill her, then her death is over-determined. Descartes was keen to point out that we may be led by experience to assume that all the body's movements were caused by the will, and that this is untrue. As we have said before, an important strand in Descartes' thought was his mechanism. In line with this many, if not most, of the human body's movements can be accounted for simply as the products of its internal material arrangements. Similarly for the movement of material bodies in general. This was the first step towards an understanding of the material world as a closed system that requires nothing more than a mechanical explanation of the events unfolding within it. Although modern science has shed the mechanistic baggage of seventeenth-century science, the idea that the world is a closed causal system has been retained and is now a fundamental assumption underlying modern science. On this view of the material world, physical causes by themselves are sufficient to bring about a physical event. We shall call this the completeness of physics. The problem with Descartes' dualism is that, if this is accepted, intentional actions, involving a bodily event such as the movement of one's leg, seems to have both a physical cause and a mental cause; both of which may be sufficient in themselves to bring the effect about. In other words the action is over-determined.

The completeness of physics and the problem of over-determination explicitly motivate the materialism of much modern philosophy of mind. The worry is not that over-determination never occurs in nature, but that it is extremely rare and Cartesian dualism would require it to be the norm with respect to a large category of physical events (i.e. those constitutive of bodily movement: behaviour). The problem arises in the context of Descartes' theory because he wished to preserve both the causal efficacy of the mind and its autonomy from the physical world. He does this by dividing the mental from the mechanical and puts the mental into a separate realm of 'inner' non-material substance. For Descartes, as Gilbert Ryle put it, 'Minds are not bits of clockwork, they are just bits of not-clockwork' (Ryle 1949, p. 21). Modern philosophy of mind is marked by the resolute rejection of this strand of Descartes' thought; but also by its acceptance of others. One that has been explicitly and widely accepted is his causalism; that psychological states make a difference to what happens in the world. Other important aspects of his thought, however, have also been accepted, albeit implicitly. For example, the larger metaphysical picture provided by the framework of the new science and, not least, in the way that many theorists assume that the essence of a psychological state is an internal fact about the person having that state. For modern theorists, therefore, there is only one kind of substance, material or physical substance as articulated by science. Consequently, they have had to confront the question; if dualism is abandoned, what is a psychological state? The only answer available, it seems, is that, in some way, it must be a state of this material substance. Different accounts of how this might be the case have dominated philosophy of mind in recent years.

SCIENCE AND SCIENTISM

A characteristic feature of much modern philosophy of mind is that it thinks that the question 'What is a psychological state?' ultimately may be answered by science. This aspiration is, as I have said, partly a consequence of its rejection of any sort of immaterialism and its implicit subscription to other Cartesian notions; but it equally shows how philosophy of mind is influenced by thinking in the philosophy of science. This brings us to the second important background development informing the current debate: the shift during the middle of the twentieth century from positivist conceptions of science to scientific realist conceptions of science. The importance of this is that the different ways philosophers have thought science operates have strongly influenced the accounts they have given of what is involved in having a psychological state.

Positivism and scientific realism differ sharply over the epistemic capabilities of science. The scientific realist believes, whereas the positivist does not, that scientific methods of investigation are capable of yielding knowledge of unobservables. Positivist conceptions of science were strongly neo-empiricist. Empiricism, broadly speaking, is the view that all knowledge of 'matters of fact and real existence' must be firmly based on, and vindicated by reference only to, sensory experience. This has sometimes led (most notably in Hume and, to a lesser extent, the positivists) to a scepticism about claims that 'go beyond' the immediate data of sensory experience. Consequently, according to positivism, scientific theories merely express regular relationships observed in the world and allow us to explain and predict natural phenomena. I say 'merely' because within the positivist framework it was not considered to be the proper job of science to go beyond the observed and postulate what is in fact unobserved, or worse still, what is in principle unobservable, entities, essences, states, or mechanisms that are thought to underlie and somehow necessitate the phenomena. All we can be sure of are the observed regularities. A corollary of this approach is that theoretical states are regarded as heuristic devices, there simply to facilitate predictions in the realm of the observed. Their status is such that they are something that can be exhaustively understood in terms of observable phenomena or can be treated as 'useful fictions'. When such positivist conceptions of science were in vogue, any legitimate science of the mind would have to conform to this framework. Consequently, we find that behaviourism was the dominant theory of the mind during this period (e.g. Watson 1913; Skinner 1953; Hempel 1980).

Those who were positivist in their philosophy of science saw psychological states as unobservable theoretical entities, postulated to explain regularities in observed behaviour, and which therefore enjoyed only the most vicarious existence. On this type of account, my intention to make a pot of tea consists in nothing more than displaying, or potentially displaying, a particular pattern of behaviour. This claim was often expressed in terms of meanings, so that the meaning of theoretical terms could be cashed out in terms of observable data. Thus Hempel wrote, 'We see clearly that the meaning of a psychological statement consists solely in the function of abbreviating the description of certain modes of physical response characteristic of the bodies of men and animals' (Hempel 1980, p. 19). So, for example, 'I intend to do *x*' simply *means* 'I am behaving, or am disposed to behave, in a specified way', where 'behaviour' indicates nothing more than 'colourless' physical movements in space and time. Among the several inadequacies inherent in this view (not least the implausibility of these semantic equivalences) is the fact that it seems to leave episodes of behaviour, even so construed, as brute occurrences. As Descartes recognised, an important aspect of our normal everyday ways of speaking about each other is that we assume that psychological states lay behind behaviour as its cause, and are not merely identical to it. Behaviourism was a theory, therefore, that many ordinary people found to be counter-intuitive and plainly wrong. But the way it bypassed causalist intuitions also became a concern for equally hard-headed materialist colleagues, and especially so as realist conceptions of science began to supersede positivism.

So, as positivism fell out of favour, so too did behaviourism. For the scientific realist, merely demonstrating that a phenomenon is an instance of an observed regularity (even if this results in the ability to make successful predictions) is not to provide an *explanation* for that phenomenon. Rather, to do this we must uncover the underlying structures or processes involved in its production and this may indeed mean postulating unobserved, or perhaps even unobservable, entities, essences, states, or mechanisms. The theoretical terms in our scientific theory are thus not simply regarded as 'useful fictions' but are interpreted as making reference to actual states in the world and providing true descriptions of how the world is, even if such states are initially identified only by their observed effects. Part of the problem for positivism was that, with the development of increasingly sophisticated observational devices, many 'useful fictions' came in time to be directly observed, and so shown to be real.[4] Hence, positivist conceptions of science proved increasingly problematic. On the realist account, the proper job of scientific investigation is to uncover the hidden essential properties of these states.

When this approach to theoretical states combines with the causalist intuitions outlined above, then it is a short step to expecting such essential properties to provide the underlying causal mechanisms. This also fits neatly with a view of scientific method in which scientific kinds are seen as natural kinds such as gold or water. Here the picture is of the world already divided into discreet kinds that we can uncover, so long as our system of classification matches the structure of the natural world. With respect to the mind, on this account of science, our psychological states may be viewed as natural kinds. As such they can feature in our causal–explanatory generalisations, explaining (and facilitating prediction of) behaviour. It then becomes the job of a scientific programme of investigation to discover what their essential characteristics are, in a way that the causal mechanisms that support such explanations are uncovered. So, just as we discovered that gold has the atomic number 79 and water the molecular structure H_2O, we may discover that being in pain, say, is C-fibre excitation. The assumption of causalism, in the context of a scientific realist framework, has therefore led to a conception of psychological states as underlying states that are causally responsible for bringing about behaviour, and whose constitutive essences are an appropriate object of scientific investigation.

Realism is probably the view closest to what we might call the 'common sense of science'; the view that science, especially in the form of the physical sciences, progressively describes the world as it really is. The conjunction of the widespread rejection of Descartes' immaterialism and the acceptance of his causalism with the recent dominance of these scientific realist attitudes thus also accounts for the commitment many philosophers have nowadays to ontological and explanatory physicalism. What this means is that, ontologically, material entities and properties are given articulation in the terms of physical science and that this mode of articulation is privileged (i.e. is seen as fundamental). Any real distinctions in the world (at least those with any real empirical import) are ones captured by the theories of physical science. What is basic, therefore, is the microworld of atomic and sub-atomic physics; the macroworld (that is, the everyday world of tables and chairs, of you and me) is ultimately the result of what obtains at the micro level. This commitment to physicalism also involves two other beliefs: first, that there is no other story we can tell about the world that is coherent enough to fulfil the role currently discharged by the theories of physical science; and second, that the explanations of physical science are both comprehensive and exhaustive. The second is an idea we have encountered already, the completeness of physics, which maintains that any physical effect has a physical cause that, in itself, is sufficient to produce that effect. Therefore, any phenomenon that can be given a physicalist characterisation can be given a *complete* causal explanation in physical terms. Physical effects have physical causes, supported by law-like generalisations that refer to physical kinds only, and whose constitutive features provide us with the requisite underlying causal mechanism.

Adherence to the common sense of science by many of those working in the field has led many outside, including other philosophers, to accuse modern philosophy of mind of being overtly scientistic. It is not always clear what this charge amounts to, other than it has a naturalising tendency, but there is some justification in the view that there often seems to be a 'veneration of science in general and physics in particular' (Lyons 1998, p. 156). As I have indicated, this veneration, in part, has its roots in a strong realist conception of science and a metaphysical preference for physicalism. There is, however, a deeper source of scientism in the philosophy of mind, something scientific realists hold in common with their positivist forebears: a deep conviction that modern science is the apogee of knowledge and rationality and its methods paradigmatic of reliable procedure. Indeed, so strong is this conviction that it sometimes seems that what is being suggested is that science is the only proper means for investigating anything: that all questions, all problems, could fall under its all-conquering microscope. The desire for this particular philosopher's stone, a flawless method for transmuting base opinion into knowledge, goes hand-in-hand with their joint aspiration for a fully systematised account of the world. In both senses, positivism and realism are products of a dominant modernist *Zeitgeist* in science and philosophy, which itself traces its lineage back through the Enlightenment to intellectual developments in the Renaissance and the Baroque.

What should we make of these scientistic claims? Well, it is certainly true that science, partly due to its unparalleled cognitive achievement and its practical benefits (in allowing us to manipulate and control the world to our advantage), is a dominant cultural force in our society. It has an allure that is hard to resist, even if we could or should (though, in any case, it is not clear what either of these would mean in practice). It is also true that philosophers, too, have their predilections and are just as prone to sweeping intellectual fashions and cultural movements as anyone else, and it is mere hubris to think otherwise. Perhaps it comes down to this: some of us have a taste for desert landscapes, others not. However, although each of these influences no doubt plays its part, if we suggest that this is all there is to it we would be doing those philosophers who subscribe to such views an injustice for, as I hope I have shown, these views are also motivated by profound philosophical worries. Nevertheless, it may be argued that, in its devotion to physics, the naturalising tendency construes 'natural' far too narrowly. It is not clear that in the philosophy of mind this approach can deliver all of what it promises and is unable to provide genuine insights into what constitutes mentality.

REDUCTIONISM AND CENTRAL STATE MATERIALISM

For physicalism, all causal–explanatory interactions, however they are expressed, have to be anchored in fundamental physical causal interactions. Within this framework the task for philosophy of mind is twofold: first, to give an account of what is involved in having psychological states that respects ontological physicalism; and, second, give an account that accommodates the causal role of the mental in a way compatible with explanatory physicalism. The task of working within these constraints currently informs much of the work in the philosophy of mind. The philosophical task involves the clearing of the conceptual ground in preparation for the mind–body problem being tackled, and ultimately solved, through empirical investigation and the application of specialised scientific knowledge and methods. In this and the following two sections we shall briefly explore this naturalising programme and show how the background assumptions adumbrated in the previous two sections inform the direction of the current debate.

There is general agreement among philosophers in this programme that the preferred method for this ground clearing is reductionist. In general terms, reductionism claims that, given two fields of discourse, there is an equivalence of either meaning or reference between the statements of the two fields so that anything explicable in terms of one field is explicable in terms of the other. In practice one of the fields of discourse is normally privileged over the other and is seen as being more basic as a means of explanation. Examples of successful reductions from the non-psychological realm are many and include the reduction of lightening to atmospheric electrical discharges, heat to mean kinetic energy, and water to H_2O. It is often characterised as a 'nothing but' claim: that, for example, water is nothing but H_2O, and so on. With respect to the specific case of the mind and body, the claim has been that anything explicable in terms of psychological entities, attributes, or descriptions is explicable in terms of physical entities, attributes, or descriptions. In other words, the psychological is nothing but the physical.

The attraction of this approach for our realist, and especially physicalist, minded philosopher is that it accords with an overall model of the way in which different levels of scientific explanation fit together. If scientific theories are not simply heuristic devices but progressively give us an accurate picture of how the world really is, then one might expect different scientific theories, even from quite different branches of science, to converge towards a systematic view of the natural world: the picture of the unity of science. Within this picture, the explanatory laws provided by 'higher level sciences' are reducible to (or derivable from) those of progressively more basic 'lower level sciences', culminating in a reduction to the laws of physics, the most basic. One reason why the lower level sciences may be considered more basic may be the greater generality, and therefore greater explanatory and predictive power, of the laws at those levels. For some, the privileging of the lower levels reflects assumptions concerning the operations of fundamental causal mechanisms. Sometimes, however, it may simply reflect the metaphysical preferences we spoke of earlier. In this scheme physics is invariably the most privileged science in recognition of the fact that it articulates the most fundamental regularities governing the natural world.

The kind of picture presented here has been given imaginative expression by Kim Sterelny. Sterelny works with the metaphor of a tree: 'The idea is that the tree is rooted in fundamental physical kinds and processes. Through various different branches, all scientific kinds depend on that taproot . . . kinds (and the laws expressed in terms of them) further out on the branches need to be explained by kinds and laws closer to the root' (Sterelny 1993, pp. 136–7) According to Sterelny, anything that cannot be incorporated into the tree (e.g. kinds that are not natural kinds) do not do genuine explanatory work. Our psychological kinds do appear to do explanatory work. If this explanatory work is to be considered genuine, then the philosophical task is to find a way to fit them onto the tree.

The simplest way such a task could be successfully completed would be if psychological states could be reduced directly to physical states. In fact, this was the option explored first, following the gradual abandonment of behaviourism (e.g. Place 1956; Smart 1959; Armstrong 1968). In this classical reductionist project, the physical states thought to be the most likely candidates were states of the brain and central nervous system. This was the view championed by the theory known therefore as central state materialism. Psychological states cause behaviour, so, for example, my desire for a refreshing drink plus my belief that tea will satisfy this desire (in conjunction with a host of other beliefs) results in my body moving in certain ways, other things being equal. These movements may be given a purely physical description and therefore, given the constraints of explanatory physicalism, are susceptible to a complete account in purely physical terms. But how are psychological causal explanations (i.e. those in terms of beliefs, desires, intentions, sensations, etc.) to be linked to physical causal explanations (those in terms of, perhaps, neurological events and processes)? The obvious move here is to suggest that they are identical: our psychological descriptions pick out just those physical kinds that feature in the relevant physical causal explanations (with neurological states regarded as being key to this). Thus, the essential characteristics of psychological states turn out to be certain sorts of physical states, so that what is involved in having a certain psychological state is simply having a certain physical state: psychological states are nothing but brain states.

The possibility of making this move depends upon a conception of states, events, or properties (whichever it is we are reducing) in which the same state, event, or property can be picked out by different, non-analytically equivalent, descriptions.

So, classical reductionism, unlike reductive behaviourism before it, did not opt for a reduction via an equivalence of meanings discoverable a priori, but via an equivalence of reference discoverable a posteriori. In other words, what is claimed is not that a given psychological description ('desires a refreshing drink') *means* the same as a given physical description ('is in neurological state x'), but that the two descriptions *refer* to the very same state, event, or property. This is so, according to this theory, not only for each individual state, etc., but also for kinds of states. The claim is not that each individual psychological state (e.g. my desire at this moment for a refreshing drink) is identical with an individual brain state. It is the much stronger claim that the type of psychological state (e.g. 'desire for refreshing drink' in general) is the same as some physical type. Therefore, whenever and wherever the desire for a refreshing drink occurs, neurological state x occurs and, equally, whenever and wherever neurological state x occurs, the desire for a refreshing drink occurs. So, it does not matter if I desire a refreshing drink today or I desire it tomorrow, the physical state underlying the desire on both occasions will be of the same kind. Similarly, it does not matter if it is me who desires a refreshing drink or if it is you that desires it; again the physical state underlying the desire in both cases will be of the same kind.

Realising this helps us make sense of the curious idea we encountered earlier; that our psychological states may be considered to be natural kinds. We noted that it was because of this that they can feature in our causal–explanatory generalisations. So, the stronger claim is needed if the causal explanatory role of our psychological states is to be accommodated. What causally explains my putting the kettle on or wincing is not just that I have a state that, respectively, happens to be a desire for a refreshing drink or a pain, but that in each case it is a state of the relevant type. Moreover, a type-to-type identity such as this offers an account of what it is to be a psychological state, that is, to be of a certain psychological kind. For each psychological kind, it claims, there will be an account, in physical terms, of what is required for a state to be of this particular kind. Thus the ambition is that we will uncover the intrinsic properties of psychological kinds and discover, say, that pain is the firing of C-fibres – in the same way that we discovered that lightening is really atmospheric electrical discharges, heat is mean kinetic energy, and that water is H_2O. And when I say 'in the same way', I mean this quite literally. Because the identity is not to be established analytically, through examining the meaning of the terms involved, it becomes the task of the scientist, and not the philosopher, to discover the identity *a posteriori* through empirical investigation (perhaps by noting, for example, a strict correlation between pain and C-fibre firings).

PROBLEMS FOR CLASSICAL REDUCTIONISM

This sort of view was predominant in the 1950s and 1960s, though it still retains some adherents today. Nevertheless, it has to confront serious objections. First, there is an objection to the reductionist claim: the distinctive features of mentality that Descartes recognised have not been adequately accommodated in an account of what it is to be a psychological state that asserts it is *nothing but* a neurological state. It is still hard to see how something as characteristically objective as, say, a neurological state has a subjective aspect; for example, how C-fibre excitation *feels* to the person in pain. Furthermore, part of what is essential for something being a belief is that it has rationalising links to other beliefs and other states; links which make it, and them, justified or unjustified, consistent or inconsistent, and so on. Surely, some would argue, it is inappropriate to describe neurological states and their relationships in these terms. These relationships are simply causal and not normative. Second, there is a methodological problem: it is not at all clear how empirical investigations can support the identity claim. After all, a substance dualist could feel perfectly at home with the discovery that strict correlations obtain between the relevant states (let's not forget that Descartes himself, as an accomplished anatomist and physiologist, was not exactly unaware of the causal relevance of the brain). We would expect such correlations to exist if the relevant states were identical; but then they would equally exist if there were merely a close causal relationship between them, so the available evidence does not force us to choose either of these options over the other. Historically, however, another methodological problem has played a more crucial role in steering philosophers away from central state materialism: the possibility, in any case, that no such correlations could ever be discovered.

Many philosophers came to the view that it was wildly implausible to suppose there will be unique one-to-one mapping between types of psychological states and types of physical states. Take a state like 'wanting to go for a walk'. Different people can be in such a state, and the same person can be in this state on quite different occasions (and in vastly different circumstances: to clear one's head, to get some exercise, to enjoy the fresh air, to think about a problem, and so on). Even a creature as physiologically different to us as a dog can want to go for a walk. It does not seem likely that the very same physical correlate is instantiated on all these occasions and in all these circumstances, even if we restrict the identification so that it is organism-specific (i.e. for an individual or species). Jaegwon Kim makes the point with reference to pain:

> Type physicalism says that pain is C-fibre excitation. But that implies that unless an organism has C-fibres or a brain of an appropriate biological structure it cannot have pain. But aren't there pain capable organisms like reptiles and molluscs, with brains very different from the human brain? . . . [M]oreover, the

neural substrates of certain mental functions can differ from person to person and may change over time even in a single individual, through maturation, learning and injuries to the brain.

(Kim 1996, pp. 69–70)

So type physicalism appears to be excessively chauvinistic; only very specific kinds of organism can enjoy mindedness. It also implies, therefore, that artificial intelligence is impossible (at least if the goal of that project is taken to be the realisation of synthetic mindedness in some non-organic medium such as silicon chips and the like). If it doesn't have a brain, it can't be in pain; or think, or desire, or hope, etc. (at least, not if it doesn't have the right sort of brain, made up of the same variety of wet stuff as our brains are). This has become known as the problem of multiple-realisation; so called because, in contrast to the chauvinism of central state materialism, it draws attention to the more plausible counter-supposition that any single kind of psychological state can have multiple kinds of physical correlates.

A number of responses to the failure of classical reductionism are available to materialist minded philosophers. One is to abandon the attempt to provide the sort of reduction we have explored so far, where a psychological type (e.g. pain in general) is identified with a physical type (e.g. C-fibre excitation in general). Instead of such type/type reductions we adopt what is known as a token/token identity theory (e.g. Davidson 1980a); tokens being discrete, individual exemplars of a type (e.g. the chair you are now sitting on is a token of the general type 'chair'). Here, therefore, the claim is the much less ambitious one that every distinct or token psychological state is identical with a distinct or token physical state. There is not necessarily any systematic link between the physical kinds of state identified with one psychological kind of state on different occasions (i.e. the type of physical state may actually differ from individual to individual, time to time, etc.). The problem with this response, crucially, is that it leaves unresolved the relation between psychological and physical properties. This means that this weaker theory cannot answer the question of what is involved in having psychological states of certain kinds, and appears to leave us with a dualism of properties. It simply does not provide a firm enough foundation for a science of the mind whose aim is to reveal the essence of psychological kinds. Moreover, in sustaining a dualism (of properties if not of substances) it retains one of the major dilemmas which was a motivation for reduction in the first place; the possibility of our behaviour being over-determined.

A completely different sort of response is adopted by eliminativist materialists. In a way, the success of a reduction can be seen as legitimating; our talk of heat, for example, is legitimate given it can be reduced to a more privileged level of description in terms of mean kinetic energy. So, if our psychological kinds cannot be reduced to more privileged physical kinds, then their role in genuine causal explanations should be called into question. On this account, explanations that invoke irreducible kinds should be eliminated and replaced by ones invoking kinds that do conform to the reductionist picture (e.g. Churchland 1981; Churchland 1986). For the eliminativist, our everyday psychological explanations (what they disparagingly refer to as 'folk psychology') do not provide us with kinds, the essence of which can be revealed by the discoveries of science, and this is so much the worse for these everyday explanations. Just as explanations of combustion in terms of the non-existent phlogiston were replaced by those in terms of oxygen, following Lavoisier's discovery of that element, so too should explanations of behaviour in terms of beliefs and desires, etc. be replaced by those in terms of a mature neuro-science. However, it is fair to say that most philosophers are not persuaded by such apparent analogies and many find eliminativism scarcely intelligible, perhaps even self-defeating – in that it seems to ask us to believe that beliefs do not exist (e.g. Rudder Baker 1987). For these theorists, if the model of reduction cannot be satisfied, the way forward is not to abandon the philosophical task of accommodating the causal role of the mental within a physicalist framework, but to revise it.

MODIFIED PHYSICALISM AND REDUCTIVE FUNCTIONALISM

Central to a reworking of this project have been attempts to formulate a minimal physicalism with help of the concept 'supervenience'. What this expresses is a non-reductive relation of dependence between higher level states, events, or properties and those at a lower level: higher level states, events, or properties are not identified with those at the lower level, but neither are they autonomous from them. The way in which the psychological supervenes on the physical is commonly explicated in terms of an indiscernibility claim. Stated simply, if two things are indiscernible with respect to their physical make-up, then they will be indiscernible with respect to their psychologies. In other words, there can be no mental difference without a physical difference. Indiscernibility may be construed as 'global' or 'local', with numerous possible positions open to occupancy on the scale between the two. At one pole, the most global, the relation connects whole families of properties or predicates and considers whole worlds that are indiscernible in physical respects to be the same in mental respects. No attempt is made to map the psychological properties of an individual onto her physical properties. At the other pole, its most local, it is a claim that concerns the psychological and physical properties of individual events or organisms. By itself, however, the indiscernibility claim is not strong enough to capture important physicalist intuitions, so it is usually accompanied by another claim: that the psychological properties are *fixed* by the physical properties. This is simply a different way of asserting the privileging of the physical we have come upon already: that physical facts, as described by our most basic physical theories, are the facts in virtue of which all true descriptions of the world are true.

It is important to grasp how supervenience differs from reduction, as the classical reductionist would also make the claim that there can be no mental difference without a physical difference. What the classical reductionist cannot claim, however, is that there can be a physical difference without a mental difference. As the two are identical, a difference in either one entails a difference in the other. Crucially, with supervenience this is not true: if two individuals, for example, are psychologically indiscernible they may be physically different. On this view, although the mental is dependent on the physical, there could be two or many more different types of physical base underlying the same psychological state (in different individuals, say, or the same individual at different times). So, as the mental remains distinct from each of its many possible physical bases, there can be physical differences without mental differences. Supervenience thus allows the possibility of multiple-realisation so that different sorts of physical organisation, perhaps even different sorts of physical stuff, may underlie mentality. Of course, this is good news for researchers in artificial intelligence as, on this model, mentality may be realisable in non-organic systems.

Accepting this model also means accepting constraints on our explanations much less demanding than those required by the unity of science model. The requirement that laws at a higher level be derivable from laws at a lower level has been shelved. Instead, psychological explanations, for example, retain a certain degree of autonomy. Although this respects the completeness of physics and rules out causal over-determination, many find these moves insufficiently robust to satisfy their physicalist predilections. They argue that the autonomy of the psychological seems to be bought at a price; that causal efficacy at this macro level is merely apparent and all the real causal work takes place at the micro, physical level. If this is so, and the psychological is not reducible to the physical, then explanatory physicalism is weakened, as the success of psychological explanations are left mysterious. Similarly, ontological physicalism is left incomplete. It seems that supervenience has allowed a form of dualism back in; albeit a dualism of properties and not of substances. Of course, it does this only in so far as the constraints of the dependency claim are met and the ontological and explanatory priority of the physical is preserved. The mental cannot simply float free of the physical. But the following questions naturally arise at this point: 'If the relation between the psychological and the physical is not one of identity, what is the nature of this dependency? Is it causal?' The answer to the second question is 'No'. Even though the mental remains distinct, it is not conceived as being so distinct that the dependency involved is causal. Some have answered the first question by suggesting the dependency is logical: if the physical base states obtain then this *entails* that the psychological states obtain. However, without some account of the mental to suggest how our psychological descriptions are made true by the physical in this way, the relation between the two remains as brute and mysterious as it did for Descartes. The puzzle is still seeing how the mere instantiation of the physical leads to the mental with its distinctive character.

This is where the theory known as functionalism comes to the fore. Functionalism, in one variety or another, is probably the most popular theory in the philosophy of mind today. One reason is that it provides a way seeing how supervenience might be true. The basic idea informing its account of the mental is that a psychological state can be individuated by means of its functional role within a network of other states so described. The 'function' involved here is causal so that, on this account, an agent is in a given psychological state (e.g. 'believes it is raining') if they are in some state that plays a specified causal role within that network. This role might be such that it causes other similar states (e.g. 'believes today has miserable weather', 'believes it is not sunny', etc.) or certain behavioural responses (e.g. takes an umbrella, avoids picnics, etc.). What functionalism does is insert an intermediate level of description, the functional level, between the psychological and the physical. The beauty of this move is that it begins to allow us to see how a physical system can instantiate psychological properties. There is no problem in grasping how we can functionally describe a physical system; think of any mechanical device, such as a car engine, for example. We could describe it in terms of its gross material composition (e.g. is made of aluminium, is of a certain structure, etc.) but it is more useful to describe it and its component parts in terms of their functions (e.g. source of motive power, combustion chamber, valve lifter, etc.). This is especially so given that engines may be made of different materials (e.g. steel or ceramic as well as aluminium) and structured in significantly different ways (e.g. rotary, transverse, etc.). These functions supervene on the engine's physical composition and structure. What is true for engines is true for any physical system underlying mentality, organic or synthetic. For the functionalist, the mistake made by classical reductionism was to try to link mental and physical properties by using the wrong level of description of the physical: it concentrated on gross material composition and not on function.

Different types of functionalism differ over how we arrive at the functional description of our psychological kinds. The one that is in most accord with the overall physicalist project we have described, with its scientific realist model of explanation, is reductive functionalism. On this account, psychological states reduce to non-mentalistic or 'topic-neutral' functional definitions discoverable by scientific psychology. These, in turn, supervene on a given physical base. So, the essence of any given psychological state is that it is an inner causal state of an organism or system with a particular functional role. If higher level psychological descriptions can be reduced in this way to an intermediate non-mentalistic functional level, and the physical is given a functional description, then we can begin to see how instantiation of the physical results in the mental. This is, however, a very big 'if'. Functionalism is probably the best attempt so far to provide a naturalising account of the mind, but it too has problems encompassing all of the mind's features in one over-arching theory. Important difficulties we encountered with central state materialism persist, most notably problems with the reductive functionalist account of what it is to be a psychological state; that is, that it is *nothing but* a functional state. Indeed, such problems persist for any attempt to reduce the psychological to something else. The functionalist story is most plausible when told of beliefs, but many feel that it leaves out a fundamental characteristic of sensations or perceptions: their subjective quality. As Descartes recognised, for the person who is in one of these states, there is something, as it is commonly put nowadays, 'what it is like to be in that state' (Nagel 1979a).[5] Considerable discussion now centres on whether any non-mentalistic description of these states, functional or otherwise, can capture this subjective feature of mentality. The worry for some is that it is conceivable, they argue, that two people might be relevantly indiscernible in their physical or functional aspects, yet one of them may be a zombie and lack an inner subjective life. This inner life is what most people are referring to when they speak of consciousness, and accounting for it has been called the 'hard problem' for the philosophy of mind and its related disciplines (Chalmers 1996).

Nonetheless, there is also a fundamental feature of states like beliefs, their normativity, which appears not to be captured by this reductionist approach. It may, as a matter of fact, be true that 'believing α' causes a further state such as 'believing β' or 'doing γ', but this is not the whole picture. It may also be true that in 'believing α' we *should* or *should not* also 'believe β' or 'do γ'. As we have already said in relation to central state materialism, part of what it is to be a belief is not just that it causes other beliefs or actions, but that it *implies* other beliefs or actions. Thus, beliefs and actions may be described as being justified or unjustified, appropriate or inappropriate, consistent or inconsistent, etc., in relation to each other. These rationalising links, it has been argued, 'have no echo in physical theory' (Davidson 1980b, p. 231). Attempts have been made to reduce them to patterns of causal transitions between physical states with certain kinds of structural features (computational models of the mind); but, arguably, these attempts ultimately rest upon an excessively narrow conception of rationality. The move makes two assumptions. The first is that such rationalising links are formally codifiable and can be spelt out as patterns that hold because of the *structure* or form of the propositions that give them expression (i.e. their syntax), rather than the *meaning* they have (i.e. their semantic content). The second is that reason is essentially calculative. Both assumptions are highly contentious. The first, formally codifying the links, awaits the outcome of a project the aim of which is to provide a naturalised account of what determines the semantic content of our thoughts. So far this project is unfulfilled and there are powerful arguments suggesting it cannot succeed. The second fails to recognise that rationality does not always consist in showing that a belief or action conforms to some objectively specifiable standard or algorithm, but in understanding what is justified or appropriate from the perspective of the agent concerned. And this requires us to recognise that, in deciding what to believe or how to act, the agent has a seemingly irreducible subjective point of view on the world with which she is engaged as an embodied agent.

PROSPECTS AND CONCLUSION

What then are the prospects for a solution to the mind–body problem? Can the naturalising project we have been examining achieve its goal of articulating a conception of the mental consistent with its investigation by natural science? How close are we to having a fully-fledged science of the mind? Theorists in the field do not divide neatly into those who are optimists and those who are pessimists. There are those who are optimistic about the achievement of these goals, though many hold a mixture of both optimistic and pessimistic expectations about the philosophical task ahead and the possibility for a scientific understanding of the mind. For example, for their own reasons and to varying degrees, some have expressed reservations about reductionist strategies (Davidson 1980c; Dennett 1978); some object to an 'objectifying tendency' in the materialist tradition that does not take the mind's distinctiveness seriously enough (Searle 1992); and others do not think a reductionist approach works across the spectrum of mental phenomena (Chalmers 1996). Then again, it is fair to say that most remain optimistic about the eventual attainment of the overall naturalising goal: the philosophical task may be difficult, but it is not impossible. On the other hand, the eliminativists are extremely pessimistic about the prospects for the philosophical task *tout court*; but this does not concern them, as they do not think this philosophical failure impacts on the development of a scientific understanding. They and their followers in the brain sciences (e.g. Crick 1994) remain resolutely optimistic that profound insights will follow discoveries in the relevant scientific fields. The optimism of others, in contrast, is tempered by the thought that a shift in scientific thinking may be required and that the solution may demand a whole new science and mathematics (Penrose 1989).

There are some outright pessimists, however. Still others, for example, even more radically, have argued that a solution requires a fundamental shift in our thinking as a whole; a shift so profound that we have no idea what it would be (Nagel 1986). Descartes himself, of course, was a pessimist of a particularly strong sort. Although he tried extremely hard to formulate a satisfactory account of the mind–body relation, in the end he thought that we are constitutionally unable to provide a complete exposition. This is because human reason is not structured in the requisite way: the task obliges us to use our intellect and imagination, but these can help us toward only a very obscure grasp of the issues (Descartes 1991, pp. 226–8). That human beings are 'cognitively closed' in this radical sort of way is an argument that has been recently revived (McGinn 1989). On this view, we are rather like a rat or a monkey trying to understand the General Theory of Relativity. The point is not that we are not clever enough, but that we have not evolved with the requisite cognitive architecture: we simply cannot think in the right sort of way. Some might even go further and argue that we may be limited by a sort of self-reflexive blindness: that there is something deeply problematic about the mind trying to comprehend itself (Hayek 1952, p. 185). If the advocates of cognitive closure are correct, neither philosophy nor science can help us find an answer.

Most theorists would regard such strong pessimism as somewhat premature and unjustifiably defeatist. Surely, we cannot rule out in advance that some more sophisticated offspring of current theories may hold the answer. It is certainly true that philosophers should be wary about legislating for the future, especially on what science will or will not deliver. Nonetheless, the depth of the impasse that faces us means that an answer is unlikely to arrive in the near future, if at all, and may not necessarily do all we want it to do if it did arrive. Jaegwon Kim suggests we are confronted with stark choices, each of which exact a high price, and each of which brings as much bad news as good news. For example, a successful reduction of the mental would solve the problem of mental causation, but would also mean that the causal powers of the mind are only apparent and depend on the causal powers of the physical base – assuming, of course, that all mental properties can be reduced. Admitting they cannot means either adopting dualism (perhaps even a Cartesian substance dualism) or going for a modified physicalism. If we stick with physicalism, we then have to choose between retaining supervenient and irreducible mental properties (but accepting, again, the causal impotence of the mental) or eliminativism (and denying the reality of these irreducible properties). Both these options, Kim argues, may be equally unpalatable and may, along with reductionism, amount to the same thing: mental irrealism. As he says, 'This should come as no surprise: we should remember that physicalism, as an overarching metaphysical doctrine about all of reality, exacts a steep price. . . . Reductive physicalism saves the mental but only as part of the physical. . . . Physicalism cannot be had on the cheap' (Kim 1998, pp. 119–20).

These choices are indeed stark; but are perhaps too stark, and are perhaps not the only choices available. In fact, with the exception of substance dualism, they are alternatives only within the limiting framework of that 'overarching metaphysical doctrine'. Earlier we mentioned Kim Sterelny's metaphor of the tree; this picture, or one very much like it, is the metaphysical framework informing much modern philosophy of mind and is the sort of thing Kim has in mind here. This framework operates largely as a tacit presupposition, and most of its proponents offer little or no defence of it other than its supposed plausibility and its centrality to physicalism. We are sometimes apt to forget the historical contingency of such frameworks and particularly so when they are as culturally dominant as this one, which is one reason why we need to rehearse their histories. We may also forget that alternative pictures may be available. In fact, twentieth century thought in general is marked by a gradual shift away from unifying metaphors such as Sterelny's tree and the dream of a fully systematised account of the world. The unity of science is no longer a universal aspiration even among scientists (though see Wilson 1998). Resisting this picture means accepting a pluralist metaphysics in which science, especially science *qua* physics, is not taken to provide a complete and exhaustive account of the material world. It also means accepting pluralism in our modes of explanation and that physicalist discourses do not play a privileged role in the material world's articulation. With respect to the mind, it means giving up on the central goal of the naturalising project; that psychological states have constitutive essences waiting to be revealed by scientific investigation, and that the task of philosophy is to facilitate this. It is important to grasp, however, that such a move is not anti-science – even if it can be construed as anti-scientism. It is simply the recognition that we should not expect empirical investigations to provide insights into what *constitutes* the psychological. This does not preclude those investigations having relevance of another kind. To establish the physical causal base for distinct kinds of psychological capacities is an important and entirely legitimate project. The proper goal, however, should be to discover what kinds of functional and physical organisation *enable* mindedness. What this sort of investigation cannot do is reveal what it is to be minded; that is, what it is to have any given psychological state. This question cannot be addressed within that project; though, *pace* eliminativists, it is one for which it needs an answer, in order to inform its investigations.

There are important reasons why we may not be able to integrate everyday psychological kinds onto a tree of scientific natural kinds; not least is the fact that they play a role in explanatory projects distinct from bringing particular instances under general regularities. They have a distinctive kind of intelligibility that is tied up with making an agent's responses to the world rational and appropriate in various kinds of ways. In other words, explanations referring to psychological kinds are not just causal explanations. Yet, as Descartes understood, they are causal explanations too and this double character is what has made them so troublesome for the modern, post-Cartesian philosopher. Much of the motivation for the metaphysical picture illustrated by Sterelny's tree are the following, related thoughts; that any genuine explanatory work is causal explanatory work, that anything that counts as real must possess causal power (which is why Kim thinks mental impotence entails mental irrealism), and that all causal explanations must be integrated into a common framework. In this way, it is argued, we can avoid causal over-determination and preserve the completeness of physics. Nonetheless, this picture works with a very restricted, almost naive realist, view of causation; that all causal interactions are really the function of properties of matter at the microphysical level. In fact, the discourses surrounding causality are themselves multifarious and cannot be forced under a single schema. It seems inappropriate for a whole range of cases, and not just the psychological, to assume that whenever we have a causal explanation it must conform to this model. For example, when we explain why a sea bird's eggs do not fall off the narrow ledge of the cliff, we do so in terms of their distinctive *shape* and not in terms of their properties at a microphysical level. So, it may be argued that psychological discourses are *sui generis* explanatory projects, which do not need legitimation from physical science, and that acknowledging their causal role does not necessarily force us into the arms of physicalism.[6]

On the other hand, nor does opting out of the physicalist framework, and recognising the distinctiveness of psychological discourses, mean having to embrace the immaterialism of Cartesian substance dualism. Supervenience is seen as the minimal position required for materialism; but, as we have seen, this claim usually has two strands. The first strand is an asymmetric indiscernibility relation where two things cannot alter in terms of their psychological descriptions without altering in terms of their physical descriptions. The second strand is a robustly ontological supplement to the first and consists in a privileging of the physical. Metaphysical pluralism may accept the first strand of the supervenience claim whilst rejecting the second. Accepting indiscernibility sets up a constraint on the relationship between psychological and physical discourses; each must be applied in ways that respect it. However, we need not take this as a consequence of the ontological priority ascribed to physicalist descriptions of the world, but rather of what Wittgenstein calls the 'logical grammar' of our psychological discourses. This is anchored in the *expressive* power of the body; not in its gross composition or functional description. The expressive power of the body requires a certain architectural form, or a certain range of architectural forms, in order to be apt for such expression. As Wittgenstein says, 'It comes to this: only of a living human being and what resembles (behaves like) a living human being can one say: it has sensations; it sees; is blind; is deaf; is conscious or unconscious' (Wittgenstein 1953, §281). It is the expressive human body, and not the body as described by physicalism, that Wittgenstein also refers to as the 'best picture of the human soul'. Such a view is a materialist position and a minimal supervenience claim helps us see how this is so. Two bodies with exactly the same microphysical structure would be perceived as expressive of the same kind of psychology. Thus, certain physical conditions are required if we are to have mentality and the mental cannot simply float free of the physical.

No doubt many will find the idea of a 'third way' as vague and unconvincing in the philosophy of mind as it is in politics, and it certainly needs filling out. Nevertheless, the stark choice Kim offers us between Cartesian immaterialism and physicalism is a false one: we can hold onto the idea that our mindedness is an entirely natural fact about us, without having to embrace reductive naturalism. The choice can be avoided by thinking beyond the framework that encompasses both options. The naturalising project itself was born out of the Descartes' division and is, in many ways, the direct inheritor of Descartes' new science. Thus, the recent history of the philosophy of mind can be seen as one side of Descartes' philosophy attempting to swallow up the other: counteracting his immaterialism by privileging the other side of his mental–physical divide. It is within this conceptual framework that modern philosophy of mind operates. When Merleau-Ponty (1962) said 'How significance and intentionality could come to dwell in molecular edifices or masses of cells is a thing that can never be made comprehensible,' he also added 'and here Cartesianism is right'. But if it is right, this should not surprise us, for it was the Cartesian turn in philosophy itself, and the metaphysical view it initiated, that was largely responsible for setting up this exclusionary division as a problem for us. Overcoming this dichotomy may require us to rethink all the categories we have inherited from that intellectual revolution and not just the mental. So perhaps Thomas Nagel is also right when he says,

> To insist on trying to explain the mind in terms of concepts and theories that have been devised exclusively to explain nonmental phenomena is, in view of the radically distinguishing characteristics of the mental, both intellectually backward and scientifically suicidal. . . .We need entirely new intellectual tools, and it is precisely by reflection upon what appears impossible . . . that we will be forced to create such tools.
>
> (Nagel 1986: 52)

We cannot say, of course, how people would use these tools on the other side of such a conceptual shift. It may be, as Nagel suggests, that a solution to the mind–body problem will be forthcoming, or it may not. It could equally be that this particular question simply ceases to have the urgency for them that it has for us. Other, perhaps new, problems may emerge. If there is any good news, then perhaps it is this: there will be plenty of philosophy left to do.[7]

EXERCISES

1 Consider the following ten statements. Which do you think are true and which do you think are false? What reasons do you have for your conclusions?

a) The mind is an autonomous entity, capable of existing separately from the body.

b) An immaterial mind can causally interact with the physical world.

c) The mind is real but causally impotent.

d) The psychological is distinct from, but nonetheless dependent on, the physical.

e) The mind is nothing more than the activity of the brain.

f) A psychological state may have more than one kind of physical basis.

g) Psychological descriptions are shorthand for complex behavioural descriptions.

h) A psychological state is nothing but a functional state of an organism or system.

i) The constitutive essences of psychological states will be revealed by science.

j) Physical descriptions are those in virtue of which other descriptions, if true, are true.

2 What is distinctive about psychological phenomena? Why might these distinctive features cause a problem for reductionist accounts of the mind?

3 What is causal over-determination? Why is it thought to be a problem for dualist theories of the mind?

4 If you think the mind is the same thing as the brain, what implications does this have for artificial intelligence research?

5 Should we, or could we, abandon our everyday psychological taxonomy (in terms of beliefs, desires, etc.) in favour of a more scientifically respectable classification?

6 Could zombies exist? How could you tell if someone was a zombie or not?

NOTES

1 At least, this is true for the philosophical tradition known as 'analytic philosophy' as opposed to so-called 'continental philosophy'. This division is slowly dissolving, though it is still true that analytic philosophy is the tradition within which most philosophy of mind, qua philosophy of mind, is conducted. That is to say, it is a fair bet that any book with this subject as its title will be in that tradition.

2 Immortality, in any case, is not guaranteed by substance dualism: additional arguments are required to show that the mind or soul continues on after the death of the body. Nor is it the case that materialism it itself rules immortality out as we may believe, as the many of the early Christians did, in the resurrection of the body.

3 The exception being thoughts about God. In the *Third meditation* Descartes argued that God must exist in order for us to have thoughts about Him.

4 Though, given what is known as the theory-dependence of observation (where what we observe depends, in part, on what theories we hold), what counts as a direct observation is not at all straightforward.

5 The question arises with any putatively minded organism or system. Less liberally, Descartes would have considered this to be true only of human beings, as this capacity involves conscious thought.

6 The nature of causality is, of course, a huge, contested subject in its own right. What we have shown here is just how much discussion in the philosophy of mind is dependent on progress in this other field.

7   Many of the points and arguments made here, especially in the last section, were developed in conjunction with my colleagues Paul Gilbert and Kathleen Lennon.

BIBLIOGRAPHY

Armstrong, D.M. (1968) *A Materialist Theory of Mind*, London: Routledge.
Block, N. (ed.) (1980) *Readings in the Philosophy of Psychology*, volume 1, Cambridge, MA: Harvard University Press.
Chalmers, D. (1996) *The Conscious Mind*, Oxford: Oxford University Press.
Churchland, P.M. (1981) 'Eliminativist materialism and propositional attitudes', *Journal of Philosophy* **78**: 67–90. Reprinted in Lyons (1995) pp. 214–39.
Churchland, P.S. (1986) *Neurophilosophy: Toward a Unified Science of the Mind-brain*, Cambridge, MA: MIT Press.
Crick, F. (1994) *The Astonishing Hypothesis*, London: Simon & Schuster.
Davidson, D. (1980a) 'Mental events', in Davidson (1980c), pp. 207–27.
Davidson, D. (1980b) 'Psychology as philosophy', in Davidson (1980c), pp. 229–39.
Davidson, D. (1980c) *Essays on Actions and Events*, Oxford: Oxford University Press.
Dennett, D.C. (1978) *Brainstorms: Philosophical Essays on Mind and Psychology*, Montgomery, VT: Bradford Books/MIT Press, and (1997) London: Penguin.
Descartes (1991) *The Philosophical Writings of Descartes: The Correspondence*, Cottingham, J., Stoothoff, R., Murdoch, D. and Kenny, A. (eds), Cambridge: Cambridge University Press.
Foster, J.A. (1991) *The Immaterial Mind: A Defence of the Cartesian Dualist Conception of the Mind*, London: Routledge.
Hayek, F.A. (1952) *The Sensory Order: An Enquiry into the Foundations of Theoretical Psychology*, London: Routledge & Kegan Paul.
Hempel, K. (1980) 'The logical analysis of psychology', in Block, pp. 14–23.
Kim, J. (1996) *Philosophy of Mind*, Boulder, CO: Westview Press.
Kim, J. (1998) *Mind in a Physical World*, Cambridge, MA: MIT Press.
Leaman, O. (ed.) (1998) *The Future of Philosophy*, London: Routledge.
Lyons, W. (ed.) (1995) *Modern Philosophy of Mind*, London: Everyman.
Lyons, W. (1998) 'Philosophy of mind', in Leaman, pp. 151–67.
McGinn, C. (1989) 'Can we solve the mind–body problem?', *Mind* **98**: 349–66. Reprinted in Lyons (1995), pp. 272–95.
Madell, G. (1988) *Mind and Materialism*, Edinburgh: Edinburgh University Press.
Merleau-Ponty, M. (1962) *Phenomenology of Perception*, C. Smith (trans.), London: Routledge & Kegan Paul.
Nagel, T. (1979a) 'What it is like to be a bat', in Nagel (1979b), pp. 165–80.
Nagel, T. (1979b) *Mortal Questions*, Cambridge: Cambridge University Press.
Nagel, T. (1986) *The View from Nowhere*, Oxford: Oxford University Press.
Neander, K. and Ravenscroft, I. (eds) (1993) *Prospects for Intentionality: Working Papers in Philosophy 3*, Research School of Social Sciences, Australian National University.
Penrose, R. (1989) *The Emperor's New Mind*, Oxford: Oxford University Press.
Place, U.T. (1956) 'Is consciousness a brain process?', *British Journal of Psychology* **47**: 44–50. Reprinted in Lyons (1995), pp. 106–16.
Popper, K.R. and Eccles, J. (1977) *The Self and its Brain*, Berlin: Springer International.

Rudder Baker, L. (1987) *Saving Belief: A Critique of Physicalism*, Princeton: Princeton University Press.

Ryle, G. (1949) *The Concept of Mind*, London: Hutchinson.

Searle, J.R. (1992) *The Rediscovery of the Mind*, Cambridge, MA: MIT Press.

Skinner, B.F. (1953) *Science and Human Behaviour*, New York: Macmillan.

Smart, J.J.C. (1959) 'Sensations and brain processes', *Philosophical Review* **68**: 141–56. Reprinted in Lyons (1995), pp. 117–32.

Sterelny, K. (1993) 'Why naturalise representation?', In Neander and Ravenscroft, pp. 133–40.

Watson, J.B. (1913) 'Psychology as the behaviourist views it', *Psychological Review* **20**: 155–77. Reprinted in Lyons (1995), pp. 24–42.

Wilson, E.O. (1998) *Consilience*, London: Little, Brown & Company.

Wittgenstein, L. (1953) *Philosophical Investigations*, Oxford: Basil Blackwell.

FURTHER READING

For an excellent and compact overview of the current debate from one of its leading players, see Jaegwon Kim (1998) *Mind in a Physical World*, Cambridge, MA: MIT Press. Worthwhile general introductions in the mainstream tradition are Jaegwon Kim (1996) *Philosophy of Mind*, Boulder, CO: Westview Press, and David Braddon-Mitchell and Frank Jackson (1996) *Philosophy of Mind and Cognition*, Oxford: Blackwell. Those that propose alternative approaches include Gregory McCulloch (1995) *The Mind and its World*, London: Routledge; Stephen Burwood, Paul Gilbert and Kathleen Lennon (1998) *Philosophy of Mind*, London: Routledge; and the slightly more accessible David Cockburn (2001) *An Introduction to the Philosophy of Mind*, Basingstoke, Hants.: Palgrave, which draws on the insights of Wittgenstein. William Lyons (2001) *Matters of the Mind*, Edinburgh: Edinburgh University Press, sets the subject in its broader intellectual context in a readable manner, and his edited collection (1995) *Modern Philosophy of Mind*, London: Everyman, is a handy and uncommonly affordable assortment of seminal papers. Extremely helpful anthologies of advanced readings are Richard Warner and Tadeusz Szubka (eds) (1994) *The Mind–Body Problem*, Oxford: Blackwell; and William Lycan (ed.) (1990) *Mind and Cognition: A Reader*, Oxford: Blackwell, now in its second edition. Samuel Guttenplan (ed.) (1994) *A Companion to the Philosophy of Mind*, Oxford: Blackwell, is an indispensable guide through the subject's more technical aspects for the serious student. The most concise yet erudite accounts of positivism and scientific realism are provided by Russell Keat and John Urry (1975) *Social Theory as Science*, London: Routledge & Kegan Paul, Chapters 1–3. Descartes' philosophy of mind can be found principally in his *Meditations on First Philosophy* (especially the 2nd and the 6th). A more thorough examination, however, requires looking at the *Discourse on the Method, Treatise on Man, Description of the Human Body*, and *The Passions of the Soul*. All of these (some in abridged form) can be found in the two volume translation by John Cottingham, Robert Stoothoff and Dugald Murdoch (eds) (1984) *The Philosophical Writings of Descartes*, Cambridge: Cambridge University Press. This translation of the *Meditations* is also available in a stand-alone volume. There is an enormous amount of material to be found online, though it can be of variable quality. The most reliable place to start is David Chalmer's annotated bibliography on his web page – http://www.u.arizona.edu/~chalmers/biblio.html

9

PHILOSOPHY OF LANGUAGE*

Alexander Miller

INTRODUCTION

Often, students coming to philosophy of language for the first time express a worry that it is boring, uninteresting, and trivial: isn't it all just about words? The short (and correct) answer to this is: no, it is not. Philosophy of language is not lexicography: it is not concerned with language as such, but with the relationships between *language*, *mind*, and *world*. Creatures like us are able to use language, whether written or spoken, to communicate about ourselves and the world that we inhabit. Indeed, many would say that this capacity of ours is the most important and distinctive of any that we possess. It is certainly one of the most amazing. David Hume once observed that

> [T]he thought can in an instant transport us into the most distant regions of the universe, or even beyond the universe into the unbounded chaos where nature is supposed to lie in confusion. What never was seen or heard of, may yet be conceived, nor is anything beyond the power of thought except what implies an absolute contradiction.
>
> (Hume 1748, p. 27)[1]

What Hume observes concerning thought also goes for language, as any reader of Stephen Hawking or J.R.R. Tolkien can attest. On reflection, though, we can see that more mundane uses of language are no less amazing. How can these marks on paper, or this sequence of perturbations in the air, mean *anything*, whether near or remote? In many ways this question – 'How is meaning possible?' – is the central question addressed in the philosophy of language. Take something as apparently simple as a proper name, such as 'Plato'. It means the famous philosopher of antiquity who taught Aristotle (doesn't it ?). Well, I can use it to mean *him*, even though he died a few thousand years before my birth. How is that possible?

The link with other central areas, such as philosophy of mind, or metaphysics, is not hard to discern. It is not only linguistic expressions that are capable of possessing meaning. Some mental states – beliefs, desires, intentions, and wishes – are also normally thought to possess meaning or content. For example, the content of my belief that Cardiff is in Wales is *that Cardiff is in Wales*. Just as the sentence 'Cardiff is more impressive than Birmingham' is *about* Cardiff, and says that it is more impressive than Birmingham, my belief is *about* Cardiff, and is to the effect that it is in Wales. This is also true of the other types of mental states mentioned. For example, I can have an intention with the content *that I will finish writing this chapter by the time the pubs open*; I can have a wish with the content *that it stops raining*; and I can have a desire with the content *that I get to the airport on time*. Philosophers call mental states such as beliefs, desires, wishes, intentions, and so on, *propositional attitudes*.[2] Just as sentences have linguistic meaning, propositional attitudes have *mental content*. Given this, and the fact that understanding a linguistic expression is itself usually held to be a mental state, it is unlikely that an investigation into the possibility of language will have no consequences for the *philosophy of mind* (and vice versa).

Language represents the world. But what does the world have to be like in order for language to be capable of representing it? Just as idealist philosophers (e.g. Berkeley) argued the world has to be in some sense *mind-dependent* in order to be represented in thought, contemporary philosophers of an anti-realist persuasion (e.g. Dummett) investigate the idea that traditional realism about the external world is somehow compromised by the fact that language as we use it represents reality. Issues about language and meaning thus lead directly to the heart of traditional *metaphysics*. Other connections emerge just as quickly. Given that our claims to knowledge are typically expressed linguistically, issues in the philosophy of language impact on traditional *epistemology*; and in *metaethics*, we try to understand the role and function of ethical language.

In what follows, I introduce the work of four very prominent philosophers of language. Gottlob Frege (1848–1925) argued that in order to understand how language can represent reality we require a distinction, within our intuitive notion of meaning, between *Sinn* and *Bedeutung* (or sense and semantic value). Frege's views are outlined on pages 264–75. Frege's distinction was famously challenged in the *theory of definite descriptions* developed by Bertrand Russell (1872–1970). Russell's theory is outlined on pages 275–81. The works of Frege and Russell that are outlined in these sections are perhaps the most important works in the whole of modern philosophy of language. Saul Kripke (1940–) and Hilary Putnam (1926–) are two highly influential contemporary philosophers whose views on language develop out of critical reflection on Frege and Russell. Kripke's attack on Russell and Frege, and his idea of a causal theory of reference, are outlined on pages

282–8; Putnam's famous 'twin-earth' thought-experiment is described on pages 288–90. A guide to further reading on Frege, Russell, Kripke, and Putnam is provided on pages 293–4, and study questions can be found on pages 290–1.

An understanding of the views of Frege, Russell, Kripke, and Putnam, forms the foundations of any study of contemporary philosophy of language. A guide for students wishing to take their study beyond these four seminal figures is given on pages 294–6.

FREGE'S THEORY OF MEANING: BEDEUTUNG AND SEMANTIC VALUE

Frege's lifelong project was that of establishing in a rigorous fashion the certainty of the truths of mathematics, particularly arithmetic. (What follows illustrates one connection between issues in philosophy of language and issues in epistemology.) In order to do this, Frege attempted to show (a) that arithmetical propositions could be translated into propositions of logic, and (b) that the arithmetical propositions so translated could be rigorously proved within a formal logical system. This project is known as *logicism*. In order to carry out (a), Frege developed a logical notation into which the propositions of arithmetic were to be translated: this notation was the forerunner of what is known nowadays as *propositional* and *predicate calculus*.

What does this project have to do with the philosophy of language? One crucial concept in logic is that of *validity*. An inference is valid if and only if there are no possible circumstances in which all of its premises are true and its conclusion is false. Obviously, Frege wished to ensure that the inferences of arithmetical propositions within his formal system were valid. Consider a simple inference, such as

13 is prime and 4 is even; therefore
13 is prime.

This formalises as P&Q; therefore, P. How do we determine whether an argument of this form is valid? One way is to use the truth-table method. The truth-table for arguments of this form is

P	Q	P&Q	P
T	T	T	T
T	F	F	T
F	T	F	F
F	F	F	F

There is only one circumstance in which the premise is true – when both P&Q are assigned the value true – and that in this case, the conclusion is also true. So there are no cases in which the premise is true and in which the conclusion is false. So the argument is valid.

What does validity have to do with semantics? Intuitively, the validity of an argument is going to depend on the *meanings* of the expressions which appear in it. That is to say, the validity of an argument is going to depend on the *semantic properties* of the expressions out of which it is constructed. In the argument above the basic expressions out of which the argument is constructed are sentences. What properties of the sentences are relevant to determining the validity of the inference? It seems as if it is the properties of *truth* and *falsity*. After all, the truth-table method works by determining the possible distributions of these very properties. So, truth and falsity look like good candidates for the semantic properties in question. Given assignments of truth and falsity to P and Q, we can work out the various assignments of truth and falsity to the premises and conclusion, and this allows us to say whether or not the argument is valid. So, validity is determined by the possible distributions of truth and falsity to the premises and conclusion, and this in turn is determined by the possible distributions of truth and falsity to the constituent sentences. Thus Frege defines *Bedeutung* (or *semantic value*) as follows:

DEFINITION: The *Bedeutung* or *semantic value* of any expression is that feature of it which determines whether sentences in which it occurs are true or false.[3]

In the case we have just looked at, the constituent expressions of the argument are the sentences represented by P and Q. Which features of these are relevant to determining whether the sentences in which they occur are true or false? Well, their truth or falsity: as shown in the truth-table, the distributions of T and F to P and Q determine the truth or falsity of the complex sentence represented by P&Q which forms the premise of the argument. Given the definition above, then, it follows that the semantic value of a sentence is its truth-value.

We have here the beginnings of an informal semantic theory: an assignment of a semantic property (truth or falsity) to the sentences of a language, which determines the validity of the inferences in which those sentences appear as constituents. Thus

THESIS 1: The semantic value of a sentence is its truth-value (true or false).

Note that in the case above, the semantic value of the complex expression represented by P&Q – its truth-value – is determined by the truth-values of the constituent sentences represented by P, Q. In general, the semantic value of a complex expression is determined by the semantic values of its parts and the way they are put together. Thus

> **THESIS 2: The semantic value of a complex expression is determined by the semantic values of its parts.**

From this, we can derive a third thesis. Since the semantic value of a complex expression is determined by the semantic values of its parts, substituting one part with another which has the same semantic value will leave the semantic value (truth-value) of the whole sentence unchanged. Thus

> **THESIS 3: Substitution of a constituent of a sentence with another which has the same semantic value will leave the semantic value (i.e. truth-value) of the sentence unchanged.**

What about expressions from syntactic categories other than that of declarative sentences? In addition, we have to consider proper names ('Cicero'), predicates ('Fat') sentential connectives ('and', 'or', 'not'), and quantifiers ('all', 'some').

Consider the sentence 'Cicero is Roman'. What feature of the proper name 'Cicero' is relevant to determining whether this sentence is true or false? Intuitively, the fact that it stands for the individual *object* which is the man Cicero: if the proper name stood for some other individual (e.g. Plato) the sentence in question might have a different truth-value from the one it actually has. So, just as the semantic value of a declarative sentence is a truth-value, the semantic value of a proper name is an object. This allows us to state the fourth thesis of Frege's semantic theory:

> **THESIS 4: The semantic value of a proper name is the object which it stands for.**

Consider the predicate expression '. . . is even'. This has a gap into which a numeral can be slotted. What is the result of slotting a given numeral into the gap? It will be a *true* sentence, if the number denoted by the numeral is even; it will be a *false* sentence, otherwise. Thus, we can view the predicate '. . . is even' as standing for a *function* from numbers to truth-values. There are also functions which take objects other than numbers as their arguments. Consider '. . . is round'. This has a gap into which a proper name may be slotted, and the value delivered will be true if the object denoted by that proper name is round, false otherwise. Thus '. . . is round' can be viewed as standing for a function from objects to truth-values. *In general, a predicate expression will stand for a function from objects to truth-values. Frege reserves the term 'concept' for a function whose value is always a truth-value.*

We can represent a function as a set of ordered pairs, where the first member corresponds to the argument of the function and the second member corresponds to the value which the function delivers for that argument.[4] Thus the function denoted by '. . . is even' can be represented by {(1, false), (2, true), (3, false), (4, true), . . . }. This set of ordered pairs is called the *extension* of the function. Intuitively, it is the extension of a predicate which determines the truth-value of sentences in which it appears. Take a subject-predicate sentence like '4 is even'. That this is true is determined by two things: first, that the numeral '4' stands for the number 4, and second, that the number 4 is paired with the value true in the extension of the function denoted by '. . . is even'. Also, thesis 3 states that the substitution, in a complex expression, of a part with some other part having the same semantic value, leaves the truth-value of the whole unchanged. We can see that this condition is met if we identify the semantic value of a predicate with a function, understood in extensional terms: the substitution of a predicate having the same extension as the predicate '. . . is even' will leave the truth-value of '4 is even' unchanged, since the identity in extension will ensure that the number 4 is still paired with the value true.

Frege also includes the logical connectives and the quantifiers within the scope of his semantic theory, since these too can be viewed as standing for functions. Indeed, the logical connectives are often called 'truth-functions' or 'truth-functional connectives'. *The reason is that these can be viewed as standing for functions from truth-values to truth-values.* Take the *negation* operator '– . . .'. This can be viewed as standing for a function of one argument, which has the following extension: {(T, F), (F, T)}. For the argument true, the value false is delivered, and for the argument false, the value true is delivered. Likewise, the connective for *conjunction*, '. . . & . . .' can be viewed as standing for a function of two arguments, which has the following extension: {(T, T, T), (T, F, F), (F, T, F), (F, F, F)}.

Frege treats the universal and existential quantifiers as standing for a special sort of function: *second-level functions*. A first-level function is a function which takes objects (of whatever sort) as arguments. A second-level function is a function which takes *concepts* as arguments. Frege viewed the universal and existential quantifiers as standing for second-level functions, taking concepts as arguments and yielding truth-values as values. Let's deal with the universal quantifier first. As usual, whenever we are formalising parts of natural language by using quantifiers, we have to specify a universe of discourse: this is the group of objects which our variables are taken to range over. Suppose that we select the group of humans {Quine, Boris Yeltsin, John Major, Bill Clinton} as our *universe of discourse*. Now consider the universally quantified sentence 'Everyone is mortal'. We can formalise this, taking 'G' to abbreviate '. . . is mortal', as follows: $(\forall x)Gx$. Frege suggested that we view the quantifier as standing for a function $(\forall x)(\ )$, which takes a concept Gx as argument and yields the truth-value T if the concept G is paired with T in its extension. The concept G will be paired with T in the extension of the quantifier if every object in the universe of discourse is paired with T in the extension of G. Similarly $(\forall x)Gx$ yields the truth-value F if the concept G is paired with F in the extension of the quantifier. And the concept G is paired with F in the extension of the quantifier if at least one object in the universe of discourse is paired with the value F in the extension of G. Thus, consider 'Everyone is mortal'. $(\forall x)(\ )$ is a second-level function, from concepts to truth-values. If the argument is the concept Gx, then the function $(\forall x)(\ )$ yields the value T if G is paired with T in its extension. In turn, G will be paired with T in the extension of $(\forall x)(\ )$ if *every* object in the universe of discourse is paired with T in the extension of G. In the case at hand, the extension of G is {(Quine, T), (Boris Yeltsin, T), (John Major, T), (Bill Clinton, T)}. We see that every object *is* paired with T in the extension of G, so that G will be paired with T in the extension of $(\forall x)(\ )$. So, finally, '$(\forall x)Gx$' is true. Note that this shows that the truth-value of the sentence '$(\forall x)Gx$' is determined by the semantic values of its parts, namely, the extension of the function $(\forall x)(\ )$, and the extension of the concept G.

Likewise, consider the existentially quantified sentence 'Someone is Russian', keeping the universe of discourse the same as in the example above. We can formalise this as $(\exists x)Hx$, taking 'H' to abbreviate '. . . is Russian'. We can then spell out how the semantic value of the existentially quantified sentence is determined by the semantic values of its parts as follows. $(\exists x)(\ )$ is a second-level function, from concepts to truth-values. If the argument is the concept Hx, then the function $(\exists x)(\ )$ yields the value T if H is paired with T in its extension. In turn, H will be paired with T in the extension of $(\exists x)(\ )$ if *at least one* object in the universe of discourse is paired with T in the extension of H. In the case at hand, the extension of H is {(Quine, F), (Boris Yeltsin, T), (John Major, F), (Bill Clinton, F)}. We see that at least one object is paired with T in the extension of H (Boris Yeltsin), so that H will be paired with T in the extension of $(\exists x)(\ )$. So, finally, '$(\exists x)Hx$' is true.

We can summarise these points about predicates, connectives, and quantifiers as follows:

> **THESIS 5: The semantic value of a predicate is a first-level function from objects to truth-values; the semantic value of a sentential connective is a first-level function from truth-values to truth-values; the semantic value of a quantifier is a second-level function from concepts to truth-values.**

FREGE'S THEORY OF MEANING: SINN AND SENSE

Frege's theory of meaning, as outlined above, trades in just one theoretical notion, semantic value. I'll now look at some of Frege's arguments for the claim that we need an additional notion, *Sinn* (or sense).

The problem of bearerless names

Consider a sentence such as 'Odysseus was set ashore at Ithaca while sound asleep'. The name 'Odysseus' has no bearer, since the character is entirely fictional. Since the name has no reference, and the semantic value of a sentence is determined by the semantic values of its parts, it follows that the sentence 'Odysseus was set ashore at Ithaca while sound asleep' has no semantic value either. So if having a semantic value were the only semantic property, we would have to say that the sentence is meaningless. But we can certainly understand the sentence: it is certainly not just meaningless gibberish. So it seems that we will have to attribute some other semantic property to the name 'Odysseus' in addition to its semantic value.

The problem of substitution into belief contexts

According to thesis 3 substitution of a part of a sentence with another expression which has the same semantic value will leave the truth-value of the sentence unchanged. But it is easy to find apparent counterexamples to this. Consider the following sentence, where Weir is a person with no knowledge about Mark Twain (except perhaps that he is the author of *Huckleberry Finn*):

(1) Weir believes that Mark Twain is Mark Twain.

This will be true, unless Weir has some very bizarre views on identity. But 'Mark Twain' and 'Samuel Clemens' have the same semantic value: they are different names for the same person. So the following, which results by substituting one of the occurrences of 'Mark Twain' by 'Samuel Clemens', should also be true:

(2) Weir believes that Mark Twain is Samuel Clemens.

But, of course, this is actually false, since Weir knows nothing about Mark Twain except that he is the author of *Huckleberry Finn*. This suggests that Frege is either going to have to give up thesis 4, that the semantic value of a name is its bearer, or thesis 3, and thereby thesis 2, the principle of compositionality. But these are both central and indispensable planks of Frege's theory of meaning. We shall see that Frege's attempt to solve this problem without giving up either of theses 2, 3, or 4, requires the introduction of another semantic property of names in addition to their having a semantic value.

The problem of informative identity statements

It took an empirical discovery in astronomy to discover that the planet Venus was both the celestial object known as 'the Evening Star' and also the celestial object known as 'the Morning Star'. Consider the state of a competent language user who is unaware of the discovery. Such a person understands the identity statement 'The Morning Star is the Evening Star', even though they do not know its truth-value. Frege's claim is that if meaning were simply identified with semantic value, this would be impossible. He argues

(3) Suppose (for reductio) that meaning is to be identified with semantic value.

(4) Understanding a sentence requires understanding its constituents. In other words, knowing the meaning of a sentence requires knowing the meanings of its constituents.

So,

(5) Understanding 'The Morning Star is the Evening Star' requires knowing the meanings of, inter alia, 'The Morning Star' and 'The Evening Star'.

So,

(6) Understanding 'The Morning Star is the Evening Star' requires knowing the semantic values of 'The Morning Star' and 'The Evening Star'.

But,

(7) The semantic value of 'The Morning Star' is the same as that of 'The Evening Star': the planet Venus.

So,

(8) Understanding 'The Morning Star is the Evening Star' requires knowing that the semantic values of 'The Morning Star' and 'The Evening Star' are the same: in other words, requires knowing that 'The Morning Star is the Evening Star' is true.

But,

(9) It is possible to understand 'The Morning Star is the Evening Star' without knowing its truth-value. So,

(10) The meaning of an expression cannot be identified with its semantic value.

So, in giving an account of meaning we are going to have to introduce some semantic property in addition to semantic value. Frege calls this additional semantic property 'Sinn' or 'sense'. But what is sense, and how does it help us to solve the three problems outlined above?

The first thesis concerning sense that I'll introduce is

THESIS 6: The sense of an expression is that ingredient of its meaning which determines its semantic value.

In addition to having semantic values, expressions also have semantic properties which determine what those semantic values are. The property which determines semantic value is the property of having a certain sense. Thus, a name has a reference – stands for a particular object – and also has a sense, some means of determining which particular object this is. For example, the sense of 'The Evening Star' is some condition which an object has to satisfy in order to count as the reference of the name. The simplest way of spelling this out would be to specify some *descriptive condition*, such as 'that object which appears in such and such a place in the sky at such and such times in the evening'. If an object satisfies this condition, then it is the reference of 'The Evening Star'. It turns out, on empirical investigation, that Venus satisfies this condition, so that the name 'The Evening Star' refers to the planet

Venus. Now, someone who knows which descriptive condition an object has to satisfy in order to count as the reference of 'The Evening Star' understands the name; but it does not follow that he knows what the reference of the name actually is. I can know that whatever object it is that appears at such and such a place in the sky at such and such a time in the evening is referred to by 'The Evening Star' without knowing which object that is: I may not have done any astronomy. Thus we also have the following thesis:

> **THESIS 7: It is possible to know the sense of an expression without knowing its semantic value.**

This thesis which allows us to solve the problem of informativeness. We first of all set out the theses:

> **THESIS 8: The sense of an expression is what someone who understands the expression grasps.**
>
> **THESIS 9: The sense of a complex expression is determined by the senses of its constituents.**

Consider Frege's Evening Star–Morning Star example. Understanding a sentence requires understanding its constituents. Together with thesis 8, this entails that knowing the sense of a sentence requires knowing the senses of its constituents. So, understanding 'The Morning Star is the Evening Star' requires grasping the senses of, inter alia, 'The Morning Star' and 'The Evening Star'. But, from thesis 7, it is possible to grasp the senses of 'The Morning Star' and 'The Evening Star' without knowing their references. So, from theses 9 and 2, it is possible to grasp the sense of the sentence 'The Evening Star is the Morning Star' without knowing its truth-value. So this explains how it is possible to understand a sentence without knowing its truth-value, which is just to explain how sentences can be informative.

The introduction of sense also enables Frege to solve the problem of bearerless names. Consider again the example of 'Odysseus'. Suppose, for the sake of argument, that the sense of this is given by some descriptive condition such as 'The hero of Homer's *Odyssey* and the son of Laertes and Antikleia'. Clearly, someone can grasp such a condition even if there actually is no object which satisfies it: someone can know what it would be for a person to be referred to by the name

'Odysseus' even if there is in fact no such person. This is even clearer in the case of a term like 'The twelve-headed student in my logic class'. I can certainly understand this term: this in part explains why I am able to understand the sentence 'The twelve-headed student in my logic class has more than two heads'. That is, I know what would have to be the case for someone to be referred to by the term, and I can possess this knowledge even though there is no twelve-headed student in my class. Thus,

> **THESIS 10: An expression can have a sense even if it lacks a semantic value.**

What follows about sentences containing bearerless names? For example, consider 'Odysseus was set ashore at Ithaca while sound asleep'. Since one of the expressions, 'Odysseus', lacks a reference, it follows from thesis 2 that this sentence itself does not have a semantic value. In other words, it lacks a truth-value: it is neither true nor false. This gives us another of Frege's theses:

> **THESIS 11: A sentence which contains an expression which lacks a semantic value is neither true nor false.**

How does Frege solve the problem of substitution into belief contexts? Frege attempts to save thesis 3 by denying that 'Mark Twain' and 'Samuel Clemens' are indeed co-referential in the relevant sort of belief context. Customarily, outside of belief contexts, they refer to the man who authored *Huckleberry Finn* and so on, as in

(11) Mark Twain was an American.

But within belief contexts they refer to the *senses* they ordinarily possess outside belief contexts (as in e.g. (11)). Frege expresses this by saying that in (11), 'Mark Twain' has its *customary reference* and *customary sense*. However, in belief contexts 'Mark Twain' refers, not to the man, but rather to the customary sense of the name. Frege expresses this by saying that in belief contexts a name refers to its customary sense, and he calls this its *indirect reference*. Since 'Mark Twain' and 'Samuel Clemens' have different customary senses and therefore different indirect references, in moving from (1) to (2) we have not actually substituted one co-referential expression for another, so that we do not really have a counterexample to thesis 3.

273

The identification of indirect reference with customary sense thus allows us to avoid the problem of substitution into belief contexts. Thus

> **THESIS 12: In a belief context, the (indirect) reference of a proper name is its customary sense.**

It is worth noting that just as thesis 2 led to thesis 3, so thesis 9 (the compositionality of sense) leads to:

> **Thesis 13: Substitution of one expression in a sentence with another which has the same sense will leave the sense of the sentence unchanged.**

This can be used to give us some clue as to what the senses of sentences are. Consider the move from

(12) John believes that London is south of Glasgow.

to

(13) John believes that electrons are negatively charged particles.

where John is aware of the elementary geography of Britain, but knows nothing about subatomic physics. Since the semantic value of a sentence is a truth-value, and since the embedded sentences in (12) and (13) have the same truth-values (T), the fact that (12) is true and (13) is false appears to generate a problem for thesis 3. Again, Frege's way round this problem is to apply (an analogue of) thesis 12. In (12) and (13) the embedded sentences do not have their customary semantic values (truth-values): within belief contexts their semantic values are their *customary senses*. But what is the customary sense of a sentence? Well, what are we referring to in using 'London is south of Glasgow' within a belief context such as (12)? Intuitively, we are referring to John's thought *that London is south of Glasgow*. That is to say, we are using the sentence to specify the *content* of a *thought*. Now, if we substitute the embedded sentence in (12) with one which expresses the *same thought* (as opposed to merely having the same truth-value), is it possible for (12) to change truth-value? If not, the identification of the sense of a sentence with the thought it expresses will respect thesis 13. The question as to the identity of thoughts is a thorny one (when does one sentence express the same thought as another?), but intuitively it looks as if the substitution of 'London is South of Glasgow' by another sentence expressing the same thought will leave the truth-value of (12) unchanged. For example, the sentence 'London is south of Glasgow' intuitively expresses the same thought as 'Glasgow is north of London', and the substitution of the latter for the former results in the true sentence

(14) John believes that Glasgow is north of London.

These considerations suggest that the sense of a sentence is a thought. It is important to note that for Frege, a thought is not something *psychological* or *subjective*. Rather, it is *objective* in the sense that it specifies some condition in the world the obtaining of which is necessary and sufficient for the truth of the sentence which expresses it. Thus

> **THESIS 14: The sense of a sentence is a thought (its truth-condition).**
>
> **THESIS 15: Sense is objective: grasping a sense is not a matter of having ideas, mental images, or private psychological items.**

RUSSELL'S THEORY OF DEFINITE DESCRIPTIONS

Bertrand Russell, in developing his 'theory of descriptions' in his famous 1905 paper 'On Denoting' (in Russell 1956), challenged some of Frege's views on the philosophy of language. In fact, Russell raised two distinct sorts of criticism of Frege. On the one hand, he accepted, in broad outline, the account of semantic value described above, but argued that Frege had gone wrong on some important points of detail. On the other, he attacked Frege's introduction of the notion of sense over and above that of semantic value. I'll consider criticisms of both sorts in this section and the next.

We saw above that Frege held the following thesis:

> **THESIS 4: The semantic value of a proper name is the object for which it stands.**

We could also view this as a *definition* of 'proper name': proper names are precisely those expressions which have objects as their semantic values. It would then be an open question whether names in natural languages such as English are proper names as thus defined. Frege clearly held that ordinary names, such as 'Aristotle' and 'Odysseus', are proper names in this sense. He also held that *definite descriptions* are proper names in this sense. A definite description is a phrase like 'the so and so'. So examples of definite descriptions would be 'the King of France', 'the unhappiest man in Washington', and 'the least rapidly convergent series'. Frege thus held that the semantic value of a definite description is the object which it stands for: the contribution which a definite description makes to the truth-values of complex sentences in which it appears is determined by the fact that it stands for a certain object.

This leaves Frege with a problem. We saw above (thesis 11) that according to Frege, a sentence which contains an expression which lacks a semantic value is neither true nor false. In addition, he held that the sense of a sentence is the thought which it expresses (thesis 14). So, since

(15) The King of France is bald.

contains an expression 'the King of France' which has no semantic value (there is no such object), it is neither true nor false. But it is meaningful, and so has a sense, and so expresses a thought. But how can a sentence with no truth-value express a genuine thought? Or, how can a sentence express a thought which is neither true nor false? This is very problematical (see Evans 1982: 23–4), and suggests that Frege's introduction of sense does not after all solve the problem of bearerless proper names.

Perhaps the easiest way into Russell's theory is to see him as attempting to find a way to avoid this problem. One way of avoiding the problem is Meinong's: the expression 'the King of France' *does* refer to an object, but a non-existent one (see Meinong (1960), first published in 1904). The King of France, even though he doesn't exist, nevertheless *subsists*. Russell attempts to avoid the problem in a way which does not involve the highly implausible postulation of non-existent, but nevertheless subsistent, objects. *Rather, Russell attempts to avoid the problem by denying that definite descriptions are proper names.* (This illustrates how philosophy of language can be crucial for issues in metaphysics and ontology). If definite descriptions are not proper names, their semantic values are not given by the objects for which they stand, so the fact that there are many definite descriptions which do not stand for an object does not lead to the problem faced by Frege. But if the semantic behaviour of definite descriptions is not to be explained in terms of their standing for objects, how is it to be explained? What are definite descriptions if they are not proper names?

In order to see Russell's answer to these questions, think about the correct translation of (15) into Frege's logical language. (15) has the grammatical form of a subject–predicate sentence. So if we were taking grammatical form as a guide to the correct translation of (15) into logical symbolism, it would come out as

(16) Fa.

A property, being bald, represented by 'F', is predicated of the King of France, represented by 'a'. We can say that in translating a sentence into Frege's logical symbolism we are attempting to capture its *logical form*: we exhibit the form of the sentence in such a way that the contributions its constituents make to its truth-value are thereby exhibited. Thus, in translating (15) by (16) we are suggesting that 'the King of France' contributes to determining the truth-value of (15) in the manner of a proper name, and 'bald' contributes in the manner of a predicate. *Russell suggests that in this instance we should not take the grammatical form of the sentence as a guide to its logical form.* In fact, the logical form of (15) is given by something quite different from (16). Russell analyses (15) by first breaking it up into three different parts:

(17) There is at least one King of France.

(18) There is at most one King of France.

(19) Anything which is a King of France is also bald.

The conjunction of (17), (18) and (19) amount to the claim that the King of France is bald. Thus, the logical form of (15) can be represented by the translation of the conjunction of (17), (18) and (19) into Frege's logical symbolism. Taking 'F' to abbreviate the predicate '. . . is a King of France' and 'G' to abbreviate the predicate '. . . is bald', this comes out as

(20) $(\exists x)((Fx \text{ and } Gx) \text{ and } (\forall y)(Fy \rightarrow x=y))$

Representing the logical form of (15) by (20) does not involve representing the King of France' as a proper name, as in (16). (Note that it is very important that we take the predicate to be '. . . is *a* King of France'. If we took it as '. . . is the King of France' we would be using the very notion we are attempting to analyse). We can represent the logical form of sentences in which definite descriptions appear without viewing those descriptions as having objects as their semantic values. But if definite descriptions do not have objects as their semantic values, what are their semantic values? *The answer to this is that definite descriptions have second-level functions as their semantic values.* In (15), the definite description 'the King of France' is translated by

(21) $(\exists x)((Fx \text{ and } . . . x) \text{ and } (\forall y)(Fy \rightarrow x=y))$

which stands for a function from concepts (first-level functions) to truth-values. Russell's criticism of Frege's view of definite descriptions can thus be summed up as follows. *Frege assigns definite descriptions the wrong sort of semantic values: Frege views definite descriptions as proper names, as having objects as their semantic values; but in fact definite descriptions have second-level functions as their semantic values.*

Note how this solves the problem of bearerless definite descriptions. Since definite descriptions are not proper names, but rather functional expressions which do not have objects as their semantic values, the failure of a definite description to stand for an object does not imply that it has no semantic value: we still have an account of how it contributes to the truth-values of complex sentences in which it appears. What, then, is the truth-value of (15)? Given the analysis into (20) we can see that it is false, since '$(\exists x)Fx$' is false (since there is no King of France).

In fact, Russell attempts to avoid the problem of bearerless names in exactly the same way, *by treating ordinary names as disguised definite descriptions.* That is, Russell claims that even ordinary names are not proper names in the sense defined by thesis 4. Consider the sentence

(22) Odysseus was set ashore at Ithaca while sound asleep.

Frege would analyse this as having the logical form given by

(23) Mb.

where 'M' translates the predicate '. . . was set ashore at Ithaca while sound asleep' and 'b' translates 'Odysseus'. Again, Russell suggests that we should not take the grammatical form of (22) as an infallible guide to its logical form. 'Odysseus' is really a disguised definite description: for simplicity, suppose that it is the definite description 'the hero of Homer's *Odyssey*'. (22) thus really amounts to

(24) The hero of Homer's *Odyssey* was set ashore at Ithaca while sound asleep.

We now analyse this in the same way that we analysed (15), using 'N' to translate the predicate '. . . is a hero of Homer's *Odyssey*':

(25) $(\exists x)((Nx \text{ and } Mx) \text{ and } (\forall y)(Ny \rightarrow x=y))$

This analysis shows that 'Odysseus' is not really a proper name. Rather, the semantic value of 'Odysseus' is the second-level function denoted by:

(26) $(\exists x)((Nx \text{ and } \ldots x) \text{ and } (\forall y)(Ny \rightarrow x=y))$

So the fact that there actually is no Odysseus does not cause problems: we can still account for the contribution 'Odysseus' makes to the truth-values of sentences containing it. The problem of bearerless names has disappeared.

RUSSELL'S ATTACK ON FREGE ON SENSE

In addition to making criticisms of detail about Frege's assignments of semantic value, Russell also developed two main criticisms of the notion of sense. The first is that the distinction between sense and semantic value is actually *incoherent*: Russell (1956: 50) describes Frege's attempt at drawing the distinction as leading to an 'inextricable tangle' and writes that 'the whole distinction of [sense] and [reference] has been wrongly conceived'.[5] But I shall not consider the argument (1956: 48–51) here: it is truly one of the most mysterious passages in twentieth-century philosophy. Instead I shall concentrate on Russell's second main line of criticism of the notion of sense. This does not involve the claim that the notion of sense is incoherent: rather, Russell tries to show that the invocation of the notion of sense is simply *superfluous*. Frege introduced the notion of sense in an attempt to solve a number of puzzles. Russell argues that these puzzles can be solved in a way which does not involve any appeal to the notion of sense, so that Frege's rationale for introducing the notion is undercut.

Frege's introduction of sense was motivated by the desire to solve three main problems: the problem of bearerless names, the problem of substitution into belief contexts, and the problem of informativeness. I have already shown how Russell attempted to solve the first of these: empty definite descriptions and ordinary names still have a semantic value because they are not actually genuine proper names, but rather have second-level functions as their semantic values. I now look at how Russell deals with the other two problems.

Recall that the problem of substitution into belief contexts was a problem because it threatened thesis 3: substituting a constituent of a sentence with another which has the same semantic value will leave the truth-value of the sentence unchanged. Consider

(27) Smith believes that the composer of *Fidelio* had cirrhosis of the liver.

Now suppose that Smith doesn't realise that the composer of Fidelio is in fact the same person as the composer of the *Moonlight Sonata*. That is, Smith doesn't know that

(28) The composer of *Fidelio* is the composer of the *Moonlight Sonata*.

Suppose that 'The composer of *Fidelio*' and 'The composer of the *Moonlight Sonata*' are proper names. Then, they have the same semantic value, since they pick out the same person, Beethoven. So we should be able to substitute 'The composer of the *Moonlight Sonata*' for 'The composer of *Fidelio*' in (27) without changing (27)'s truth-value. But in fact the substitution results in the false

(29) Smith believes that the composer of the *Moonlight Sonata* had cirrhosis of the liver.

So it looks as if we have a counterexample to thesis 3.

Russell wants to hold on to thesis 3, so he tries to explain away the apparent counterexample. In order to show how he attempted to do so, it will be best first to restate the problem in slightly more formal terms. On the assumption that definite descriptions are genuine proper names, we can (partially) translate (27) into logical symbolism as follows, where 'a' translates 'the composer of *Fidelio*' and 'F' translates the predicate '. . . has cirrhosis of the liver':

(30) Smith believes that Fa.

Taking 'b' to abbreviate 'the composer of the *Moonlight Sonata*', (28) gets translated as:

(31) a = b

And (29) gets translated as

(32) Smith believes that Fb.

The counterexample is now clear: we substitute into the true (30) on the basis of the true (31) and get the false (32) as a result.

Russell's response to the problem is basically this: (30), (31), and (32) misrepresent the logical form of (27), (28), and (29), and when we see their true logical form, we'll see that there is simply no scope for the sort of substitution which takes us from (30) and (31) to (32). For Russell, 'the composer of Fidelio' is not a proper name. Rather, it gets treated in the same way as 'the King of France', so that the logical form of (27) is more accurately captured by

(33) Smith believes that $(\exists x)((Gx \text{ and } Fx) \text{ and } (\forall y)(Gy \to x=y))$

where 'G' stands for the predicate '. . . is a composer of *Fidelio*'. The logical form of (28) is given by

(34) $(\exists x)(Gx \text{ and } Hx \text{ and } (\forall y)(Gy \rightarrow x=y) \text{ and } (\forall z)(Hz \rightarrow x=z))$

where 'H' abbreviates the predicate '. . . is a composer of the Moonlight Sonata'.

Now whereas (31) allowed us to substitute into the true (30) to obtain the false (32), (34) simply does not allow us to substitute into (33): (33) and (34) are simply not of the right logical form to allow a substitution, so a fortiori, there is no possibility of a substitution which takes us from a true sentence to a falsehood. Alternatively, the logical form of (29) is given by

(35) Smith believes that $(\exists x)((Hx \text{ and } Fx) \text{ and } (\forall y)(Hy \rightarrow x=y))$

This is false, but it cannot be reached by substituting into (33) on the basis of (34). Thesis 3 is safe. Note that since Russell views natural names as disguised definite descriptions, he can apply this solution of the problem to cases which involve natural names rather than explicit definite descriptions.

Russell is thus able to solve the problem of substitution into belief contexts without invoking the notion of sense. But what about the problem of informativeness? Recall from the section on Russell's theory of definite descriptions that Frege argued for the introduction of sense on the basis of a reductio argument: if the only semantic property that could be ascribed to expressions was possessing a semantic value, then it would not be possible to understand a sentence and yet fail to know its truth-value. Now, a crucial step in the reductio was premise (7): the semantic value of 'The Morning Star' is the same as that of 'The Evening Star', namely, the planet Venus. Russell will reply that this presupposes that 'The Evening Star' and 'The Morning Star' are proper names, expressions which have the objects they stand for as their semantic values. But this is false. Natural names are disguised definite descriptions, and have second-level functions, rather than the objects they pick out, as their semantic values. The fact that 'The Evening Star' and 'The Morning Star' both pick out the same object thus does not entail that they have the same semantic value, and Frege's argument is blocked: the assumption that the only semantic property of an expression is its possession of a semantic value does not imply that one can never understand a sentence without knowing its truth-value. So on Russell's account the problem of informative identity statements doesn't get a chance to arise.

Overall, then, Russell claims he can deal with the various puzzles that led Frege to introduce the notion of sense, while relying only on the notion of semantic value.

KRIPKE'S ATTACK ON FREGE AND RUSSELL

Thus far, in discussing Frege we have taken the sense of a proper name to be a *descriptive condition*. There is considerable doubt as to whether this is the right way to interpret Frege. Dummett, for instance, writes:

> All that is necessary, in order that the senses of two names which have the same referent should differ, is that we should have a different way of recognising an object as the referent of each of the names: there is no reason to suppose that the means by which we effect such a recognition should be expressible by means of a definite description.
>
> (1981a, pp. 98–9; see also Evans 1982, p. 18)

In this chapter, however, I will assume that for Frege the sense of a proper name is given by a descriptive condition: if the objections which depend on this assumption are cogent, this shows that it is a matter of urgency for a defender of Frege to have an alternative, fully worked-out notion of sense. But investigating the possibility of such an alternative is beyond the scope of this chapter. And Russell, unlike Frege, is explicit on the question: he takes ordinary proper names simply to *abbreviate* definite descriptions. This seems a bit strong, though. Do we really want to hold that 'Aristotle' abbreviates e.g. 'the pupil of Plato and the teacher of Alexander the Great' in the way that 'BBC' abbreviates 'British Broadcasting Corporation'? It seems more plausible to take Russell to be claiming that 'Aristotle' is *synonymous* with e.g. 'the pupil of Plato and the teacher of Alexander the Great'. It is against this idea that Kripke develops his first objection to what he calls 'the Frege–Russell view of proper names'.[6]

Kripke argues that if we accept the claim that 'Aristotle' is in this way synonymous with a complex definite description, we end up committed to some highly implausible claims about Aristotle. In order to spell out Kripke's argument, I need to introduce the distinction between *necessary* and *contingent* truth.

Consider a true sentence such as '2+2=4'. Could things have turned out in such a way that this would have been false? It seems not: there are simply no possible situations in which the sum of 2 and 2 is not 4. Likewise for 'All bachelors are unmarried': there is no way there could have been a married bachelor. Philosophers attempt to capture this feature of '2+2=4' and 'All bachelors are married' by saying that they are *necessary truths*. Sometimes this notion is glossed as follows: a necessary truth is one which is true, not only in this, the actual world, but also in *all logically possible worlds*. '2+2=4' and 'All bachelors are unmarried' contrast with 'Bill Clinton was US president in 1997' or 'Napoleon lost the battle of Waterloo'. Although these are actually true, we can conceive of logically possible situations in which they are false: there are logically possible worlds in which Clinton was not US president in 1997, and there are logically possible worlds in which Napoleon *won* the battle of Waterloo. 'Bill Clinton was US president in 1997' and 'Napoleon lost the battle of Waterloo' are *contingent truths*. They are true in the actual world, but not in all possible worlds.

There is another distinction which is related to the distinction between necessary and contingent truth, but which must also be distinguished from it. An *analytically true* sentence is one which is true purely in virtue of the senses of its constituents, in virtue of some synonymy relation holding between them. 'All bachelors are unmarried males of marriageable age' would be an example of an analytic truth: its truth is settled by the fact that 'bachelor' and 'unmarried male of marriageable age' are synonymous. An example of a *synthetic* truth would be 'George W. Bush was President of the USA in 2001'. This is true, but not *purely* in virtue of the senses of the constituent expressions. The relationship between the necessary-contingent and analytic-synthetic distinctions is a matter of some controversy. Philosophers are generally agreed that all analytic truths are necessary, but not all philosophers hold that all necessary truths are analytic. Kant, for example, held that arithmetical truths such as '2+2=4' are necessary but synthetic (Frege disagreed with Kant on this, and held that arithmetical truths are analytic).

Kripke's objection to taking 'Aristotle' to be synonymous with a description like 'the pupil of Plato and teacher of Alexander the Great' is quite simple: if we take the sense of the name to be given by this description, then certain sentences that are intuitively only contingently true turn out to be necessarily true. Suppose that the sense of 'Aristotle' is given by 'the pupil of Plato and teacher of Alexander the Great'. Then consider the sentence

(36) Aristotle was the pupil of Plato and the teacher of Alexander the Great.

Since the sense of 'Aristotle' is *given* by 'the pupil of Plato and the teacher of Alexander the Great' this sentence is true, and, moreover, true purely in virtue of facts about sense. In other words, it is analytically true. But if it is analytically true, it is also necessarily true, true in all logically possible worlds. But surely it is at most a contingent truth: we have no trouble in conceiving of situations in which Aristotle was taught by someone other than Plato and did not himself teach Alexander the Great.

So, if the sense of 'Aristotle' is given by the description, (36) would be a necessary truth. But (36) is not a necessary truth, it is at most a contingent truth. So the sense of 'Aristotle' cannot be given by the description.

According to Kripke, this is a manifestation of the fact that ordinary proper names, unlike definite descriptions, are what he calls *rigid designators*: where a rigid designator is an expression which refers to the same individual in every possible world in which that individual exists. Definite descriptions are non-rigid designators since their reference can change from possible world to possible world: 'the US president in 2001' in one world refers to George W. Bush, in another to Al Gore, and in yet another to Hilary Clinton. So it is unlikely that the sense of an ordinary proper name could be given by some complex definite description.

Kripke introduces an important distinction which may, on the face it, allow the Frege–Russell view to deflect this objection: between taking a definite description to *give the meaning* of a proper name and between taking a definite description to *fix the reference* of a proper name. Suppose the view is not that 'Aristotle' is synonymous with 'the pupil of Plato and the teacher of Alexander the Great' (so that the latter would give the meaning of the former), but rather that the reference of 'Aristotle' is fixed via the property of being the pupil of Plato and the teacher of Aristotle. The idea is that 'Aristotle' refers, in the actual world, to whoever possesses that property. But the property is a contingent property of whoever possesses it: since we are not taking the definite description to give the meaning of the name, there is no suggestion that the individual concerned has to possess that property in any (let alone all) of the possible worlds distinct from the actual world. So if we take the Frege–Russell view to be the view that definite descriptions fix the reference of ordinary proper names rather than give their meanings, Kripke's first objection appears to be neutralised.

Although, as we'll see, Kripke objects to the idea that in general the reference of an ordinary proper name is fixed by some associated definite description, there are cases where he thinks it is plausible to view reference as fixed by a definite description. And these cases have some important consequences. I introduced above the concepts of necessity and contingency. Another important distinction often drawn in philosophy is that between a priori and a posteriori truths. An a priori truth is one that can be known independently of sense-experience, an a posteriori truth is one that cannot be known independently of sense-experience. Kripke points out that 'In contemporary discussion very few people, if any, distinguish between the concepts of statements being a priori and their being necessary' (1980, p. 34). Kripke argues against this identification: the concepts of necessity and contingency are *metaphysical* concepts, whereas the concepts of the a priori and a posteriori are *epistemological*: the latter are concerned with our *knowledge*, whereas the former are not. In fact, Kripke argues that there may actually be statements which, although only contingently true, may nevertheless be a priori (1980: 54–7). Take the standard metre-rod, S, in Paris. Suppose we use 'the length of S at t' to fix the reference of 'one metre'. Since there are possible worlds in which the length of S was different at time t, the statement 'S is one metre at t' expresses only a contingent truth: but because we have used the length of S at t to fix the reference of 'one metre' at t, the sentence is a priori true. Thus we have a statement which is a *contingent a priori truth*.

In general, though, Kripke thinks that we cannot plausibly view definite descriptions as fixing the reference of ordinary proper names. On this sort of view, to simplify greatly, a speaker would be viewed as referring to an individual in virtue of that individual's uniquely satisfying some complex definite description, though there is now no suggestion that the definite description somehow gives the meaning of the name. Kripke uses two types of example to show that, in general, this is not a correct account of how the reference of names gets fixed. First of all, the fact that an individual satisfies a complex definite description associated with an ordinary proper name is not *sufficient* to ensure that someone using the name refers to that individual. Take the name 'Gödel', and suppose that its reference is fixed by the definite description 'the man who proved the incompleteness of arithmetic'. Kripke asks us to imagine the following sort of (purely fictional) situation:

> Suppose that Gödel was not in fact the author of [the proof that arithmetic is incomplete]. A man named 'Schmidt', whose body was found in Vienna under mysterious circumstances many years ago, actually did the work in question. His friend Gödel somehow got hold of the manuscript and it was thereafter attributed to Gödel. On the view in question, then, when our ordinary man uses the name 'Gödel', he really means to refer to Schmidt, because Schmidt is the unique person satisfying the description, 'the man who discovered the incompleteness of arithmetic'.
>
> (1980, pp. 83–4)

If the reference of 'Gödel' were fixed by the relevant definite description, then in this scenario the ordinary man would actually be referring to Schmidt and not Gödel, because it is Schmidt and not Gödel who uniquely satisfies the description. Kripke finds this consequence implausible:

'[S]ince the man who discovered the incompleteness of arithmetic is in fact Schmidt, we, when we talk about 'Gödel', are in fact always referring to Schmidt. But it seems to me that we are not. We simply are not' (1980, p. 84). Kripke argues likewise that it is not *necessary* for an individual to uniquely satisfy a definite description associated with a name in order for the individual to be referred to by uses of that name. Take the name 'Richard Feynman'. The ordinary speaker, it seems, can certainly use this name to refer to Richard Feynman, as when I say to my father 'Richard Feynman will present his programme at 8 p.m. this evening'. But there seems to be no description, associated by me with the name, which Feynman uniquely satisfies. And the same thing seems to hold of the name 'Cicero':

In fact, most people, when they think of Cicero, just think of a famous Roman orator, without any pretension to think either that there was only one famous Roman orator or that one must know something else about Cicero to have a referent for the name. Consider Richard Feynman, to whom many of us are able to refer. He is a leading contemporary theoretical physicist. Everyone here [Kripke is speaking in a seminar at Princeton University] (I'm sure!) can state the contents of one of Feynman's theories so as to differentiate him from Gel-Mann. However, the man in the street, not possessing these abilities, may still use the name 'Feynman'. When asked he will say: well he's a physicist or something. He may not think that this picks out anyone uniquely. I still think he uses the name 'Feynman' as a name for Feynman.

(1980, p. 81)

Thus, according to Kripke it is neither sufficient nor necessary for an ordinary proper name to refer to an individual that the individual in question satisfy some definite description associated with the name: in general, the reference of a proper name is not fixed by some associated definite description.

Just as Kripke argues that there may be contingent a priori truths, he argues also that there may be necessary a posteriori truths. This is a consequence of his claim that many ordinary proper names are rigid designators, in other words stand for the same individual in every possible world in which that individual exists. Then, for example, 'Hesperus is Phosphorus', if it expresses a truth, expresses a necessary truth, even though there is no way, other than empirical investigation of some sort, of establishing that it is in fact true. Kripke explores the implications of this result for views in the philosophy of mind, in particular the materialist 'identity theory', in Lecture III of Kripke 1980.

KRIPKE'S CAUSAL THEORY OF REFERENCE

How, then, is the reference of a proper name, in general, fixed? Kripke proposes to replace the Frege–Russell view with the following alternative picture:

Someone, let's say, a baby, is born; his parents call him by a certain name. They talk about him to their friends. Other people meet him. Through various sorts of talk the name is spread from link to link as if by a chain. A speaker who is on the far end of this chain, who has heard about, say, Richard Feynman, in the market place or elsewhere, may be referring to Richard Feynman even though he can't remember from whom he first heard of Feynman or from whom he ever heard of Feynman. He knows that Feynman is a famous physicist. A certain passage of communication reaching ultimately to the man himself does reach the speaker. He then is referring to Feynman even though he can't identify him uniquely . . . a chain of communication going back to Feynman himself has been established, by virtue of his membership in a community which passed the name on from link to link.

(1980, p. 91)

Note that the cases where the description theory of names is plausible as a story about reference-fixing are those in which the object is originally christened with the name. In some cases this will be via ostention ('I call this baby "Kirsty"'), but in others it may be by description (the Chief Inspector announces "Jack the Ripper' refers to whoever committed the last three Whitechapel murders'). This only applies to the first link in the chain: after the first link, causal considerations come to the fore.

Kripke admits that this picture is only a rough one, and expresses some doubt himself as to whether it can be refined into a set of necessary and sufficient conditions for reference (1980, p. 96). Indeed, he explicitly disavows the ambition to construct an alternative 'theory' of reference at all. But the picture is already sharp enough to admit of potential counterexamples. The name 'Arthur Schopenhauer' was given, we may suppose, to the distinguished pessimistic philosopher by his parents in some initial 'dubbing' or 'baptismal' ceremony. The name has finally reached me via a long causal chain, reaching back through time to this initial baptismal act. Does it follow, then, that when impressed by my dog's doleful countenance I start to call him 'Arthur Schopenhauer' I refer to the distinguished philosopher and not to my Springer Spaniel? Of course not: and Kripke adds a simple clause to his account designed to deal with this sort of example:

> An initial 'baptism' takes place. Here the object may be named by ostension, or the reference of the name may be fixed by a description. When the name is 'passed from link to link' the receiver of the name must, I think, intend when he learns it to use it with the same reference as the man from whom he heard it.
>
> (1980, p. 96).

When, in throwing the ball over the dog's head I shout 'Go fetch it, Schopenhauer!', my intention is not to use it with the same reference as my teacher Professor Schaper, from whom I originally picked up the name. So there is no real counterexample.

Even with the addition of the clause that the receiver intend to use the name with the same reference as the person from whom he learned it, though, other counterexamples can be found. Gareth Evans, in his 1973 work (Kripke's lectures were originally published in 1972), cites the following example from Isaac Taylor's 1898

287

book *Names and their History*: 'In the case of "Madagascar" a hearsay report of Malay or Arab sailors misunderstood by Marco Polo . . . has had the effect of transferring a corrupt form of the name of a portion of the African mainland to the great African island' (quoted in Evans 1973, p. 11).

Suppose that the use we moderns make of 'Madagascar' can be traced back to Marco Polo. Then, since we intend to use the name with the same reference as Marco Polo, and since Marco Polo presumably intended to use it with the same reference as the native, it follows that in our contemporary use of 'Madagascar' we refer not to the island, but to the relevant portion of the African mainland. This example clearly calls for some more sophisticated revisions in Kripke's causal picture.

PUTNAM, TWIN-EARTH AND EXTERNALISM

Kripke and Putnam argue that just as 'Hesperus' rigidly designates Hesperus, a kind term such as 'water' rigidly designates a kind of stuff. And just as 'Hesperus is Phosphorus' expresses a necessary truth which is nevertheless a posteriori, 'Water is H_2O' expresses a necessary truth which is discoverable only via empirical investigation. In discovering that water is H_2O, we are discovering the essence of water. Simplifying greatly, just as Hesperus rigidly denotes an individual – the planet Venus – which stands in a certain sort of privileged causal relationship to our uses of 'Hesperus' (in that there is a causal chain leading back from our current uses to an event in which the planet was christened with the name 'Hesperus'), 'water' rigidly denotes a scientifically identified kind which stands in a certain sort of privileged causal relationship to our perceptions of the features used in the initial baptism to fix the reference of 'water'. We could sum up this fact about 'water' as follows. The superficial features of water include the fact that it is clear, odourless, thirst-quenching, falls from the sky, fills rivers and lakes, and so on. '(W) "water" refers to that kind of stuff which is dominantly causally responsible for our perceptions of co-instantiations of the superficial features.'

It follows that, for English speakers, 'water' denotes H_2O, since that is in fact the kind of stuff which is relevantly causally responsible. This shows that 'water', as we use it, is a *natural kind* term. If we discovered a substance with the same superficial features as water, but with a different underlying molecular structure, that substance would not be water, the superficial similarities notwithstanding. A test we can apply to a term X to see whether it denotes a natural kind is to ask whether it is possible for there to be 'fools-X', stuff with all the superficial features of X but which is nevertheless not actually X. 'Gold' is thus a natural kind term since not only is 'fool's gold' possible, there actually is such a substance (iron pyrites).

Hilary Putnam devised an ingenious argument designed, as he put it in his 1975, to show that 'meanings just ain't in the head', or to establish a form of what is nowadays known as *externalism*, which uses this account of the semantics of kind terms such as 'water'. This is the now famous argument involving the thought-experiment of 'twin-earth'. In this section, I'll outline the argument, using some of the Fregean terminology introduced in the sections on Frege's theory of meaning, pp. 264–75.

Earth and Twin-Earth are here taken to be distant parts of the same possible world. A and B are atom-for-atom doppelgangers. H_2O and XYZ are substances with different molecular structures, but which are indistinguishable in point of superficial observable characteristics: for both, these are exactly the same as water on Earth. Putnam wants to argue that although A and B are atom-for-atom doppelgangers, they are in different mental states precisely because the molecular structures underlying 'water' on each of their planets are different. Since what they mean is determined in this way, not by the structure of their brains (these, we are supposing, are identical) it follows that 'meanings just ain't in the head'. It is best to break the argument down into the following distinct steps:

(37) A and B live in a different environment: A lives in an H_2O environment, and B lives in an XYZ environment.

(38) If competent speakers of A's language were to come across things with the superficial characteristics of H_2O, but which had underlying molecular structure XYZ, they would, after reflection on these facts about molecular structure, judge that 'water' does not apply to them. Likewise, if competent speakers of B's language were to come across things with the superficial characteristics of XYZ, but which had underlying molecular structure H_2O, they would, after reflection on these facts about molecular structure, judge that 'water' does not apply to them. (This follows from (W) above.)

(39) Given (37) and (38), A ought to apply 'water' to the things in his environment with the superficial characteristics of water, and ought to refuse to apply 'water' to the things in B's environment with the superficial characteristics of water. And given (37) and (38), B ought to apply 'water' to the things in his environment with the superficial characteristics of water, and ought to refuse to apply 'water' to the things in A's environment with the superficial characteristics of water.

(40) But (39) is incompatible with the thought that the extensions of '. . . is water', as used by A and B, are identical.

So given (37) and (38), we get (39), given (39) we get (40). So given (37) and (38) we get

(41) The predicate '. . . is water', as used by A and B, has different extensions.

(42) The sense of '. . . is water' determines its extension (from Frege's thesis 6 together with the fact that the semantic values of predicates – functions – are extensional: see pp. 267–8 above).

(43) Grasping the sense of '. . . is water' is just a matter of being in a certain psychological state.

(44) Psychological states are 'psychological states in the narrow sense': states whose attribution to a subject entails nothing about his environment.

(45) As far as psychological states in the narrow sense are concerned, A and B are identical (since they are atom-for-atom doppelgangers).

(46) Given (42), (43), (44), and (45), the extensions of '. . . is water', as used by A and B, are identical.

(47) Contradiction (from (41) and (46)).

Therefore

(48) not-(43). In other words, grasping the sense of '. . . is water' is not just a case of being in a certain psychological state: it implies a certain relationship to things in one's physical environment. As Putnam puts it 'meanings just ain't in the head'.

This view, that the nature of an agent's mental states is in this way closely bound up with the nature of that agent's physical environment, has come to be known as *externalism*, and is one of the most hotly debated views in contemporary philosophy of mind.[7]

EXERCISES

1 Identify the suppressed premise in the argument of Frege's concerning informative identity statements, pp. 269–75. Is that premise plausible? Choose your own examples to show that Frege's argument generalises to the cases of sentences and predicates.

2 Can Frege use the sense–reference distinction to explain why 'The Evening Star is The Evening Star' is *uninformative*?

3 Use Russell's theory of definite descriptions to write out the logical form of 'The unhappiest man in Washington is a philosopher'.

4 If, as Russell thinks, neither ordinary proper names nor definite descriptions are genuine proper names, what sorts of expression are genuine proper names? (Hint: see 'The Philosophy of Logical Atomism', in Russell (1956)).

5 Show that Russell's theory of descriptions fails to solve the problems of substitution into

belief contexts and informative identity statements. (Hint: use the fact, mentioned in the section Frege's theory of meaning: bedeutung and semantic value, pp. 264–9, that functions are extensional. If you get stuck, see Miller 1998, pp. 70–2).

6 Can Kripke's objection to taking 'Aristotle' to be synonymous with 'the pupil of Plato and the teacher of Alexander the Great' be assuaged by the *cluster* theory of proper names? See Searle (1958). What would Kripke say about this?

7 Do Kripke's examples of 'Gödel', 'Cicero', and 'Feynman' really show that their reference is not fixed via associated definite descriptions?

8 Can you think of any other cases, like Kripke's 'Jack the Ripper' example, in which the reference of a proper name is plausibly fixed by a definite description?

9 Construct a counterexample of your own to Kripke's causal theory of reference. How would you amend Kripke's theory to avoid Evans's 'Madagascar' counterexample? (For Kripke's own remark on this, see 1980, p. 163).

10 Does 'blue' refer to a natural kind?

11 In the section on Putnam, twin-earth and externalism Putnam rejects premise (7), and concludes that grasping the meaning of 'water' is not (just) a psychological state. But could one hold on to (7) and reject one or more of the other premises instead? (Hint: see essay 13 of McDowell 1998 for one such approach; for discussion, see Miller 2002).

NOTES

* For advice, thanks to John Shand, Peter Sullivan and Roger White.

1 Of course, Hume actually goes on to argue that our capacity for thought is constrained by his theory concerning the association of 'ideas' and 'impressions'.

2 'Propositional attitude' was coined by Bertrand Russell. It is relatively easy to see the reason for this term. A belief consists in taking a certain sort of attitude (the 'belief-attitude') to a proposition or thought: so having the belief that Cardiff is in Wales consists in taking the 'belief-attitude' to the proposition *that Cardiff is in Wales*. Likewise, having a desire for a glass of beer consists in taking the 'desire-attitude' to the proposition that you are having a glass of beer, etc.

3 'Bedeutung' is often translated as 'reference' or 'meaning'. I have chosen 'semantic value' in place of these, since Frege's notion has a precise definition which applies to types of expression – e.g. predicates – which we would not normally take as referring to anything in the ordinary sense of reference.

4 We need to distinguish between an *ordered pair* and a *set*, represented by the use of curly brackets {, }. A set is a collection of objects, where the order of the objects is irrelevant to the identity of the set. Thus, {1, 2} is the *same* set as {2,1}. In the case of an ordered pair (represented by normal brackets), the order does matter. So (1,2) is a different ordered pair from (2,1).

5 Russell uses 'meaning' for 'sense' and 'denotation' for 'semantic value'.

6   I will use 'the Frege–Russell view' in the same way as Kripke, whilst bearing in mind that the attribution of the view, to Frege at least, is unwarranted.

7   It is opposed by internalism. The distinction between internalism and externalism in the philosophy of mind is a different distinction from the distinctions with the same name in epistemology and moral psychology.

BIBLIOGRAPHY

Anscombe, G.E.M. (1959) *An Introduction to Wittgenstein's 'Tractatus'*, London: Hutchinson University Library.

Ayer, A. (1946) *Language, Truth, and Logic*, 2nd edn, New York: Dover.

Ayer, A. (ed.) (1959) *Logical Positivism*, Glencoe, IL: Free Press.

Beaney, M. (ed.) (1997) *The Frege Reader*, Oxford: Blackwell.

Blackburn, S. (1984) *Spreading The Word*, Oxford: Oxford University Press.

Burge, T. (1979) 'Individualism and the mental', *Midwest Studies in Philosophy* **4**.

Cain, M. (2001) *Fodor*, Cambridge: Polity Press.

Chomsky, N. (1986) *Knowledge of Language*, New York: Praeger.

Davidson, D. (1984) *Inquiries Into Truth and Interpretation*, Oxford: Oxford University Press.

Devitt, M. (1989) 'Against direct reference', *Midwest Studies in Philosophy* **14**.

Devitt, M. and Sterelny, K. (1987) *Language and Reality*, Cambridge, MA: MIT Press.

Divers, J. (2002) *Possible Worlds*, London: Routledge.

Donnellan, K. (1966) 'Reference and definite descriptions', *Philosophical Review* **75**.

Dummett, M. (1978) *Truth and Other Enigmas*, London: Duckworth.

Dummett, M. (1981a) *Frege: Philosophy of Language*, 2nd edn, London: Duckworth.

Dummett, M. (1981b) *The Interpretation of Frege's Philosophy*, London: Duckworth.

Dummett, M. (2001) 'Gottlob Frege', in A. Martinich and D. Sosa (eds) *A Companion to Analytic Philosophy*, Oxford: Blackwell.

Evans, G. (1973) 'The causal theory of names', reprinted in Evans 1985.

Evans, G. (1982) *The Varieties of Reference*, Oxford: Oxford University Press.

Evans, G. (1985) *Collected Papers*, Oxford: Oxford University Press.

Evnine, S. (1991) *Donald Davidson*, Palo Alto, CA: Stanford University Press.

Fodor, J. (1987) *Psychosemantics: The Problem of Meaning in the Philosophy of Mind*, Cambridge, MA: MIT Press).

Frege, G. (1980) *The Foundations of Arithmetic*, 2nd edn, trans. J.L. Austin, Oxford: Blackwell.

Goldberg, S. and Pessin, M. (eds) (1996) *The Twin Earth Chronicles*, London: MA Sharpe.

Grice, H.P. (1989) *Studies in the Ways of Words*, Cambridge, MA: Harvard University Press.

Hale, B. and Wright, C. (eds) (1997) *A Companion to the Philosophy of Language*, Oxford: Blackwell.

Hookway, C. (1987) *Quine*, Cambridge: Polity Press.

Hume, D. (1748) *An Inquiry Concerning Human Understanding*, Indianapolis, IN: Bobbs Merrill 1977.

Kenny, A. (1973) *Wittgenstein*, London: Penguin.

Kripke, S. (1980) *Naming and Necessity*, Oxford: Blackwell.

Kripke, S. (1982) *Wittgenstein on Rules and Private Language*, Oxford: Oxford University Press.

Lemmon, E. (1964) *Beginning Logic*, London: Nelsons University Paperbacks.

Lyons, J. (1977) *Noam Chomsky*, revised edition, Harmondsworth: Penguin.

McCulloch, G. (1989) *The Game of the Name*, Oxford: Oxford University Press.

McDowell, J. (1998) *Meaning, Knowledge, and Reality*, Cambridge, MA: Harvard University Press.

McGilvray, J. (1999) *Chomsky: Language, Mind, and Politics*, Cambridge: Polity Press.

Meinong, A. (1960) 'The theory of objects', in R. Chisolm (ed.) *Realism and the Background of Phenomenology*, Glencoe, IL: Free Press.

Miller, A. (1998) *Philosophy of Language*, London: Routledge.

Miller, A. (2001) 'Michael Dummett', in A. Martinich and D. Sosa (eds) *A Companion to Analytic Philosophy*, Oxford: Blackwell.

Miller, A. (forthcoming) 'Rule-following and externalism', *Philosophy and Phenomenological Research*.

Miller, A. and Wright, C. (eds) (2002) *Rule-Following and Meaning*, London: Acumen.

Noonan, H. (2000) *Frege*, Cambridge: Polity Press.

Putnam, H. (1975) 'The meaning of "meaning"', in his *Mind, Language, and Reality*, Cambridge: Cambridge University Press.

Quine, W.V.O. (1953) 'Two dogmas of empiricism', in his *From A Logical Point of View*, Cambridge, MA: Harvard University Press.

Quine, W.V.O. (1960) *Word and Object*, Cambridge, MA: MIT Press.

Russell, B. (1919) *Introduction to Mathematical Philosophy*, London: Allen & Unwin.

Russell, B. (1956) *Logic and Knowledge*, London: Routledge.

Russell, B. (1978) *The Problems of Philosophy*, Oxford: Oxford University Press.

Searle, J. (1958) 'Proper names', *Mind* **67**.

Smith, B. (1992) 'Understanding language', *Proceedings of the Aristotelian Society* **LXXXXII**.

Stenius, E. (1960) *Wittgenstein's 'Tractatus'*, Oxford: Blackwell.

Strawson, P. (1950) 'On referring', *Mind* **56**.

Thornton, T. (1998) *Wittgenstein on Language and Thought*, Edinburgh: Edinburgh University Press.

Weiner, J. (1999) *Frege*, Oxford: Oxford University Press.

Weiss, B. (2002) *Dummett*, London: Acumen.

Wittgenstein, L. (1958) *Philosophical Investigations*, trans. G.E.M. Anscombe, Oxford: Blackwell.

Wittgenstein, L. (1961) *Tractatus Logico-Philosophicus*, trans. D. Pears and B. McGuinness, London: Routledge.

Wright, C. (1993) *Realism, Meaning and Truth*, 2nd edn, Oxford: Blackwell.

FURTHER READING

On Frege, Russell, Kripke and Putnam

It will be clear from the sections on Frege's theory of meaning above that a study of Frege's philosophy of language builds on a knowledge of the language of elementary propositional and predicate calculus. If you don't already have this, a good logic textbook, such as Lemmon 1964, is essential. The key essays by Frege relevant to the discussion above are 'Function and Concept', 'On Concept and Object', 'On Sense and Meaning', and 'The Thought'. These are collected in Beaney (1997). Frege's logicist programme is introduced in *The Foundations of Arithmetic* (Frege

1980). The sections above are expanded in Miller (1998), chapters 1 and 2. Weiner (1999) is a useful, concise introduction to Frege, which is good at placing Frege's philosophy of language in the context of his logicist programme in the philosophy of mathematics. Noonan (2000) is also useful. The most important contemporary interpreter of Frege is Michael Dummett. See Dummett (1981a), especially the Introduction and chapters 1, 5, 6, and 19; Dummett (1981b); and Dummett (2001). For an interpretation that diverges sharply from Dummett's, see Evans (1982) and McDowell (1998), essay 8.

The relevant key works by Russell are 'On Denoting' and chapter 6 of 'The philosophy of logical atomism', both in Russell (1966); and also chapter 16 of Russell (1919) and chapter 5 of Russell (1978). The sections above are expanded in Miller (1998), chapter 2. See also Strawson (1950), Donnellan (1956), Blackburn (1984) chapter 9, McCulloch (1989) chapters 2 and 3.

The work of Kripke and Putnam has given rise to a huge secondary literature. This consists largely of monographs and journal articles, most of which will be of scant use to the student with little prior experience in the philosophy of language. Kripke (1980) is demanding, but largely written in an easygoing, informal manner (it is a transcript of some talks), so that is as good a place to start as any. Dummett (1981a) raises some objections in the appendix to chapter 5 of his, and Evans (1973) discusses Kripke's causal alternative to Frege and Russell; but both the Dummett and the Evans are hard going, though worth the effort if you can manage it. I found the discussion of Kripke and Dummett in chapter 4 of McCulloch (1989) helpful. For more demanding expositions, see the papers by Stalnaker and Stanley in Hale and Wright (1997). For an introduction to necessity and contingency, see Divers (2002). Kripke's work on reference forms the departure point for the 'direct reference' theorists: see Devitt (1989). For the best introductory book on the internalist–externalist debate see the excellent and clearly written Thornton (1998). John McDowell provides a version of externalism which is radically different from Putnam's (see McDowell 1998, essays 7–13, and exercise 15 below). For a collection of essays on the twin-earth argument, see Goldberg and Pessin (1996). Tyler Burge's (1979) offers another argument for a form of externalism. The leading contemporary internalist is perhaps Jerry Fodor. See e.g. Fodor (1987). For a good introduction to Fodor, see Cain (2001).

What to read next

General

For an overview, see Miller (1998). For a collection of 'critical survey' type articles, many by leading contemporary philosophers, see Hale and Wright (1997). Blackburn (1984) is an excellent introduction showing how the philosophy of language can impact on other central areas in philosophy.

Logical Positivism

Ayer (1946) and the articles collected in Ayer (1959) are the best place to start. Miller (1998), chapter 3, provides an overview.

Quine

Quine's philosophy grows out of an attack on the logical positivist theory of meaning: for an excellent account of this see Hookway (1987). The most important pieces by Quine are his (1953) and (1960) chapter 2. Miller (1998), chapter 4, provides a commentary and more detailed advice on further reading.

The Early Wittgenstein

Wittgenstein (1961), first published in 1921, is perhaps the most elusive yet famous philosophical work of the twentieth century: it grows out of, but ultimately diverges from, the work of Frege and Russell. For an introductory commentary, see the opening chapters of Kenny (1973). See also Anscombe (1959) and Stenius (1960).

The Later Wittgenstein

The central text is Wittgenstein (1958). Although questionable as exegesis, the most stimulating secondary work is Kripke (1982). For the ensuing literature, see Miller (1998) chapters 5–6, and the papers in Miller and Wright (2002).

Grice's Programme

Grice attempts to explain linguistic meaning in terms of speaker's intentions and linguistic conventions. The classic paper is his 'Meaning', reprinted in Grice (1989). For critical discussion and advice on further study, see Miller (1998) chapter 7, and the paper by Avramides in Hale and Wright (1997).

Davidson's Project

This takes off from the idea of a formal theory of truth and utilises Tarski's work on truth. Davidson's key papers are collected in Davidson (1984). Evnine (1991) is a very useful book-length introduction. See also Miller (1998), chapter 8.

Chomsky

Chomsky's work on theoretical linguistics impacts on the philosophy of language at several places. You could start with Chomsky (1986), then Lyons (1977) and McGilvray (1999). An article which very helpfully places Chomsky's work with respect to contemporary philosophy of language is Smith (1992).

Realism and Antirealism

The idea that metaphysical issues can be resolved in the philosophy of language receives its most famous exposition in the work of Michael Dummett. See e.g. essays 1, 10, 14, and 21 in Dummett

(1978). These make hard reading. For more accessible treatments, see the introduction to Wright (1993) and the essay by Hale on 'Realism and its oppositions' in Hale and Wright (1997). For an introductory book on Dummett, see Weiss (2002). For an introduction totally opposed to Dummett's approach see Devitt and Sterelny (1987). See also Miller (1998) chapter 9, and Miller (2001).

10

PHILOSOPHY OF SCIENCE
Alexander Bird

INTRODUCTION

The central concerns of the philosophy of science as a whole divide into two areas. One of these areas, perhaps the traditionally more dominant side, encompasses such questions as: Is scientific knowledge possible? If so, how? What methods of reasoning do scientists use? What is the role of observation and experiment in scientific reasoning? Are theories justified that concern entities and processes that cannot be observed? This area is where philosophy of science overlaps with epistemology, the theory of knowledge.

The second area is situated where philosophy of science overlaps with metaphysics. Here we are concerned not with whether and why our theories amount to knowledge, but instead we focus on what our theories are about – in the most general terms. For example, the world contains *laws of nature* and is divided up into different *kinds* of things. Almost all scientific theories concern one or other of these two general features of the world – or at least their subject matter will reflect these features. Associated with features is the fact that most theories attempt to *explain* some phenomenon or other. These are metaphysical topics.

In this chapter we shall look first at the second area, metaphysical philosophy of science, before returning to the first, epistemological philosophy of science.

THE METAPHYSICS OF SCIENCE

I mentioned three key components in the metaphysical part of the philosophy of science: laws of nature, natural kinds, and explanation. We can see these all operating together in John Dalton's atomic hypothesis. The starting point is the obvious fact that chemists deal with different substances. The stuff of chemistry divides naturally in to different chemical kinds, which for the most part remain or can be made to remain as they are and distinct from one another. The task of the chemist is to discover by what processes these kinds will react to produce other kinds – and to enquire into why they do so. In the process of investigating the reactions that they undergo, it was discovered that substances would react together only in fixed proportions; and in the case of gases the proportions, when measured by volume, were always ratios of small whole numbers. In reacting hydrogen with oxygen we find that they will combine without residue to form water if we use exactly twice as much hydrogen as oxygen. But if we deviate from this proportion then some hydrogen or some oxygen will be left over unreacted. So we have an experimentally discovered law: the law of constant proportions. Dalton's explanation for this was that the basic constituents of chemical matter are atoms, a different kind of atom for each chemical element. When substances react they do so because atoms combine in small clusters – molecules. The molecules are the basic form of the compound substance. So that substance will contain the elements in exactly the proportion that the elements occur in the compound molecule. Hence a *law of nature* (the law of constant proportions) governs *kinds* at one level (laboratory substances), is *explained* by the existence of kinds at another level (atoms and molecules).

In the next three sections we shall look at these components in detail. What exactly does it mean to explain a phenomenon? What is the relationship between explanations and causes and laws of nature? What for that matter are laws of nature? Where does our sense that the world divides into different kinds of thing come from? Is it a reflection of the division of the world into natural kinds, or does it reflect more human interests and categories?

EXPLANATION

The explanation of phenomena such as the law of constant proportions is a characteristic and indeed central task of science. The nature of scientific explanation raises a range of philosophical problems and controversies. A very basic one asks whether science really should be engaged in explanation at all. One view, associated with *positivist* philosophy of science, is that to seek explanations in terms of hidden processes is just so much mystery-mongering and that science should aim solely to describe carefully the various regularities to be found in the observable phenomena. Dalton's atomic hypothesis was attacked on those grounds and the related ground that even if the phenomena are explained by hidden processes we could never know what those processes really are (because, for example, we could never have good reason to choose between different possible underlying explanations). We shall return to positivist philosophy of science later. Another problem raised by the notion of explanation concerns the variety of explanation. We are all familiar with *causal* explanation, a form of explanation found in the physical sciences. But in biology we also find explanation through *natural selection*. We can explain why giraffes have long necks by citing the adaptive advantage a long neck gives an animal, enabling it to reach a greater range of leafy food. This seems different from causal explanation, since an adaptive advantage does not cause a giraffe to have a long neck; what causes a giraffe to have a long neck is its genes. We might ask whether behind this difference in kind of explanation is an unity in the underlying mechanism. For example, it is plausible to suggest that whenever one can give a correct natural selectionist explanation that is only because a more complex causal explanation is also available: mutations cause certain giraffes to have longer necks which cause them to eat more than other giraffes which in turn causes those giraffes to have more offspring, and so on.

Whether this constitutes a reduction of selectionist explanation to causal explanation is a question for philosophers of biology; similar questions arise in the philosophy of psychology and in other areas of science. A form of explanation that is perhaps most common in physics is *nomic* explanation – explanation in terms of the laws of nature. We will see an attempted unification with causal explanation here too. In the sixteenth century Johannes Kepler discovered that the planets rotate about the Sun in ellipses, rejecting centuries of conviction that planetary motion was essentially circular. A century later Isaac Newton was able to explain Kepler's discovery. All objects, the planets included, obey a universal law of gravitation and basic laws of motion. Newton deduced from his laws the fact that a small object rotating under gravity around a much more massive one will travel in an ellipse. In a different case physicists can now give a full explanation of why an aeroplane wing generates lift. We take certain general laws concerning the motion of the air (or any fluid). These laws, plus a description of the particular shape of the aerofoil allow us to deduce that there will be a difference in pressure between the lower and upper sides of the wing, which in turn means that there will be an upwards force on the wing. These two examples suggest a general pattern for explanations involving laws of nature: from a statement of certain relevant laws plus a statement concerning the particular conditions surrounding the phenomenon in question we *deduce* the facts we want to explain. Diagrammatically this can be represented thus:

from	laws;	e.g.	laws of gravitation and motion; the Sun is much more massive than the planets
	particular conditions		
we deduce	the facts to be explained		the planets travel in ellipses with the Sun at one focus

The idea that we can explain a phenomenon by showing how it is in instance of a law or several laws is known as the *covering law* model of explanation. The particular version we have been looking at is the *deductive–nomological* version, where the phenomenon is deduced from the laws (plus other relevant conditions).

The originator of the deductive–nomological version of the covering law model, Carl Hempel (Hempel 1965, 1966), extended this idea to cases where explanations do not permit us to deduce that the phenomenon in question will occur but nonetheless make it *likely*. Subatomic events, such as the decay of an atomic nucleus, are inherently probabilistic. This means that we can never deduce that such an event will occur, and so no deductive–nomological explanation is available. It might be thought that we may nevertheless explain why some atomic explosion occurred by citing the laws and circumstances that make it likely. This is the *probabilistic–statistical* (or *inductive–probabilistic*) version of the covering law model. The laws still make the phenomenon expected, but only with a high degree of probability rather than certainty. We can see a connection between the covering law model of explanation and prediction. If we know the explanation of an event, then we could have predicted it in advance. If we had known the laws of gravitation and motion before we had ever observed the planets, then we would have been able to expect them to travel in ellipses. If we knew that a compound consists of molecules made up of a few atoms, then we would expect the reaction producing this compound to require precise proportions of the reagents. Conversely, according to Hempel, if we can predict an event then we are in a position to explain it once it has occurred.

One immediate problem with this view is that it seems we can explain things with information that is insufficient to permit prediction. An unfortunate baggage handler at London's Heathrow airport once contracted malaria from a mosquito which has travelled from overseas attached to some luggage. We can explain why he got malaria – he was bitten by a mosquito. But this is not enough to allow us to predict in advance that he would. We cannot deduce that he gets malaria, for not all mosquitoes carry malaria, and not all bites from infected mosquitoes lead to malaria. The fact that it was unlikely that he would get malaria is consistent with the fact that we can explain why he did after the event. So explanation does not seem, after all, to require that we deduce the fact to be explained. To a great extent this observation can be reconciled with the covering law model of explanation by distinguishing complete from incomplete (or so-called 'elliptical') explanations. A complete explanation is one that gives all the laws and conditions required to deduce the phenomenon to be explained (or to make the phenomenon highly likely). An incomplete explanation supplies just part of a complete explanation. A complete explanation of the baggage handler's malaria would include the fact that the mosquito was infected, the fact that the bite was in a certain place, the fact that the baggage handler had a physiology susceptible to malarial infection, and other such facts that altogether, along with the relevant biological and biochemical laws, would allow us to deduce that he would contract malaria. The explanations we give in most circumstances are incomplete, leaving out facts that are not of especial interest or facts about which we are ignorant. In fixing upon the mosquito bite we are focusing on only a part of the complete explanation, but an especially salient part. As this case suggests, the idea of an incomplete explanation allows us to link nomic to causal explanation. A causal explanation is an incomplete explanation where we have chosen to cite one of the salient conditions, such as the mosquito bite, rather than any of the laws.

A number of further problems beset the covering law model and its various forms. One such problem concerns the probabilistic–statistical version. Some philosophers argue that a complete explanation that shows only that some event is likely (rather than certain) does not really explain it; after all, that does not explain why it happened rather than did not happen. On this view inherently probabilistic events cannot be explained. At best we can explain why they were likely to occur, not why they actually occurred.

Different problems face both versions of the covering law model. Peter Achinstein gives this example, concerning an unfortunate Mr Jones who ate a pound of arsenic and died shortly thereafter (Achinstein 1983):

from the law	everyone who eats a pound of arsenic dies within 24 hours;
and condition	Jones ate a pound of arsenic
we deduce	Jones dies within 24 hours

We would certainly have been able to predict Mr Jones' death from the law and condition given. However, this does not, in this case, explain his death. For just after eating the arsenic and while still in good shape, Mr Jones left his house and was run down by a bus. Not every correct prediction translates into a correct explanation. This suggests that there is more to explanation than just being able to deduce the phenomenon from laws and conditions.

The preceding problem can be called the problem of pre-emption. Another problem concerns the asymmetry of explanation. If A explains B then B cannot explain A. But the deductive pattern of deductive–nomological explanation does not show this asymmetry. It seems that we may explain why the pressure in a syringe increased by 50 per cent when we pushed in the plunger by one third using a deductive-nomological explanation:

from law	under conditions of constant temperature, PV=constant;
and conditions	the temperature remained constant,
	the volume decreased by one third
we deduce	the pressure increased by 50 per cent

But note that the following also fits the pattern:

from law	under conditions of constant temperature, PV=constant;
and conditions	the temperature remained constant,
	the pressure increased by 50%
we deduce	the volume decreased by one third

It looks as if we can also explain the decrease in volume by citing the change in pressure – but that is clearly the wrong way round.

One way out of both the pre-emption and the asymmetry problems would be to suggest that an explanation should mention something known to be a cause of the phenomenon to be explained. But that seems too easy an escape. First, this would prevent us from using this model of explanation to tell us what causal explanation is – for it would now assume we understood causal explanation already. Second, one might expect similar problems to arise when trying to give an independent account of what causes are (and indeed similar problems do arise). So this 'solution' just moves the problem elsewhere. As regards the problem of asymmetry one might want to add the proviso that the explaining conditions should precede the phenomenon to be explained in time. This would work but again it might be too easy a solution. For what determines the direction of the arrow of time? One plausible answer is that it is the direction of causation. So we could not assume we know what the direction of time is without circularity.

Another approach is to look at the bigger picture. We knew that the poison did not explain Jones' death because we knew that the bus did. If we had looked at Jones' physiology we would have seen that the chain of events that normally lead from ingesting poison to death had not been completed. Similarly, we knew that the change in the gas pressure did not cause the change in volume in the syringe, because we knew that it was that the experimenter's pushing on the plunger that caused the volume to change. So perhaps the way to discern explanations is to see how the proposed explanation fits into a larger pattern of explanations. We shall see one way how this might work in the next section of this chapter. Hempel's covering law model might still be part of the picture, since all the explanations will have to conform to it. But merely fitting that model won't be enough – integration with other explanations will also be required. However, even this approach is unlikely to be enough, because at the most basic level some of these problems will refuse to go away. One basic idea in Hempel's model might still be right – that to explain some fact fully is to show how it is the *instantiation* of some law or combination of laws of nature. That is to say, that the fact is an instance of that law in action, as when a falling stone is the law of gravity in action. However, what our examples have shown is that being deducible from a law does not show that a fact is indeed an instantiation of the law. In fact it may not be possible to give a perfect account of when laws are instantiated, or, correspondingly, of when one event causes another.

LAWS OF NATURE

Even if we cannot say exactly what it is for a fact to be an instance of a law, for a fact to show a law in action, we may at least be able to make some progress by investigating the concept of law itself. That is what this section is about. At the beginning of this chapter I mentioned the law of constant proportions. This was discovered as a result of careful laboratory measurements taken by chemists such as Jeremias Richter. The observed fact that substances reacting together in laboratory experiments do so in fixed proportions was taken to be a sign of a universal fact, that *all* chemical substances always react together in fixed proportions. So perhaps this is just what a law of nature is, an *universal regularity*. This is the simplest and perhaps initially most attractive view of what a law of nature is. Some laws may not seem to be fully universal. Kepler's laws of planetary motion were formulated to describe the motions of planets in the Solar System, not any other planetary system. However, even Kepler's laws are general to the extent that they tell us how the planets move at any time, not, for example, just when they are being observed. Furthermore, thanks to Newton, we know that any planetary system will obey Kepler's laws, so long as the gravitational effect of the planets on each other is negligible compared to that of their sun. Newton showed that Kepler's laws hold if and only if the Sun and each planet exert a force on each other that is attractive, that acts along the line joining them, whose strength is proportional to the product of the two masses and is inversely proportional to the square of their separation. If this is generalised from the Sun and planets to all masses whatsoever we get Newton's law of universal gravitation. As its name suggests, this law is truly universal: currently we believe that it holds everywhere and for all times. Some physicists suggest that the law is not truly universal, claiming that the so-called gravitational constant is not constant after all – the strength of the force of gravity is changing over time. But even if this is true, we would expect there to be some underlying law that shows why the gravitational constant should change. That underlying law would be genuinely universal.

It is wise to note some ambiguity in our language. Strictly speaking Kepler's laws do not hold of our Solar System, since inter-planetary forces mean that there is some deviation from those laws. Does that mean that, strictly speaking Kepler's laws are not laws at all? Or does it mean that although still laws, those laws are strictly false? Similarly, if we discovered the gravitational 'constant' to be changing, would that mean that Newton's law of gravitation is not a law after all, or that it is a law that is false? Both ways of speaking are correct. One way means by 'law' some general proposition or statement, something which can be asserted by people, be believed, and found, in due course, to be wrong (or right). The other way takes 'law' to be referring to the objective features of the world we are trying to uncover. On the latter view a law is just *there* making the world behave in the way that it does, independently of whether we know or believe it to be there. Since we are at this point doing metaphysics, it is more useful to reserve the term 'law' for this objective notion, and use 'law statement' for the other way of speaking. Then we can say that law statements are attempts to describe the laws that there actually are.

So far we have formulated the view that a law (an objective law) is just a universal regularity is the way nature behaves. But some reflection suggests that this cannot be all there is to being law. A coincidence is two events happening together or in close succession. A *mere* coincidence is such a co-occurrence that is purely accidental – nothing connects the two events. Too many coincidences and we begin to suspect that they are not mere coincidences and that the kinds of event are in fact related. Conspiracy theorists tend to think that there are very few repeated mere coincidences – they see sinister connections where there is just the co-occurrence of independent happenings. A rational person must accept that mere coincidences can be repeated. If the coincidence is repeated again and again, it may be reasonable to suppose that there is some connection. But one should still admit that a repeated mere coincidence can happen, even if it is unlikely. (And we know that unlikely events do happen – which is why people hope to win lotteries). Now imagine that a chain of mere coincidences constitutes a fully universal regularity – it has no exceptions. To make this clearer, imagine that on some busy London bus at some particular moment all its passengers are people who that evening have Italian food for dinner. That could happen by sheer fluke. Now imagine that something akin to that happens on a comic scale. Would that cosmic coincidence be a law? You would think not – it would be a mere coincidence, a fluke, an accident. And the occurrences of laws are just not that sort of thing – occurrences of laws are not accidental; they have to happen the way they do.

There could be a universal regularity that is merely a cosmic coincidence, not a law. So a law must be more than just any universal regularity. It must be a non-accidental universal regularity. But what do we mean by 'non-accidental'? This is a tricky question, since we cannot simply reply that a regularity is accidental if it does not come about as the result of a law – since the notion of law is precisely the one that we are ultimately trying to explain. Our explanation would be circular. There are two standard responses to this problem. I shall look at one solution in detail. It notes that we could say without immediate circularity that an accidental regularity is one that does not come about as a result of an underlying or basic law. Kepler's laws are non-accidental, since they can be explained by Newton's law of gravitation, the law that underlies them. But to avoid circularity, we must be able to give a satisfactory explanation of what an *underlying* or *basic* law is. What features do we think the basic laws should have? For a start, a basic law (such as Newton's) explains other regularities that are non-basic laws (like Kepler's laws) as well as individual events (such as the behaviour of a comet or space vehicle); but the basic law does not itself get explained. How much should be explained by the basic laws? If the world is deterministic then the basic laws should between them explain every individual event. In fact the world is not deterministic; individual events such as the nuclear decay of a radioactive atom do not happen as the inevitable result of the existence of a law. Even so, the probability of that atom's decaying is subject to a law of nuclear physics. So at least the probabilities of events should be captured by the laws. In general as much information as possible about the occurrence of individual events should be captured by our basic laws. Another feature of the way basic laws operate is illustrated by the explanation of Kepler's laws or of the motion of a comet. To give a full explanation we need not only Newton's law of gravitation, we need Newton's laws of motion as well. The laws operate together to explain events and regularities. And if we are talking about the motion of charged particles, we will have to introduce further basic laws. So we expect our basic laws to form an integrated system. Lastly, we note that the history of science shows that the laws we uncover as we get closer to our basic laws are fewer in number, more general in scope, and simpler in form. For example, before Kepler and Newton, the behaviour of objects in the universe were thought to be governed by different laws for heavenly objects (the Sun, planets, etc.) from the laws for earthly objects. Furthermore, the mathematically quantified laws for the motions of the planets were very complicated (both in Ptolemy's Earth-centred system and in Copernicus' Sun-centred system). Kepler then showed how the laws governing the planets could be reduced to three simple laws, while Newton further simplified matters by introducing the single even simpler law of gravitation, which with the laws of motion explain the behaviour not just of planets but (in part at least) of all objects whatsoever. The various sciences have a multiplicity of non-basic laws, but physicists have shown how to reduce the underlying laws of physics to just three laws (gravity, the electro-weak force and the strong nuclear force), and hope to unify even these. So our conception of law seems to include the thought that the basic system of laws should not only seek to encompass as many phenomena as possible, but should also be as simple as possible and should integrate into a system. A god-like mind should be able to deduce all the non-basic laws from these basic ones. And so the *systematic* account of what a law is says that a law is either basic, in which case it is one of the regularities of nature that is part of an integrated system of regularities, which is optimal in the sense of capturing as many facts, actual and potential, as possible while also being as simple as possible (Lewis 1973, pp. 72–7). Or the law is non-basic, in which case it can be derived from the basic ones. We can now see why cosmic accidental regularities don't get to be laws. This is because we would not expect them to help explain many things, and so we would not want them as part of our basic system. At the same time we cannot derive the accidental regularity from the basic laws. We can explain the individual events making up the accidental regularity but we cannot give a unified explanation for all of them together. Return to the case of the bus passengers; we know that this is just an accident because we can give an explanation of why each passenger ate Italian food, and the explanations will be independent of one another and independent of the bus journey.

The systematic account of laws has its critics. For sure, they say, it looks as if *our* universe is governed by a system of well-integrated simple laws of great scope. But things did not have to be that way. There is no contradiction in supposing that an universe could exist with many complicated laws that do not integrate well but act largely independently. Furthermore, one could imagine that by fluke there occurred an accidental regularity in that world which would very much improve the simplicity and power of the system of supposed basic laws for that world, if it were added to that system. But that would not make the accidental regularity a law. A really amazing coincidence could still be a mere coincidence without being a law (it only looks like a law). A different sort of problem with the systematic account, and indeed with any account that thinks of laws as some kind of regularity, is that it doesn't do justice to the thought that laws explain things. A regularity, even a basic one, is just a collection of resembling co-occurrences. In what sense does the collection of such co-occurrences explain why any particular co-occurrence happened? The worry is that the natural answer is: none at all. It may be a botanical regularity that all toadstools are poisonous. But that does not explain why some particular one poisoned me when I ate it. For an explanation we want something behind the regularity, something that can itself explain the regularity, and therefore something which is not the regularity itself. These critics suggest that we should not focus on individual events or facts, nor on collections of them (i.e. not on regularities). What we should focus upon are *properties*. These critics have a particular conception of what a property is. Properties are what they call *universals*, entities that exist, in some sense, in their own right, more or less independently of their belonging to specific objects. We can then think of laws as relations among properties. So we can think of the property *black* as being a universal – all black things share one and the same property. And it can relate to other properties in a law of nature: for example, being black makes something heat up more quickly when irradiated than being white does.

Thinking of laws as relations among properties has the advantage of making it plausible that laws explain individual facts and events as well as regular co-occurrences of events. That blackness is related to heating explains why all black things heat up quickly. The law is not the regularity but stands behind the regularity. The relation between properties is often called *nomic necessitation*. We can think of nomic necessitation as something like causation (after all, it is reasonable to say that being coloured black causes rapid heating). However that is not very helpful at explaining what 'nomic necessitation' means, especially if we aim, as well we might, to explain causation in terms of laws/nomic necessitation. We can often explain what property or relation we are thinking of by explaining what it does: *black* is the property that makes things appear black to normal observers, or is a property that makes things heat up rapidly; *being heavier than* is the relation that explains why some thing take more force to lift or accelerate than others. What would explain the relation of *nomic necessitation*? To reply 'it is the relation that relates properties in laws' is clearly going to be circular if we want to use the concept of nomic necessitation in explaining what laws are.

I'll mention one last view of laws that differs importantly from both the systematic regularity and the nomic necessitation views. This view at least shares this with the nomic necessitation view, that it takes properties to be of fundamental importance. But the nomic necessitation view thinks that properties exist independently of one another and might be conjoined in any combination. It might be that in some other possible universe, white things heat up more rapidly than black, or that colour and heating are not connected at all. The *dispositionalist* view of properties and laws notes something important from the previous paragraph, that properties can be specified by their causal or functional role. Perhaps these roles are *essential*. That is, to say what a property is, is to say what causal role it fulfils. It might, for example, be the role of *being negatively charged* that things with this property repel one another and attract things with the property of being positively charged. So, necessarily, negatively charged objects repel one another. If some objects with property *P* failed to repel one another, *P* would not be negative charge. If so, then the law that negatively charged objects repel just follows from the existence of the property of negative charge. We do not need a separate account of laws (see Mumford 1998). One intriguing aspect of this view is that it makes the laws of nature hold in all possible worlds (where the property exists). This appears to conflict with an intuition that the laws of nature could have been different from what they actually are. However, it is unclear just what weight we should put on this intuition.

NATURAL KINDS

The things and stuffs we find in this world divide into different kinds. Some differences in kind are due to the fact that the things in question are made by us for different purposes, knives are different from forks, tables from chairs, buses from trains, because these items have been designed with different functions in mind. Much of science proceeds upon the assumption that there are also natural divisions of things into kinds – animal species, chemical elements, kinds of subatomic particles, and so forth. The central philosophical problem surrounding natural kinds asks what it is that divides things into natural kinds. The parallel with kinds of artefacts is unlikely to be helpful, since that would suggest that natural kinds are divided by virtue of being designed for a purpose. Although that answer might be congenial to some religious views, it is inadequate if we seek a natural rather than a supernatural explanation of the existence of natural kinds. Another outlook that sees a close analogy to artefactual kinds regards the division of things into kinds as reflecting human interests, even if natural objects are not designed by us. For example, the greengrocer's division of produce into fruit and 'vegetables' reflects a culinary perspective, and hence tomatoes and cucumbers are not regarded as fruit, even though they perform the same seed-bearing role as apples and strawberries. We think that there is a natural botanical division as well as the culinary one, but can we be sure that this is not just a matter of a different anthropocentric perspective?

One way we might ensure that we achieve a natural division with our concepts is to provide careful definitions of our kind concepts in terms of purely scientific properties: the definition of 'fruit' as 'the seed bearing part of a plant' seems to be scientifically respectable in a way that 'sweet-tasting part of a plant' does not. This however just postpones the problem. For the definitions will succeed in picking out natural divisions only if the terms employed in the definitions themselves reflect genuinely natural kinds, in this case 'seed' and 'plant'. Any definition must refer to properties that things may or may not have and these properties must be natural properties if the definitions are to define natural kinds. But the question, what makes a property a natural property is no advance on the question, what makes a kind a natural kind.

There are two ways of tackling this problem, both of which make progress towards an answer. The first approach points out that we would expect humans to have some innate ability to perceive difference in kinds. This is because such an ability would have been required by our ancestors in coping with the environment in which they found themselves. An individual who cannot spot the differences between a lion and an antelope or between a poisonous plant and nutritious one will not survive for long in the African savannah. Looking at the other end of the evolutionary chain, even single-celled creatures respond differently to different kinds of chemicals in their environments. So natural selection will confer on us at least some ability to detect differences in natural kinds. Building on this initial innate ability we can develop means of detecting yet further kinds. For example, natural selection has given us the ability to see different colours. This may not be enough to tell the difference between two different chemical substances which look exactly the same; but those substances may burn to produce flames with different colours, and so this test will allow us to know of another natural division.

The second approach denies that our kind concepts work by having precise verbal definitions of the sort envisaged. Take as a simple example the concept of 'water'. Today we might employ a scientific definition: 'compound with formula H_2O'. But that water is H_2O was a discovery made in the nineteenth century about stuff that people were already calling 'water'. So before the discovery, the term 'water' must have been referring to water even without the benefit of such a definition. Saul Kripke and Hilary Putnam have argued that it is plausible that no definition was available then that could have successfully picked out precisely water (Kripke 1980; Putnam 1975). This is because in a limited state of chemical knowledge the best definition of water would have been something like 'a colourless, tasteless liquid that boils at 100°C and freezes at 0°C'. Now imagine that on some other planet superficially like Earth there is a colourless, tasteless liquid that boils at 100°C and freezes at 0°C, and which is found in the places where water is found on Earth. However this stuff is not H_2O but has some other formula, say XYZ. On the accepted assumptions that what 'water' refers to hasn't changed since the eighteenth century and that water is precisely H_2O, it follows that XYZ is not water and never has been. However, had people in the eighteenth century employed the supposed definition of water ('a colourless, tasteless liquid that boils at 100°C and freezes at 0°C') then XYZ would have passed their definition and would have been water. Hence it follows that in the eighteenth century neither this nor anything else like it was the *definition* of water. (This argument from Putnam and others from Kripke are discussed in more detail by Alexander Miller in his chapter in this book on the Philosophy of Language.)

So it seems that in the eighteenth century people were able to refer to water without having a definition of water. That itself should be no great surprise, for not every word can have an informative, non-circular verbal definition. Indeed it is plausible that most do not. But if a verbal definition is not what gives the concept of water its content, what does? The proper names of people provide an useful analogy here. Proper names don't have verbal definitions. People get their names in naming ceremonies. Other people may get to know the name by being introduced to the person in question, or by having them pointed out. But we can use a name to refer to someone we have never met nor seen. In such a case, what makes that name refer to them is the fact that our use of the name is linked, via the use of the name by other people, all the way back to the person who bears that name. So we can explain that what ties the use of a name to the person is an initial naming ceremony followed a series of causal connections between one person and another. Often such connections will be reinforced by 'repetitions' of the naming ceremony, as when someone is introduced by name.

Something similar may be regarded as happening with common kind names, such as 'water'. At some time in the past something like a naming ceremony took place when our ancestors agreed to use 'water' (or some predecessor of that word) to refer to the stuff they found around them, which they could see and point to. That links our use of 'water' to the stuff water. That link is reinforced (rather more strongly that the original link) by the fact that as children we are introduced to the word 'water' in connection with samples of water. Since we are not linked in this way to any samples of XYZ, our word does not refer to XYZ. A similar story may be told about many other natural kind terms. According to this view of how we refer to natural kinds, we can do so without being able to describe them definitively. Perhaps we need a conception of 'kind of stuff' so that we can pick out water/H_2O (but not XYZ) when we say 'water is this kind of stuff'. The pointing ('this') and the notion of stuff will be enough to permit reference to a single natural kind. Of course not *all* natural kinds can be identified this way – subatomic particles are not easily pointed to. But we can nonetheless forge a similar sort of connection with them via their effects. We can see the light emitted by a gas in the cathode ray tube or the traces in a cloud chamber. This may not count as seeing electrons, but we can say 'electrons are the things that explain these effects'. In yet more sophisticated cases we might have to articulate some theory in which a kind of thing or stuff is postulated to explain some phenomenon – as neutrinos were postulated to explain the 'missing' mass in beta decay.

It is reasonable to suppose that, speaking generally, there are natural kinds. The structure that there is in the universe, which requires both difference and sameness, would not be possible without natural kinds. The laws of nature govern the behaviour of entities according to the kinds of thing that they are. Natural kinds are those kinds that play a part in genuine explanations of natural phenomena. But not all the kind terms that occur in language are natural kind terms. So what, we asked, distinguishes genuine natural kind terms from other linguistic expressions? What reason do we have to suppose that they really do reflect naturally occurring divisions among things? The first part of the answer was that the meanings of some words are attached to our innate perceptual discriminatory abilities. We would expect for evolutionary reasons that these should pick out real rather than imagined differences between things. But not all differences in kinds will be perceptual. The second part of the answer suggests that our terms refer to natural kinds because the way our language works. On the (reasonable) assumption that there are indeed natural kinds, the function of certain terms is to latch onto the natural kinds that there are. This latching on occurs independently of our discriminatory abilities. In some cases we are in direct contact with a kind. If we inaugurate the use of the word 'water' by saying 'water is this stuff' pointing at what happens to be H_2O, then water is H_2O and not XYZ, even if we cannot tell H_2O and XYZ apart. In other cases we are not in direct contact with the kind. But we may know about the phenomena that a kind explains. In such cases a kind term may be introduced by an explanatory theory. If we say 'neutrinos are the particles whose emission explains the missing mass of beta decay' then 'neutrino' refers to that kind of particle (if there is such a kind) even when we had not worked out any way of detecting neutrinos.

In the last case, either the word 'neutrino' will pick out the natural kind of neutrinos – if the theory is true – or it will pick out nothing at all – if the theory is false. Knowing whether 'neutrino' successfully refers will depend on knowing whether the theory of neutrinos is true or false. Knowledge of the truth of theories is the subject of the next part of this chapter.

THE EPISTEMOLOGY OF SCIENCE

The theories and hypotheses of science can be highly contentious. Yet at the same time we regard much of science as constituting a solid body of knowledge. The key to moving from disagreement to settled opinion is the gathering of evidence, typically in the form of observations and the outcomes of experiments, that will *confirm* one particular hypothesis. The epistemological part of the philosophy of science starts from this relationship between evidence and hypothesis: when does evidence confirm a hypothesis?

Confirmation

Enumerative (or *Humean*) *induction* provides the simplest account of confirmation. Enumerative induction takes hypotheses to be universal generalisations: all light travels in a straight line in a vacuum, all plants contain chlorophyll, and so on. Its account of confirmation says that universal generalisations like these are confirmed by the observation of repeated particular cases that exemplify the relationship in question. If our experiments reveal that on all the many occasions on which we have traced the path of light in a vacuum we have found the path to be a straight line, then the hypothesis that *all* light travels in a straight line in a vacuum is confirmed.

Enumerative induction may be elaborated by adding that the degree or strength of confirmation is greater if the number of individual confirming instances is large and if they have come from a variety of different circumstances. Another elaboration confirms statistical hypotheses. A statistical hypothesis might say that 85 per cent of people with colitis will suffer from anaemia. This is confirmed by the evidence that 85 per cent of the patients we have observed to have colitis also had anaemia. Even with such elaborations, the core of the inductivist account of confirmation is simple: observational evidence confirms those hypotheses that say that what has not been observed will be like what has been observed.

The fact that enumerative induction can be summed up as 'more of the same' shows that it can confirm only hypotheses concerning observable features of things. We can confirm 'all Fs are Gs' only if we can observe particular things to be both F and G. This is an important limitation of enumerative induction. For many hypotheses in science concern unobservable properties. Scientists construct hypotheses concerning the nature of subatomic particles; they regard these as being confirmed by (amongst other things) the observation of the traces revealed in bubble chambers. If there is such confirmation, it cannot be explained by enumerative induction.

Another account of confirmation is able to avoid this problem. Carl Hempel's *hypothetico-deductive* model of confirmation says that an observation confirms a hypothesis if that observation is deducible from the hypotheses (in conjunction with other known facts). Consider Einstein's general theory of relativity, which says that the path of a light ray can be bent by gravitational force (or, more precisely, that mass will bend space-time, which in turns means that a light-ray will take a curved path). Sir Arthur Eddington deduced from Einstein's theory the curved path that light from a star should take when bent by the mass of the Sun. From this Eddington deduced the position at which the star should appear to be in the sky. In 1919 he made the relevant observations during a solar eclipse. These observations were in close agreement with the deductions from the theory. By deducing what was actually observed from Einstein's theory, the latter was confirmed. When presented schematically,

from	hypothesis;	e.g.	the general theory of relativity;
			facts about the position of stars,
	particular known conditions		Earth, and Sun
we deduce	observation		the star is to be observed in such-and-such a place during the eclipse

and thus confirm the hypothesis

we can see the parallel between Hempel's deductive–nomological model of explanation and his hypothetico-deductive model of confirmation (see above).

The hypothetico-deductive model doesn't require us to reject enumerative induction. Instead, it is able to include it because the particular case is deducible from the hypothesised general case. From the hypothesis that all plants contain chlorophyll and the condition that this organism is a plant, we can deduce that this plant contains chlorophyll. If investigation reveals that the plant does contain chlorophyll, then the hypothesis is confirmed. Thus evidence that confirms a general hypothesis, according to enumerative induction, also confirms it according to the hypothetico-deductive model of confirmation. The strength of the latter is that it goes beyond enumerative induction.

Despite its advantages, hypothetico-deductivism suffers from objections, the best known of which is the paradox of confirmation. Hypothetico-deductivism says that any observed fact deducible from a hypothesis confirms that hypothesis. The paradox of confirmation suggests that some such facts do not confirm a hypothesis. Let us imagine that we are investigating the hypothesis that all colitis patients suffer from anaemia. In line with hypothetico-deductivism we are able to confirm this by considering colitis patients, deducing that they should have anaemia and then observing accordingly that they do indeed have anaemia. Imagine that we now turn our attention to another individual (call her Jane). In this case, before testing Jane for colitis we test first her for anaemia and discover that she does not have anaemia. Notice that from our hypothesis 'all colitis patients have anaemia' and the fact 'Jane does not have anaemia' we can deduce 'Jane does not have colitis'. So we now test for colitis and find accordingly that Jane does not have colitis. According to the hypothetico-deductive model, the observation that Jane does not have colitis should confirm the hypothesis that all colitis patients have anaemia, because that observation was deduced from the hypothesis (in conjunction with another previously known fact). But that seems to be a mistake. How can a perfectly healthy person, Jane (who happens to be a nurse not a patient), confirm a hypothesis about people with colitis?

Hempel's own response to the paradox was to say that Jane does indeed confirm the hypothesis, but only to a very small degree. But this is unsatisfactory. For one thing, it reveals a weakness in the model, in that it tells us nothing about the strength of confirmation evidence can give. Why should Jane the healthy nurse be weak evidence while Jim an anaemic colitis sufferer be strong evidence? The model doesn't tell us. A more significant concern is that Jane might indeed be evidence *against* the hypothesis. Imagine that we find that Jane is far from anaemic yet we find that she has strong signs of incipient colitis. So although she does not have colitis, she might easily soon have colitis. That might make us think that if it is possible to be close to having colitis while being far from anaemic, then it might be possible to actually have (mild) colitis without being anaemic. If so, the hypothesis is false.

I noted the structural similarity between Hempel's hypothetico-deductive model of confirmation and his deductive–nomological model of explanation. In effect, Hempel is saying that a piece of evidence confirms a hypothesis precisely when that hypothesis would, if true, explain the evidence. This relationship between confirmation and explanation can be retained even if we are forced to discard Hempel's accounts of what confirmation and explanation actually are. *Abductivism* places this relationship at the centre of its account of confirmation. According to abductivism, a hypothesis is confirmed to the extent that it provides or is part of a good (potential) explanation of the evidence. The best confirmed hypothesis is one which provides the best putative explanation. If investigation reveals several conceivable explanations of the known phenomena but one is not only a good explanation in itself but clearly better than its rivals, then we may be in a position to infer that this hypothesis, the best putative explanation, is in fact the actual explanation and so is true. Abductivism, for obvious reasons, is also known as *Inference to the Best Explanation*. We have already seen abduction at work. The reason that Dalton believed in the existence of unseen atoms was that this hypothesis provided the best explanation of the observed phenomenon of the law of constant proportions. Later evidence, such as the existence of isomerism, also provided confirmation of the atomic hypothesis. Isomers are distinct substances, which have different physical or chemical properties, but which share the same chemical formula and so are compounds with the same proportions of chemical elements. On the atomic hypothesis this is easily explained, since the same set of atoms might combine in different structures to form molecules with different properties. For instance they may form molecules which are mirror images of one another and so will refract light in different directions. Other phenomena, for example Brownian motion (the rapid random motion of dust particles on the surface of a liquid, observable with a microscope), could also be explained by the existence of atoms and molecules. The explanatory power of atomism provides confirmation of its truth.

Abductivism provides us with an answer to the paradox of confirmation. The hypothetico-deductivism told us that the healthy nurse confirms the hypothesis that all colitis patients have anaemia. Abductivism tells us that evidence is relevant to a hypothesis if it bears on the explanatory power of that hypothesis. Since the healthy nurse is irrelevant to the explanatory power of the hypothesis that colitis is causally related anaemia, it provides no confirmation. The hypothetico-deductive model of confirmation is mistaken. Not everything deducible from a hypothesis confirms that hypothesis. This ties in with what we discovered about explanation. According to the deductive-nomological conception of explanation we can explain an event by deducing its occurrence from a law. But we saw that this was wrong, thanks to the example of Mr Jones, whose death was deducible from the law that a pound of arsenic is fatal but not explained by that law (being explained by the bus instead). Correspondingly, Mr Jones' death does not confirm the hypothesis that a pound of arsenic is fatal. Abductivism also gives the right answer to the puzzle of the individual who is on the verge of colitis but who is far from anaemic. Hempel's defence against the paradox of confirmation was to assert that cases such as the healthy nurse do provide confirmation, albeit only slight confirmation. Abductivism shows why this is not weak positive evidence but may be strong negative evidence. Cases where colitis patients have anaemia support the hypothesis that all colitis patients are anaemic, since that evidence supports one or more explanatory hypotheses linking the two conditions (e.g. that colitis causes anaemia). However, the existence of a case of near colitis without signs of anaemia undermine such explanations. For example, if colitis causes anaemia, one would expect patients on the verge of colitis (those who will have colitis soon if not treated immediately) to show signs of anaemia also. So when all evidence is taken into consideration, hypotheses that suggest a strong causal link between colitis and anaemia (strong enough to say *all* colitis patients have anaemia) now seem less powerful explanations.

SCEPTICISM AND SCIENCE

Inductivism and hypothetico-deductivism offer *formal* accounts of confirmation. When considering the deductive validity of an inference what matters is only the logical form of the components of the inference. For example consider the deduction: all colitis patients have anaemia; John is a colitis patient; *therefore* John has anaemia. One can see that the conclusion follows deductively from the premises just by considering the structure of the inference. One does not need to know anything about John, nor about colitis or anaemia. We can replace John by Jane, being a colitis patient by being a consultant surgeon and anaemia by high-blood pressure, and we have an inference that has the same form and is equally valid: all consultant surgeons have high blood pressure; Jane is a consultant surgeon; *therefore* Jane has high blood pressure. Since such inferences are valid in virtue of their form we can represent them all schematically: all Fs are Gs; S is an F; *therefore* S is a G. Whatever we put in place of S, F, and G, the inference will be valid. Inductivism proposes a formal account of confirmation, schematically: all observed Fs are Gs *confirms* all Fs are Gs. This relationship of confirmation is supposed to hold whatever F and G are. More sophisticated versions of inductivism have sought to develop a formal inductive logic to mirror deductive logic. Similarly hypothetico-deductivism proposes a formal account of confirmation: if E is deducible from H and known conditions C then E *confirms* H. Since deduction is formal and no restrictions are put on E, H, and C, this relationship is formal also.

Is this assumption right, that confirmation is a formal relationship? Nelson Goodman has shown that it is not (Goodman 1954). We can invent a new adjective *grue* which is defined as follows:

> X is grue = either X is green and observed before midnight on 31 December 2050
> or X is blue and not observed before midnight on 31 December 2050

So an emerald observed today is grue, while a blue sapphire dug up for the first time in 2051 will also be grue. It follows from this definition that anything seen until today which is green can be counted as grue. So, in particular, all observed emeralds are grue. The rule of enumerative induction says: the fact that all observed Fs are Gs confirms the hypothesis that all Fs are Gs (for any F and G). If we put 'emerald' for 'F' and 'grue' for 'G' we have: the fact that all observed emeralds are grue confirms the hypothesis that all emeralds are grue. We have seen that it is true that all observed emeralds are grue. Now that the hypothesis is confirmed: all emeralds are grue. This covers *all* emeralds, whether observed or not. Which means that an emerald which is first mined and seen in 2051 is grue, according to the definition of 'grue'. It says that when something is grue, if it has not been observed before midnight on 31 December 2050, then it is blue. So this emerald, first seen in 2051, should be blue. What Goodman's example has shown then, is that enumerative induction allows us, using the term 'grue', to infer that emeralds first seen after 2050 will be blue. But it seems clear that the observation of green emeralds does not confirm the hypothesis that emeralds are grue and its corollary that emeralds first seen after 2050 are blue. So it looks as if, depending on which vocabulary we use, we can use any evidence to confirm any hypothesis about the future, however bizarre. Furthermore, when we use our ordinary predicate 'green' inductivism tells us that the same evidence (observed green emeralds) confirms the (more reasonable) hypothesis that all emeralds are green. So inductivism tells us that the same evidence supports both of two inconsistent hypotheses. It is easy enough to show that hypothetico-deductivism suffers from exactly the same problem. The assumption that led to this conclusion was that confirmation is formal, that the quality of an inductive (or hypothetico-deductive) inference would depend only on the structure of the inference and not on the vocabulary used. Goodman's new riddle of induction shows us that there is no formal account of confirmation. (It is worth noting that abduction need not suffer from Goodman's riddle, since one might think that a proper account of explanation – unlike Hempel's covering law model – is not formal or that the qualities of a good explanation cannot be accounted for in formal terms.)

The lack of a formal account of confirmation raises a question for the justification of any inference we make on the basis of what we take to be confirming evidence, and thus for the kinds of inference we habitually make in science. It seems that confirmation is not a matter of *deductive* logic, because one cannot deduce, for example, the existence of atoms from the law of constant proportions. But if confirmation is not formal then an *inductive* logic will not exist and cannot be the basis of confirmation. Either way, there cannot be an a priori account of confirmation: pure reason cannot tell us when evidence confirms a hypothesis. In which case, is it experience that tells us when a hypothesis is confirmed? Could experience be what tells us that certain inductive inferences justify their conclusions, or that an inference to the best explanation is likely to lead to a true belief?

Imagine that you use a certain form of inductive inference on a regular basis, and that hitherto it has yielded conclusions that you have subsequently found to be true. This experience might seem to be a source of justification for your use of such inductive arguments and hence a source of justification for the conclusion of such arguments. However, the form of this justification of the use of induction is itself inductive: this argument has the form 'inductive arguments (of this kind) have been successful until now; therefore inductive arguments (of this kind) are in general (past, present, and future) successful.' If the supposed justification for induction is inductive then that justification is circular and no justification at all. Analogous remarks can be made with respect to any account of confirmation that seeks justification through experience.

The argument that the attempt at justifying induction is doomed to failure, in particular the observation that an appeal to experience will be circular, was first advanced by David Hume (Hume 1739). Hume himself believed that people do actually infer, on the whole, in accordance with naive enumerative induction, regarding this as a product of human nature, which tends to habituate itself to repeated occurrences of events. Subsequent philosophers have held his argument to show that induction cannot lead to a rationally justified belief in a hypothesis, and that by extension evidence cannot ever confirm a hypothesis it does not deductively entail. In particular, we cannot be justified in believing any scientific hypothesis, since no such hypothesis will receive any confirmation.

This might seem inevitably to lead to the conclusion that science as a whole is irrational. But Sir Karl Popper instead denied that induction is the foundation of scientific reasoning. More generally he denied that the relationship between evidence and hypothesis is one of confirmation. Believing both that Hume's problem of induction was insurmountable and that science is rational, Popper sought to develop an account of science free from induction (or any other kind of confirmation) (Popper 1959). Recalling our hypothesis that all colitis patients are anaemic, Popper's rejection of induction means that no matter how many colitis patients we observe all of whom have colitis, this evidence does not confirm our hypothesis. But were we to find a colitis patient who did not have anaemia, we would know immediately that the hypothesis is false. It is a matter of deductive logic that if one colitis patient is not anaemic, then it is false that all colitis patients have anaemia. According to Popper the relevant relationship between evidence and hypothesis is not the confirming of a hypothesis by positive evidence but is the refuting of a hypothesis by negative, falsifying evidence.

Popper's *falsificationism* characterises the process of scientific progress as *conjecture and refutation*. First the scientist constructs a bold hypothesis – a conjecture. Then he or she deduces observable consequences from it. So far this is similar to hypothetico-deductivism. But instead of seeking agreement between the predictions and what is observed, the falsificationist looks for sources of possible *disagreement*. The scientist constructs severe tests of the theory in an attempt to refute it. If the test does provide a refutation – a disagreement between what the conjecture predicts and what is observed – then progress of some sort has been made. We know the conjecture is false. At this point the process of conjecture and refutation recommences with a new conjecture. Even if a hypothesis succeeds in resisting the most stringent tests, given the rejection of confirmation, we never have any reason to think that the evidence shows a hypothesis to be true. A hypothesis of the latter kind is *well-corroborated*. But, says Popper, corroboration should not be confused with confirmation.

Popper's falsificationism has had many critics. At the bottom of their criticism is a rejection of the scepticism that is implicit in Popper's refusal to countenance confirmation. A picture of science without confirmation might appeal, for example, to physicists who regard Newtonian physics as refuted by Einstein after centuries of remarkable corroboration. On the other hand, it seems highly implausible to say that neither Harvey's theory that blood circulates not Crick and Watson's double-helical model of DNA have not had any confirmation from our observations and experiments. These are hypotheses that are not only well-confirmed but sufficiently well-confirmed as to be known to be true. Even in the case of changing physical theory, most physicists would want to claim that we are getting closer to the truth – our theories are showing increasing *verisimilitude*. But without confirmation we cannot claim even to have evidence for improved verisimilitude. This degree of scepticism seems incompatible with depicting science as rational. Furthermore, it undermines Popper's falsificationist alternative. For Popper accepts that observation in science is not a matter of uneducated sensation; rather an observation is itself the outcome of a process that draws upon scientific findings. To decide whether a patient is anaemic or not, we have to carry out certain tests which will themselves presume a certain amount of theory (concerning the constituents of blood and their function). But if no theory ever gets confirmed then because we rely on theory in the generation of statements like 'John has colitis' or 'Jane is not anaemic' those statements lack confirmation also. And if we cannot rely on such statements, we cannot rely on their use in falsifying hypotheses such as 'all colitis sufferers are anaemic'. If we cannot have confirmation we cannot have falsification either.

REALISM AND ANTI-REALISM

What is the aim of science? We have just seen one answer, that science aims at true theories – or at least at theories with increasing verisimilitude. This is the view of the realist. But the anti-realist argues that this cannot or should not be the aim of science. The anti-realist limits the aim of science to generating true observational consequences. A theory can yield accurate predictions even if it is itself false. We assess theories through their observational predictions and consequences. A theory may say something about an unobservable reality (subatomic particles, for instance). But we cannot directly evaluate that part of a theory. So we can directly assess a theory's observable consequences but not its unobservable component. Hence the most we should expect from a well-confirmed theory is that it be accurate in what it says concerning observable phenomena, not that it should be true in respect of unobservable things.

Anti-realist interpretations of theories have had a historically ancient pedigree. When Nicholas Copernicus' revolutionary thesis that the Sun is at the centre of the planetary system, not the Earth as Claudius Ptolemy had held, was published in his *On the Revolutions of the Spheres*, the theologian Osiander wrote a preface to that book explaining that the new theory should not be seen as aiming to state truths about the planets, but rather as seeking to provide an improved basis for computing their positions in the night sky as observed from the Earth. In propounding an anti-realist interpretation of Copernicus's work, Osiander was influenced not only by the conflict between the new theory and religious teaching but also by the conflict with current beliefs in physics. The view that theories do not aim at presenting true pictures of reality but instead are devices for making accurate predictive computations is known as *instrumentalism*.

Earlier I explained that the chemist John Dalton had proposed invisible atoms and unobservable modes of their combination as the best explanation of the experimental law of constant proportions. Many of Dalton's contemporaries and successors rejected the atomic hypothesis as pointless speculation on the grounds that is could never be confirmed. Chemists such as Sir Benjamin Brodie considered that chemical theories should confine themselves to articulating testable laws concerning quantities and operations which could be observed or performed in the laboratory. (Even so, the law of constant proportions ensured that the hypothesis was very helpful to chemists in devising chemical equations. Hence the atomic hypothesis was widely used by chemists who, taking an instrumentalist attitude, did not actually believe it.)

Brodie's thoroughgoing rejection of atomism was influenced by *positivism*. Positivism was a philosophy espoused by the French philosophers Henri de Saint-Simon and Auguste Comte in the early part of the nineteenth century, building on the empiricism of British philosophers such as Hume and Locke. Positivists regarded speculation concerning the unobservable as pointless and unscientific metaphysics. Science should aim only at establishing correlations among observable phenomena. The positivism of Saint-Simon and Comte was taken up by German-speaking philosophers in the latter part of the nineteenth century and early in the twentieth. The Vienna Circle group of philosophers, working in the 1920s, advocated a principle of verification according to which the meaning of a sentence is the way in which it is verified. What a sentence means is shown by the method by which we decide whether it is true. When combined with the positivist view that the only way to decide the truth of any (non-logical) proposition is on the basis of observational experience (e.g. one's sensations), the principle of verification yields the conclusion that the meaning of any sentence is equivalent to some claim about what one may observe or experience. So, in particular, any theoretical claim in science is really just about observations and sensations. Accordingly, a claim about atoms *appears* to say something about unobservable micro-entities, but in truth it is at best only a statement about the sorts of observations one might make in a laboratory.

If apparently theoretical statements are really about observable things, then it ought in principle to be possible to translate the theoretical statements into purely observational ones. This turned out to be impossible to do. So some positivists developed an alternative view according to which theoretical statements are, strictly speaking, not about anything at all. Hence theories cannot properly be said to be true or false. But we can still deduce observational predictions from them. Predictive utility is the measure of a theory, not truth. Either way, the positivists held that there must be a part of scientific language that is purely observational. For example, if theoretical statements are (as on the earlier view) reducible to statements about observations, it must be that there is some language for discussing observations which is itself free from any element of theory. The idea that there is a pure 'observation' language has since been discredited. Ludwig Wittgenstein attacked the idea that there could be a 'private language' of sensation terms defined by their user directly by association with his or her experiences. Various philosophers have argued that all our scientific language is to some extent theoretical (for example, Maxwell 1962). Furthermore there seems no clear dividing line between what is observable and what is not. The term 'gene' was introduced by Wilhelm Johannsen to name the mechanism whereby biological characteristics are passed from generation to generation. Genes were at that time unobservable, theoretical entities. But now with high powered microscopes and the techniques of DNA sequencing, genetic material can be observed and manipulated. The unobservable has become observable.

Recent empiricists, such as Bas van Fraassen, have rejected the positivist idea that theoretical talk is different in kind from observation talk (van Fraassen 1980). And he accepts that there is a spectrum from observable to unobservable. Many theories postulate the existence of highly unobservable entities with unobservable properties, while our evidence is all at the observable end of the spectrum. Van Fraassen's *constructive empiricism* points out that many different theories about unobservables will have the same consequences as regards observables. Our evidence is like seeing the tip of an iceberg; lots of differently shaped icebergs might have similarly shaped tips; hence we cannot know from looking just at the tip of some iceberg what it looks like beneath water. Similarly van Fraassen argues that we cannot know from just our observable evidence which the true theory about unobservables is. The best we can hope for is a theory which is *empirically adequate* – one which generates true predictions about observables. This reminds us of Osiander's preface to Copernicus' planetary theory – stating that his theory was just a vehicle for accurately calculating the visible positions of planets. So van Fraassen agrees with the positivists that the aim of a theory is to yield accurate predictions. But they disagree in their views regarding what theories are about. The positivist thinks that a theory is either strictly speaking about our observations and instruments or is really about nothing at all. Van Fraassen thinks that there could be electrons, neutrinos, and other subatomic particles and that our theories do attempt to describe such things. Only, he argues, we simply have no reason to suppose that they are successful in this respect.

Realists reject positivism and empiricism about theories. Against the positivists, they claim that our theories are genuinely about unobservable entities, and against empiricists such as van Fraassen, realists hold that if there is enough evidence we can know those theories to be true. Realists have been successful in defeating positivism, primarily because the theory–observation distinction could not be maintained in the way the positivists required. This is now accepted by other anti-realists, such as van Fraassen. As regards the debate between realism and van Fraassen's constructive empiricism, a key issue centres on the ability of abductive inference to yield knowledge. Realists will claim that we know that electrons exist, since their existence is the best explanation of many phenomena, such as chemical bonding, cathode rays and static electricity. More generally, many realists will claim that without a realist view of science, the success of science would be a miracle. In other words, the best explanation of the predictive and technological success of science is that science has, by and large, given us true theories.

Unsurprisingly, Van Fraassen rejects inference to the best explanation as an admissible mode of inference, at least when hypotheses concerning the unobservable are concerned. His main criticism is that because there are infinitely many possible competing hypotheses that might fit a given set of observational evidence, we have little chance of even thinking of the one true hypothesis. So even if abduction can select the best hypothesis *among those considered*, the chances are slim that this hypothesis is true. Furthermore, why should we think that the best explanation is more likely to be true? In his novel *Candide*, Voltaire makes fun of the philosopher

Leibniz in the character of Dr Pangloss. Like Leibniz, Pangloss believes, in the face of disaster, that this the actual world is the best of all possible worlds. Similarly we may ask, why should this world be one in which the best explanations tend to be true? Might not the world be one where poor explanations are very often true and good explanation tend to be false? For example, we think that to be a good explanation, a hypothesis should be simple and powerful, should unify diverse phenomena, and should give us an intellectually satisfying insight or understanding of the nature of things. But might not the world be a complicated place, where diverse phenomena are indeed diverse and not unified, where the true nature of things is not intellectually satisfying? If the world were like that, then an inference to the best explanation would lead us to get things wrong. It might be thought that the success of science shows that abductive inferences tend to lead to the truth. That is to say, the best explanation of the success of science is the fact that the world is after all a place where simple, powerful, unifying, and satisfying explanations tend to be true. That looks to be a case of using abduction to justify abduction, in which case we have another instance of Hume's problem.

RELIABILIST EPISTEMOLOGY AND THE PHILOSOPHY OF SCIENCE

To conclude, I shall describe how many philosophers of science now think that we should tackle the most general epistemological problems in the philosophy of science. In this area we should expect the philosophy of science to draw upon advances in general epistemology. There the refutation of scepticism draws upon 'externalist' epistemology – epistemology that says that the world may play a part in enabling us to know things; justified believing does not depend solely on the way we organise our beliefs from an internal perspective. Among philosophers of science a favoured form of externalist epistemology is *reliabilism*. (Externalist epistemology and reliabilism are discussed in more detail in Alan Goldman's chapter in this book on Epistemology.) According to reliabilism a person knows something when they have a true belief brought about by a reliable process: a process that generally delivers true beliefs. What makes this 'externalist' is that what makes a process reliable is whether the world is such a process that brings about true beliefs and not false ones. It does not matter whether or not the person in question knows that the process is reliable. (The process is reliable as a matter of fact in the 'external' world, but may not be *seen* to be reliable from the internal perspective of the thinker's mind.) For example, a perceptual process like seeing can let us have knowledge of our surroundings so long as it is reliable, even if we do not know that it is reliable. The same goes for the sorts of belief-forming process employed in science. Some such processes involve enumerative induction. These can give us knowledge so long as they are reliable. That is, if we live in a world where the laws of nature make nature regular in the relevant respects, then an inductive belief-forming process can be knowledge-yielding. If I hypothesise that all acids will turn my test solution red, and have discovered that a wide variety of acids do indeed turn it red, then my conclusion that the hypothesis is true will be knowledge if nature is indeed uniform in this area. The sceptic claims that we must justify our use of induction in order to be able to use it to get knowledge. This the externalist denies; the latter says that I don't need to have proven first that nature is uniform to get knowledge from induction.

This sort of scientific use of induction is not so very far from the pre-scientific inductive learning from experience that we all employ every day. Our disposition to make inductions of a simple sort is innate, another product of evolution and natural selection. Since creatures, especially humans, have to live in a diversity of environments, not all useful knowledge can be innate. We have to be able to learn. But a disposition to learn that made faulty inductive inferences would be no advantage. So we are born with a disposition to infer inductively, and furthermore this disposition is accompanied by an innate sense of when inductions are likely to be successful, that is we are disposed to make induction in circumstances when nature is relevantly uniform. The lesson of Goodman's new riddle of induction was that we cannot infer inductively with just any old property that comes to mind. The properties in question have to be natural ones. As suggested when discussing natural kinds, another of our innate abilities is the ability to distinguish at least some natural kinds and properties. Our inductive disposition is a disposition to infer with respect to these kinds and properties and not with respect to others.

Our scientific inferential practices go well beyond these basic inductive capacities, which are shared to some degree with many animals. But science nonetheless builds upon these capacities. One respect in which science seems to go well beyond simple induction is in our ability to make sophisticated abductive inferences (inferences to the best explanation). Quite what the nature of inference to the best explanation is, and when we may expect it to deliver knowledge, are questions of current debate. Just as we have an intuitive sense of when inductions are likely to be reliable, it may be that scientists acquire, through long experience, a sense of just when abduction is likely to be reliable. Whatever answers we come up with, externalist epistemology tells us that we do not need to worry about general problems of induction. So long as our abductive dispositions are reliable they can be knowledge yielding. In particular, if they are reliable, then our use of inference to the best explanation to generate beliefs in electrons, neutrinos and other unobservables, in fact generates knowledge of these things. So externalist epistemology applied to abduction allows us to respond to anti-realist scepticism as well.

CONCLUSION

For much of its history the philosophy of science has been dominated by empiricism. With its emphasis on observation as the basis of knowledge and understanding in science it has been a fruitful doctrine in encouraging an experimental and investigative approach to science. Empiricism does however also limit the ambitions of science. We saw that empiricism in the guises of positivism, instrumentalism, and constructive empiricism rejects the view that science can uncover the hidden natures of things. All we can hope to know concerns the observable features of the world. Empiricism even limits our conception of what there is in the world. Positivism denied that we could even talk about genuinely theoretical, unobservable things. Elsewhere we encountered the regularity conception of laws of nature. The empiricist thinks of laws as just regularities in the way things are, while the anti-empiricist wants to think of laws as something deeper – laws are what stand behind regularities and explain why they exist.

It is fair to say that empiricism is no longer the dominant philosophy of science. Most philosophers of science think that there are indeed hidden natures to things and that science has the ability to give us knowledge of them, even if there are debates about quite how it does so. Nonetheless there persist powerful traces of empiricism, such as the conviction that scientific evidence is ultimately observational and that the laws of nature are contingent. It remains a task for philosophy of science to decide whether these are lasting legacies or residues that will ultimately wither.

EXERCISES

1 How does explanation differ from 'prediction after the event'?
2 What is a law of nature? Is it any more than just a regularity found in nature?
3 Are there really *natural* kinds? What (if anything) makes green things form a natural kind but not grue things?
4 When does evidence confirm a hypothesis? What is the relationship between confirmation and explanation?
5 What are the grounds for scepticism concerning knowledge of (a) things we could observe but have not observed yet, and (b) things we cannot observe? Do we have a response to such scepticism?

BIBLIOGRAPHY

Achinstein, Peter (1983) *The Nature of Explanation,* Oxford: Oxford University Press.

Goodman, Nelson (1954) *Fact, Fiction and Forecast*, Atlantic Highlands, NJ: Athlone Press.

Hempel, Carl (1965) *Aspects of Scientific Explanation*, New York: Free Press.

Hempel, Carl (1966) *Philosophy of Natural Science*, Englewood Cliffs, NJ: Prentice-Hall.

Hume, David (1739) *A Treatise of Human Nature,* London.

Kripke, Saul (1980) *Naming and Necessity*, Cambridge, MA: Harvard University Press.

Lewis, David (1973) *Counterfactuals*, Oxford: Blackwell.

Maxwell, Grover (1962) 'The ontological status of theoretical entities', in Herbert Feigl and Grover Maxwell (eds) *Minnesota Studies in the Philosophy of Science, Vol. III*, Minneapolis: University of Minnesota Press.

Mumford, Stephen (1998) *Dispositions*, Oxford: Oxford University Press.

Popper, Sir Karl (1959) *The Logic of Scientific Discovery*, London: Hutchinson.

Putnam, Hilary (1975) 'The meaning of "Meaning" ' in *Philosophical Papers, Vol. II Mind, Language and Reality*, Cambridge: Cambridge University Press.

van Fraassen, Bas (1980) *The Scientific Image*, Oxford: Oxford University Press.

FURTHER READING

Much of this chapter relates to my book *Philosophy of Science* (London: Routledge, 1998). A useful collection of readings that connect well with my book and this chapter is to be found in Martin Curd and Jan Cover *Philosophy of Science* (London: Norton, 1998). Good introductions to the philosophy of science include James Ladyman *Understanding Philosophy of Science* (London: Routledge, 2002), John Losee *A Historical Introduction to the Philosophy of Science* (Oxford: Oxford University Press, 4th edition, 2001), and Carl Hempel *Philosophy of Natural Science* (Englewood Cliffs NJ: Prentice-Hall, 1965). The latter is out-of-date in many respects but is nonetheless a very clear and stimulating introduction to the subject. Hempel's work is still a starting point for most discussions of scientific explanation. David-Hillel Ruben's *Explaining Explanation* shows how matters have progressed, and the collection edited by Ruben Explanation (Oxford: Oxford University Press, 1993) contains key papers by Hempel, Railton, and others. On laws of nature I recommend David Armstrong's *What is a Law of Nature?* (Cambridge: Cambridge University Press, 1983). W.V. Quine's 'Natural Kinds' in his *Ontological Relativity and Other Essays* (New York: Columbia University Press, 1969) is a centrally important paper on that subject. The problems of inductivism are forcefully articulated by Sir Karl Popper in his *Logic of Scientific Discovery* (London: Hutchinson, 1959) along with his falsificationist alternative. For hypothetico-deductivism we may return to Hempel's *Philosophy of Natural Science*. Goodman's new riddle of induction is introduced in his *Fact, Fiction and Forecast* (Atlantic Highlands, NJ: Athlone Press, 1954). The many issues surrounding abductivism/inference to the best explanation are very clearly addressed in Peter Lipton's *Inference to the Best Explanation* (London: Routledge, 1991). On realism and anti-realism you cannot do better than Stathis Psillos' *Scientific Realism* (London: Routledge, 2000). A good collection of important papers in the philosophy of science that deals mainly with the realism debate is David Papineau (ed.) *The Philosophy of Science* (Oxford: Oxford University Press, 1996).

11

POLITICAL PHILOSOPHY

Dudley Knowles

INTRODUCTION

Political philosophy has a unique standing within the domain of philosophy. From an analytical perspective it is a by-way, a branch of ethics which investigates that portion of our lives wherein citizens interact with each other through the medium of the state. It is a normative study, examining values such as freedom and justice, together with the institutional structures which manifest or deny them. From a historical perspective, it has been amongst the central concerns of the great dead philosophers as it has been the central focus for some of the most impressive philosophical work of modern times. Any list of the great books of philosophy would include Plato's *Republic* and Aristotle's *Politics*, Hobbes's *Leviathan*, Locke's *Second Treatise* and Rousseau's *Second Discourse* and *Social Contract*, Hegel's *Philosophy of Right*, a selection of the work of Marx, including the first volume of *Capital*, and Mill's *On Liberty*, as well as, amongst contemporary writings, Rawls's pre-eminent *A Theory of Justice*. This should be puzzling at first sight, but a moment's reflection will dispel the mystery. No-one can escape the clutches of the state. Daily, it demands things of us and these demands are often pressing and onerous, sometimes lethal. They force the most docile of citizens to review the credentials of the state, the extent of its proper powers, the constitutional form of its decision-making powers, and the nature of justice, its distinctive virtue. The only discipline which can promise illumination when these problems press hard is that of philosophy, so it should be no great surprise that the finest philosophers have bent their minds to the task.

The citizen who is commanded to obey the law, to pay her taxes or enlist for military service has often challenged the legitimacy of these requirements and the coercive state apparatus of police, courts and prisons which backs them up. This prompts the *first question* of political philosophy: does the state have a legitimate claim to authority?

As citizens review the state's claim to authority, they may enquire into the propriety of the procedures whereby laws are made – and in modern times they will insist that these procedures be democratic, though there will be much dispute about what counts as genuine democracy. This suggests, as a *second question* that the political philosopher will naturally ask: how should the state be constituted?

When citizens going about their daily business or indulging their pleasures find that some activity is forbidden them, they may question not the legitimacy of the state's claim to authority but rather the proper extent of the state's coercive powers. They will ask how far the liberty or the rights of the citizens constrain the activities of the state. Such thoughts set up the *third question* that political philosophers will investigate: what are the limits of the (democratic) state's business; correlatively, what is the private sphere of the citizen, the sphere of personal liberty?

Most theorists who defend the state will point to its role in establishing a framework of liberty, in demarcating citizens' rights the better to protect them. A central site of conflict between citizens who assert their rights is that of private property. Citizens who challenge any given allocation will find themselves seeking principles of just distribution which the state is charged to enforce, taxing some, transferring wealth to others, in the name of utility, fairness, equality, needs or desert, to list a few of the criteria which have grounded claims of justice. This is the topic of the *fourth question* that political philosophy must address: What principles determine a just allocation of goods and services?

Thus far I have isolated four main questions as the central concerns of political philosophy. It would be a mistake to think that these questions are independent of each other. They are not, as we shall see. It would be an error, too, to believe that these questions exhaust the agenda of the political philosopher. They don't. It is easy to think of political issues which give rise to philosophical questions which don't map straightforwardly onto the problems I have claimed are central. Sometimes this is because our ethical perspective is limited to what we see as present-day concerns; we regard some formerly urgent questions as settled. So, unlike philosophers from Aristotle to Rousseau, we do not discuss the legitimacy of slavery, although our contemporary ethical and political world-view is in good measure a legacy of this controversy. Sometimes our philosophical concerns are parochial in a sociological, almost geographical, sense, although this parochialism has historical antecedents. Thus very few Western philosophers nowadays see a philosophical problem in the relations of Church and State. We are tight-lipped (and often quietly contemptuous) when confronted with the reality of theocratic regimes.

By contrast, other philosophical issues seem so entangled in the exigencies of the present that it is hard to decide how far they are independent of the central concerns of political philosophy as I have represented them or how far they represent a novel approach to the same old questions. Thus in recent years, political philosophers have been much engaged with problems of nationalism, multi-culturalism, ethnicity and race. It is tempting to see this congeries as a new item to add to the old agenda. Nation-states were ever the product of historical contingency, fashioned through wars and alliances, dynastic unions and family squabbles, federation and secession. Cultural unity was always the exception rather than the rule, but this was frequently concealed behind the singular voice of the state which constructed a unitary tradition that enlisted or enforced a common allegiance. In the modern world, we add to the sources of national variety, transportation and immigration and describe the modern state as either a patchwork or a melting-pot. I shall mention these issues briefly at the end of the chapter.[1]

Thus far I have characterised political philosophy in terms of four questions I have deemed central, and, by implication, as the range of answers that have been given to them. Obviously, there are other ways in which the subject may be approached. Since political philosophy is a branch of ethics, concerned with the rights and wrongs of human conduct, by way of interrogation, explanation and instruction, one could cast its subject-matter as the application of a range of normative theories which govern this domain. Thus one might investigate the credentials of, say, natural law, utilitarianism, social contract, Kantian autonomy, Hegelian communitarianism and Marxist science. All of these theoretical approaches have valuable insights to contribute, but I cannot think of an effective way to review them which would not introduce massive redundancy into the consideration of central issues. (What does each have to say about problem x, problem y, problem z?)

A different methodology would summarise the history of the subject, beginning with the political philosophers of Ancient Greece and taking the subject up to the present day, traversing the Roman philosopher, those of the Middle Ages, the great philosophers of the seventeenth century and the Enlightenment, and the giant figures of the nineteenth century. So long as the student is alert to continuities and discontinuities of subject-matter, which is to say, can contextualise and legitimately extrapolate from historical texts as appropriate, all would be fine. In fact, I think this Plato-to-Nato approach is quite the best way to study political philosophy since the preoccupations of the parochial present inhibit the kind of wide-ranging reflectiveness that the best political philosophy exhibits. But it won't do here, since first, I want to motivate your study of the subject; second, the material could not be satisfactorily condensed.

Yet another approach to political philosophy would be to select the chief *values* adduced in political debate and subject these to analysis and evaluation. This has the great virtue of concentrating on the terms we apply when we engage in political debate or, more likely, judge the affairs of the day as these are presented to us in newspapers, radio or TV. We are all connoisseurs in political judgement; none of us would deny ourselves a capacity upon which we can reflect freely. Thus we might consider in turn utility and efficiency, liberty (or freedom), rights, authority and obligation, distributive justice, and democracy. (Perhaps, following the discussion above, one might add nationalism and multi-culturalism, and no doubt there are others.) As it happens, I think this approach is just about captured by a discussion of the questions I have highlighted as central. These *are* the values you will be interrogating as you pursue your studies in political philosophy, and I can think of no better way to motivate your investigation of them than to address the four questions I have singled out.

QUESTION 1: DOES THE STATE HAVE A LEGITIMATE CLAIM TO AUTHORITY?

Or

DO CITIZENS HAVE A MORAL OBLIGATION TO OBEY THE LAW, OR A DUTY OF ALLEGIANCE?

Some say these are different questions. They may well be right. I shall treat them as the same question. Some say these questions are philosophically incoherent, of the same stripe as: is health a good thing? That is, they insist that one who asks the question does not properly understand the concept of the state, or of the law, or of allegiance. They insist that 'the state' means 'she who is to be obeyed', that 'law' means 'the commands of she who has to be obeyed', that 'allegiance' means 'the attitude of those who understand these things'. But they are wrong, since there will always be impertinent individuals (liberals, on one account) who ask how these insistencies are to be defended – in which case some (obviously controversial) story must be told about the meanings on which such claims rely. So the good old philosophical question about the grounds of authority, obedience and allegiance is still open.

Others deny that the state can make any claim to legitimacy. This is the anarchist view – quite the noblest position in political philosophy since it attributes to persons the capacity to behave well without their deliberations being corrupted by the coercive apparatus of the state. Anarchism has the great virtue of appealing to decent people who can recognise themselves in the portrayal of universal human nature as sociable, cooperative, trustworthy, and regularly altruistic. Unfortunately, the best of men and women may not see their fellows in this light. So they may demand a kind of self-protection that they cannot achieve for themselves. They may demand a state, not because *they* may violate other persons' rights, but because *others* may violate theirs. Since it is a credulous fellow who will refuse this demand for their own part, and a dangerous woman who will insist that others are wrong to insist on such protection, the anarchist view has found few friends. But it does not reflect well on the opponents of the anarchist that they have neither the self-confidence nor the trust in others that anarchism requires.

Anarchism is a permanent possibility within political thought, even if it is an unlikely goal of genuinely practical political activity. At its core are generous claims about human nature which are difficult to vindicate but humiliating to refute. And the anarchist has a dialectical strategy which puts his claims beyond the reach of swift rebuttal. If his opponent counters the picture of helpful co-operation which the anarchist paints with a Hobbesian portrayal of humans as menacing and untrustworthy (Hobbes 1985: ch.13), the anarchist can agree that matters do look to be so. But this is the fault of the state, which diminishes our moral stature by teaching us to ask, not which conduct is virtuous, but rather which vices can we indulge with impunity. In conditions of anarchy we would not engage in the self-interested cost–benefit analysis on which the state relies to keep its citizens on the straight and narrow path. We would do what we judge to be right.

Suppose we reject anarchism. What arguments may convince citizens that they have an obligation to obey the sovereign state? One of the strongest derives from Hume, a proto-utilitarian claim asserted directly against the anarchist to the effect that mankind has discovered over time that the state is the most efficient means of securing peace and stability in the face of tendencies towards conflict which cannot be eliminated in the modern world. Justice (by which Hume means the property system administered by the state) 'derives its existence entirely from its necessary *use* to the intercourse and social state of mankind' (Hume 1975: Sect. III, Part I, p. 186). (Of course, the anarchist will reply that the cure is worse than the disease.) Hume's argument needs careful handling, but roughly it amounts to the claim that we should explain and endorse our feelings of allegiance to the state on the grounds of the perceived utility of the contrivance. To be acceptable, this claim needs to be underpinned by some version of utilitarian or mutual advantage theory. And then it must fit the facts.

Hume's theory was developed in response to the most influential accounts of political obligation available in his day – those which derive citizens' obligations from their consent. It is easy to see why consent arguments proved attractive. Philosophically, the strategy is hard to dispute. If you are rational, well-informed and uncoerced, your consent to government implies an obligation to obey. Politically, this source of obligation commends itself because it is grounded in the citizen's own will (as against unattractive alternatives – the might or the natural patriarchal authority or the divine endorsement of the sovereign). But once this plausible thought is teased out it looks harder and harder to defend. If we are speaking of actual consent, when was it given? Suppose, what is probably false, that consent was given in some historical contract – how does that bind the contractors' successors who were not party to it? Who nowadays has given their explicit consent? Perhaps a few naturalised citizens who have signed on the dotted line, but no more than these.

Maybe citizens have consented tacitly, as Locke believed. Tacit consent is real enough, as witnessed by the obligations of those who accept drinks purchased for them in a round. So what are the marks of the tacit consent that citizens are supposed to attest? Locke gives two answers (Locke 1960, §§119–22). First, tacit consent is witnessed in the behaviour of citizens who do not dissent in the obvious way, by selling up their property and departing for pastures new. In his essay 'Of the Original Contract', Hume (1963, p. 462) argued, correctly, that this was a silly way to describe the condition of most citizens (which is not to say that the right to emigrate is not a significant human right). Second, tacit consent is attributed to citizens who receive benefits from the state, notably security in their persons and possessions, but the list of goodies could be extended. Does the simple (and unrequested) receipt of benefits entail an obligation to the benefactor? The quick answer is 'No': no-one can impose obligations merely by conferring benefits. The more subtle answer is 'Perhaps', but we should note that this requires prior acceptance of a convention (as in the case of drinkers in a pub who understand that if rounds are being bought, they should pay their turn) to the effect that reciprocity is appropriate in the circumstances. In the case of the state, and the obligations it seeks to establish, the existence of such a convention is just what is in dispute.

A final answer, which was not available to Locke, witnesses tacit consent in the conduct of those who vote in democratic elections. This claim should be given qualified endorsement, since I take it that those who vote in elections generally signal their willingness to abide by the outcome. This is a convention of democratic participation which voters should understand. But the qualifications are obvious: this argument cannot capture the consent of those who, understanding the convention, either don't vote or spoil their papers. And in the modern world of book-length party manifestos, it is too much to suppose that voters must buy the whole package. And it would be irrational for voters to commit themselves to accepting policies which have not been thus advertised.

There are other arguments for an obligation to obey the state which proceed from the fact of citizens' receipt of benefits. I like the argument from gratitude which some have identified in the voice of the personified Laws of Athens in Plato's *Crito*. When put clearly, this states first, that citizens ought to feel grateful to the state for the benefits provided, and next, that the proper response of those who do feel gratitude is the assumption of the duties of citizenship. Both of these claims are evidently controversial, but one who advances them has not committed an elementary philosophical blunder.

The state is ambitious. It seeks to capture all citizens in the net of obligation. Consent arguments cannot achieve this since there will always be bloody-minded individuals who receive no benefits and do not vote, taking themselves off to the wilds of Montana or wherever, living an isolated and self-sufficient existence. Such a creature, Militia Man, is the bane of theories of political obligation. Since most arguments for the authority of the state advance from a conditional premise: if citizens . . . (do x, believe y, claim z), then they have a duty to . . . (obey the law, pay taxes, join the armed forces), the first clause, the antecedent of the conditional, is always open to repudiation. If this is so, and if Militia Man is not also a utilitarian, the task of refuting the sceptic about political obligation remains open.

QUESTION 2: HOW SHOULD THE STATE BE CONSTITUTED?

Nowadays, one might think, there is only one answer to this question: the legitimate state must have a democratic constitution, settling policy disputes by voting, each adult citizen having equal power in the decision procedure. This is a simple model of democracy which will serve for the purpose of investigating the credentials of democracy. To the degree that actual constitutions (historical or contemporary) depart from this model, we can say that the ideal of pure democracy is compromised. Since this ideal has found critics as well as supporters, and since the political world recognises other ideals which may conflict with that of democracy, for example liberty and human rights, it remains to be seen whether such compromises are to be applauded or criticised. A necessary first step in any investigation is to examine arguments for and against the democratic ideal.

The most elegant argument for democracy has its origins in the work of the utilitarian philosopher, Jeremy Bentham. Assume that voters take a view on which, of alternative policies, is in their best interests and then register their preference in a vote. It follows, if a majority decision wins, that more people will be suited than frustrated. Automatically, algorithmically, the majority decision secures the greatest happiness aggregated across the community of voters. Bentham's utilitarianism fixed the right policy as the policy which maximised happiness, understood as the balance of pleasure over pain, amongst those affected by it. Bentham's philosophical psychology claimed that individual persons are in the best position to know what is in their own best interests, and knowing it, will pursue it. It follows that a democratic system of making policy decisions can guarantee what other systems are unlikely to deliver: the greatest happiness of the greatest number, to cite his formula.

This argument contains many hostages to fortune, not least the assumption that the impact of any one person's vote will outweigh the effort of voting in any tolerably large constituency. But it has the interesting property that challenges to it, say in respect of persons' knowledge of their own interests, may reveal an autocratic and paternalistic temper. It often works, particularly amongst small groups of people with a decision to take. It is a good argument to keep in mind, if not one to apply wholeheartedly.

The most persuasive arguments for democracy are Rousseauian in spirit. In *The Social Contract*, subtitled 'Principles of Political Right', Jean-Jacques Rousseau claimed that democratic decisions express the *general will*. By this he meant that citizens voting in a democracy agree on values of freedom and equality as well as requiring the protection of their persons and property. Think of these values as comprising the common good. When making decisions, a democrat will ask, not what benefits *me* most, but what best promotes the common good, values to which *we*, collectively, subscribe. Persons who value freedom and equality will find these values exemplified in a constitution that grants each citizen an equal right of participation. Citizens who participate actively as voters will take decisions in accordance with the principles that underwrite the democratic constitution. Those values which dictate that a democracy is the only constitution which satisfies the principles of political right will be expressed directly in laws which bespeak the general will. So, if you value equality and freedom, as Rousseau insists you must, you will accept only a democratic sovereign, you will actively promote these values through your participation as a citizen in the making of laws, and you will accept your subjection to these laws along with all other citizens.

This is the core of the doctrine of the general will. It has its origin in the liberal insistence that all persons are free and equal. Its upshot is the spirit of collectivism or communitarianism that seeks to identify the state as a unity of persons expressing a common set of values. Thus it displays a necessary tension within political life between the ethical demands of individuals and the coercive impositions of the state to which they feel allegiance. Rousseau's ideals have found widespread acceptance. Indeed they probably explain why it is commonly believed that democracy is the only game in town. Which is not to say that the issue of the proper constitution is settled, as any careful reader of *The Social Contract* will soon recognise.

First, the detail of the institution of democracy as Rousseau described it will be challenged. Rousseau envisaged a direct democracy, believing it would be irrational for those who value freedom and equality to hand over law-making powers to a delegated body, an assembly or parliament. And this, for many, is impractical since it would be appropriate only in the smallest city-state where all citizens could attend the forum. But perhaps this condition is anachronistic in the modern world. Citizens could vote by modem in frequent referendums. But who would set the agenda and fix the terms of popular debate? Not political parties: Rousseau hated 'factions' quite as much as the arch-anti-democrat Plato hated demagogues. Presumably these tasks would fall to the executive or civil service which Rousseau ironically dubs the 'government'. But then the government is either large, honest and inefficient, or small, efficient and corrupt.

Rousseau thus neatly opens up a political question which is with us still concerning the democratic credentials of representative institutions. The enemies of democracy, amongst whom Plato in the *Republic* is pre-eminent, are confident that democracy is the rule of the ignorant and easily led. Who would take decisions aboard ship by polling the crew? Or for that matter, who would travel on a ship which elects its captain? Defenders of democracy will not be impressed by the nautical analogies, but they may be willing to concede a role for professional politicians who are elected (and thrown out) periodically on the basis of their personal or party credentials and performance. The sure way of aligning the individual interests of the politicians (which make them susceptible to corruption) with the interests of their constituents is to have regular elections – yearly elections in the opinion of James Mill (the father of John Stuart Mill) in his *Essay on Government*.

My own judgement on these matters is that the democrat should grant the necessity of representative institutions, permitting a cadre of professional or semi-professional people to conduct the main business of national and local government in an efficient and stable fashion. On the other hand, the democrat should not concede politicians any moral expertise, and should not expect them to have a more refined conscience than their fellow citizens. (These are not qualities which they have the gall to trumpet when they parade before party selection committees or solicit the vote of the electorate.) So citizens should press that so-called 'free votes', when representatives vote according to their consciences and do not follow party discipline, signal issues that should be decided by popular vote in a referendum. If the instincts of the well educated jib at this proposal, they should examine the sources of their anxiety: are they concerned that decisions should be taken by members of an elite with which they identify, or are they worried that the task of moral and political education has not been effected in their communities? The true democrat believes that all fellow citizens are entitled to whatever resources are necessary in order to give them the opportunity to deliberate carefully about the governance of their communities. At the heart of the recent movement for 'deliberative democracy' is the strong valuation of a culture of well-informed, popular decision-making on the basis of values citizens believe are defensible.

Rousseau would have recognised the cogency of this conclusion – that democracy needs a bottom line of values to which all subscribe. Indeed the major flaws in his practical proposals derive from his insouciance concerning the detail of these values and the rigour with which he believed they should be indoctrinated and policed (to the point of establishing a civil religion to prescribe its major tenets and a regime which imposes the death penalty on recalcitrants). The more tolerant and optimistic modern variant is the conception of 'public reason' elaborated as the currency of political debate in John Rawls's *Political Liberalism*. Articulated by Rawls as a kind of common denominator of value systems (roughly, philosophical and religious conceptions of the good life), this has found few friends.

But no democrat should reject all such prospectuses. Not least because they should recognise the practical urgency of settling the question of how far explicitly non-democratic parties should be able to avail themselves of democratic methods of proselytisation (on the basis of, say, freedom of conscience, freedom of thought and discussion, freedom of association). To be blunt and parochial: should Glasgow City Council lease Partick Burgh Hall to the National Front for political meetings? To be philosophical and woolly: should democrats permit the exploitation of democratic freedoms by those committed to the destruction of these freedoms? I say: No; but this bare assertion highlights the philosophical task of elaborating in full dress the principles which democrats must defend.

The history of the last century (the Weimar Republic, post-Tito Yugoslavia) should alert us to the dangers of democracy. At the beginning of the nineteenth century, Alexis de Tocqueville, writing in *Democracy in America*, diagnosed this specific problem as the 'tyranny of the majority'. In truth, he presaged two problems: the first, the one most conspicuous to him after his brief but well-informed and prescient study of the United States, was a problem of democratic temperament. Taking decisions, alongside others, for ourselves and our neighbours, we shall take too close an interest in our neighbours' business. The culture of equality will be realised in a regime of conformity. As they used to say, 'Mrs Grundy' will rule. This problem of social intrusion and personal intolerance was what exercised John Stuart Mill, one of de Tocqueville's earliest and most influential readers.

But Mill also identified a different problem, which he stressed in the first chapter of his essay *On Liberty*. To put the problem in modern terms, if a democratic regime is riven by antecedent allegiances, if there are majority and minority groups fixed by religious affiliation, racial or ethnic origins, or tribal or caste divisions, these divisions will be reproduced and accentuated as members answer all political questions put in the democratic forum by considering 'What's best for *us*?', or worse 'How can we put *them* in their place?' Democracy can emphasise entrenched social divisions and legitmise tyranny. Worse, it can be the cause of civil war.

I think these are facts attested by current affairs as well as history, facts which cannot be denied. In which case we need to look for constraints on the exercise of democratic power which will avoid the excesses which democratic decisions can spuriously legitimate. This takes us to our third question.

QUESTION 3: HOW FAR SHOULD THE COERCIVE ACTIVITY OF THE STATE BE CONSTRAINED BY THE FREEDOM OR RIGHTS OF THE CITIZEN?

The *locus classicus* which answers this question is John Stuart Mill's essay *On Liberty* (1859/1910). The question is straightforward, given the diagnosis of the problem: What is the proper sphere of the state's interference in the lives of its citizens? What is the state's business? Mill thought, with too much optimism, that 'one very simple principle' would serve to answer these questions:

> That principle is, that the sole end for which mankind are warranted, individually or collectively, in interfering with the liberty of action of any of their number is self-protection. That the only purpose for which power can be legitimately exercised over any member of a civilised community, against his will, is to prevent harm to others.

> (Mill 1910, pp. 72–3)

This is Mill's famous 'Harm Principle'. He offers it as a necessary, if not quite sufficient, condition on legitimate interference, not only by the state, but by society at large; it is a constraint on intrusive neighbours as much as over-busy legislators. It doesn't quite work as a sufficient condition, since legal interference, in particular, is always costly, and the costs of extending police powers may be greater than the benefits achieved by prohibiting the harm.

The virtue of Mill's proposal is that most readers, I surmise, will grant that the harmfulness to other people of a type of conduct is a *prima facie* reason for stopping it. If it turns out that erecting radio masts in cities is a cause of cancer, opponents can bank a very strong reason for banning them. If radio masts are suspected of causing such harm, these suspicions constitute very good reason for investigating the technology to establish whether or not harm is caused. Mill's principle, it should not be forgotten, directs us towards asking sensible questions and conducting appropriate enquiries.

This is not to say that it has not encountered philosophical difficulties. It was early objected by Fitzjames Stephen, in *Liberty, Equality, Fraternity*, that all actions do or may cause harm to others. But this is bluster. Most actions of most people do not in fact harm others. The law will concentrate on those *action-types*, all (or a significant proportion of) *tokens* of which are harmful. I may cause harm by cleaning my teeth in some Chaplinesque scenario, but we shouldn't conclude that teeth-cleaning is harmful. Assault and battery by contrast will always be harmful. It is no weakness of Mill's proposal that there will turn out to be many grey areas wherein the severity or probability (or, indeed, tolerability) of harm is difficult to establish. Mill's question may be exactly the right one to ask, albeit difficult to answer.

More worrying is the vagueness of the concept of harm. Physical harm is no doubt central, but what of mental harm? Can persons be harmed without knowing that they are harmed? Careful readers of Mill have unearthed the likelihood that he envisaged significant damage to persons' security interests as the type of harm to others which may legitimately be prevented, what may otherwise be called violations of their rights. This does not settle the question of what rights persons may be supposed to have (Mill himself, in *Utilitarianism* ch. V, insisted that this will be a judgement of utility), but it links usefully to another way of thinking concerning the limits of government action – the tradition of natural or human rights.

On this account persons possess rights against each other. The most important of these are claim rights: negatively, rights against interference; positively, rights to the provision of goods and services, but we should note that this is a very imperfect classification. Rights claims constrain the state in two conspicuous ways. First, it is the task of the state to protect persons in the exercise of their rights (and indeed the necessity of such protection grounds one important argument for citizens' accepting the authority of the state). Second, states must not themselves violate the rights of their citizens. We have seen that it is perfectly possible for a democratic regime to fail its citizens by taking majority decisions which make rights violations permissible or by themselves violating the rights of a minority of citizens.

This suggests another way of limiting the power of the state – by establishing a bill or charter of rights that permits independent, generally judicial, review of legislative and executive action and in consequence makes an authoritative judgement that rights be protected or that laws which violate them be struck down, however pure their democratic credentials. Such constitutional protection for rights evidently needs to be entrenched in a fashion that leaves them less vulnerable to repeal than ordinary legislation, though nothing can give them immunity against the interpretative powers of the judiciary which upholds them.

It is not easy to judge whether the harm principle and the rights principle amount to different standards. Defenders of the harm principle need to construct a specification of harm, and may well incorporate a theory of rights in that specification, arguing that the harms which citizens need to be protected against are violations of rights. Defenders of a rights principle will employ a specification of rights (there is no shortage of lists and declarations to choose from) which itself needs justification – and a natural way to think of many rights violations is as conspicuous harms.

Mill's proposal, as I have argued, seems to pose the right question to legislators who envisage prohibitions: what harm does it do? But it is not easy to see how it could be given constitutional entrenchment against majority decisions. It will have to serve as a moral principle which democratic regimes are persuaded to accept. Charters of rights, by contrast, have operated as effective constitutional devices serving to protect citizens from the state and each other. The major weakness of this device is the lack of any clearly defined decision process for scrutinising candidate rights. At the moment we suffer from rights inflation, with new rights being claimed each week. (A recent example: adults conceived in a process of artificial insemination by donor, AID, have the human right to know the identity of the sperm donor.) Practically, if not philosophically, it seems that we must rely on a cadre of imperfect adjudicators, i.e. the judiciary, to determine whether newly discovered rights are worthy of respect.

At this point it is worth mentioning briefly the difficulty of the project of giving a satisfactory philosophical grounding for rights claims. The simplest derivation of rights was offered by Locke. Since we find ourselves on earth as trustees of the purposes God laid down for us, we need the wherewithal to execute these purposes. Hence we may claim, on grounds of natural law, rights to life, health, liberty and possessions, as well as the supplementary right to punish those who violate these rights (Locke 1960, §§6–7). The argument is spare but cogent, but the theistic premises are too controversial to provide satisfactory grounding. Many philosophers have sought a secular equivalent, substituting for God's purposes a requirement of the possibility of effective autonomous rational agency. This proposal is Kantian in spirit; in modern times it has been worked out in most detail by Alan Gewirth (1978, 1982, 1996), but the supposedly *logical* derivation of rights which he provides has found little favour. Mill's utilitarian strategy is even less favoured than the Kantian one; many argue that a distinctive feature of rights claims is that they outweigh, even 'trump', calculations of utility.[2] (This has the unfortunate consequence of placing out of court considerations of public interest in adjudicating putative rights of the sort claimed by the AID beneficiary mentioned above.) Given the ubiquity and importance of claims to rights in the modern world, if any problem has the distinction of being the most urgent in modern political philosophy it is that of explaining systematically the grounds of such claims.

Suppose, though, that we have in place a principle which reins in the state to the exercise of its proper function, that of the prevention of harm or the protection of rights. Are there any other grounds that may be advanced to justify state interference? Mill evidently thought not; the harm principle, we recall, is the 'sole end', the 'only purpose' of legitimate interference. But other candidate principles have been advanced.[3]

To discuss these alternative or supplementary principles, we must assume that some of the conduct which their application renders susceptible to prohibition is not harmful nor does it violate rights. Otherwise the harm or rights principles will serve. The first candidate is often dubbed 'legal moralism'. It states that the immorality or moral wrongness of conduct is generally good grounds for stopping it through legislation or other coercive social instruments. The second candidate is 'offence'; it is claimed to be sufficient ground for interference that conduct is widely offensive. I invite the reader to pursue these for herself. It is challenging to find examples of kinds of action which are agreed to be harmless, which yet are immoral or offensive and which, on these latter grounds alone, may properly be prohibited. In your deliberations, bear in mind the state's willingness to legislate against any kind of conduct if it believes a sufficient majority of the public would support such restrictions on liberty, and note, too, that charges of immorality and offensivness are uttered in a loud public voice. So expect to find cases regularly reported in the newspapers. (A tip for researchers: local government is even keener to introduce prohibitive rules than parliaments. Councillors elected on the basis of national policy often find themselves the guardians of public morals and the last defence of the easily offended – and they relish the roles.)

Paternalism – the prevention of harm to self, as against harm to others – poses clear philosophical problems, since paternalistic policies non-controversially aim at the promotion of persons' well-being. With children we are all paternalists; we force the child to take the nasty-tasting medicine though he would rather not, being ignorant of the good it will do him or judging falsely that avoiding the bad taste is a greater good than getting better. State paternalism which coerces grown-ups is a different kettle of fish. Mill detested it since he judged that it denied the fundamental tenet of his liberalism, that rational adults are best able through trial and error to fashion a suitable life for themselves, that the denial of their autonomous capacity to think through what is the best thing for them to do turns them into moral dwarfs, incapable of independent thought and action.

The state, however, is desperate to do good, to create better people. It forces us to be prudent by penalising those who do not wear seat-belts in cars. It forces us to be cautious by banning the consumption of beef on the bone. It forces us to be healthy by enacting drug control policies. Let us concede what, in particular cases like drugs legislation we probably should not concede, that such policies do good. They save lives. Is this sufficient justification for paternalistic legislation? We should beware an easy acceptance of this claim. Few of us would think it the state's business to ban high-altitude mountaineering on grounds of its extreme danger – a one-in-nine chance of death. Mill would insist: why not just tell people, who may otherwise be ignorant, of the danger they court, much as smokers are bombarded with health warnings? Paternalistic state policies should stick in the craw of the intelligent, rational adults who are reluctant to make sweeping judgements about the incompetence of their fellows. But it is a good philosophical exercise to work one's way through the arguments for and against this practice since they reveal our deepest assumptions about the value of individual liberty. It is no bad thing to ask the paternalist what assumptions are being made about the populace for whom they are legislating, and whom they are treating like children.

The major weakness of Mill's harm principle concerns interventions which are necessary for the effective pursuit of public policy, for the efficient promotion of public goods. We generally distinguish a tax from a prohibition, but taxes are demanded with provision for punishment in case of evasion. Taxes on earnings and spending constrain our freedom to dispose of our income as we see fit, whatever the use to which the taxes are put. So a diminution of freedom is the price we pay for defence and personal security, for public parks and lighthouses, for educating children, treating the sick, feeding and housing the poor. It is unnecessary mental gymnastics to equate the provision of a good with the prevention of harm, and if we believe that all or some of these goods should be provided by the state on the basis of universal taxation, the harm principle should be supplemented to permit coercive tax collection.

This opens up a different set of questions: what is the role of the state in the provision of public goods? *Libertarians* accept only a minimal state, restricted to the functions of the night-watchmen, maintaining security by policing the streets, guarding the city gates, and keeping the prisons, in other words: law and order and defence. This is an extreme position, eloquently defended in modern times in Robert Nozick's *Anarchy, State and Utopia*. Most citizens (and political philosophers) grant the state a wider role through the provision of services and the re-distribution of goods. This leads on nicely to our final question.

QUESTION 4: WHAT PRINCIPLES DETERMINE A JUST ALLOCATION OF GOODS AND SERVICES?

'There is more than one kind of justice', as Aristotle saw (Aristotle 1925, Bk V, 1130b). Plato, in the *Republic*, distinguished justice as a quality of persons and justice as a quality of states. (This latter has an echo in modern times in the work of John Rawls, whose theory of justice, though markedly different from Plato's, is similarly an account of what it is for a state to be well-ordered.) There is the justice which is the proper response to wrong-doing, as achieved by punishment or compensation, variously described and classified as retributive, corrective, or commutative justice. And there is justice in distribution, which offers an account of how benefits (income and wealth, plus the direct provision of services, such as healthcare and education), and burdens (chiefly taxation) should be allocated and charged for amongst the community. There are other conceptions of justice, too: some wider in scope than any of these (to each his due), some narrower (equity, as respected in courts of law). In what follows we shall be considering justice in distribution, but this is the place to give readers *a philosophical health warning*: whenever you come across the terms 'justice' or 'injustice', 'just' or 'unjust', try to establish what meaning they are being given and what context is framing their use. (And perhaps this is also the place where the same caution should be extended to the use of terms designating other grand political values such as liberty and equality.)

If justice in distribution concerns the proper allocation of goods and services an appropriate place to start our inquiry is with your use of this book. How can you defend it? To simplify massively, you will have bought it, borrowed it, have been given or bequeathed it. Traditionally the rules of property concern first acquisition and contract, with riders concerning the rectification of injustice. Thus Hegel's discussion of 'Abstract Right', which takes private property as the paradigm personal right, has sub-sections discussing successively 'Property', 'Contract' and 'Wrong' (Hegel 1991, §§34–104). Exactly the same structure is reproduced in Robert Nozick's 'Entitlement' theory of justice in *Anarchy, State, and Utopia* (Nozick 1974, pp. 150–3). A holding is just if it can be vindicated by principles of just (first) acquisition, principles of just transfer or by an iteration of such principles.

I don't see how this can be denied. How else might you defend your claim to the proper use of this book? So the important questions concern the principles governing just acquisition and just transfer. Original acquisition is a real problem. What was the original state of things prior to the institution of private property? Two answers are possible: either goods were owned by nobody – things were ownerless – or things were owned, inclusively, by everybody – everyone had the right to use the goods of the earth. Either way, it has proved notoriously difficult to ground rules which establish first ownership, since any such rules must deny to individuals, who hitherto could claim legitimate access to the land or its crop, access that they legitimately enjoyed. The simple thought is this: no matter what *you* do by way of skill or effort or ingenuity, how can you dump on *me* a duty not to use what was previously available?

John Locke sees this problem and heroically struggles to solve it (Locke 1960, ch. V). The thrust of his argument, though the detail is massively disputed by commentators, is that one who owns his labour and mixes it with the land, thereby improving it, deserves the premium of exclusive use. This complex argument has not found much support. The notion of mixing one's labour is mysterious, but so is the idea of desert (or at least the idea that one person's desert can impose a duty on someone else). In the background of Locke's theory is the idea that private property is a useful, indeed necessary, institution – otherwise 'Man had starved'.[4] This idea should not be derided, though it is hard to derive from it principles which determine who exactly has a claim on what. You might think, if you live in the West, that disputes concerning first ownership don't matter. Everything is owned by somebody although the origins of private claims are crimes or con-tricks hidden in the mist of times. But we can safely forget about all this ancient history. We should think about what has happened since.

There are two objections to this: the first, which arises periodically in Australia or the USA, and doubtless elsewhere, concerns genuinely aboriginal rights, rights which were ceded by conquerors, documented in contracts or by treaty but, following early violation, have been ignored ever since. What to do about these? There will be a fudge, but at least one element of the fudge will be a (very rudimentary) respect for original rights, amounting at least to a day in court. More important, if not more difficult, is the problem of what to do with state or otherwise communal assets in societies where it is correctly judged that only the transformation into a private property regime will prevent starvation. Lately in Russia and elsewhere, this process has seen the triumph of the spiv and the gangster, characters well represented in the formerly higher echelons of the Party. But how can the transformation take place in largely rural China? How can the forests of Brazil or India be sustainably exploited to the advantage of indigenous inhabitants? How can the state both protect the assets from destructive local use and keep out the multi-national timber companies? These questions cannot be answered unless we develop a neo-Humean utilitarian theory. Some form of private or exclusive community property is necessary, otherwise man will continue to starve, despite the riches of the natural resources and the profits others extract from their use. I cannot see any a priori theory based on autonomy or rights that will serve.

At this point we should listen to a sceptical voice which insists that a prescriptive philosophical theory of social justice is a mirage. The best we can do is to endorse the system of property rights we find in place. This argumentative strategy has two variants. Hume tells us that justice is an artificial virtue, which is to say that our natural sentiments have nothing to say on the matter. All depends on the efficiency in point of utility of human conventions and contrivances. We should expect that the property regime that is operative at the time of writing is the best humans to date can manage. No formulaic rule of justice, such as equality or the distribution of goods in accordance with virtue, will produce anything but chaos. This elegant conservatism doesn't work for most human beings, who curse the fact that their societies have not achieved the level of well-being so visible in OECD nations.

The second species of denial of principles of social justice derives from the work of F.A. Hayek (Hayek 1960, 1982, vol. 2). Whereas Hume was prepared to accept a status quo which could be supposed to represent mankind's best efforts, Hayek insists that he is no conservative. He identifies a free market system as the most efficient way of organising economic life. Further, as against totalitarian alternatives, it respects mankind's aspirations to freedom. It is a moot point how far Hayek's ideas contributed to the spirit of unregulated capitalism and the hostility to public ownership which infused the policies of the Thatcher administrations (and which undermined a valuable ethos of public service). But there can be no doubt that Hayek's insistence that the value of social justice is a mirage is hard to square with policies that are intended to improve the welfare (health, education, a settled home, employment opportunities, comfort in old age) of the worst-off in otherwise wealthy societies. Maybe this would not matter if the richest societies did not harbour conspicuous pockets of desperate poverty, of deprivation which ensures that a significant proportion of children are born to fail. But since these facts cannot be denied, social justice remains an ideal which is worth articulating.

If it is the fact of dire need which is the most powerful motivation for the construction of a theory of justice which presents an alternative to the status quo, then it looks as though a standard relating to the provision for needs is the most obvious requirement of justice. This is my belief, but I cannot claim that it has found much favour.[5] Major difficulties have been encountered by those who have tried to explain justice as responsiveness to needs. It is quite straightforward analytically to distinguish needs from wants generally, but it is hard to draft a specification of basic needs which is sufficiently precise and uncontentious to fund a theory of justice. Are needs objective, in the sense of being identifiable regardless of the beliefs of those who suffer them, or are they subjective, identifiable only through the felt responses of those who are deprived? Are needs universal, attributable to all members of all societies at all times, or are they relative to a range of modes of social circumstance. Do kids in the prosperous West need the latest trainers if they are not to be psychologically damaged through loss of street-cred? Do their parents need televisions so that they can discuss soap operas with their peers (or the programmes of political parties with their fellow electors)? What exactly or approximately is the level of infant mortality or average life expectancy within a society which is recognisable as a denial of the most basic need?

For some, these are problems no sooner stated than the standard of need is abandoned as a principle of justice. By contrast, I think these questions should frame the agenda of political philosophers who are concerned about justice; this for one simple reason: whilst the problem of justice within a nation state is plausibly addressed by a range of competing theories (so that one might believe the debate to be endless and irredeemably contaminated by entrenched political views), I believe that the articulation of standards of needs is the only way of thinking about international justice, justice between nations. Famine, appalling infant mortality, low levels of literacy: these (and plenty of other Third World) evils import an urgency which demands justice as much as charity. Which is to say that justice must address the conditions of basic need. But we should move on.

Another historically important criterion of justice is desert. Any distribution is just if folks are allocated the benefits and burdens they deserve. Desert seems to be a rock-bottom moral principle which is resistant to further analysis – and certainly the grounds of desert are mysterious. Many would accept that the person who works harder deserves more pay, but the prettiest baby deserves the Bonny Baby prize at the village fête. Whether the grounds of desert are effort or beauty, intelligence or willingness to do dirty work, many have worried about how comparative judgements in different domains can yield cardinal measures of reward, and many more have worried that the natural lottery, the graces of nature and favourable nurture, may be the ultimate source of the differences that ground differential desert. I suspect that judgements of desert are ineliminable, but they yield a very controversial theory of distributive justice.

For some, justice is a matter of equality. Formally this may be true, since as Amartya Sen pointed out, many theories of justice propose equality of something: so that, as he claimed, the problem of justice is often one of 'Equality of What?' (Sen 1992, pp. 12–17). Sen may be right, but his thesis concerns the *form* rather than the *content* of the theories it embraces (and I cannot see that Humean conservatism, as against classical utilitarianism, can be yoked within its reach). And so each candidate specification of equality (equal concern, equal respect for rights, equal utility, equal primary social goods, basic capability equality, to name leading contenders) has to be defended on its merits.

We can (massively over-)simplify our discussion by supposing that the goods to be distributed are wealth and income, and so the proposal is that a just distribution is one that allocates equal wealth and income to all. Departures from equality are unjust. I shall give one historically important argument for this claim and register two objections. The argument for equality is better seen as an argument against significant inequality and derives from Rousseau. Inequalities of wealth and income are criticised first because of their psychological effects, second because of their social consequences. Psychologically, a condition of inequality demeans the independent standing of all parties: 'If rich, they stood in need of the services of others; if poor, of their assistance' (Rousseau 1973, p. 86). Rousseau's insight has been expanded and articulated in a variety of ways and contexts, most notably by Hegel in his celebrated 'Master–Slave Dialectic' (Hegel 1977, §§189–96), itself appropriated by critics of capitalism, proponents of feminism, opponents of colonialism – indeed anyone hostile to specific modes of institutional domination and servitude. This line of criticism of inequality has very great power, as its empirical foundations reveal. The rich are corrupted by their power to command; the poor are blighted by the necessity of service. Workers under the exploitative regime of capitalism are alienated from their labour power as well as from its products. Even capitalist owners are alienated, alongside their workers, from their 'species being', their distinctively creative human nature. And everyone is alienated from everyone else as community is dissolved by the disciplines of capitalistic competition (Marx 1977, pp. 77–87). But is this true of all inequalities of wealth and income? Or, as careful readers will ask, what degree of inequality is 'significant' as specified above?

344

The answer must be: that degree of inequality which is psychologically debilitating in the terms described. But note Rousseau's powerful implication. Inequalities of wealth are swiftly transformed into inequalities of social status, as class differentials are distilled out of the economic system. Class differentials, in turn, are transformed into inequalities of political power. *In extremis*, even democracies are corrupted as individuals manipulate the mass media by the purchase of newspapers, radio and television. A democracy which tolerates politically potent inequalities of wealth is a democracy in name only. In substance, it amounts to rule by the rich and (therefore) powerful.

This amounts to a prescription for rough or approximate equality, a proscription of such inequalities as in practice reduce citizens to bullies or ciphers. The vagueness in the principle is no weakness, since an insistence on precise equality has unfortunate consequences.

Suppose we were to make such a demand, requiring an exact equality of wealth and income. And suppose Wilt Chamberlin (a famous basketball player) comes to town, asking fans to pay 25 cents extra on the normal gate money to fund his appearance. Plenty of folks willingly do so, hence lucky Wilt is a rich man at the end of the season. The just state, if justice equals equality, will insist that the consequent inequality be remedied, that Wilt's post-equality increment be taxed, i.e. confiscated to the treasury. But why so? The folks who paid their allocated equal income to see Wilt could have spent the money 'on going to the movies, or on candy bars, or on copies of *Dissent* magazine, or of *Monthly Review*' (Nozick 1974, pp. 160–4). Nozick's conclusion is that liberty upsets patterns. Whatever *pattern* of holdings is specified as just – equality is a clear example – it can only be maintained by continuous interference with citizens' freedom to dispose of their earnings. Any reader with left-wing leanings should regard this argument as a severe test.

A second challenge to strict equality is made by asking whether it is a good thing that equality be achieved by levelling down, by e.g. confiscating all wealth and income above the level of the poorest. Egalitarianism has a kindly face when it issues proposals for levelling up. But if equality itself is a value, regardless of the value of the goods distributed to each, it should not matter whether this is achieved by levelling up or down.

That distributive justice is a matter of levelling up, as far as is practicable, is an implication of John Rawls's famous Difference Principle which states that 'social and economic inequalities are to be arranged so that they are . . . to the greatest benefit of the least advantaged' (Rawls 1972, p. 302). It is not possible in this compass to give even a flavour of Rawls's work, which is surely the most significant contribution to political philosophy of the twentieth century. Rawls basic achievement is to have elaborated a fresh way of thinking about the problem of justice. To dub it a 'social contract theory' is to understate its novelty and overemphasise its affinity with the traditional social contract thinkers. Rawls claims that the search for principles of social justice (which embrace all principles determinative of the well-ordering of states, not simply principles of just distribution) must respect a condition of fairness if they are to command agreement: 'justice as fairness' is the term that encapsulates Rawls's theory. Fairness is a matter of impartiality in our deliberations about justice and concomitantly of equality, of granting all citizens equal standing. And this is achieved by placing ourselves in a hypothetical (i.e. artificially constructed) position, the Original Position, behind a Veil of Ignorance which disbars us from using any information which may lead us to favour our own case as we specify the principles. From this stance, we would seek to maximise the well-being of the worst-off group, since we may find ourselves to be a member of it.

Rawls's theory has proved massively controversial. I invite you to pursue the controversies further. But before I close this chapter, I want to spring a surprise, to introduce a question which I didn't advertise in the agenda. Thus far, all of the questions posed have been addressed to an imagined reader whose philosophical temperament enables her to tackle each question on its merits: which is to say, to philosophically dissociate herself from the actual practices of her political community (which may demand allegiance willy-nilly, which may recognise a non-democratic sovereign which accepts no principled restrictions on its authority and determines its own conception of justice) while she investigates principles which may lead to a critical judgement of that society.

It is an obvious truth that all persons nowadays find themselves to be citizens of a state which demands their allegiance and commands them in the forms and details of proper obedience. The questions that I have posed as the agenda of the political philosopher require that citizens detach themselves in thought from the prescriptions of allegiance and examine these, as it were, *externally*, as a foreigner or a Martian might be placed when they inspect the credentials of an actual state. But, it has been insisted, this stance is impossible. We find ourselves to be the creatures of the communities we inhabit, endorsing its values (and its regime).

It follows, in the modern world, that we find ourselves to be citizens of a nation-state with traditional values inscribed in law and positive morality. Or else we find ourselves members of some cultural (ethnic, racial, or religious) sub-group which challenges the demands of moral identity which the nation state articulates. Either way, we find that our identity is determined by political or social allegiances from which we cannot detach ourselves. We find that we *cannot* (as true citizens) or that we *must* (as faithful members or true believers) question the authority of the state. But we cannot do this as bare *individuals*, for there are none such. We are all of us entrammelled, embroiled, enlisted, engulfed, encumbered, or as philosophers say, constituted by our occurrent allegiances (Sandel 1984).

So we are all, as citizens of the United Kingdom or the United States, nationalists; or we are Pakistani-British, or Episcopal Scots, or Black Americans, or Franco-Algerians or whatever. In the modern world, the permutations are uncountable.

The range of configurations of individual identity, as attested by persons who find themselves to be members of groups, sects, races, religions and nation-states is both obvious and impressive – as are the conflicts (personal as well as interpersonal) to which these affiliations give rise. The liberal does not believe that such affiliations are, of themselves, irrational, but he does believe that the demands which affiliation requires are open to question, that natives or recruits be able to demonstrate themselves unwilling. The opponents of liberalism in this domain must say that such external inspection is epistemologically impossible or morally impertinent. For them, questions such as: is nationalism a good thing? is religious observance optional? is tribal loyalty escapable?, cannot be investigated by true believers, because they suppose a detachment, hypothesise a standpoint of enquiry, that is unattainable.

I close this chapter by asking readers whether they think this is true. I will give you some clues to begin your enquiry: is this argument appealing simply to the facts of the matter concerning psychological limitations or inhibitions on philosophical enquiry? If so, if this is at bottom an empirical claim, is it true or false? Or is there a deeper argument motivating this criticism of liberalism? One thing is certain: your first-shot answer is not likely to settle this question of political philosophy, just as it is unlikely to satisfy others. If you are a real philosopher, that is.

EXERCISES

I have organised this essay around a number of questions. The questions that follow are intended to induce philosophical reflection on issues of more immediate practical import, but they are questions that cannot be answered without reflection on the philosophical problems in the background. And inevitably, reflection on them will prompt further questions for you to investigate.

1   Is it always morally wrong to disobey the law?
2   Do those who vote in referendums or elections commit themselves to accept the majority decision?
3   Is it legitimate for a government to use the criminal law to prevent citizens harming themselves?
4   Are those who ask fellow citizens to contribute towards the satisfaction of their basic needs seeking charity or demanding their rights?
5   Is nationalism a virtue or a vice?

NOTES

1   Two recent books which tackle these issues concerning social affiliation are Kymlicka 1995 and Miller 1995.
2   The slogan 'Rights are trumps' is owed to R. Dworkin 1978. A first class anthology of modern articles on the foundations of rights is found in Waldron 1984. A defence of the utilitarian account of rights is provided by Sumner 1987.
3   The most thorough treatment of these questions in modern times is found in the work of Joel Feinberg: initially and briefly in Feinberg 1973, then in the four volumes of *The Moral Limits of the Criminal Law*: 1984, 1985, 1986, 1988.
4   I am extending the scope of the argument Locke (1960) uses against consent as a ground of private property at ch. V, §28. My view is that (local) consent is the *only* acceptable ground of privatisation of the commons.
5   I recommend, for those who wish to take the topic further, R. Plant 1991, ch. 5, for an excellent textbook treatment; D. Wiggins 1987, pp. 1–57 for a seminal, if difficult, essay; and D. Braybrooke 1987 for a heroic attempt to confront all the objections.

BIBLIOGRAPHY

Aristotle (1925) *Nichomachean Ethics*, trans. W.D. Ross, Oxford: Oxford University Press.
Aristotle (1946) *Politics*, trans. E. Barker, Oxford: Clarendon Press.
Braybrooke, D. (1987) *Meeting Needs*, Princeton, NJ: Princeton University Press.
Dworkin, R. (1978) *Taking Rights Seriously*, London: Duckworth.
Feinberg, J. (1973) *Social Philosophy*, Englewood Cliffs, NJ: Prentice Hall.
Feinberg, J. (1984, 1985, 1986, 1988) *The Moral Limits of the Criminal Law* (4 vols) *Harm to Others*, *Offense to Others*, *Harm to Self*, and *Harmless Wrongdoing*, New York: Oxford University Press.
Gewirth, A. (1978) *Reason and Morality*, Chicago: University of Chicago Press.
Gewirth, A. (1982) *Human Rights: Essays on Justification and Applications*, Chicago: University of Chicago Press.
Gewirth, A. (1996) *The Community of Rights*, Chicago: University of Chicago Press.
Hayek, F.A. (1960) *The Constitution of Liberty*, London: Routledge & Kegan Paul.
Hayek, F.A. (1982) *Law, Legislation and Liberty*, London: Routledge & Kegan Paul (published in 3 vols, 1973, 1976, and 1979).
Hegel, G.W.F. (1977) *The Phenomenology of Spirit*, trans. A.V. Miller, Oxford: Clarendon Press [first pub. 1807].
Hegel, G.W.F. (1991) *Elements of the Philosophy of Right*, ed. A.W. Wood, trans. H.B. Nisbet, Cambridge: Cambridge University Press [first pub. 1821].
Hobbes, T. (1985) *Leviathan*, ed. C.B. Macpherson, Harmondsworth: Penguin (first pub. 1651].
Hume, D. (1963) *Essays*, Oxford: Oxford University Press [first pub. 1741/2].
Hume, D. (1975), *An Enquiry Concerning the Principles of Morals* [1751] in D. Hume, *Enquiries*, ed. L.A. Selby-Bigge, Oxford: Clarendon Press.
Kymlicka, W. (1995) *Multicultural Citizenship*, Oxford: Clarendon Press.
Locke, J. (1960) *Second Treatise of Government*, in Locke, *Two Treatises of Government*, ed. P. Laslett, Cambridge: Cambridge University Press [first pub. 1690].

Marx, K. (1977) *Economic and Philosophical Manuscripts* in K. Marx, *Selected Works*, ed. D. McLellan, Oxford: Oxford University Press.

Marx, K. (1979) *Capital*, (3 vols) trans. D. Fernbach, Harmondsworth: Penguin [vol. I, first pub. 1867].

Mill, James (1992) *Essay on Government*, in J. Mill, *The Political Writings*, ed. T. Ball, Cambridge: Cambridge University Press [first pub. 1819].

Mill, J.S. (1910) *On Liberty*, in J.S. Mill, *Utilitarianism, Liberty, Representative Government*, London: Dent, Everyman's Library [first pub. 1859].

Miller, D. (1995) *Nationalism*, Oxford: Clarendon Press.

Nozick, R. (1974) *Anarchy, State, and Utopia*, Oxford: Blackwell.

Plant, R. (1991) *Modern Political Thought*, Oxford: Blackwell.

Plato (1955) *The Republic*, trans. H.P.D. Lee, Harmondsworth: Penguin.

Rawls, J. (1972) *A Theory of Justice*, Oxford: Clarendon Press.

Rawls, J. (1993) *Political Liberalism*, New York: Columbia University Press.

Raz, J. (1986) *The Morality of Freedom*, Oxford: Clarendon Press.

Rousseau, J.-J. (1973) *A Discourse on the Origin of Inequality* [1755] and *The Social Contract* [1762] in *The Social Contract and Discourses*, trans., ed. and revised by G.D.H. Cole, J.H. Brumfitt and J.C. Hall, London: Dent, Everyman's Library.

Sandel, M. (1984) 'The procedural republic and the unencumbered self', *Political Theory* **12**: 81–96; repr. in Goodin, R.E. and Pettit, P. (eds) *Contemporary Political Philosophy: An Anthology* (1997) Oxford: Blackwell.

Sen, A. (1992) *Equality Reconsidered*, Oxford: Clarendon Press.

Stephen, J.F. (1967) *Liberty, Equality, Fraternity*, ed. R.J. White, Cambridge: Cambridge University Press [first pub. 1863].

Sumner, L.W. (1987) *The Moral Foundations of Rights*, Oxford: Clarendon Press.

Tocqueville, A. de (1969) *Democracy in America*, trans. G. Lawrence, ed. J.P. Mayer, New York: Doubleday [first trans. 1835]

Waldron, J. (1984) *Theories of Rights*, Oxford: Oxford University Press.

Wiggins, D. (1987) 'Claims of Need' in *Needs, Values, Truth*, Oxford: Blackwell, pp.1–57.

FURTHER READING

Most of the great books of political philosophy have been referred to in this essay. You will generally find that they are published in several editions. The great reward of studying the primary sources is that they prompt your critical responses at every turn. The richness of their ideas will outstrip the most thorough commentaries on them. But everyone needs short-cuts, if only for swift reference. Useful summaries of authors' views as well as brief expositions of the central topics and concepts of political philosophy will be found in a range of dictionaries and encyclopaedias of philosophy. I recommend the ten-volume *Routledge Encyclopaedia of Philosophy* and R. Scruton (1982) *A Dictionary of Political Thought*, London: Macmillan. For more substantial coverage of the great dead modern political philosophers, I recommend Iain Hampsher-Monk (1992) *A History of Modern Political Thought: Major Political Thinkers from Hobbes to Marx*, Oxford: Blackwell. J. Coleman (2000) *A History of Political Thought from Ancient Greece to Early Christianity*, Oxford: Blackwell, is a good guide to the classical authors. M.H. Lessnoff (1999) *Political Philosophers of the Twentieth Century*, Oxford: Blackwell, brings the story up to date.

Recent introductory books on political philosophy include D. Knowles (2001) *Political Philosophy*, London: Routledge (in which I elaborate many of the ideas sketched here); J. Wolff (1996) *An Introduction to Political Philosophy*, Oxford: Oxford University Press (from whom I have borrowed the elegant order of exposition of topics selected in this essay); W. Kymlicka (1990) *Contemporary Political Philosophy: An Introduction*, Oxford: Oxford University Press; R. Plant (1991) *Modern Political Thought*, Oxford: Blackwell; J. Hampton (1997) *Political Philosophy*, Boulder, CO: Westview. References to further reading on the problems I have raised should cascade from these sources.

R.E. Goodin and P. Pettit (eds) (1993) *A Companion to Contemporary Political Philosophy*, Oxford: Blackwell, is a good compendium of essays on the central 'isms, concepts and values of political philosophy. R.E. Goodin and P. Pettit (eds) (1997) *Contemporary Political Philosophy: An Anthology*, Oxford: Blackwell, is a thick and wide-ranging collection of excerpts and essays representing some of the best modern work in the subject. In point of general interest and unusual range of sources, the best modern anthology is M. Rosen and J. Wolff (eds) (1999) *Political Thought*, Oxford: Oxford University Press.

12

AESTHETICS

Colin Lyas

PRELIMINARY: AESTHETICS AND PHILOSOPHICAL AESTHETICS

It essential from the outset to be aware of the difference between aesthetics and philosophical aesthetics. The former has to do with the ways in which we respond aesthetically to natural objects and to works of art. Thus, an aesthetic response to nature might be expressed by saying that a sunset is beautiful or the Grand Canyon sublime. And an aesthetic response to a work of art might be expressed in similar ways, as when one finds, too, a lyric by Schubert or Joni Mitchell beautiful or *Citizen Kane* and *King Lear* sublime. Such responses, which have their roots in the way in which we, from early infancy, respond both to the sensory textures of the world, its colours, fragrances and sounds, and to such humanly constructed things as simple rhythms, nursery rhymes, fairy stories and cradle songs, are the material of aesthetics.

Much great art may be intellectually as well as emotionally demanding, but in their earliest manifestations there is nothing particularly intellectual about many of our aesthetic responses. They are a bedrock upon which any more developed aesthetic life is founded. We start by dancing to simple rhythms, being enraptured by simple stories and being entranced by colour. As we mature intellectually and emotionally, experience and practice lead us to a greater range and depth in aesthetic experience and the power to make finer discriminations within our preferred experiences, be they of rap or of Rachmaninov. But if we concede that our aesthetic capacities can develop, we ought also to concede that this development can be arrested. Too-narrowly focused educational systems, allied to such things as the brutalising effects of poverty and ignorance, discourage the sustained exercise, and with it the continued development, of those innate aesthetic capacities.

The various forms of aesthetic life can be taken up into the intellectual life. This happens when we study such things as the history of art and the history of the ways people have responded to nature. Again one might study the sociology of art, asking, for example, what kinds of societies produced what kinds of art and why they did so (as a Marxist might ask why, say, the novel as a form of literature should have appeared just when it did). Again one might ask questions about the psychology of art, leading, for example, to the kinds of speculations about artistic creativity prompted by Freud's psychological theories. To these we may add, first, practical aesthetics (the kinds of things done in colleges of art, music, and drama) and, second, the various more or less formal ways in which one might study, pursue and enjoy art in order to increase one's capacities for response. All these are part of that huge whirl of activity called 'aesthetics'.

Yet none of these is philosophical aesthetics. And that is why it is essential, from the outset, to stress the differences between aesthetics and philosophical aesthetics. Indeed, were we simply to call our subject 'aesthetics', as opposed to 'philosophical aesthetics', we might encourage the view that some greater practical competence in appreciation of the arts and of nature might be the fruit of its study, so that one's ability to make the right sorts of noises in the Tate Modern, for example, would thus be enhanced. If that is the object of the reader's study, a better way to achieve it would be to haunt such places as galleries and concert halls.

But what then is philosophical aesthetics? And what are its problems? And why am I prepared to say that its study, although not an express route to the acquisition of aesthetic capacities, is nonetheless of great importance for the understanding of certain of our responses to art and nature?

To understand this we must understand what the word 'philosophical' in 'philosophical aesthetics' is doing. That word is itself controversial, since one of the fundamental questions in the history of philosophy is what the scope and limits of that discipline should be. What follows is one kind of answer.

We can think of at least two sorts of questions. One sort requires us to find out something new. That sort of question, in its more sophisticated forms, gives rise to the empirical sciences. Think of wondering whether and why a red sky at night is invariably a harbinger of fine weather. But not all questions are like this. Mathematical questions aren't. One does not have to undertake an observational study of triangles to know that all of them have angles that add up to 180 degrees. More especially, philosophical questions, and, therefore, questions in philosophical aesthetics, seem not to be the kinds of empirical questions that might be studied by science (including psychological or sociological enquiries, if they are indeed scientific). Examples from philosophical aesthetics may make this clear.

Thus, some people agree that Barry Manilow is a great singer. Some don't. Here are some empirical questions: what correlation is there between thinking he is a great singer and (a) income (b) number of university degrees (c) political allegiance (d) gender and (e) being the child of separated parents? These are empirical questions and to answer them we will have to do some field research. But now consider the question: 'Regardless of how many people do or don't think he is a great singer, who, if anyone, is *right* in thinking that he is, or is not, a great singer?' Empirical study[1] might tell me that a certain kind of elite takes it upon itself to *say* from its point of view what is right and wrong in aesthetics. But that empirical enquiry will not answer the question whether what this elite claims is right is right. Consider again the sociology of art. A sociologist may be able to tell me whether this or that social group called something or other 'art', but, as some of the storms about *avant garde* art in this century have reminded us, this does not settle the question whether those who call something 'art' are right so to do.

A final set of considerations: we know we are moved, and sometimes deeply moved by natural scenes, objects and events. The effects of such things: 'the round ocean and the living air', 'the proud music of the storm', 'the purple hush of twilight time', are rightly celebrated in the literature of nature. And art, too, moves us, and moves us deeply. For many of us this is most familiar as an experience had when listening to music, when, as Eliot put it in *Four Quartets*, the music is heard so deeply it is not heard at all but 'you are the music'. It is possible to be blankly moved by such things. But then, for many, the insistent question arises as to why such things move us so deeply. This is the question that puzzled Benedick in *Much Ado About Nothing*, who, hearing a viol playing (strung as they were with animals' intestines), could not understand how sheep's guts should haul the souls out of human beings.

The kinds of puzzlements here are typically philosophical. Each of us can tell the time, waste time, ask the time, keep to time and die because of time. Again we can ask what someone has in mind, have a mind to so something, grieve that someone loses his or her mind, admire an able mind and keep something in mind. So we operate wonderfully well with the words 'mind' and 'time'. Yet, as St Augustine noted, which of us, including great philosophers, can easily answer the question 'what is mind' or 'what is time'. These are philosophical questions, arising when something familiar to us becomes enigmatic. So, too, in philosophical aesthetics. I often unhesitatingly call a scene 'beautiful'. But if I am asked 'What is beauty?' I seem at loss. Again, you and I might have not the least inclination to disagree that *Breaking the Waves* is a deeply impressive film. We might think that this is true, if anything is. And, yet, we might not know what to say to someone who, disagreeing with us, claims that such judgements are totally subjective.

Reflecting on these matters we might come to understand why some have said that philosophy, and hence philosophical aesthetics, is a second, or higher order activity. On the first floor are the responses that we make to art and nature. But we can reflect at a higher remove on these first level responses, and when we do so puzzlements can arise, say about objectivity. To engage with those puzzles is to do philosophy. We do not have to do philosophical aesthetics. Keats, indeed, thought it best not to do so, since, he claimed, cold philosophy would simply 'unweave the rainbow' and remove the mystery of art (a task, indeed, recently essayed, taking his title from Keats, and with typical modesty, by Professor Dawkins[2]). So, we might simply and unreflectively seek to reap the rewards of the enjoyment of art and nature. Good luck to those that can! For myself, I am touched by another thought. For one of the things that can disturb me is being aware of something that I cannot articulate, as when I stumble into inarticulacy when trying to make a point at a meeting, or find myself unable to say to someone how I feel about them. Then somebody puts into words for me what I cannot articulate and I feel a relief. Croce, indeed, thought that this was one of the central things that made art central to us, echoing Pope's remarks that poetic wit gives us 'what oft was thought but ne'er so well expressed'. Think, in this connection, of how, for many, e.e. cummings' 'somewhere i have never traveled' (quoted to memorable effect by Michael Caine in *Hannah and Her Sisters*) might enable someone to articulate and give voice to a hitherto dumb feeling of love. Or think of the way in which Becket's *Waiting for Godot* might seem to sum up for someone a whole feeling about life, as, for Bernstein, from the age of fourteen, Mahler's music seemed to do. So, too, I might feel deeply about art and nature and not be able to say why. So I am led to reflect on those experiences. Until my reflections lay my puzzlement to rest, I will not feel that I really understand art, nature and my relation to them. That understanding, were I to attain it, might reveal the importance and centrality of the experiences of art and nature in human life. And that, in turn, that might enable more cogent things to be said to (doubtless to be ignored by) the utilitarian philistines who run the educational systems of this and many other lands, and for whom aesthetic interests are peripheral to central vocational concerns. To ask why I am so moved by art or nature is ultimately to ask what art and nature are, and that kind of higher order question (what is courage, love, virtue, justice) is precisely where philosophy began (some say mistakenly) with Socrates.

ART AND NATURE

We get philosophical aesthetics, then, when we are puzzled by and reflect on the spontaneous ongoing activities that constitute our aesthetic dealings with art and nature. The 'and' suggests that we ought to distinguish the philosophical aesthetics of nature and the philosophical aesthetics of art. And indeed I think one must. True, sometimes what we are interested in when we are interested in art is just the sort of thing that we might be interested in when we look at nature. The American novelist James Lee Burke remarks, in one of his books, on a colour of the sky as 'such a deep, heart wrenching blue that you felt you could reach up and fill your hand with it like bolls of stained cotton'. But one can be as struck by the quality of the blue in the paintings of Yves Klein. And I might be moved in the same way by the formal perfection of a spiral shell and the intricate plot of the Japanese film *The Ring*. Colours, shapes, forms and sounds, then, can engage me whether I find them in art or in nature. But it is equally true that some of the things I might be moved by in nature are not the things that could be found in art (the size of nature), and equally, some of the things for which I most value art, could not be found in nature. (For example, the remark, 'how cleverly and wittily that portrait captures a facial expression' could not be made of the reflection of a face in a pond).

For this reason one influential account of the subject matter of philosophical aesthetics is simply wrong. Monroe Beardsley, in a standard textbook, defines philosophical aesthetics as the philosophy of criticism, that is, higher order reflection on the things that people say about art.[3] But such a definition simply leaves aside questions about the kinds of aesthetic experiences that we have with nature.

One reason for privileging the philosophy of art over the philosophy of nature stems from Hegel and involves the view that our fundamental aesthetic experiences come from art, so that those we have in the presence of nature are derivative from those more primary dealings with art works. This is a view espoused also by Croce and, more recently, by Wollheim.[4] (A striking attempt to homogenise the response to nature and the response to art is to be found in the work of Savile.[5])

We can indeed treat nature through the eyes of art, so that we might look at a sunset and say 'How Turneresque'. This option is not available to us prior to the existence of or prior to a knowledge of Turner's distinctive mode of painting. But our aesthetic capacities, in one very good sense of the term 'aesthetic', are not all dependent on our acquisition of a capacity to respond properly to art. I suspect Wordsworth was stirred by nature before he made art out of those stirrings, and a small child, ignorant of art, entranced by colour or rhythm seems to me to be having aesthetic experiences.

Two main things have happened recently that subvert any easy attempt to define philosophical aesthetics as the philosophy of art.

The first is the major revival of the study of the aesthetics of nature as an important sub-section of the philosophical aesthetics. One reason for this is a suspicion (the rightness of which does not concern me) that nature, with its flora and fauna, has not been respected as valuable in itself as opposed to valuable only as instrumental to human purposes. Another reason has been a recognition that our responses to nature simply are philosophical interesting, that is to say, puzzling in the way in which I have earlier attempted to explain. Hence there has been a rich literature in very recent years on the aesthetics of nature. This began with a notable paper by Ronald Hepburn[6] and has been carried forward by writers such as Alan Carlson and Arnold Berleant.[7]

The second main thing to subvert any easy amalgamation of the aesthetics of nature and the aesthetics of art has been the simple realisation that one of the traditional subjects of aesthetics, namely, beauty, is not solely a province of art. Indeed, in such earlier enquiries as Socrates' glorious engagement with the matter in *The Symposium* (a drinking party of which there never has been the like) beauty, far from being understood through its association with art, was important because beauty was thought of as a reflection of, and, through its infusion into the visible universe, a magnet drawing us towards God himself. Hence, it has recently been trenchantly argued[8] that a concentration on art may entirely ignore the tradition of interest in aesthetic beauty access to which comes as much from the natural world as from the artistic.

Beauty was indeed, for a long time a central concept in aesthetics. Its disappearance from aesthetic literature was encouraged by two related developments. The first was a retreat from the idealist tradition instituted by Hegel and culminating, in aesthetics, in the work of Gentile and Croce in Italy and Bosanquet and, influentially still, Collingwood[9] in England. That tradition did indeed make the investigation of beauty central to its enquiries.

Idealism was the prevailing philosophy in England for nearly a hundred years, lasting, through such remarkable and still influential figures such as Bradley, well into the twentieth century. It was, however, substantially subverted in the early work of Russell and Moore. When Idealism was subverted, idealist aesthetics, with its analysis of such super-concepts as the concept of beauty, seemed undermined also.

Second, in the place of idealism came something strikingly smaller scale. Idealism had talked about big theories, such as the theories of beauty (a title, indeed, of a collection of readings by the idealist aesthetician Carritt). Two reactions then occurred. One, to be found in Passmore's 'The dreariness of aesthetics'[10] was a reaction to what seemed high-faluting and interminable discussions of large-scale issues, such as the nature of beauty, apparently little related to the actual practice of aesthetics. (One finds an early forerunner of that distaste in Tolstoy's great classic *What is Art*[11].) Second, sensing that not much progress was being made with the big notions, like 'beauty', attention turned the study of smaller scale, more down to earth notions, where, it is thought, some more progress might be made. Hence Austin's claim that we might leave aside for a while the analysis of words like 'beauty' and try to make progress by examining such notions as the dainty and the dumpy. Wittgenstein was a major influence in this. For it was he who advocated an attention to the words that we actually use in making our aesthetic judgements, 'beautiful' being only one, and not the most common one, of these. To readers used to high sounding discussions of terms like 'beauty', the cool tone of Sibley's classic 'Aesthetic concepts',[12] still a wonderful example of how far reaching humbler-looking enquiries can be, must have come as an extraordinary breath of a different air.

For whatever reason, for a long period of time dating from the 1950s, 'beauty' tended not to be much discussed, nor, since beauty was one of its main claims to attention, were nature, and aesthetic responses to nature, much discussed. This has now begun to change. As I write evidence is emerging that not merely that nature is becoming a central object of philosophical aesthetics, but that beauty is now again being thought of as a central player on the stage. An entire issue of one of the central journals has been devoted to the subject and an influential aesthetician, Noel Carroll, writes that 'beyond the world of academia, artists and art critics have heralded a return to aesthetics, often couched in the language of beauty'.[13] In this, aesthetics goes back to its roots.

PHILOSOPHICAL AESTHETICS AS THE PHILOSOPHY OF ART

For all that the aesthetics of nature and, more especially the analysis of the beauty of nature has become a prominent topic of recent discussion, the predominant topics in more recent philosophical aesthetics have concerned problems in the philosophy of art. In what follows, somewhat artificially, I divide these problems into three (admittedly overlapping) categories. The categories I propose are The Definition of Art, The Value of Art, and a category of More Specific Problems about art in general and about the individual arts.

THE DEFINITION OF ART

The definitional question What is Art? is asked for at least two reasons. First, there is the wish, as part of the process of relieving puzzlements about to which I have earlier referred, to understand what art essentially is. But in addition, in recent years, the extraordinary range of things which have been offered in art, emblematic of which are the urinal exhibited by Duchamp under the title *Fontaine*, the *4'33"* of silence offered by John Cage and, more recently, the exhibition by Tracey Emin of her bed, has caused further puzzlement. One wants to know whether and why one should allow such things into the fold of art. A question (which is indeed the title of an excellent book) seems insistently to rise: 'But is it art?' (Or, to use the title of another equally interesting book, *Art or Bunk?*).[14]

Many answers have been offered to the general question 'What is Art?' Some, Croce, Tolstoy and Collingwood, have claimed that art is expression. The artist produces a work of art which is the expression of the emotion, belief or attitude that the artist felt and wished to articulate. That view accords with the fact that some artists have testified to creating their works according to this prescription. Others, and here Fry and Bell are exemplary, have claimed that the question whether something is or is not properly to be called 'art' is a matter of whether it exhibits certain kinds of formal relations.[15] Again, that view gets plausibility from the fact that formal relations within a picture are a source of delight to us.[16] Yet again there are those, of whom Dewey,[17] and later, influenced by Dewey, Beardsley are important examples, who argue that a work of art is something that yields a certain distinctive kind of experience (called by Dewey the 'consummatory' experience). And in favour of that view is the fact that we do seem to be powerfully and distinctively affected by art. A further important category of definitions attaches the notion of art to objects which require us to exercise our imaginations.[18] Various things encourage this position. Think of someone going to a play, or reading a novel or watching a film, none of whose characters ever existed and none of whose scenes or events actually took place. The object of attention is a work of the imagination and the delight we take in it is the delight in exercising our imaginations in revelling in the make-believe world of the work.[19] Such a view also has affinities with theories, as advocated by Schiller (and more recently Derrida), of art as a kind of play, and Schopenhauer's view that art frees us from the everyday activity of willing to which we are generally chained. The view seems, indeed, to accord with the intuition that imagination is in the creation of art, a view memorably expressed by Shakespeare when he speaks of the imaginative poet as 'giving to airy nothings, local habitation and a name'. Finally, in a line of thinking that originates with Kant, and was notably revived by Bullough, there are those who define the aesthetic as a kind of disinterested, contemplative attention to the world.[20]

Philosophical aesthetics was often conducted in terms of these accounts of art, with one person advocating one theory and dismissing others and so on seriatim, ad infinitum and ad nauseam. That, indeed is what led some to talk of the 'dreariness' of aesthetics.

Sometime in the late 1950s this internecine warfare faded. The reason is simple to explain. For consider, the argument went, what each of these theories undertook to do. Each attempted to state a condition which was necessary and sufficient to art. The condition was meant to be necessary: that is to say, nothing could be art which failed to meet this condition. And the condition was meant to be sufficient, which is to say that if something exhibited this condition, then that was enough to make it art. So, an expression theory, say, asserts that if something is to be art, it necessarily must be an expression, and if it is an expression, that is enough to make it art. The traditional discussion consisted in finding cases of art which are not expressions (thus defeating the claim that being an expression is necessary to art) and finding cases of expression which are not art (thus defeating the claim that expression is sufficient to make something art). So, too, for the other theories.

But then something happened to make this whole procedure seem wrong. This was the gradually dissemination of some posthumously published remarks by Wittgenstein about definition. For in his *Philosophical Investigations*,[21] Wittgenstein seemed to cast doubt on the notion that one could define something in terms of necessary and sufficient conditions. The most commonly quoted example is the definition of the word 'game'. For Wittgenstein, claimed, there is nothing that all the things we call games have in common which would serve as a necessary and sufficient condition for something's being a game. All we have is a complex of overlapping features, in the way in which, to use another of Wittgenstein's examples, a single rope need have no single strand running through its entire length. If, to use another of his examples, we think of the resemblances between the members of a family, there need be no one feature which all share. Rather there might be a pool of features, some of which, in overlapping ways, belong to some of the family, some to others. It might even be that although, when we see the whole family assembled, we can see the resemblances between them all, we might also see that two members of the family have no features in common. So it was argued, there need be no features common to all and only the things we call 'art'. Rather there might be at best a pool of art-relevant features permuted in different ways among the different things we call 'art'. This was indeed the burden of a famous paper by Morris Weitz which, for a while, seemed to end the search for accounts of art in terms of necessary and sufficient conditions.[22]

I say 'for a while', because the search for a way of determining the status of some of the more outré candidates for the status of art was to produce a different kind of definition of art in terms of necessary and sufficient conditions. That definition took its departure from the notion, introduced by Arthur Danto of an 'Art World'.[23] The Art World consists of producers, historians, dealers, purchasers, curators, and the like, of art. The activities of such people give the notion of art the sense and life it has. That thought, indeed, is related to the later philosophy of Wittgenstein. For on that account, any word, be it 'pot', 'art' or 'God', gets its meaning by having a living use. If we wish to know what that meaning is, then we have to examine the use that word has in the lives of those who see some point in deploying it.

The notion of the 'art world' as a kind of institution seems to have suggested to George Dickie 'The Institution Theory.'[24] Dickie deploys a notion that figured prominently in the work of the philosopher J.L. Austin, that of the performative utterance. For consider, what makes it the case that a baby is a baptised member of a Christian community. No visible change in the infant occurs. What makes it the case that the child is a baptised member of the Christian community is that someone, acting on behalf of the Christian community, confers that status on the child. By parity of reasoning, as Danto had argued, what marks something off as a work of art need be nothing in its appearance. (Duchamp's ready-mades were simply ordinary things brought into a gallery.) Why not then, Dickie suggests, suppose that something is art if someone, acting on behalf of the art world, confers on it a certain status, by, say, bringing it into a gallery, and thus offering it as candidate for appreciation. So the question whether 4'33" is a work of art is decided affirmatively, in that it has attained a place in the art world. Tracey Emin's bed, by the same argument, is an art work because she, acting on behalf of the art world, has made it an object of contemplation.

Dickie's account has stirred substantial discussion. Some have asked who, in the art world, occupies the authorised role occupied by the priest in baptismal ceremonies. Others have thought that bestowing an art-authenticating role on some dubious clique called 'the art world' is a recipe for elitism. More powerfully, some have claimed that the institutional definition is unilluminating. What someone who is puzzled by *Fontaine*, or 4'33" wants to know is not whether some people have called it 'art' (we all knew that), but why they have done so. Merely to say that it becomes art because someone has bestowed that status on it is to leave out the only interesting question, which is why someone would have wished to do that.

Although discussion of the institution theory continues, the earlier kinds of definition that I mentioned, those cast in terms of expression, form and the like, seem not now to be a substantial topic for discussion. My guess is that this will change. First, a central reason why such definitions are not discussed is that Wittgenstein is thought to have shown the folly of seeking definitions in terms of necessary and sufficient conditions. But it is quite unclear that he intended any such thing, and, anyway, that notion of 'family resemblance' and the role it was meant to play in Wittgenstein's analysis of language use is quite unclear. Second, there is evidence that some of the usual suspects were somewhat hastily written off. Here the perennial favourites are definitions in terms of expression and imagination. Scruton's recent book on music, for example, shows how much mileage there might be in a resuscitation of the notion of expression as a central feature of art.

THE VALUE OF ART

It is useful to divide the discussion of this matter into an investigation of two main areas. There is first the question of the important benefits, if any, we obtain in our wider lives from encounters with works of art. Second there is the question of the intrinsic values that we assign to a work of art when we appraise it critically.

The benefits of art

Some, of course, have queried whether art is in any way a good thing. The most striking, and much the most readable, is Plato, who, in Book 10 of the *Republic* urges that poets and painters be banished from the ideal state. One reason is that the kinds of stories told by poets feed and water the passions, these being somewhat unruly elements of the psyche which need to be kept under. Again, poets and painters tend to give the wrong impression of important things like the Gods. These charges are echoed today when anyone argues that Hollywood films not only water the wrong passions but suggest the wrong sorts of models to follow. More interesting is the claim, not to be divorced from Plato's general philosophy, that painters tell lies. For truth in assertion has to do with what is really the case. But, on Plato's account, the painter and novelist gives us imitations of reality rather than reality itself. Indeed, since on Plato's account real objects, such as beds and chairs, are themselves only second-hand copies of the pure Forms of the bed and the chair as they exist in some true reality, the painter is two removes from that true reality, offering copies of copies. Even divorced from Plato's general philosophical theories there is something of lasting interest here. For one might well ask why we need pictures of beds, or whatever, when we have perfectly good beds to look at. (Why do those of us with relatives like that, need *The Royle Family* or *Roseanne*?) Hence the lasting problem of the point of representational art.

Aristotle's *Poetics*, of which we have only fragments of the part dealing with tragedy, are taken to be a rejoinder to his master, Plato, and to stake out a defence of the utility of art, one that is still being deployed as I write. In the *Poetics* appears a passage, the deeply enigmatic nature of which, has not prevented most aestheticians from offering exegeses. Writing of the effect of a tragedy Aristotle suggests that it provokes pity and fear in order to bring about a 'catharsis' of those emotions. This has, rightly or wrongly, been read by some as the view that a fictional work of art engages our emotions and, through that engagement, exercises and so educates our emotional life. For the kinds of exercises of emotion with which we are concerned with in responses to art are the kinds of responses in which our judgements of behaviour are expressed, for example, contempt, approval and delight. So the exercise of emotions afforded by art is a kind of training, thought to be an important means to the acquisition of a right moral character. (Leavis certainly thought so.) This defence of the value of art relates art to morality.

Aristotle also speaks of truth as a special value in art. For he suggests, again somewhat enigmatically, that whereas history tells us particular truths, the kinds of truths we learn from a work of art are general. That locates another defence of the value of art, one which assigns a role to art as a means to understanding the truth.

Truth

Here I mention three matters:

1 Propositional truth in art

First, one great problem in philosophy has been the truth status of propositions which do not refer to any real thing. Thus 'The present Prime Minister is a charlatan' seems arguably either true or false. But 'the present President of the United Kingdom is a charlatan' seems neither true nor false. The problems here were raised in their modern form by Russell and are central to contemporary philosophical logic. Works of art often get involved with these matters because many of them are fictional and so involve statements about fictional characters, as when Kafka memorably begins by telling us that, after a night of troubled sleep, Gregor Samsa awoke to find that he had turned into a giant insect. There is much debate about the proper analysis of fictional statements. In part this can be left to philosophical logicians. But it cannot be entirely so left because of a conundrum posed by Colin Radford about responses to fictions.[25]

2 Responses to fictions

If I am afraid of something I must believe that it exists and is threatening. Thus if I believe that there is a burglar in the house, I have good reason to be afraid. If I toe-stubbingly and timorously explore my property and find no such intruder exists, I cannot now be rationally afraid of him or her. But now, I sit in my seat in the Essoldo Cinema and watch the Blob approaching on the screen and I am scared stiff. But I know that the Blob does not exist. Or I grieve for the Jess of *Breaking the Waves*. Yet I know there is no Jess. And since to feel an emotion towards what one knows does not exist is defined as irrational, isn't my emotion to fiction then simply irrational. This matter goes deep into many aesthetic issues.[26]

3 Plausibility

Next, there are some nice problems about truth, plausibility and belief in art. Coleridge remarked that art involves a willing suspension of disbelief. This is sometimes possible, as when I go along with the extraordinary things that happen to Alice in Wonderland, or engage with Gregor Samsa. But it is not always possible. A picture of a salmon swimming up-river in the wrong season is likely to jar the cognoscenti. More importantly, is it to be supposed that I can suspend my disbelief sufficiently to make Katherine's catalogue of the duties of a wife in the *Taming of the Shrew*, or D.W. Griffiths' racism in *The Birth of a Nation* seem aesthetically enjoyable?[27]

What truths, then, can a work of art give me? Some (Beardsley and Isenberg) say 'none'. A proposition is entitled to be assessed for its truth only if seriously asserted, and, so they argue, the propositions of a work of art are not seriously asserted but are imaginary propositions meant to be enjoyed imaginatively. I doubt this is a fair description of what Dickens is up to in attacking Chancery in *Bleak House*. Others have argued that, for some of the arts, truth cannot be an issue because such works anyway lack propositional content. (How can a piece of music be true or false? Or a painting of a cornfield?)

Yet one does think, sometimes, that one has learned something from a work. (In his remarkable *Crazy* – which may have found a new kind of philosophical voice – Benjamin Lebert remarks that 'literature is where you feel you could put a little mark under every line because it's true'.[28])

I have tried the following way forward. There seem, as I said earlier, to be two kinds of truths. Some are the kind we might find out by investigation. A work of art might provide something along those lines, as when the heist movie *Rififi* proved, accidentally, to be of assistance to Brazilian safe crackers, or as when *Casablanca* suggested new possible seduction gambits to one of Woody Allen's characters. However, I doubt the greatest works of art are into the game of passing on new factual information. But there are other kinds of truths, such as those in mathematics, which seem not so much to be known as the result of new empirical discoveries, but to be found out by thinking out the implications of what we already know. The truths I seem to come to possess through art may be of that order. They come to me with an air of familiarity and are greeted with comments like 'that's how it is with me'. For one can know something without being able to be clear what one knows and without being able to express it. And then a work of art might make me see by giving me the means to articulate how it already is with me. And since to be inarticulate about one's inner life can be painful, and since clarity about our inner lives can be so important to us, whatever gives us that clarity can seem, too, important. (And this is why I lean to expression theories of art, since in their most sophisticated forms they seek to do justice to our needs to express and articulate what we struggle to express and articulate.) But to understand the nature of some, at least, of these truths we need to look at art and morality.

Morality

That brings me to the other defence of the value of art, which treats art as a means to the education of the moral life. (The study of the connection between art and morality is now one of the growth areas of aesthetics.[29])

The first thing to be said is that such an education is unlikely to come from heavily didactic works which have a blatantly obvious design on us. (A good question here is why Bunyan's *Pilgrim's Progress* gets away with something like that, while the equally felt message of the abominable *Rules of Engagement* repels.) That said I am pulled two ways.

On the one hand, I am acutely aware that works of fiction do have a moral effect. One striking case is the parable of the good Samaritan. Who, Christ is asked, is my neighbour? And he does not answer 'the one who lives next door' or 'all your work mates'. He gives a fictional account of a man who fell among thieves, at the end of which he asks the audience who was the neighbour of that man. And the audience now knows. That this is a power of fiction has been powerfully and vividly exemplified in the moral philosophy of Peter Winch.[30] And the kind of revelation here seems to me to be of a piece with the kind that I spoke of in talking of truth. We seem to have implicit in us a moral understanding which needs to be brought to light, and works of art can do this for us. Further, a work of art, such as *Oedipus*, can present us with situations which we are unlikely confront in our lives and hence can stretch the implications of our moral imaginations.

On the other hand I have doubts about the morally educative force of art. For the account I have given speaks of drawing out the implications of our moral commitments. That seems to me to presuppose that we have that morality already implicit in us. If we do, then a work of art can bring it out. But what comes out depends on what is already in. We already have to be morally educated for that illuminative education to work. Someone said to me recently how strange, if art is so civilising, that countries replete with culture, could have produced such things, to take from a rich possible list, as the massacre of Amritsar, the Holocaust (with the orchestras of the camps playing the great classics), the events of Mai Lai, and the travails of Fascism. How odd, if art is morally educative, that Heidrich should have loved Mozart. I add, further, that I find it inconceivable that someone brutalised by ignorance, poverty and mental and physical cruelty could be educated by art. And that is quite apart from the problems raised by the possibility of alternative moralities not to our taste. A neo-nazi skinhead may watch an 'oy' band and feel that this has entirely articulated how it is and ought to be for everyone. The fascist mob orator fulfils and articulates the inchoate life of his audience. Those[31] who talk of works of art as giving the emotions a good work-out seem to have some art-independent method of deciding which emotions ought to undergo these callisthenics. But that suggests a way of assessing morality that does not come from art.

The critical values of art

Art is valued. That gives rise to three questions. First, for what particular qualities is it valued. Second, what is the structure of evaluation. And third, what degree of objectivity that attaches to these evaluations.

1   The range of appraisal terms

As to the first, it is unlikely that the terms of appraisal we use of works of art will be confined to a few terms of which 'beautiful' is a standard case. We praise wit, elegance, grace, dynamism, perceptivity, originality, vigour, sass, irony, formal qualities such as balance, tact, skill and many more.

2   The structure of criticism

More interestingly, reflection on the very many kinds of things we say in the course of our critical appraisals reveals that criticism has a structure. Consider the claim 'what gives it balance is this patch of red in the left corner'. Here it is clear that the balance in some way depends on the patch being where it is. But it is equally obvious that someone, lacking experience, could see the patch and not see that it contributed to the balance of the composition. For that reason, Sibley ('Aesthetic concepts', op. cit.), in a famous paper, argued that aesthetic qualities, such as balance, are dependent upon and emergent from, but not entailed by the presence of non-aesthetic qualities, such as being a red patch in this or that position. Moreover one cannot, he thought, deduce the fact that the composition is balanced merely by seeing the red patch, even if the red patch is what contributes to the balance. We have to see the balance for ourselves. Aesthetics is a perceptual matter. Once we have seen a feature, then we can try to see on what non-aesthetic features it depends. But to see those features is not to see the balance.

3   Subjectivity and objectivity

But, now, the question arises whether these judgements about a work are objective. Some, Hume notably, have asserted that such judgements are subjective. For they express the feelings of the perceiver rather than, as objective judgements do, refer to properties in the work. And if two people disagree in their sentiments that is the end of the matter. That, for Kant, gave rise to a fundamental question. For we do seem to be expressing our sentiments when we say how a work affects us. Yet at the same time we speak as if we were talking about the work itself. We say that it is graceful, elegant, moving, witty and so on. His question was how that personally-based judgement could be a judgement with a claim to objectivity.

Kant's answer is best approached through the secondary literature.[32] Here I mention a not dissimilar line that originates in the work of Sibley.[33] For on Sibley's account, since aesthetics is a perceptual matter, we cannot prove our aesthetic judgements by reasoning someone into seeing the merits of the work, any more than we could prove that something is red by reasoning someone into seeing its redness.

The temptation then is to say that if critical judgements cannot be proved by reasoning, then they are not reasonable judgements. Here Sibley remarks that reasoned proofs are not the only ways in which we can get people to see or notice things. For aesthetics is a perceptual matter. We want to see, hear, notice what there is to be seen, heard and noticed in works of art. So the kinds of things we can do are the kinds of things we do when we try to help someone to see something. These are discussed in the second half of Sibley's influential 'Aesthetic Concepts', and range from simply drawing someone's attention to something to the use of rich metaphors. For, if I can get someone to see the rain by directing attention to the rain, why can't I get someone to see the compositional power of Van Eyck's *The Arnolfini Portrait* by directing attention to it?

Aesthetics then, is perceptual in the way in which the colour language is perceptual. The last part of Sibley's discussion, therefore, trades on the fact that we do think that we are talking about things (and not just about ourselves) when we say that the grass is green or the sky blue. Whether or not that claim stands up to sceptical scrutiny in philosophy, in ordinary life we act as if these matters were objective. And Sibley's claim is that aesthetic perception is as objective as that. Like colour perception, it rests upon a certain kind of agreement in judgements among those who respond to aspects of the world and of the things in it.

That reference to a kind of agreement is related to Kant's thought that there ought to be some kind of universality of response underlying objectivity in aesthetics. That, in turn, is related to another important set of thoughts recently offered by Ted Cohen.[34] For talk about objectivity which suggests that some kind of infallible proof procedure ought to be available if a matter is to be called 'objective', and talk of subjectivity as a kind of failure of that requirement, is not helpful in aesthetics (and morality) though it might serve our purposes in scientific and mathematical matters. Cohen offers the notion that what we seek in aesthetic discussions is community. If I come out of the pictures and say to you 'I liked that', this is not a subjective end-it-all remark but an invitation to share our thoughts. If you did not like the film some kind of rift opens between us and community is lost. To talk and find some possible common ground is to re-establish that community. But nothing can guarantee that we will succeed, and the world is a remarkable arena of criss-crossing and overlapping communities in which universality might not be a thing coherently to be sought. Think of the way in which two people who agree on Mozart might come apart with respect to Mahler.

SOME OTHER GENERAL PROBLEMS

Hitherto, we have been dealing with two central problems about art generally, the nature of art and the value of art. There are other problems which embrace the arts generally. I mention two.

Ontology

First, as befits any discipline which is properly philosophical, there are ontological problems, problems about what there is and what sort of thing something is. Here a central problem has been the ontological status of the work of art, what sort of thing a work of art is.[35] Thus, a painting or sculpture might seem to be a physical thing. A poem or a novel certainly is not. Though copies of books are physical things, the things of which they are copies are not. In the literature the latter are called 'types' of which the former are 'tokens'. (Consider, to begin to get a grasp on this, that in the sentence 'the cat sat on the mat', the same word, 'the', appears twice. So we have two tokens of the same type.) Musical works, such as symphonies raise equally intriguing problems. The symphony I hear is a physical thing, at least insofar as it impinges acoustically upon my ear. Yet a quite different interpretation can seem to be an interpretation of one and the same symphony. There are interesting questions as to how far an interpretation may go and still be an interpretation of the same work. Is a transcription of Beethoven's *Fifth Symphony* for the piano the same work? Is Disney's *The Waterboy*[36] an interpretation of the theme of Harold Lloyd's *The Freshman*, or a simple copy? Should we talk of the performance of a symphony as a token of a type? Does that type exist eternally only waiting from some composer to discover it? Or does it come into existence when created by a composer. These questions have a purely theoretical interest, but they are not entirely theoretical (as the litigation over *The Waterboy* shows). One, not entirely theoretical, question is what our aims are in restoring works of art. Another might be about the latitude a director or conductor has in performing a work. Again there are questions about whether copies of a painting can be as aesthetically valuable as the original, and, a question raised by Adorno, what painting might be like in an age of mass production. More recently Currie has shown that the kinds of things works of art are might have a bearing on the ways we should deal with them. His suggestion (earlier made by Merleau-Ponty) that a work of art is a kind of performance might have far-reaching consequences for the ways in which we go about judging a work of art.[37] (We would, as with any performance, have to take into account, intentions, how the agent conceived the action, the possibilities open to the agent, and so forth.)

Realism

Ontological questions may also be in the offing when questions about realism or objectivity are raised. One might ask, again, whether the properties attributed to a work are really there in the way in which one thinks of squareness as a real property of objects in the world. Against that there is a view (associated in very different forms, with Goodman, Margolis and Krausz)[38] that since a work of art exists only when given an interpretation by a human being, aesthetic objects and their properties are constructed by us (constructivism) and are not in the fullest sense independent of critical contexts or human interpretations.

Author and intentions

A second overarching question about works of art, the subject of a vast literature, is whether everything we ought to be interested in when we are interested in a work of art for itself can be ascertained independently of knowledge of or reference to the artist, and the cultural/historical circumstances of the artist who created it. A particular case of this is the claim that the intentions of the author are irrelevant to the consideration of the work. That view has been the subject of passionate debate, though for different sorts of reasons, in both Anglo-American and in Franco-German philosophy.

Three strands for further consideration are:

1 Meaning and intention
   First, there is the meaning argument, certainly to be found in Beardsley, Barthes and Derrida. If a word has a meaning, it cannot rely on its speaker's intentions for that meaning, if only for the entirely simple reason that when I speak I use words which had a meaning long before I was born and which will continue to have a meaning long after I have gone. Whether this entails an absolute separation between meaning and intention is quite unclear.[39] It is worth remarking also that Beardsley thought the separation of meaning from intention was compatible with there being something we could call 'the meaning' of the work, whereas, more radically, Derrida denied that there could be any such thing.

2 Artist and work
   Second, Beardsley and Wimsatt suggested that an artist is one object, the work of art produced by that artist is another object. (The work of art, they say, is detached from the author at birth and goes about the world beyond his [sic] power to intend or control it.) But it is the task of critics and appreciators of works of art to talk about works of art and not about something else. So, given that the artist, in being a separate thing from the work is 'something else', it follows that the critic and appreciator should not refer to the artist when talking about the work. But whether this absolute separation of author and work is intelligible has been contested.[40]

3 The death of the author

Sartre, Barthes, Derrida and Foucault have argued 'the death of the Author' on the grounds that to allow the author to control the meaning of the work is not only incoherent (for the reason given in 1 above) but wrong in promoting the author to a dictatorial, controlling status that improperly impinges on the freedom of the reader to interpret as he or she chooses. Hence we have Barthes' memorable slogan that the death of the author is the birth of the reader. (But the more radical, and probably more consistent line, taken by Derrida, is to deny anyone authority over the interpretation of a work.) Again, too, it is not clear (particularly if we adopt the kind of view to be found in Currie) that the entirely true claim that the artist is not the best judge of what he or she has done in the work, rules out the claim that to judge the work is, in part at least, to judge the author's performance in that work.

PROBLEMS ABOUT INDIVIDUAL ART FORMS

Beyond the general problems about art, each of the arts yields its specific aesthetic problems. The following are three examples.

Tragedy

Beginning with Aristotle there have been problems about tragedy. One such problem is why, given that the content of tragedy is so wracking (think here of *King Lear* and *Oedipus*), we involve ourselves so intensely with what is so distressing. Schopenhauer, who greatly valued tragedy, claimed that tragedy portrayed accurately the nothingness of life and helps us resign ourselves to our own cessation (a view rudely dismissed by Nietzsche, a notable reflector on tragedy, as 'resignationism'.)

Musical expression

Music is rich in material for aesthetic reflection, not the least because of the vigorous debate about what music is, whether, for example, tonality is definitive of music. One problem, however, is perennial.

We use expressive terms when we speak of music. We might call a tune 'happy', a pavanne 'grave', a march 'mournful', a cadenza 'angry' and a song as 'sad'. Two analyses of these idioms do not work. One is the claim that in using such expressive terms we are talking of the feeling or emotion felt by the composer of the music, which he or she has put into the work. However, it is far too easy to imagine cases in which we feel that the work has an expressive quality but would be loath to attribute that quality to the composer. Thus, we could imagine a lugubrious funeral march, composed for a dead monarch by a composer who was delighted to get the commission, enjoyed every moment of the writing, felt no particular grief for the monarch and watched the effect of his music on the audience with smiling satisfaction. So we cannot simply analyse the claim that music has an expressive quality as the claim that the composer of the music transferred that quality from his or her bosom to the music. Another alternative is to say that on hearing the music the audience comes to feel in a certain way, which is then assigned to the music as its cause. But that seems even more implausible. Let the case be one in which the music is called 'sad'. Is it true that when I hear such music I call it 'sad' because it makes me feel sad? Sad about what? Not the music (although I might be, as Wittgenstein was with Mahler, sad that someone would apparently have wasted his time composing it.) And would we go to listen to music if it really made us sad (or angry or bitter and so on)?

The first issue, now, is whether those two theories really are non-starters. (Some, such as Wollheim, have hinted that this might not be entirely obvious. Is it, do you think?) Second, granted they are non-starters, the question is what the proper analysis is of musical expression. One suggestion made by Tormey[41] is that when we call music 'expressive' we are doing something like what we do when we say that the face of a bloodhound looks lugubrious. We do not think that the dog has to be sad for its face to look so. Hence, when we say that music is sad, it is the look on its face, so to speak, that is sad. We can enjoy contemplating this in the way we might contemplatively take an interest in the kind of quality of sadness to be found on the look of a face. More radically Hanslick, in a famous piece of writing, has sought to eliminate the problem by eliminating talk of the emotional expressiveness of music as ill-founded. There are outstanding discussions of this problem by Scruton and an informative recent paper by Levinson. Davis has written a complete study of the literature on this matter.[42]

Representation

One of the central topics in the visual arts has been the nature and place of representation in painting. Here there are two problems.

1   The nature of representation
    One is how the notion of representation is to be analysed. Goodman has vigorously argued that representation cannot be analysed as resemblance, if only because John can resemble Jim, being his twin, without representing

him. It is, on Goodman's account also mysterious how the picture of a unicorn can resemble a unicorn, there being no such thing.[43] This attempt to sever representation and resemblance has been vigorously challenged. Wollheim has introduced into the discussion that notion of seeing-in. Just as we can see a cloud as a camel so we can see a camel in a configuration of lines and colours. More than this is needed however. For, Wollheim points out, one might see battles in the glowing embers without the embers representing battles. For us to have representation, he thinks, what we see in a work must somehow match an artistic intention that we should see just that.[44]

2   The relevance of representation

There have been equally vigorous arguments over the place of representation in art. Plato, as we have seen, admitted that painting could be representational but thought that a bad thing. More strikingly Bell (*Art*, op. cit.) thought the representational elements of a painting to be entirely irrelevant. To take an aesthetic attitude to a painting we must ignore anything representational. One reason Bell gave seems entirely specious. For he remarked that photography had given us such good representations that painters need not bother with that sort of thing anymore.[45] Is the argument here one to the effect that since photographers can now produce representations, painters, can be made redundant? To which one might reply, why need anyone be made redundant? And, if someone must be, why must it be the painter? The further reason why Bell thought representation eliminable was that he thought an aesthetic interest should confine itself to shapes, colours, lines and objects in three-dimensional space. Leaving aside the fact that to represent a three-dimensional object, however abstract, on a two-dimensional picture plane is to engage in representation, it is simply not the case that we can grasp all the relevant formal relations of a picture without reference to what is represented. The composition of Stubbs' masterly *Racehorses Belonging to the Duke of Richmond Exercising at Goodwood* can only be grasped if one follows the line across the painting, but one can only do that if one recognises and follows the direction of a represented pointing hand and a represented steady gaze.

SOME THINGS HAPPENING NOW

Traditional philosophical aesthetics, as outlined above is now under attack from at least three directions.

Race and gender

First, it has been observed that the canon of the great masterpieces traditionally discussed in anglophone philosophical aesthetics contains largely the products of whitish European males. In reaction to this, as with parallel discussions in ethics, two strands are discernible. One is a strand which argues that what women and/or non-Caucasians have been excluded from is something (art making) that is all right as it is. The situation is to be redressed by admitting more people to the activity. The more radical claim is that the traditional ways of doing things are (moderate form) all right, but not the only way, since other genders and other cultures have it in them to produce other kinds of art, as worthy of attention as the traditional masterpieces. Alternatively (radical form), it is asserted the traditional ways of doing things are not all right at all. In being exclusive, they are flawed and repressive. The examination of these claims is an important part of the agenda of contemporary aesthetics.

Cultural relativity

It has become apparent that other civilisations have produced extraordinarily powerful works, which seem, at first sight, quite unlike the works produced in Europe between 1400 and 1900, the period, it is often claimed, in which a canon of masterpieces was laid down. This fact had already imposed itself on Picasso through that acquaintance with African tribal art which left so stark a mark on *Les Demoiselles d'Avignon*. And Picasso was most certainly not alone. But with increasing knowledge, the creative activities of other cultures press on us more and more. They present two sorts of challenges. First, we call what, say, aboriginal Australians produced 'art'. But what do we mean by that? Are we assuming that they were doing what Rembrandt was doing? And were they? Are we simply forcing these works into our categories? Second, a point much explored by the great philosopher Peter Winch in such works as 'Understanding a Primitive Society', how much of the works of another culture can we understand? Is another culture ultimately impenetrable by us? Or, hopefully, are these works a way in which we can broaden ourselves by understanding something other than ourselves. So ethno-aesthetics becomes a vital topic. (And, as Winch would have pointed out, even our own national sub-cultures can be enigmatic to us.)

The philosophical challenge to 'High Art'[46]

Finally, philosophical aesthetics has traditionally been pursued by reference to examples taken from what is called 'High Art'. But that leaves untouched the things read, watched, danced to, drawn by, a huge range of the human race. It leaves out (to take a minimal selection from a vast field) rap, hip-hop, garage, Puff Daddy and Celine Dion, soap operas, graffiti, films, and rave dancing. Hence the question arises as to whether these forms of aesthetic behaviour have an equal claim on the attention of aestheticians and philosophers. One form this has taken is the enquiry into the claims of mass art, an enquiry which begins, as all good philosophy would, by asking want exactly we mean when we use that phrase.[47] And then there is the issue of whether some of the forms of popular culture have as much claim on us as the traditional forms of High Art, Shusterman, indeed, making just that claim for rap music.[48]

EXERCISES

Think what your views now are on these questions:

1 Could you think of reasons why some controversial piece of modern art has a rightful claim to be called 'art'?
2 Have you been tempted to think of music as expressive? Think critically about the kinds things you might mean by this.
3 How could knowing something about an artist bear on your opinion of the merit of a work produced by that artist?
4 Do you have any views as to why we are so powerfully affected by natural scenes, objects and events?
5 Why do we treat things produced in other cultures as art?
6 Are some of the products of popular cultures art? Are some of them great art?

NOTES

1 See, for example, Bordieu, P. and Darbel, A., *The Love of Art* (Stanford: Stanford University Press, 1990).
2 Dawkins, R., *Unweaving the Rainbow* (London: Allen Lane, 1998).
3 Beardsley, M.C. *Aesthetics* (New York: Harcourt Brace and World, 1959).
4 Croce, B., *The Aesthetic* (Cambridge: Cambridge University Press, 1992) and Wollheim, R., *Art and its Objects*, second edition (Cambridge: Cambridge University Press, 1980).
5 Savile, A., *The Test of Time* (Oxford: Oxford University Press, 1982).

6 Hepburn, R., 'Contemporary aesthetics and the neglect of natural beauty' in *Wonder and Other Essays* (Edinburgh: Edinburgh University Press, 1984).

7 The most accessible way into these recent departures is via some of the essays in Kemal, S. and Gaskell, I. (eds), *Landscape, Natural Beauty and the Arts* (Cambridge: Cambridge University Press, 1993). See also the very accessible material in the special issue of *The Journal of Aesthetics and Art Criticism* (Spring, 1998).

8 Kirwan, C., *Beauty* (Manchester: Manchester University Press, 1999). See also the symposium, 'Beauty Matters', in the special issue of *The Journal of Aesthetics and Art Criticism* (Winter, 1999).

9 Collingwood, R.G., *The Principles of Art* (Oxford: Oxford University Press, 1938).

10 Passmore, J., 'The Dreariness of Aesthetics', in Elton, W. (ed.), *Aesthetics and Language* (Oxford: Blackwell, 1954).

11 Tolstot, L., *What is Art?* (London: Bristol Classical Press, 1994).

12 To be found in Barrett, C. (ed.), *Collected Papers in Aesthetics* (Oxford: Blackwell, 1965).

13 Carroll, N., 'Art and the domain of the aesthetic', *British Journal of Aesthetics* **40**, 2 (2000).

14 Tilghman, B., *But is it Art?* (Oxford: Blackwell, 1984) and Ground, I., *Art or Bunk?* (Bristol: Bristol Classical Press).

15 Bell, C., *Art* (London: Chatto, 1920).

16 A modified version of formalism has recently been defended by Nick Zangwill in 'Defusing anti-formalist arguments', *British Journal of Aesthetics* **40** (2000).

17 Dewey, J., *Art as Experience* (New York: Capricorn, 1958).

18 Scruton, R., *Art and Imagination* (London: Methuen, 1974).

19 Some such view is to be found in Walton, K., *Mimesis as Make-Believe* (Cambridge, MA: Harvard University Press, 1990).

20 Bullough, E. '"Psychical distance" as a factor in art and as an aesthetic principle', *British Journal of Psychology* **5**, 1912.

21 (Oxford: Blackwell, 1953).

22 Weitz, M., 'The role of theory in aesthetics', *Journal of Aesthetics and Art Criticism* **15** (1956): 27–35.

23 Danto, A., 'The Art World', *Journal of Philosophy*, **XLI** (1964).

24 The first, and most frequently discussed version of this is to be found in Dickie, G., *Art and the Aesthetic* (Ithaca: Cornell University Press, 1974).

25 Radford, C., 'How can we be moved by the fate of Anna Karennina?', *Proceedings of the Aristotelian Society*, supp. vol. 49 (1975)

26 Yanal, R., *Paradoxes of Emotion and Fiction* (University Park, PA: Pennsylvania State University Press, 1999)

27 Day, J.P., 'Artistic verisimilitude' *Dialogue*, **1**, 1&2 (1962).

28 Lebert, B., *Crazy* (London: Hamish Hamilton, 2000).

29 Levinson, J. (ed.), *Aesthetics and Ethics* (Cambridge: Cambridge University Press, 1998).

30 Winch, P., *Ethics and Action* (London: Routledge and Kegan Paul, 1972) and *Trying to Make Sense* (Oxford: Blackwell, 1987).

31 Feagin, S., *Reading with Feeling* (Ithaca: Cornell University Press, 1996).

32 See Lyas, C., *Aesthetics* (London: Routledge, 1998), chapter 2.

33 A full outline of this work is to be found in Lyas, C., *Aesthetics* (London: Routledge, 1998), chapter 6.

34 Cohen, T., 'Some philosophy, in two parts' in T. Cohen *et al.* (eds), *Pursuits of Reason* (Lubbock: Texas Tech Press, 1993).

35 For a good survey see Hanfling, O. (ed.), *Philosophical Aesthetics* (Oxford: Blackwell, 1992).

36 Summary of story: Despite being the constant target of gross jokes and public humiliation from the university football team players he serves, lowly water boy Bobby Boucher loves his job and thinks dispensing water to dehydrated athletes is life's greatest calling. However, when he is unceremoniously fired, for no reason other than pure ineptitude, Bobby gets a chance as a player for the neighboring down-and-out team. US CD California 00 CV 11517.

    Suzanne Lloyd Hayes, as trustee of the Harold Lloyd Trust *v.*The Walt Disney Company.

37 Currie, G., *The Ontology of Art* (London: Macmillan, 1989).

38 For references and discussion see Stecker, R., 'The Constructivist's Dilemma', *Journal of Aesthetics and Art Criticism* **55** (1997): 43–52.

39 See Lyas, C., 'Wittgensteinian Intentions' in G. Iseminger (ed.), *Intention and Interpretation* (Philadelphia: Temple University Press, 1992).

40 Lyas, C., 'Personal qualities and the intentional fallacy' in Vesey, G. (ed.), *Philosophy and the Arts* (London: Macmillan, 1972).

41 Tormey, A., *The Concept of Expression* (Princeton: Princeton University Press, 1971).

42 Scruton, R., *The Aesthetics of Music* (Oxford: Clarendon Press, 1997); Levinson, J., *The Pleasures of the Aesthetic* (Ithaca: Cornell University Press, 1998); Davies, S., *Music Meaning and Expression* (Ithaca: Cornell University Press, 1994).

43 Goodman, N., *Languages of Art* (Indianapolis: Indiana University Press, 1976).

44 Wollheim, R., *Art and its Objects*, 2nd edn (Cambridge: Cambridge University Press, 1983), supplementary essay 5.

45 Film and photography have become vehemently interesting topics. For an exciting ride see the essays on these subjects in Scruton, R., *The Aesthetic Understanding* (Manchester: New Carcanet, 1973).

46 On which, see the special issue of *The Journal of Aesthetics and Art Criticism* (Spring, 1999) devoted to popular culture.

47 Carroll, N., *The Philosophy of Mass Art* (Oxford: Oxford University Press, 1998).

48 Shusterman, R., *Pragmatist Aesthetics* (Oxford: Blackwell, 1992).

FURTHER READING

The notes will expand your reading on the particular topics mentioned. I have tried to confine these end notes to things that might be understood by a beginner prepared to put in some work. Some further things are worth mentioning.

Encyclopedias

General philosophy

We are, recall, dealing with philosophical aesthetics. I have mentioned terms like 'realism' and 'ontology', which are philosophical terms. You can check these in general encyclopedias of philosophy. The greatest is Edward Craig's magisterially edited *Routledge Encyclopedia of*

Philosophy (which has much on aesthetics in it). A more pocket-friendly (both in size and price) guide is Antony Flew's *The Dictionary of Philosophy* (London: Pan, 1979).

Aesthetics

There is the mighty, four volume *Encyclopedia of Aesthetics* edited by Michael Kelley (Oxford: Oxford University Press, 1999). More handy is Cooper, D. (ed.), *A Companion to Aesthetics* (Oxford: Blackwell, 1992). These contain easily accessible material on most of the topics I have covered. The year 2001 saw publication of Gaut, B., and Lopes, D. (eds), *The Routledge Encyclopedia of Aesthetics*.

Histories

Read the history of Aesthetics. A start can be made with the survey in Dickie, G., *Aesthetics* (Indianapolis: Pegasus, 1971). A fuller version is Beardsley, M., *Aesthetics from Classical Greece to the Present Day* (New York: Macmillan, 1966). More recently there has been Bredin, H. and Santoro-Brienza, L., *Philosophies of Art and Beauty* (Edinburgh: Edinburgh University Press, 2000). For individuals see the encyclopedias above.

Introductions

These proliferate but I mention:

Carroll, N., *Philosophy of Art* (London: Routledge, 1999).
Graham, G., *Philosophy of the Arts*, second edition (London: Routledge, 2000).
Lyas, C., *Aesthetics* (London: Routledge, 1998).

Journals

Both the *British Journal of Aesthetics* and *The Journal of Aesthetics and Art Criticism* contain accessible material.

Web sites

Try these:

Aesthetics on Line (http://www.indiana.edu/~asanl)
For discussion, email majordomo@indiana.edu with the message 'subscribe Aesthetics'.

13

PHILOSOPHY OF RELIGION
W. Jay Wood

INTRODUCTION

Few questions have so engaged philosophical attention as those surrounding religion. We shall survey the central concerns of the philosophy of religion by focusing on two sets of questions, those surrounding the rationality of religious belief, and those asking about the nature of God. Do we have good reasons for thinking that God exists? Do the requirements of good intellectual conduct require that believers have evidence? These and related questions ask what sorts of intellectual requirements, if any, religious believers must satisfy in order to believe rationally. Assuming that God exists, our second set of questions asks what is he like?[1] Throughout the chapter, we shall note how scepticism concerning religion has influenced the arguments and discussion in the philosophy of religion by posing powerful objections against God's existence and against certain understandings of his nature.

IS IT REASONABLE TO BELIEVE THAT GOD EXISTS?

Suppose that God exists, that he is your loving creator, and that your deepest fulfilment now and in the life to come depends upon your being rightly related to him. If this were true, it would be no trivial matter, but one of incalculable weightiness. But what reasons do we have for thinking this supposition is true? At a dinner meeting of the Voltaire Society, a group of Oxford undergraduates once asked Bertrand Russell, a famous atheist philosopher then in his mid-eighties, the following question:

> Suppose you have been wrong about the existence of God. Suppose that the
> whole story were true, and that you arrived at the Pearly Gates to be admitted

by Saint Peter. Having denied God's existence all your life, what would you say to . . . Him? Russell answered without a moment's hesitation. 'Well, I would go up to Him, and I would say, "You didn't give us enough evidence".'[2]

Russell's retort raises a number of important questions. Is there adequate evidence to show that God exists? Do we have an obligation to try to conform our beliefs as best we can to the evidence as we see it? One could read into Russell's remark an implicit belief policy to the effect that one ought to believe only those claims that enjoy the support of adequate evidence. So another question is, 'Must all of our beliefs enjoy the support of adequate evidence before we accept them?'

Evidentialism is the philosophical view that all our beliefs must be supported by adequate evidence if they are to be responsibly held. The philosopher W.K. Clifford put the thesis this way: 'It is wrong always, everywhere, and for anyone, to believe anything upon insufficient evidence.'[3] And at first blush, this position may strike one as eminent good sense. Suppose, for instance, that your financial broker telephones you claiming to have identified an ideal investment for your hard-earned savings. When you ask your broker why she thinks this is a sound investment, she mumbles something about the alignment of the stars and planets and other astral portents. You probably wouldn't heed the advice, and you'd most likely get another broker. Indeed, in so many walks of life, medicine, business, engineering, law, etc., we think it prudent to form our beliefs only in accordance with the preponderance of evidence. Now one might argue that religion should be treated no differently than these other concerns, that one should have ample evidence before accepting religious claims. Indeed, since the personal costs of accepting religious beliefs may be quite high, perhaps a matter should be treated with an extra measure of intellectual caution.

The sentiments of Russell and Clifford can be formulated into what sometimes is called 'the evidentialist objection to religious belief'. In brief, the objection claims that the canons of good intellectual conduct require that we support all our beliefs with adequate evidence. Further, if we lack sufficient evidence to support the claim that God exists (or any other belief for that matter), and if we are to conduct our intellectual lives reasonably and responsibly, then we ought not to believe it. Those who believe that God exists must therefore be judged guilty of intellectual impropriety. In what follows, we consider a number of responses to this challenge.

Historically, philosophers belonging to the tradition of natural theology have expressed robust confidence that the evidentialist's demands can be met. Natural theologians claim that we have evidence aplenty for thinking that God exists, indeed enough to prove decisively that he exists! The approach of natural theology is 'natural' in two senses: 1) the evidence forming the basis of its arguments is available to us simply by using our native, in-born powers of reason, faculties such as perception, introspection, and inferential reasoning; 2) our reason need only turn to nature, to the world around us, in order to find compelling evidence that supports theism.[4] This tradition is famous for a trio of so-called proofs for God's existence: the teleological, cosmological, and ontological arguments. These arguments admit of many variations, only a few of which will be surveyed here.

The teleological argument, also called the design argument, has attracted tremendous attention since it is grounded in a widespread human experience – that of beholding the complexity, grandeur, and apparent design of the world around us. Surely, our initial sentiments suggest, all this could not have arisen by accident, but must be the work of an intelligent agent, and who better than God to produce a universe of such scale and intricacy? William Paley, an eighteenth-century philosopher and theologian, likened the world to a watch. Suppose one were to stroll along the shore and there discover lying on the sand a beautiful gold pocket-watch ticking away in perfect time. Even if we had no prior acquaintance with watches, no one upon finding the watch would suppose it had been accidentally assembled by the waves and tossed onto the beach. We think an object of such complexity and apparent purpose – call it a teleological mechanism – could not have come about accidentally, but could only have come about as the handiwork of some intelligent agent. Indeed, experience uniformly teaches us that when we find teleological mechanisms whose parts appear to have been framed and put together with a purpose – cameras, computers, and cars being good examples – that they were the handiwork of creative agents, and didn't happen by accident. The world around us, says Paley, should intensify such thoughts, for its subtlety, complexity, and size far surpass that of a watch. For when we see similar effects, we reasonably infer similar causes. When a doctor sees a patient displaying the same symptoms as those she recently diagnosed in another patient, she reasonably supposes the same cause. So, too, with signs of teleology.

David Hume, a famous eighteenth-century philosopher and sceptic, criticised arguments like Paley's to devastating effect in his *Dialogues Concerning Natural Religion*. Hume's criticisms focus on three concerns. First, he thought the analogy drawn between a watch and the world a weak one. We know too little about the universe as a whole to say with any confidence that it, like the watch, is marked by teleology throughout; perhaps chaos reigns in the outermost parts of the universe. Imagine going into an immense warehouse filled with countless shelves of books stretching from floor to ceiling. If you were to inspect the first shelf of books and note that they are alphabetically arranged, you could not with any confidence suppose the rest were so arranged. Contemporary science, however, gives us reasons that Hume did not have for thinking that the laws of nature are uniform throughout the universe.

Even if we grant that the universe resembles a watch by being ordered throughout, the argument still fails to establish the existence of the omniscient, omnipotent, omnibenevolent God of theism. If like effects presuppose like causes, then we cannot affirm God's present existence, his unity, his infinity nor, more disturbingly, his goodness. To appreciate Hume's point, consider the pyramids and the Great Wall of China; impressive as these artifacts may be, we know that their designers were not infinite in power, are no longer living and, given the lives sacrificed in their construction, were hardly benevolent. Now consider the universe: by strict parity of reasoning, we likewise do not have grounds for believing in the unity of the world's designer, its present existence, nor its infinite powers. More disturbingly, given the natural disasters that routinely plague us, and the cataclysmic 'heat death' that many scientists say awaits all living things, we have inadequate reason to believe in the designer's goodness. Our universe, if designed, is something of a jalopy, lurching down the road in fits and starts, and far from the sleek, stylish, smooth-running Rolls Royce we'd expect of an infinite God.

Finally, foreshadowing Charles Darwin, Hume surmised that there might be 'hidden springs and principles' within nature that could account for her organisation and development. Evolutionary theory names and describes Hume's 'hidden springs and principles', explaining the existence and behaviour of living things by the twin principles of random genetic mutation and natural selection. Very roughly, natural organisms occasionally undergo random genetic mutations, some of which prove favourable for survival in their particular environment. When these changes make them better able to elude predators and compete for scarce resources, then their genetic material, rather than that of their competitors, has a stronger chance of being passed along to future generations. Nature's work scarcely resembles a watchmaker's, however. Richard Dawkins describes nature's processes thus: 'It has no mind and no mind's eye. It does not plan for the future. It has no vision, no foresight, no sight at all. If it can be said to play the role of watchmaker in nature, it is the *blind* watchmaker.[5] According to Dawkins, 'The universe we observe has precisely the properties we should expect if there is, at bottom, no design, no purpose, no evil and no good, nothing but blind, pitiless indifference. . . . DNA neither knows nor cares. DNA just is. And we dance to its music.'[6]

Recent variations on the design argument may help to revive its fortunes. One variation turns on the work of cellular biologist Michael Behe and mathematicianphilosopher William Dembski,[7] who argue that cells, among other things, are irreducibly complex machines that could not have arisen in the way evolutionary theory suggests. To understand the concept of an irreducibly complex machine, consider a mousetrap. It is a very simple device, consisting of a spring, a hammer, a triggering device, and a platform to hold the parts in place. The important point is that if you take away any one of the parts, the mousetrap won't function at all.

It works only with every part present, or it doesn't work at all. So it is with cells, say these thinkers. They couldn't have acquired their various parts over millions of years by random processes; for without all their parts present, they not only wouldn't perform the function of cells, but there would have been no functional biological precursor from which they could evolve.

A second variation on the design argument, sometimes called the 'fine-tuning' argument, emphasises how our world shows every appearance of having been extraordinarily adjusted to allow for human life. For example, had the explosion at the big bang been stronger or weaker by one part in 10^{60}, then the universe would either have expanded too fast or collapsed back on itself making life impossible. If gravity had been stronger or weaker by some infinitesimal degree, had the level of radiation from the sun been minutely greater than it is, had the structure and forces binding the atom been at all different, then life would not have been possible. According to proponents of the fine-tuning argument, the fact that all these physical constants allow for life is best explained as the fine-tuning of an intelligent agent.

Finally, writers such as C.S. Lewis, Richard Taylor and, most recently, Alvin Plantinga, offer variations of an argument designed to show that the reliability of human reason can't be adequately explained as the outcome of accidental evolutionary processes, but is better explained as the work of a divine agent. If the mechanisms of the evolutionary process are truly random and blind, as Richard Dawkins suggests, fitting us merely to pass on our genes, then why suppose that the human mind has evolved as an instrument able to reason in a reliable, truth-conducive fashion? Richard Taylor nicely illustrates the point here. Suppose, he says, that while travelling by train we gaze out of the window and see dozens of large boulders arranged on a hillside spelling out the words 'The British Railways welcomes you to Wales'. Now it is conceivable, though improbable, that the rocks simply fell into that configuration over hundreds of thousands of years. After all, nature sometimes produces strange and marvellous phenomena. But if you supposed the arrangement of the rocks to be entirely random and accidental, you would be unjustified in supposing that they conveyed a truthful message about your proximity to Wales. You cannot simultaneously see the arrangement as purely accidental and truth-conducive. Likewise, if the arrangement of the molecules in our brains is entirely accidental, we cannot suppose that the mental operations it makes possible are truth-conducive. If our minds are unreliable, then we cannot trust its outputs to tell us the truth about the world. And as Alvin Plantinga reminds us, among the deliverances of reason that we would have reason to doubt is the truth of the evolutionary theory. So to assume that our capacities for thought arose from random evolutionary processes is to be handed a defeater for a justified belief in the evolutionary process!

Cosmological arguments attempt to show that God is needed to explain not just the world's order, but its very existence. One historically important form of cosmological argument is the prime mover, or Kalam argument, the latter arising from the work of medieval Islamic scholars.[8] Briefly, the argument says that the world's history cannot extend into the infinite past, but must have had a first cause, whom proponents claim is God. In order to see why ours cannot be a beginningless universe, we must distinguish the concept of an actual infinite series of objects from a potentially infinite one. A collection is actually infinite if a part of it equals the whole of it. For example, the series of natural numbers '1, 2, 3, . . .' is equivalent to the series of even numbers '2, 4, 6 . . .' even though the natural numbers contain all the even numbers. For any natural number we pick out, we can map an even number onto it without fear of the first series outstripping the resources of the second. A potential infinity is a finite collection to which we can add indefinitely. So, a 10-metre length of rope can theoretically be divided into half, and into half again, indefinitely without reaching the last division. This does not mean that we have actually succeeded in littering the floor with an infinite number of rope pieces. Crucial to the Kalam argument is the claim while actual infinities may exist as theoretical entities in the mind, they cannot be said actually to exist without absurd consequences. Suppose we had a library with an actually infinite number of books. As an actual infinity, it cannot be enlarged. But suppose we were to tear the first page out of the first four hundred books, slap a title page and binding on them, and add it the library. According to mathematics, I would not have succeeded in adding anything! Nor would I add to the number of books if I repeated this process a million times, and this seems counterintuitive. But the proponent of a beginningless world is saying that we have an actual infinite series of events stretching into the past. This has the counterintuitive consequence that the universe will grow no older even if a million years is added to it. Since it appears absurd to say the history of the universe is an actually infinite series, we should hold that the universe had a beginning, and was brought into being by God. Even if we grant, as contemporary cosmology does, that our universe does not extend into the infinite past, critics of prime mover arguments deny that this requires us to postulate God's existence. We can see this by looking at a different form of the cosmological argument, the 'argument from contingency'.

Everything with which we have daily commerce – rocks, trees, chairs, people, and even the sun and stars – are the kinds of things whose non-existence is possible. They are, in a word, 'contingent'. To be sure, we may not be on hand to witness a mountain range reduced to dust, or a star go supernova, but we know that such things happen. The fact that everything making up the universe is contingent invites us to ask: Why are there now, and why should there have ever been contingent entities? Since all contingent objects might never have existed, why is there something rather than nothing at all? And even if contingent objects should begin to exist, they needn't have persisted in being; why should not all contingent things, like the dinosaurs, have become extinct by now? Theists argue that God's creating and sustaining activity best explains the existence of a contingent world. Critics wonder why we have to answer the question of the world's existence. Explanations (at least those typically invoked by science) for empirical phenomena are usually constructed with reference to the causal powers and influence of objects within the universe, existing in space and time. But the cosmological arguer wants an explanation for why the universe itself exists, including all its laws and spatio-temporal and causal relations, and this sort of explanation cannot be given, says the critic. That is why many philosophers, such as Bertrand Russell, deny that explanations for the universe's existence are available; it is, according to such critics, a brute fact susceptible to no further explanation.

The ontological argument is the least intuitively obvious of the aforementioned trio of arguments. At the heart of the argument lies the concept of 'metaphysical necessity'. To say that something is necessarily the case is to say that it is impossible that it be otherwise. 'Logical necessity' is a notion we are familiar with in logic and mathematics. Squares do not just happen to have four equal sides and four equal angles; it is impossible for them to lack these features and still be squares. Four-sidedness is an 'irremovable' or essential property of being a square. Some philosophers argue that things in the world, natural kinds, and not just propositions and abstract mathematical concepts, have essential properties which make them the kinds of things that they are. Philosophers such as Saul Kripke, for instance, have argued that in order for something to be water it must necessarily have two hydrogen and one oxygen atoms. Other things may look and feel like water, but they aren't water if they lack the right essential properties. According to classical theism, God, too, has necessary properties. He doesn't just happen to be wise, he is essentially wise. He couldn't be God and lack perfect wisdom. The same is true of his goodness, his power and, what is more pertinent to the ontological argument, his very existence. If God is an unsurpassably great being, then he can't resemble contingent entities by being the sort of thing who can die, or who depends on something else for his existence. So being unsurpassably great requires that God, if he exists, exists necessarily.

One might protest that, so far, we have succeeded only in linking conceptually the notions of God and necessary existence, but we haven't shown that anything in the world answers to this description. But what could stand in the way of a necessarily existing being actually having existence? A necessarily existing being could fail to exist only if it is impossible that such a being exists. But as proponents of the argument insist, it is not impossible that God exists. It is, in other words, possible that God exists. So, if it is possible that there exists a being who couldn't fail to exist, then he must exist. To use the language of possible worlds, if we say that it is possible that a necessary being exists, then we are admitting that there is a possible world where there resides a being whose essential nature is to exist in every other conceivable world. Once one grants such a being existence in one possible world, one is forced to admit his existence in every other possible world.

Critics of the argument, and they are many, claim that it advances only by some philosophical sleight of hand or some abuse of ordinary language. Kant claimed that 'existence' is implicit in our acts of predication, and doesn't itself function as a predicate. If we ascribe the property of 'redness' to the apple, it would be most peculiar to follow that up with 'and what's more, the apple exists!' To use existence as a predicate, then, is to abuse the conventions of normal language use. Advocates of the argument counter that this may be true of simple existence, but it is not true of the property of 'necessary existence'. Critics that are more recent have questioned an assumption crucial to all formulations of the ontological argument, namely, that it is possible that God exists. Richard Gale, for instance, argues that the presence of morally unjustified evil in the world logically precludes God's existence; in other words, because evil exists, it is impossible that God exists.[9] According to Gale, the phenomenon of human suffering shows that there is no possible world in which God exists.

Thus far, it seems obvious that the traditional arguments of natural theology have failed to prove God's existence to a considerable number of intelligent, and we may suppose, fair-minded folks. Even some of natural theology's most ardent supporters, such as Richard Swinburne and St Thomas Aquinas, are quick to acknowledge its limitations. Even if we can establish by argument that God exists, we cannot establish the great bulk of what constitutes monotheistic orthodoxy. Moreover, we can't establish by argument alone the central doctrines of monotheism's variants: that Jesus is God incarnate, or that there will be a general resurrection of the dead, for example. Moreover, said Aquinas, most persons are, with respect to time, ability, and inclination, unsuited to the rigours of natural theology. 'If the only way open to us for the knowledge of God were solely that of reason,' wrote Aquinas, 'the human race would remain in the blackest shadows of ignorance.'[10] While the traditional proofs may offer evidence enough to convince someone that theism is not unreasonable, the general consensus among philosophers is they don't show theism to be the *only* reasonable view, still less that such arguments can coerce belief in others. But for reasons we will see below, most of our considered judgements and reasonable beliefs about most subjects are held on the basis of reasons we find convincing but not coercive; we know that others of equal intelligence and good will see matters differently to how we do.

Because many philosophers are sceptical that one can find decisive and compelling arguments for theism, some thinkers have instead tried to support theism by offering an overall cumulative case.[11] The general strategy here is not unlike that used in a courtroom. Suppose a prosecutor argues before a jury that the defendant did indeed commit the murder, and offers as her sole piece of evidence that the defendant owned the gun used in the crime. One could hardly expect the jury to be convinced on such scant evidence. But suppose the prosecutor also points out that the only finger prints found on the weapon were those of the defendant, and that the defendant had argued vehemently with the victim just the day before. These additional pieces of evidence would indeed bolster the case for the defendant's guilt. Suppose further, that two eyewitnesses swear under oath that they saw the defendant commit the crime. With each additional piece of evidence, the case for guilt grows stronger. (We've all seen enough detective shows, however, to realise that even such powerful evidence can be refuted; perhaps the eye-witnesses are in cahoots to frame the defendant.) Of course the total case against the defendant must be assessed in the light of the defence attorney's arguments and alibis offered on behalf of the accused. The job of jurors is to evaluate the evidence for and against the accused and reach a verdict. So it is with theism, say proponents of cumulative case arguments. Theists offer an array of evidence, which, while not proving God's existence beyond a shadow of a doubt, nevertheless gives one convincing grounds for believing that God exists.

Religious experiences are frequently cited as providing powerful evidence for God's existence and an important part of any cumulative case for theism. Religious experiences vary in kind and level of specificity. Bernardette Soubirous purportedly saw a vision of the Virgin Mary at Lourdes, and St Paul is said to have heard the voice of Jesus on the road to Damascus. Mystics attest to experiences of the divine that transcend all the distinctions we use to describe experiences of the sensory world, and thus defy description. Perhaps the most common type of religious experience, however, is what is sometimes characterised as a perceptual, but non-sensory experience of God. One commonly hears religious believers testify to the following sorts of experiences: feeling that God was present to one in worship, sensing that God disapproved of one after one treated another unfairly, sensing God's majesty upon gazing into the night sky, or sensing God's peace in the midst of personal crisis. These experiences give rise to what William Alston calls 'manifestation beliefs'; the beliefs that are formed in one on the basis of God's having manifested himself in these ways.[12] On what basis could we judge such experiences veridical? And if they are veridical, what sort of evidential force do they carry?

Many theists argue that religious experiences provide adequate intellectual grounds for thinking that God exists. They urge, first, that we do not impose a stricter standard to judge such experiences than we do to evaluate beliefs formed by perceptual experience. With respect to both, say advocates, we should exercise the principle of charity; we should treat such experiences as veridical unless we have overriding reason to think otherwise. In short, we should judge religious experiences as innocent until proven guilty. Second, we should not think that people whose belief in God is grounded in religious experience must necessarily reason in strict logical fashion from the experience to the belief – although one could do that – any more that we reason in step-by-step fashion from our seeing a house in our field of vision to the belief that there is indeed a house before us. Rather, the experience simply prompts a belief to be formed in us in what is sometimes called a 'cognitively spontaneous' and non-inferential way. Still, critics are quick to point out that we do have reasons for thinking religious experiences guilty rather than innocent. We turn to a few of the more commonly cited objections.

Critics contend that religious experiences of the sort mentioned above can be explained as arising from natural rather than supernatural causes. We might suppose that such experiences are the product of mental illness or psychological malad-justment. Sigmund Freud is famous for having dismissed religious experiences as so much 'wish-fulfilment'.[13] Belief in God is a natural psychological response, says Freud, to the inadequacies of our earthly fathers to protect us from the 'crushingly superior forces of nature'. In short, religion is merely a psychological coping mechanism that helps us to confront accidents, illness, and a death we cannot prevent. Now Freud is right that we sometimes cope with adversity by way of wish fulfilment. Imagine a mother who answers a knock at her door only to discover two army officers bearing the personal belongings of her son, killed in action. The mother, shocked and overwhelmed by the report, refuses to believe that her son is dead. Perhaps, she reasons, the eyewitness reports of his having been killed were mistaken. Perhaps it was only someone who closely resembled him. Perhaps he simply lost his identifying dog tags, and is still alive in a prisoner of war camp. Clearly, the mother's belief that her son is still alive is not grounded in the facts, but in some psychological coping strategy.

Is believing in God in response to religious experiences just like the mother's belief? First, let us note that many Christian thinkers have claimed that humans were created by God to have a natural God-ward orientation. According to these thinkers, we are psychologically constituted so that we can only find genuine fulfilment as persons when rightly related to God. So to be told by Freud that we have a natural psychological propensity to seek security and happiness in God is not something with which theists ought automatically to disagree. In fact, it's just what we should expect if we have been created by God with an impulse to seek him. The genesis of a belief does not in itself show it to be false or even unjustified. But how are we to differentiate Christian belief in God from the mother's belief that her son is still alive? Clearly, we know that someone's belief has arisen from wish-fulfilment when it is obviously false, massively disconfirmed by the evidence, or is the kind of belief we have strong inductive reasons for believing is generally due to wish-fulfilment. The mother's belief can reasonably be so described. But, says the theist, no one has shown that theism is false or massively disconfirmed by the evidence. Nor do we have inductive reasons for supposing that religious beliefs as a whole are generally due to wish fulfilment. The only basis, then, for claiming that theistic belief is the product of wish fulfilment is the assumption that there is no God; but this assumption begs the question against the theist.

Two other often-cited reasons for discounting the evidential value of religious experiences are closely connected. First, critics often note the incompatible, even contradictory, claims about God to which religious experiences sometimes give rise, no doubt due in part to the different cultural circumstances of those who testify to such experiences. Some Buddhists, for instance, experience ultimate reality as impersonal, whereas Christians claim to experience a personal God. Some think that their religious experiences point to a polytheistic deity, whereas others take the deity to be monistic. This much is plain: God cannot be one and many, personal and impersonal at the same time and in the same respect. Critics draw the conclusion that the contradictory nature of religious experiences has the net effect of 'cancelling each other out'; one ought not look to such experiences to provide rational support for religious belief. Second, critics contend that the phenomenon of ongoing, unresolved disagreement about the content of religious experiences among persons we may presume are equally pious and sincere also undercuts the evidential support such experiences offer. If two eyewitnesses, equally well situated when observing a crime, disagree about whether the robber was alone or had accomplices, one might suppose that, on the basis of the eyewitness testimony alone, one should withhold judgement about the matter. So too the disagreements among practitioners of the world's religions also counsel that we do not look to religious experiences to provide rational grounds for belief in God. Do the critic's conclusions undercut the evidential value of religious experiences?

Let us grant for the moment that religious experiences are indeed coloured by the cultural backgrounds of those who have them, and that these experiences have given rise to incompatible accounts of divine reality. Why suppose, however, that this fact robs all religious experiences of their evidential value? After all, one might argue, all experiences are somewhat 'theory-laden'. The contribution of one's background occurs in both a direct and indirect way. It is widely acknowledged, for instance, that scientists with different theoretical backgrounds sometimes disagree about what they are 'seeing' when looking at astronomical data; they have different 'Gestalts', as it were. Less directly, two paleontologists can look at an identical fossil record, but owing to different theoretical assumptions, reach incompatible conclusions about why the dinosaurs died. But we don't think that the holders of these incompatible scientific beliefs are irrational. Since it would be inappropriate to impose a harsher standard on religious beliefs than we apply to other areas of inquiry, we must deny that the fact of their being theory-laden, even when this gives rise to incompatible interpretations, automatically robs them of their evidential value. Moreover, some studies suggest that young children, who have not been as significantly shaped by the theories their cultures have about religion, tend to offer more uniform descriptions of their religious experiences. As we mature, we tend to encode our experiences in the symbol system of a particular culture in order more easily to recall and communicate the experience's content.[14]

What might defenders of religious belief say about the long-standing disagreements over what, if anything, religious experiences show about God? Does protracted disagreement undermine the rationality beliefs grounded in such experiences? Hardly. After all, most academicians hold views while fully aware that others of equal intelligence and training hold different views. This is the norm rather than the exception in philosophy, for example. One philosopher may, consequent upon much reflection, hold that humans are entirely material beings, while another equally reflective philosopher may hold that humans are not merely material. Two economists may survey the same data and hold different beliefs about the effect on the economy of another cut to the prime lending rate. Similar disagreements hold amongst psychologists, political scientists, and so on. If unresolved disagreement, by itself, bars us from holding the disputed beliefs in a rational manner, then most academicians are irrational in a great deal of what they believe. But this is an unpalatable conclusion; rather, we should reject the principle which requires that only those beliefs are rational which are not the subject of protracted disagreement.

The phenomenon of morality offers another piece of evidence cited by theists as an important part of any cumulative case. Consider the following widespread, if not universal phenomena: there is no culture that lacks a sense of right and wrong, good and bad, just and unjust. In addition, there is the pervasive phenomenon of sensing that one has failed to live by the demands of the moral law, however conceived, and that one has thereby incurred guilt, or stain, or fault, or blemish, or the like. As a result, people everywhere attest to there being a 'moral gap' between the kinds of persons they are and the kinds of persons they ought to be. This in turn leads to the universal phenomenon among cultures of seeking ablution, cleansing, forgiveness, etc.[15] Still further, there is widespread unanimity among developed cultures, concerning fundamental moral precepts: incest is wrong, cowardice is wrong, one should act justly toward those in one's community, and so on.[16] These common moral judgements are what some philosophers call first principles of the natural law: elemental moral truths that we apprehend through reason. How shall we explain these phenomena? Theists, obviously, will argue that the best way of accounting for these features of human experience is that God, himself a being perfect in moral goodness, has created us as moral beings. His moral nature is thus the ground or basis for our judgements about right and wrong, justice and injustice. This is not the only explanation, however.

Some evolutionary theorists have cited the principle of natural selection as an alternative to the theistic explanation of the phenomenon of morality. We have a better chance of insuring the survival of the human gene pool if we don't marry our sisters, murder and steal from one another and if, in general, we follow such rules as make for organised communities of any sort. In short, there is a socio-biological explanation for the phenomenon of morality. And the similarities in moral precepts among literate cultures are easily explained as the result of similar socio-biological needs among humans. We all need to eat, sleep, procreate, and conduct business in predictable, relatively safe environments, so it is no wonder that there is similarity in our moral precepts. Does a purely naturalistic explanation suffice to explain moral phenomena?

Consider the world Bertrand Russell thinks we inhabit as described in his famous essay 'A free man's worship': 'Brief and powerless is man's life on earth. On him and all his race, the slow sure doom falls pitiless and dark. Blind to good and evil, reckless of destruction, omnipotent matter rolls on its relentless way'.[17] On Russell's naturalist view, we are but 'accidental collocations of atoms'; all human loves, beliefs, thoughts, and feelings, 'all the noonday brightness of human genius, are destined to extinction in the vast death of the solar system'.[18] Theists and naturalists disagree about whether a world such as the one Russell thinks we inhabit is an adequate basis for explaining and motivating the moral life. In *Crime and Punishment*, Dostoevsky writes 'if God does not exist, all things are permissible'. He means to suggest, I think, that a godless universe fails to motivate the moral life adequately. He was sensitive to the curious incongruity of admitting, on the one hand, that we are accidental products of a universe that will destroy us and, on the other hand, believing that we should exercise self-control, be generous and kind to others, master our fears and act courageously, and strive to meet the rigorous demands of the moral life. Why not simply yield to anger, injustice, envy, cowardice, and laziness? Why not eat, drink, and be merry, for tomorrow we die? Immanuel Kant, one of natural theology's greatest critics, nevertheless felt compelled to posit God's existence in order to motivate and preserve morality. For he recognised that in this life, morality doesn't always pay. Sometimes the just are persecuted for their justice, and robber barons that dispossess widows and orphans sleep like babies and live to a ripe old age. Kant thought we must postulate God's existence to satisfy the practical concern of justice being meted out in the life to come.

Let us take stock of the argument thus far. The cumulative case reasoner has offered in support of theism evidence from fine-tuning, the contingency of the universe, religious experience, and moral arguments. To this, theists could add, among other things, the evidence of alleged miracles, answers to prayer, personal transformation, and relevant historical data. Cumulative case reasoners claim that this collection of evidence makes it more probable than not that God exists. And if God's existence is more probable than not, more likely to be true than false, then it is certainly rational to believe that he exists.[19]

We have noticed that there is an inescapable interpretive or subjective element to assessing the force of evidence. Religious believers often cite as evidence for their belief in God experiences and other beliefs that their critics simply don't acknowledged as acceptable evidence. Not only do people disagree over what counts as acceptable grounds, they disagree over the 'weightiness' or significance of the grounds we do acknowledge. Jurors that disagree about a defendant's guilt may not disagree that the testimony given by the prosecution's star witness is relevant to the case; they disagree instead as to its significance, some investing it with tremendous import, others with less. Disagreements about the saliency of evidence are legion, arising in debates about history, aesthetics, exegesis, morals, law, the natural sciences, even a boxing match, and indeed anywhere for which interpretive judgement is called.

How are disagreements about saliency settled? Indeed, why do they arise at all? Typically, we invite our interlocutor to look again and see whether he or she is not as impressed as we are by what we take to be some crucial piece of evidence. Sometimes new evidence arises that throws the original evidence in a new light. Unfortunately, some of our disagreements revolve around issues buried in the past, for which we cannot reasonably expect dramatic new evidence to emerge.

We puzzle not only about how disagreements over saliency are settled, but why they occur at all. Why should our standards of evidence be so variable? The reasons here are numerous and complex. No doubt our finitude, and the limitations imposed by our cultural, historical, and linguistic perspectives play a large part. Another factor is training. If I lack training in radiology, I might stare directly at an X-ray, but not see the black and white patterns before me as evidence that the patient has a tumour.

I want also to suggest that whether or not we are suitably positioned to see and appreciate the evidence for a particular view depends on what kinds of persons we are: whether we are morally and intellectually virtuous or vicious.[20] A long-standing tradition reaching as far back as Plato and Aristotle suggests that our cognitive powers cannot function as they ought, if they are not appropriately connected with emotions and concerns that have been trained to virtue. Consider someone whose intellectual character is marked by gullibility, superstitiousness, or willful naiveté. Contrast this person with someone in whom discernment, prudence, and love of truth have taken deep root. The latter individual is more likely than the former to discern evidence and to assess its probative force aright. Further, moral virtues and vices often bear upon our pursuit of the truth. If I am a racist, it is likely that I will depreciate the evidence given in defence of some person of colour, and estimate too high the evidence offered by the prosecutor. So, we see that in religion, and in many other areas where we seek to know the truth and hold justified beliefs, that our ability to see and appreciate evidence for some claim depends on what sorts of persons we are.

So far, we have assumed that in order for theists to be justified in believing that God exists, they must have an argument, which shows theism likely to be true. Some theists, however, question whether one's believing in God requires evidence to be reasonable. Why think that faith commitments must pass muster before the bar of reason in order to be justifiably believed? Two developed positions, Pascal's pragmatic argument and Alvin Plantinga's 'reformed epistemology', argue that belief in God can be rationally acceptable without the benefit of argumentative support.

Blaise Pascal, the brilliant seventeenth century French mathematician, scientist, and philosopher, posed the question: 'God is or he is not. But to which side shall we incline? Reason can decide nothing here.'[21] According to Pascal, human reason alone can tell us neither what God is like, nor whether he exists. Reason's impotence in divine matters stems partly from the gross disparity between our finite cognitive faculties and the infinite being about whom we inquire. Therefore, we are in a state of evidential equilibrium with respect to theism. One might suppose that reason's council in such cases would be that we suspend judgement, that we adopt agnosticism regarding God's existence. And such council would be right if the only reasonable basis for accepting a belief is that it enjoys the support of evidence. Pascal, however, thought that while there may not be evidence sufficient to show that theism is true, there are nevertheless *practical* or *prudential* reasons for believing. Suppose God exists, and that only by believing in him will we gain heaven or some other tremendous benefit. Pragmatic considerations bearing on our personal well-being counsel that we believe. As Pascal puts it, by believing in God, 'If you gain, you gain all; if you lose, you lose nothing.' Consider an analogy. Suppose while at a casino, you espy a lone croupier off in the corner flipping a coin into the air. You wander over and ask what kind of game one plays at her table. 'Heads or tails,' comes the response. 'What do I get if I guess correctly?' 'A million dollars,' she says. 'And what does it cost to play?' you ask. 'Nothing,' she replies. Although one has no more reason for thinking that heads or tails will come up, who wouldn't take advantage of that wager? Even if it cost you a thousand dollars a toss, you'd still think the risk negligible compared to what you stand to gain if you guess correctly. (Agnostics should note that no winnings go to those who stand on the sidelines and refuse to play the game.) The stakes in religion are still greater, Pascal thinks, for if one believes in God and it turns out that God exists, then one gains eternal happiness.

As we've already seen, many philosophers deny that reason is impotent to determine if theism is true. But even if Pascal is correct about reason's inability to tip the evidential scales one way or the other, many philosophers nevertheless judge pragmatic arguments to be an inadequate basis for licensing belief. First, Pascal's wager offers no council as to what sort of God we should believe in. Since reason can tell us nothing about God's nature, why bet on monotheism? Perhaps the most practical thing would be to hedge one's bets and embrace polytheism. Second, it seems that prudential reasons can license, at best, a kind of tentative faith, a faith always on the lookout for evidence that might settle the matter of theism's truth decisively. Yet the great monotheistic religions recommend that we believe in God with full devotion, a posture pragmatic reasons can't seem to underwrite. Can Pascalians rebut such objections?

To address the 'many gods' objection, Pascalians ask us to recall that our deliberations about God's existence and nature lie behind a veil that reason cannot penetrate. Can prudential considerations guide us on how to wager? Well, among the gods that might exist, there are those that dispense rewards only if believed in, and those who dispense rewards even if not believed in. It makes sense to bet on the former, since we will suffer no loss by failing to believe in the latter. And among the gods who reward only when believed in, there are those that are limited in goodness, power, and wisdom, and those that aren't. Since nothing can frustrate the intention of an almighty God to dispense rewards, and something could potentially frustrate the will of a weaker deity, it makes sense to bet on an all-powerful God. And if one adds that there are independent a priori reasons for thinking that there can't be more than one omnipotent being, then the God of monotheism looks like the best bet. The second criticism is based on the assumption that we cannot commit ourselves whole-heartedly to beliefs grounded in prudential considerations alone. Is this correct? Suppose a doctor tells you that you have only a 50/50 chance of recovering from some illness. Suppose too, that you know that people who believe unreservedly that they will recover have a higher likelihood of recovering from illness. Would it not make sense to believe as fervently as possible that one would recover?

Alvin Plantinga advances the view that belief in God can be 'properly basic', that is justifiably held in the absence of argumentative support.[22] First, note that all persons hold some beliefs in this basic way. Examples include one's belief that the future will be like the past, that one's senses reliably tell us the truth about our physical surroundings, that one's memory and other cognitive faculties work in a reliable fashion, that there are other minds; we don't adduce evidence for such beliefs before accepting them. We are psychologically so constituted, that when we have the requisite sorts of experiences, we simply find the corresponding belief formed in us spontaneously and non-inferentially. When someone greets me on the street, I immediately respond, as to another person; I do not deliberate first about whether what I take to be a person is really a clever automaton or holographic projection. Plantinga claims that our belief in God, like our belief in an external world, can be accepted in the same basic way. A belief in God can be the immediate and non-inferential response to experiences such as observing the majestic grandeur of a mountain range, beholding the star-studded sky above, feeling that God disapproves of one's having treated someone unfairly, or feeling that God is comforting one in times of trial. These experiential circumstances serve as the occasions for coming to believe that God exists without the benefit of explicit reasoning.

Plantinga's position should be distinguished from fideism, the view that religious beliefs ought solely to be matters of faith, and that we cannot or should not endeavour to support them with reason. On the contrary, Plantinga thinks that one's taking God's existence as properly basic can itself be viewed as a function of reason, but not *reasoning*. He thinks that humans have a '*sensus divinitatus*', an innate disposition to believe in God in response to a wide range of experiential circumstances. If there is such a cognitive faculty, and if it operates reliably in the environment for which it was intended, then one's belief may be said to have warrant, that quality, enough of which, when added to true belief yields knowledge.

We have so far surveyed a variety of strategies theists employ to show that belief in God is rationally justifiable. But we have neglected to consider what is thought by many to be the strongest piece of counter-evidence against theism – the problem of evil or human suffering. 'Moral evil' refers to the suffering, physical and emotional, that we unjustly inflict on one another, theft, murder, rape, and acts of terrorism being representative examples. 'Natural evils' refer to the suffering we endure at the hands of nature, diseases, earthquakes, tornadoes, and pestilence being obvious examples. Now if God were perfect in wisdom, power, and goodness, why would he permit us – and animals for that matter – to suffer so? Surely he is powerful enough to deter any suffering we might experience. Furthermore, reasons the critic, if he is perfect in goodness, he would surely wish to alleviate our suffering. Yet intense, widespread suffering persists. If all suffering were deserved or were accompanied by some evident compensatory good, we might then reconcile it with God's goodness and power. According to critics of theism, however, much suffering, that of infant children and animals for instance, is undeserved, and no such compensating good offsets it; it is unmitigated, or gratuitous suffering.

What, precisely, does the phenomenon of suffering show? Some critics of religious belief argue that suffering makes it impossible for theism to be true, since if God did exist, he would both want and be able to eliminate all human suffering. Since evil abounds, it shows conclusively that God does not exist, thereby making belief in God irrational. Others critics argue, more modestly, that the phenomenon of human suffering shows that God's existence is unlikely. More modest still is the position of William Rowe who, as a self-described 'friendly atheist', believes that, on balance, the amount and severity of human suffering makes theism improbable. He believes that a theist who sizes up the evidence differently might nevertheless be rational in accepting theism. Let us examine, however, the various responses theists have made to the problem of human suffering.

The term theodicy signifies an attempt to reconcile the perfect justice and goodness of God with human suffering, and admits of both a strong and weak sense.

In its strong sense, theodicies purport to explain why God permits all the specific evils we experience, whereas in its weaker sense, theodicies – or defences as they are sometimes called – attempt only to offer plausible reasons a perfectly good and powerful God might have for permitting us to suffer. Recently, philosophers friendly to theism have tended to restrict themselves to 'defences' or theodicies in only the weak sense, since whatever God's precise reasons may be for allowing us to suffer, they no doubt turn on goods and purposes that he is realising throughout history and throughout the whole of creation. But we simply aren't privy, and couldn't be as finite knowers, to the complex balance of goods and evils being realised throughout all of time and creation. So even if God has justifying reasons for allowing evil, it's not clear that we could fathom them in all their detail.

The limitations of the human perspective bear also on claims that our world has gratuitous or pointless evil. Critics of theism insist that while we may not occupy a 'God's eye' point of view concerning the possible reasons for evil, we are nevertheless not entirely in the dark about what such reasons might be. Moreover, since the our limited human perspective is the only one from which determinations about the rational propriety of religious belief may be made, we have no choice but to avail ourselves of such evidence as comes within our purview. And if, from our human standpoint, we can't see any countervailing goods that would provide morally justifiable reasons for God's allowing us to suffer as we do, then we cannot but judge theism to be rationally unacceptable.

This last inference, however, is precisely where theists urge caution. From the claim 'I don't see any countervailing goods for God's permitting us to suffer', may one legitimately infer 'there are no countervailing goods'? Consider some analogous cases:

a) I don't see any milk in the refrigerator, therefore there isn't any.
b) A chess novice declares, 'I don't see any way for Kasparov to win the chess game, therefore there isn't any way for him to win.'
c) I've never seen aliens, therefore there aren't any.[23]

In each case, the reasoner employs what is sometimes called a 'noseeum' inference: since I can't see some phenomenon, it doesn't exist. But clearly, there are legitimate and illegitimate 'noseeum' inferences. The first is clearly legitimate, since our repertoire of perceptual faculties and the proximity of the refrigerator's contents make it reasonable to think that if there were some milk, it would be within view. The second is clearly illegitimate. The tyro is in no position to assert that because he can't see any manoeuvres available to a chess grand master, there aren't any. His skills aren't suitably developed to make such an inference reasonable. What about the last example? Does the fact that I haven't seen any aliens give me good reason to think there aren't any? Here we might counsel withholding judgement, since we simply don't know anything about aliens. For all we know, they may wish to remain undetected, or not to associate with species they consider inferior. Which case does the religious sceptic's most closely resemble? If failing to see countervailing goods is on a par with the chess novice, then clearly, we should consider that God might have reasons for allowing evil that we fail to grasp. If, however, we are agnostic about the detectability of countervailing reasons, we can't rule out decisively the possibility of there being such reasons.

So what, then, are the countervailing reasons most often cited for God's allowing us to suffer? One of the most famous efforts at reconciling the goodness and justice of God with our suffering is the free will defence, variations of which having been offered by Alvin Plantinga, Richard Swinburne, and John Hick, among others. If God is unsurpassably great, as theists suppose, what could possibly be his reason for creating us? Aquinas claims that 'we show reverence to God not for his benefit, since creatures can add nothing to the fullness of glory he already has in himself, we do it for our benefit, so as to subject our spirit to him and perfect it.'[24] On Aquinas's view, if God created us, it isn't because he is lonely, needy, or in some sense incomplete; he creates us not to receive a benefit but to confer one. And what might that benefit be? Many theists suggest it is to draw us into friendship with himself, wherein our highest beatitude consists. But if God wishes to draw us into friendship with himself, one with genuine mutuality, then he must make us free with respect to himself. God cannot coerce our friendship and have it be genuine; if we enter into friendship with God, it must be voluntary. But in order for us to respond to God voluntarily, we must be created with freedom of the will, which leaves open the possibility that we will refuse God's overtures to us. For God cannot create us free and simultaneously guarantee that we will choose friendship with him. We might instead exercise our freedom to reject his offer and rebel against his plans and purposes for us. And according to the free-will defender, a great deal of the suffering we experience is attributable to human malevolence and rejecting God's purposes for us.

If, for reasons scientific, philosophical, or theological, one believes that humans lack the requisite sense of freedom of the will, then one will not find the free will defence plausible. Critics of the free will defence raise additional worries. Why does God permit humans to abuse their creaturely freedom to the degree that they do? It is reasonable to suppose a perfectly competent parent won't intervene to settle every sibling squabble; it's good for children to learn to work such matters out on their own. But when one sibling grabs the kitchen meat cleaver with malevolent designs upon her older brother, we think that freedom to settle such matters on their own comes to an end. In fact, we'd blame any parent who wouldn't intervene in such a situation. Why hasn't God, the critic of religion asks, done more to circumscribe the range within which our free choices take place? Theists respond by claiming that there are no clear lines of demarcation separating permissible and impermissible uses of freedom. Moreover, were God to circumscribe the scope of our freedom, and the evils to which it can give rise, we would lose other valuable goods.

According the 'greater good' defence, God will not allow us to suffer unless it is indispensable for our achieving some equivalent or greater good we are better off having than lacking, and for which our suffering is necessary. Many theists argue that our suffering through this 'vale of tears' is necessary for us to cultivate moral virtues such as compassion, forbearance, generosity, and courage, traits that ideally suit us for this life and for friendship with God. What would it mean to be compassionate in a world where there were no tears, generous in a world with no want, courageous in a world where one could not suffer a scratch? Better a world, then, that contains suffering and the opportunity for virtue, than a world that contains neither. Suffering makes possible other important goods for which it (or the possibility thereof) is a necessary condition. Richard Swinburne argues that our freedom is a great good that allows us to be deeply and meaningfully responsible for one another's welfare and the welfare of the world. God allows us the good of co-operating with him in being genuine agents in the world, entrusting to us the care of one another and the world. But our genuine agency makes it possible for us to neglect the care of others, thereby contributing to the misery of others. Moreover, for us to be responsible agents, we must be able to form rational judgements concerning the likely effects of our actions. This, in turn, requires that God govern the world in accordance with regular natural laws that make such judgements possible. But these same natural regularities also make possible tidal ebbs and flows, shifting plates, and a self-balancing ecosystem that occasionally leads to human and animal suffering.

Philosophers disagree about the respective merits of the arguments for and against theism based on suffering. They disagree about what concerns should be most salient in such determinations. Perhaps this is why philosophers such as William Rowe, himself an atheist, does not think that the problem of evil is sufficient to show that no theists can be rational in their belief.

IF GOD EXISTS, WHAT IS HE LIKE?

If God exists, it naturally leads one to ask what sort of being he is. Questions about God's nature can be motivated by both theistic and non-theistic motives. In his *Proslogion*, Anselm of Canterbury prays to God asking 'Lord, You give understanding to faith, grant me that I may understand, as much as You see fit, that You exist as we believe You to exist, and that you are what we believe you to be.'[25] Anselm takes metaphysical investigations into God's nature to follow naturally upon one's desire to know the object of one's devotion better. Critics of theism urge careful study of the metaphysics of theism as a way of showing that the concept of an omnipotent, omniscient, and omnibenevolent being is incoherent, and if incoherent, unbelievable. Regardless of one's motivation, metaphysical investigations into God's nature are philosophically rich in their own right, shedding light on the nature of necessity, being, time, and a host of other concepts of general metaphysical interest.

How do we gain knowledge of God, or settle disputes about his nature? Jews, Christians, and Muslims, point to God's special revelation of himself, either in holy writings or to appropriate authorities, as the best source for informing our judgements about God's attributes and his dealings with creation. In addition to special revelation, many theists think there is a 'general revelation' made to all humans, that allows us to discern truths about God's existence and his nature.

Three approaches characterise most philosophical efforts to depict God's nature by relying on reason alone. 'Creation theology' begins with the common theistic assumption that God is the creator and sustainer of the universe, and reasons 'backward' to determine what traits such a creator must possess to accomplish these ends. Obviously, a creator and sustainer of the world would have to possess tremendous power and intelligence as well as the ongoing will to preserve it in being. David Hume would no doubt remind us, however, that such an approach alone cannot help us to fix the fine points of our theology. Among other things, we cannot by creation theology alone determine if God is perfect in goodness, more or less likely to communicate with us, or what steps humans should take to be rightly related to him. 'Comparative theology' tries to forge a composite portrait of God by examining the central insights gleaned about him from the world's major religions. Unfortunately, the world's religions say incompatible things about God, for example, that God is one and that God is many. The disagreements dividing the world's religions thus give us grounds for suspecting that reason cannot establish any substantive 'lowest common denominator' conception of God. 'Perfect being theology' depicts God's nature simply by reflecting a priori on what must be true for God to be the maximally perfect being: as Anselm expresses it, 'the being than which no greater can be conceived.'[26] If God is the being than which no greater is possible, it follows that he is unsurpassably great in wisdom, power, or goodness, and in every other property that contributes to an exalted status. But in what does such perfection consist? Philosophers disagree at many points about the nature of a maximally perfect being. Is it more perfect for God to be able to experience emotions or to be 'impassible', as many medieval theologians believed? Will a perfect God control every event that occurs or does God display greater power by coordinating his actions with those of genuinely free creatures? Can a perfect God change in any way or allow his actions to be 'conditioned' or affected by those of his creatures? Our conflicting intuitions about the nature of a perfect being suggest the limitations of providing a determinate picture of God based on a priori reason alone. Most likely we test our convictions about God's nature (or the incoherence thereof) through a kind of 'reflective equilibrium' that involves the ongoing modification of our views in the light of our encounters with the thinking of others, especially as those opinions vary with our own.

How powerful is God? As the old schoolyard question asks, 'Is he powerful enough to make a stone so big that he'd be unable to lift it?' Before turning to this question, we must consider some preliminary matters. First, recall the point made earlier that God's unsurpassable greatness requires that he embody every perfection essentially; that is, the perfections God has he cannot fail to have and still be God. If there was a tremendously powerful being who was also dimwitted and mean, then that being, however impressive his power, would not be God. Second, our judgements about the extent of God's power must be assessed in the light of his total nature, his goodness, wisdom, immateriality, and so on. So, our question might be put more carefully by asking 'What does it mean to be perfect in power, while simultaneously possessing all the other attributes characteristic of divinity?' Finally, humans, equipped with finite cognitive faculties cannot hope to plumb the depths of the divine nature. While we cannot know God exhaustively, however, it does not follow that we can know nothing of God. The philosophical tradition that has given rise to reflections about God's nature has largely assumed that our minds are not utterly impotent to discover truths about his nature.[27]

Traditional theists frequently offer two qualifications concerning God's perfect power. First, as Thomas Aquinas argued, being omnipotent doesn't require that God be able to bring about states of affairs that are logically contradictory or incompatible with other parts of his nature. For instance, God, who is the perfection of all being, cannot make it such that he both exists and doesn't exist simultaneously, for that would be contrary to his nature. According to Aquinas, when one utters a contradiction, one doesn't successfully identify a coherent state of affairs, so one hasn't actually pointed out something that God can't do; one has only spouted gibberish. One might protest: 'Shall the power of an infinite God be circumscribed by human logic?' Could not, as Descartes seems to in his correspondence with Mersenne, claim that God is above logic and in fact invents all necessary truths? If God had wanted to, on this view, he could have made it such that I am simultaneously over six feet tall and under six feet tall. Setting aside the fact that we can't impart any sense to such strings of words, numerous other problems beset this view. For instance, if God were able to do what to us is contradictory, then his wisdom, and the rest of his nature for that matter, must remain utterly inscrutable to us. Moreover, if God is inscrutable, then he is not the sort of being one can look to for guidance or count on to keep his promises. The second limitation on divine power – if it is a limitation at all – is that the scope of God's power be understood in the light of his other attributes. God is perfect in power, consistent with his being all-knowing and perfectly good.

Our earlier discussion of the free-will defence reveals another interesting limit on divine power. Not only cannot God do the logically impossible, there are logically *possible* states of affairs that God cannot 'strongly actualise' or directly bring about. For example, if I am genuinely free with respect to a wide range of morally significant actions, then whether I choose to act in a morally appropriate or inappropriate manner is up to me. If God necessitates my choices, then I'm not genuinely free. God can, to be sure, control whether or not I ever come to exist, as well as the morally significant situations in which I find myself. But he can't, consistent with my freedom, make me free and guarantee that I won't choose in a morally inappropriate way. So, we see that if God creates a world containing creatures with libertarian freedom, then there are further restrictions on divine power.

But what about the stone? Some technicalities aside, philosophers offer several solutions. One solution suggests that God can in fact create such a stone, but it poses a problem for him only if he decides to create it. Were he to create the unliftable stone, it would, ironically, be his last act as an omnipotent being. But as long as he refrains from this particular action, he remains omnipotent. This solution, however, goes against the widespread theistic belief that God possesses his attributes essentially. Another solution points out that God's creating a stone so heavy he subsequently won't be able to lift it logically reduces to 'The being that can lift anything can create something he cannot lift.' Since it is no slight on omnipotence not to be able to bring about the incoherent, we really have no paradox of the stone.

To say God is omniscient is to claim that he knows of every truth that it is true, and of every falsehood that it is false. But what should be included within the scope of 'every truth'? Does God have exhaustive knowledge of the future? Does he, for example, know from all eternity everything I will ever think or do? Does He have knowledge of alternative futures – futures that would have come about had free creatures made different choices to the ones that they did make?

One of the main philosophical challenges posed by saying that God is omniscient rests not with the claim itself, but with its alleged implications for human freedom. If God knew from the foundation of the world that I will go to the zoo tomorrow, then it looks as though I'm not free to act otherwise than as God foreknows. Plainly, God cannot be omniscient and be mistaken in his belief that I will go to the zoo. Moreover, most of us think that the past is fixed and unalterable; past events are, to use common terminology, 'accidentally necessary.' Not even God can now undo the fact that Winston Churchill was Prime Minister during the Second World War. So if God knew in the past that I would go to the zoo tomorrow, and he cannot be mistaken, then it seems impossible that I act otherwise than as God knows. To claim I could act otherwise, say, by going to the movies instead, appears to entail either that I can cause God to have a false belief, or that I have power to change the past and what God has always believed, claims that traditional theists cannot concede. And if I cannot act otherwise than as God knows I will act, then I am not free. So to affirm with classical theism that God is omniscient seems to require that we deny humans are free to choose amongst alternative courses of action.

Richard Swinburne has argued that the view of foreknowledge just articulated interferes with God's freedom as well as ours. If God knows infallibly from the foundation of the world every decision he will make, then he too is not free to deviate from what he infallibly knows. In order to accommodate the traditional belief that God is free, Swinburne limits God's knowledge to all propositions about the past, present, and only those propositions about the future which are physically necessitated by the past.

> That God is omniscient only in the attenuated sense would of course – given that he is perfectly free and omnipotent – have resulted from his own choice. In choosing to preserve his own freedom (and to give freedom to others), he limits his own knowledge of what is to come. He continually limits himself in this way by not curtailing his or men's future freedom.[28]

God could have exhaustive knowledge of the future simply by decreeing all that will ever occur, though he refrains from this for freedom's sake.

Luminaries such as Augustine, Anselm, and Aquinas, claim that the problem of divine foreknowledge and human freedom is a pseudo-problem insofar as it suggests that God be in time. Strictly speaking, God does not have *fore*knowledge. If God is outside of time, he is aware only of one eternal present, a single unvarying glance of all that ever happens. No moment of time is any less available to his gaze than another. Merely to observe an event occurring, however, is not thereby to cause that event to happen. From my vantage point atop a hill, I may observe two cars on the winding road below me headed inescapably toward a collision, but my presently seeing this unfold does not cause it to be so. If this analogy is apt, then neither does God's observing the events of history unfold efficiently cause those events. Many thinkers are reluctant to avail themselves of this solution, however, as positing a God outside of time poses additional problems for notions of providence, prayer, and other sorts of divine–human interaction.

Some philosophers, following remarks in Aristotle's *On Interpretation*, hold that God is in time but lacks knowledge of the future because, strictly speaking, there are no true statements about the future for God to know. And if there are no truths about the future, then one doesn't depreciate divine omniscience to say God doesn't know them. Why would someone say there are no truths about the future? One analysis of what it means to say a proposition is true holds that there are truth bearers and truth makers. A truth bearer, such as the proposition 'Stonehenge is in England' is made true by Stonehenge's actually being in England. By contrast, the proposition 'Prince Harry will have four children' has no corresponding truth maker, no current state of affairs to make the proposition true. Philosophical and theological problems beset this simple analysis of statements about the future. First, many other true statements we make, such as the universal generalisation that 'All crows are black' is not grounded in any current state of affairs, since the generalisation is about all crows, past, present, and presumably future. Second, this proposal runs counter to the traditional theistic claim that God not only knows the future, but prophesies to humans that certain events will take place.

Is there a way to keep both divine foreknowledge and a robust account of human freedom? Following suggestions from the late medieval philosopher William of Ockham, some philosophers argue that not all statements about the past are, strictly speaking, irrevocably true in a way that makes them accidentally necessary.[29] They distinguish between what are called 'hard facts' about the past and 'soft facts' about the past, only the former being accidentally necessary. Consider the proposition 'The First World War began in 1914'; it is strictly about the past, and no one, not even God, can alter its being true. Now consider the claim 'The First World War began eighty years before I took my wife on a cruise.' This claim is only partially about the past, since it is about how some fact in the past is related to what is now within my power. I can make this claim, partially about the past, true by picking up the telephone and booking a cruise for my wife and myself. Statements of the form 'God knew that S would do A', do not express irrevocably true hard facts about the past, but soft facts, whose truth is contingent on my free actions now or in the future. So it is false that God's having forever known about what I will do tomorrow is accidentally necessary in the sense that puts them beyond my counterfactual power.

One final, ingenious solution for reconciling divine omniscience and human freedom stems from the work of another late medieval philosopher, Luis de Molina and, appropriately enough, is called 'molinism'. Molinism's robust account of divine omniscience describes three aspects to God's knowledge. First, and logically most prior, is the knowledge God has by his very nature an essentially omniscient being. This 'natural knowledge' encompasses knowledge of everything that it is logically possible to bring about as well as knowledge of all necessary truths, such as the truths of logic and mathematics. God's 'free knowledge' consists of the knowledge God has owing to his decision to bring about some particular creation scenario. Of course God was free either to create or not to create and, what's more, free to select from amongst an impressively wide array of creation scenarios. But once he selects one, then he has 'post-volitional' knowledge of all the truths characterising the world he has selected. But after God's natural knowledge, and logically prior to his free knowledge, is what Molina called God's 'middle knowledge', for it is between the others in the logical progression of God's thinking about what to create. (There is no temporal progression, since God is outside of time, according to Molina.) By his middle knowledge, God knows what philosophers call 'the counterfactuals of freedom'. These propositions state, for every possible free creature God could create, and every free situation it confronts, how that creature would exercise its libertarian freedom. In addition to knowing the actual future, God knows possible futures that would have come about had his creatures made different choices, or if he had populated the world with different free creatures. This knowledge gives God meticulous, providential control over creation, for by knowing all the possible free creatures, and all the choices they would make in any free situations they confront, God was able to select just those free agents whose free choices coincided with his purposes.

Advocates of divine middle knowledge think it confers theological and philo-sophical advantages. Suppose you receive simultaneous scholarship offers from three different universities of equivalent stature. Suppose further that you pray to God, asking him to guide you to that university which will contribute to your enjoying the best overall collegiate experience. If God had only simple foreknowledge, that is, the ability to look into the actual future, all he can do is tell you about the choice you in fact will make. If God has middle knowledge, however, he can see how your life would have unfolded had you chosen differently, and can thus better answer your prayer. The doctrine of divine middle knowledge also offers a solution to the apparent injustice of those theological perspectives that require one to hold certain doctrines as a necessary condition for enjoying eternal beatitude. How are babies who die in infancy or remote people who have never heard the required doctrines to qualify for the afterlife? The molinist has a ready answer: God knows how such persons would have chosen had they heard the requisite teachings.

Despite its apparent advantages, critics have not spared molinism, attacking both its philosophical coherence and alleged theological advantages. Perhaps the most oft-cited objection to molinism is the so-called 'grounding objection'. What makes the counterfactuals of creaturely freedom true? How can there be a truth about what university my tenth child will select, since I don't have a tenth child? What makes statements about possible but non-existent creatures true? Recall our earlier discussion about truth bearers and truth makers. According to truth maker theory, truth bearers such as propositions, are made true by states of affairs in the world. But there are no states of affairs, or truth makers, that make claims about my tenth child and other non-existent beings true. Since we've no way to understand how such claims could be true, we can't make sense of what it would mean for God to know them. Advocates of molinism counter by claiming that they are more confident that there are true counterfactuals of creaturely freedom than they are of the theory which requires that counterfactuals have grounds, or truth makers. Moreover, as we saw earlier, we express many sorts of propositions whose truth doesn't depend on the world being a certain way. Negative existentials, for instance, like the claim 'there are no dinosaurs', is true, but not because it is grounded in the way the world is now.

Critics of Molinism also claim that the doctrine places unacceptable limitations on divine creativity. For according to Molinism, counterfactual truths of human freedom are not made true by God but by us, otherwise they would not be truths of freedom. So when God goes to create the world, he does not make the contingent truths about creaturely freedom; they're already true independently of God's creative activity, and all God can do is select which among the array of truths he wishes to instantiate. It is as if God goes to the divine workshop to make a world, and finds many of the raw materials available for his use are already in place. He is at liberty to use them or not, or to use only those that suit his purposes, but he's stuck with the materials on hand. Some find this an unacceptable limitation on both divine power and freedom. Perhaps these limitations would be acceptable if molinism delivered all its alleged benefits. Consider our earlier example about choosing a university. If it is a free choice, then presumably God knew from the foundation of the world which university you'd choose. In fact, he instantiated you knowing in advance that you'd make the particular choice you do. So what good does it do you if God knows that you'd have been happier had you chosen differently. He has created you precisely because he already knew how you'd exercise your freedom. So it doesn't appear that molinism even delivers one of its vaunted benefits.

Having now surveyed some of the philosophical matters concerning God's omnipotence and omniscience, we turn finally to God's omnibenevolence. According to the moral argument for God's existence, surveyed earlier, God's essential goodness serves as the ground of human moral precepts. We also considered the very serious challenge to God's goodness posed by the problem of evil. Theists, as we saw, argue that God's perfect goodness does not consist in his granting our every wish, like some fabled genie, but in arranging the world to be conducive to our ultimate and deep flourishing. In order to deepen our understanding of both these points, we turn to a dilemma about God's relationship to morality posed by Plato's dialogue *Euthyphro*. In a discussion about the nature of true piety, Euthyphro asks if an action is pious just because God commands it, or whether God commands only that which is pious. (For our purposes, we can substitute 'morally good' for 'pious'.) If the former, then God's commands appear arbitrary; he could just as well have commanded that torturing innocent children is morally obligatory. But if the latter, then it would seem God's commanding it is superfluous to its being good; it was good already and didn't need God's command to be so. And if God commands that which is good independently of his commands, it would seem there is some power independent of God to which he is beholden.

Divine command theorists embrace the first horn of the dilemma, claiming that an action acquires its status as right or wrong in virtue of having been commanded by God. This not only makes God's commands seem arbitrary, but also it evacuates the concept of good of all its meaning when applied to God. For if God's actions are good no matter what he does, simply in virtue of the fact that it is *he* who does them, then to say that God is good is devoid of content and becomes tautologous, on a par with 'God is God'. To say that God issues commands about good and bad actions by some standard independent of himself not only threatens God's aseity (his independence of all of creation), but works against the moral argument's claim that our morality is somehow grounded in God.

As often happens with dilemmas, the wisest course lies not with either extreme, but somewhere in the middle. To recall a point made earlier, we must understand the divine attributes, not in isolation, but in conjunction with and as modified by the totality of God's character. God is not powerful, *simpliciter*, but powerful as befits his wisdom and goodness. To say that God is perfect in goodness is to say that God's moral character embodies every moral perfection to the highest degree possible. This would mean that God is, among other things, loving, compassionate, just, and forgiving, all traits readily ascribed to God by theism. And if God is essentially good, then there is indeed a standard from which he cannot deviate – the grain of truth in the second horn of the dilemma – but that standard is not independent from him but ingredient in his very nature. The first horn of the dilemma also contains a grain of truth, to wit, that the moral standards that are in force throughout creation are in some way up to God. For suppose God had never decided to create anything. There would then have been no use for commands to honour him as creator. Or suppose that God had created only spiritual beings such as angels. Then commands against adultery and gluttony would obviously make no sense. The moral commands that have force in the created order, then, reflect the particular creaturely natures God has chosen to instantiate, and the particular conditions of their creaturely flourishing. In going between the horns of Euthyphro's dilemma, we have agreed that the particular moral precepts that have force in creation are partially up to God and the kinds of beings that he elects to create. But we have denied that God could create creatures and then command those things which would undermine their creaturely flourishing. But this isn't to hold God accountable to a standard outside himself, but merely to require that he act consistently with his essentially loving character.

We have looked only briefly at the three properties most commonly ascribed to God, omnipotence, omniscience, and omnibenevolence, and some of the philosophical concerns these ascriptions generate. We have not touched upon many of the other traits often ascribed to God: simplicity, impassability, and immutability, to name but a few. If theists are correct, then this life does not exhaust but is only a foretaste of that beatific vision wherein our greatest happiness resides.

EXERCISES

1 Does the belief that God exists satisfy the standards of good intellectual conduct as you understand them? Might not reasonable people have intellectual standards different than your own?

2 To what extent, if any, are our native cognitive powers suitable to discover truths about God?

3 Do the latest findings of contemporary science provide more or less confirmation for theism?

4 Is belief in God necessary to motivate and inform the moral life? How might the contours of the moral life vary depending on whether it is or is not rooted in theism?

5 Must we experience suffering in order to grow into morally mature, responsible persons? Could God have so arranged the world that we become such persons without ever experiencing suffering?

6 Can one find meaning in life if, with Bertrand Russell and Richard Dawkins, one views human existence as an 'accidental collocation of atoms?'

7 Theists portray God as a divine person, perfect in wisdom, power and goodness, who created and guides his creation. Practitioners of other religious traditions disagree. How do you explain the varying accounts of God's nature among the world's religions?

NOTES

1 Some religions, such as most branches of Buddhism, don't teach that God exists. Nor do the paradigm examples of religious experience in Buddhism have to do with a supernatural person. To simplify matters, therefore, I shall restrict my focus to the sorts of experiences and claims common to the world's great monotheistic religions, Judaism, Christianity, and Islam. All three affirm that God is the unsurpassably great creator of the heavens and earth. I shall also adopt the dominant practice of these traditions by referring to God with masculine pronouns.

2 The philosopher John Searle, who was present at the dinner, recounts this story in *Mind, Language, and Society: Philosophy in the Real World* (New York: Basic Books, 1998), pp. 36–37.

3 W.K. Clifford, 'The Ethics of Belief,' anthologised in *Philosophy of Religion*, 2nd edn, Hasker *et. al.* (eds) (Oxford: Oxford University Press, 2001), p. 85.

4 'Theism' says there is a personal God who providentially guides and interacts in various ways with his creation. 'Deism' is the view that a supremely powerful being created the world, but thereafter left it to run of its own accord; he does not intervene in its affairs.

5   Richard Dawkins, 'The blind watchmaker', in *The Blind Watchmaker: Why the Evidence of Evolution Reveals a Universe Without Design* (New York: W.W. Norton and Company, Inc., 1986.)

6   Richard Dawkins, *River Out of Eden: A Darwinian View of Life* (New York: Basic Books, 1995).

7   See *Darwin's Black Box: The Biomechanical Challenge to Evolution* (New York: Free Press, 1996), by Michael Behe, and William Dembski's *The Design Inference: Eliminating Chance Through Small Probabilities* (Cambridge: Cambridge University Press, 1998).

8   I am indebted here to William Lane Craig's article 'The Kalam version of the cosmological argument', in Kelly James Clark (ed.), *Readings in the Philosophy of Religion*, (New York: Broadview Press, 2000). Readers wishing for a more complete explication and defence of the argument can consult Craig's *The Kalam Cosmological Argument* (Eugene, OR: Wipf and Stock Publishers, 2000).

9   See Richard Gale's *On the Nature and Existence of God* (Cambridge: Cambridge University Press, 1991), pp. 204–5.

10 St Thomas Aquinas, *Summa Contra Gentiles* 1.4.4 (Notre Dame, IN: University of Notre Dame Press, 1975), p. 67.

11 A very clear example of cumulative case reasoning can be found in chapter 3 of Basil Mitchell's book *The Justification of Religious Belief* (New York: Seabury Press, 1973). Also see Richard Swinburne's *Is There a God?* (Oxford: Oxford University Press, 1996).

12 William P. Alston, *Perceiving God* (Ithaca, New York: Cornell University Press, 1991).

13 Sigmund Freud, *The Future of an Illusion*, translated by W.D. Robson-Scott (Garden City, NY: Anchor Books, 1964). See especially chapters 3 and 4.

14 Caroline Franks Davis's *The Evidential Force of Religious Experience* (Oxford: Oxford University Press, 1989), makes this point in chapter 6, on 'Experience and interpretation'.

15 These phenomena are discussed in interesting detail by Paul Ricoeur in *The Symbolism of Evil* (Boston: Beacon Press, 1967), especially chapters 1–3.

16 In the index of his *Abolition of Man*, C.S. Lewis compares the basic moral precepts found in the *Analects* of Confucius, the *Vedas*, Roman civil law, the Jewish Torah, Hammurabi's Code, and the ancient Egyptian Book of the Dead. What he finds is that disagreement on fundamental moral precepts is the exception rather than the norm.

17 Bertrand Russell, 'A Free Man's Worship', in *Mysticism and Logic* (London: George Allen and Unwin, 1917), p. 56.

18 *Ibid.*, p. 47.

19 Because it is difficult to specify with precision theism's degree of probability, some theists prefer to support their belief with a close cousin of the cumulative case argument, what is sometimes called an 'argument to the best explanation'. Here theists claim that their hypothesis, rather than naturalism or some other explanatory framework, best explains phenomena such as design, intelligent life, religious experiences, etc.

20 See my book *Epistemology: Becoming Intellectually Virtuous*, especially chapter 8, for more about intellectual virtues and vices, and their connection to emotions and other aspects of our character.

21 Blaise Pascal, *Pensées* (New York: E.P. Dutton and Co., Inc., 1958), p. 66.

22 For a full account of Plantinga's views see his *Warranted Christian Belief* (Oxford: Oxford University Press, 2000).

23 Similar examples are used by Daniel Howard-Snyder in his 'God, evil, and suffering,' in

Reason For the Hope Within, ed. Michael Murray (Grand Rapids, MI: Eerdmans Publishing Company, 1999).

24 St Thomas Aquinas, *Summa Theologiae, A Concise Translation*, ed. by Timothy McDermott (Westminster, MD: Christian Classics, 1989), p. 400.

25 Anselm of Canterbury, *Proslogion, in Anselm of Canterbury: The Major Works*, ed. by Brian Davies and G.R. Evans (Oxford: Oxford University Press, 1998) p. 87.

26 Thomas V. Morris's *Anselmian Explorations* (Notre Dame: University of Notre Dame Press, 1987), and Katherin Rogers' *Perfect Being Theology* Edinburgh: Edinburgh University Press, 2000) are both illustrative of perfect being theology, and interesting for the different conclusions they reach.

27 A minority strain within the Western philosophical tradition – recall the quote cited from Pascal's *Pensées* – denies that our unaided, finite faculties can discern anything of the divine nature. If God does not reveal himself to us in a special way, our only path is the *via negativa*, the way of remotion, which restricts us to saying only what God is not.

28 Richard Swinburne, *The Coherence of Theism* (Oxford: Oxford University Press, 1977), p. 176.

29 For an excellent overview of the solutions offered by contemporary philosophers, see Linda Zagzebski's *The Dilemma of Freedom and Foreknowledge* (Oxford: Oxford University Press, 1991).

FURTHER READING

The Problem of Evil, ed. by Marilyn McCord Adams and Robert Merrihew Adams (Oxford: Oxford University Press, 1990). A balanced anthology that introduces readers to the general lines of argument on the topic. Also excellent, but somewhat narrower in focus are *The Evidential Argument from Evil*, by Daniel Howard-Snyder (Indianapolis: Indiana University Press, 1996) and *Divine Hiddenness*, ed. by Daniel Howard-Snyder and Paul K. Moser (Cambridge: Cambridge University Press, 2002).

Perceiving God, the Epistemology of Religious Experience by William P. Alston (Ithaca: Cornell University Press, 1991). A thorough, formidably argued examination of religious experience and the grounds of its justification.

Our Idea of God: An Introduction to Philosophical Theology by Thomas V. Morris (Vancouver, British Columbia: Regent College, 2002). An engaging, clearly written exploration of God's nature and the attributes most often ascribed to him.

A Companion to the Philosophy of Religion, ed. by Philip Quinn and Charles Taliaferro (Oxford: Blackwell Publishers, 1997). An outstanding reference work that includes contributions from the leading philosophers of religion as they address all the central concerns in the philosophy of religion.

Warranted Christian Belief by Alvin Plantinga (Oxford: Oxford University Press, 2000). Arguably the most thorough and clearly written treatment of epistemological concerns as they bear on issues in the philosophy of religion.

Is There a God? by Richard Swinburne (Oxford: Oxford University Press, 1996). One of Britain's outstanding philosophers of religion addresses the most fundamental question raised in the philosophy of religion. Suitable for beginning students in philosophy.

14

CONTINENTAL PHILOSOPHY
Simon Glendinning

INTRODUCTION

Since the 1970s – but not before – there have been undergraduate and graduate university courses in philosophy in the English-speaking world which have gone by, or include, the title 'Continental Philosophy'. Why it came about at that time that some courses came to be so called is reasonably clear, although, as we shall see, it was in some ways a rather odd choice. In order not to beg too many questions about that oddness, I want first to give the reason for the introduction of this title in a rather roundabout way. The reason, prosaically speaking, was this. In the English-speaking world there were (and still are) a number of professional philosophers with a serious working interest in ideas and arguments developed by authors whose work was (and largely remains) not at all well regarded by most mainstream 'analytic' philosophers. The course titles which were typically being used to teach the work of such authors included, among others, 'Phenomenology', 'Existentialism', 'Hegel and Marx', 'Hermeneutics' and 'Critical Theory'. These were all quite different (if typically overlapping) courses, but they were all beginning to look like explorations of authors and themes with increasingly more historical interest than contemporary relevance. By this I mean that the ideas at the heart of such courses were being challenged by many of those whom they most deeply influenced. New trends and new thinkers were emerging that could not be happily included in courses going under those old titles. We can be even more precise here, for there is near universal agreement that the changeover to the new title occurred in order to enable teachers in the English-speaking world to include in the syllabuses of their various courses authors whose work was coming to be known, as Simon Critchley puts it, by 'the rather unhelpful and approximative labels' of 'post-structuralism', 'post-modernism' and 'French feminism'.[1] 'Continental philosophy', an appropriately vague category that was already to hand, provided the convenient catch-all for courses covering both the old and the new.

I say that this convenient choice was, nevertheless, in some ways odd. This is, in part, because the new title – along with the rather unhelpful approximative labels that I have just mentioned – did not emerge from within the movements in philosophy that the new courses were aiming to cover.[2] As we shall see, the reason why this title was to hand in the first place is that it had for some time served philosophers from the analytic movement as the name for a supposedly highly distinctive non-analytic tradition in contemporary Western philosophy. This title, with its vagueness and availability proved suitably vague and available to be appropriated by teachers of those courses which aimed to cover authors whose work was not part of the analytic canon. Unfortunately, this choice of title has given rise to a seriously misleading impression, an impression which up until then only analytic philosophers had been seriously impressed by: namely, that there really is a more or less coherent philosophical lineage or philosophical tradition that might fairly be called 'the Continental tradition in philosophy'.[3] In my view there is no such thing, and one of the aims of this chapter will be to provide a defence of this view.

THE USUAL SUSPECTS

Let me say straight away that even if I am right that the title 'Continental Philosophy' gives rise to a seriously misleading impression of a more or less coherent philosophical tradition, that is not intended to suggest that teachers of courses going by that title cannot have a perfectly clear idea of the thinkers and themes that they want to cover, and an equally clear idea of how those thinkers and themes relate to each other. The possibility of providing a coherent overview at this point is not, in my view, in the least impossible since the teachers of such courses will always be selective, and, as I have already indicated, the basic raison d'être for the new title was to enable teachers to take on board recent developments and challenges to the ideas and arguments which they had been exploring under the old titles.[4] Nevertheless, I am saying that it is not seriously credible to suppose that one can offer a coherent overview of 'Continental philosophy' as a whole or *as such*, at least in so far as that overview is intended to enable us to see 'what distinguishes it from analytic philosophy'. As we shall see everyone knows one cannot provide such an overview. Unfortunately, this has not stopped many from trying to give one. Following Cora Diamond (on another topic) I will call this 'chickening out'.[5] And as we shall see, it is still rather common.

All complications apart, however, there remains one fundamental and irreducible feature of this strange scene: namely, the presence of a more or less stable collection of thinkers that comprise what I will call 'the usual suspects'. This is the set of thinkers that will typically be drawn from in the selections that are taught in courses under the title 'Continental Philosophy', and they are for that reason (and in my view for that reason alone), appropriately called 'Continental philosophers'. It will always help students embarking on a course in Continental philosophy to know who they are and to have an idea of what their most significant contribution to philosophy is usually taken to be. So in this section I will provide some details on this score.

There is a kind of irony to the idea of giving a list of the usual suspects. For there is a well known joke that suggests that the distinction between analytic and Continental philosophy resides in the fact that the former deals with 'problems' and the latter deals with 'proper names'.[6] Actually, I like this way of putting things very much. It is not, one should emphasise, a pointer towards a true empirical generalisation. If it was it would just be false and wilfully so. Rather it is simply a delightful verbal caricature. And it caricatures 'both sides' equally, and equally pointedly and equally distortingly. The fact that the caricature itself does not fit happily into either side further reminds us that the distinction it posits is one that is best captured by a caricature. Only this form of representation captures the sense in which there really are sides here and in which there are two sides – both ideas I take to be false if taken as generalisations. Even so, however, the editor of one recent *Companion to Continental Philosophy*, Simon Critchley, was forced to take it quite seriously when it transpired that his own 'principle of selection' was precisely one of 'organizing the *Companion* by proper names'.[7] However, it strikes me as significant that, in fact, this principle is not appropriate only to one side of the supposed divide. On the contrary, as Critchley himself went on to note, the 'easiest and most minimal' way of distinguishing analytic and Continental philosophy is, on both sides, through proper names. Here is Critchley: 'What matters here is which tradition the philosopher feels part of, knowing who counts (and perhaps more importantly, knowing who doesn't count – sometimes without knowing why) as an ancestor or an authority, who's in and who's out.'[8]

We might at this point simply ask: Who, then, is 'in' as far as Continental philosophy is concerned? But Critchley's parenthetical point about it being more important knowing who is 'out' should not be passed over too quickly, especially with regard to the Continental collection. For, as I shall indicate later, with the exception of Kant, the list of the usual suspects, the list at the bottom of all the complex issues I have touched on so far, is formed entirely from thinkers who are typically regarded as 'out' by (self-authorised) analytic philosophers. I take this as the major motivation for supposing that the impression of internal unity within the category of Continental philosophy is seriously misleading. For, to make use of a nicely ambiguous way of putting things, in my view, this is a unity that is *forged by exclusion*. That is (apart from Kant), this collection of authors forms a distinct set simply by their being regarded, one and all, as *not* part of analytic philosophy. In my view, then, the category of 'Continental philosophy' is, in its origins at least, part of analytic philosophy in a very strong sense: it is, as it were, the defining 'not part' of analytic philosophy.

So we need to bear in mind that the list of the usual suspects is fundamentally a list of those who are 'out'. And we should note, too, Critchley's claim that philosophers may not know why someone counts as 'out'. They are very unlikely to have read them *well* if they are. Finally, I would want to insist, that there is no earthly reason why any one of the names that figure in the list we are about to look at might not figure in the list of those who are cited as 'an ancestor or an authority' for particular philosophers who feel or declare themselves as belonging to the analytic tradition – many of them will have been whether they have read them or not.

Enough said. Here is a decent selection of the usual suspects, not the 'A list' but rather a reasonably comprehensive listing (by date of birth) of 'Continental philosophers' (and the major not-simply-philosophical comrades who they care about) since Kant:[9]

Kant, Immanuel (1724–1804), German philosopher, almost universally ranked as the most important thinker of modern times. The keystone of Kant's 'critical philosophy', his transcendental idealism, is presented in his *Critique of Pure Reason* (1781), also known as the first *Critique*. The central idea of Kant's idealism is that the structure of objectivity of all objects of experience (spatio-temporal particulars in nature) has its source in the structure of subjectivity, in a priori conditions for the unity of subjective representations. Kant's ethical ideas, in particular his conception of human beings as worthy of unconditional respect, are the logical outcome of his belief in the fundamental freedom of the individual as stated in his *Critique of Practical Reason* (1788), also known as the second *Critique*. In the *Critique of Judgement* (1790), also known as the third *Critique*, Kant attempts to construct a bridge between the faculties of the understanding (whose concern is knowledge of *nature*) and reason (whose concern is *freedom*). Specifically, it deals with the capacity to make aesthetic and teleological judgements.

Fichte, Johann Gottlieb (1762–1814), German philosopher. Fichte was a proponent of an idealist theory of reality and moral action and, along with Friedrich Schelling and G.W.F. Hegel, was one of the most important figures in the philosophical movement of German idealism. In Fichte's view, we can either try to explain consciousness in terms of the activity of the objective world upon human beings, or explain the objective world in terms of the activity of consciousness. Fichte argued that only the second option is compatible with human freedom. Fichte's works include *The Science of Knowledge* (1794; trans. 1970), *The Science of Rights* (1796; trans. 1869), *The Science of Ethics as Based on the Science of Knowledge* (1798;

trans. 1907), and *Addresses to the German Nation* (1808; trans. 1922). His most accessible work, introducing his basic ideas in deliberately plain and simple language, is *The Vocation of Man* (1800; trans. 1956).

Schleiermacher, Friedrich Ernst Daniel (1768–1834), German theologian, who is often called the father of the hermeneutic tradition. Hermeneutics is defined by Schleiermacher as the 'art of understanding' where its object is any 'foreign' or 'strange' discourse that aims to communicate thoughts. His greatest contribution on this subject, published under the title *Hermeneutics: the Handwritten Manuscripts* (1977), was constantly reworked by Schleiermacher but never prepared for publication.

Hegel, Georg Wilhelm Friedrich (1770–1831), German philosopher, who became one of the most influential thinkers of the nineteenth century, and the self-appointed apogee of German idealism. A major feature of Hegel's writing is his interest in the philosophy of history and the history of philosophy. Almost all Hegel scholars accept that, for Hegel, historical considerations are integral to his philosophical concerns and were not items tacked on to some non-historically conceived approach to philosophy. *The Phenomenology of Spirit* (1807; trans. 1910) is usually thought to be his most important work. Hegel published over a period of several years *The Science of Logic* (1812, 1813, 1816; trans. 1929). In 1817 he published in summary form a systematic statement of his entire philosophy entitled *Encyclopedia of the Philosophical Sciences in Outline* (1817 rev. edn 1827, 1830; trans. 1959). The last full-length work published by Hegel was *The Philosophy of Right* (1821; trans. 1896), although several sets of his lecture notes, supplemented by students' notes, were published after his death.

Schelling, Friedrich Wilhelm Joseph von (1775–1854), German philosopher, and one of the leading figures in the movement of German idealism. Throughout his career, Schelling sought an equilibrium between the demand for a theoretical system, which ties him to the rationalist metaphysicians of the eighteenth century, and the demand for freedom, through which he anticipates the emergence of existentialism. It has also been suggested that the shape of argument in Derrida's 'deconstruction' bears striking similarities to those found in Schelling's writings. Schelling's many works include *System of Transcendental Idealism* (1800), *Ideas for a Philosophy of Nature* (1803), *Of Human Freedom* (1809), and *On the History of Modern Philosophy* (1827).

Schopenhauer, Arthur (1788–1860), German philosopher. While mercilessly hostile to German idealism, Schopenhauer's work is deeply Kantian in character, based on the duality of appearances and thing-in-itself, a duality mirrored in the fundamental dualism of his 'system', that of world as representation and world as will. His principal work, *The World as Will and Representation* (1819; trans. 1883), outlines the essential unity of metaphysics, ethics and aesthetics.

Feuerbach, Ludwig Andreas (1804–72), German philosopher, who appealed to principles of psychology to explain orthodox religious belief and developed one of the first German materialistic philosophies. Feuerbach was a pupil of Hegel's. In his chief work, *The Essence of Christianity* (1841; trans. 1854), Feuerbach stated that the existence of religion is justifiable only in that it satisfies a psychological need; a person's essential preoccupation is with the self, and the worship of God is actually worship of an idealised self.

Kierkegaard, Søren Aabye (1813–55), Danish philosopher, whose concern with individual existence, choice, and commitment profoundly influenced modern existentialism. Many of his works were originally published under pseudonyms. He applied the term 'existential' to his work because he regarded philosophy as the expression of an intensely examined individual life, not as the construction of a monolithic system in the manner of Hegel, whose work he attacked in *Concluding Unscientific Postscript* (1846; trans. 1941). In his first major work, *Either/Or* (2 vols, 1843; trans. 1944), Kierkegaard described two 'stages' of existence: the aesthetic and the ethical. In his later works, such as *Stages on Life's Way* (1845; trans. 1940), Kierkegaard proposed a third stage, the religious, in which one submits to the will of God, but in so doing finds authentic freedom. In *Fear and Trembling* (1843; trans. 1941) Kierkegaard focused on God's command that Abraham sacrifice his son Isaac. Other major writings include *The Concept of Dread* (1844; trans. 1944), *The Present Age* (1846; trans. 1940) and *The Sickness unto Death* (1849; trans. 1941).

Marx, Karl (1818–83), German political philosopher and revolutionary, co-founder with Friedrich Engels of scientific socialism and, as such, one of the most influential thinkers in modern history. In 1847 Marx and Engels were commissioned to formulate a statement of socialist principles. The programme they submitted was the *Communist Manifesto*. The central propositions of the *Manifesto* embody the neo-Hegelian theory, later explicitly formulated in his *Critique of Political Economy* (1859), called the dialectical materialist conception of history, or historical materialism. The *Economic and Philosophical Manuscripts* (1844) is perhaps Marx's most influential philosophical contribution, but his greatest work of political philosophy and economy is undoubtedly *Capital* (vol. 1, 1867; vols 2 and 3, edited by Engels and published posthumously in 1885 and 1894, respectively; trans. 1907–9).

Dilthey, Wilhelm (1833–1911), German philosopher of history and culture, whose theories have especially influenced theology and sociology. Dilthey saw himself as heir to Kant's critical philosophy, and conceived his life's work as a Critique of Historical Reason. That is, where Kant provided an epistemological foundation for the natural sciences, Dilthey aimed to establish the epistemological foundations for those disciplines concerned with meaning, value and purpose: what he called the 'human sciences'. Dilthey's hermeneutic theory of historical understanding was presented in a number of books, and in greatest detail in *The Formation of the Historical World in the Human Sciences* (1910).

Nietzsche, Friedrich Wilhelm (1844–1900), German philosopher, and one of the most provocative thinkers of the modern period. His influence has been all pervasive, most obviously in his pronouncement of the death of God, his 'aristocratic' critique of traditional 'slave' morality, his diagnosis of modernity in terms of its 'nihilism', and his call for 'a transvaluation of all values'. A prolific writer, he wrote several major works, among them *The Birth of Tragedy* (1872; trans. 1967), *Daybreak* (1881; trans. 1974), *The Gay Science* (1882; trans. 1974), *Thus Spoke Zarathustra* (1883–85; trans. 1961), *Beyond Good and Evil* (1886; trans. 1973), *On the Genealogy of Morals* (1887; trans. 1967), *The Antichrist* (1895; trans. 1968), *Ecce Homo* (1908; trans. 1968), and the controversially edited notes published posthumously as *The Will to Power* (1901; trans. 1910).

Brentano, Franz (1838–1917), German philosopher and psychologist. In 1874 Brentano wrote his most famous work, *Psychology From an Empirical Standpoint* (trans. 1973). In the same year he became a teacher in Vienna. Among the students present at his lectures were Sigmund Freud and Edmund Husserl. Brentano is most famous for his 'intentionality' thesis: 'Every mental phenomenon is characterised by what the Scholastics of the middle ages called the intentional (or mental) inexistence of an object.' 'Inexistence' here does not mean 'non-existence' but 'existence within the mind'. The thesis thus asserts that all conscious phenomenon are characterised by their being a consciousness *of* some mental content: a contentful (mental) accusative is always included within the description of any mental act.

Cohen, Hermann (1842–1918), German-Jewish philosopher, and one of the founders of the Neo-Kantian school at Marburg. Cohen is noted for his commentaries on Kant, written over some 40 years, notably his *Kant's Theory of Empirical Knowledge* (1871).

Freud, Sigmund (1856–1939), Austrian physician and founder of psychoanalysis. His hugely influential book *The Interpretation of Dreams* was first published in

1900. Freud's work effected a radical complication or 'decentering' of classical psychology. Freud claims that ordinary actions are often determined by networks of motives far more extensive and complex than we normally realise. Moreover, many everyday desires arise, in part, from motives which are *unconscious* residues of encounters with significant persons and situations from the past, reaching back into infancy.

Saussure, Ferdinand de (1857–1913), Swiss linguist. Saussure is best known for his *Course in General Linguistics* (1916; trans. 1959), a text which was constructed from his lecture notes and other materials after his death. He is often called the father of structuralism. Saussure made explicit the implications of a structuralist approach to language which claims that language is a *system of differences*, not a collection of word-atoms or other 'positive terms'. He made a series of theoretical distinctions which became the foundation of structuralist linguistics, for example between *langue* (the system of language) and *parole* (events of speech), and a conception of the sign as a two-sided unity comprised of a signifier (acoustic image) and a signified (concept).

Bergson, Henri (1859–1941), French philosopher. Bergson is probably best known for his 'vitalism', an evolutionary and deeply biological theory of knowledge and the intellect. His theory tends to favour natural instincts 'moulded on the very form of life' over the intellect. The latter is, he says, 'characterised by a natural inability to comprehend life'. Bergson's philosophy is contained in four major books: *Time and Free Will* (1889), *Matter and Memory* (1897), *Creative Evolution* (1907), *The Two Sources of Morality and Religion* (1932); and two smaller books: *Laughter* (1937) and *Duration and Simultaneity* (1922). Two books of collected essays are also published: *Mind Energy* (1919) and *An Introduction to Metaphysics: The Creative Mind* (1934).

Husserl, Edmund (1859–1938), German philosopher, and founder of phenomenology. His first book, *Philosophy of Arithmetic* (1891) was roundly criticised by Frege for its supposed 'psychologism', and his mature writings, beginning with the *Logical Investigations* (1900–1; trans. 1970), are far more clearly resistant to that charge. The 'Fifth Logical Investigation' is famous for introducing the notion of intentionality (with explicit reference to Brentano) as central to the understanding of consciousness and mental content. His later writings develop within a more or less Kantian point of view. His major works of such 'transcendental phenomenology' are, *Ideas: A General Introduction to Pure Phenomenology* in 1913 (trans. 1931) and *Cartesian Meditations* (1931; trans. 1960).

Cassirer, Ernst (1874–1945), German philosopher, born in Poland. A great admirer of Kant's critical philosophy, Cassirer was a leading figure in the Marburg Neo-Kantian school. Cassirer's works include *The Problem of Knowledge* (3 vols, 1906–20) and *The Philosophy of Symbolic Forms* (3 vols, 1923–9).

Buber, Martin (1878–1965), German-Jewish philosopher, who developed a philosophy of encounter, or dialogue. His most widely known work, *I and Thou* (1922; trans. 1937), is a concise expression of his philosophy. His other main book, *On Judaism* (1923; trans. 1967), established his intellectual leadership of the German-Jewish community.

Hartmann, Nicolai (1882–1950), German philosopher and one of the central figures in the Marburg Neo-Kantian school. His works include *Plato's Logic of Being* (1909), *Ethics* (1926; trans. 1932), *New Ways of Ontology* (1943; trans. 1953), and *Aesthetics* (1953).

Jaspers, Karl (1883–1969), German philosopher, one of the originators of modern existentialism, whose work influenced modern theology and psychiatry as well as philosophy. His major works include, *General Psychopathology* (1913; trans. 1963), *Psychology of World Views* (1919), and *Philosophy and Existence* (1938; trans. 1971).

Lukács, Georg (1885–1971), Hungarian Marxist philosopher. Lukács's major writings on literature and philosophy incorporates ideas from the German sociologist Max Weber into traditional Marxist analyses. He is best known for his book *History and Class Consciousness* (1923; trans. 1967). This book was to influence many later Marxists and critical theorists, particularly its discussion of alienation.

Bloch, Ernst (1885–1977), German philosopher and social theorist. Somewhat misleadingly regarded as part of the movement of critical theory, Bloch's work incorporates elements of Hegelian Marxism, phenomenology, literary expressionism, Kierkegaardian existentialism, hermeneutics, secular–theological utopianism and a Schelling-influenced philosophy of nature. His work spans the period from 1919, when he published *Spirit of Utopia* to 1974 when he wrote his last major book *Experimentum Mundi*. Other major works include *The Principle of Hope* (1954), *Atheism in Christianity* (1968) and *Natural Law and Human Dignity* (1961).

Heidegger, Martin (1889–1976), German philosopher, who developed a radically new form of phenomenology, and is widely regarded as one of the most original philosophers of the twentieth century. His most important and influential work is

Being and Time (1927; trans. 1962). Fundamental to Heidegger's thought is his claim that the metaphysical tradition fails to do justice to the 'ontological difference', to the difference that is between entities and the Being of entities. *Being and Time* is dominated by an analysis of the Being of the entity that can grasp (or fail to grasp) this difference; the entity that we are, and which Heidegger calls *Dasein*. His later writings explore, among many other topics, questions concerning art and technology, and the idea of the end of philosophy.

Marcel, Gabriel (1889–1973), French Roman Catholic existentialist philosopher, who insisted that individuals can only be understood as embodied and involved in specific situations. Marcel proposes a fundamental distinction between the body as something possessed (like property or equipment), and the body as something that one is; a distinction between having and being a body. The main thrust of his view is to deny that the fundamental experience of one's body is the experience of 'having' something. His ideas are developed in a number of books, including *Creative Fidelity* (trans. 1964) and *Tragic Wisdom and Beyond* (trans. 1973).

Gramsci, Antonio (1891–1937), Italian Marxist thinker and activist, one of the founders of the Italian Communist party. Deepening traditional Marxist ideas on ideology, Gramsci's influence has continued through his *Prison Notebooks*, first published between 1948 and 1951.

Benjamin, Walter (1892–1940), German writer, Marxist theorist, and aesthetician. Closely identified with (but not a member of) the Frankfurt School, Benjamin is best known for his essays 'The Work of Art in the Age of Mechanical Reproduction' in *Illuminations* (1931; trans. 1968), and 'The Author as Producer' (1934; trans. 1966).

Horkheimer, Max (1895–1973), Jewish-German philosopher and social theorist. Director of the Institute for Social Research in Frankfurt ('the Frankfurt School'), and inaugurator of the 'critical theory' of society. The basic feature of critical theory is the refusal absolutely to separate fact from value. It understands that all theoretical projects, including its own, necessarily serve, and are shaped by, social interests and exist in particular social contexts. However, for Horkheimer critical theory is to be distinguished from sceptical relativism by its insistence on the possibility of sustaining truth claims. See entry on Adorno for major publication details.

Marcuse, Herbert (1898–1979), German-American philosopher, closely identified with (but not a member of) the Frankfurt School. His social philosophy is outlined in *Eros and Civilization* (1955) and *One-Dimensional Man* (1964). One of the most distinctive aspects of Marcuse's work is the extent to which it embodies a distinctively reciprocal reception of Heidegger's phenomenology and of Marx's historical materialism.

Gadamer, Hans-Georg (1900–2002), German philosopher. In his development of a philosophical hermeneutics in his major work *Truth and Method* (1960), Gadamer claims to follow his former teacher Heidegger in conceiving understanding as 'the basic motion' of our existence. The idea here is that understanding is not essentially a theoretical posture that we might try to achieve or adopt now and then, but is something that we 'are' and 'do' all the time. However, according to Gadamer this structure of being cannot be reduced to a technique or a set of rules: it is, as Schleiermacher said, an 'art', one connected to knowledge, but not accounted for by the idea of method. Among his other numerous books are *Philosophical Hermeneutics* (trans. 1976), *Reason in the Age of Science* (trans. 1976), and *The Relevance of the Beautiful and Other Essays* (trans. 1986).

Lacan, Jacques (1901–81), French psychoanalyst. Lacan's major volume of writings, *Ecrits* (1966; trans. 1977) is famous for providing a structuralist reading of Freudian theory. His most significant thesis concerns the importance of understanding language to understanding the workings of the unconscious. Adopting ideas from Saussure, Lacan argues that the unconscious is 'structured like a language'.

Adorno, Theodor Wiesengrund (1903–69), German philosopher and social theorist. Most closely associated with the Frankfurt School, although he did not become a member until the 1940s. In 1938 he emigrated to the United States, where he worked with Horkheimer on *Dialectic of Enlightenment* (1947) and other books. Adorno and Horkheimer returned to teaching in Frankfurt in 1951. Articulated in terms of a Marxist account of society, the central concern of Adorno's philosophy is the problem of how to think about (and engage with) the world in a culture that inhibits critical reflection on, and conceptualisation of, that world. His key publications after the War include *Minima Moralia* (1951), *Jargon of Authenticity* (1964) and *Negative Dialectics* (1973).

Sartre, Jean-Paul (1905–80), French philosopher, and leading exponent of modern existentialism. In 1938 he published his philosophical novel *Nausea* (trans. 1949), and in 1943 he published a play, *The Flies* (1943; trans. 1946), as well as his major philosophical *Being and Nothingness* (1943; trans. 1953). That work sets out to develop a rigorously anti-phenomenalist phenomenology of 'human reality'. Some of his more accessible 'existentialist' views were popularised in *Existentialism and Humanism* (1946; trans. 1948). Sartre's later philosophical work *Critique of*

Dialectical Reason (1960; 1976) shifted his emphasis from individual freedom to a Marx-influenced theory of the subject as an actor who is always historically and socially conditioned. Sartre's other main works include the series of novels *The Roads to Liberty*.

Arendt, Hannah (1906–75), German-born American-Jewish political scientist and social commentator, noted for her writings on totalitarianism and Jewish affairs. Arendt received wide acclaim for her book *Origins of Totalitarianism* (1951), and held appointments at the University of California at Berkeley, Princeton University, and the University of Chicago. Among her many other writings are *The Human Condition* (1958), *Between Past and Future* (1961), *On Revolution* (1963), and the controversial *Eichmann in Jerusalem* (1963), based on her reports of the Nazi war trials.

Levinas, Emmanuel (1906–95), born to Lithuanian-Jewish parents but later naturalised French citizen. Levinas published the first full-length study of Husserl's work in French (in 1930), and as a co-translator of Husserl's *Cartesian Meditations* played an important role in introducing phenomenology into France. In his early work on Husserl the influence of Heidegger is already marked, and Levinas's methods and themes remain throughout deeply indebted to Heidegger's analysis of *Dasein* in *Being and Time*. However, he also asserts that his work is 'governed by a profound need to leave the climate of [Heidegger's] philosophy'. Of greatest significance in this movement away from Heidegger is Levinas's defence of the primacy of ethics (the relation to the other) over ontology. His principle works include *Time and the Other* (1948; trans. 1987), *Totality and Infinity* (1961; trans. 1969) and *Otherwise than Being* (1974; trans. 1981).

de Beauvoir, Simone (1908–86), French philosopher and novelist and advocate of existentialism. In her first novel, *She Came to Stay* (1943; trans. 1949), de Beauvoir explored the existentialist dilemmas of individual freedom, action, and responsibility. Later novels dealt with the same themes; among these are *The Blood of Others* (1944; trans. 1948) and *The Mandarins* (1954; trans. 1956), for which de Beauvoir received the Prix Goncourt. De Beauvoir's is best known for her existentialist treatment of sexual difference in *The Second Sex* (1949; 1953). The existentialist thesis that one is responsible for oneself is also advanced in her series of autobiographical works, notably *Memoirs of a Dutiful Daughter* (1958; trans. 1959) and *All Said and Done* (1972; trans. 1974). *Adieux: A Farewell to Sartre* (1984) is a memoir about her long-time colleague and life partner Sartre.

Merleau-Ponty, Maurice (1908–61), French philosopher, whose existential phenomenology of the body opened a new field of philosophical investigation. His first important work was *The Structure of Behaviour* (1942; trans. 1963), a critique of behaviourism. His major work is *Phenomenology of Perception* (1945; trans. 1962) which tries to cut a path between the twin prejudices of empiricist-realism and intellectualist-idealism in the philosophy of perception. A number of essays on art, film, politics, psychology, and religion have been collected in *Sense and Nonsense* (1948; trans. 1964). At the time of his death, he was working on a book, *The Visible and the Invisible* (1964; trans. 1968), in which he argues that the whole perceptual world has the sort of organic unity he had earlier attributed to the body and to works of art.

Lévi-Strauss, Claude Gustave (1908–), French anthropologist and leading proponent of the structuralist approach in social anthropology. Among his books are: *Elementary Structures of Kinship* (1962); his autobiography, *Tristes Tropiques* (1964); and *The Savage Mind* (1966).

Camus, Albert (1913–60), French novelist and moralist, regarded as one of the finest philosophical writers of modern France. Camus's first published novel was *The Outsider* (1942; trans. 1946). This work and the philosophical essay on which it is based, *The Myth of Sisyphus* (1942; trans. 1955), have clear connections with existentialist thought, although he had serious differences of opinion with Sartre. Of the plays that develop existentialist themes, *Caligula* (1944), produced in New York in 1960, is one of the best known.

Ricoeur, Paul (1913–), French philosopher. In his numerous writings on hermeneutics and phenomenology Ricoeur attempts to do justice to a call for textual objectivity and yet remain open to what texts may have to teach us about the construction of such objectivity. Ricoeur's hermeneutics represents his attempt to retain both science and art, whilst disallowing either an absolute status: 'Hermeneutics seems to me to be animated by this double motivation: willingness to suspect, willingness to listen.' Ricoeur has made significant contributions to debates in phenomenology, philosophy of language, philosophy of psychoanalysis, social theory, moral, political and legal philosophy. Among his best known writings are *Freud and Philosophy: An Essay on Interpretation* (trans. 1970), *The Conflict of Interpretations: Essays in Hermeneutics*, *The Rule of Metaphor* (trans. 1974), *Time and Narrative* (3 vols, trans. 1984–8), *Lectures on Ideology and Utopia* (trans. 1986), and *Oneself as Another* (1992).

Barthes, Roland (1915–80), French literary critic and social theorist. His book *On Racine* (1964) was a landmark attempt to apply structuralist theory to literary works, claiming that the elements of such works are constituted in their relation to other textual elements. Today he is best known for his striking essays on and semiotic analyses of the codings that command our daily life in *Mythologies* (1957; trans. 1972). Some of his other works available in translation are *Elements of Semiology* (1965; trans. 1967), *S/Z* (1970; trans. 1974) and *The Pleasure of the Text* (1973; trans. 1976).

Althusser, Louis (1918–90), French political philosopher, and leading structuralist Marxist theoretician. International attention came to Althusser with the publication in 1965 of *For Marx* (trans. 1969) closely followed, again in 1965, by *Reading Capital* (trans. 1970). His anti-empiricist and anti-humanist arguments set the terms of the Marxist philosophical debate during the 1970s. Of major significance is *Essays on Ideology* (1984) in which Althusser develops the idea that history is a 'process without a subject', and that social structures have priority over individual human beings who are, in the process of socialisation, 'interpolated' as subjects, constituted *as* such in and by the dominant ideology of any given period.

Deleuze, Gilles (1925–95), French philosopher. Deleuze is widely credited with inaugurating the post-structuralist movement with his 1962 book *Nietzsche and Philosophy*, as well as providing its definitive text, the 1972 *Anti-Oedipus* (co-written with Felix Guattari). The critical motif of production pervades his thought, and he defined his work in philosophy as 'the art of forming, inventing, and fabricating concepts' which attempt to give an account of (quasi-Kantian) transcendental conditions of the empirical realm in terms which are 'essentially pre-individual, non-personal and a-conceptual'.

Lyotard, Jean-François (1925–98), French philosopher. Lyotard came to prominence with the publication of *The Postmodern Condition: A Report on Knowledge* (1979; trans. 1983) an explication of the idea of the postmodern and its relation to modernity. Along with the French social theorist Jean Baudrillard, Lyotard is often hailed (or condemned) as a 'high priest' of the postmodern world. His most important book, however, is *The Differend*, (trans. 1988) composed between 1973 to 1983, which investigates disputes where one of the interlocutors is divested of the means to argue. A case of a 'differend' between two parties takes place when the 'regulation' of the conflict that opposes them is done in the idiom of one of the parties, and where the wrong suffered by the other is not signified in that idiom.

Foucault, Michel (1926–84), French philosopher. In *Madness and Civilization* (1965), Foucault traced how, in the Western world, madness came to be thought of as mental illness. In *The Birth of the Clinic* (1973) he analyses the emergence of the modern concept of physical illness. In *The Order of Things* (1970) he focuses on the different epistemic conventions that make up the historical a priori or 'episteme' of different historical periods. In *Discipline and Punish* (1975) he investigates the way social power can come to constitutively order the lives of individuals by training their bodies, in much the way that basic training may discipline and prepare a person to be a soldier. His last three books, *History of Sexuality, Volume I: An Introduction* (1976), *The Use of Pleasure* (1984), and *The Care of the Self* (1984), are parts of an unfinished genealogy of sexuality.

Habermas, Jürgen (1929–), German sociologist and philosopher, widely known as the leading exponent of 'second generation' critical theory. Habermas's central claim – that human language and human communication in general already contain implicit intersubjective norms – is a development of Adorno's critique of traditional theory. However, for Habermas early critical theory conceded too much ground to the scepticism which it wished to contest, and he insists that universally valid norms governing communicative action can be isolated and stated. This is the project of his own *Theory of Communicative Action* (trans. 1987). His other major works include *Toward a Rational Society* (trans. 1971), *Knowledge and Human Interests* (trans. 1971), *Legitimation Crisis* (trans. 1976), *The Philosophical Discourse of Modernity* (trans. 1987) and *Facts and Norms* (trans. 1996).

Derrida, Jacques (1930–), French-Algerian philosopher, whose work introduced the idea of 'deconstruction' into contemporary thought and culture. Derrida's first published work was a long introduction to his own translation of Husserl's short essay *The Origin of Geometry* (1962), but he burst onto the international scene in 1967 with the publication of three major books which introduced the deconstructive reading of philosophical theories and assumptions: *Speech and Phenomena* (trans. 1973), *Of Grammatology* (trans. 1977), and *Writing and Difference* (trans. 1978). Derrida's most famous claim is that the predicates traditionally thought to belong only to writing belong, in fact and in principle, to every species of sign whatsoever, including speech. Derrida's output is prodigious: some of his other major works include *Margins of Philosophy* (1972), *The Post Card* (1980), *Of Spirit* (1987), 'Force of Law' (1989), *The Other Heading* (1991), *Specters of Marx* (1993) and *Politics of Friendship* (1994).

Irigaray, Luce (1930–), Belgian-born philosopher, psychoanalyst and linguist. In the 1960s Irigaray trained as a psychoanalyst, attending Lacan's seminars, and her work remains indebted to Lacanian theory. Her second successful doctoral thesis (the first was in linguistics) was published in 1974 as *Speculum of the Other Woman* (trans. 1985) which includes a major essay and critique of Freud's account of female sexuality and subjectivity. In *Marine Lover* (trans. 1991) and *Forgetting the Air* (trans. 1983), Irigaray devotes her attention to Nietzsche and Heidegger respectively. The ambiguity in the title of her earlier book *This Sex Which Is Not One* (1977; trans. 1985) nicely captures Irigaray's challenge to the dominant understanding of women's sexuality. Some of her most important other philosophical essays are collected in *An Ethics of Sexual Difference* (1984; trans. 1993).

Kofman, Sarah (1934–94), French philosopher. Kofman wrote on a wide range of philosophical figures, but it is Nietzsche who dominates her critical writings. Her books are only slowly becoming available in English, and among her three books on Nietzsche only *Nietzsche and Metaphor* (1972; trans. 1993) has been translated. The two books which placed her on the feminist map are *The Enigma of Woman: Woman in Freud's Writings* (1980; trans. 1985) and *Le respect des femmes (Kant et Rousseau)* (1982), the latter raises the question of the applicability of Kant's categorical imperative to women and argues that Rousseau's exhortations that women conform to their nature have the effect of both normalising and naturalising women's subordination to men.

Kristeva, Julia (1941–), Bulgarian-born French psychoanalyst and linguist. Kristeva has written articles on poetic language, semiotics, psychoanalysis, and narrative. Her first collection of these, *Séméiotikè: Recherches Pour une Sémanalyse*, was published in 1969, followed by *Le Texte du Roman* (1970), and *La Révolution du Langage Poétique* (1974), in which she explores the notion of subjectivity in language and history. Kristeva became a practising psychoanalyst in 1979, and has since written books and articles on a variety of topics and in various literary forms.

Le Doeuff, Michele (1948–), French philosopher. Le Doeuff's work questions the boundaries of philosophy, while insisting upon philosophy's importance. She is critical of professional philosophers' neglectful attitude to science, and argues that disputes within sciences are often philosophical. In her most well-known book *Hipparchia's Choice* (trans. 1991) she critically investigates philosophy's claim to achieve a pure clarity. In her view, philosophy is inevitably shaped by language, metaphor, and power relations, including gender relations.

MOVEMENTS IN THE STREAM

Among the many things that stand out in this list is the fact that not all the 'proper names' are professional philosophers. Philosophy (in general) is arguably the most richly interdisciplinary of all the humanities disciplines, but the serious interest in psychoanalysis, history, politics and literature shown by a number of the philosophers on this list is certainly striking. However, this is by no means true of all, and while I hope these entries will prove useful, the listing as a whole is still fairly misleading. In particular, what it struggles to show is the extent to which the authors named on it are, and are not, 'close' to each other, philosophically speaking. As I have indicated, the usual suspects can often be quite helpfully grouped into more or less separate clusters of coherence; more or less distinct streams, movements and schools within the vast reservoir of Western thought. And those unfamiliar with the standard groupings need to know what they are (those who are already familiar with them might be surprised to see who was, in fact, a contemporary or near contemporary with whom). Some of the standard groupings are more helpful and informative than others. (The brief notes provided on each of the titles should give a fair impression of the rigour of a given grouping.)[10] And the fact that there are no authors from the grouping 'analytic philosophy'[11] on this list multiplies the problems. A basic point that I will return to shortly is that while there are numerous thematic and methodological convergences among the figures typically designated as 'Continental philosophers', there are also, and equally importantly, numerous thematic and methodological divergences and differences to be found too. Indeed, there are a number of figures on the list who are far closer to figures typically designated as 'analytic philosophers' than they are with most of the figures on the 'Continental' list. As one observer notes 'Husserl has more in common with Frege than with Nietzsche, and Habermas more in common with Rawls than Marx'.[12] Nevertheless, with all this borne in mind, let us list the major movements and commonly identified groupings among the 'Continental philosophers', again starting with Kant.

Kantianism   Central to Kant's critical philosophy is the distinction between things considered as they are 'in themselves' and things conceived in so far as we are conscious of them, 'appearances'. Kant claims that we can know nothing whatsoever about things in themselves, but only as they appear to us. Appearances (empirically real things) are understood as structured by the ways in which we must represent and think about them, conditions ultimately grounded in the conditions of unity of the self-conscious subject itself (the 'unity of apperception'). Major representative: Kant.

German Idealism   Kant's immediate followers were dissatisfied with two aspects of his idealism. The first is the notion of the thing in itself. The second is the lack of systematicity. The former was regarded as a dogmatic remnant from transcendental realism. The latter concerns the fact that Kant does not begin from a self-evident first principle and derive everything from this. It is true that Kant arrived at an ultimate condition of knowledge in the unity of apperception, but what was required by his followers was that philosophy should *begin* with something like this principle. Otherwise concepts and distinctions will be introduced before they have been accounted for. Major representatives: Fichte, Schelling, Hegel.

Hermeneutics   For hermeneutists we always bring certain presuppositions or 'prejudices' to a reading of a text, to a dialogue or argument with another, or to an experience. While some of these count as prejudices in the pejorative sense and may be eliminable, in general they are regarded as presuppositions which make knowledge and understanding possible and are not only a limitation. It is only from the perspective of projecting a God's eye view that the necessity of such 'prejudices' counts as a failing or a lack. The inevitability of prejudices in every investigation, including an investigation of prejudices, gives rise to the dynamic (non-vicious) 'hermeneutic circle' where, in understanding and interpretation, part and whole are related in a circular way: in order to understand the whole it is necessary to understand the parts and vice versa, and as one's understanding of a part develops or changes this will 'feedback' into one's grasp of the whole. Major representatives: Schleiermacher, Dilthey, Heidegger, Gadamer, Ricoeur.

Philosophy of Life   What unites these authors is their concern to rearticulate the account of the relation between human beings and the world they inhabit in order to show the limits of theoretical reason, and to undermine the picture of mental life as primarily cognitive, rational and conceptual. Philosophers of life place great stress on concrete and organic processes, which is allied to the idea that life is not to be grasped by theoretical systematicity, as supposed by the German idealists. This does not mean that such thinkers give up all attempts to being systematic but that the unity they seek is a 'concrete whole' (e.g. 'my life'), not a theoretical construction (e.g. 'a rational mind'). Major representatives: Schopenhauer, Nietzsche, Bergson.

Young Hegelians   Following Hegel's death in 1831 two antithetical Hegelian schools developed: the so-called 'Old' Hegelians and the 'Young' Hegelians, later also categorised as 'Right' and 'Left' Hegelians. Both groups agreed with Hegel that 'what is rational is actual and what is actual is rational', but they differed over its significance. In the view of the Young Hegelians it might be the case, *in principle*, that the actual is rational, but *in fact* it most assuredly is not. Nevertheless, they were alike convinced in a 'second creation' to come; that is, an unquestioned eschatological belief that a new order was imminent defines the outlook (and for some the appeal) of the Young Hegelians. The group found its first leader in Ludwig Feuerbach. While deeply indebted to Hegel, Feuerbach's philosophy is characterised by its rejection of Hegel's abstract idealism. Feuerbach's call for a 'new basis of things' was intended to restore real significance to 'man and his world'. Major representatives: Ludwig Feuerbach and Karl Marx, but also Bruno Bauer, Edgar Bauer, Moses Hess, Karl Schmidt, Arnold Ruge, Max Stirner.

Philosophy of Existence   Like philosophers of life, philosophers of existence or 'existentialists' advocate an understanding of what is concrete and particular rather than what is abstract and universal. If philosophy is understood as the systematic study of universal and general truths, then philosophy of existence is the anti-philosophical movement *par excellence*. One of the most influential practitioners of suspicion about systematic philosophy was Kierkegaard in his resistance to Hegel's grandiose efforts at absolute thought. Kierkegaard accuses Hegel of building a great mansion without doors, in which the human being is left to live in the outhouse. It is in the realisation of the way in which existence is situated beyond the reach of systematic and formal logical impositions that a wide range of existential critiques of philosophy have been advanced. The lived reality of 'being in the world' is usually what philosophers of existence mean by 'existence'. Since Sartre (who claimed to be following Heidegger) the idea that human beings are 'self-creative' (or that, for human beings, 'existence precedes essence') has become a common slogan of existentialist philosophy. Major representatives: Kierkegaard, Nietzsche, Buber, Jaspers, Heidegger, Marcel, Sartre, Merleau-Ponty, de Beauvoir, Levinas, Camus.

Phenomenology   Kant's influence on phenomenology is all pervasive. Although Kant did not make use of the term in his main works, his emphasis on the unifying and structuring function of consciousness, as exemplified by the unity of apperception, set the stage for Brentano's discussion of the intentionality of consciousness, and Kant's ongoing concern about the relation between the phenomenal and noumenal realms provides a crucial point of departure for many subsequent phenomenological discussions of the being of the phenomenon that appears. While phenomenology is a historical movement in modern Europe with various more or less continuous themes (intentionality, empirical realism, description not explanation), Heidegger preferred to explain the title by tracing its etymology to its Greek roots, in which it signified 'to let that which shows itself be seen from itself in the very way in which it shows itself from itself'. One can see why Heidegger called the idea of 'descriptive phenomenology' a tautology, but it is important to note that the 'phenomena' of phenomenology are not phenomena in the ordinary sense (things, beings). Heidegger explicitly recalls the Kantian notion of forms of sensible intuition when he notes that his concern as a phenomenologist is not with those phenomena encountered within experience but with what makes any such encounter possible. The phenomenon of phenomenology is thus 'that which already shows itself in the appearance as prior to the "phenomenon" as ordinarily understood'. Major representatives: Brentano, Husserl, Jaspers, Heidegger, Gadamer, Sartre, Levinas, Arendt, Merleau-Ponty.

Marxist Political Philosophy A central tenet of Marxist philosophy is that the ways in which many social divisions express themselves (e.g. gender and racial divisions) are dependent on the differing historico-economic and economic-class circumstances in which they occur. Some have found this to be an overly reductive conception of social reality, others suggest that to grasp such divisions within economic contexts is not to undervalue them. Nevertheless, the history of Marxism in Europe is a history of attempts to either create a synthesis of Marx with other thinkers or to deepen the understanding of the social and ideological 'infrastructure' in order to over come its apparent economism. Georg Lukács's interpretation of Marx's notion of alienation owes much to Weber's idea of the increasing rationalisation of society. The Italian communist Antonio Gramsci stressed the role of ideology in civil society in the construction of political hegemony. The appeal of Marxism is that it gives powerful intellectual backing to irreducibly normative responses to the iniquities of the modern capitalist world, and thus gives grounds to the hope that a system which *ought* to disintegrate *will* eventually do so. Major representatives: Marx, Lukács, Gramsci, and also Friedrich Engels, the Frankfurt School, later Sartre, Althusser.

Neo-Kantianism While phenomenology developed the ontological implications of Kantianism, with Heidegger in particular insisting that Kant's goal was knowledge of 'what it is to be an object' (knowledge of the Being of objects), the neo-Kantians stressed the epistemological implications, seeking in the first Critique a 'theory of knowledge' and a philosophy of science. The connections to phenomenology are, however, much greater than is often acknowledged. Cassirer, for example, claims to provide a phenomenology that centres on the power of human symbolisation. It is, he argues, our ability to symbolise our experience that has lead to the flowering of human culture, whether in art or in science. Many of the neo-Kantians were concerned to give an account of the ultimate unity of the natural and the human sciences, typically through transcendental analyses of the constitution of all 'objects' of human concern whether scientific, aesthetic or moral. Major representatives: Hermann Cohen, Ernst Cassirer, Nicolai Hartmann, and also Paul Natorp and Heinrich Rickert.

Freudian Psychoanalytic theory A central theme in Freud's understanding of human psychology is the theory of wishfulfilment. In many cases, he claimed, desires are pacified not through a real action which satisfies it (e.g. the desire for a drink of water being pacified by drinking water) but a kind of short-circuiting of this route in which the mind produces a pacifying representation of satisfaction for itself (e.g. the desire for a drink of water being pacified for someone who is asleep by her dreaming that she is drinking water). Moreover, in Freud's view the goal of many of our most constant and basic desires is not realistic satisfaction but representational pacification. Such desires are typically expressed in a symbolic or metaphorical form, a feature of Freud's account which was to be deepened and developed by the French psychoanalyst Jacques Lacan. Major Representatives: Sigmund Freud, Jacques Lacan, but also a significant influence on the Frankfurt School and Critical theory.

Structuralism   'What is structuralism?' Roland Barthes asked in 1963: 'Not a school, not even a movement (at least not yet), for most of the authors ordinarily labelled with this word are unaware of being united by any solidarity of doctrine or commitment. Nor is it a vocabulary.' Nevertheless, there is a unifying vision that connects the various authors convinced by the work of Saussure in linguistics: namely, that the fundamental features of human life – those to be found in language, but also in kinship and society, in literature, and in psychology – are relational and structural rather than intrinsic or substantial. That is, they cannot be discovered by looking at factual elements given to observation and perception but only by looking beyond these to the relations that constitute them. These structures may be hidden from view, but the phenomena that are open to view emanate or flow from these hidden forms. The concern to explore networks of relationships that unite and form structures thus gives analytical priority to wholes and totalities rather than particular individuals and concrete events. Major representatives: Saussure, Lacan, Lévi-Strauss, Barthes, Althusser.

Frankfurt School and Critical Theory   Critical theorists have attempted to develop interdisciplinary collaboration between philosophy and the human sciences in ways which question the nature and limits of the division of intellectual labour which has so powerfully determined their relationship in the modern era. Critical theorists do not share substantive social, historical or conceptual theses, nor a common method. What unifies them, however, can be gleaned in their shared title: their commitment to theoretical work which is '*critical*' – in contrast to traditional 'descriptive' theories which claim to be able to separate fact and value – and to develop criticisms that are '*theoretical*' – in contrast to sociological relativism which suppose that truth claims are simply decided by whether or not they serve the right social interest. The Institute for Social Research was opened in Frankfurt by Felix Weil, the Marxist son of a grain millionaire, in 1924. The Institute initially had strong ties to the Soviet socialist model and aimed to advance the study of Marxism in Germany. Following the appointment of Horkheimer to the directorship in 1930 its leading members were almost uniformly critical of the Soviet Union, while remaining deeply attached to Marx's own work. Of those who are typically given the title of major representative in this grouping, some bear it fairly – Horkheimer, Adorno, Habermas – others rather less fairly – Bloch, Benjamin, Marcuse.

Lacanian Psychoanalytic theory   A central feature of Lacan's inheritance of Freudian theory is the effort to expose psychoanalytic discourse to theoretical developments within the human sciences, in particular, to merge psychoanalysis with philosophy, linguistics and anthropology. His seminars and papers contain complex references to Hegel, Heidegger and Lévi-Strauss as well as (more famously) Saussure. Central to Lacan's account of our lives as individual 'subjects' is his view of our entry into language, which is taken to have three interdependent and interpenetrating 'registers': the symbolic, the imaginary and the real. The symbolic order is the order of signs 'bound together by specific laws' (the prohibition of incest is a socio-symbolic law for Lacan.) The imaginary realm is the field wherein ideas (or, more precisely, illusions) of individuality are maintained. And the real, not to be confused with standard conceptions of reality, is what is not representable in discourse at all: it is a dimension of existence behind and beyond anything that can be grasped by signs and symbols, and is resistant to symbolisation. Irigaray has argued that the dominance of the symbolic order by signs of masculinity and the father figure means that the experience of the specifically feminine subject is generated through her relation to the real rather than the symbolic order. Major representatives: Lacan, Irigaray.

Post-Structuralism   In my view this group has the greatest chance of being thought of as made up of 'Continental philosophers' in a significant sense: for they all have affinities with, relationships to and a serious working interest in a great number of the authors cited as the usual suspects – but without being part of one of the schools or movements that are usually associated with them. They have debts all over the place, including for some, debts to analytic philosophy. The authors in this group are predominantly contemporary French philosophers, and their work is typically as much 'post' Kantian, 'post' phenomenological, 'post' existentialist, 'post' Marxist, 'post' Freudian, as it is 'post' structuralist. It is because of the dominance of structuralist themes in French philosophy in the 1960s and 1970s, and the reaction against that dominance by a new generation of French thinkers, that gave rise to the current title. A better title might have been 'recent French philosophy' except for the fact that soon enough it won't be recent and many thinkers who are of significance to this generation are not French: Paul de Man, Judith Butler, John Sallis and, in general, the leading 'Continental philosophers' in Britain and America, are part of this loose network of authors who are hard to place except in the 'who's in and who's out' sense outlined above. Major representatives: Deleuze, Foucault, Lyotard, Derrida, French feminism.

French Feminism   This title, like the previous one, is a peculiar invention. In fact it is a kind of microcosm for 'Continental philosophy' as a whole, except that its originators were more well-meaning. Created by an Anglo-American readership, the title oversimplifies by creating the misleading impression of homogeneity between diverse (although exclusively female) thinkers who live in France. Le Doeuff, for example, finds little to praise in Irigaray's work. One commentator notes that these days 'the indignity and deceptiveness of this sort of homogenization is widely recognised'.[13] This is spot on and precisely what I would like to see more widely recognised about the collection of the usual suspects of 'Continental philosophy' as a whole.

CHICKENING OUT: ON HOW NOT TO READ THE LISTS

In collections such as this one, the chapter on Continental philosophy typically stands as 'an irritable and slightly swollen appendix'[14] to the other chapters in the book, and typically comes somewhere – would you know it – near the end . . . Anyone trying to put together such a chapter is bound to face a peculiar challenge trying to squeeze it all in without oversimplifying too much. However, he or she must also face a more peculiar problem of principle, that I want now to face up to directly. David West puts it starkly right at the outset of his opening chapter to his *Introduction to Continental Philosophy*. There is, he warns, 'a possible objection to our whole enterprise': namely, 'that the isolation of a separate tradition of Continental philosophy is contentious or even perverse'.[15]

As should be clear from my comments at the end of the entry on 'French feminism' above, I am convinced that this objection is fundamentally sound. In my view, the real perversity is to suppose that there is some way (or distinctive set of ways) of going on in philosophy which would seriously merit the title 'Continental philosophy'. However, if it is not to fly in the face of the entrenched, familiar and stubbornly undeniable reality of what Simon Critchley calls the '*de facto* distinction between analytic and Continental philosophy'[16] this point requires careful development and presentation. I will try to do so below, but despite some complexities, the basic truth can be simply stated, even if it is extremely difficult to keep one's head above the water trying to adhere to it. Everyone can see it. Here is Critchley:

It would not take a genius to realize that there are grave problems with the *de facto* distinction between analytic and Continental philosophy. . . . Continental

It may prove helpful to draw a 'map' of the preceding descriptions by using the list of 'movements in the stream' to make groupings among the list of 'the usual suspects'. The rough 'map of France' produced below is formed by date-of-birth on the vertical axis and a more or less entirely arbitrary but hopefully schematically helpful distribution along the horizontal axis.

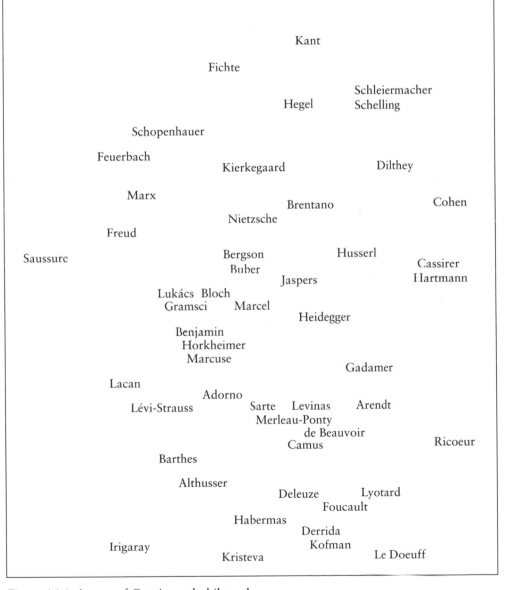

Figure 14.1 A map of Continental philosophy

philosophy is a highly eclectic and disparate series of intellectual currents that could hardly be said to amount to a unified tradition. As such, Continental philosophy is an *invention*, or more accurately, a *projection* of the Anglo-American academy onto a Continental Europe that would not recognise the legitimacy of such an appellation – a little like asking for a Continental breakfast in Paris.

(Critchley 1998, p. 5)

And here is West:

There is no single, homogeneous continental tradition. Rather, there is a variety of more or less closely related currents of thought. . . . In fact, continental philosophy began life as a category of exclusion. Until recently the analytical philosophy prevailing within the English-speaking countries of the West . . .has almost completely ignored work produced on the continent of Europe since Kant – or, in other words, continental philosophy.

(West 1996, pp. 1–3)

The difficulty of keeping the basic truth in view is very clear in West's comments here. He knows that there is no genuinely unified tradition of 'Continental philosophy', and he wants to acknowledge that the category originates within analytic philosophy as a term of exclusion. But to exclude something is not at all the same gesture as merely to ignore it, and it is utterly distorting to suppose that analytic philosophy can be even remotely accurately described as ignoring work produced on the continent of Europe since Kant. Indeed, the origins of analytic philosophy are profoundly Germanophone.

So let's get things straight first with regard to the point about exclusion. Although I cannot go into the sometimes astonishing historical and institutional details,[17] in my view, the basic idea here is that during the rise of the analytic movement, as part of that movement's developing self-understanding, the again already available, and again already not-simply-geographical category of 'Continental philosophy' came to function for analytic philosophers as the repository for all that is philosophically 'alien' to 'properly philosophical' inquiry as such. That is, Continental philosophy came to be regarded as consisting of all that is *philosophically foreign to philosophy*.[18] It is, that is to say, that which threatens philosophy from within, and so represents what *must* be excluded by a serious professional discipline.

In my view this means that the very process, or becoming, of the designation – the emergence of the idea of 'a radical distinction' or 'gulf' between 'analytic and Continental philosophy' – involved the false personification of what is, in fact and in principle, *philosophy's own interminable possibility*: the possibility of the kind of philosophical failure or emptiness most famously figured as the Sophist. In this way it came to pass that for self-authorised analytic philosophers, the analytic movement appeared to be an essentially healthy philosophical home, the home of clarity, logical rigour and intellectual honesty. And Continental philosophy, by essential contrast, came to be regarded as the home of obscurity, rhetorical excess and bonnet polishing, of 'wool-gathering and bathos' as Stanley Rosen has put it.[19]

I will say more about this attempt to expel what cannot be intelligibly expelled towards the end of this chapter, but I find it quite extraordinary that, having just acknowledged the point about exclusion and acknowledged the basic truth that there is no isolable tradition of Continental philosophy, West immediately goes on to say that his book will be about 'thinkers who, in one way or another, work in an identifiably continental mode'.[20] As I say, I call this 'chickening out'. Perhaps surprisingly, given the forceful way in which he states the basic truth, Critchley chickens out too. That is, even while noting as clearly and as starkly as possible that 'there is simply no category that would begin to cover the diversity of work produced by thinkers as methodologically and thematically opposed as Hegel and Kierkegaard, Freud and Buber, Heidegger and Adorno, or Lacan and Deleuze',[21] Critchley will nevertheless go on to insist that there is a way of 'dislodging the stereotypes' that can show 'how, after all, the analytic/Continental distinction [can] be drawn',[22] a possibility he affirms even more confidently with the claim that 'the notion of Continental philosophy can, indeed, be well defined and constitutes a distinct set of philosophical traditions and practices with a compelling range of problems'.[23]

It would, indeed, make things easier if it were so. And, of course, the mere fact that 'Continental philosophy' was not, in its origins, named 'from the inside' does not by itself mean that it is not so. Perhaps it could have been the case that there was a movement or a distinct set of movements to be identified, and analytic philosophers identified it. Analytic philosophers may loathe it, 'ignore' and 'dismiss' it, others, on the other hand, may come to find it 'compelling', comprising a well-defined set of philosophical traditions and practices that contains 'some of the best of what has been thought on the philosophically most fertile territory on the globe for the past two hundred years'.[24] On this hypothesis the attitude is irrelevant, what matters is that there is, as West puts it 'an identifiably continental mode' of doing philosophy. And . . .isn't there?

This is where it gets hard to keep one's head up, hard not to chicken out. Remember, all that one has to keep clearly in view, if one is not to chicken out, is the basic truth that there is simply no category that would begin to cover the diversity of work produced by thinkers as methodologically and thematically opposed as those who are held within this one. So why do we wind up wanting to say that nonetheless there is, for all that, a distinctive 'Continental tradition' or that there is 'an identifiably Continental mode' of doing philosophy? In my view, two reasons are powerfully operative here. First and foremost, anyone who has found their time *well spent* with thinkers who are largely 'ignored' (to use the weakest possible expression) by the analytic movement, will quite rightly think of that experience as inseparable from their sense of what philosophy is and can be. Second, there is no doubt that the various 'currents of thought' that are brought together under the title 'Continental philosophy' *are* 'more or less closely related' to each other.

If that is all one wants to say, fine. But that is not all that many people want to say. Many want to say that there is, after all, a distinctive 'Continental tradition', distinctive because certain things are true of it that are not true of the analytic tradition. For example, Critchley suggests that one crucial mark of what he calls 'the Continental tradition' is that it would 'refuse the validity of the distinction between philosophy and the history of philosophy operative in much of the analytic tradition'.[25] Straightened out this means: many philosophers, some of them who call themselves analytic philosophers but most of them not, do not accept a distinction that many who call themselves analytic philosophers accept. You do not need the idea of a distinctive Continental tradition to make the point, and in many ways it makes things worse if you do. For example, if you do you will have to preface the point, as Critchley does, by saying that one is speaking 'in doubtless unjustifiably general terms'. And one will have to hedge about and concede that accepting the validity of this distinction is true only of 'much' of the analytic tradition.[26] These ways of speaking – speaking 'roughly' and speaking in terms of 'many' or 'most' or 'much' – are not preliminary to a more rigorous specification but are congenital to this situation. And that way of speaking may on occasion be excusable or at least extremely hard to avoid – if, say, you are speaking to an interviewer from the BBC or CNN. But that does not prevent it from being unjustifiable and so, ultimately, misleading; it doesn't mean that, fundamentally, it is not chickening out.

I think it is deeply significant that 'Continental philosophy' as an isolable category has its origins in and is part of the conceptuality of analytic philosophy. The peculiar difficulty this fact throws up for us today is consistently to acknowledge that what is non-arbitrary about the specific collection of thinkers gathered together under this title is not something that can be unearthed through reading their work. So what can be gathered by reading them? The remainder of this chapter will attempt to develop some thoughts on this.

TOWARDS THE END

I have suggested that there are two basic reasons why we tend to think that there is or must be a distinctive 'tradition of Continental philosophy' as distinguished from the analytic tradition. In conjunction with the fact that the collection of usual suspects is not an absurd hodgepodge of utterly unrelated authors, the main reason here is, I have suggested, that having found one's time well spent with a thinker or thinkers who are considered 'out' by the analytic movement, the experienced interest in that encounter strongly suggests the idea that there is or must be, after all, this other way of doing things, this alternative way of going on in philosophy. What seems to me right about this is that, in the light of this experienced interest, one cannot, as Stephen Mulhall has put it, but find the 'picture of the essence of philosophical writing to which [analytic philosophers] officially cleave as open to question'.[27] Indeed, once that picture has been challenged, the apparent modesty of the standard analytic evaluation of 'what it is for such writing to be well shaped and disciplined',[28] and so ultimately the apparent modesty of its inheritance of the subject called 'philosophy', can come to seem deeply immodest and distorting. As I say, that 'result' is extremely suggestive of the idea that there is an alternative 'non-immodest' or 'non-distorting' line of inheritance available for more open-minded or less desiccated readers. However, it seems to me important that one can fully affirm the result without needing to affirm the idea that there is such an alternative at all. Indeed, the result itself strongly suggests that the very idea of inhabiting a philosophically 'healthy home', a stand-point in philosophy which has successfully expelled such immodesty and distortion, is precisely what one needs to avoid.

It will help to remind ourselves at this point why it is that the origins of the distinction between analytic and Continental philosophy are not at all irrelevant to the status of the movements thereby distinguished. As I have indicated, the idea here is that during the rise of the analytic movement the category of 'Continental philosophy' came to be represented as that which contains all that is philosophically foreign to philosophy, and so, therefore, to be represented as what must be excluded by a 'healthy' philosophical culture. I have called this the false personification of philosophy's own interminable possibility of failure, the attempt to evade the possibility that what one is doing might just be a kind of spinning in the wind or wool-gathering. In recalling this argument Stella Sandford (a reader of the usual suspects who is far less uncertain about the idea of a distinctive 'Continental tradition' than I am) interestingly adds '(analytic)' into the phrase where I simply talk about 'philosophy's interminable possibility of failure'.[29] That addition (perhaps unintentionally but still conveniently) holds on to the idea that one might inhabit a fold in philosophy that would have overcome that threat. And there, in my view, the danger lies. Indeed, as I see things the problems really begin as soon as there is, as Geoffrey Bennington has put it, a 'fold of philosophers' who 'believe they really are philosophers and know what philosophy is and how to do it'.[30] Ultimately, then, in my view Sandford's affirmation of a 'self-determined' version of 'Continental philosophy', a version that would have freed itself from the 'disparaging' analytic idea of it,[31] represents a 'fold' only marginally less problematic than its self-authorised analytic opponent, and certainly has not escaped the threat of emptiness.

I will still say 'marginally *less* problematic', however, since, as things stand, and as Bennington is careful to note, the outbursts of 'war-driven rhetoric' of 'denunications and even smears' which marks the 'discussion' between insiders and outsiders to such 'folds' today are 'rather massively the case on the "analytic" side'.[32] And I take it that this is particularly closely connected to the philosophically 'alien' status of the 'Continental philosopher' as constructed by the analytic movement. As Bennington notes, 'nothing is more like a holy war than the war of what perceives itself as reason against what it perceives as unreason'.[33] Nevertheless, it cannot be ignored that a war declared by the other can have the (perhaps desired) effect of uniting (or, as I put it earlier, *forging* a unity as) *its* opponent. Indeed, one can anticipate that for the vast majority of readers of the usual suspects there will be occasions when the felt need to countersign that declaration of war from the 'Continental' side is all but irresistible. As will become clear, I do not regard myself as somehow free of such 'gulf-effects'. Moreover, it would be utterly naive to think one could totally control them. Much as it pains me to acknowledge it, it would not be altogether surprising if at least some of those countersignatures, or (why not?) all of them on some occasion, took woolgathering to be an honourable or at least somehow excusable way of going on.

In the end, this is why I think that (despite my qualifications) chickening out on the question of 'the very idea of Continental philosophy' is not *essentially* more responsible than going in for the kind of (downright pernicious) constructions of 'Continental philosophy' that have been (and in some quarters remain) typical of the analytic movement. For, again, the point is that as soon as someone attempts to identify something as a healthy or philosophically responsible philosophical home, for example, as soon as someone 'appropriates' the title 'Continental philosophy' to name what they regard as the site of the most fertile movements in contemporary philosophy, a distinctive tradition with its own distinctive principles, even 'first principles',[34] not only would that be no guarantee at all that one had freed oneself from the threat of having a 'good conscience', it would actually promote the reverse, for it assumes that this kind of 'health' could be instituted in a tradition, a method, an approach, a style, an idiom, or some mode of inheriting 'philosophy', which has successfully expelled the threat of emptiness. But that threat, I want to say, belongs (*qua* threat) to the condition of any philosophising 'worthy of the name' whatsoever: it is not just something that we occasionally fall into (in falling away from philosophy proper) and from which a tradition (any tradition) might secure us protection.

It might be fitting to close with a few words connecting these points to the future inheritance of 'Continental philosophy' as I see it. I have no doubt that there will be a continued and indeed one might hope growing line of readers and students spending their time and finding their time well spent with one or other or some of the usual suspects. I expect to be very much among them. However, for reasons that will become clearer in a moment, it seems to me more or less inevitable that each of these readers will be riven by a conflict between two kinds of response to their experience, responses that could be figured as that of the 'ender' and that of the 'bender' respectively. The ender is the one who knows (what is in any case obvious) that the very idea of a 'Continental philosophical tradition' is 'contentious or even perverse', and so will be inclined to work with a certain lack of interest in securing or maintaining the idea of the analytic/Continental division. On the whole, I tend to be an enthusiastic ender. Another, and perhaps the most well-known, British reader of usual suspects who gives clear expression to an ender response is Simon Critchley. For along with his already witnessed tendency to chicken out, Critchley also presents Continental philosophy 'as a self-description' which is, as he puts it, only 'a necessary – but perhaps transitory – evil of the professionalisation of the discipline'.[35] Moreover, it is clear to Critchley that this transitional period may be coming to an end. For apart from Derrida, who is, as he says, 'still very much going strong', there is, in his view, nothing special going on in 'Paris or Frankfurt' at the moment, and it would be a serious mistake to 'expect any new prince(sse)s from over the water'.[36] For Critchley then, and for myself too, one should not ignore the path into the future which aims to cultivate ways of going on which will encourage our philosophical culture to overcome, as he puts it, 'a distinction which has become tiresome'.[37]

This is not, however, the point of view that Critchley (or I for that matter) will endorse at every turn. There is this other kind of response, the response of the bender, which always comes along too. The bender response demands that we acknowledge the real world gulf or, at the very least, real world 'gulf-effects', holding apart many readers of the usual suspects and many analytic philosophers, and the bender is (at least on occasion) willing to appropriate the title 'Continental philosophy' in order to do so. When they are most confident (or most resigned) they know they are fated to remain 'perverted' in the eyes of most analytic philosophers, and they may well see attempts to find ways of working without the distinction as little more than an expression of 'a fawning need for Oxbridge acceptance', a need that they have 'long ago dispensed with'.[38]

I think these two responses, that of the ender and that of the bender, struggle within the breast of everyone who has become a serious reader of the usual suspects.

For such readers cannot but find themselves embroiled in an inescapable, and rather singular, double demand or double bind.

On the one hand, the ender (in us) will insist that while one has to be careful not to fly in the face of the de facto distinction, it is equally important to acknowledge philosophical differences that do.[39] In doing so one cannot but come to see a deeper, one might say, 'constitutional difference' in philosophy: namely, between those who do and those who do not think they know what (inheriting) philosophy (philosophically) is. This difference is 'constitutional' because, of course, we are all inheritors here, and as such we all inherit the endless task, the endless risk, of inheriting philosophy philosophically, of making what we do normative for 'philosophy'. And we do so, everyone of us, as soon as we open our mouths to speak or put pen to paper. In the clear and decisive 'Oh, yes' and 'Oh, no' of a philosopher at home in his or her institutional fold, anxiety may be almost imperceptible. Yet, while one can never simply do without philosophical institutions and their histories, the essential *existential risk* that is inherited with the (inherited) words 'I, *philosopher*, say . . .' will survive as such today only as long as it can survive without the immodesty of an institutional guarantee – whether analytic or Continental.

On the other hand, however, one only needs to imagine talking about such 'existential risks' to a hard-nosed analytic philosopher to see one's utter inability to remain simply 'philosophical' through and through. And the bender (in us) will want to insist that even if one should never seek out or take refuge in an institutional guarantee, one is also never simply free of some institution or other either. Everyone who 'in their own way' inherits 'philosophy' is always also and willy-nilly situating themselves (deliberately or not, consciously or not) with respect to going institutions, valuations and folds. And whether one likes it or not, invites it or not, or resists it or not there are always police waiting in the wings, ready to intervene to place every(other)one.[40]

And so today, *even in the absence of a tradition to inherit*, anyone who has found their time genuinely well spent with one or other or some of the usual suspects is a potential inheritor (whether they like it or not, invite it or not, resist it or not) of the going *institutional risk* that is inherited with the (inherited) words 'This *Continental philosopher* says . . .', words which I know are there for any one to take (or, indeed, refuse[41]) in my own case as soon as I open my mouth to speak or put my pen to paper. No doubt whether or when or how one might want to take them on for oneself will remain the singular 'existential-institutional' question for every reader of the usual suspects for some time to come.[42]

EXERCISES

1 Are there *any* compelling grounds for distinguishing between 'analytic' and 'Continental' philosophy?

2 What is the relationship between Hegel's absolute idealism and Kant's transcendental idealism?

3 Does Husserl's appeal to the idea of the 'lived-world' mark a significant departure from Kantian transcendentalism?

4 What reasons are there for accepting Heidegger's claim that 'being-with others' is a constant structural feature of human existence?

5 Explain and critically discuss Merleau-Ponty's claim that 'consciousness is in the first place not a matter of "I think that" but of "I can"'.

6 Critically examine Derrida's claim that the predicates traditionally thought to belong only to writing belong, in fact and in principle, to every species of sign whatsoever, including speech.

NOTES

1 Simon Critchley, 'What is Continental philosophy?', p. 2.

2 The turn-of-the-last-century German philosopher Edmund Husserl is usually credited with inaugurating the modern philosophical movement known as 'Phenomenology'. Can we say that those engaged in the philosophical developments which led some teachers in the English-speaking world to feel the need to change course titles 'inaugurated a movement' of 'Continental philosophy'? I do not want to simply dismiss that idea, but I will certainly want to complicate it in what follows.

3 In an attempt to avoid such misleading impressions a growing number of courses today (mine included) go by the title 'Modern European Philosophy'. But placing the 'Continental' collection under that (or some other) title only hides and does not resolve the problems.

4 Incidentally, the same sort of internal transformation has also gone on within analytic philosophy – in that case, roughly speaking, from a post-empiricist to a post-Kantian phase – but for various reasons a change in title has not, on the whole, seemed necessary or desirable to most (self-authorised) analytic philosophers.

5 See Cora Diamond, 'Throwing away the ladder'. In this essay Diamond suggests that readers of Wittgenstein's early philosophy who attempt to hold on to the idea that his self-declared 'nonsense' nevertheless gestures at genuine 'features of reality' are guilty of 'chickening out' (p. 181).

6 The joke is made in print by Richard Rorty in *Contingency, Irony and Solidarity*, p. 81. The idea is that one way of delineating analytic from Continental philosophy is that the former is primarily concerned with philosophical problems – the nature of meaning, our knowledge of other minds, the intentionality of consciousness, etc. – while the latter simply discusses what other people have written.

7 See Critchley, op. cit., p. 2.

8　Ibid., p. 9.

9　In constructing these entries I have made extensive use of the survey essays in *The Edinburgh Encyclopedia of Continental Philosophy*, ed. S. Glendinning.

10　On this point I would ask that readers who are just skimming the entries on these 'movements in the stream' pay particular attention to the observations made in the final two groupings.

11　It should be noted that this grouping, which is, as I am trying to show, of peculiar significance for the grouping 'Continental philosophy' as such, is in some ways simply another movement in the stream of Western thought. Moreover, its identity is no more secure than any other mentioned here. Indeed since it has a constitutive relation to what is strictly speaking a distorting projection of its own, its identity is far from problem free. (That is, there is no reason why a legitimate heir to analytic philosophy might want to affirm that, strictly speaking, there is no analytic philosophy.)

12　See Brian Leiter's 'Note on analytic and Continental philosophy' in his annual 'Gourmet Report' published by Blackwell at http://www.blackwellpublishers.co.uk/gourmet.

13　Stella Sandford, 'Johnny Foreigner', p. 45.

14　Critchley, op. cit., p. 13.

15　David West, *An Introduction to Continental Philosophy*, p. 2.

16　Critchley, op. cit., p. 3.

17　For a detailed treatment see my 'What is Continental Philosophy?' in *The Edinburgh Encyclopedia of Continental Philosophy*, S. Glendinning (ed.).

18　One should not forget, of course, that the category is *also* a geographical one, so that references to work by the usual suspects as 'alien' or 'foreign' can (and often do) carry national as well as philosophical connotations.

19　Cited in Critchley, op. cit., p. 7.

20　West, op. cit., p. 1.

21　Critchley, op. cit., p. 6.

22　Ibid., p. 8.

23　Critchley, *Continental Philosophy: A Very Short Introduction*, p. ii.

24　Critchley 'What is Continental Philosophy?', p. 14.

25　Ibid., p. 10.

26　Ibid., p. 10.

27　Stephen Mulhall, *Inheritance and Originality*, p. 1.

28　Ibid.

29　Sandford, op. cit., p. 43.

30　Geoffrey Bennington, 'For the sake of argument (up to a point)', p. 38.

31　Sandford, op. cit., p. 43.

32　Bennington, op. cit., p. 41.

33　Ibid.

34　Sandford, op. cit., p. 44.

35　Critchley, *Continental Philosophy: A Very Short Introduction*, p. 48.

36　Ibid., p. 125.

37　Ibid., p. 126.

38　Sandford, op. cit., p. 43.

39　Lively benders are thus typically those readers of the usual suspects who are most likely to de-emphasise the sometimes deep theoretical and conceptual differences between them, and so are those most likely to chicken out. I have already noted a number of divergent 'movements in the stream' but it is also worth mentioning a further, and in my view particularly deep and powerful undertow in the waters of the contemporary philosophical culture, one which is sometimes thought to sit squarely over the analytic/Continental division but which, in reality, does not: namely, between those who do and those who do not see philosophy as importantly continuous with or in the service of science. For an immensely interesting interpretation of the analytic/Continental distinction which conceives it in terms of this undertow, see David Copper's 'Analytic and Continental philosophy' in *Proceedings of the Aristotelian Society* **XCVII** (1994) and his 'Modern European philosophy' in *The Blackwell Companion to Philosophy*, N. Bunnin and E.P. Tsui-James (eds), Oxford: Blackwell (1996). The proximity of the analytic/Continental division to the undertow is nicely illustrated by Heidegger's representation of the 'extreme counter-positions' of the '"philosophy"' of our day': '[Carnap → Heidegger]' (cited in Critchley, op. cit., p. 104). While one could obviously argue the point in both directions, it seems to me that one can sustain the parallel (as Cooper does) only if one reads analytic philosophy today as far more 'Carnapian' than it actually is.

40 Lively enders are thus typically those readers of the usual suspects who are least affected by or who most want (or need) to forget the 'in the world' conditions of philosophical identification. The point here is that the ('conceptual') ender response no less than the ('institutional') bender response is always also engaged in a 'political' strategy, and is so even (perhaps especially) at the moment when it seems to transcend such vicissitudes in order to speak purely 'conceptually' or 'philosophically'. An ender, even if not 'fawning for Oxbridge acceptance', certainly look like someone who wants to get on better with the institutionally dominant analytic movers and shakers, and no doubt appearing in the world as an ender may make you more employable – around here these days. However, even if you are lucky enough to have a job, you will be very unlikely to be working alongside many (if any) departmental colleagues with a serious working interest in your work, and, moreover, you will in any case have a serious dearth of places to publish it and a critical shortage of avenues of financial support for your 'conferences' and 'research'. At least the bender response is prepared for this kind of glass ceiling, more alive, theoretically and practically, to the facts about institutional prejudices. No reader of the usual suspects can work in philosophy in the English-speaking world and be blind to the prejudices against them.

41 Nicely illustrating the generality of my point about 'police' placing those who do not (want to) place themselves, it is worth noting that (in what might also pass as a passing complement) Sanford represents me as belonging to the philosophical fold (over there) who work 'in the thriving non-xenophobic analytic and post-analytic scene' (Sanford, op. cit., p. 43).

42 I am particularly grateful to Simon Critchley, Fiona Hughes, Stella Sandford and John Shand for their comments on drafts of this chapter.

BIBLIOGRAPHY

Bennington, Geoffrey (2001) 'For the sake of argument (up to a point)', in S. Glendinning (ed.) *Arguing with Derrida*, Oxford: Blackwell.

Critchley, Simon (1998) 'What is Continental philosophy?', in S. Critchley and W. Schroeder (eds) *A Companion to Continental Philosophy*, Oxford: Blackwell.

Critchley, Simon (2001) *Continental Philosophy: A Very Short Introduction*, Oxford: Oxford University Press.

Diamond, Cora (1996) 'Throwing away the ladder' in *The Realistic Spirit*, Cambridge, MA: MIT Press.

Glendinning, Simon (1999) 'What is Continental philosophy?', in S. Glendinning (ed.) *The Edinburgh Encyclopedia of Continental Philosophy*, Edinburgh: Edinburgh University Press.

Mulhall Stephen, (2001) *Inheritance and Originality*, Oxford: Oxford University Press.

Rorty, Richard (1989) *Contingency, Irony and Solidarity*, Cambridge: Cambridge University Press.

Sandford, Stella (2000) 'Johnny Foreigner' in *Radical Philosophy* **102** (July/Aug).

West, David (1996) *An Introduction to Continental Philosophy*, Cambridge: Polity Press.

FURTHER READING

There are now two compendious surveys of all the major thinkers and themes mentioned in this chapter, both with strengths and weaknesses:

Critchley, Simon and Schroeder, William (eds) (1998) *A Companion to Continental Philosophy*, Oxford: Blackwell.

Glendinning, Simon (ed.) (1999) *The Edinburgh Encyclopedia of Continental Philosophy*, Edinburgh: Edinburgh University Press.

There is no substitute for reading the texts of one or other or some of the usual suspects, but there are a growing number of books covering thinkers and themes introduced in this chapter that address readers with a largely Anglophone 'analytic' philosophical background. These include:

Glendinning, Simon (1998) *On Being With Others: Heidegger–Derrida–Wittgenstein*, London: Routledge (1998).

Guignon, Charles (1983) *Heidegger and the Problem of Knowledge*, Indianapolis, IN: Hackett.

Hammond, Michael, Howarth, Jane and Keat, Russell (1991) *Understanding Phenomenology*, Oxford: Blackwell.

Held, David (1980) *Introduction to Critical Theory: Horkheimer to Habermas*, Berkeley: University of California Press.

McCulluch, Gregory (1994) *Using Sartre*, London: Routledge.

There are also a number of books that, without chickening out (too much), try to situate many of the thinkers and themes introduced in this chapter in a wider historical and philosophical context. In my view the best are:

Pippin, Robert (1999) *Modernism as a Philosophical Problem*, Oxford: Blackwell.

Solomon, Robert (1988) *Continental Philosophy Since 1750*, Oxford: Oxford University Press.

Finally, a truly excellent history of the phenomenological movement that deserves the widest possible audience is:

Denoon Cumming, Robert (1991–2001) *Phenomenology and Deconstruction* (four volumes), Chicago: University of Chicago Press.

INDEX